Culture, Thought and Belief
in British Political Life since 1800

Culture, Thought and Belief in British Political Life since 1800

Essays in Honour of Jonathan Parry

Edited by Paul Readman and Geraint Thomas

THE BOYDELL PRESS

© Contributors 2024

All Rights Reserved. Except as permitted under current legislation
no part of this work may be photocopied, stored in a retrieval system,
published, performed in public, adapted, broadcast,
transmitted, recorded or reproduced in any form or by any means,
without the prior permission of the copyright owner

First published 2024
The Boydell Press, Woodbridge

ISBN 978 1 83765 018 7

The Boydell Press is an imprint of Boydell & Brewer Ltd
PO Box 9, Woodbridge, Suffolk IP12 3DF, UK
and of Boydell & Brewer Inc.
668 Mt Hope Avenue, Rochester, NY 14620–2731, USA
website: www.boydellandbrewer.com

A CIP catalogue record for this book is available
from the British Library

The publisher has no responsibility for the continued existence or accuracy of
URLs for external or third-party internet websites referred to in this book, and
does not guarantee that any content on such websites is, or will remain, accurate
or appropriate

Contents

List of Figures and Tables		vii
Contributors		ix
Acknowledgements		xi
Introduction		1
Paul Readman and Geraint Thomas		

Part I: Writing Modern British History

1	*Parry Passu*: Jonathan Parry in European Echo	17
	Michael Bentley	
2	G.M. Trevelyan, Landscape and the Writing of History in England, *c.*1870–*c.*1950	38
	Paul Readman	

Part II: Nation

3	The Image of the Country House in Victorian Political Culture	61
	James Thompson	
4	Hugh de Sélincourt, *The Cricket Match*, and Englishness between the Wars	82
	Matthew Cragoe	
5	Nation and Union in the Career of David Lloyd George	102
	Geraint Thomas	

Part III: Ideas Over Time: Narratives of Change

6	Politics, Rhetoric and the Serial Fluctuations of 'Small State' Ideology in the Long Nineteenth Century and After	123
	Boyd Hilton	
7	The Socialist Lives of Beatrice Webb and Margaret Cole	143
	Helen McCarthy	
8	'Great Contemporaries' but Guarded Friends: Winston Churchill and G.M. Trevelyan Revisited	164
	David Cannadine	

vi   *Contents*

9   What Happened to Political Nonconformity?   190
      Philip Williamson

Part IV: Institutions

10   Liberalism, the Law and Parliament in Modern British Politics   213
      Ben Griffin

11   The Backbenchers of the Nineteenth-century Commons: Activity
      and Accountability in the Age of Reform   233
      Kathryn Rix

12   Lord Salisbury as Modern Political Man, *c.*1880–1902   252
      Tom Crewe

13   Edward the Caresser: Monarchy and Religion in the Reign of
      Edward VII   272
      Michael Ledger-Lomas

Part V: Britain in the World

14   Irish Realities and British Liberal Self-deception: The Reaches and
      Limits of British Liberal Constitutionalism   295
      John Bew and Paul Bew

15   Latin America and British International Thought, 1880–1920   310
      Alex Middleton

16   Cambridge Beginnings, Oxford Departures: 'Liberal Education'
      and Imperial Legacies, 1945–70   330
      Susan D. Pennybacker

17   The Curious Case of Wales's Statue to Henry Morton Stanley   349
      Joanna Lewis

      Jonathan Parry: List of Publications   371
      Index   378
      Tabula Gratulatoria   387

Figures and Tables

Figures

2.1   Caspar David Friedrich, *Der Wanderer über dem Nebelmeer* [*The Wanderer Above the Sea of Fog*] (*c.*1818). © bpk / Hamburger Kunsthalle, SHK / Elke Walford.   48

3.1   'The Calm Before the Storm: A Sketch at Dalmeny on Saturday, April 3', *Illustrated London News*, 4 Apr. 1880. © *Illustrated London News Ltd*/Mary Evans.   64

3.2   'The Review of Lancashire Rifle Volunteers in Knowsley Park – the Earl and Countess of Derby Leaving Knowsley Hall for the Review', *Illustrated London News*, 15 Sept. 1860. © *Illustrated London News Ltd*/Mary Evans.   70

3.3   'Wet Monday at Hawarden', *Judy*, 23 May 1888. By permission of the British Library.   74

3.4   'English Homes: Stoke Park', *Illustrated London News*, 21 Nov. 1896. © *Illustrated London News Ltd*/Mary Evans.   76

3.5   'Hawarden Castle, the Seat of the Right Hon. William Ewart Gladstone, M.P.', *Illustrated London News*, 20 July 1889. © *Illustrated London News Ltd*/Mary Evans.   77

3.6   'Mr Chamberlain's Favourite Hobby', *Illustrated London News*, 19 Dec. 1903. © *Illustrated London News Ltd*/Mary Evans.   80

4.1   'This *is* nice darling; now you'll be able to enjoy the cricket with us', *Punch*, 30 July 1930. Amélie Deblauwe / Reproduced by kind permission of the Syndics of Cambridge University Library.   95

4.2   'No, darling, Daddy can't talk to you now; wait until he's dropped this one!', *Punch*, 8 May 1935. Amélie Deblauwe / Reproduced by kind permission of the Syndics of Cambridge University Library.   96

7.1   The partnership at work: the newly-wed Webbs photographed at their first home in Hampstead, north London, *c.*1894. © National Portrait Gallery.   155

7.2   The Coles at home: Margaret and Douglas in their study in Hendon, north London, 1938. © National Portrait Gallery.   156

11.1   'H.B.' [John Doyle], *March of Reform*, 1833. Lithograph. © National Portrait Gallery, London.   234

12.1	Tom Merry [pseud. William Mecham], 'One Flag, One Leader, One Voice!', *St Stephen's Review*, 25 Apr. 1891. © Mary Evans Picture Library.	268
17.1	Jeff Buck / Statue of H.M. Stanley, Denbigh / CC BY-SA 2.0	351
17.2	Llywelyn2000 / H.M. Stanley Sculpture, St Asaph / CC BY-SA 4.0	364

Table

11.1	Turnover of MPs at General Elections, 1820–32	235

The editors, contributors and publisher are grateful to all the institutions and persons listed for permission to reproduce the materials in which they hold copyright. Every effort has been made to trace the copyright holders; apologies are offered for any omission, and the publisher will be pleased to add any necessary acknowledgement in subsequent editions.

Contributors

Michael Bentley is Senior Research Fellow in Historiography at St Hugh's College, Oxford and Emeritus Professor of Modern History at the University of St Andrews.

John Bew is Professor of History and Foreign Policy at the Department of War Studies, King's College London.

Paul Bew is Emeritus Professor of Irish Politics at Queen's University Belfast and a crossbench peer in the House of Lords.

Sir David Cannadine is Dodge Professor Emeritus of History at Princeton University, a Visiting Professor of History at the University of Oxford, and the General Editor of the *Oxford Dictionary of National Biography*.

Matthew Cragoe is Head of the School of Professional Studies, Science and Technology at Goldsmiths, University of London.

Tom Crewe is Contributing Editor at the *London Review of Books* and winner of the 2023 Orwell Prize for Political Fiction.

Ben Griffin is Associate Professor in Modern British History at the University of Cambridge and a Fellow of Girton College.

Boyd Hilton is Emeritus Professor of Modern British History at the University of Cambridge and a Fellow of Trinity College.

Michael Ledger-Lomas is a Visiting Research Fellow at King's College London and the author of *Queen Victoria: This Thorny Crown* (Oxford, 2022).

Joanna Lewis is Professor in the Department of International History at the London School of Economics, where she is also Director of the Centre for Women, Peace and Security.

Helen McCarthy is Professor of Modern and Contemporary British History at the University of Cambridge and a Fellow of St John's College.

Alex Middleton is Fellow in History at St Hugh's College, Oxford.

Susan D. Pennybacker is the Chalmers W. Poston Distinguished Professor of European History at the University of North Carolina, Chapel Hill.

x   *Contributors*

Paul Readman is Professor of Modern British History at King's College London.

Kathryn Rix is the Assistant Editor of the *House of Commons, 1832–1945* project at the History of Parliament.

Geraint Thomas is Fellow and Director of Studies in History at Peterhouse, University of Cambridge.

James Thompson is Professor of Modern British History at the University of Bristol.

Philip Williamson is Emeritus Professor of Modern British History at Durham University.

Acknowledgements

The essays in this volume received their first outing at a two-day symposium in honour of Jonathan Parry, held in Peterhouse in September 2022. The event was generously funded by Peterhouse and Pembroke College, Cambridge, to whom we offer our sincerest gratitude, and benefitted greatly from the support and enthusiasm of the late Saskia Murk Jansen and Miri Rubin. We wish to thank all those who attended and participated, including Michael Middeke of Boydell and Brewer, whose enthusiasm for the volume has been a source of encouragement, as well as the two anonymous referees for their valuable comments. Lastly, we would like to thank the honorand himself – for his own assistance with organising the symposium (and for enduring the limelight for two days), for his generous support since, and above all for his ongoing example.

Introduction

Paul Readman and Geraint Thomas

In recent decades, assessments of the state of modern British political history have been legion.[1] Often seen as conservative in both their method and choice of subject matter – focused on political parties, the structures and operations of government and the conduct of foreign policy – its practitioners can easily be presented as occupying the rearguard rather than the van of trends in historical research. Occasionally the field is described as being in 'crisis', eroded by the challenges of postmodernism, cultural history and the lure of successive methodological 'turns', of which the linguistic, material, affective and environmental stand out only as some of the most obvious examples. It is certainly true that political history, once widely regarded as exerting some primacy over other historical sub-disciplines – dealing as it does with state power, after all – has now irrevocably lost this status. Its curricula offerings can appear fusty and dry to undergraduates in comparison with competing attractions on course lists.

Yet while there is some truth in this picture, much of it is a mirage. British political history may no longer be *primus inter pares*, but it retains a great deal of vitality. It is also more varied and innovative than ever before.[2] Far from retreating behind the ramparts of a Dryasdust positivism, its exponents have sallied forth to engage with new currents of thought, new philosophical and epistemological approaches, new themes and emphases – new ways, in short, of understanding the worlds and workings of modern British politics. To take

[1] See, for example, Susan Pedersen, 'What Is Political History Now?', in David Cannadine (ed.), *What is History Now?* (Basingstoke, 2002); Paul Readman, 'The State of Twentieth-century Political History', *Journal of Policy History*, 21 (2009), 219–38; Jon Lawrence and Alexander Campsie, 'Political History', in Stefan Berger, Heiko Feldner and Kevin Passmore (eds), *Writing History: Theory and Practice* (3rd edn, London, 2020), 323–42; Alex Middleton, 'The State of Modern British Political History?', *Parliamentary History*, 38 (2019), 278–85; special issue, 'The Future of British Political History', *Political Quarterly*, 94 (2023), 159–35.

[2] David Brown, Robert Crowcroft and Gordon Pentland, 'Introduction', in Brown, Crowcroft and Pentland (eds), *Oxford Handbook of Modern British Political History 1800–2000* (Oxford, 2018), 1–2.

perhaps the most obvious example, consideration of the politics of gender now looms much larger than previously, extending far beyond the issue of women's suffrage, now definitively a 'classic' topic on undergraduate reading lists – for all that that subject remains the focus of much stimulating scholarship and debate.[3] Themes of nation, race and empire, too, are now staple fare for the modern British historian, thanks in large part to the efforts of those scholars who have insisted on the impact of imperialism at home, on politics as well as society and culture.[4] In more methodological a vein, what became known as the 'New Political History' – much of which also addressed these themes – acknowledged the implications of the linguistic turn, drawing more attention to the role of language, rhetoric and ideas in the formulation of policy, the business of governance, the construction of political identities and the outcome of elections.[5] And while few have gone as far as Patrick Joyce in supplying rigorously postmodernist readings of (political) discourse as integral to regimes of 'liberal governmentality',[6] other historians have been equally innovative in their choice of tools with which to excavate the meaning and significance of political language. Perhaps most notably, some have turned to quantitative techniques – in part derived from digital humanities or corpus linguistics – in

[3] For outstanding examples of work of this kind, see Kathryn Gleadle, *Borderline Citizens: Women, Gender and Political Culture in Britain, 1815–1867* (Oxford, 2009); Ben Griffin, *The Politics of Gender in Victorian Britain: Masculinity, Political Culture and the Struggle for Women's Rights* (Cambridge, 2012); and Robert Saunders, '"A Great and Holy War": Religious Routes to Women's Suffrage, 1909–1914', *English Historical Review*, 134 (2019), 1471–1502.

[4] Seminal works in this 'New Imperial History' include John M. MacKenzie, *Propaganda and Empire* (Manchester, 1984); Antoinette Burton, *At the Heart of Empire: Indians and the Colonial Encounter in Late Victorian Britain* (Berkeley: CA, 1998); Catherine Hall, *Civilising Subjects: Metropole and Colony in the English Imagination 1830–67* (Oxford, 2002).

[5] For historiographical commentary on this approach, see Dror Wahrman, 'The New Political History: A Review Essay', *Social History*, 21 (1996), 343–54; Lawrence and Campsie, 'Political History', 332–5; and – for some coruscating critique – Michael Bentley, 'Victorian Politics and the Linguistic Turn', *Historical Journal*, 42 (1999), 883–902. Foundational texts for the New Political History include James Vernon, *Politics and the People: A Study in English Political Culture* (Cambridge, 1993) and Jon Lawrence and Miles Taylor's edited collection, *Party, State and Society: Electoral Behaviour in Britain since 1820* (Aldershot, 1997).

[6] See esp. Patrick Joyce, *The Rule of Freedom: Liberalism and the Modern City* (London, 2003), and for a recent assessment of his oeuvre as a whole, Robert Colls, 'Post-modern Pat: The Work of Patrick Joyce', *Cultural and Social History*, 13 (2016), 135–48.

Introduction 3

order to analyse the content of politicians' election addresses and speeches.[7] We now have a much more sophisticated understanding of the ideas and issues at play in political debate, and also their (often intersectional) relationship with various constructions of identity, whether rooted in class and gender, locality and nation, or race and empire.

So, modern British political history is vibrant and diverse. Its historiographies and topics of debate are well developed, and its practitioners are often creative and subtle in their methodological approaches – even if not all work in the field (including some of that deemed seminal) has been as careful, rigorous or attentive to the importance of literary expression as one might wish.[8] The impact of the linguistic turn has helped ensure that crude class-based analysis of political change has now definitely been consigned to the historiographical dustbin – for all that it was never as dominant as many of its detractors alleged. At the same time, we are also now largely free of narrow institutional histories, whether of political parties, pressure groups or arms of government – for all that penetrating analysis of the workings of the British state and constitution remains worthwhile and much needed.[9] Yet not everything in the garden is rosy. The fecund profusion of historiographical vegetation is entrancing, but – as many convenors of undergraduate courses can doubtless testify – in it the wanderer can easily get lost. As the editors of the *Oxford Handbook of Modern British Political History* (2018) admit, the field as a whole is lacking in 'coherence' – an assessment ironically borne out by the content and structure of their unwieldy 33-chapter volume.[10] More specifically, while the (relatively) recent emphasis on language, rhetoric, ideas and representations is all to the good, it has tended to promote a curiously disembodied and abstracted kind of history-writing, one in which discourse is often disconnected from people, and their practice of the business of politics, with all its manoeuvring, compromises and complexity. And if the recent 'material', 'biographical' and 'emotional' turns may have done something to correct this, it remains a prominent feature of much scholarship.[11]

[7] Joseph S. Meisel, 'Words by the Numbers: A Quantitative Analysis and Comparison of the Oratorical Careers of William Ewart Gladstone and Winston Spencer Churchill', *Historical Research*, 73 (2000), 262–95; and for a more sophisticated methodological approach, see the recent work of Luke Blaxill, in particular his 'Quantifying the Language of British Politics', *Historical Research*, 86 (2013), 313–43 and *The War of Words: The Language of British Elections, 1880–1914* (Woodbridge, 2020).

[8] For powerful evidence of such shortcomings, see Bentley, 'Victorian Politics and the Linguistic Turn'.

[9] A point made in Pedersen, 'What is Political History Now?', and still valid today.

[10] Brown, Crowcroft and Pentland, 'Introduction', 1.

[11] For examples of the latter, see Martin Francis, 'Tears, Tantrums, and Bared Teeth: The Emotional Economy of Three Conservative Prime Ministers, 1951–1963',

4   *Paul Readman and Geraint Thomas*

This book seeks to address these problems by emphasising – and through its constituent essays demonstrating – the value of an approach that foregrounds the importance of ideas to modern British political life; but one that does so while connecting these ideas, and the discourses in which they were embedded, to the day-to-day practice of politics, the decisions of policymakers, the shaping of political allegiances and the business of government. In this aim, it is inspired by the work of Jonathan Parry, who for more than forty years has continued to innovate a distinctive approach to the writing of modern political history – one which seeks, as he put it in describing a key aim of his book, *The Politics of Patriotism* (2006), to address the question of 'how historians can best capture the complex dynamic of political history and especially the relation between political tactics, languages and ideas'.[12]

Parry's work, of course, is usually squarely placed in the category of 'high political' history. This may be correct, insofar as such categorisations are of any use, but it can and has led to misunderstandings – not least because of the negative associations that are often attached to high political history more generally. Practitioners of this approach, it is frequently alleged, are excessively interested in the minutiae of political manoeuvre on the part of Westminster figures, exaggerate the role of self-interest and expediency in the decision-making of these same figures, and show unjustifiable, even contemptuous, disdain for the significance of popular and radical politics. Politics is thus reduced to a game for entitled elites, jockeying for position in the corridors of Westminster, the salons of Belgravia and the drawing rooms of country houses.

As with all caricatures, there is some truth in the picture drawn. The focus on elites – what Maurice Cowling once called 'the politicians who mattered' – cannot be denied,[13] and the counterpart to this is a relative lack of emphasis on extra-parliamentary agitations, popular radicalism and the like. And it is certainly also true that the impact of popular politics – on shaping policy and influencing the passage of legislation – has been downplayed, with the case of the Second Reform Act being one notable example.[14] Furthermore, the painstaking and precise reconstruction of the cut and thrust of political machinations, covering often very short time periods, has led to work the value and

---

Journal of British Studies, 41 (2002), 354–87 and Emily Robinson, 'The Authority of Feeling in Mid-Twentieth Century English Conservatism', *Historical Journal*, 63 (2020), 1303–24.

[12] Jonathan Parry, *The Politics of Patriotism: English Liberalism, National Identity and Europe, 1830–1886* (Cambridge, 2006), x.

[13] Maurice Cowling, *The Impact of Labour 1920–1924: The Beginning of Modern British Politics* (Cambridge, 1971), 3.

[14] Maurice Cowling, *1867: Disraeli, Gladstone and Revolution: The Passing of the Second Reform Bill* (Cambridge, 1967).

Introduction 5

argument of which is sometimes obscured by bristling thickets of rebarbative detail.[15] At worst, and occasionally with good reason, high political history, like diplomatic history, can be seen as presenting elite politics as a world hermetically sealed off from its wider social, cultural and intellectual contexts.[16] This, at any rate, remains often the received wisdom, the impression given – even, perhaps inadvertently, by scholars admiring of the approach.[17]

It is, however, to an important extent an inaccurate impression. While it might have suited its detractors to present all work in the high politics mould as conforming to the stereotype sketched above, even the most trenchant of its practitioners were – more often than not – notably attentive to the role played by language, rhetoric, belief and ideas. As has been recognised by commentators both within and outwith the high political tradition, Cowling is an outstanding case in point.[18] Some, indeed, have even seen his work as anticipating the preoccupations of the New Political History.[19] As Susan Pedersen noted in 2002, Cowling was acutely aware that 'all politicians after 1832 lived by the word' – and this awareness is apparent from any serious consideration of his work, which sought not only to document the tactical tussles at the top of the greasy pole, but the complex interplay of these tussles with ideals, doctrine and thought.[20]

---

[15] See, for examples of this kind of work, Andrew Jones, *The Politics of Reform, 1884* (Cambridge, 1972) and A.B. Cooke and John Vincent, *The Governing Passion: Cabinet Government and Party Politics in Britain, 1885–86* (Brighton, 1974).

[16] Thus, for Cooke and Vincent – though not for Parry – the Liberal split over Irish Home Rule had little to do with ideology at all. Cooke and Vincent, *Governing Passion*; cf. J.P. Parry, *Democracy and Religion: Gladstone and the Liberal Party 1867–1875* (Cambridge, 1986), 437–9 and Jonathan Parry, *The Rise and Fall of Liberal Government in Victorian Britain* (New Haven & London, 1993), 295–303.

[17] See, for example, Robert Crowcroft, 'Maurice Cowling and the Writing of British Political History', *Contemporary British History*, 22 (2008), 279–86, esp. 280.

[18] Lawrence and Campsie, 'Political History', 325–6; Readman, 'State of Twentieth-century British Political History', 232 and 'Speeches', in Miriam Dobson and Benjamin Ziemann (eds), *Reading Primary Sources* (2nd edn, London, 2020), 241; Philip Williamson, 'Maurice Cowling and Modern British Political History', in Robert Crowcroft, S.J.D. Green and Richard Whiting (eds), *The Philosophy, Politics and Religion of British Democracy: Maurice Cowling and Conservatism* (London, 2010), 126–7, 138–40; Alex Middleton, '"High Politics" and its Intellectual Contexts', *Parliamentary History*, 40 (2021), esp. 168, 171–2.

[19] David Craig, '"High Politics" and the "New Political History"', *Historical Journal*, 53 (2010), 453–75.

[20] Pedersen, 'What is Political History Now?', 41–2. As Cowling himself made clear, high politics, in his definition, was 'primarily a matter of rhetoric and manoeuvre': *Impact of Labour*, 3–4.

6   *Paul Readman and Geraint Thomas*

Political action, leadership and the business of government were conditioned by considerations of personal and party advantage, but also by ideas.

Yet if high political history was never an idea-free zone, Parry's specific achievement – and one to which the essays in this book pay homage – was to widen its scope, to go beyond the parameters delineated by Cowling. Proceeding along lines similar to those followed by other members of the so-called 'Peterhouse School', such as Michael Bentley and Philip Williamson, Parry aimed – as he put it in one of his relatively rare explicit statements of methodological intent – to 'rework the traditional "high political" approach on a broader canvas, marrying a properly sophisticated account of political practice with a due attention to the importance of contemporary ideas and values'.[21] This meant reconstructing the 'thought-worlds' of politicians,[22] taking due cognisance of the wider intellectual context in which they operated. It meant (as many historians, astonishingly, still do not) taking seriously the role of religious belief to modern British politics, the significance of which he demonstrated to magisterial effect in his first book.[23] More generally, it meant understanding the interrelationship between wider cultural currents and the landscape and practice of politics, and – crucially – recognising that the most politically consequential of the ideas carried by these currents were not necessarily those that might be seen as the most intellectually advanced or canonical. Thus, for all that John Stuart Mill (for instance) might have been a great philosopher, recognition of the quality of his thought should not lead to overestimations of its political significance, relative to other ideological influences. As Parry put it, with pleasing tartness, in an early essay,

> Once half-baked versions of German Idealism or Tractarianism had been fashioned by 'second-rate' followers of, say, Carlyle or Newman, and had been transmitted to a comparatively large market with the aid of a facile pen, they were likely to be far more potent than the abstract, academic philosophy of many self-consciously 'radical' thinkers, which might only reach a small circle of admirers.[24]

Parry's, then, is an understanding of the political significance of ideas that situates them not in the context of other texts – as in the 'Cambridge

---

[21]   Parry, *Politics of Patriotism*, 31. For Williamson and Bentley's contributions in this vein, see esp. Philip Williamson, *Stanley Baldwin: Conservative Leadership and National Values* (Cambridge, 1999); Michael Bentley, *Lord Salisbury's World: Conservative Environments in Late-Victorian Britain* (Cambridge, 2001).

[22]   Parry, *Democracy and Religion*, 47.

[23]   Parry, *Democracy and Religion*.

[24]   J.P. Parry, 'The State of Victorian Political History', *Historical Journal*, 26 (1983), 469–84, at 472.

Introduction   7

School' of the history of political thought associated with Quentin Skinner, J.G.A. Pocock and John Dunn – but in the context of political *practice*. It is an understanding, moreover, that involves sensitivity not only to the subtleties of ideological positions, but also to the personalities and life experiences of the politicians who adopted them. Such a sensitivity to the people behind the discourse is one notable way in which Parry's work can be distinguished from that of the New Political History, and is beautifully demonstrated by his work on Benjamin Disraeli, Lord John Russell, John Buchan and other figures, but is also apparent across his oeuvre as a whole.[25] It is an emphasis that doubtless owes much to the influence of his doctoral supervisor, Derek Beales (the apt title of whose *festschrift* was *History and Biography*), as well as to Cowling, for whom 'political activity was... very much a matter of personality, of individual temperaments, concerns, purposes and aversions'.[26]

As perhaps most apparent in his more biographically-focused work, Parry's history-writing has paid considerable attention not only to the cultural hinterland of political practice, but also to 'culture' itself – whether this be the fiction of Buchan and Disraeli, the archaeological excavations of A.H. Layard in the Ottoman Middle East, or the often abstruse content of Victorian theological debate.[27] This dimension of his work, apparent also from the content of the courses he taught at the University of Cambridge,[28] is reflected in the chapters that make up the present volume. More generally, however, the essays follow Parry by taking ideas seriously, but not detaching these ideas from political personalities or their practice of politics, while at the same emphasising the significance of the wider intellectual and cultural context in which politics took place. The book as a whole thus demonstrates the utility of an approach that

[25] J.P. Parry, 'From the Thirty-nine Articles to the Thirty-nine Steps: Reflections on the Thought of John Buchan', in Michael Bentley (ed.), *Public and Private Doctrine: Essays in British History Presented to Maurice Cowling* (Cambridge, 1993), 209–35; 'Past and Future in the Later Career of Lord John Russell', in T.C.W. Blanning and David Cannadine (eds), *History and Biography: Essays in Honour of Derek Beales* (Cambridge, 1996), 142–72; *Benjamin Disraeli* (Oxford, 2007). See also the entertaining biographical notes in Parry, *Rise and Fall*, 319–34.

[26] Williamson, 'Maurice Cowling and Modern British Political History', 125.

[27] Parry, 'From the Thirty-nine Articles to the Thirty-nine Steps'; *Disraeli*; 'Disraeli, the East and Religion: *Tancred* in Context', *English Historical Review*, 132 (2017), 570–604; 'Henry Layard and the British Parliament: Outsider and Expert', in Stefania Ermidoro and Cecilia Riva (eds), *Rethinking Layard 1817–2017* (Venice, 2020), 155–70; *Democracy and Religion*; 'Christian Socialism, Class Collaboration, and British Public Life after 1848', in Douglas Moggach and Gareth Stedman Jones (eds), *The 1848 Revolutions and European Political Thought* (Cambridge, 2018), 162–84.

[28] Among them 'The British and Europe, 1815–1906', 'Culture Wars in Mid-Victorian England 1848–59', and 'The British and the Ottoman Middle East, 1798–c.1850'.

places culture, thought and belief at the heart of any satisfactory understanding of British political history since 1800.

In pursuit of this aim, the chapters have been organised around themes reflective of some of the key preoccupations of Parry's work to date. The first two attend to the practice of writing modern British history and call up two very different cognitive contexts to illustrate the conscious as well as the less conscious experiences that shape the historical mind. In proposing 'comparative historiography' as a subject capable of extracting parallels and absences in authorial awareness, Michael Bentley re-assembles the 'subterranean structures' of British and European scholarship on nineteenth-century Liberalism as they operated in the period during which Parry published his three volumes on English Liberalism. The imperatives and forces that shaped the Liberal environment – political economy, religious establishment and pluralism, state-formation, nationalism, bourgeois and aristocratic interests – had a degree of commonality that was Europe-wide. Yet its treatment by historians resulted in bifurcation, typically along national lines, giving us distinct historiographies of which Parry's is one. Reflecting in part the national distinctiveness of the British experience – industrial precocity, an aristocratic reform tradition in the shape of the Whigs, a unitary centre at Westminster – Parry's formulation of British (or English) Liberalism also reflected his own 'situational distinctiveness' as a working historian. If this is apparent only in retrospect, the historian nonetheless occupies a present whose bearing upon historical thinking and writing can, if so desired, form the subject of methodological reflection of an acutely conscious kind. We see this in the case of George Macaulay Trevelyan, the subject of Paul Readman's chapter. Like many of his (largely Liberal) contemporaries, Trevelyan's love of walking did much to refine his historical sensibility beyond the confines of archive and library, so much so that he evangelised its value as a tool that might be seen as carrying anthropological potential. It sharpened the skill of observation and fostered an 'empathetic imagination' with which to recall and interpret the past. A century on from Trevelyan, Readman claims the writing of British history stands to benefit from 'integrating direct experience of landscape and place into our historical practice.'[29]

For Parry, as for Trevelyan, the 'nation' has remained perhaps the ultimate subject of concern for any faithful understanding of political life in modern Britain – indisputably important as the object of political designs and as the chief stage on which politicians and their various interlocutors performed. Treated not as a primordial or nativistic entity, but as a phenomenon susceptible to multiple constructions and contestations, it emerges in Parry's work as something highly situational in the nineteenth and early twentieth centuries.

---

[29] For a sympathetic example, in miniature, see Jonathan Parry, 'Life on Sark', *London Review of Books*, 45 (18 May 2023).

Introduction 9

Radicals, Whigs and Tories staked their separate claims to the guardianship of the 'national interest' by condemning as corrupting influences the factions and parties to which their opponents were perceived to belong. But as parliament underwent reform and the party system became more widely accepted after 1832, patriotic rhetoric grew less fevered, and there emerged a shared – if not consensual – prescription of patriotism that prioritised the defence of constitutional ideals. Indeed, for Parry, 'the most important development in the whole century was the sense, from about 1850, that the nation was broadly united as a political community – that patriotism had real depth and strength'.[30] The reach and potency of this idea of the nation reflected the myriad ways in which seemingly non-political sources articulated its qualities to the public, through symbolism – as Parry has shown in the case of the monarchy[31] – and through metaphor, as discussed by James Thompson and Matthew Cragoe in the present volume. In Thompson's chapter, the English country house, as visually represented in the Victorian illustrated press, is shown to have attracted analogies with the British constitution and the English nation. In Cragoe's study, it is village cricket, the subject of novelist Hugh de Sélincourt's best-seller, *The Cricket Match* (1924), that provides the metaphor – representing the more inward-looking national self-image that proliferated after the Great War and the avowedly non-sectional, cross-class claims of Baldwinite Englishness.

Almost any conception of the nation was of course a contested conception of the nation, and nothing disrupted the trajectory of mid-Victorian patriotism more than Irish nationalism and Gladstone's response to it.[32] The place of another 'Celtic' nation, Wales, within the 'British' political nation is the subject of Geraint Thomas's chapter, which takes as its focus the career of David Lloyd George. As Thomas shows, Lloyd George recognised the value of his Welsh-nationalist and British-Unionist identities in forging a distinct political persona for himself at home and abroad. However, his assessment of the benefits and disbenefits of the Anglo-Welsh union for Wales was nonetheless grounded in a concern with those ideals of representative government that were integral to mid-Victorian patriotism.

The third section considers the role of ideas in political life. Like Parry, the authors conceive of 'ideas' not as canonical monoliths carrying theoretical definitions but as doctrines constituted of objectives and prejudices and, to borrow R.G. Collingwood's definition of political history, that 'thought which

---

[30] Jonathan Parry, 'Patriotism', in David Craig and James Thompson (eds), *Languages of Politics in Nineteenth-century Britain* (Basingstoke, 2013), 69–71.

[31] Jonathan Parry, 'Whig Monarchy, Whig Nation: Crown, Politics and Representativeness, 1800–2000', in Andrzej Olechnowicz (ed.), *The Monarchy and the British Nation, 1780 to the Present* (Cambridge, 2007), 47–75.

[32] Parry, *Rise and Fall*, 292–303; 'Patriotism', 84–6.

occupies the mind of a man engaged in political work.[33] The relationship between ideas and political practice emerges as something more-or-less mutually constitutive. As Boyd Hilton demonstrates in his survey of the career of 'small state' ideology in the two centuries since Pitt the Younger, the process of promoting and implementing a policy was rarely secure against the unknown impact of political contingencies. Yet seldom did it lack political opportunity. 'The shrewdest politicians sought to manipulate... incoherent happenstances in a particular direction' through rhetoric. In doing so, they endowed 'ideas' with explicable meaning, nurturing public doctrines that came to carry their own distinctive set of claims, interests, associations and traditions over time and across generations. If the public evolution of policy in this way highlights the importance of circumstance, Helen McCarthy and David Cannadine, in their chapters, demonstrate the extent to which the personal political commitments and identities of some notable late-Victorian figures were forged from their intellectual relationships and friendships. In her exploration of the intergenerational friendship that bound Margaret Cole and Beatrice Webb to one another, and to socialism, McCarthy shows the importance of intimacy and loyalty to our understanding of political action. The friendship between Winston Churchill and G.M. Trevelyan, the subject of Cannadine's chapter, was marked less by intimacy or political action. Yet as their correspondence reveals, the two Edwardian Liberals shared and perpetuated a distinctive cultural world. Defined by a profound devotion to Britain's national history, and to their dynastic connections to it, this worldview carried Victorian conceptions of good political leadership – as culturally attuned to the past as much as the present – into the mid-twentieth century.

The afterlife of Victorian political ideas is also evident in Philip Williamson's chapter on political nonconformity. Although chapel adherence and partisan (Liberal-aligned) nonconformity declined after 1906, especially in England, the free churches wielded considerable political agency in the interwar years – the result of denominational leaders skilfully positioning themselves within the burgeoning landscape of non-party voluntary associations; and doing so, crucially, with encouragement from the Church of England as well as Baldwin as Conservative leader. By the 1940s, nonconformity occupied an uncontested place in the national establishment. This development could be said to represent the fulfilment of a key idea of Liberal government according to Parry, namely its 'notion of religion as a broad, modern and essentially undogmatic creed capable of speaking to and uniting the whole nation.'[34]

---

[33] R.G. Collingwood, *An Autobiography* (Oxford, 1939; 1978), 110.

[34] Parry, *Rise and Fall*, 4; see also Jonathan Parry, 'The Disciplining of the Religious Conscience in Nineteenth-century British Politics', in Ira Katznelson and Gareth Stedman Jones (eds), *Religion and the Political Imagination* (Cambridge, 2010), 214–34.

Introduction   11

The same 'integrating' motive was responsible for framing nineteenth-century Liberal attitudes towards the institutions of state, the focus of our fourth section. 'If nineteenth-century Liberalism meant anything', according to Parry, 'it meant a political system in which a large number of potentially incompatible interests... were mature enough to accept an over-arching code of law which guaranteed each a wide variety of liberties'. Such maturity required public acceptance of political institutions and 'popular acquiescence in legislation'.[35] Signifying the rejection of 'Old Corruption', the project of institutional reform hitherto propelled by Radicals was increasingly embraced by the emerging Liberal party in the decades after 1832. As Ben Griffin and Kathryn Rix show in their chapters, the result was the introduction of powerful and far-reaching new norms to the relationship between the nation's political institutions and its people. Griffin explores the concerted efforts of nineteenth-century politicians to demarcate law and politics as separate and discrete areas of governance. By removing judges from government and from the House of Commons, not only did they disentangle the incestuous legal-political formations that operated in the eighteenth century; they succeeded in establishing, over time, a mutual system – marked by a 'non-political' judiciary and a 'non-judicial' parliament – that dominated until the re-juridification of British politics witnessed in our own time. The same period saw the emergence of a 'culture of accountability' around parliament itself, especially the activities of MPs in the Commons. As Rix argues, from the 1830s, the reporting of debates, recording of divisions and publication of parliamentary papers signalled a proliferation of 'official information', the circulation of which transformed communication between Members and their constituents and facilitated greater public scrutiny.

The emphasis on institutional reform faded markedly in the second half of the nineteenth century – the result, as Parry sees it, of a 'significant shift in *perceptions* of the legitimacy of the state'.[36] How did this shift come about? Tom Crewe, in his chapter, suggests that political celebrity could itself ascribe legitimacy to institutions. Robert Gascoyne-Cecil, the third marquess of Salisbury, who famously opposed the 1867 Reform Act, was an unlikely celebrity. Yet through the construction and projection of his political persona, and the consequent sense of familiarity engendered in the public who encountered him on the platform and in the media, the Conservative aristocrat rendered democracy a fit and engaging institution for the resolution of popular grievances. Yet, if elite personalities could project, they could also be projected onto. Michael

[35] Parry, *Rise and Fall*, 3, 6.

[36] Jonathan Parry, 'The Decline of Institutional Reform in Nineteenth-century Britain', in David Feldman and Jon Lawrence (eds), *Structures and Transformations in Modern British History: Essays for Gareth Stedman Jones* (Cambridge, 2011), 164–86, at 165 (emphasis added).

Ledger-Lomas demonstrates this with reference to the monarchy, exploring how multiple and diverse religious leaders in Britain and the empire succeeded in ascribing 'piety' to King Edward VII. This marked a striking, and perhaps unexpected, continuity with the religiosity projected onto his mother, Queen Victoria. More than that, in illustrating the reputation of monarchy as 'protector of religion' – Protestant and non-Protestant, established and dissenting – Ledger-Lomas reconstructs an important component of the 'rationality' that underpinned popular acquiescence in monarchy.

The fifth and final section turns to Britain in the world, reflecting the preoccupations of Parry's two most recent monographs. In *The Politics of Patriotism* he charted the connection between domestic and foreign issues and its role in fostering a nationalistic yet progressive form of popular Liberalism in the mid-nineteenth century. 'The constant articulation of pride in the values that Britain projected to the world' – constitutionalism, tolerance, fiscal accountability, free trade, Christian humanitarianism – 'helped to define [the state's] purpose and underpin state legitimacy to a broader public at home'.[37] Except, of course, in Ireland. As argued in John and Paul Bew's chapter, British Liberal constitutionalism, avowedly assimilationist and self-defined in contradistinction to the spectre of continental autocracy, could neither accommodate separatist rebellion nor justify coercive legislation. Faced with this existential dilemma, the Irish question became for Gladstone a question about 'the destiny of liberalism' itself. His solution – Home Rule for Ireland – prompted him retroactively to view the Anglo-Irish union as a regrettable anomaly, a contortion made possible only by what the Bews identify as a degree of self-deception within Liberal minds by the 1880s. The following chapter, by Alex Middleton, explores the growing interest in Latin America evident among the British political class at the turn of the twentieth century. Like Parry's study of British incursions into and cultural engagement with the Ottoman Middle East a century earlier,[38] he traces the intellectual contexts in which Latin America – and South America more broadly – acquired additional geopolitical significance in the light of Great Power naval rivalry and US imperial ambitions.

In contrast to the largely 'informal' nature of Britain's involvement in the Middle East and South America, the distinct legacies of Britain's 'formal' empire make up the theme of the final two chapters. Susan D. Pennybacker investigates the lives of individuals, born or raised in India and South Africa, who received their higher education in Oxford, Cambridge and London in the decades after

---

[37] Parry, *Politics of Patriotism*, 387, 389.

[38] Jonathan Parry, *Promised Lands: The British and the Ottoman Middle East* (Princeton, 2022); also 'Steam Power and British Influence in Baghdad, 1820–1860', *Historical Journal*, 56 (2013), 145–73 and 'The Land Between Rivers', *History Today*, 73 (2023), 28–39.

1945. Though these elite institutions imparted the conventions and discourses of British political culture, they also afforded fertile contexts for the 'altered and self-questioning commitments' that shaped these individuals' subsequent political activism within the former empire. Joanna Lewis considers the case of the statue erected in Denbigh in 2010 to commemorate the Victorian imperial figure, Sir Henry Morton Stanley (1841–1904), who had been born in the town. As Lewis's chapter suggests, the delay in public recognition can be read as symptomatic of the relative absence of imperial consciousness in Welsh rural life as well as a response to Stanley's ambivalence about his Welsh heritage.

Part I

Writing Modern British History

Chapter 1

Parry Passu: Jonathan Parry in European Echo

Michael Bentley

It seems a hard thing to celebrate our dedicatee by talking about everyone else. Jonathan Parry's extensive work in nineteenth-century British history demands consideration in its own terms and within its own parameters. It stretches from an early concern with the nature of Liberal high politics to a broadening focus on the cultural history of British public life, a concern most evident in his short study of Disraeli.[1] It encompasses Europe and the Middle East as formative contexts for the development of British politics and policy,[2] to be sure, but the centre of gravity in all that Parry has produced remains firmly Anglocentric and anglophone. Why, then, think about correspondences and contradictions within European historiography in relation to that oeuvre? The risk beckons of claiming parallels or contrasts that suggest at best indulgence, and at worst irrelevance. As in substantive historical criticism, however, one might, in reviewing a period of historiography, point to levels of analysis that take one beyond – or, perhaps better to say *below* – authorial horizons to drill down into subterranean structures apparent to nobody at the time of writing. Professional historians know what they are saying when they say it. They do not, because they cannot, know what they are *doing*. The doingness appears only in retrospect when it finds a location within contexts far from consciousness at the moment of creation. Perhaps readers will forgive a personal anecdote by way of illustration. Many years ago I led a seminar at Columbia University in New York by offering thoughts on what I saw as family resemblances and joint perceptions between French historiography at the beginning of the twentieth century, epitomised in Charles-Olivier Carbonell's study of proto-*Annaliste* tendencies, and the emergence in the United States during the same period of moods that led towards the 'New History'

---

[1] Jonathan Parry, *Benjamin Disraeli* (Oxford, 2007).

[2] Jonathan Parry, *The Politics of Patriotism: English Liberalism, National Identity and Europe, 1830–1886* (Cambridge, 2006); *Promised Lands: The British and the Ottoman Middle East* (Princeton, 2022).

18   *Michael Bentley*

proclaimed by James Harvey Robinson, Charles Beard and others.[3] Those two national persuasions occurred almost entirely without conscious mutual interaction; it was as though a tectonic plate somehow connected them, one whose shifts helped propel a slide towards the sociological and anthropological in historical awareness. A person present in the seminar, the distinguished historian of Japan, Carol Gluck, then pointed out, to general fascination and bafflement, that precisely the same tendencies at precisely the same time had characterised Japanese historiography. What on earth (literally) could have been going on?

One way of thinking about experiences of this kind emerges if we propose the existence, as I intend here, of a subject we rarely acknowledge, still less investigate. Let us call it 'comparative historiography'. And since this essay seeks to situate Parry's work within that frame it may make sense to offer a short excursus about what this form of analysis involves in order to defend its plausibility.

The idea of 'comparative history' needs no defence. It has a long pedigree reaching back to Pirenne's famous address to the Brussels international congress in 1923.[4] In the audience that day, one attendee took away its lessons and resolved to apply them, as he did with great brilliance; so when we think of comparative history as a successful genre we think at once of Marc Bloch and, for example, the way he brought to the history of field systems in France the questions he had raised about enclosure of fields in England – the background to his Oslo lectures in 1928 which gave rise to one of his best books.[5] That tradition has borne much fruit and it has become omnipresent in our own historical world as global comparative history, or in 'transnational history, 'entanglement history' and the fashion for *histoire croisée*. Yet this style of enquiry turns on conscious extensions of historical method to revisit geographical correspondences by pursuing the conscious intentions of historical agents: it travels across the ground rather than beneath it. Comparative *historiography* works differently by situating itself within a particular period or genre of historical thought and writing, rather than with overt historical events, and it seeks a level of explanation below authorial awareness or intention. It can only work at its fullest potential in the light of retrospect to reveal structures and persuasions operating beyond contemporary consciousness. It imports one significant aspect from Bloch's comparative history: its explanatory method. Historians have their customary toolbox of questions – when, what, how, who

---

[3]   Charles-Olivier Carbonell and Georges Livet (eds), *Au Berceau des Annales: le milieu strasbourgeois* (Toulouse, 1983); James Harvey Robinson (ed.), *The New History: Essays Illustrating the Modern Historical Outlook* (New York, 1912).

[4]   Henri Pirenne, 'The Comparative Method in History', *5th International Congress of Historical Sciences* (Brussels, 1923), much reprinted.

[5]   Marc Bloch, *Les caractères originaux de l'histoire rurale française* (Oslo, 1931).

and above all, why? To Bloch we owe the comparative question which lends the enquiry its greatest power: not why? but rather why *not*? This gives comparative historiography its penetration and logic. If in culture A we notice an historiographical formation P, then why in culture B, which resembles A in many of its characteristics, do we *not* discern P but instead Q? How do we account for such presences and absences?

Maybe Parry's European echoes now appear less far-fetched. For attempting to locate those subterranean, tectonic structures within historical accounts of nineteenth-century Liberalism may throw some illumination on both sides of the Channel.[6] It will do so, moreover, as much through contrast as similitude. A fatal assumption, one all too common among evangelists of comparative study, begins with the mistake of seeing the point of comparison to detect resemblance when its sharpest perceptions often derive from the lack of one. Distinctiveness is a virtue; it does not have to flush down the pan of 'exceptionalism', an idea which itself feeds from an unsavoury attachment to 'processes' and underlying conditioning from modernisation theory or its pre-modern equivalents. The point has particular force when directed at the work of a single historian when sceptical observers may feel that the result of a comparative treatment will somehow dilute the singular distinction of the subject. Quite the opposite: one is not considering distinction, which in Parry's case needs no elaboration, but rather location, context and contrast. And the point of the exercise is that it throws light both on the subject of study and on his or her comparators among whom the oeuvre may be placed. As the wonderful Welsh wizard of historiography, Rees Davies, once remarked, comparative questions 'serve to make our historical antennae more sensitive, especially to those features of respective "national" histories which we often take for granted and do not begin to explain.'[7] We emerge from our comparative questions with three, we hope for four, dimensions providing depth and width and an enhanced sense of temporality that better represents all participants. It is a 'big ask' but, once we stop asking, the past whispers no reply.

The Liberal Trilogy

Applying this logic to Parry's case demands a thorough reading of his books with a view to abstracting their overall thrust, their undertows of exposition and approach, their choice of method. To do this with all of them would lead

---

[6]   Upper-case Liberalism is often hard to separate from lower-case liberalism, especially in the European context. In this essay, lower-case is used only when it explicitly relates to thought and doctrine rather than political formations.

[7]   R.R. Davies, 'In Praise of British History', in Davies (ed.), *The British Isles 1100–1500: Comparisons, Contrasts and Connections* (Edinburgh, 1988), 21.

20   *Michael Bentley*

to incoherence since Parry has thought and written about nineteenth-century England for almost forty years; the later work, with its emerging cultural focus and the recent turn towards foreign policy, does not readily compress into the earlier for comparative purposes.[8] What follows will reflect, therefore, solely on three books published in the two decades from 1986 to 2006. They present a trilogy intended to provide a history of British, mostly English, Liberalism between 1830 and 1886 and they manifest a number of key ingredients suitable for reading across time and space.[9]

First, the periodicity of the trilogy is entirely consistent, running from the Whig accession to power in 1830 to the impact of the Third Reform Bill and Gladstone's move towards Home Rule in 1886. Parry made this period his own and saw within it a particular coming-into-being among the complications of English high politics. Complications he certainly accepted: who could not amid the fissiparousness of the Whig-Liberal party, its endless trimming and negoti-ation? He did not wish to decaffeinate high politics by pretending that it could be explained through the 'beliefs' of participants, as in a chapter of Trollope or Galsworthy. Ringing in his ears, even twenty years *après la lettre*, John Vincent's conclusion that the Liberal party amounted to no more than 'a coa-lition of convenience, not the instrument of a creed',[10] would have made Parry think twice about making Liberal 'ideology' (whatever that meant) a causal agent in political explanation. '[I]t is no longer possible' he wrote in the first volume, 'to assume a simple connection between an individual's ideas and his political activity.'[11] But that did not mean ruling out a complex connection and he made its tracing his purpose. He went beyond Vincent, as he did beyond Maurice Cowling's *1867* and then Cooke and Vincent on *The Governing Passion*, in seeing English Liberalism as a *thing*: an emerging identity recognised by its adherents who knew by association and instinct what it was and what it meant in what Germans might call a *Deutungsmuster*.[12] And, whatever it meant, the English Liberal party transcended faction, sect and wing in its sense of what a

---

[8]   See esp. the study of *Benjamin Disraeli*, where Parry takes to task those histori-ans who have remained sceptical about 'integrat[ing] his ideas with his practice' (p. 123); and *Promised Lands* devoted to British foreign policy towards the Middle East in an earlier period.

[9]   J.P. Parry, *Democracy and Religion: Gladstone and the Liberal Party, 1867–1875* (Cambridge, 1986); *The Rise and Fall of Liberal Government in Victorian Britain* (New Haven & London, 1993); *Politics of Patriotism*.

[10]   J.R. Vincent, *The Formation of the British Liberal Party, 1857–1868* (Harmond-sworth, 1972 [1966]), 290.

[11]   Parry, *Democracy and Religion*, 3.

[12]   Maurice Cowling, *1867, Disraeli, Gladstone and Revolution: The Passing of the Second Reform Bill* (Cambridge, 1967); A.B. Cooke and John Vincent, *The Governing Passion: Cabinet Government and Party Politics in Britain, 1885–1886* (Brighton, 1974).

Liberal government ought to be for, why it mattered and how to go about persuading 'the people' – its people – that they should support the project.

Nor need conceding the absence of a creed imply the lack of a *mission* in the most centralised and mature state in Europe, one still struggling to govern itself, not through 'democracy', which nobody wanted, but through representative institutions. Parry presents England's nineteenth century as a unique polity partly because of its advanced state-formation in relation to most countries in Europe: a crucial point which again can be read sideways in thinking about liberalism in Spain with its early *trienio* (1820–23), in France governed by the consequences of Napoleonic statecraft, in the Low countries with 1830 as their benchmark, and in the German lands looking for their own unified state after 1848. Liberal mission in England takes the form, in Parry's hands, of attempting to educate and elevate its imagined constituency. Certainly they espoused 'capacity' as a criterion for Liberal citizenship but not, as a recent study suggests, to defend or ringfence their existing constituency but rather to expand it through the promulgation of values and especially through religion and church simply because 'it was only religious issues which *were* able to link the world with which the politically interested public was concerned to the high political world.'[13] Consequently it was legitimate and desirable for the state to give moral guidance, just as it was part of Gladstone's success that he came to be seen as a spiritual as much as a political leader.[14] These values dominated the first volume of the trilogy and penetrated the second in ways that would have been more obvious from Parry's original title which Yale University Press chose to reconfigure. *Learning to Govern the People* may not have enhanced the sales promised by *The Rise and Fall of Liberal Government* but it would better have addressed the volume's point and direction. It might also have introduced a thesis open to comparative study.

The third volume of Parry's trilogy seemingly differs from its predecessors in providing a reception-history of events in Europe. Little time is spent on European events themselves: 'British debates about world affairs were insular.'[15] We do not acquire much knowledge of the Low Countries' coming to independence in 1830, or of the 1848 revolutions, or of the Risorgimento, or of the impact of Bismarck on Denmark and Austria, or of the Franco-Prussian war and the Commune. Instead, these events find their way into the patterns and discourse of English high politics and then become re-emitted at a new wavelength to the Liberal constituency as justification for a specifically Liberal form of nationalism which Palmerston did much to embody. We remain within

---

[13]   Parry, *Democracy and Religion*, 53 [original emphasis]. Cf. Alan S. Kahan, *Liberalism in Nineteenth-century Europe* (Basingstoke, 2003).

[14]   Parry, *Democracy and Religion*, 448, 452.

[15]   Parry, *Politics of Patriotism*, 5, 399.

'the political strategies, tactics and languages pursued by Liberals of the Parliamentary class.'[16] But I want, perhaps provocatively, to suggest that *all* parts of the trilogy take the form of a reception history. For in the treatment of domestic politics as much as in considering foreign stimuli, Parry conceives Westminster as a hub for receiving environmental and peripheral messages, imperatives, requests and threats which those active in high politics then re-emit at their chosen wavelength in a language of persuasion. It goes without saying that this procedure renders the trilogy Anglocentric and comes close to assuming a certain exceptionalism. No criticism of Parry is intended, granted his objectives, in reporting that the result is also anglophone. The excellent bibliographies appended to each volume contain, on a cursory glance, only one item published in a language other than English. Whether that matters will only appear from a comparative sense of how European texts about liberalism conduct themselves.

These operational issues – *modes d'emploi* – take us to the final element in Parry's trilogy which calls for abstraction and comparison: the question of method. Among a largely unconceptual and unselfconscious cohort of historians, Parry stands out for his interest in conceptual matters and historical method in relation to the study of high politics. He sees himself as heir to English traditions running two or two and a half decades deep,[17] and he wants to go beyond them in widening the net of high-political evidence to encompass intellectual and religious currents that the austerities of Cowling and Vincent had tended to exclude. He confesses to an interest in rhetoric: not as a 'situational' requirement as Cowling had contended but as a form worth studying in its own right, partly for the limits and opportunities it established in political action but also and increasingly throughout the trilogy out of a wish to reinstate belief and conviction as causal agencies in political behaviour. So 'prejudices and "ideas"' should not disappear from political histories; historians should pay more attention 'to the intellectual setting in which political activity takes place.'[18] They should seek a 'conception of the integrating function and rational nature of politics.'[19] They should understand that policy had its origins 'in terms of values as well as strategy.'[20] It would be stimulating to know whether European historians echoed that imperative in their own encapsulations of nineteenth-century liberalism.

An historian wanting to make sense of Parry's oeuvre will need to ponder these and other elements among the books that he has written. An

---

[16] *Ibid.*, 30.

[17] Parry, *Democracy and Religion*, 1; *Rise and Fall*, 17–18.

[18] Parry, *Democracy and Religion*, 3.

[19] Parry, *Rise and Fall*, 7.

[20] Parry, *Politics of Patriotism*, 5.

historiographer, on the other hand, needs no less urgently to consider the books that he has not. He has not written a history of liberal political thought from Bentham to T.H. Green and given great space to John Stuart Mill. He has not written an account of liberal political economy that would make Cobden, Bright and the League as significant as Russell, Palmerston or Gladstone. He has not, unlike the previous generation of scholars, written a regional or local account of Liberal party politics demonstrating the strength or waywardness of provincial objectives. He has not grounded Liberal politics in a systematic study of demography with a stress on the eternally rising middle classes in order to lend nineteenth-century liberalism its social anchorage. Evading these aspects of liberal history made, of course, complete sense within Parry's own schemata. Political thought had never been a central interest in any case, and he wanted to locate Liberal identity in looser constellations of ideas and practices. Political economy did not warm his cockles either, not only because the drift of the trilogy runs away from that theme as a causal element but also since, during Parry's period of composition, other scholars were pursuing that theme with some distinction: Norman McCord, Tony Howe and Frank Trentmann come at once to mind.[21] If he did not turn to regionalism (nor to a major incorporation of Scotland, Wales and Ireland), then one could say that the approach had been given a strong airing after 1970 and that it would in any case have been counter-thematic for Parry to dwell on the extra-parliamentary in a study seeking to emphasise the centralisation of a mature Liberal state. Equally, to dwell on horizontal structures in Victorian society, and especially that of class, would likewise have cut across the grain. Class and vertical sections such as the Church appear constantly in Parry's books but they do so as elements in an integrative, rather than a fissiparous, function in political life, a place where sensitive leadership from the centre 'could succeed in reconciling tensions and subordinating sectional pressures'.[22]

If these four absences draw no blood from Parry's presentation of Victorian liberalism, then what is the point of dwelling upon them or raising them at all? For one simple reason that might interest a comparative project: those four absences constitute the four preponderant *presences* in all German and much Spanish, Italian, Belgian and Dutch images of nineteenth-century Liberalism. Perhaps the time has come to wonder why.

---

[21] Norman McCord, *Free Trade: Theory and Practice from Adam Smith to Keynes* (Newton Abbot, 1970) and *The Anti-Corn Law League, 1838–1846* (London, 1958); Anthony Howe, *Free Trade and Liberal England, 1846–1946* (Oxford, 1997); Frank Trentmann, *Free Trade Nation: Commerce, Consumption, and Civil Society in Modern Britain* (Oxford, 2008).

[22] Parry, *Rise and Fall*, 8.

24   *Michael Bentley*

Liberal histories in Europe intertwine three narratives unfamiliar in Britain. First of all, virtually every state, both in Europe and throughout Central and South America, possesses a *liberation* narrative. This normally has its anchorage in French or Austrian domination and occupation. Release from what was seen as bondage, in 1813, 1820, 1830 or 1860 generated a second story in the acquisition of a *national* narrative celebrating a sense of independent identity. Third, a concentration on internal governance in these 'new' nations and emerging states constructed a *constitutional* narrative intended to show progress towards limiting arbitrary power of monarchs and promoting the idea of parliamentary stewardship. This took inspiration from the French revolutionary constitution of 1793, never implemented and abrogated by the Directory and Napoleon, and later the Cadiz constitution of 1812 after which liberalism itself could come into focus as no more than 'une pensée de la constitution.'[23] Because of that plaited history of advance, each strand teleological in a different way, liberal histories written in the nineteenth century do not reduce to a single trajectory but demand a wider perspective than may seem obvious. In the twentieth century a further complication appeared in a retrospect of philosophical enquiry and context. It no more escaped teleology than had its predecessors and showed a remarkable degree of consistency in its content. By the time that Parry had moved forwards in his thinking about how to present British Liberalism, continental scholars had already formulated a firm, not to say sclerotic, impression of what liberalism was, where it came from and why it died. They saw it as an entity, to be sure, but their liberalism took the form, first and essentially, of an intellectual, philosophical and doctrinal configuration, not as a collective noun for Liberal practices.

European Perspectives

Like their constitutions, European historians of liberalism saw its best expression in texts; and the texts did not vary significantly. From Brussels to Bogatá, everything began with John Locke and particularly the second 'Treatise on Government' and his 'Essay Concerning Human Understanding', both of which dated from 1689.[24] The German case proved particularly pressing in a culture saturated from philosophical approaches to mundanity. One of its exponents in Parry's period, Lothar Gall, had edited some years earlier a well-known text called simply *Liberalismus*.[25] A second and unchanged edition appeared,

---

[23] Nicolas Roussellier, 'Libéralisme et institutions', *Mélanges de l'école française de Rome*, 114 (2002), 629.

[24] E.g. Ricardo Vélez Rodríguez, *Liberalismo y conservatismo en América Latina* (Bogatá, 1978), 9–10, 72.

[25] Lothar Gall, *Liberalismus* (Cologne, 1976).

significantly, in 1980. A collection of texts from a variety of locations – an English perspective was included in Bullock and Shock on *The Liberal Tradition* which had run into criticism in Britain since at least 1969[26] – it began with four extracts from theoretical or philosophical sources. In the following year, 1981, Gall and a collaborator edited four volumes of texts intended to ground liberalism in Europe as a form of political thought and their rollcall of actors merits recall. The first instalment considered liberty (Locke, Mill, Ritchie and Hobhouse) and state formation (Locke, Kant, Dahlmann, Bastiat); the second liberty plus democracy (Tocqueville, Guizot, Pareto); the third nation and empire (Locke, Mazzini, Hobson, Weber) and political economy with the 'social question' (Adam Smith, Malthus, Sismondi, Mill and Lloyd George!); the fourth discussed *fin de siècle* liberalism in, weirdly, Escott, Naumann and Hobhouse again.[27] This list matters in lending insight into how German scholars have tended to envisage Liberalism as a phenomenon better described (in lower case) as liberal theory. When an American historian of German Liberalism approached his subject at the end of the 1990s, his intellectual experience – he had been taught by Hayek at Chicago and had translated Mises – played directly into that supposition. 'At the centre of my work,' he wrote, 'stands political philosophy'. Systems of political thought, he continued, may not have a decisive effect on political action but they exercise none the less 'a powerful and independent influence on how historical events play out'.[28] Rarely in the German understanding of European Liberalism does this assumption not appear.

Other national perspectives of course arise. In an authoritarian culture such as nineteenth-century Spain, the idea of liberalism in the first half of the nineteenth century might become 'a fear-inspired concept' that traded on its Other of royal despotism.[29] In France one finds a greater acceptance that Liberalism, once 'un discours sur les libertés civiles', had by end of century

---

[26] Alan Bullock and Maurice Shock, *The Liberal Tradition from Fox to Keynes* (London, 1956). The use of 'traditions' as an analytical device met its Waterloo in Quentin Skinner's 'Meaning and Understanding in the History of Ideas', *History and Theory*, 8 (1969), 3–53 and had been targeted within Liberal historiography by the present writer among others: see Michael Bentley, *The Liberal Mind 1914–1929* (Cambridge, 1977). Gall's volume contained texts dating mostly from the 1950s and 1960s.

[27] Lothar Gall and Rainer Koch (eds), *Der europäische Liberalismus im 19. Jahrhundert: Texte zu seiner Entwicklung* (Frankfurt-am-Main, 1981). The final noun ('Development') speaks volumes for teleology.

[28] Ralph Raico, *Die Partei der Freiheit: Studien zur Geschichte des deutschen Liberalismus* (Stuttgart, 1999), xiv. [My translation.]

[29] Fidel Gómez Ochoa, 'El liberalismo conservador español del siglo XIX: la forja de una identidad política 1810–1840', *História y política*, 17 (2007), 37–68.

become 'un art politique de gouverner' in terms closer to Parry's English depiction.[30] One could agree that the idea of liberalism always remained 'un terme polysémique à la signification plurielle';[31] but it still seemed a requirement to trace the origins of liberal thought to the fifteenth and sixteenth centuries before embarking on the inevitable John Locke. Everywhere liberalism in its nineteenth-century format displayed a 'classical' mode with an Enlightenment flavour leading to a transitional mode of accommodation with industrialisation and proto-democracy and then ending with a vision of 'social liberalism' in which the working classes became at once the opportunity and ruin of Liberal politics. And this progress, for such it was, became a thing of texts in political thought far more than a catalogue of administrations and leading personalities in the parliamentary arena, where one existed at all.

Instead of seeing political leaders as crucial to the development of Liberal politics, with the partial exception of Thorbecke in the Netherlands, continental commentators turned rather to economic and social process as a generating element. It would be fatuous to deny the presence of economic and social transformation in the West during the nineteenth century: industrialisation became universal (though at different rates and in different periods); technological change revolutionised communication, both physical and social; relations between urban and rural societies altered in their relative strength to effect or prevent change. In writing the history of Liberalism in Parry's period, however, a difference in stress followed. For those shifts continued to be seen as causal, and not merely concomitant, in explanations of Liberal origins, success and failure. Where these things evaded explanation at the level of political thought and philosophy, they became intelligible on the ground, as it were, as the products of economic environment and social response. Historians tended, therefore, to follow that signpost in writing their accounts of Liberalism in its rise and seeming fall; and their narratives revealed their pilgrimage. First, economic protection had a grip on economic priority for much of the century after 1830 as nascent industrialisation made demands which Liberal politics could not ignore without danger. Most manifest in the German lands in the era of the *Zollverein*, it also arose in the Iberian countries where Spanish early-liberalism marked a conservative future by resisting free trade and market politics while Portuguese politics had protection and the demands of political economy at its centre.[32] A contrasting case occurred in the Netherlands – 'probably an exception in Europe' – where economic liberalism attracted a particular power

---

[30] Roussellier, 'Libéralisme et institutions', 630.

[31] Serge Bernstein, introducing a special issue on 'Le Libéralisme et les libéralismes en Europe', *Mélanges de l'école française de Rome*, 114 (2002), 667.

[32] For the Spanish case, see Gabriel Paquette, 'Romantic Liberalism in Spain and Portugal *c*.1825–1850', *Historical Journal*, 58 (2015), 481–511 esp. 486–8; and for Portugal

and social Liberalism became its child.[33] Second, this orientation towards economic process coloured periodisation. Parry could relax within Britain's industrial precocity from 1830. European historians looked to the period beyond 1870 when their industrial revolutions gathered pace, and beyond 1890 in the Italian case – fractured as the country was by an advancing north and a backward *mezzogiorno*. Their high-point of Liberal politics thus came late after Parry's constellation had already run into the sands of Irish nationalism. In Italy, indeed, the adjective *liberale* attached itself less to doctrine or economic structure but to a *period* relating to the half century after 1861.

Large-scale social and economic processes of this kind, married to peculiarities in the nature and rate of state-formation, brought with them the peril of generalisation. One way of dealing with that pointed towards writing the history of individual 'nations', during a period in which nationalism and liberalism informed one another, and tracking their internal conversations. Yet that, too, worked less well when the nation had yet to become self-conscious, when identities still struggled to express themselves, when political structures did not reflect those broader categories and trends on which historians wanted to remark. Go closer to the ground, became a recommendation from research directors of hundreds of Master's and doctoral students; come down from the stratosphere and show the application of those diffuse environments in a case study. Go regional; go local. So just at the time when Parry lifted the eyes of readers to consider the operation of Liberalism as a coherent national event with its energy-centre at Westminster, European scholarship of Liberalism as an embodied political presence carried its enquiry to a sometimes-literal coalface: the shopfloor, the factory, the trade union, the local council, the churches, the locations and practices of a place-specific and evolving *Bürgertum*.

Northern Europe furnished the most prominent examples of this regional historiography. When Lothar Gall's *Liberalismus* appeared, he stressed, even then, the need for a disintegrative method: the history of Liberalism, he insisted, had to consist in according each version of Liberalism 'a specific temporal and spatial frame'.[34] He intended those frames to be national. In 1992, however, when Gall was editor of the *Historische Zeitschrift*, he persuaded the then-guru of German Liberal historiography, Dieter Langewiesche, to compile a collection of papers from a *Tagung* on regional Liberalism in Germany and to publish the result as a *Beiheft* of the *HZ* which appeared in 1995.[35] Langewiesche's

---

specifically, Maria de Fátia Bonifácio, *Seis Estudos sobre o liberalismo Português* (Lisbon, 1991) in which several studies have economic protection at their centre.

[33] T.J. Boschloo, *De productiemaatschappij: Liberalisme, economische wetenschap en het vragstuk der armoede in Nederland 1800–1875* (Hilversum, 1989), 272–3.

[34] Gall, *Liberalismus*, 10.

[35] Dieter Langewiesche (ed.), *Liberalismus und Region* (Beiheft 19, Munich, 1995).

introduction to the volume lacked evangelism; he produced a tentative defence of a regional approach but worried about its penetration in a period dominated by state-formation and nationalism.[36] Yet the striking aspect of his collection comes with its narrowness of comparison and multiplicity of local detail. One might expect the treatment of Prussia, Saxony or Thuringia. But a concentration on Frankfurt, Baden, Munich, Kurhessen, Hamburg, Bremen, Hanover and Breslau suggests a finer filter, and this at a time – one year after the publication of Parry's *Rise and Fall* – when English historiography had moved away from a regional model. It said something, of course, about a need to offset the sheer dominance of Bismarckian Prussia and marked a drift to emphasising the experience of south-western Germany, the 'Hochburg des vormärzlichen Liberalismus', which turned out not so *hoch* as to prevent the *Kaiserproklamation* happening elsewhere.[37] The flood of regional and urban studies of Liberalism in Germany, Belgium, the Netherlands and northern France threatened to drown national imperatives for a time, with Liberalism in Nuremberg, Liberalism in Ghent, Liberalism in Groningen and, more quaintly, Liberalism in Le Havre which generated a style of politics unlike that even of its immediate neighbours.[38] At what point does regionalism in nineteenth-century political history thus descend to a methodological *pointillisme* of parish pump and market cross?

Southern Europe did not escape it, though its units proved larger. Spain's conversation with Catalonia hardly demanded much amplification and a millennial study brought the latter's unique liberalism into focus by silhouetting Barcelona's lawyers and their role in generating a conservative version of Liberal politics.[39] Yet regional particularities ran far beyond this famous disparity as they had done for centuries; and, although historians of Liberalism wanted to continue a tradition of celebrating the 'projecto Liberal que se articuló a partir de la Constitución de 1812', an imperative emerged in conceding that in this sphere as in every other, Aragon was not Andalusia, nor Castile Galicia.

---

[36] *Ibid.*, 1–4.

[37] See Frank Möller, 'Historische Erinnerung und politische Vision: die Idee des Kaisers in deutschen Liberalismus 1815–1871', in Dieter Hein, Klaus Hildebrand and Andreas Schulz (eds), *Historie und Leben: der Historiker als Wissenschaftler und Zeitgenosse* (Munich, 2006), 659.

[38] Petrus Müller, *Liberalismus in Nürnberg 1800 bis 1871* (Nuremberg, 1990); Emile Lamberts, *Kerk en Liberalisme in het Bisdom Gent 1821–1857* (Louvain, 1972); Gerrit Voerman, *Het Liberalisme in Groningen* (Groningen, 1995). Cf. Pierre Ardaillou's scepticism about the larger picture even across Normandy – 'il faut se méfier des visions générales' – in Ardaillou, 'Ni rouge, ni blanc, mais bleu: le libéralisme républicain havrais au XIXe siècle', *Études Normandes*, 49 (2000), 80.

[39] Stephen Jacobson, 'Droit et politique dans l'Espagne au XIX siècle: les avocats barcelonais et les particularités du libéralisme catalan', *Genèses*, 45 (2001), 4–26.

Gossamer threads could still hold the story together by proclaiming that local and regional peculiarities developed in tandem with nation-making and not in contradiction to it, but it seems awkward all the same to conceive of a national Liberalism of the kind Parry identified in England.[40] Colonial territories in Central and Latin America broke out of that account by involving their liberation narrative and seeing national divergence in state and institutional development within an overarching story of freedom from the metropole.

Italy meanwhile had succeeded, apparently, in achieving a Risorgimento and a national, unified, liberal state from 1861. The success was delusional. A blatant problem stood before the pioneers of Italian nationhood in the *mezzogiorno*, a huge area of the south in which, then as now, many inhabitants could not understand what neighbours from a nearby village were saying, and a region dominated by primitive agriculture unlikely to spawn liberal ideas of progress. So when Marco Minghetti wanted to offer his provinces 'l'esempio del *self-government* inglese', he whistled for the wind.[41] From the start, Italian proto-liberalism had its distinctive geography in leaders who self-identified as piemontesi, lombardi, toscani or emiliani before they saw themselves as Italians.[42] Even after the achievement of 'unity', Rome remained a conclave in both senses; the Veneto still languished in the shadow of Vienna; Sicily or Calabria might as well have been in the Balkans for all they could offer to the new Italian state. To talk of class in a Gramscian fashion still obsessed the Italian universities in the 1980s and 90s but the sheer fact of nobility – 'le radici aristocratiche' – as formative of Italian liberalism brooked little denial. Aristocratic values more than class conflict gave rise to a liberal sensibility that owed little to a 'borghesia commerciale e industriale', whether it were rising or not.[43]

Liberalism as a disembodied doctrine; Liberalism as a prescription from prevailing political economy; Liberalism as a collective noun for a pattern of local and regional particularities: these elements constitute three of the four 'absences' in Parry's formulation of the idea. The fourth unites and renders coherent what might otherwise seem inchoate. For nothing more characterises European tonality in its various renderings of liberal harmonies than a plangency about social and economic dynamics acting as the *fons et origo* of Liberal politics. This operates as an essential, not accompanying, characteristic:

---

[40] Josep Ramon Segarra i Estarelle, 'Liberalismo, História y provincialismo en las decadas centrales del siglo XIX', in *Las escalas del passado* (IV Congreso de história local de Aragón, 2005), 141.

[41] Quoted in Raffaele Romanelli, *L'Italia Liberale (1861–1900)* [Bologna, 1979], 39. His proposal died in the Italian Chamber.

[42] *Ibid.*, 17.

[43] See the vigorous lecture by Ettore Cuomo, *Il liberalismo europeo: il modello politico classico* (Naples, 1990).

essential because causal. On this series of assumptions, liberalism arose from a specific set of economic and social environments; it then, in upper-case, congealed into a form of practice intended to preserve itself by appealing to the interests and constituencies which those environments had favoured; it encouraged the confidence and representation of its own slice of bourgeoisie; it thrived when its exclusiveness matched its social power; it fell into desuetude when exclusion failed and the working classes emerged as a political force with their own very different ambitions and political strength. Looking back on this declared trajectory, European historians of liberalism and Liberal politics sang from the same sheet, regardless of their location. The world of nineteenth-century Liberalism could survive on this reading only so long as its urban and class foundation persisted or, in those regions where no such social base existed, so long as its leaders could find ways of masking the difficulty through a rhetoric of organic advance.

Northern Europe had the easier time in asserting *Bürgertum* as the social base of Liberalism. Some of this derived from the power and heritage of the town in northern European culture – a thought implicit since Pirenne – and the apparatus of councils and local functionaries, plus the undoubted urban control of an industrialising society, helped propel the *Bürger* to centre-stage in historical accounts. In Parry's period the most striking example of this assertion emerged in a Bielefeld research seminar in 1986/7, the moment of Parry's first book. An original focus on 'Bürgertum, Bürgerlichkeit und bürgerliche Gesellschaft', which carried the stamp of Jürgen Kocka, slid noiselessly, in the hands of Dieter Langewiesche, towards a publication now reading *Bürgertum und Liberalismus im 19. Jahrhundert*.[44] This in turn encouraged an editorial volume in the following year reflecting more generally on Liberalism as a German problem.[45] Kocka identified that problem at the outset; it arose from the postulated relationship between German Liberalism and the rise of a *Bürgertum*: 'ein zentrales Problem'.[46] Langewiesche in his own text acknowledged the existence throughout Europe of 'starken regionalen Differenzierungen', to be sure, and he warned against any attempt to reduce the basis of trans-European Liberalism to some 'eternal foundations'; but the undertow continued because, for all the geographical and social complications, Liberalism was 'a bürgerliche movement'.[47] They – the *Bürger* – had supplied the linkage between town, the wider society and an emerging state as unification ran forward and presented 'a major factor' in developing a public sphere that would bring together a familiar

---

[44] Dieter Langewiesche (ed.), *Bürgertum und Liberalismus im 19. Jahrhundert: Deutschland im europäischen Vergleich* (Göttingen, 1987).

[45] Dieter Langewiesche (ed.), *Liberalismus im 19. Jahrhundert* (Göttingen, 1988).

[46] Kocka in his Foreword to *ibid.*, 10.

[47] Langewiesche, in *ibid.*, 17

lifestyle and status, on the one hand, and the idea of establishing their own form of hegemony [*Herrschaftsraum*], on the other.[48] Dutch social structures may have been different but an historian of Liberalism there imagined the objectives of Liberalism in the 1850s and 1860s as a society resting on equal suffrage among a responsible, property-owning [*gegroede*] *Bürgertum*.[49]

One explanation for this stress on an urban bourgeoisie as the location of Liberalism, apart from the usual nod towards modernisation theory, consists in the operation of its Other: the European nobility. Their social and sometimes financial prominence tended not to lead in the direction of political – in the sense of parliamentary – involvement; their world revolved far more around monarchy as an ally in the project of limiting democratic incursions; their 'liberalism', in so far as they embodied it, extended only to modest constitutional reform. Such thoughts applied especially to central and southern European states: to Austria whose society during the *Vormärz* often still reflected semi-feudal structures;[50] or to Spain with its *hidalgo* instincts; or to Italy where unification and the establishment of the Liberal state owed more to aristocratic notables than popular pressure. Reflecting on the status of Germany's *Bürgertum*, David Blackbourn has reminded historians of the Western middle classes that '[t]he stakes for our view of Liberalism are high' if the German case (with its catastrophic termination in 1933) becomes the test of normality in nineteenth-century development.[51] But the stakes become no lower when casting an eye over the function, or lack of one, of Europe's aristocracies in the formation and progress of Liberal politics and their relationship, or lack of one, to an urban middle class and its Liberal agenda. A study of Italian *borghesia* after 1861 pointed vaguely to a Liberal involvement which never became the focus as it might have done in one considering German or Dutch politics.[52] A reworking of Spanish liberalism in 2001, in light of the 'cultural turn', reacted against the usual picture of local domination by *caciques* and presented a picture of the café, the press and the novel better representing liberalism than

---

[48] See Dieter Hein, 'Die Bürger zwishen Stadt, Staat und Nation: historische Erinnerung und politische Identität in Deutschland 1800–1850', in Hein et al, *Historie und Leben*, 673–4. This Festschrift for Lothar Gall can be supplemented by a collection of his essays on the same theme: Lothar Gall, *Bürgertum, liberale Bewegung und Nation* (Munich, 1996).

[49] Henk te Velde, *Gemeenschapszin en plichtsbesef: Liberalisme en Nationalisme in Nederland* (Groningen, 1992), 15.

[50] See Helmut Reinalter, *Anfänge des Liberalismus und der Demokratie in Deutschland und Österreich 1830–1848/9* (Frankfurt-am-Main, 2002), 271–91, esp. 277.

[51] David Blackbourn, 'Reflections on James J. Sheehan and the Writing of Modern German History', in Hein et al, *Historie und Leben*, 153.

[52] See Alberto M. Banti, *Storia della borghesia italiana: l'età liberale* (Rome, 1996).

32   Michael Bentley

constitutions or parliaments.[53] A similar thrust in the following year distanced itself from modernisation theory with its rising middle class and argued that in Spain, at least, liberals showed themselves capable of moulding and responding to social structures of a distinctive character.[54] In so far as Spain followed 'normal' development, it occurred only at a tectonic level in patterns of expanding suffrage found 'in Victorian England or the Germany of Bismarck'.[55]

Home Environments

Victorian England preoccupied European historians of Liberalism quite as much as the internal dynamics witnessed in their own states – if only as a space of contrast and antinomy. The Liberal environment presented by Parry in his trilogy was familiar to them. What he did with it was not. Perhaps the foregoing illustrations may help explain why not.

Periodicity, Parry's first benchmark, defied sharing because state formation and the bedding-in of a parliamentary system happened later in Europe. The focus of much European writing on Liberalism in the 1980s and 1990s resolved on the period after 1870, and in some cases after the 1890s, when historians turned the problematic of a Labour- and proletarian- challenge, compelling in Europe, into a re-reading of English politics to replicate (implausibly) the same mood. 'New Liberalism' held their attention as a response, in their eyes, to an assault from the Left, and the British authors they wanted mostly to quote – Collini, Emy, Freeden, Weiler, Bellamy – not only reflected their chosen period but represented it through political thought and doctrine and thus pulled the British situation closer to their own paradigms.[56] They did not quote Parry; they did not quote Peter Clarke;[57] they missed a style of historiography which portrayed Liberalism with a future despite the coming of a Labour Party in 1906. Parry's own period, beginning in 1830, looked more like an Enlightenment

---

[53]   Cf. essays by Juan Francisco Fuentes and Jean Louis Guereña in Fuentes and Luís Roura (eds), *Sociabilidad y liberalismo en la España del siglo XIX: homenaje a Alberto Gil Novales* (Lleida, 2001), 207–37.

[54]   Jesús Millán, 'La doble cara del liberalismo en España: el cambio social y el sub-desarollo de la ciudadanía,' *Mélanges de l'école de Rome*, 114 (2002), 695–710.

[55]   *Ibid.*, 697.

[56]   Stefan Collini, *Liberalism and Sociology: L.T. Hobhouse and Political Argument in England 1880–1914* (Cambridge, 1979); Michael Freeden, *The New Liberalism* (Oxford, 1978); H.V. Emy, *Liberals, Radicals and Social Politics, 1892–1914* (Cambridge, 1973); Peter Weiler, *The New Liberalism* (New York, 1982); Richard Bellamy, *Victorian Liberalism* (London, 1990).

[57]   P.F. Clarke, *Lancashire and the New Liberalism* (Cambridge, 1971); *Liberals and Social Democrats* (Cambridge, 1978). For a discussion of the issues, see Michael Bentley, *The Climax of Liberal Politics* (London, 1987), 128–52.

deposit, often labelled 'classical liberalism', than a harbinger of something closer to home. Spanish authors could relate to a premature burst of liberal enthusiasm from their own, lamented *trienio*; but that had gone the way of absolutism. French understanding, when it (rarely) escaped from the École des Hautes Études en Sciences Sociales and the accretions of *Annalisme* with its demotion of all political history to the status of the *événementielle*, sang in harmony. Bédarida, sole prophet in many ways, evaded *Annalisme* but not much else; he was happy to portray Victorian Liberalism as a nationalistic phenomenon, '[c]omme l'a souligné Élie Halévy' and then tell a story beginning with a founding father (Bentham, apparently) and trundling onwards through Cobden, Bright and Mill. Nobody deserved encomium more than Peel ('période brillante et féconde') whose fecundity attached to promoting free trade. Laissez-faire was Bédarida's watchword and he made it a Victorian theme.[58] German patriotism, meanwhile, confused English conditions with those precipitated by the twin-determinants of unification and Bismarck. Wolfgang Mommsen, in typical muscle-bound mood, saw no great difference between these Liberalisms. Both began, he wrote, from a reform movement with market-oriented economic tendencies – we have seen that some Liberalisms actually *opposed* such tendencies – and both wanted to bring other classes into the system. The differences were just two: precocity on the part of English Liberalism, and aristocracy, which German society could not match as a Liberal ingredient since it had 'kein Äquivalent für die englischen Whigs.'[59]

A second radiation from Parry's conception of English Liberalism concerned religion and the Liberal imperative to make of the party and its identity a form of political church. In a publication at the millennium, he and Stephen Taylor argued thus:

> [T]he weakness of ecclesiastical authority, and the absence of uniformity, have not prevented religion from playing a large part in political life in the past... A parliamentary Church... has performed a central role in defending the freedom, and the peculiarities, of the English.[60]

Those peculiarities escaped much of European scholarship. One German dissertation did capture a sense of 'Kulturprotestanismus' in a study of Berlin, Mannheim and Bremen, and evoked a Liberalism that was Protestant, 'aber

---

[58] Francois Bedarida, *L'Ère victorienne* (Paris, 1974), 70–4.

[59] Wolfgang J. Mommsen, 'Einführung: Deutscher und britischer Liberalismus: Versuch einer Bilanz', in Langewiesche, *Liberalismus in 19. Jahrhundert*, 211–22. He saw in early German Liberalism a *Bildungsschicht* but seems not to have seen it also in England (p. 215).

[60] Jonathan Parry and Stephen Taylor, 'Introduction' to Parry and Taylor (eds), *Parliament and the Church, 1529–1960* (Edinburgh, 2000), 13.

nicht dogmatisch manchesterlich', one which held for a time but then became asymmetrical: Liberals remained Protestant but by no means all Protestants remained Liberal.[61] In one nation, however, the echoes resounded with greater clarity in nineteenth-century historiography. Belgium, indeed, constitutes a closer sister to English experience in this regard than perhaps anywhere else in Western Europe. Partly this reflects a profound division between Catholic and Protestant societies and its relation to the long-standing success of Liberal politics there. Geographically speaking, the Liberal vote fractured between Wallonia, where it predominated, and Flanders and Brussels, where it remained a significant minority. Yet the crucial divide was not geographical but denominational; the fragile concordat between Catholics and Liberals agreed in 1828 came rapidly under strain and escalated under the papacy of Pope Pius IX (1846–78), when ultramontane attitudes gained ground.[62] The question turned on whether the state had the right to determine national, and especially educational, policy in its wider ramifications or whether, as ultramontanes insisted, the Church should lead the state in such matters. Powerful in the south of the country and led by Bishop Sterckx and Catholic theologians in Ghent and Louvain, they drew heavily on the ideas of the French thinker, Lammenais, in his ultra period, and manifested aggression over control of the schools.[63] So Parry's concern with the Irish Universities Bill in *Democracy and Religion* strikes an immediate chord in Belgium's Liberal crisis during the so-called *schoolstrijt* of 1878–84 concerning the issue of what could be taught in schools.[64] Of course differences existed, not least in the analysis, common to Belgium and the Netherlands, of vertical divisions in society – the so-called *verzuiling* – which cut across both electoral and ecclesiastical politics. Uniting the historiographies at a deeper level, however, the possibility, indeed urgency, persisted of 'missionary' or 'moral' politics to embrace a democratising polity preoccupied by representation of frictional interests. Somewhere beneath the North Sea, two tectonic plates slid closer.

Suggesting that Parry's trilogy contains between its lines a form of reception history does not, by contrast, travel at all for the patent reason that the place of a national parliament in Britain, one housing both bourgeoisie and nobility

---

[61] Gangolf Hübinger, *Kulturprotestantismus und Politik: zum Verhältnis von Liberalismus und Protestantismus im wilhelmischen Deutschland* (Tübingen, 1994), 8–10.

[62] See, in particular, Hervé Hasquin and Adriaan Verhulst (eds), *Le Libéralisme en Belgique: deux cents ans d'histoire* (Brussels, 1989).

[63] E. Lamberts, 'Het ultramontanisme in België, 1830–1914', in Lamberts (ed.), *De Kruistocht tegen Liberalisme* (Louvain, 1984), 39–41; Veronique A. Adriaens, *Liberalisme op et Zuid-Ostvlaamse platteland in de 19e eeuw* (Ghent, 1991), 10–11.

[64] Parry, *Democracy and Religion*, 33–68; *Rise and Fall*, 266–8. For the schoolstrijt, see André De Vries, *Flanders: A Cultural History* (Oxford, 2007), 35.

and capable at Parry's hands of absorbing conflict at the centre of the state, finds little echo. Rudolf Muhs's contention that the German parliament displayed by comparison a greater and more precocious 'Parlamentarisierung der Staatsgewalt' seems, in this light, hard to understand; and Bismarck's capacity to attract state power to himself makes it no more plausible.[65] A more general persuasion among European historians of Liberalism dwells on the *failure* of Liberal politics to assimilate and ride out social and economic challenges through parliamentary activity, a thought that they import into British conditions. So an Italian author, preoccupied by the theoretical problem of liberals handling the rise of organised political parties – he begins with Duverger and Ostrogorski – sees in Joseph Chamberlain's Birmingham caucus and his successors a silver bullet for English Liberalism rather than a peripheral noise to be accommodated at the centre.[66] Or one might point to a German investigation of Liberal reactions in England to industrialisation and the rise of a working-class presence. Erlangen's Karl Heinz Metz offered in 1985, on the eve of Parry's opening volume, an account that can stand for many others in its comprehensive vision and contentions. Industrialisation means Thomas Carlyle: he begins there. Then we have political economy: Adam Smith and Bentham. Then we get the rise of a social politics (Chadwick, Nassau Senior, Brougham and a nod to Vincent's *Formation of the Liberal Party*); then we advance to *Arbeiterliberalismus*, a 'central event in the development of British liberalism' which distinguishes it, the author contends, 'from that of continental Europe'. Then comes New Liberalism, seen at the end of a line drawn from Bright, via Mill, to Churchill and Lloyd George. And all the time Liberals were working 'under the shadow of an emerging labour party', because the relationship between the middle class and the working class was '*presumably* the most important sphere of social relations during this time'.[67] Much rests on that presumption and nothing that Parry wrote over the following twenty years lent it confirmation as an ingredient in Liberal politics. Social relations and their conflicts could be absorbed, not weakly contested, within a parliamentary culture that turned on the language of mission, elevation and national cohesion.

A final proposal extracted from Parry's trilogy, that political language should be studied for its own sake and from a more generous posture adopted in face of the relationship between what politicians said and their behaviour

---

[65] Rudolf Muhs, 'Deutscher und britischer Liberalismus im Vergleich', in Langewiesche (ed.), *Liberalismus im 19. Jahrhundert*, 236.

[66] Gaetano Quagliarello, 'Il liberalismo e i partiti politici (1867–1989)', in *Mélanges*, 616.

[67] Karl H. Metz, 'Liberalismus und soziale Frage: liberales Denken und die Auswirkungen der Industrialisierung im Großbritannien des 19. Jahrhunderts', *Zeitschrift für Politik*, 32 (1985), 384, 392 [emphasis added].

within and without parliament, fed from a context distinctively English in the 1970s and 1980s. It involved a reconceptualisation of 'high politics' as both subject and method when approaching 'the structure of political action',[68] and Parry extended its meaning to think about forms of language that may have connected the high-political world with a wider one populated by intellectuals, journalists, churchmen and the entire social formation known to Coleridge as the 'clerisy'. European scholarship did not draw from that tradition and its presentation of Liberal politics remained concentrated on the history of political parties and their leading exponents. The so-called 'linguistic turn' of the 1970s and beyond altered that orientation to some extent. Taken more seriously and dispersed more broadly than in Britain, the Parisian intellectual revolution fomented by Foucault, Barthes, Derrida and others led indirectly to a genre of writing that attended to parliamentary language in particular.[69] So far as the history of 'Liberalism' is concerned, the idea of a systematic *Semantik* provoked by the term reached its apogee, also in Parry's period, in Jörn Leonhard's vast book about it, though that study retained, for all its geographical width, a visible German base.[70] Postmodern styles and their adoption in English Victorian studies remained partial – Jon Lawrence, Patrick Joyce, James Vernon – though some American influence persisted.[71] One might reasonably suppose that Parry himself did not need to comment on the linguistic turn. Surprisingly, he did: though only and inevitably in French.[72] But he gave the turn a turn of his own. He did not want to evoke the capacity of words to constitute a nineteenth-century world, in a Foucauldian sense, but rather to ask whether 'discursive phenomena' located within parliamentary institutions proved *representative* of a real word beyond them. He continued to seek a bridge between a world within and a word without. His language may have been new; his point was not.

[68] The phrase, much repeated, comes from Cooke and Vincent, *Governing Passion*, 3–22.

[69] For some comments see Michael Bentley, 'Parliamentary History: An Oblique Glance', *Parliamentary History*, 40 (2021), 228–44.

[70] Jörn Leonhard, *Liberalismus: zur historischen Semantik eines europäischen Deutungsmusters* (Munich 2001). This work covers styles of discourse in France, Germany, Italy and England. Parry does not enter the index; Langewiesche gets 14 entries.

[71] Jon Lawrence, *Speaking for the People: Party, Language and Popular Politics in England 1867–1914* (Cambridge, 1998); Patrick Joyce, *Democratic Subjects: The Self and the Social in Nineteenth-century England* (Cambridge, 1994); James Vernon, *Politics and the People: A Study in English Political Culture, c.1815–1867* (Cambridge, 1993). A sardonic descant appeared in Michael Bentley, 'Victorian Politics and the Linguistic Turn', *Historical Journal*, 42 (1999), 883–902.

[72] Jonathan Parry, 'Recent Developments in Victorian Political History', *Revue d'histoire du XIXe siècle*, 37 (2008), 71–86.

* * *

What this engagement with Parry's trilogy has implied is that the plural nature of nineteenth-century Liberalism invites the possibility of lateral thinking and geological speculation. Some years ago, a student of Spanish political thought asked the question, 'Are there "hidden" or "parallel" histories of liberalism that merit reconstruction?'[73] This essay points to a few. It does not do so in order to proclaim a false correspondence between English political historians of the 1980s and 1990s and their European counterparts. It is comfortable over denying one. It does not want, equally, to sever all relations between Parry's work and those continental historians who spent his period trying to make sense of English Liberalism. It happily reports divergence. It does not, emphatically not, seek to assert superiority or inferiority in the various perceptions thus reported. Let a thousand flowers bloom. Yet it does contend that there existed, below authorial horizons and the traditions that delineate them, a substrate of perception and method which it helps understanding to excavate. Context contains more than text; it points to deeper things in the world which no writing wants to acknowledge yet which none can entirely escape. Maybe all of us who write professionally as historians should try harder to listen for their reverberations even as we write, instead of listening over the shoulder, many years hence, for their faint and distant echo. There are naturally some dangers in mis-diagnosis, in false retrieval. Perhaps, however, we stand in greater danger without a diagnosis and lacking any theory of what might be retrieved. In thinking, *pari passu*, about Jonathan Parry's oeuvre, we do not think less of his writing and achievement. We discover, rather, a second level of encomium and explanation by identifying within his intellectual distinction a situational distinctiveness.

---

[73] Gabriel Paquette, Introduction to a special issue of *History of European Ideas*, 41 (2015), 153–65.

Chapter 2

G.M. Trevelyan, Landscape and the Writing of History in England, c.1870–c.1950[1]

Paul Readman

This essay is about the relationship between history-writing and landscape. More specifically, it is about the ways in which historians' experience of landscape related to their intellectual endeavours. The category of historians I have in mind here are small but not necessarily large L liberal figures, of the kind that dominated the English tradition of historiography between the later nineteenth and mid-twentieth centuries. My case study is the most widely read historian of them all: George Macaulay Trevelyan. Yet notwithstanding his extraordinary popularity, by the 1950s Trevelyan's vivid, impressionistic and unashamedly narrative form of history found little favour with academics increasingly drawn to rigorous critical analysis, quantitative method and theory-driven conceptualisation. Trevelyan had become 'the last Whig historian': his work was a relic of a patriotic and complacently teleological approach to the past which, in university circles at least, had happily been superseded.[2] This view remains the orthodoxy, despite David Cannadine's 1992 biography, a book that some have seen as an unsuccessful 'rescue operation' on an unpleasantly nationalist, even virulently imperialist, dead white man.[3] For Bill Schwarz, Cannadine's attempted rehabilitation of Trevelyan was not simply ill-advised; it was 'a kind of scandal'.[4]

It was nothing of the sort, of course, and like many of Jonathan Parry's former students I am disinclined to make moralising judgments on history or

[1]   My thanks to Chad Bryant and Geraint Thomas for their comments on various versions of this essay.

[2]   J.M. Hernon, 'The Last Whig Historian and Consensus History: George Macaulay Trevelyan, 1876–1962', *American Historical Review*, 81 (1976), 66–97.

[3]   David Cannadine, *G.M. Trevelyan* (London, 1992); Bill Schwarz, '"Englishry": The histories of G.M. Trevelyan', in Catherine Hall and Keith McClelland (eds), *Race, Nation and Empire* (Manchester, 2010), 117–32.

[4]   Schwarz, '"Englishry"', 117.

G.M. Trevelyan, Landscape and the Writing of History in England   39

history-writing. Cannadine was right to take Trevelyan seriously as a historian. And while Trevelyan's scholarship might fall short by modern academic standards, his life and work have useful things to tell us, even now. As David Gange has pointed out, Trevelyan's responsiveness to landscape has lessons for environmental historians, underlining to them the importance of getting out of the archive and into the field.[5] I agree, but I would go further: what follows will show that Trevelyan's topographical sensitivity has lessons of wider applicability – not just for environmental history, but history more generally. One reason why this is the case is that Trevelyan was far from alone. As this essay will suggest, affective and embodied engagement with landscape was a common feature of mainstream history-writing in England between the later nineteenth and mid-twentieth centuries.

Landscape and Historical Evidence

For Trevelyan, walking was essential for his wellbeing: as he told his brother in 1904, his 'health, though good, requires country, exercise, mountains, at frequent intervals; and my life, my youth, my soul crave for them with a yearning as to their food'.[6] It helped him get his thoughts in order; it was essential to his creative process. In this he was not unusual. Many writers, scientists, artists and musicians have attached importance to walking as a means of intellectual stimulation: Wordsworth, Coleridge, Darwin, Nietzsche and Vaughan Williams are just some examples.[7] But historians' on-foot engagement with landscape shaped their thought in distinctive ways. The locational particularity of history – *this* happened *there* – gave particular places particular significance.

For Trevelyan, the uplands of Northumberland were especially significant. His childhood home was Wallington Hall; in later life he had a house of his own, Hallington Hall, a few miles away. Both places were bases for country excursions into the moorlands to the north and west. This was wild, windswept landscape, the openness of which was suggestive of freedom to a liberal like Trevelyan – as, indeed, open landscapes often were to other liberal-minded intellectuals, not least those associated with commons preservation.[8] Dotted

---

[5]   David Gange, 'Retracing Trevelyan? Historical Practice and the Archive of the Feet', *Green Letters*, 21 (2017), 246–61.

[6]   G.M. Trevelyan to C.P. Trevelyan, 11 Nov. 1904: Trevelyan (Charles Philips) Archive, Newcastle University [hereafter CPT], 237/55–62.

[7]   For excellent discussion of the significance of walking to English literary intellectuals, see A.D. Wallace, *Walking, Literature and English Culture: The Origins and Uses of Peripatetic in the Nineteenth Century* (Oxford, 1994).

[8]   This is not to deny that the cause of landscape preservation could not also appeal to conservatives, but the origins of the movement can very largely be traced back to

with castles, fortified towers and ancient monuments, Northumberland was also redolent of an excitingly vicissitudinous past – not least centuries of cross-border conflict – but the ruined quality of much that remained was happily suggestive of progress towards present-day Anglo-Scottish unity: Britain had progressed from the troublous days of moss-troopers and border reivers. Trevelyan's sense of what he called 'the whole pageant of history' – its drama, poetry and continuity – was derived from his experience of this landscape, from solitary walks that 'captivated my soul and enhanced my historical interest and imaginings'.[9] It was a landscape in which discrete pieces of information about the past were not simply preserved, as flies in amber, but one whose palimpsestic features embodied history as narrative. It was a landscape that told a story.

Trevelyan was not the only historian to draw inspiration from Northumberland. It had been an important influence on the young Mandell Creighton, who served as vicar of Embleton between 1875 and 1884 and whose burgeoning historical talents had, like Trevelyan's after him, been sharpened by walks in a landscape 'full of inexhaustible interest' whose 'striking history' of 'constant struggles' could be read in its features.[10] Mutatis mutandis, other landscapes exerted similarly formative influences on other historians. For the medievalist F.M. Powicke, who had an old farmhouse in Eskdale, the Lake District was vital in shaping his historical sensibility. As Powicke's colleague R.W. Southern remembered, 'He saw the whole scene' around his adoptive Cumberland home 'bathed in an historical light: the houses and fields, the church and the paths along which the dead were brought from outlying settlements, the Roman camp and the network of roads and defences of which it formed part, provided him with endless opportunities for reflection'.[11] The ineluctably historical quality of landscape inspired Powicke; indeed he was drawn to the Lake District by the work he did early in his career for a *Victoria County History* article on Furness

---

Victorian liberalism. See M.J.D. Roberts, 'Gladstonian Liberalism and Environment Protection, 1865–76', *English Historical Review*, 138 (2013), 292–322. Of course, by the interwar period, many of those whose intellectual formation was broadly liberal gravitated towards the Conservatives, including Trevelyan himself, for whom Stanley Baldwin's lyrical ruralism exerted a considerable appeal, chiming with his active involvement with the National Trust.

[9] G.M. Trevelyan to Mary Trevelyan (G.M.T.'s daughter), 10 Sept. 1926: Moorman (Mary) Archive, Newcastle University [hereafter MM], 1/4/14/29; G.M. Trevelyan, *An Autobiography and Other Essays* (London, 1949), 25–6.

[10] Louise Creighton, *The Life and Letters of Mandell Creighton* (2 vols, London, 1904), vol. 1, 176; Mandell Creighton, *The Story of Some English Shires* (London, 1897), 13, 22.

[11] R.W. Southern, 'Sir Maurice Powicke 1879–1963', *Proceedings of the British Academy*, 50 (1964), 302.

Abbey, the sight of the ancient sheepwalks tracking over the fells evoking the monastic life of the past and making a lasting impression on him. Another Lake District example is that of R.G. Collingwood, whose whole approach to history – and indeed his influential philosophy of history – owed much to the out-of-doors topographical education in Lakeland heritage he received from his father, the polymath artist and antiquarian William Gershom Collingwood.[12]

Landscape gave historians solace and inspiration, as well as – at least sometimes – opportunities for companionship with likeminded people. No doubt, too, it also provided opportunities for restorative recreation – the mountaineering exploits of J.H. Clapham and James Bryce, among others, spring to mind here.[13] But for many, including those like Trevelyan for whom it also provided such opportunities, much of its significance lay in its storied quality. Landscape offered access to the past: it supplied evidence for the crafting of narratives and the shaping of arguments. We are now very familiar with the spatial turn, and accounts of its genesis often reach back to landscape historians such as W.G. Hoskins and Maurice Beresford, or – in a rather different vein – the *Annales* school in France.[14] The practice of social anthropologists, geographers and archaeologists have encouraged modern-day historians to undertake on-foot observation of the materiality of the landscape, to read in its contours, field lines and other features the interaction of human beings with the environment over time. For many landscape and environmental historians, such traces have as much evidentiary significance as documentary sources.

But this approach has a longer and more diversely originated heritage than often appreciated. As Marc Bloch acknowledged, the practice of what he called 'reading history backwards' from the present-day landscape had been a feature of the work of an older generation of English historians of medieval society, among them Frederic Seebohm and F.W. Maitland.[15] But even in the late nineteenth century, topographical sensitivity was not confined to scholars of the Anglo-Saxon village community. Some idea of its prevalence is given by the examples of three prominent historians of liberal sympathies – Edward

---

[12] Vicky Albritton and Fredrik Albritton Jonsson, *Green Victorians: The Simple Life in John Ruskin's Lake District* (Chicago, 2016), 149ff.

[13] Trevelyan recalled that as a Fellow of King's College Cambridge from 1898, Clapham 'found salvation as a mountaineer': Trevelyan, *Autobiography*, 216–17. For Bryce, see Paul Readman, 'Walking and Environmentalism in the Career of James Bryce: Mountaineer, Scholar, Statesman, 1838–1922', in Arthur Burns, Chad Bryant and Paul Readman (eds), *Walking Histories: 1800–1950* (Basingstoke, 2016), 287–318.

[14] W.G. Hoskins, *The Making of the English Landscape* (London, 1955); M.W. Beresford, *The Lost Villages of England* (London, 1954); Peter Burke, *The French Historical Revolution: The Annales School, 1929–89* (Cambridge, 1990).

[15] Peter Burke, 'The Annales in Global Context', *International Review of Social History*, 35 (1990), 426.

Augustus Freeman, John Richard Green and James Bryce. In different ways, all were convinced of the imbrication of geography and history: for Bryce, the former was the 'key to' or 'foundation of' the latter.[16] Green thought similarly, the value he placed on geography being attested to by his co-authorship, with his wife and fellow-historian Alice Stopford Green, of a *Short Geography of the British Islands*.[17] All these historians saw personal engagement with landscape as vital to the business of history. Landscape not only inspired; it also informed. As Freeman wrote in his *Methods of Historical Study*, 'the finished historian must be a traveller; he must see with his own eyes the true look of a wide land; he must see too with his eyes the very spots where great events happened; he must mark the lie of a city, and take in... all that is special about a battle-field... You cannot... fully take in the history of the world, its lands and its cities, except by working at each historic spot on the spot itself'.[18]

In this, Freeman was as good as his word: even when afflicted with gout, he was relentless in his commitment to on-foot visits of the places that featured in his histories, not least his monumental *Norman Conquest*.[19] And as is clear from his correspondence, these visits were an integral part of his research method. They were made, as he put it, 'to store my mind', to shed 'new light'.[20] Likewise plagued with indifferent health, Green was similarly energetic. Although he has been portrayed as reacting against the antiquarian tradition,[21] his on-foot observation of the landscape had real affinities with that of, say, William Hutton, whose pioneering 1802 *History of the Roman Wall* drew much on his experience of walking the length of it.[22] Green was adamant, as he told Freeman, that historians – or English historians at any rate – must continue to 'live in the free human air' and not 'sink into mere "paper chasers"' after the fashion of Ranke.[23] His notebooks contain detailed descriptions of the places

---

[16] James Bryce, 'The Importance of Geography in Education. I', *Journal of Geography*, 1 (1902), 145; 'The Importance of Geography in Education. II', *Journal of Geography*, 1 (1902), 207. See also E.A. Freeman, *The Methods of Historical Study* (London, 1886), esp. 296ff.

[17] A.S. and J.R. Green, *A Short Geography of the British Islands* (London, 1879).

[18] Freeman, *Methods*, 314–15.

[19] 'Freeman was always at his best when in the field': James Bryce, 'Edward Augustus Freeman', *English Historical Review*, 7 (1892), 499.

[20] Freeman to Dean Hook, April 1867, and to William Boyd Dawkins, 25 July 1867: W.R.W. Stephens (ed.), *The Life and Letters of Edward A. Freeman* (2 vols, London, 1895), vol. 1, 381, 389.

[21] John Burrow, *A History of Histories* (London, 2009 [2007]), 501–3.

[22] William Hutton, *The History of the Roman Wall* (London, 1802).

[23] Green to Freeman, 26 Feb. 1876, in Leslie Stephen (ed.), *Letters of John Richard Green* (London, 1901), 427.

he visited,[24] a good part of the history of which he gleaned not from books, or even local archives, but pedestrian exploration.

This sensitivity to the legibility of the past in place and landscape informed Green's major works, not least his *Short History of the English People* (1874), a publishing sensation which – until the appearance of Trevelyan's *English Social History* nearly seventy years later – was by far and away the bestselling single volume history of England. Green's *Short History* is shot through with vivid topographical description and bears compelling testimony to his reading of history through landscape. A visit to the Isle of Thanet in 1870, where he walked the coastline around Ebbsfleet, convinced him that this was the place where the Saxons first made landfall in the fifth century: quite apart from what the *Anglo-Saxon Chronicle* might say, it was clear from the lie of the land.[25] Similarly, Green's account of the background to the Norman Conquest begins with a description of the Normandy countryside, a walk through which, he tells his reader, 'teaches one more of the age of our history which we are about to traverse than all the books in the world'.[26] Green's attentiveness to landscape and place increased still further in his later work, not least in his last book, *The Making of England*, which made extensive and more systematic use of archaeology and geography.[27] It was an approach that had considerable influence, not just on Freeman, but also on younger historians such as Kate Norgate, whose own topographical sensitivity – amply evident in her *England under the Angevin Kings* (1889) – owed much to Green's example and encouragement.[28]

It is in this tradition of topographically engaged history-writing that Trevelyan should be placed. As with Freeman and Green before him, Trevelyan thought history did not merely give meaning to place; place also gave meaning to history. As 'witness' to the past, landscape was rich grist to the historian's mill. Some of this grist was evidentiary in character, providing information as important as that which might be collected from documentary sources. For Trevelyan, this was particularly true of battlefields, the exploration of which was an enduring fascination – one that had been nurtured by his father George

---

[24] Notebooks of J.R. Green, British Library, Add. MSS 40169–71; for a good example, Add. MSS 40171, vol. 3, 11–13.

[25] J.R. Green, *A Short History of the English People* (London, 1992 [reprint of 1st edn, 1874]), 7. For Green's first-hand impressions of the landscape, see his letters to Freeman (3 Feb. 1870) and W. Boyd Dawkins (6 Feb. 1870), in Stephen, *Letters of Green*, 243–4

[26] Green, *Short History*, 69.

[27] J.R. Green, *The Making of England* (London, 1881); also Green, *The Conquest of England*, ed. Alice Stopford Green (London, 1883).

[28] Kate Norgate, *England under the Angevin Kings* (2 vols, London, 1889); Green to Norgate, 18 June 1877, in Stephen, *Letters of Green*, 470–1.

Otto and his upbringing in Northumberland, a martial landscape *par excellence*, with its many sites of cross-border conflict.[29] From boyhood onward, Trevelyan's correspondence was replete with descriptions of battlefields he had visited on foot: Waterloo, Sedgemoor, Culloden, Gibraltar, to name but a few.[30] Even walking expeditions to the Alps offered opportunities for examining sites of conflict.[31] Such activity was enjoyable in itself, but also fed into his historical writing, one prominent feature of which is its topographically precise but vividly dramatised handling of warfare and military campaigns. The trilogy of books on *Garibaldi* (1907–11) is a case in point.[32] The inspiration for this project, one that made Trevelyan's name as an historian as well as being expressive of his liberal sympathies at the time, was directly derived from personal experience of the Italian landscape. Work on these books involved what Trevelyan called 'much out-of-door exploration'. This included walking the route of Garibaldi's retreat in the company of his friend Hilton Young, whose photographs were used to illustrate the first volume; traversing Sicily – again on foot – to help him with the second; and, for the final volume, walking the battlefields north of Naples in company with J.L. and Barbara Hammond, themselves historians whose work was topographically engaged to a high degree (most strikingly in their writings on enclosure).[33] As with Freeman and Green before him, personal experience of the places he wrote about was vital to Trevelyan's craft; it stocked his mind with material, with 'facts and thoughts'.[34]

And such 'facts and thoughts' also informed Trevelyan's monumental *England under Queen Anne* (1930–4), another trilogy, and one he came to regard as 'the chief historical work of my life'.[35] Like the *Garibaldi* volumes, the books in this series – covering among other things the campaigns of the

---

[29] G.M. Trevelyan, *Sir George Otto Trevelyan* (London, 1932), 134–5; Trevelyan, 'The Middle Marches', *Independent Review*, 5 (1905), 231–40.

[30] G.M. Trevelyan to C.P. Trevelyan, 16 April 1892, CPT 236/12–19; G.M. Trevelyan to Mary Trevelyan, 2 June 1922, MM 1/4/10/5; G.M. Trevelyan to Mary Trevelyan 26 March 1928, MM 1/4/16/3; Mary Moorman, *George Macaulay Trevelyan* (London, 1980), 64–5.

[31] G.M. Trevelyan to G.O. Trevelyan, 6 Aug. 1896: Trevelyan (George Otto) Archive, Newcastle University [hereafter GOT], 89/24–6.

[32] G.M. Trevelyan, *Garibaldi's Defence of the Roman Republic* (London, 1907); *Garibaldi and the Thousand* (London, 1909); *Garibaldi and the Making of Italy* (London, 1911).

[33] Moorman, *Trevelyan*, 101–8; Trevelyan, *Autobiography*, 31–3. For the Hammonds, see S.A. Weaver, *The Hammonds* (Stanford: CA, 1997).

[34] G.M. Trevelyan to his mother, Caroline Trevelyan, 12 Nov 1908: GOT 100/17.

[35] Trevelyan, *An Autobiography*, 46; *Blenheim* (London, 1930); *Ramillies and the Union with Scotland* (London, 1932); *The Peace and the Protestant Succession* (London, 1934).

G.M. Trevelyan, Landscape and the Writing of History in England

duke of Marlborough – involved a good deal of military history, not least the Battle of Blenheim (1704), to which Trevelyan devoted a whole chapter rich in topographical detail gleaned from his own observations.[36] Other less significant engagements received similar treatment. His account of the 1704–5 siege of Gibraltar, for example, owed much to walks taken over the Rock, the rugged landscape of which was vividly described in the book.[37] More thoroughgoing still in its topographical precision was Trevelyan's treatment of the Battle of Vigo Bay (1702), which relied heavily on his own exploration of a wild estuarial coastline (during which he found a fort stormed by the British 'buried now amid trees'), his in-situ sketch of the locale providing the basis for the map included in the book.[38]

But while the influence of what J.H. Plumb called Trevelyan's 'very strongly developed topographical sense' can be seen most obviously in his handling of military history, it was not confined to this quarter of his endeavours.[39] It is observable throughout his writing, from the panoramic survey of England that opens his *Queen Anne* trilogy, to passing vignettes and thumbnail evocations of particular landscapes.[40] The latter are legion: the 'trackless wastes of grass "bent", heather and wet moss-hag' of Elizabethan Redesdale and North Tyne; the 'perfection of rural loveliness' attained by the eighteenth-century Lake District; the lonely sublimity of the fens, 'over which the rising and setting sun and the glories of cloudland were often watched by solitary men' such as 'Squire Cromwell... and the yeomen farmers who became his Ironsides', and in whose 'wide spaces... each... had felt himself to be alone with God, before ever they joined to form a regiment'.[41]

Landscape and the Historical Imagination

Trevelyan's topographical sense had a deeper significance still, however: it stimulated the historical imagination. Few would deny that the writing of history involves the exercise of imagination, and with this the intuition and empathy

---

[36] Trevelyan, *Blenheim*, 378ff.

[37] G.M. Trevelyan to Mary Trevelyan, 26 March 1928, MM 1/4/16/3; Trevelyan, *Blenheim*, 407–15.

[38] G.M. Trevelyan to Mary Trevelyan, 4 Apr. 1928, MM 1/4/16/7; Trevelyan, *Blenheim*, 268–73.

[39] J.H. Plumb, *G.M. Trevelyan* (London, 1951), 18–19.

[40] Trevelyan, *Blenheim*, ch. 1.

[41] G.M. Trevelyan, *English Social History* (London 1944 [1942]), 153, 236; *Blenheim*, 36–7.

satisfactorily to understand human experience in the past.[42] But the *visual* dimension to this is less often appreciated. As the social anthropologist Tim Ingold has shown, human imagination is rooted in our perceptions of the outside world or, to put it another way, the pictures we make of the outside world.[43] This is implicit in the etymology of the word imagination: the Latin 'imaginari' means 'to picture to oneself'. It follows that the exercise of the historical imagination – as an integral part of human imagination more generally – involves visualisation, picture-making, the 'seeing' of or into the past from our position in the present. As Bryce told an Historical Association audience in 1907, 'the true qualification of the historian' was 'to be able to see the past as if it was the present, and to be able to look at the present as if it was the past'; the good historian was capable of detachedly discriminating, clear-sighted observation, the study of human experience over time being akin to 'look[ing] through a long vista, to see clearly the trees nearer, and to see the trees receding at the end of the vista until one gets only an outline and cannot see the small boughs'.[44] Lord Acton had this quality of mind, Bryce felt, recalling one occasion when 'in his library at Cannes', Acton

> expounded to me his view of how... a history of Liberty... might be written... He spoke for six or seven minutes only; but he spoke like a man inspired, seeming as if, from some mountain summit high in air, he saw beneath him the far-winding path of human progress from dim Cimmerian shores of prehistoric shadow into the fuller yet broken and fitful light of modern time. The eloquence was splendid, but greater than the eloquence was the penetrating vision... It was as if the whole landscape of history had been suddenly lit up by a burst of sunlight.[45]

Bryce's imagery here is revealing, the master historian being figured as a mountaineer subjecting a summit view to his penetrating gaze, and by doing so rendering it intelligible and meaningful. It is a metaphor that was also invoked by

---

[42] As the philosopher Ernst Cassirer put it in 1944, while historians work with verifiable facts and evidence, 'the last and decisive act [of the historian] is always an act of the productive imagination... The great historians... are empiricists; they are careful observers and investigators of special facts; but they do not lack the "poetic spirit". It is the keen sense for the empirical reality of things combined with the free gift of imagination upon which the true historical synthesis or synopsis depends': *An Essay on Man* (New Haven, 1972 [1944]), 204–5.

[43] Tim Ingold, 'Ways of Mind-Walking: Reading, Writing, Painting', *Visual Studies*, 25 (2010), 15–23.

[44] *Address by the Right Hon. James Bryce on the Teaching of History in Schools* (London, 1907), 4, 7.

[45] H.A.L. Fisher, *James Bryce* (2 vols, London, 1927), vol. 1, 336–7.

G.M. Trevelyan, Landscape and the Writing of History in England 47

others, including Trevelyan,[46] and more recently by John Lewis Gaddis in a series of lectures on *The Landscape of History: How Historians Map the Past*. In these lectures, later published as a book, Gaddis suggested that 'the past is a landscape and history is the way we present it',[47] and that historians therefore need vantage points, like that occupied by the Wanderer in the famous painting by Caspar David Friedrich – a painting which frames Gaddis's whole discussion and adorns the cover of his book (see fig. 2.1).[48] 'If you think of the past as a landscape', Gaddis writes, 'then history is... that act of representation that lifts us above the familiar to let us experience vicariously what we can't experience directly: a wider view'.[49]

Gaddis was correct to emphasise the visual quality of historical imagination, but his figuring of history as a landscape from which the historian ought to be elevated is a different perspective from that taken by historians like Trevelyan, Bryce and Green. These historians did not just see landscape as a metaphor *for* history; their embodied engagement with the outside world was a crucial means of accessing the past, of realising it, of bringing it to life *as* history. Visiting historical sites did not only furnish additional evidence, it also released the springs of historical imagination. Thus, when Green visited Chateau Gaillard, the fortress on the Seine that Richard I had built to protect his lands in Normandy, he did not just obtain information about its site and features (used to vivid effect in the *Short History*), he also realised the longer-term significance of King John's failure to prevent its capture by the French. The loss of the castle meant not just the end of English rule in Normandy, but also liberalising constitutional upheaval at home: 'The interest that attaches one to the grand ruin on the heights of Les Andelys is that it represents the ruin of a system as well as of a camp. From its dark donjon and broken walls we see not merely the pleasant vale of Seine, but the sedgy flats of our own Runnymeade'. His epiphany on the battlements was, he told Freeman, 'one of the great impressions of my life'.[50] For Trevelyan, too, landscape had an imaginative bearing on his history-writing.

---

[46] "'The curtain of cloud", he said, "that hides the scenes of the past is broken here and there, and we have magic glimpses into that lost world which is as actual as our own"': *George Macaulay Trevelyan: An Address Given in Trinity College Chapel on 17 November 1962* (by J.R.M.B.), copy in CPT 244/65–73.

[47] John Lewis Gaddis, *The Landscape of History: How Historians Map the Past* (Oxford, 2002), 33.

[48] It is also, incidentally, a painting which I first encountered as a student on Jonathan Parry's long-running 'Specified Subject' paper on 'The British and Europe, 1815–1906', a course which dealt as much with culture as it did with politics, and which had more influence on my formation as an historian than anything else I can remember doing at Cambridge. I still have the reading list in my filing cabinet.

[49] Gaddis, *Landscape*, 5

[50] Green, *Short History*, 113–14; Stephen, *Letters of Green*, 407, 409.

Fig. 2.1. Caspar David Friedrich, *Der Wanderer über dem Nebelmeer* [*The Wanderer Above the Sea of Fog*], c.1818. Oil on canvas.

G.M. Trevelyan, Landscape and the Writing of History in England   49

His letters are well stocked with attestations as to the capacity of landscape to make the past real in the mind of the present-day observer. A 'wonderful coast walk' from Ballantrae to Stranraer in summer 1899, for example, transported him back to the seventeenth century. As he told his mother, the sight of ships 'flying out from Stranraer… off into the distance towards a low black line – the unhappy land [of Ireland]' brought to mind the 'ships bearing Scotchmen to Ireland' in the reign of James I. 'One imagined oneself a Galloway shepherd watching the… fleet rolling up Ryan Bay, bearing the first Pilgrim Fathers of British Ireland to their work of good and evil, fateful and fated men'.[51]

As with Green's thoughts on visiting Chateau Gaillard, such reflections were not mere flights of fancy on Trevelyan's part, but important to his craft. As he said in another letter to his mother, written during a walking trip to southern Scotland at a time when he was working on an article on the 8th Earl of Lauderdale and the Scottish Whigs, 'seeing the country does not always *give* you ideas, but *helps* you to them by making you feel the thing'.[52] This affective engagement with the past through landscape – 'making you feel the thing' – was a function of Trevelyan's oft-stated conviction that history was not about 'scientific deduction' but about imagination.[53] Thus, in order to 'recover… our ancestors' real thoughts and feelings', the historian needed facts and knowledge, but 'also insight, sympathy and imagination of the finest, and last but not least the art of making our ancestors live again in modern narrative'.[54] And one key means of effecting such feats of recovery, Trevelyan thought, was through direct contact with storied landscape. It was not enough to rely on documentary research. 'To be perfect', the historian 'must know and feel what kind of men they were who climbed the terraces at Calatafimi or stormed the rifle-pits on Missionary Ridge; who marched up to the stockade at Blenheim to the sound of fife and drum; who hacked at each other that evening on Marston Moor' – and this meant visiting such places in person.[55] Moreover, in bringing the historian closer to the lived experience of people in the past, doing so enabled fuller appreciation of the contingency of history, its human quality, its irreducibility to narrowly deterministic or scientific modes of explanation. The course of events was shaped less by the workings of abstract social or economic forces than by the actions of individual men and women in specific locational

---

[51]   G.M. Trevelyan to Caroline Trevelyan, 6 July 1899, GOT 92/8.

[52]   G.M. Trevelyan to Caroline Trevelyan, 19 June 1900, GOT 93/12.

[53]   G.M. Trevelyan, *Clio, a Muse* (London, 1914 [1913]), 9–10; see also Trevelyan, 'The Latest View of History', *Independent Review*, 1 (1903), 395–414, and Cannadine, *Trevelyan*, 190–2.

[54]   Trevelyan, *Clio*, 17.

[55]   *Ibid.*, 29.

50   Paul Readman

contexts: this was a liberal, humane perspective on the past. As Trevelyan explained:

> Chance selected this field out of so many, that low wall, this gentle slope of grass, a windmill, a farm or straggling hedge, to turn the tide of war and decide the fate of nations and of creeds. Look on this scene, restored to its rustic sleep that was so rudely interrupted on that one day in all the ages; and looking, laugh at the 'science of history'. But for some honest soldier's pluck or luck in the decisive onslaught round yonder village spire, the lost cause would now be hailed as 'the tide of inevitable tendency' that nothing could have turned aside![56]

Trevelyan's historical sensibility, then, was inseparably connected with landscape. Conceiving of history less as a science than a literary art, his experience of places rich in historical association was a powerful spur to his empathetic imagination, and a vital means by which the past was realised through his writing. Deep into the era of professionalisation, the imagination of many historians was similarly roused. Green, Freeman and Bryce have already been mentioned. Other, later, examples include the medievalist Eileen Power, to whose memory Trevelyan dedicated his *English Social History*. As Maxine Berg has shown, a crucial formative experience for Power was her encounter with the landscape of India and China on a travelling fellowship in 1920–21, which gave her what she called 'flashbacks' to the world of medieval Europe. A walking tour in the Western Hills of China proved particularly important in Power's Orientalist recovery of the European past in the present-day landscape of the East, the monasteries she visited seeming akin to those of the Middle Ages. This experience – and the fellowship more generally – charged Power's historical imagination, having what Berg judges to be 'a very significant impact on her choice of subjects' and the way she wrote about them.[57]

Powicke is another example. A contemporary of Power's, he shared with her an imaginative approach to the medieval past. Like her, his writing brought to life places – and people in those places – with a romantic intensity. He could do a lot with scanty material, and his doing so was at least in part based on a conviction that 'the faculty of imagination' was crucial to history. This was a lesson he had learned from A.L. Smith, his tutor at Balliol College Oxford (and, perhaps significantly, an exponent of an outdoorsy approach to pedagogy).[58]

---

[56]   *Ibid.*, 27–8.

[57]   Maxine Berg, *A Woman in History: Eileen Power 1889–1940* (Cambridge, 1996), 99–110, at 110.

[58]   Smith felt 'muddy boots' a prerequisite of undergraduate teaching, a good deal of which he seemed to do while out walking with his pupils: R.L. Patterson, 'Smith, Arthur Lionel', *Oxford Dictionary of National Biography*.

G.M. Trevelyan, Landscape and the Writing of History in England   51

'Imagination is the only key that can unlock the past', Smith taught Powicke, because in order 'to make discoveries... the thoughts of men in the past must once more become thinkable to us'.[59] Only by exercising imagination could the past be made real; only thus, according to Powicke, could the historian 're-capture the thoughts and moods of the men who listened to Beowulf and the sagas, the Chanson de Roland, the story of Alexander or Arthur, the *gestes* about Charles the Great and his companions, or about forgotten warriors of the Welsh Marches'.[60] This has affinities with R.G. Collingwood's influential injunction that the practice of history involves the 're-enactment' of the thoughts of people in the past: hence his famous dictum that 'all history is the history of thought'.[61] Doing the work of re-enactment also implied judicious appreciation of the dramatic force of history, without which, Collingwood once said, one could 'never be an historian'.[62] Collingwood's emphasis on the role of imagination in re-enacting the 'drama' of history was shared by Powicke – and also, for that matter, by Trevelyan, who was swept up in the interwar enthusiasm for historical pageantry (he played Chaucer in the 1922 Berkhamsted pageant), and whose *English Social History* was arranged, as he explained, 'as life is presented on the stage, that is to say by a series of scenes divided by intervals of time'.[63]

As Carolyn Steedman has pointed out, the dramatic re-enactment of the past gives rise to a sense of its 'perpetual presentness'.[64] In this way, history is made poetic; the past is lost yet still lives. This was the perspective of Powicke and Trevelyan, both avid readers of poetry.[65] As the latter wrote to his daughter Mary in 1926, 'It *is* not – yet it *is*, that world of the Time Past'; and it was 'the romance of that which devotes us to history'.[66] The simultaneous is- and is-nottedness of the past derived from its tangibility in the places of the present, from the associational value of landscape. As Powicke explained in a lecture of 1947, the

---

[59]   F.M. Powicke, *Three Lectures Given in the Hall of Balliol College, Oxford in May 1947* (Oxford, 1947), 9–10; A.L. Smith, *Frederic William Maitland* (Oxford, 1908), 19–20; M.F. Smith, *Arthur Lionel Smith* (London, 1928), 157–8.

[60]   Powicke, *Three Lectures*, 46.

[61]   R.G. Collingwood, *The Idea of History* (Oxford, 1994 [1st ed. 1946]), 215.

[62]   W.H. Day, *History as Re-enactment: R.G. Collingwood's Idea of History* (Oxford, 1995), 94, 173, 226–7, at 226.

[63]   Moorman, *Trevelyan*, 202; Trevelyan, *English Social History*, xi.

[64]   Carolyn Steedman, *Poetry for Historians* (Manchester, 2018), esp. 7, 182, 209, 229 (at 209).

[65]   Indeed, for the agnostic Trevelyan, what he called 'the Bible of English poetry' took the place of religion: G.M. Trevelyan to C.P. Trevelyan, *c.* 1902, CPT 237/2–6.

[66]   G.M. Trevelyan to Mary Trevelyan, 5 Sept. 1926, MM 1/4/14/28.

peculiar poetic emotion... which we feel in Fountains Abbey or on the field of Naseby is very complex. There is, of course, the sense of beauty, often of the beauty of age... But mingled with the sense of beauty is the knowledge that certain shadowy figures, or vaguely understood institutions, which attract us actually had presence there, and also that, if we desire to know more, we must make a particular kind of effort. The effort helps to form the poetic imagination in history.[67]

Trevelyan was similarly vocal as to 'the poetry of history' being rooted in 'the quasi-miraculous fact that once, on this earth, once, on this familiar spot of ground, walked other men and women, as actual as we are to-day, thinking their own thoughts, swayed by their own passions, but now all gone, one generation vanishing after another, gone as utterly as we ourselves shall shortly be gone like ghost at cock-crow'.[68] Indeed, his powerful sense of the poetry of history being linked to specific locales helps explain his support for preservationist causes such as the National Trust.[69] The spoliation of landscape rich in historical associations was abhorrent not simply because it involved the spoliation of recreational amenity. It was abhorrent because it destroyed the 'presentness' of the past in that landscape; it made the past less accessible, less recoverable, less easy to imagine; and in doing so it made history less poetic.

Given their emphasis on the poetic character of the historical imagination, it should be no surprise that Powicke and Trevelyan saw history and literature as closely related: attempts to separate them were 'unnatural and injurious'.[70] Just as historians contributed to literature, so writers of poetry and fiction contributed to history. And one key means by which they did so was through their engagement with landscape, whether this be Wordsworth's Lake District, or the Sussex of Kipling's *Puck of Pook's Hill*, or Housman's Shropshire. For Powicke, the writer who best appreciated the poetic quality of history was Thomas Hardy, about whose 'Wessex in every clod and stone there linger[ed] "associations enough and to spare – echoes from songs of ancient harvest days, of spoken words and of sturdy deeds"'.[71] Trevelyan's hero in this respect was Sir Walter Scott, whose writings had done so much to invest the Northumbrian Borderland with storied romance. As evident not least in his engagement with this landscape, Trevelyan felt Scott understood better than many historians that men were produced by their 'special environment' – that they were

---

[67] Powicke, *Three Lectures*, 71–2.

[68] Trevelyan, *An Autobiography*, 13.

[69] For which see Cannadine, *Trevelyan*, 153–8.

[70] G.M. Trevelyan, *A Layman's Love of Letters* (London, 1954), 1; F.M. Powicke, 'The Poetic in History', *History*, 2 (1913), 175–87.

[71] Powicke, *Three Lectures*, 72–3. The quotation is from Thomas Hardy, *Jude the Obscure* (New York & London, 1895), 9.

G.M. Trevelyan, Landscape and the Writing of History in England   53

products of specific times and places. In so articulating this understanding, Scott 'revolutionized the scope and study of history itself', sweeping aside the model that had been established by Edward Gibbon – a model that failed to acknowledge 'the extent to which the habits and thoughts of men, no less than the forms of society, differ from country to country and from age to age'.[72]

Trevelyan's reading of Scott accords with the assessment of later scholars: Scott certainly did revolutionise the practice of history, through his fictional quite as much as his non-fictional writings. But Trevelyan's emphasis on Scott's historicism – his understanding of human experience as 'richly variegated' depending on context – stands out as particularly significant for our purposes here.[73] It indicates what might be termed a liberal-environmentalist mode of thought, one attentive to individual human experience of and interaction with the physical, lived-in world.

Trevelyan's liberal-environmentalism was also reflected in his engagement with another one of his literary heroes, George Meredith, on whom he published a book in 1906.[74] Meredith appealed to Trevelyan for a range of reasons, perhaps most obviously on account of his being a writer who 'spent much of his best years... in long cross-country walks in communion with woods, fields and hills, with sun, wind and stars'.[75] A profound engagement with nature, rooted in individual experience, dominated his poetry. For Trevelyan, this confirmed his own sense of the spiritual importance of contact with nature – and natural beauty – in the context of urban-industrial modernity. The importance of this contact derived from the earth being what he called the 'mother' of humankind: 'Man's spirit and brain, no less than his body, says Mr. Meredith, are earth-born. We are not dropped down from Heaven above. We are autochthonous'.[76] Humanity, in short, was *of* the earth – or, to put the same thought in the words of one modern-day anthropologist, 'persons and environment are mutually constitutive components of the same world'.[77] This point of view, which certainly calls into question jibes about Trevelyan's thought lacking sophistication, gave further impetus to his preservationist convictions, since it implied that to safeguard valued landscapes was to protect some of the core attributes of humankind itself. As he put it in his introduction to the National Trust's *Record of Fifty Years' Achievement* (1945), the preservation of natural

---

[72] Trevelyan, *Autobiography*, 200–1.

[73] *Ibid.*, 200–2.

[74] G.M. Trevelyan, *The Poetry and Philosophy of George Meredith* (London, 1906).

[75] Trevelyan, *Layman's Love of Letters*, 106ff, at 117.

[76] Trevelyan, *Meredith*, 114–15.

[77] Tim Ingold, 'Culture and the Perception of the Environment', in Elisabeth Croll and David Parkin (eds), *Bush Base: Forest Farm: Culture, Environment and Development* (London, 1992), 50–1.

beauty was 'a matter of preserving a main source of spiritual wellbeing and inspiration... We are literally "children of the earth", and removed from her our spirit withers'.[78]

But Trevelyan's liberal-environmentalism does not just tell us about his support for the preservation of landscape; it also tells us about his practice as an historian. Trevelyan's conception of humanity as being of the earth – as living *in* the world not *on* it[79] – does much to explain the centrality of landscape to his writing. Indeed, it suggests prescriptions for the writing of history more generally. These prescriptions are as valid now as they ever were, not least because of the resilience of cognitivist assumptions that humans impose their cultural designs on an 'external' reality of 'nature'. If humanity is 'earthborn', as Trevelyan put it, then history cannot satisfactorily be written without taking account of human experience of and interaction with the physical, lived-in world. And to do this, the historian cannot rely merely on documentary evidence. To paraphrase R.H. Tawney, she or he needs a stout pair of boots.[80] These boots are needed to walk the landscape to gain both factual knowledge of and imaginative insight into the past. The importance of doing this has long been recognised by historians of landscape, but it is applicable to all forms of history, since human experience happens in space as well as time.

Indeed, the practice of *walking* the landscape is particularly important. Many of the historians discussed in this essay were keen walkers, and to their names could be added many more. The popularity of walking with historians is telling. Walking is not just a means of relaxation, or a congenial context for thinking and sociability; it is also a means of understanding the past through embodied encounter with storied ground. As Ingold has argued, the land is 'not so much a stage for the enactment of history, or a surface on which it is inscribed, as *history congealed*'.[81] As such, we need to adopt what Ingold, drawing on Heidegger, Bourdieu and others, calls a 'dwelling perspective', one in which

> the landscape is constituted as an enduring record of – and testimony to – the lives and works of past generations who have dwelt within it, and in so doing, have left something of themselves... the landscape tells – or rather *is* – a story... It enfolds the lives and times of predecessors who, over the generations, have moved around in it and played their part in its formation.

[78] G.M. Trevelyan, 'Introduction', in James Lees-Milne (ed.), *The National Trust* (London, 1945), xi.

[79] Cf. Tim Ingold, 'Culture on the Ground: The World Perceived Through the Feet', *Journal of Material Culture*, 9 (2004), 333.

[80] 'What historians need is not more documents but stronger boots': Tawney as quoted in W.K. Hancock, *Country and Calling* (London, 1954), 95.

[81] Tim Ingold, *The Perception of the Environment* (London, 2000), 150.

G.M. Trevelyan, Landscape and the Writing of History in England

To perceive the landscape is therefore to carry out an act of remembrance, and remembering is not so much a matter of calling up an internal image, stored in the mind, as of engaging perceptually with an environment that is itself pregnant with the past.[82]

Something like this perspective was adopted by historians such as Freeman, Green and Trevelyan. It was a perspective that drew heavily on embodied, on-foot, experience. Walking made possible a particular sort of historical knowing, its relatively slow speed enabling the careful observation of landscape and the imaginative appreciation of place.

In a sense, this was nothing new. Pedestrianised forms of historical knowing had been a feature of the older antiquarian tradition.[83] This tradition had more influence than is sometimes supposed, deep into the twentieth century. Its reach extended into the rapidly professionalising universities, as exemplified by figures such as Charles Henderson (1900–33), whose amazingly detailed self-directed research into Cornish ecclesiastical antiquities, old bridges and rivers laid the foundation for academic appointments, first at University College Exeter and then at Corpus Christi College, Oxford.[84] As his obituary notices emphasised, Henderson was an enthusiastic walker, and like his eighteenth- and nineteenth-century antiquarian forebears he did much of his research on foot, making in-situ notes and drawings; this also gave him a keen sense of the way in which landscape features such as the river Tamar had shaped Cornish history.[85] Even when his interests moved beyond Cornwall to the history of eighteenth-century Europe, close topographical observation remained central to his method.[86] One Oxford colleague noted after Henderson's untimely death that his 'mind was never absent from his surroundings', his powers of observation enabling him to 'see the past in the present'.[87]

Like Trevelyan and other more celebrated historians, Henderson's envisioning of the past through engagement with the present-day landscape was as much an imaginative act as it was about noting down recondite information about the relics of distant times. It expressed something fundamental about the practice of history – what Collingwood described as the 're-enactment of past

---

[82] *Ibid.*, 189.

[83] Paul Readman, 'Walking, and Knowing the Past: Antiquaries, Pedestrianism and Historical Practice in Modern Britain', *History*, 107 (2022), 51–73.

[84] Henderson's papers are held in the Courtney Library at the Royal Institution of Cornwall, Truro.

[85] *West Briton*, 28 Sept. and 5 Oct. 1933 (cuttings in Courtney Library); Charles Henderson and Henry Coates, *Old Cornish Bridges and Streams* (Exeter, 1928).

[86] As evident not least from his travel diaries: Henderson papers, Courtney Library.

[87] W.F.R.H., 'Charles Henderson', *Pelican Record*, 21 (Dec. 1933), 87–8: copy in Courtney Library.

experience' in the mind of the historian.[88] Indeed, Collingwood's own anti-quarian leanings are worth recalling here. The schooling he received from his father in the antiquities of Lakeland led him to archaeology as well as history, and he duly succeeded him as President of the Cumberland and Westmoreland Antiquarian and Archaeological Society. In this capacity, and in works such as his *Archaeology of Roman Britain*, Collingwood represented the British anti-quarian tradition – what Mortimer Wheeler later described as 'that long and distinguished line of amateurs... who for three centuries or more had sustained the study of British antiquities as an inevitable and engrossing study of the educated mind'.[89] Collingwood's antiquarianism complemented his philosophy of history, since the re-enactment of past experience cannot be divorced from the locational context of that experience. Thus 'To write the history of a battle, we must re-think the thoughts which determined its various tactical phases: we must *see the ground of the battlefield as the opposing commanders saw it*, and *draw from the topography* the conclusions that they drew: and so forth'.[90] Trevelyan, surely, would have concurred.

* * *

It remains true that works such as Green's *Short History* and Trevelyan's *English Social History* are far from perfect, if judged by modern professional standards. Yet their writers understood something important – that knowledge is learned through whole-body encounters with the world, that 'thinking is inseparable from doing'.[91] Just such a rejection of the cartesian mind/body dualism has much preoccupied social theorists. Jean Lave's fieldwork-based research on the anthropology of cognition, for example, is a compelling demonstration of how knowledge is more a 'process of knowing' in the world, and less 'a factual com-modity or compendium of facts'. Cognitive activity is to an important extent 'physical', whether this be 'searching' for a particular item in a supermarket, 'getting the point' of a lecture, or 'digging' a rock concert.[92] And while Lave's

---

[88] Collingwood, *Idea of History*, esp. 215–19, 282–302.

[89] R.G. Collingwood, *The Archaeology of Roman Britain* (London, 1930); Tony Birley, 'Collingwood as Archaeologist and Historian', in David Boucher and Teresa Smith (eds), *R.G. Collingwood: An Autobiography and other Writings: With Essays on Collingwood's Life and Work* (Oxford, 2013), 290.

[90] Cited in Marnie Hughes-Warrington, *'How Good an Historian Shall I Be? R.G. Collingwood, the Historical Imagination and Education* (Exeter, 2003), 55 [emphasis added].

[91] Ingold, *Perception of the Environment*, 162.

[92] Jean Lave, *Cognition in Practice* (Cambridge, 1988), esp. 171–5, 181–2, at 175, 182. See also Mark Johnson and George Lakoff on the embodied basis of metaphor and cognitive activity more generally: Johnson, *The Body in the Mind* (Chicago, 1987) and

work was focused on everyday cognition – specifically the arithmetic calculations of shoppers – its conclusions are applicable to all forms of thought. As she explains, 'the unique, the nonroutine... the creative novelty, the scientific discovery, major contributions to knowledge' are all 'constructed in dialectical relations between the experienced lived-in world and its constitutive order – in practice'.[93] If we accept this – that cognition is embodied – then it follows that the necessarily cognitive business of doing history cannot be separated from whole-person experience, and that historians should recognise this inseparability in their practice. To paraphrase Tim Ingold, we need to think with our feet as well as our heads.[94]

No doubt this is easier and more interpretatively fruitful for some kinds of history. Subjects where the written source base is scanty are more likely to have us reaching for our walking boots and leaving our desks to keep company with anthropologists and archaeologists – as, for example, Naomi Standen has done in her work on medieval eastern Eurasia.[95] But, I would suggest, personal experience of the places we write about is valuable to *all* forms of historical inquiry. If Collingwood is right that all history is the history of thought, and if we reject the cartesian mind/body dichotomy and accept the ineluctably embodied nature of cognition, then thinking historically means thinking with all our senses. It means integrating direct experience of landscape and place into our historical practice, or at least acknowledging the power of its influence on our historical practice. Among other things, but often in association with walking (since the slow speed of walking permits it to be done with special profit), this means looking around us – and it means looking not just at paintings, photographs and other typical examples of 'visual' sources.[96] Yet historians are often bad at looking. Non-textual evidence, especially when it is garnered from our own direct sense impressions, seems unreliable, unsusceptible to independent verification, impossible to footnote. To the now thoroughly professionalised historian, written records appear a more secure basis for supporting arguments, for providing proof. And as Raphael Samuel pointed out some time ago, 'modern conditions of research seem to dictate an almost

---

Embodied Mind, Meaning and Reason (Chicago, 2017); Lakoff and Johnson, *Metaphors We Live By* (Chicago, 1980) and *Philosophy in the Flesh* (New York, 1999).

[93] Lave, *Cognition in Practice*, 190.

[94] Ingold, 'Culture on the Ground'; 'Ways of Mind-Walking'.

[95] Naomi Standen, 'Colouring Outside the Lines: Methods for a Global History of Eastern Eurasia, 600–1350', *Transactions of the Royal Historical Society*, 6th ser., 29 (2019), 27–63.

[96] Ludmilla Jordanova, *The Look of the Past* (Cambridge, 2012).

complete detachment from the material environment'.[97] This was a prescient observation; thanks to the internet, there seems less need than ever to leave the study.

But whatever the reasons for this persisting and perhaps increasing detachment from the outside world, further reflection on the practice of Trevelyan and the other historians discussed in this essay may give new momentum – and perhaps add a new dimension – to the much vaunted but by no means all-conquering 'spatial' and 'material' turns. These historians knew that a great deal could be learnt from personal (and typically on-foot) experience beyond archive and library; they knew, to quote James Bryce, that an important adjunct to 'mere book knowledge' was 'direct personal knowledge' of the landscape and places of which the past was constitutive.[98] What might be termed their chronotopic sensitivity provided them with information – field lines, settlement patterns, defensive positions and so on – but, more crucially, it stimulated their historical imagination. It made the past live in the present; it made the past real – fully, richly, and humanly known.

[97] Raphael Samuel, *Theatres of Memory*, Vol. 1: *Past and Present in Contemporary Culture* (London, 1994), 269.

[98] Bryce, 'Importance of Geography in Education. I', 148.

Part II

Nation

Chapter 3

The Image of the Country House in Victorian Political Culture

James Thompson

The literature on the English country house is compendious, ranging from the building to the destroying of country houses, and paying lavish attention to gardens, art collections and gilded consumption, not forgetting the occasional physics laboratory.[1] The substantial historiography of the British and Irish aristocracy has had much to say about country houses, not least their cost.[2] In recent years, important work has focused on the links between country houses, empire and the history of slavery – charting connections that, as Margot Finn rightly notes, were familiar to nineteenth-century observers, not to mention some twentieth-century historiography.[3] The fall and rise of the

---

[1] Terence A.M. Dooley, *Burning the Big House: The Story of the Irish Country House in Time of War and Revolution* (New Haven, 2022); James S. Donnelly Jr., 'Big House Burnings in County Cork during the Irish Revolution', *Éire-Ireland*, 47 (2012), 141–97; Simon Schaffer, 'Physics Laboratories and the Victorian Country House', in Crosbie Smith, Jon Agar and Gerald Schmidt (eds), *Making Space for Science: Territorial Themes in the Shaping of Knowledge* (Basingstoke, 1998), 149–80; Mark Girouard, *Life in the English Country House: A Social and Architectural History* (New Haven, 1978).

[2] F.M.L. Thompson, *English Landed Society in the Nineteenth Century* (London, 1963); David Spring, 'The English Landed Estate in the Age of Coal and Iron: 1830–1880', *Journal of Economic History*, 11 (1951), 3–24; David Cannadine, *The Decline and Fall of the British Aristocracy* (New Haven, 1990) and *Aspects of Aristocracy: Grandeur and Decline in Modern Britain* (London, 1994); Mark Girouard, *The Victorian Country House* (London, 1979).

[3] Stephanie Barczewski, *Country Houses and the British Empire* (Manchester, 2014); Stephanie Barczewski, 'Country Houses and the Distinctiveness of the Irish Imperial Experience', in Timothy G. McMahon, Michael de Nie and Paul Townend (eds), *Ireland in an Imperial World: Citizenship, Opportunism and Subversion* (London, 2017), 25–48; Madge Dresser and Andrew Hann (eds), *Slavery and the British Country House* (Swindon, 2013); Jessica Moody and Stephen Small, 'Slavery and Public History at the Big House: Remembering and Forgetting at American Plantation Museums and

country house in English culture has received distinguished treatment.[4] The significance of the country house in the history of 'heritage' has been sharply debated, notably in the 1980s.[5] The history of the country house clearly cannot be described as a 'neglected subject'.

Debates about country houses and heritage have been deeply concerned with questions of national identity.[6] Recent decades have seen a broader interest in histories of 'Englishness'.[7] Much of this writing has been primarily cultural in its orientation. 'Englishness' has also been an important theme in the work of Jonathan Parry, but approached chiefly through political history. In a series of publications, Parry has explored the politics and language of patriotism in nineteenth- and twentieth-century Britain, particularly, though not exclusively, in relation to liberalism.[8] The persistence of a 'Whig' model of the constitution, and its relationship to national identity, have been central to this body of work.[9] This chapter takes a topic – the country house – for which there is an extensive and valuable literature in cultural history, and examines it through

---

British Country Houses', *Journal of Global Slavery*, 4 (2019), 34–68; Margot C. Finn, 'Material Turns in British History: IV. Empire in India, Cancel Culture and the Country House', *Transactions of the Royal Historical Society*, 6th ser., 31 (2021), 1–21; *Illustrated London News*, 8 Nov. 1890, 590; Raymond Williams, *The Country and the City* (London, 2016 [1973]), 150.

4   Peter Mandler, *The Fall and Rise of the Stately Home* (New Haven, 1997).

5   Raphael Samuel, *Theatres of Memory, Vol. 1: Past and Present in Contemporary Culture* (London, 2012); Peter Mandler, 'Nationalising the Country House' in Michael Hunter (ed.), *Preserving the Past: The Rise of Heritage in Modern Britain* (London, 1994); Robert Hewison, *The Heritage Industry: Britain in a Climate of Decline* (London, 1987); Patrick Wright, *On Living in an Old Country* (London, 1985).

6   Stephanie Barczewski, *How the Country House Became English* (London, 2023), 10–11.

7   Paul Readman, *Storied Ground: Landscape and the Shaping of English National Identity* (Cambridge, 2018); Peter Mandler, *The English National Character: The History of an Idea from Edmund Burke to Tony Blair* (New Haven and London, 2006).

8   Jonathan Parry, *The Politics of Patriotism: English Liberalism, National Identity and Europe, 1838–1886* (Cambridge, 2006); 'Patriotism', in David Craig and James Thompson (eds), *Languages of Politics in Nineteenth-Century Britain* (Basingstoke, 2013), 69–92; 'Whig Monarchy, Whig Nation: Crown, Politics and Representativeness, 1800–2000', in Andrej Olechnowicz (ed.), *The Monarchy and the British Nation 1780 to the Present* (Cambridge, 2004), 47–75; 'Nonconformity, Clericalism and "Englishness": The United Kingdom', in Christopher Clark and Wolfram Kaiser (eds), *Culture Wars: Secular-Catholic Conflict in Nineteenth-century Europe* (Cambridge, 2003), 152–80; 'The Impact of Napoleon III on British Politics, 1851–1880', *Transactions of the Royal Historical Society*, 6th ser., 6 (2001), 147–75; 'Disraeli and England', *Historical Journal* 43 (2000), 699–728.

9   Parry, *Politics of Patriotism*, 15; 'Whig Monarchy, Whig Nation', 66.

The Image of the Country House in Victorian Political Culture   63

a more political lens. In doing so, it seeks to reflect upon themes – the nature of political leadership, the construction of political personae, the projection of values – that recur through Parry's writings.[10]

Amidst the vast body of work on country houses, limited attention has been paid to the political significance and uses of the nineteenth-century country house, though biographies teem with details of country house weekends and encounters. In histories of the press and of high politics, the country house serves as a stage for the exchange of news and gossip, the forging of alliances and the flying of kites.[11] But it remains a suitably expensive background to such carefully traced manoeuvres, rather than an object of analysis. This chapter examines the place of the country house in Victorian political culture – 'its role and symbolism' – paying particular attention to its visual representation.[12] As the illustrated press burgeoned from the 1860s, representations of politics and politicians proliferated. In 1880, the *Illustrated London News* featured an aged Gladstone at Dalmeny, in a picture entitled 'the calm before the storm' (fig. 3.1).[13]

Country houses could be presented as both sites of elite political exchange and as affording moments of private respite amidst the rigours of public life. For opponents of the status quo in Britain and Ireland, the big house could be a potent symbol of oppression that required a literal dismantling.[14] The image of the country house thus offers both a way into the relationship between 'popular' and 'elite' politics in the nineteenth century, and a window onto the image of 'politics' itself.

Historians have long argued – to quote David Cannadine paraphrasing Mark Girouard – that 'country houses were not fetish objects, inhabited by implausibly nice and exquisitely civilized people: they were fundamentally machines for a power elite to live in'.[15] Half a century ago Raymond Williams stressed the view 'from the outside looking in' at buildings that constituted 'a visible stamping of power, of displayed wealth and command: a social dispro-portion that was meant to impress and overawe'.[16] As 'bastions of power, as

[10] J.P. Parry, *Democracy and Religion: Gladstone and the Liberal Party, 1867–1875* (Cambridge, 1986); Jonathan Parry, *The Rise and Fall of Liberal Government in Victorian Britain* (New Haven & London, 1993); *Politics of Patriotism*.

[11] A.B. Cooke and John Vincent, *The Governing Passion: Cabinet Government and Party Politics in Britain, 1885–86* (Brighton, 1974); Stephen Koss, *The Rise and Fall of the Political Press in Britain* (London, 1990).

[12] Parry, 'Whig Monarchy, Whig Nation', 48.

[13] *Illustrated London News*, 4 Apr. 1880, 353.

[14] Dooley, *Burning the Big House*, 9–10; Brian Friel, *Aristocrats* (Loughcrew, 1980), 43.

[15] David Cannadine, *The Pleasures of the Past* (London, 1997), 266.

[16] Williams, *Country and the City*, 151.

Fig. 3.1. 'The Calm Before the Storm: A Sketch at Dalmeny on Saturday, April 3', *Illustrated London News*, 4 Apr. 1880.

The Image of the Country House in Victorian Political Culture 65

expressions of wealth, and as assertions of status', these houses always served a political function, supplying a 'citadel from which a landed family superintended its economic affairs, organized its political activities, and proclaimed its social position'.[17] Their later twentieth-century domestication as a heritage of idealised 'homes' can distract from their more political role in the nineteenth century.[18] As Antony Taylor has traced, there was a lively tradition of hostility to aristocracy in nineteenth-century Britain.[19] Country houses were sites for demonstrating for Chartists in England; from the 1880s, Irish nationalists targeted the biggest houses and landowners especially.[20] In 1872 the *Irish Examiner* took the very splendour of English country houses and their surroundings, in a country neither artistic nor blessed with much natural beauty, as clear evidence of the power of money and of the misrule of Ireland.[21] As Parry has noted, the volunteers of the early 1860s were entertained on country estates.[22] In holding picnics in the grounds of stately homes, Primrose Leaguers mobilised the symbolic power of the country house, advancing a particular, and contested, view of the social and political order.[23] The links between formal politics and the country house were both various and deep.

The chapter is in two parts. The first examines the invocation of the country house as metaphor, and as infrastructure, for politics in Victorian Britain. It ranges from the use of grounds to host volunteering in the 1860s to Primrose League lantern lectures in the 1890s, exploring the contested political resonances and uses of country houses. The second section draws upon the burgeoning pictorial press to trace how the country house figures in political cartoons and reporting. It then turns to the place of politics in the often extensively illustrated guides to country houses that proliferated in the media from the 1880s, linking these to the development and nature of political celebrity.

---

[17] Cannadine, *Decline and Fall*, 693.

[18] Wright, *On Living in an Old Country*, 11; on their political role in the nineteenth century, see Barczewski, *How the Country House Became English*, 21.

[19] Anthony Taylor, *Lords of Misrule: Hostility to Aristocracy in Late Nineteenth and Early Twentieth Century Britain* (Basingstoke, 2004).

[20] Mandler, *Fall and Rise*, 39; Rolf Loeber *et al.*, *Art and Architecture of Ireland Vol. IV: Architecture 1600–2000* (Dublin, 2015), 384.

[21] *Irish Examiner*, 13 Dec. 1872, 2.

[22] Parry, 'Impact of Napoleon III', 165.

[23] Patricia Lynch, *The Liberal Party in Rural England, 1885–1910* (Oxford, 2003), 57; Martin Pugh, *The Tories and the People 1880–1935* (London, 1985), 31.

Political Metaphor and Infrastructure

Important work on the history of the country house in Britain has emphasised the divisions in nineteenth-century views, and located the 'cult' of the country house well into the post-1945 period.[24] The evidence from Victorian political culture aligns with this interpretation, not least in the lack of reverence in the caricatures of the weekly press. The heyday of identification of the country house with notions of 'Englishness' was a later phenomenon. Such identifications were not, however, unknown in the nineteenth century, though, nor were they invariably laudatory.[25] They often assumed a specifically political form. Editorialising on 'Conservative Progress' in 1858, the *Armagh Gazette* approvingly quoted Lord Derby on the nature of the times. In a well-known speech, Derby argued that a Conservative ministry would not be hostile to change, but would recognise that 'we live in an age of constant progress – moral, social, and political... when knowledge is daily more and more widely diffused' and that 'our constitution itself is a result of perpetual changes'. He went on to develop, in revealing terms, an analogy between the constitution and the 'the venerable old country-house of England' that had been

> formed... by successive occupants, with no great regard to regular architectural uniformity or regularity of outline, but adding a window here, throwing out a gable there, and making some fresh accommodation in another place, as might appear to suit, not the beauty of the external structure, but, what is of more importance, the convenience and comfort of the inhabitants. [26]

The metaphor rested precisely upon a willingness – recognisable amongst nineteenth-century country house owners – to make changes, and to do so with a focus on 'convenience and comfort' above 'the beauty of the external structure'.[27]

The analogy with the constitution linked the country house to a central aspect of nineteenth-century conceptions of politics.[28] The constitution was

---

[24] Mark Girouard, *Town and Country* (New Haven, 1992), 9; Mandler, *Fall and Rise*, 245; Mandler, 'Nationalising the Country House', 113.

[25] Barczewski, *How the Country House Became English*, 22, 33, 304–5.

[26] *Armagh Guardian*, 12 Mar. 1858, 4.

[27] Girouard, *Victorian Country House*, 8.

[28] James Vernon (ed.), *Re-reading the Constitution: New Narratives in the Political History of England's Long Nineteenth Century* (Cambridge, 1996); Parry, *Rise and Fall*; James Thompson, *British Political Culture and the Idea of 'Public Opinion'* (Cambridge, 2013); Anna Clark, *Scandal: The Sexual Politics of the British Constitution* (Princeton, 2013).

The Image of the Country House in Victorian Political Culture 67

integral to the politics of patriotism, and to discussions of national character.[29] The country house could serve as a shorthand for English wealth in critiques of its origins and basis. In doing so, the *Irish Examiner* noted that 'scattered through the country houses... there are treasures of art almost rivalling those of Italy... the product of... superabundant money'. For the *Examiner*, 'the lawns... glorious Woods... blazing parterres, and charming verdure, such as no country probably, whatever its natural capacity can rival' were proof of how money had brought 'fertility and grace and variety out of the soil'. The paper proceeded to note how 'when Englishmen are boasting of the remarkable freedom and good Government of their country, the name of Ireland has been incessantly thrown in their teeth', arguing that Ireland had 'revenged herself for the misrule from which she suffered by being an incessant source of peril and humiliation to her proud sister'. It compared the political challenge to English forms of governance supplied by Ireland to the social challenges of trade unions and agricultural labour, finishing with a denunciation of those 'who rely exclusively on political economy' and discounted 'men's feelings' preferring 'the table of averages', implying these were characteristically English failings.[30]

The connections between politics and the social embodied in the county house were elaborated rather differently by the prolific journalist and writer T.H.S. Escott.[31] Escott took 'the country house, as an institution, situated in that extensive borderland where politics and society meet' to be common to both Liberals and Conservatives.[32] His fullest account of 'the country-house system' offered an extended paean to country houses as 'centres of social or political life and interest', and as sites and symbols of political continuity and social integration.[33] Its political significance was conveyed by a geographically-specific variant of the constitutional analogy: 'the English constitution, as Disraeli once put it, was born in the bosom of the Chilterns; the country-house system was cradled in the valley of the Medway'.[34] A sharp inversion of this conception of the country house was expressed by William Cobbett. Cobbett's greater enthusiasm for parks than houses was widespread in nineteenth-century commentary, as was his interest in the sources of wealth – viewed by Cobbett through the lens of Anti-Semitism.[35] For Cobbett, 'the war and paper system' had placed the 'good houses' in the hands of a new 'gentry, only now and then residing

[29] Parry, *Politics of Patriotism*; Mandler, *English National Character*.
[30] *Irish Examiner*, 13 Dec. 1872, 2.
[31] Mandler, *Fall and Rise*, 130.
[32] T.H.S. Escott, *England: Its People, Polity and Pursuits* (London, 1885), 342.
[33] T.H.S. Escott, *Society in the Country House* (London, 1907), 17, 84, 150, 485.
[34] *Ibid.*, 150.
[35] John W. Osborne, 'William Cobbett's Anti-Semitism', *The Historian*, 47 (1984), 86–92, at 87.

at all, having no relish for country-delights, foreign in their manners, distant and haughty in their behaviour, looking to the soil only for its rents, viewing it as a mere object of speculation, unacquainted with its cultivators, despising them and their pursuits, and relying, for influence, not upon the good will of the vicinage, but upon the dread of their power'.[36] As historians of the eighteenth century have shown, country houses could be perceived as markers of illegitimate and troubling wealth, notably if owned by 'nabobs'.[37] The representative function of the country house continued to feature in prominent works of political criticism. In Matthew Arnold's *Culture and Anarchy*, the 'beautiful and imposing seat' in the country served to distinguish the aristocracy from the middle-class by providing 'a great fortified post of the Barbarians'.[38] From a rather different perspective, W.H. Mallock set his conservative meditation on 'culture, faith and philosophy' in an English country house, and parodies of it borrowed the location to undercut the supposed profundity of his protagonists.[39]

The country house was also, though, part of the infrastructure of politics, as the Victorian press made clear. The movements of elite politicians constituted a form of 'political news'. The return of ministers from their country houses to attend parliament was reported as part of the rhythms of the political year.[40] The *Cork Constitution* was unimpressed in 1895 with the Tory Lord Norton for hosting Gladstone, suggesting his 'devotion amounts to a sort of religion'.[41] In 1856 the *Berkshire Chronicle* reported that 'some importance is attached to the visit of Lord Palmerston to Woburn Abbey, the seat of the Duke of Bedford', noting the role of the Abbey as 'the rendezvous of the leading Whigs when in political difficulties'.[42] Such visits were also opportunities (not always accepted) for the mobilising of local supporters to pay tribute, as Bedfordshire Liberals sought to do in 1866 when Gladstone visited the same house.[43] Country houses were presented as both sites for informal discussions within a political and media elite, and spaces of encounter – often ritualised – between leading

[36] William Cobbett, *Rural Rides – Vol. I*, ed. G.D.H. and Margaret Cole (London, 1930), 34.

[37] Finn, 'Material Turns', 14–15; Tillman W. Nechtman, *Nabobs: Empire and Identity in Eighteenth-Century Britain* (Cambridge, 2010).

[38] Matthew Arnold, *Culture and Anarchy and other Writings*, ed. Stefan Collini (Cambridge, 1993), 106.

[39] W.H. Mallock, *The New Republic: Culture, Faith and Philosophy in an English Country House* (London, 1877); *Punch*, 'A Few Days at a Country House', 22 and 29 Sept. 1877, 124–5, 133–6.

[40] *Irish Examiner*, 6 Apr. 1888, 3.

[41] *Cork Constitution*, 4 Sept. 1895, 5.

[42] *Berkshire Chronicle*, 13 Dec. 1856, 4.

[43] *Bedfordshire Mercury*, 22 Sept. 1866, 4.

The radical press reported at length on pilgrimages to Hawarden – as in the visit of two thousand Liberals from the Potteries in 1888 – when, *Reynolds's* noted, a vase was presented to Mr and Mrs Gladstone with 'a symbolical figure of Liberty holding in one hand the scales of Justice and in the other a broken chain' along with Homer, Dante, and 'an historian' recording deeds done in the name of freedom.[45] Country house visiting could be incorporated into the culture of early socialism: Archibald Gorrie wrote in the *Clarion* newspaper on behalf of the Leicester Fabian Society, the Leicester branch of the Social Democratic Federation, and the Leicester Anarchist Communists, advertising the joys of an outing 'to Rowsley in Derbyshire, in order to visit Chatsworth and Haddon Hall Communists'.[46] In Ireland the country house was also considered as a source of armed power; the *Cork Examiner* mocked its more conservative counterpart the *Constitution* for imperilling the Irish gentry's 'reputation for hospitality' with its obsession with 'hand-grenades, swan-shot, and rifle bullets'.[47]

Through the course of the nineteenth century, the notion of 'politics' was contested and expanded in processes both reflected and constituted through the media.[48] This had implications for the political role of the country house in a period that saw growing demands for extra-parliamentary speechmaking, increases to the electorate and often raucous public politics embracing new forms of communication.[49] As a venue for politics, the country house's capacity to link changing conceptions of public and private was crucial to its efficacy. That the Lancashire Rifle volunteers gathered at Knowsley Park in 1860 rendered it a site of active citizenship, as well as providing excellent material for large-scale drawings in the illustrated press, including the 'the Earl and Countess of Derby leaving Knowsley Hall' (fig. 3.2).[50]

---

[44] Cannadine, *Pleasures of the Past*, 104; Mandler, *Fall and Rise*, 83, 213.

[45] *Reynolds's News*, 26 Aug. 1888, 5.

[46] Working Class Movement Library, Frow-Box 116 Scrapbook XXII.

[47] *Cork Examiner*, 21 Sept. 1865, 2.

[48] Jose Harris, 'The Transition to High Politics in English Social Policy, 1880–1914', in Michael Bentley and John Stevenson (eds), *High and Low Politics in Modern Britain*, (Oxford, 1983), 58–79; James Thompson, 'The Political Press', in David Finkelstein (ed.), *The Edinburgh History of the British and Irish Press, 1800–1900* (Edinburgh, 2020), 526–45.

[49] Jon Lawrence, *Electing Our Masters: The Hustings in British Politics from Hogarth to Blair* (Oxford, 2009); James Thompson, '"Pictorial lies"?: Posters and Politics in Britain, 1880–1914', *Past and Present*, 197 (2007), 177–210; Tom Crewe, 'Political Leaders, Communication, and Celebrity in Britain, c.1880–1900' (unpublished PhD diss., Cambridge, 2015).

[50] *Illustrated London News*, 15 Sept. 1860, 243.

Fig. 3.2. 'The Review of Lancashire Rifle Volunteers in Knowsley Park – the Earl and Countess of Derby Leaving Knowsley Hall for the Review', *Illustrated London News*, 15 Sept. 1860.

The Image of the Country House in Victorian Political Culture   71

Profiling Wycombe Abbey – 'neither old... nor an Abbey' – in 1895, the *Illustrated London News* found the growth of religious tolerance evident in the 'great lawn continually lent by Lord Carrington for gatherings of Dissenters of various denominations, all free to choose their own day and demonstrate on the grass to their heart's content.'[51] The blending of public and private was apparent in the practice of hosting visiting dignitaries, as in 'the garden party for the Shah at Hatfield House' in 1889, pictured in a contrasting foreground of guests in black and white with 'the seat of the Marquis [sic] of Salisbury' looming in the background.[52] For a garden party in 1891 welcoming 'Orange delegates', special trains were put on from London to Hatfield with guests 'shown over the house' before strolling through the 'beautiful grounds' and listening to speeches.[53]

The combining of public and private, domestic and political, was integral to Primrose League fêtes held in the parks of well-known country houses that Martin Pugh rightly notes were designed to 'innoculate [sic]... against the Radical characterization of the aristocracy as aloof, absentee and exploitative'.[54] The Primrose League enthusiastically embraced lantern slide lectures in the 1890s, recommending their use in 'small villages and towns'.[55] Alongside paeans to empire and Navy, the League's offerings included lectures on the Stately Homes of England, Westminster Abbey, and the Land of William the Conqueror.[56] The country house was co-opted into the League's broader understanding of history and politics. Its slides were part of a wider growth in the circulation of images of country houses at the close of the nineteenth century. Much of that imagery was rooted in the lively world of the illustrated comic press, and reveals a far from reverent approach to country houses and their occupants.

Picturing and Politics

There was a significant expansion of illustrated weeklies from the 1860s across a number of cities, including London, Manchester, Birmingham and Dublin.[57] The emergence of these periodicals – whether chiefly comic like the Liberal *Fun*

---

[51]   *Ibid.*, 5 Oct. 1895, 434.

[52]   *Ibid.*, 13 July 1889, 'Supplement'.

[53]   *Evening Herald*, 24 Apr. 1893, 3.

[54]   Pugh, *Tories and the People*, 31.

[55]   *Primrose League Gazette*, Jan. 1895, 4.

[56]   *Ibid.*, Dec. 1895, 3; James Thompson, *Seeing Politics: Visual and Political Culture in Britain, c.1867–1939* (forthcoming).

[57]   Ian Cawood and Chris Upton, 'Joseph Chamberlain and the Birmingham Satirical Journals, 1876–1911', in Ian Cawood and Chris Upton (eds), *Joseph Chamberlain: International Statesmen, National Leader, Local Icon* (Basingstoke, 2016), 176–210.

(1861), Conservative *Judy* (1867) and radical *Tomahawk* (1867), or news-based like *The Graphic* (1869) – both reflected and fostered an expanded audience for politics.[58] Portraiture and caricature were central forms of representation for these new periodicals. In the often sharply partisan comic press the country house served a distinctly political function. Much like the motifs of caricature – John Bright's hat, Joseph Chamberlain's monocle, Gladstone's axe – it acted as a signifier for a politician, ideal for mocking pretension and hypocrisy and for the manufacture of (sometimes dire) puns. *Fun* enjoyed referring to Disraeli as 'the great Hughenden lover of justice'; Salisbury was repeatedly the 'Lord' or 'Master' of Hatfield; whilst the Hatfield Street Ragged School appeared as a running gag in the 1880s in a paper keen to satirise Conservative claims on social reform.[59]

As befits a complex and self-conscious political culture, the comic press mused upon the uses of the country house as backdrop for political publicity. In an 1878 piece on 'photographic foibles', *Fun* claimed to be 'astonished' that Mr Gladstone's 'famous tree-felling photograph' had not been 'followed more generally'. Why not, it asked, 'a series of likenesses', including 'Lord Beacons-field, attired as a country squire, prodding one of his Hughenden pigs with his walking stick, Lord Cairns, with gun at his shoulder… the Right Hon. John Bright… making a cast for a big salmon; Lord John Manners, his "eye in fine frenzy rolling", dashing off the lines of a new heroic poem; and the Marquis [sic] of Hartington taking long odds against a dark colt for the Derby?'[60] *Judy* was equally alert to developments in political communication, but from an opposing perspective. It was busy in 1875 bemoaning Gladstone's tendency for telegraphing domestic speeches given at Hawarden to the press, while the following year it contemplated his enthusiasm for 'cutting things down… national churches, trees'.[61] The latter, of course, provided much copy, including a 'tree-mendous sensation' in which the trees of Hawarden conduct emergency meetings in the face of Gladstone's mania for felling them.[62]

The expansion of the political nation in the 1880s had its counterpart in the further spread of imagery within the press. In the decade in which Madame Tussaud's – full of waxwork politicians – found a new home, the visualisa-tion of political celebrity intensified.[63] Responding to the cult of the Grand Old

---

[58] Thompson, 'Political Press'.

[59] *Fun*, 1 Aug. 1877, 54; *Fun*, 9 Nov. 1872, 191; *Fun*, 6 June 1883, 246; *Truth*, 28 Aug. 1884, 327.

[60] *Fun*, 25 Sept. 1878, 133.

[61] *Judy*, 3 Nov. 1875, 22 and 24 May 1876, 59.

[62] *Judy*, 12 Sept. 1883, 132.

[63] Pamela Pilbeam, *Madame Tussauds and the History of Waxworks* (London, 2002).

The Image of the Country House in Victorian Political Culture   73

Man in which Hawarden played a significant part, *Judy* increasingly incorporated the castle into its cartooning. In 1883 it mockingly featured the 'temple of peace' inside Hawarden as the site for the Gladstonian holiday – one the Liberal leader would spend 'racking his brains for some new device to set the world agog' – combining the inevitable imagery of tree-felling, with mocking references to demonstrative religiosity, Ireland and radicalism.[64] It subverted the conventional pose of the statesman at his desk, casting Gladstone as wild-haired, slouchy, yet dangerously dynamic. The established device of politics as horserace was deployed in 1888's 'Wet Monday at Hawarden' where a power-crazed Gladstone – his hair inscribed with 'self-admiration' – is portrayed as reluctantly travelling to the country house when all he really wants is a return to Downing Street (fig. 3.3).[65]

The house featured again in 1890 in a cartoon that returned to Gladstone's love of sending postcards, and which presented the development of the house by the addition of 'a strong, fireproof room' for correspondence, as a further instance of hubris.[66]

It is important to recognise the satirical uses to which country house imagery could be put, and the ways in which it could be incorporated into the political exchanges of the partisan comic weeklies, along with its more predictable use as a stage for social comedy.[67] Images of country houses were also, however, a feature of the more earnest illustrated newspapers and magazines. Peter Mandler has traced the spread of 'country-house profiles' in 'end-of-the-century journalism' across illustrated publications like the *Graphic*, *Sketch*, *English Illustrated Magazine* and *Illustrated London News*. He emphasises the attention paid to famous occupants, and the use of photography to give a 'slick, modern gloss', arguing that even the *Illustrated London News* – 'long an exponent of the Olden Time sense of heritage (and a bastion against photography)' – concentrated in its series on 'English Homes' on 'the achievements of the current occupants.'[68]

Certainly, the *Illustrated London News*'s long sequence on 'English Homes' across the 1880s and 1890s included many houses with significant political links – and made much of those links. It was not without its assessments of 'national character', albeit these were not entirely lacking in irony. Its article on Sandringham in 1887 remarked that 'we English flatter ourselves that we are, above all things, a very plain, homely people, disliking show and ceremony, and always placing comfort before magnificence', though it went on to argue that

---

[64] *Judy*, 3 Oct. 1883, 162.

[65] *Judy*, 23 May 1888, 246.

[66] *Judy*, 30 Jan. 1889, 54.

[67] For instance, *Punch*, 21 June 1899, 291.

[68] Mandler, *Fall and Rise*, 130, 433.

Fig. 3.3. 'Wet Monday at Hawarden', *Judy*, 23 May 1888.

The Image of the Country House in Victorian Political Culture   75

'the country house of the Prince of Wales' was an 'example of its occasional truth', for it was 'more than anything a home'.[69] The series did contain elements of revivalism – the visitor to Powderham Castle was likely, the reader was told, to find themselves wishing for 'the restoration of the Courtenay Family to the great place they once held in local and even national history'.[70] It was also suspicious of 'the British Classic' as an architectural style.[71] It operated with a notion of the 'picturesque' in which grounds, gardens and sky played as large a role as houses.[72] It could be quite offhand about the 'besetting sin of old houses' as in the entry on Stoke Park: 'it was damp'.[73] The entry on Knowsley quite cheerfully noted that 'everywhere, as in many an historic English home, the old and new are side by side'.[74]

The spread of photography was evident in the *Illustrated London News* when it replaced the traditional drawings with photographs of new MPs after the 1895 general election. The growth of photographic imagery was, however, accompanied by an expansion across the press in the use of cartoons, and the relationship between the two was complex.[75] In 'English Homes', considerable use was made of layering multiple drawings, including circular images, in ways that recall the photographic, even snapshot (fig. 3.4).[76]

The multi-perspectival approach was adopted for Studley Royal. Here the focus was on Lord Ripon's 'devotion to duty'. In keeping with the motif of 'the calm before the storm', the paper noted that 'the walk of a mile or so from Studley Royal to the Abbey is one that its owner often makes... A man who lives in the hurly-burly of modern politics may easily find refreshment in recalling the tranquillity of others [monks]... who lived simple and separated lives in days of long ago'.[77]

The country house could be invoked as a symbol of county and of the political past, as in the entry for Wentworth Woodhouse that proclaimed 'we are in Yorkshire', though attention to the busts of Fox and Burke came a clear second to Stubbs's portrait of the racehorse Whistle-Jacket 'rearing magnificently at the universe'.[78] More common, though, was invocation and imagery of the

---

[69]   *Illustrated London News*, 1 Jan. 1887, 26.

[70]   *Ibid.*, 21 Jan. 1899, 88.

[71]   *Ibid.*, 8 Sept. 1888, 284.

[72]   See, for example, Cobham Hall in *Ibid.*, 27 Oct. 1888, 490–4.

[73]   *Ibid.*, 22 Nov. 1896, 675.

[74]   *Ibid.*, 9 Aug. 1890, 174.

[75]   Thompson, *Seeing Politics*.

[76]   For instance, Stoke Park in *Illustrated London News*, 21 Nov. 1896, 674; Elizabeth Edwards, *The Camera as Historian: Amateur Photographers and Historical Imagination* (Durham: NC, 2012), 70–1.

[77]   *Ibid.*, 15 Oct. 1898, 554.

[78]   *Ibid.*, 8 Sept. 1888, 284.

Fig. 3.4. 'English Homes: Stoke Park', *Illustrated London News*, 21 Nov. 1896.

Fig. 3.5. 'Hawarden Castle, the Seat of the Right Hon. William Ewart Gladstone, M.P.', *Illustrated London News*, 20 July 1889.

78   James Thompson

country house as a manifestation of a particular politician, offering a more respectful parallel to the approach of the comic press. In its coverage, including photographs, of Hughenden in 1893, the *Illustrated London News* conceived the whole house through Beaconsfield ('everything... has been kept just as it was in Lord Beaconsfield's time'), noting the political paraphernalia, including 'mementoes of his election for Shrewsbury – huge blue banners with the words "For Queen and Country," and a jug of blue Shropshire ware, whose legend, "All Friends round the Wrekin," commemorates the fact that the leading twelve members for Shropshire were all Conservatives'.[79]

This process of house and occupant symbolically merging was, though, most evident for Hawarden. Colin Matthew argued that Gladstone spent less time there than often thought, viewing himself as a guest in the home of Mrs Gladstone.[80] The representation, however, was different: the *Cavan Weekly* insisted in 1882 that 'Hawarden is his house in the sense in which Harley Street cannot be, and Downing Street certainly is not', whilst the *Illustrated London News* captioned its drawing of the house, 'the seat of the Right Hon. William Ewart Gladstone' (fig. 3.5).[81]

The Belfast-based *Witness* in 1876 stressed Gladstone's labours – 'arithmetical feats which no cabinet minister has ever surpassed' – as well as the 'air of easy and natural luxury which forms the principal charm of the English [sic] country house proper' as distinguished from 'comfortless vastness' abroad and suburban pretension at home.[82] The study, with its writing tables for different purposes, its busts of 'old comrades, rivals, and famous friends', recurred in the many pictorially descriptive passages devoted to it, and in the imagery, including after Gladstone's death.[83] It was precisely the currency of this linkage between Gladstone and Hawarden that underpinned, as we have seen, the evolving satire of the anti-Gladstonian press. And, as Ruth Windscheffel has shown, it is important in recovering the construction of the Gladstonian persona to recognise the force of opponents' caricature: the feminising portraiture she examines has its counterpart in the presentation of the hyperactive world of Hawarden as exemplifying a form of destructive hysteria.[84] However, much

---

[79]   *Ibid.*, 22 Apr. 1893, 498.

[80]   H.C.G. Matthew, *Gladstone, 1809–1898* (Oxford, 1997), 608–9.

[81]   *Cavan Weekly News and Advertiser*, 14 Apr. 1882, 4; *Illustrated London News*, 20 July 1889, 85.

[82]   *The Witness*, repr. from *The World*, 8 Sept. 1876.

[83]   *Illustrated London News*, 20 July 1889, 82; *Lloyd's Weekly Newspaper*, 29 May 1898, 6.

[84]   Ruth Windscheffel, 'Politics, Portraiture and Power: Reassessing the Public Image of William Ewart Gladstone', in Matthew McCormack (ed.), *Public Men: Masculinity and Politics in Modern Britain* (Basingstoke, 2007), 123–42.

The Image of the Country House in Victorian Political Culture   79

as Gladstone's physical prowess – and the axe-wielding is unavoidable here – and his aquiline features helped to balance his intellectual accomplishments, similarly Hawarden was presented as both dignified and efficient, the very embodiment of a politician 'as methodical as he is energetic' for whom 'no day departs without having its work fully accomplished'.[85]

The genre of the politician-at-home piece emerged in late nineteenth-century interview journalism. It was, as with the use of photographs by politicians, quickly parodied: *Punch* ran a mock 'Statesmen at Home' series from 1889.[86] By the century's end, the genre of political portrait had merged in some journalism with a lifestyles-of-the-rich-and-famous approach to photography, as in *The Sphere*'s coverage of the homes (the plural is important here) of the Earl of Rosebery. There could be a distinct awkwardness to the combination, evident in the final sentence that predicted that 'in matters of Empire the policy of Lord Rosebery will continue to be advocated by the able and ardent though limited section of the party which looks for light to the brilliant nobleman who lives in Berkeley Square, and whose houses at Mentmore, at Epsom; and at Dalmeny are pictured in THE SPHERE'.[87]

In its 'sketch' of Joseph Chamberlain's political career at the start of the Tariff Reform campaign, the *Illustrated London News* incorporated 'illustrations of his home life and pursuits'. Drawn 'during an interview at Highbury', the imagery was that of a country house created in an urban setting, featuring 'a picturesque bit of the grounds: the lake'. Chamberlain was shown 'in conversation with his head gardener' in a wooded glade, complete with a highly alert dog. Labelled 'relief from fiscal warfare', this was very much a depiction of home as refuge from the demands of public life. His 'favourite hobby' was represented in a full-page drawing of the 'orchid-house' where he is conversing with his 'head orchid-gardener', cigar in hand (fig. 3.6).

The pressure of public life was, however, also felt within the home: 'the hard-worked leisure of an ex-minister' showed him in his study dealing with 'the enormous correspondence' of the fiscal campaign. In picturing 'a man of business in the most acutely modern sense', endowed with 'great executive ability', the newspaper also drew upon an established visual vocabulary for representing the statesman at work. Both the orchids, and the repeatedly visible monocle, acted as visual signifiers for the political celebrity proclaimed in the text rumination on Chamberlain's 'fascinating audacity'. Mobilising old and new – the article noted Chamberlain's 'curious facial resemblance to Pitt' before remarking on their marked differences – the combination of word and

---

[85] *Cavan Weekly New and Gen Advertiser*, 14 Apr. 1882, 4, reprinted from *Harper's*.
[86] For example, *Punch*, 26 Oct. 1889, 202 and 25 Jan. 1890, 48.
[87] *Sphere*, 10 March 1900, 235.

Fig. 3.6. 'Mr Chamberlain's Favourite Hobby', *Illustrated London News*, 19 Dec. 1903.

image cast Chamberlain (and his home) as masculine and modern.[88] In the visual culture of politics in the late nineteenth and early twentieth centuries, the comic and the serious were often intertwined. The supplement devoted to Chamberlain also included cartoons by Harry Furniss of Chamberlain 'in the guise of various birds and animals', including a Landseer-ian stag above 'some notable specimens' of the work of Francis Carruthers Gould, billed as 'his great pictorial opponent'.[89] Chamberlain's self-consciousness about his persona was fully matched by the illustrated press's sense of its own importance, but both were right to recognise that the visual was integral to turn-of-the century political culture.

* * *

The apogee of the country house as cultural phenomenon came in later years. Its status was less secure, more contested and in some respects more political in the nineteenth century than it was in the later twentieth century. In nineteenth-century political culture, the country house was both a metaphor and practical infrastructure for doing politics. While for some, the 'country house system' was a benign miracle akin to the English constitution, for others – particularly in Ireland – it was the physical embodiment of alien and oppressive rule. In the flourishing world of visual satire, the political country house acted as a signifier for, and encapsulation of, its occupier. Within the illustrated press as a whole, it also figured as a place of refuge from the rigours of an increasingly professionalised and busy political life, with its insistent demands on time, energy and lung capacity. Yet, as well as a space to think, the country house was also a place for incessant reading and writing. Similarly, alongside its function as a place for an integrated elite of politicians and journalists, it was a stage on which 'high' and 'low' politics met, whether for picnics, meetings or protests. Houses could be incorporated into the fashioning of political personae, and the building of political celebrity. In the intermingling of 'public' and 'private', of striving and retreat, the image of the country house offers insights into the visualisation of leadership, into conceptions of 'the hurly burly of modern politics', and into changing imaginings of politics itself through the nineteenth century.

[88] *Illustrated London News*, 19 Dec. 1903, 'Supplement'.
[89] *Ibid.*, vi.; Charles Geake and F. Carruthers Gould, *John Bull's Adventures in the Fiscal Wonderland* (London, 1904).

Chapter 4

Hugh de Sélincourt, *The Cricket Match*, and Englishness between the Wars

Matthew Cragoe

In 1924, the novelist Hugh de Sélincourt published a little volume entitled *The Cricket Match*. It marked a departure from his usual, more serious literary productions, books that interrogated the relationship between the sexes and urged more liberal attitudes to female sexuality.[1] *The Cricket Match* belonged to another world entirely. It described in detail a single day in the life of a village, Tillingfold, when its cricket team played and triumphed over neighbours and arch-rivals, Raveley. Light-hearted yet insightful, it caught the imagination of the contemporary cricket-reading public and has been republished many times in the last hundred years. The book's success made de Sélincourt an important commentator on cricket in the interwar years.

De Sélincourt was by no means the first novelist to write about the game. Indeed, the buffoonery of village cricket had provided an irresistible target for storytellers ever since Charles Dickens's Pickwickians stumbled into Dingley Dell; the somewhat absurd sketch of the game by A.G. Macdonnell in *England, Their England* (1933) demonstrated that the tradition was flourishing a century later. In *The Cricket Match*, however, de Sélincourt found a new way to discuss the village game. He refused to treat his characters as a cast of clowns. Instead, he delineated them with the skill he would have brought to bear on the figures in a 'serious' novel, exploring their personalities, circumstances and aspirations. What was offered to the reader was a group of sympathetic three-dimensional figures, engaged in a common enterprise. The approach lent the book a universal quality: de Sélincourt captured with uncanny precision the range of emotions that all cricketers experience before, during and after a game, at whatever level they are playing.

However, as this chapter will demonstrate, re-reading *The Cricket Match* at the remove of one hundred years suggests there was more to the book's success than simply a keen psychological reading of the game. It also offered insightful reflections on contemporary society. De Sélincourt used his focus on a single

---

[1] Malcolm Pittock, 'Hugh de Sélincourt: A Forgotten Anti-War Novelist', *Cambridge Quarterly*, 41 (2012), 476–91.

Hugh de Sélincourt, The Cricket Match, and Englishness   83

cricket match as a means to explore issues like social class and community in the village; it became a vehicle to celebrate ways of being 'male' and, ultimately, 'English' at a time when war had stripped away many of the old certainties on which society had rested before 1914, and when mass democracy posed unknowable dangers to traditional ways of life.

Hugh de Sélincourt

Hugh de Sélincourt was born in 1878, the tenth child of Charles de Sélincourt, who ran a very profitable fabric importing business.[2] Hugh attended Dulwich College and Oxford University and then turned his hand to literary pursuits – presumably with some sort of income from family coffers. He became drama critic for the *Star* and later literary critic for the *Observer* – a role he gave up in 1914.[3] In 1907 he published his first novel, *A Boy's Marriage*, and seven more followed before the outbreak of war. What part he played in the war is not clear, though he does not appear to have served.[4] He did, however, write several acerbically anti-war novels during the conflict, highlighting both the futility of war and the unthinking hypocrisy of those who supported it when other people's lives were being sacrificed for their own principles.[5]

After the war, de Sélincourt and his wife Janet moved to a house named Sand Pits in the hamlet of Thakeham, near Storrington in the Sussex Downs. He clearly enjoyed the experience of living in a village. His surviving diary for 1924 suggests that while he worked hard at writing he pursued an active life beyond his study walls. He was a keen walker, a voracious reader and an avid gardener, working long hours digging, planting and rolling the gardens alongside Ted, his gardener. He also enjoyed a busy social life, with people calling into Sand Pits on a regular basis; he himself would often drop in and have 'tea with the Teds', as he affectionately called the gardener's family, or play billiards at the Storrington Village Hall of whose committee he was a member.[6] He and Janet were on good terms with the Aggs family who purchased Little

---

[2]   Charles, the illegitimate child of an English mother and a member of the French court, moved back to England on his father's death and was naturalised in 1859: TNA, HO/188/2862.

[3]   De Sélincourt's niece, Dorothy, married A.A. Milne while his elder brother Basil was an essayist and novelist who married bestselling American novelist Mary Douglas Sedgwick. Two other siblings pursued academic careers: Ernest was a Wordsworth specialist who became Professor of Poetry at Oxford (1928–33) and then Deputy Head of Birmingham University; Agnes became head of Westfield College.

[4]   Pittock, 'Hugh de Sélincourt', 476.

[5]   *Ibid.*, 482–3.

[6]   West Sussex Record Office, de Sélincourt MSS 1/2.

Thakeham, a superb Lutyens house, in 1919, and he also developed a very close friendship with Vera Pragnell, who had set up The Sanctuary, a Utopian community on 27 acres of Sussex heathland, in 1923.[7]

Woven through his life in the village was cricket. A keen schoolboy cricketer, he had dropped the game after leaving Dulwich, and it was not until he moved to Sand Pits that his old interest reasserted itself. Introduced to the Storrington club by Ted, he played throughout the interwar years and was captain for most of the 1920s. *The Cricket Match*, which was written at the end of the 1923 season, draws heavily on his experiences of the village and its team. Indeed, both the village and several of the characters were recognisable to contemporaries when the book appeared in 1924.[8]

Storrington was a large village. In 1921 it had about 1,200 residents, having recovered from a late nineteenth-century decline occasioned by the railway passing it by. The village was a shopping and service centre for the surrounding district, with drapers, shoemakers, butchers and solicitors; it even had a bank which opened for two hours twice a week. Cricket was played on the Recreation Ground, a piece of land acquired under the powers given to the new Parish Council established in 1894. In the book, though, these political and economic considerations are allowed to fade into the background and the village is re-christened Tillingfold, a name evoking the tilled land and folded sheep typical of Downland agriculture. It was in this bucolic setting that the cricket match to which the novel is devoted took place.

The Cricket Match

De Sélincourt was still a relatively new arrival in Storrington when he wrote *The Cricket Match*. He was part of that influx to rural districts in the 1920s and 1930s tracked by historians such as Jeremy Burchardt.[9] His 'outsider' status allowed him to bring a critical eye to the scenes he surveyed, even as – like so many other in-migrants in this period – he romanticised the rural community

---

7 Clive Webb, 'Utopian dreams, Earthly Realities', *History Today*, 73 (Jan. 2023) <https://www.historytoday.com/archive/history-matters/utopian-dreams-earthly-realities> (accessed 4 Sept. 2023).

8 As often commented upon in reviews: e.g. 'The Cricket Match: A Village Epic', *Worthing Gazette*, 4 June 1924, 10. De Sélincourt dedicated later cricketing volumes to the team or individual players.

9 Jeremy Burchardt, 'Historicizing Counter-urbanization: In-migration and the Reconstruction of Rural Space in Berkshire (UK), 1901–51', *Journal of Historical Geography*, 38 (2012), 155–66.

of which he was now a part.[10] De Sélincourt was conscious of this, and in the novel cast himself as Paul Gavinier, captain of the cricket team, and has him reflect how his French-sounding name set him apart from his fellows.

The book opens with an immersive sensory portrait of day-break in Tillingfold: the sights, sounds and smells that made it real – the 'picturesque cottages', the sound of the train passing five miles away that emphasised the village's remoteness, the smell of the 'sweet air touched by the savour of the sea on the far side of the Downs'.[11] But his real interest is the people and the community and attention turns quickly to life in the village itself. Tillingfold is, of course, Storrington in the thinnest of disguises, and much of what de Sélincourt claims for it can be verified in the columns of the contemporary press. Particularly striking is the extent to which many of the amenities in the village depended on voluntary activities and the contributions and leadership of the wealthier members of society. Thus, in Tillingfold as in real-life Storrington, the rich families subscribed to events such as the Flower Show, became vice-presidents of the Village Room or the Cricket and Football Clubs (subscribing accordingly), and served on the Parish Council. The existence of such recreational and associational facilities were, as Keith Snell has written, signs of community flourishing, especially when bonded with the local government of the parish, the legal manifestation of local belonging.[12]

Yet de Sélincourt was not blind to the fact that life was hard for many in Tillingfold, and that the sense of dissatisfaction it engendered was pregnant with mischief for his ideal of settled community. The second chapter foregrounds the different realities experienced by members of the Tillingfold cricket team. First, we encounter Sid Smith, who lives in a small house with his wife and a 'blinkin' swarm o' kids'.[13] The family is poor, and his primary concern on the morning of the match is the state of his 'forlorn, soiled [cricket] trousers': he begs his wife to do what she can to make them presentable while he goes out to work for the morning. After a breakfast comprising 'two large slices of bread and dripping at the corner of the kitchen table', he sets out on the three-mile walk to his work, as a hod-carrier to a bricklayer.

---

[10] Kristin Bluemel, 'The Regional and the Rural', in James Smith (ed.), *The Cambridge Companion to British Literature of the 1930s* (Cambridge, 2019), 160–1.

[11] Hugh de Sélincourt, *The Cricket Match* (London, 1924) [hereafter *TCM*], 9–10.

[12] K.D.M. Snell, *Parish and Belonging: Community, Identity and Welfare in England and Wales, 1700–1950* (Cambridge, 2006), 499, 504: Jeremy Burchardt, '"A New Rural Civilisation": Village Halls, Community and Citizenship in the 1920s', in Paul Brassley, *et al.* (eds), *The English Countryside Between the Wars: Regeneration or Decline?* (Woodbridge, 2006), 26–35.

[13] *TCM*, 23.

86   Matthew Cragoe

Sid's experience – and his dissatisfaction with his lot – is contrasted with that of the young man in the local great house, Edgar Trine. He is brought morning tea in bed, served by the 'neat housemaid', Kate, and some comedy ensues as he directs her to choose which of his five pairs of whites he will wear.[14] On rising he comes down to a fine breakfast involving freshly sliced ham, and his mother announces that she's delighted he's playing for the village: "'With all this discontent that's about nowadays, it is so good for them all", she says: "'I am sure we all ought to mix with the people far more than we do". Edgar's assumption that his class position entitles him to lead is also made clear, as he remarks: 'Best cricket going, village cricket... Real keenness. Oh, I'm all for village cricket. If I were down here more, I wouldn't mind running the show.'[15]

The third character to whom we are introduced is John McLeod, Secretary and Treasurer of the Tillingfold Cricket Club. His role in the novel is to exude contentment with his lot and empathy with his fellow villagers. As he tells his wife: 'I've always had the luck, Maria. Here we are. Nice little house in a beautiful village.' On this particular morning he gets his breakfast in bed: coffee, toast, two boiled eggs and several rashers of bacon. As ever, he is hugely appreciative: 'The height of luxury... Waited on like a lord. Breakfast in bed! Well, I never. No man ever had such a wife!'[16] After she has cleared away his breakfast things, however, he finds himself dwelling on all the 'incomprehensibly unnecessary unhappiness... he knew existed in the beautiful village: the crossness, the unkindness, the gossip'. "'Ah, they've not all had your luck, my boy", he said to himself to appease his anger. "Suppose you had to shovel rubble all day like Sid Smith, where'd your temper be of an evening; or to do any other work you couldn't fancy, with another chap bossing you all the time".[17]

The characters of Sid, Trine and John McLeod are not to be read solely in class terms; they also stand for different visions of community. McLeod represents the best of the existing community; a long scene early in the book concerns the long-awaited delivery of some smart blue caps for the cricket team, and their distribution. However, McLeod realises that Sid probably cannot spare three shillings for such a thing and so contrives a way to give him the cap; Sam sees through this, identifies the true cause of the gift and feels a mixture of pleasure at having the cap and humiliation at not being able to pay for it.[18] It is a suggestion, perhaps, that the older system of the better off looking after the poor through well-intentioned charity is no longer a straightforward thing. A similar point is made in relation to Trine: his easy assumption of leadership

---

[14] *TCM*, 25.
[15] *TCM*, 27.
[16] *TCM*, 30.
[17] *Ibid.*
[18] *TCM*, 72–6.

jars, and, we are made privy to the struggles that Gauvinier has in actually getting an XI together and then managing their individual foibles, pridefulness and petulance.[19] De Sélincourt seems to say that the days when the lord of the manor snapped his fingers and the community fell into line were long gone.

The figure of Sid is perhaps the most engaging. His life is hard and his burdens are many; de Sélincourt's focus throughout the novel is on how cricket, and the sense of community it engenders, can save such a man from the siren song of socialism. For class envy is not absent from the village. Early in the novel we meet another member of the XI, Tom Hunter, a local mechanic who has never been the same since coming back from the War and grumbles about everything including the cliquishness of the committee that runs the club. He is juxtaposed with an interesting 'outsider' character, Waite, a stockbroker from Beckenham who is clearly a very good cricketer and, visiting the village, gets a game. When another teammate, Bannister, praises Waite's batting, de Sélincourt inserts this short dialogue:

> 'Look at the chance for practice these gents get,' Tom, who was apt to be sore on this subject, rather crossly remarked.
>
> 'You always takes what chances there are, eh?' said Bannister, who thought Tom slack in attending practice.

Bannister's rejoinder is important because it highlights how de Sélincourt elaborates class tensions in order to knock them down. The detailed drawing out of the characters, the exploration of their hopes and feelings, represents the players as a community of individuals, each with his own skills, opportunities and hardships, bound together as cricketers; they are not just creatures of class.

In this, of course, de Sélincourt reflects the time-honoured notion that cricket was essentially classless – that lords and labourers could and did play happily alongside one another, and that the everyday distinctions that set them apart were subsumed within a larger sporting unity when they stepped onto the field.[20] In Tillingfold de Sélincourt records how each player, 'as he came to the ground, got slowly caught up in the spirit of the game, emerging... from the habits of worry and care; as each man was given the chance not too frequently offered in modern life of living for a time outside himself, with a common purpose, in which he took a genuine interest.'[21] And later in the game as the action

---

[19] *TCM*, 47.

[20] Anthony Bateman, *Cricket, Literature and Culture: Symbolising the Nation, Destabilising Empire* (Farnham, 2009), 7; Matthew Cragoe, 'The Parish Elite at Play? Cricket, Community and the 'Middling Sort' in Eighteenth-Century Kent', *History*, 102 (2017), 45–67.

[21] *TCM*, 93–4.

reaches a crescendo of excitement, Gauvinier revels 'in the good feeling that emanates from eleven men, joined together for a common end. And all the men forgot themselves and were happy in this good feeling, the most tonic, healthful feeling that exists.'[22]

A particularly good practical example of this spirit of unity – and its limits – comes later in the novel, when Sid is bowling and persuades a Ravely batsman to send up a catch that Trine takes. As the team celebrates together, de Sélincourt notes, 'There was no disparity at all between the two men now. They were just two men in flannels.' Yet de Sélincourt recognises that this on-field fellowship is potentially transient. The next evening, he writes, Trine would not understand the rather surly salute he would get should he pass Sid on the road at the end of a working day, when poor Sid was exhausted and Trine was simply going home on his chestnut mare to change for dinner.

The experience of that fellowship on the field was nevertheless important in de Sélincourt's estimation, and it was supplemented by other factors which, collectively, helped the individuals playing the game to overcome their differing material circumstances and place identity with community over that with class. In de Sélincourt's story, several interlocking processes worked together to create connection rather than division. The first of these was the sense of manliness gained from playing cricket.[23] Several characters are singled out,[24] but the idea was most fully realised in relation to Sid Smith.[25] De Sélincourt's description of Smith walking to the wicket draws it out in detail:

> Sid Smith walked slowly, proudly, happily towards the wicket. On the cricket ground he felt sure he was a man, a fact which the difficult circumstances of his life obscured at other times, for he worked under a skilled labourer and felt, when he felt anything, more like the other fellow's extra arm than a separate entity; and at home – though of course he could assert himself at times and feel a bully... he was really more like one of four children... Neither at work nor at home, somehow, did he ever feel a man – the kind, good-natured creature he persisted in dimly imagining he ought to be.

On the cricket field, however, he achieves that status.

A second context was the sense of long continuity represented by the game in the village. The experience of playing cricket binds together players across generations – both on and off the field. Early in the book we are introduced

---

[22] *TCM*, 231.

[23] Anthony Bateman, 'Performing Imperial Masculinities: The Discourse and Practice of Cricket', in Rainer Edif and Antony Rowland (eds), *Performing Masculinity* (London, 2010), 78–94.

[24] *TCM*, 41, 132.

[25] *TCM*, 139–40.

to Storrington's rotund and rather elderly umpire, Sam Bird. He had played cricket for Tillingfold before many of the players' parents 'had begun to walk out together', and he knew the name and deeds of every man who had played cricket 'within the last forty years and more'. His presence on the field was matched by the gaze of former players on the boundary's edge. When the latest recruit to the village XI, fifteen-year-old Horace Cairie, pulls off a brave stop, it catches the eye of the aged Mr Hodkiss, who had been Storrington's leading batsman over thirty years ago.[26] 'I do like to see a young one slippy in the field', he announces to no-one in particular: 'That's a good little lad, that is; a good little lad.'[27] And this leads into a passage of reflection which ties the current scene playing out in front of his eyes into the dim and distant past, fifty or sixty years before, in the same village.

> And memory took him back with all the ease imaginable to the many, many years ago when he himself was a keen little nipper, playing among men, winning his spurs; took him back (so strong is the power of fellow-feeling) so vividly and so swiftly and so completely that, could he have caught a glimpse of himself, he would not have recognised as himself the queer, bent, wrinkled, fattish chap on the bench, old now, so old.[28]

If cricket thus represented a strong bond between generations of players, it also provided a focal point for expressions of communal identity. In *The Cricket Match*, spectators from the village turn up in surprising numbers to watch the game and are active participants throughout. De Sélincourt makes repeated reference to the way in which they not only uttered catcalls and shouted things like 'Good old Jim!' or 'Well hit, mate!', but at times of particular excitement would burst into chanting. Thus, as the game approached its climax, and young Horace took an extraordinary catch, the crowd found its voice: 'And now the old catch, to the tune of the church chimes, broke out round the ground in steady earnest: "Play up Tillingfold; play up, Tillingfold".'[29]

The image of cricketers being urged to 'Play up!' by their fellow villagers to the tune of the village church bells is a powerful testament to the notion that the game embodied the whole community at an almost mystical level, that it was – as Gauvinier reflects – 'a perfect little work of art, in which the whole community took part'.[30] Indeed, as Ross McKibbin has suggested, cricket had a greater social reach and unifying impact than any other sport in interwar England, precisely because it was 'played and followed throughout the country

[26] *TCM*, 130–1.
[27] *TCM*, 231.
[28] *Ibid.*
[29] *TCM*, 243; cf. David Matless, *Landscape and Englishness* (London, 1998), 66.
[30] *TCM*, 90.

by all social classes and by both men and women'.[31] Other games, notably football, were undoubtedly played by more people, but in de Sélincourt's estimation the two games were not comparable. Indeed, in *The Cricket Match* football is presented as a symptom of the disruption that the war had caused to village life. Before the match, the umpire Sam Bird comes across a group of lads kicking a football around on the field and reflects that much has changed: 'The lads have all run wild... There's no doing anything with them. Some say it's due to their fathers being away at the war, and I may say that I am of the same opinion also'.[32]

De Sélincourt readily admitted the attractions of football for youngsters: 'Off with your jackets: four decent goal posts ready at once... The more the merrier. No old 'uns need apply. Dribble and hack and punt and charge about. Sweat and enjoy yourselves'.[33] Cricket by contrast required huge amounts of kit and always involved someone looking over your shoulder, saying '"Oh, you ought to play with a straight bat" or "Keep your right leg still, my boy" or "Watch the ball" or "Where's that left elbow now?"'. It drained all the spontaneity from the game. However, it was precisely this aspect, of the game's lore and craft being handed down from one generation to the next, that de Sélincourt felt made cricket a superior pastime than football. The process of intergenerational transmission, bridging differences of age and class as it moulded the next generation of players who would represent the village on the cricket field fostered both the cohesion and continuity of the community. It was something that had been imperilled by the war having removed so many men from the villages.[34]

The Cricket Match was thus more than a simple fable about a day of sport. De Sélincourt used cricket as a vehicle to explore a vision of a community bound together by time and tradition, qualities which trumped other divisions. In doing so, as the next section suggests, he fashioned a distinctive new vision for village cricket, one that would come to enjoy enormous popularity between the wars.

Village Cricket and Community

Cricket emerged from the First World War with one of its major narratives severely compromised. Before 1914, it was common for commentators to dwell on the game's ability to develop character, and particularly those traits which

---

[31] Ross McKibbin, *Classes and Cultures: England, 1918–1951* (Oxford, 1998), 332.

[32] *TCM*, 83–4.

[33] *TCM*, 80–1.

[34] The war's impact on cricket was often explored by interwar writers. See Bateman, *Cricket, Literature and Culture*, 64–9; Randall Stevenson, *Literature and the Great War, 1914–1918* (Oxford, 2013), 190–1.

would make a boy into a soldier worthy of defending the empire in its colonial wars. Sir Henry Newbolt's well-known poem *Vitaï Lampada*, with its juxtaposed scenes of a hard-fought school cricket match in verse one, and a desperate military encounter in some far-flung foreign field in verse two, with the repeated exhortation to 'Play up! Play up! And play the game!', is perhaps the best-known example of the genre.[35]

As the poem's third and final verse reminds us, however, the poem merely codifies a message that was being taught at all the great public schools in England at this time: that cricket and service to the nation went hand in hand. The message was actively proselytised by those such as the author and public speaker E.W. Hornung. As the historian of Uppingham School, Malcolm Tozer, has written, men like Hornung promoted the idea that cricket was 'a training ground for life, and service to the Empire was the ultimate test'.[36] At Radley, it was said 'the playing fields became as important as the chapel'.[37]

When war broke out in 1914, cricket and cricketers visibly 'played the game'. It was noted how enthusiastic the nation's cricketers were to enlist for the armed services. As Simon John has shown, the wider cultural context within which the type of people who played cricket made them especially susceptible to the 'swell of patriotism' which accompanied the outbreak of war.[38] The decision of the MCC to abandon first-class cricket for the duration of the war also stood in contrast to the refusal of the Football Association to contemplate such a move.[39]

Yet long before the war ended, its terrible toll had begun to make the pre-1914 claims for the martial value of cricket sound hollow. *Punch* began to feature spiky pieces like that from 1917 in which a stand of young willow trees who, prior to the war, objected to being 'maimed' in order to supply young men with cricket bats, eventually contribute to the war effort by supplying artificial limbs for soldiers maimed at the front – young men who will now never play cricket.[40] It was little wonder, therefore, as Alison Light has remarked,

---

[35] Jonathan F. Vance, *Death so Noble: Memory, Meaning, and the First World War* (Vancouver, 1997), 97.

[36] Malcolm Tozer, 'A Sacred Trinity – Cricket, School, Empire: E.W. Hornung and his Young Guard', in J.A. Mangan (ed.), *The Cultural Bond: Sport, Empire, Society* (Abingdon, 1992), 17–18; J.A. Mangan, 'Muscular, Militaristic and Manly': The British Middle-Class Hero as Moral Messenger', *International Journal of the History of Sport*, 13 (1996), 38–47; Simon John, 'A Different Kind of Test Match: Cricket, English Society and the First World War', *Sport in History*, 33 (2013), 19–48.

[37] Keith A.P. Sandiford, 'England', in Brian Stoddart and Keith A.P. Sandiford (eds), *The Imperial Game: Cricket, Culture and Society* (Manchester, 1998), 16.

[38] John, '"Different Kind of Test Match"', 23–4.

[39] *Ibid.*, 26.

[40] *Punch*, 18 July 1917, 44.

92   Matthew Cragoe

that after 1918 the 'kind of supremacist glorification of nationhood which had inspired the imperialist endeavour in the late nineteenth century' quickly disappeared.[41] It was replaced by a new 'national idea' where the English appeared as a home-loving, private people 'more inward-looking, more domestic and more private'.[42] 'Self-effacement' was elevated to the status of a national virtue.

The new, inward-looking Englishness was associated with an embrace of the pastoral.[43] An explosion of interest in exploring the countryside during the interwar years, whether on foot, or by bicycle or car, testified to the contemporary thirst for experiencing the rural at first hand.[44] The suburbs, meanwhile, offered people a chance to (almost) live the dream. As Kristin Bluemel has noted, the middle classes, in particular, eagerly consumed both the quasi-rural opportunities offered by the new suburbs around major towns and cities and the 'outpouring of novels about regional and rural Britain' that reflected the deep concern of writers with the ideal of rural community.[45] Unsurprisingly, as Jonathan Parry, in a youthful foray into the twentieth century, has discussed, politicians picked up on the theme and sought to turn it to party advantage.[46] No one was more master of the art than the Conservative leader Stanley Baldwin, who reaffirmed and updated the party's traditional association with the countryside, offering wistful portraits of a unifying rural Englishness that was the birthright of all English citizens, and was the antithesis of the base materialism and class conflict allegedly offered by the Labour Party's socialism.[47] If

[41]   Alison Light, *Forever England: Femininity, Literature and Conservatism between the Wars* (Oxford, 1991), 8–11.

[42]   *Ibid.*, 8–9.

[43]   Alun Howkins, 'The Discovery of Rural England', in Robert Colls and Philip Dodd (eds), *Englishness: Politics and Culture, 1880–1920* (London, 1986), 62–88.

[44]   Matless, *Landscape and Englishness*, 62–100.

[45]   Bluemel, 'The Regional and the Rural', 160–1. Even detective fiction was touched by this impulse: K.D.M. Snell, 'A Drop of Water from a Stagnant Pool? Inter-war Detective Fiction and the Rural Community', *Social History*, 35 (2010), 25–7.

[46]   Jonathan Parry, 'The Quest for Leadership in Unionist Politics, 1886–1956', *Parliamentary History*, 12 (1993), 296–311.

[47]   Matthew Cragoe, 'Conservatives, "Englishness" and "Civic Nationalism"', in Duncan Tanner *et al.* (eds), *Debating Nationhood and Governance in Britain, 1885–1939: Perspectives from the Four Nations* (Manchester, 2006), 192–210; John Ramsden, *Politics in the Age of Balfour and Baldwin* (London, 1978), 208–10; J.H. Grainger, *Patriotisms, 1900–1939* (London, 1986), 86–103. Though cf. Ross McKibbin, who cautions against taking Baldwin's views as representative of all grassroots Tory sentiment: 'Class and Conventional Wisdom: The Conservative Party and the "Public" in Inter-war Britain', in McKibbin, *The Ideologies of Class: Social Relations in Britain, 1880–1950* (Oxford, 1990), 270. For the Labour Party and cricket, see Stephen G. Jones, *Sport, Politics and the Working Class: Organised Labour and Sport in Interwar Britain* (Manchester, 1988), 76.

this held only limited appeal for grass-roots Tories who wanted strong foreign policy and tax cuts to revive industry, it did help mould that 'living, spiritual counter-atmosphere' that appealed to the broader electorate and secured the Conservative Party a near monopoly on power between the wars.[48]

As the nation's self-image changed, so did cricket's. While the notion that cricket's great purpose was to train young men for the imperial battlefield was heard much less frequently after 1918,[49] and was openly criticised in *Punch* (which insisted in 1920 that the great purpose of games like cricket should be recreation, not martial preparation),[50] cricket retained its status as the 'national sport'. As *The Times* put it in 1920, 'cricket has probably had a greater share than any other of our national sports in making England what it is'.[51] Now that England was to be defined by its local, pastoral associations, the valorisation of the village game was a logical step.

In *The Cricket Match*, de Sélincourt did precisely this, weaving together community and cricket in an authentically pastoral setting.[52] Glory was to be found not on some foreign field, but on the local village green. The war, of course, was always there in the background. There was the unfortunate mechanic, Tom Hunter, who had endured 'trench fever and poison gas' during the conflict and now only occasionally – as during the match – 'appeared the keen, kind and very bashful Tom Hunter he was intended to be'; there were the little boys playing football, apparently for want of the instruction in cricket they would have received as a matter of course had the war not taken all the men away to the front; there was even the cricket pitch itself, which had apparently only just been brought back to a semblance of its pre-war self, as if the very soil on which the community stood had taken half a decade to recover from the conflict.[53]

But if the effects of the war were visible in the novel, so too were the redemptive elements of community and cricket itself. The way the team represented the village was carefully constructed. The wide range of social classes and ages comprehended within the XI demonstrated the reach of the game, something emphasised by the way the community itself came down to watch and engage in the contest.[54] The one-ness of the team and the community was

---

[48] Parry, 'Leadership in Unionist Politics', 304–5.

[49] 'Revival of the Annual Dinner', *Grantham Journal*, 13 Dec. 1919, 2; Bateman, *Cricket, Literature and Culture*, 55–9.

[50] 'Epilogue', *Punch*, 29 June 1921, 517–18.

[51] John, '"A Different kind of Test"', 20.

[52] Cf. Duncan Stone, 'Suburbanization and Cultural Change: The Case of Club Cricket in Surrey, 1870–1939', *Urban History*, 44 (2017), 44–68.

[53] *TCM*, 41, 132, 251.

[54] *TCM*, 242–3.

underscored in the closing scenes, when the team melted back into the village to drink, dance and socialise with friends before making their way home.[55] And throughout the novel there was de Sélincourt's emphasis on cricket's unique ability to lift men above the immediate circumstances of life and instil a spirit of communal purpose all by itself.

The columns of *Punch* illustrate the contours of this newly domesticated village cricket well. Before the war, the magazine had had some sport with rustics playing cricket, highlighting either their buffoonery or – in the case of the famous 'Spinner' cartoons – the precocious ability of an unlettered village boy to unsettle his betters on the cricket field.[56] In the interwar years, however, the humour changed. Cartoonists strove to capture the sense of community associated with the game. A nice example from 1935 depicted a vicar talking with one of his parishioners and remarking that he sees her husband has been selected to be the umpire for Saturday's cricket match; 'Yes, 'e is Sir', she replies: 'E's quite ignorant of the game, Sir, but they know 'e'll be fair.'[57] While this picks up on the vagaries of village umpiring – a long-running joke in *Punch* – the exchange highlights the cardinal English virtue of fairness. Faith in that principle was the bedrock of everything else in these idealised communities.[58]

Gender provided another hook on which to hang a joke. In pre-war cartoons, women were sometimes depicted at cricket matches mistakenly calling 'umpires' 'vampires' or something similar. In the interwar period, however, they are regularly presented as being at ease in less formal suburban or village settings and the humour derives from their possessing a slightly different, more social or domestic, set of priorities from their cricket-playing spouses.

A typical example from 1930 (fig. 4.1) showed a wife and her friends sitting comfortably at the boundary's edge in deck chairs, and the wife saying to her despondent husband, trailing off the field having been dismissed by the first ball of the match: 'This *is* nice darling; now you'll be able to enjoy the cricket with us'.[59]

Another cartoon from 1935 (fig. 4.2) showed a somewhat panic-stricken fielder trying to get into position under a ball that had been skied to him near

---

[55] *TCM*, 249–56.

[56] *Punch*, 8 June 1904; 403; 9 Aug. 1905, 95; 15 May 1907, 347.

[57] *Punch*, 10 July 1935, 53.

[58] See Jonathan Duke-Evans, *The History and Significance of Fair Play: An English Tradition* (Oxford, 2023) for the sporting basis. For its wider embedding in popular culture, Rohan MacWilliam, 'Radicalism and Popular Culture: The Tichborne Case and the Politics of "Fair Play", 1867–1886', in Eugenio F. Biagini and Alastair J. Reid (eds), *Currents of Radicalism: Popular Radicalism, Organised Labour and Party Politics in Britain, 1850–1914* (Cambridge, 1991), 57–60.

[59] *Punch*, 30 July 1930, 116.

Fig. 4.1. 'This *is* nice darling; now you'll be able to enjoy the cricket with us', *Punch*, 30 July 1930.

Fig. 4.2. 'No, darling, Daddy can't talk to you now; wait until he's dropped this one!', *Punch*, 8 May 1935.

the boundary, while in the background his wife restrains their little son and says 'No, darling, Daddy can't talk to you now; wait until he's dropped this one!'[60]

Whatever the virtue of the humour, the cartoons demonstrate the way in which cricket on the village green was, as Ross McKibbin has written, 'a social mainstay of English rural life and ideally suited to its rhythms' by the 1930s.[61]

When dealing with rural cricket, many articles in *Punch* positively wallowed in the romantic nostalgia of Baldwinite Englishness and were quick to decry anything that might threaten it.[62] The practice employed in some villages of importing 'outsiders' to help the team win league matches was heavily criticised, for example, as it undermined the organic nature of local community.[63] More often, however, the threat was political. For much of the period, the threat was deemed to come specifically from the left wing of politics: organised labour, 'Class War', Bolshevism, and 'the doctrine of *class-consciousness* as taught by the Socialist party in its infant seminaries' were familiar bêtes noires.[64] The particular point which stuck in Mr Punch's craw was that the socialists did not appreciate the beneficial effects of healthily competitive sport for the community and – by extension – the nation. This point spawned regular cartoons and satirical articles: a barber in 1924 speculating about the cricketing prospects for the forthcoming season, assuming the 'socialists' did not dig up all the wickets for allotments; a story in 1930 describing the confusion into which a Russian collective village was thrown when instructed by Moscow to play a competitive cricket match – something that in their eyes would set man against man and 'play into the hands of the Capitalist Governments, which seek to divide the workers'; another in 1933 describing how the Russians took over Britain after a great war in 1943 and obliterated all games because of their 'bourgeois principles'.[65]

The sentiment evoked by *Punch* chimed with the views of those who promoted village cricket at the grass roots level. The Vicar of Waterlooville, Hampshire, for example, told diners at their annual cricket club dinner in 1927

---

[60] *Punch*, 8 May 1935, 562.

[61] McKibbin, *Classes and Cultures*, 333.

[62] See, e.g., 'Bonham's Day', *Punch*, 22 July 1925, 76–7, about a modern game played on Halfpenny Down, home of the fabled Hambledon team.

[63] 'How we shall spend out Summer?', *Punch*, 26 Apr. 1933, 466–7; Stone, 'Suburbanization and Cultural Change', 63; Derek Birley, *A Social History of English Cricket* (London, 1999), 217–20.

[64] 'Class War', *Punch*, 12 Nov. 1924, 534. In the later 1930s, Nazi Germany was similarly decried.

[65] 'The Adaptable Barber', *Punch*, 2 Apr. 1924, 349; 'Cricket in Russian', *Punch*, 26 May 1930, 612; 'Footballerina', *Punch*, 1 Jan. 1933, unpaginated front material.

that in the same way as a village without a spiritual centre was dead, so was a community without sports clubs. He promised he would do all he could to promote sport in the parish, 'because he felt sport had made England what it was'. 'Nations such as Russia and China that did not play cricket', he went on, 'did not play the game in the larger sense.'[66] As *Punch* put it in 1938, 'They don't play cricket in Totalitarian countries.'[67]

The cult of village cricket thus became widespread during the interwar years. For all the glamour of Test and County cricket, it came to be recognised as the game's most authentic form. As the *West Sussex Gazette* remarked when reviewing a reissue of *The Cricket Match* in 1931, the book 'deals with the cricket we see most of in Sussex; the cricket which really counts for most in the heart of the game; and the cricket which has to be kept alive if the game remains the national English game.'[68] Hugh de Sélincourt made a similar point in his book *Moreover* (1934): 'without us', he wrote, 'there would be no county cricket: no Test Matches.'[69] The same thing was often said by professional cricketers when they visited local clubs to deliver prizes at annual dinners and the like. Even Douglas Jardine, England captain during the controversial Bodyline series with Australia in 1932–3, was prepared to acknowledge that the village green 'was the natural home of cricket'.[70] De Sélincourt became known as its primary exponent.

The Impact of *The Cricket Match*

The Cricket Match was published in summer 1924 and garnered favourable notices. Many reviewers were struck by the skill with which the characters were drawn. *Punch* remarked that 'All the Tillingford [sic] players and several of their rivals are drawn with so nice a skill that one seems to know them not only on the cricket field but also in their daily life', while the *Gentlewoman* felt the book was 'full of the charm of real Sussex village life'.[71] The *Yorkshire Post*, which went on to make it one of their Books of the Year,[72] admired his use of cricket as a peg for his 'suggestive sketches' of village life, and added that 'some of his men and women are thought-provoking people in this new day'.[73]

---

[66] 'Village Cricket', *Hampshire Telegraph*, 14 Jan. 1927, 4.

[67] 'Epilogue', *Punch*, 194, 29 June 1938, 727–8.

[68] 'Reviews', *West Sussex Gazette*, 30 Apr. 1931, 6.

[69] Hugh De Sélincourt, *Moreover: Reflections on the Game of Cricket* (London, 1934), 49.

[70] Quoted in 'Expert Instructions', *Punch*, 2 Dec 1936, 642.

[71] *Punch*, 18 June 1924, 679–80; *Gentlewoman*, 31 July 1926, 31.

[72] *Yorkshire Post*, 3 Dec. 1924, 24.

[73] 'The Cricket Match', *Yorkshire Post*, 11 June 1924, 4.

The *Daily Herald*, meanwhile, considered it much more than a 'well-written cricket-yarn': 'it is full of shrewd and sympathetic comment on the game of life no less than the game of cricket'.[74]

The Cricket Match propelled de Sélincourt into a new phase of his literary career. While his serious novels garnered some critical attention, his cricket writing gained him a dedicated readership. The book went through several editions and was added to Cape's Travellers collection in 1928. More books flowed from his pen, and he became acknowledged as the village game's literary voice. Encomiums rolled in. Not only did Baldwin profess himself an admirer but J.M. Barrie wrote to tell de Sélincourt he was 'an ardent lover' *of The Cricket Match*, adding, 'I envied you the writing of this book'. It was, he said, 'the best story about cricket or any other game that was ever written'.[75]

De Sélincourt's writing started to appear regularly in published anthologies, such as *A Cricket XI* (1927). The other authors in this volume – Charles Dickens, P.G. Wodehouse, Thomas Hughes, E.W. Hornung and Mary Russell Mitford – show the literary company he was keeping. In 1935 he was included in another collection, *Bat and Ball*, edited by Thomas Moult, which, besides the illustrious Neville Cardus (the *Manchester Guardian*'s cricket correspondent and acknowledged doyen of interwar cricket writers), included contributions from Douglas Jardine, Hedley Verity, Maurice Tate, and "Plum" Warner – some of the great names of contemporary cricket.[76] One imagines that inclusion in the second collection pleased de Sélincourt the more. He was delighted to learn that *The Cricket Match* had been enjoyed by a number of leading Australian and England cricketers, and spent fifteen pages of *Moreover* describing an evening he spent with Jardine in London.[77] He was a 'wholly small boy' throughout, he recorded. In the later 1930s, he also began to feature regularly on the radio, talking about cricket.[78]

De Sélincourt's assimilation into the canon of cricket writing occurred very quickly. His approach, while psychologically compelling, chimed with the emphasis on community and the pastoral prevalent in this period. Through the medium of village cricket, de Sélincourt portrayed village society as many imagined it had been in the past and could be in the future – classless, friendly, intimate – 'men of varying social standing united into one happy family by the claims of cricket', as one critic put it.[79]

---

[74] 'Village Cricket', *Daily Herald*, 18 June 1924, 7.

[75] Letter from J.M. Barrie, Aug. 1930, Sélincourt MSS 1/1.

[76] 'Sport with the Lid Off', *Bystander*, 28 August 1935, 41. He was often mentioned alongside Cardus: see, e.g., 'Unhappy Cricket', *Graphic*, 30 Aug. 1930, 334.

[77] De Sélincourt, *Moreover*, 57, 67–82.

[78] 'Week-end Wireless', *North Wilts Herald*, 16 Aug. 1935, 10.

[79] 'Literature', *Montrose Standard*, 15 May 1931, 6.

100   Matthew Cragoe

The fact that de Sélincourt played village cricket added authenticity to his books. He remained Storrington's leading bowler throughout the interwar years, was a useful middle order batsman and a decent slip fielder. Perhaps more significantly, in light of his writing, was the way he conducted himself – the way he 'played the game'. As the club chairman, Col. H.V. Ravenscroft, of the Abbey, Storrington, put it when making a presentation to de Sélincourt in 1930, 'the good name for sportsmanship in cricket which Storrington enjoyed was largely due to the efforts of Mr de Sélincourt and his association with the club'.[80] He certainly laboured as hard off the field as he did on it to ensure the club was successful, working tirelessly at tasks such as rolling the pitch during the week to get the wicket ready for the weekend's game, attending club meetings, and encouraging other – especially younger – players. A particularly good example of this was at the Storrington club dinner in 1928 when a star-studded panel of cricketing guests, including two of Sussex's England players – Arthur Gilligan (who captained England in Australia, 1924–5) and Maurice Tate – joined the party. Addressing this august assembly, de Sélincourt drew the attention of the great and the good to the youngest member present:

> I can assure these gentlemen that I have never played in such keen cricket as in Storrington, and such men as Jack Quait, who at the age of 16, can make fifty runs against a good side, should be encouraged, and we are proud of him. It is magnificent to sit at supper with such men as we have with us to-night.[81]

What that can have meant to young Quait it is impossible to know, but the spirit in which these remarks were uttered was typical of de Sélincourt. This was the older generation reaching down to the younger, creating those vertical bonds through the fellowship of cricket which were one of the buttresses of local community, and therefore of society more widely.

* * *

At one hundred years' remove, *The Cricket Match* still works as a piece of writing. The story is exciting and well told, while the psychological insights into cricketing ring as true today as they did in 1924. Equally, the book struck a deep contemporary chord of longing – for a vision of Englishness residing in ordered, homogenous village communities, distant from the war and the divisions of industrial society. De Sélincourt clearly felt that himself and was part of the movement of people out of cities into the countryside at this time. Like many others who made that move, he was concerned to promote the ideals

---

[80] 'Cricket Club Presentation', *West Sussex Gazette*, 17 July 1929, 4.
[81] 'Gilligan and Tate at Storrington', *Worthing Herald*, 18 Feb. 1928, 2.

of rural communality that had brought him to Sussex – and the idealisations of community in *The Cricket Match* are a major part of its appeal. However, by marrying this idea with cricket, de Sélincourt managed to forge anew the association between the game of cricket and the prevailing idea of what it meant to be English in terms acceptable to a generation traumatised by the shock of the First World War. On the village green, cricket was once again the 'national game'.

Chapter 5

Nation and Union in the Career of David Lloyd George

Geraint Thomas

Welsh nationality has survived two thousand years in spite of every human effort to crush out its vitality. The strongest governing forces in the world have successively attempted to crush it, to coax it, and even to pray it out of existence. The Roman, the Saxon, and Dane, the Norman, and lastly the race which is a blend of all have waged an intermittent warfare against Welsh nationality for twenty centuries, and still, after all, here we are... claiming the same measure of Welsh national self-government as our forefathers fought and died for hundreds of years ago.

So declared David Lloyd George in Aberystwyth in December 1896.[1] The speech was typical of the nationalist message carried by the Liberal MP for Caernarfon Boroughs to all parts of Wales following his by-election victory in 1890. The valorisation of national survival in the face of a succession of invasive civilisations lent his speeches a note of romantic and nativistic pride. But it served a definite political and legislative ambition also, as stated by the Cymru Fydd Society whose programme he championed, namely 'to secure a National Legislature for Wales, dealing exclusively with Welsh affairs, while preserving the relations with the British Parliament upon all questions of Imperial interest.'[2] Lloyd George devoted his backbench career in the 1890s to the cause of Welsh Home Rule, energetically touring both north and south Wales with the aim of mobilising mass support, organising Liberal endorsement and cultivating press backing, while in parliament he convened a group of sympathetic Liberal MPs – a self-styled 'Independent' or 'Welsh National' party – to bring pressure to bear on the Liberal leadership.[3]

Yet, as Prime Minister, Lloyd George not only abandoned but resisted self-government for Wales. He did so in the face of renewed calls from Welsh

[1] Herbert du Parcq, *Life of David Lloyd George* (4 vols, London, 1912), vol. 1, 146.

[2] *Home Rule for Wales: What Does it Mean?* (London, 1888), containing the 'Constitution and Rules of the Cymru Fydd Society', 2.

[3] Kenneth O. Morgan, *Rebirth of a Nation: A History of Modern Wales* (Oxford, 1981), 112–18.

Nation and Union in the Career of David Lloyd George   103

and Scottish home rulers, alongside Unionist advocates of a UK-wide federal solution to the urgent situation in Ireland, who urged him to place 'Home Rule All Round' at the centre of the government's programme of post-war reconstruction. His response was skilfully to stonewall such representations, commissioning a Speaker's Conference on devolution in 1919 and receiving multiple deputations on the subject, to which he responded with lip service. This reflected his fundamental reappraisal of the Union by this time, which engendered in him a defiant unionism that was nowhere more starkly displayed than in his policy towards Ireland. For all that he had supported Gladstone's policy of Irish Home Rule and would become the only Prime Minister to date to preside over a break-up of the Union, following the Anglo-Irish Treaty and the founding of the Irish Free State in 1922, between 1919 and 1921 he sought to defend the Union with military force. Comparing the righteousness of the Unionist cause to that of the North in the American Civil War, he confided to one political ally that he could see 'no alternative but to fight it out... A republic at our doors is unthinkable'.[4]

It is tempting to read this transformation as a case of opportunistic inconsistency. After all, testimonies to Lloyd George's unscrupulousness are legion. Writing to his future first wife during their courtship, he made clear that his 'supreme idea is to get on' and if necessary 'to thrust even love itself under the wheels of my Juggernaut'.[5] Over subsequent decades his devious methods as a minister, his association with the press barons, his sale of honours, all contributed to a reputation for crookedness and cynical opportunism successfully exploited by Stanley Baldwin and Ramsay MacDonald and immortalised by John Maynard Keynes, who saw in him simply a 'love of power', a 'final purposelessness': 'Lloyd George is rooted in nothing; he is void and without content; he lives and feeds on his immediate surroundings'.[6] His pursuit of a federalist solution to the Irish question, in the form of Home Rule All Round, has been interpreted as a scheme intended primarily to secure for himself the leadership of a centrist patriotic bloc amid 'the flux of parties and issues' that characterised Edwardian politics.[7]

---

[4]   *Lord Riddell's Intimate Diary of the Peace Conference and After, 1918–1923* (London, 1933), 290.

[5]   *Lloyd George Family Letters, 1885–1936*, ed. Kenneth O. Morgan (Cardiff, 1973), 14.

[6]   John Maynard Keynes, *Essays in Biography* (London, 1933), 36. On how Baldwin presented himself in contradistinction to Lloyd George, see Philip Williamson, *Stanley Baldwin: Conservative Leadership and National Values* (Cambridge, 1998), 228–31.

[7]   David W. Savage, "'The Parnell of Wales has become the Chamberlain of England": Lloyd George and the Irish Question', *Journal of British Studies*, 12 (1972), 108.

But to read Lloyd George's eventual unionism as the product of cynical careerism is to simplify a more complex and interesting reality. As Jonathan Parry has shown, perhaps most acutely in his treatment of that other opportunistic outsider of Westminster folklore, Benjamin Disraeli, most political lives were animated by some coherence of outlook.[8] Hardly any politician could escape formative influences on their worldview. These included upbringing and education; attachment to some prevailing or as yet unattained set of political, social or cultural conditions; perceived threats, historical and current; and networks of contacts, political and otherwise, representing shared sympathies and exchange of knowledge. Even where a political leader's behaviour and policies were 'reactive', they therefore constituted a broadly comprehensible response in the service of a broadly coherent agenda.

For all his celebrity as a domestic social reformer, Lloyd George lived his political career grappling with questions of nationhood and statehood, at home and abroad and in peace and war. As Welsh nationalist and Irish Home Ruler, vocal critic of the Boer War, lead negotiator with Irish Nationalists on behalf of the Asquith government, member of the Council of Four at Versailles, an architect of the League of Nations, sponsor of constitutional reform in India, and active world statesman in the 1920s and 1930s – he was rarely disengaged from the predicaments of nations, states and borders.[9] He travelled widely in Europe and the Americas and had contact – which he frequently cultivated – with leading political figures and academic experts drawn from nationalist, unionist and federalist traditions, among them Michael Davitt, James Bryce, Lionel Curtis, Alfred Milner and Jan Smuts. Yet we still lack a distillation of

---

[8] Jonathan Parry, *The Rise and Fall of Liberal Government in Victorian Britain* (New Haven & London, 1993); 'Past and Future in the Later Career of Lord John Russell', in T.C.W. Blanning and David Cannadine (eds), *History and Biography: Essays in Honour of Derek Beales* (Cambridge, 1996), 142–72; 'Disraeli and England', *Historical Journal*, 43 (2000), 699–728.

[9] Though an evolving constant, spanning his whole career c. 1890–1945, this feature of Lloyd George's career emerges in rather disaggregated form in the literature, reflecting how historians have proceeded episodically – attending primarily to the narrative of Lloyd George's foreign policy – and with a focus on the years 1914–22. See, for example, Norman Davies, 'Lloyd George and Poland, 1919–1920', *Journal of Contemporary History*, 6 (1971), 132–54; George W. Egerton, 'The Lloyd George Government and the Creation of the League of Nations', *American Historical Review*, 79 (1974), 419–44; Margaret Macmillan, *Peacemakers: The Paris Peace Conference and its Attempt to End War* (London, 2001), esp. ch. 4; Alan Sharp, 'From Caxton Hall to Genoa via Fontainebleau and Cannes: David Lloyd George's Vision of Post-war Europe', *Diplomacy & Statecraft*, 30 (2019), 314–35; Andrzej Nowak, *The Forgotten Appeasement of 1920: Lloyd George, Lenin and Poland* (London, 2023).

Nation and Union in the Career of David Lloyd George 105

Lloyd George's understanding of 'nation' and how this framed his attitude towards the Union.

A single essay cannot consider the full range of Lloyd George's interventions on the Union. The aim of this essay, instead, is to examine important contexts that help to make his transition to unionism comprehensible in the critical period between his first forays as a political campaigner in the 1880s and his second term as prime minister following the First World War.

A Welsh Worldview

Lloyd George's early life is familiar enough, thanks to over fifty biographies, that the most formative influences of his upbringing can be summarised briefly. Born in Manchester in January 1863, he moved aged eighteen months to the village of Llanystumdwy in south Caernarfonshire, where together with his widowed mother and siblings he lived under the guardianship of his maternal uncle, Richard Lloyd. Here he received a distinctively Welsh upbringing of the kind that never shaped a British prime minister before or since. The home was Welsh-speaking, teetotal and godly. The Disciples of Christ chapel, the centre of Richard Lloyd's career as a well-known lay preacher, served as a place of worship for the young Lloyd George as well as a means of education and self-improvement through Bible study and the Eisteddfod – all through the medium of the Welsh language. He received his formal education in the one school available to him, the Anglican elementary school. As he later liked to recall, it was here that he first rebelled against the 'English' establishment – the 'English' church and the 'English' squire – by refusing to attend school services in the parish church and refusing to recite the catechism on the squire's inspection.[10]

If this distinctively Welsh upbringing is commonly viewed by historians as the source of his 'outsider' status, his conception of nationhood was formulated within a political-intellectual hinterland that also demands examination. In a survey of how Victorian political thinkers emphasised geographic and population size as well as cultural 'greatness' as key to legitimating nationality, Georgios Varouxakis identifies a shift away from an early nineteenth-century tradition of defending small nations to a conception of 'nationalism as positive only when it led to larger units.'[11] While such discourse reflected primarily on developments in continental Europe, it also created a framework for

[10] du Parcq, *Life*, vol. 1, 16–18.

[11] Georgios Varouxakis, 'Great Versus Small Nations: Size and National Greatness in Victorian Political Thought', in Duncan Bell (ed.), *Victorian Visions of Global Order: Empire and International Relations in Nineteenth-century Political Thought* (Cambridge, 2007), 154.

understanding the place of the Celtic nations relative to England, and therefore the merits and demerits of union. It is possible to extract three main claims from this discourse with which Lloyd George, as will be shown, was familiar.

The first is John Stuart Mill's civilisational argument. Mill famously held that the progress of civilisation involved the absorption of backward nations by energetic and civilised nations. He denied a firm correlation between size and greatness of civilisation, but argued that the United Kingdom, like France, exemplified circumstances in which a civilised majority population could absorb minorities to the latter's advantage. Without such absorption, the Welshman, like the Breton in France, would find himself 'sulk[ing] on his own rocks, the half-savage relic of past times, revolving in his own little mental orbit, without participation or interest in the general movement of the world.'[12]

A second claim was that a nation's prestige in the world, and hence its legitimacy, depended in large part on cultural greatness, which Matthew Arnold defined as culture that 'excite[d] love, interest, and admiration' in those nations lacking it. Arnold viewed with approval the extent of cultural consciousness in Welsh society and contrasted it with the 'Philistinism' that beset England; yet, as a nation 'disinherited of political success', Wales's prospects demanded that it embrace amalgamation with England.[13] 'An Englishman, with his country's history behind him, descends and deteriorates by becoming anything but an Englishman', whereas Welshmen, like Irishmen, were elevated by their nation's 'amalgamation' with England. That being so, claims to nationality should not be permitted to develop 'too far', even in nations demonstrating cultural vibrancy, since the indiscriminate indulgence of the principle of nationality imperilled 'that natural and beneficial union of conterminous or neighbouring territories into one great state, upon which the grandeur of nations and the progress of civilisation depends.'[14]

A third claim insisted that larger polities delivered more efficient government. Surveying the rise of two new 'great states' on the continent, Walter Bagehot argued that, in addition to enjoying enhanced geopolitical security, large nations optimised the mental resources required for successful governance. 'The many small governments of Italy and Germany waste far more of the highest class of mind upon the work of government than the two single

---

[12] John Stuart Mill, *Considerations on Representative Government* (London, 1861; 1884 edn), 122.

[13] Matthew Arnold, *The Study of Celtic Literature* (London, 1867), vii.

[14] Matthew Arnold, *Culture and Anarchy* (London, 1869; 1889 edn), 12 and *England and the Italian Question* (London, 1859), 11, 14; see also Varouxakis, 'Great Versus Small Nations', 141–4.

large states which will replace them.' The same applied to 'England' – a designation which he, like most Victorians, took to include Wales.[15]

This Victorian preoccupation with categorising 'the nation' formed an important backdrop to Lloyd George's early career in that it provided a means of placing vernacular experiences of Wales's particularity into a more theorised, comparative understanding of modern nationhood. The Welsh press played a crucial part in facilitating this. In the second half of the century, about 250 Welsh or bilingual periodicals were published in addition to the English-language newspaper press, a proliferation driven in part by the immense spread of denominational weeklies and the emergence of a nonconformist reading public. Modelled on English periodicals like *The Edinburgh Review*, the content was typically literary, theological and antiquarian. However, in the final third of the century, following Gladstone's Midlothian campaign, it came to feature more systematic coverage of foreign affairs, with the nonconformist ministers and literary figures who dominated the genre fostering readers' familiarity with the struggles of national and religious minorities elsewhere, notably in the Habsburg and Ottoman empires, and in doing so drawing implicit and explicit lessons for Wales.[16] Consequently, the *South Wales Daily News* considered Welshmen not only 'as well informed as to foreign and Colonial politics as the ordinary Englishman', but particularly susceptible to a didactic and moralising framing of the national question.[17]

One reason for this was that a discourse of civilisational progress in which small nations were excluded produced uncanny echoes of the notorious 1847 official report on education in Wales. Commissioned by the government through the Committee of the Privy Council on Education, the three commissioners – all non-Welsh speaking and Anglican – concluded that the Welsh language and the prevalence of nonconformity accounted for Wales's backwardness as a nation. Of the Welshman, they remarked: 'His language keeps him under the hatches, being one in which he can neither acquire nor communicate the necessary information. It is a language of old-fashioned agriculture, of theology, and of simple rustic life, while all the world around him is English.'[18] This state-sanctioned insult was deeply felt by many in mid-century Wales, including Richard Lloyd and the residents of Llanystumdwy, where

---

[15] Walter Bagehot, 'The Gains of the World by the Last Two Wars in Europe', *Economist* (18 Aug. 1866), 966.

[16] Huw Walters, 'The Welsh Language and the Periodical Press', in Geraint H. Jenkins (ed.), *The Welsh Language and its Social Domains, 1801–1911* (Cardiff, 2000), 359, 363, 374.

[17] *South Wales Daily News*, 10 Jan. 1896, 3.

[18] *Reports of the Commissioners of Inquiry into the State of Education in Wales, Part I* (London, 1847), 3.

108 Geraint Thomas

the commissioners deemed the village school to be particularly deficient. The hurt lived long in the inherited memory of Lloyd George and his generation, renewed as it was by exposure to those metropolitan polemics on progress and nationhood.[19]

These polemics had an evident effect on Lloyd George's thinking about Wales's place within the Union, as discussed in the next section. But they also had a performative function. As a budding platform orator and parliamentary hopeful, Lloyd George had more reason than most of his Welsh compatriots to subject the metropolitan wisdoms of the day to critical attention. This can be seen in two ways. First, doing so was integral to the project of forging a public profile for himself – a profile that needed to be authoritative on the national question as well as popular with the Welsh public. He understood that popularity could depend to a considerable degree on deference to authority – that is, authority displayed not by social status but through mastery of argument. As a professional solicitor already making a name for himself as an effective courtroom advocate and cross-examiner, he knew the reputational value to be garnered from being able to demolish seemingly inviolable cases through cogent argument. His preparation involved extensive reading beyond the periodical press. In addition to famous works of English literature, including the plays of Shakespeare, Carlyle's *Sartor Resartus* and Disraeli's *Tancred*, he read constitutional and national histories by Edmund Burke and A.M. Sullivan, whose nationalist *Story of Ireland* (1867) left a particular impression.[20] Secondly, it served the needs of Cymru Fydd. Under his influence in the 1890s, the society retreated from its metropolitan, self-consciously intellectual origins to become a popular movement in the towns and counties of Wales. By immersing himself in the metropolitan mindset, Lloyd George was able to acquaint Welsh audiences with a caricatured version of it, thereby framing the case for self-government with a mocking portrayal of the high priests of Unionism: 'Their eyes sweep over empires and continents, Wales is but a speck in their mental landscape… Such colossal intellects would be lost upon so modest a programme as that of our society, and Heaven preserve you from such superior persons.'[21]

Wales and the Union

One challenge facing Welsh Home Rulers was the peculiar nature of the Anglo-Welsh Union. Whereas the Acts of Union with Scotland in 1707 and Ireland in 1801 were ratified by contracting parliaments, the Laws in Wales Act 1536

---

[19] William George, *Richard Lloyd, Criccieth* (Caerdydd, 1934), 11–12.

[20] du Parcq, *Life*, vol. 1, 37; William George, *My Brother and I* (London, 1958), 128–9.

[21] *Western Mail*, 2 Dec. 1896, 6.

necessarily lacked any such elective basis, since Wales was already annexed and, since the thirteenth century, had been without a parliament or parliamentary representation in Westminster. Welsh constituencies were created in 1536 for representation in the English House of Commons, among them Lloyd George's Caernarfon Boroughs; but no representative assembly existed by which the Union could have been negotiated and ratified nor subsequently challenged on constitutional grounds.[22] The Anglo-Welsh Union therefore represented a fundamentally different phenomenon from the Scottish and Irish unions, which by contrast became the subject of comprehensive study and debate among political and legal thinkers up to the twentieth century.[23] Not until the age of home rule itself was the Welsh Union treated as a subject meriting jurisprudential academic interest, and even then it proved limited and too late to shape the context in which Lloyd George campaigned in the 1890s.[24] As a result, advocates of Welsh self-government operated without the aid of an established, albeit contested, vocabulary of modern statehood of the kind bequeathed to their Scottish and Irish counterparts.

One response was to align with Irish and especially Scottish home rulers in pursuit of Home Rule All Round. Frustrated by the Liberal leadership's prioritisation of the claims of the Irish Nationalists following the 1892 general election, Lloyd George began to cooperate closely with Henry Dalziel, the newly elected Liberal MP for Kirkcaldy Burghs. Like Lloyd George, Dalziel was already known as a radical nationalist in his native home.[25] During the parliaments of 1892–95, the two members moved several resolutions calling on the Liberal government to establish devolved legislatures;[26] and in opposition from 1895 they made Home Rule All Round a regular topic of discussion among members of the Radical Committee of Liberal MPs, which included Sir Charles Dilke and Henry Labouchère.[27]

The other response was to construct a case for Welsh self-government. This encompassed distinct causes, notably church disestablishment, land reform, temperance and education, each with a particular set of grievances and

---

[22] J. Gwynfor Jones, *Wales and the Tudor State: Government, Religious Change and the Social Order, 1534–1603* (Cardiff, 1989), ch. 1.

[23] Colin Kidd, *Union and Unionisms: Political Thought in Scotland, 1500–2000* (Cambridge, 2008); Alvin Jackson, *The Two Unions: Ireland, Scotland and the Survival of the United Kingdom, 1707–2007* (Oxford, 2011).

[24] E.g., Ivor Bowen, *The Statutes of Wales* (London, 1908); William Llewellyn Williams, 'The Union of England and Wales', *Transactions of the Honourable Society of Cymmrodorion: Session 1907–08* (1909).

[25] Frederick J. Higginbottom, *The Vivid Life: A Journalist's Career* (London, 1934), 204–5.

[26] *Hansard*, 29 Mar. 1895, vol. 32, cc. 523–60.

[27] *Family Letters*, 99, 101–2 (18 Feb.; 3, 6, 24 Mar. 1896), 111 (3 June 1897).

demands, which made the wider campaign contingent on political conditions, including the progress of individual policies. However, there was one overarching refrain in Lloyd George's speeches throughout the 1890s: that is, the cause of 'good government' and the role of the Union in impeding the realisation of its benefits in Wales. This same cause, according to Jonathan Parry's seminal study, constituted the driving mission of Victorian Liberalism in the decades before 1886. According to Parry, British Liberals conceived of representative government as responsive and rational. It responded to popular grievances, not by conceding to sectional interests but by parliament assenting to 'settled opinion', itself wrought through 'prolonged deliberation' by MPs and signifying the 'closest approximation' of public opinion. In turn, popular acquiescence in legislation helped to ensure political stability. Crucially, this model of representative government also had an important 'integrating' function, not least within the Union, insofar as it placed all four nations under the same rules of responsive and rational government and thus 'idealise[d] parliament as a truly national body'.[28]

It was against the backdrop of this Liberal ideal that Lloyd George criticised the Union in its unitary form as an impediment to good government in Wales. He did so with three principal arguments. The first was that Westminster had proved singularly incapable of integrating the settled will of the Welsh nation into its legislative programme. It was with the intention of projecting this settled will that he sought to organise Cymru Fydd into a popular movement. Speaking at the launch of the Cardiff branch in 1894, he set out the context as follows:

> Let us not forget that as far as the main items in our programme are concerned they have maintained a prominent part in the national hopes for the last fifty years. The great fathers of Welsh Liberalism all fought for these identical ideals. In reading their speeches and writings there is nothing so pathetic as the imminence with which they regarded the realisation of their dreams. But two generations have passed away not having received the promise.[29]

Making the same observation in the Commons, he warned of the potential consequences. 'One regrettable result of the present system was that before a small nationality in the kingdom could get its grievances attended to it had to resort to something in the nature of lawlessness', as the Scottish Crofters Act and the Irish Land Acts demonstrated.[30]

---

[28] Parry, *Rise and Fall*, 3–9.

[29] du Parcq, *Life*, vol. 1, 143; *Western Mail*, 5 Oct 1894, 6.

[30] *Hansard*, 29 Mar. 1895, vol. 32, cc. 533–4.

Second, he argued that Westminster's unresponsiveness to Wales stemmed from England's undue predominance over parliament and government. The failure to enact Wales's political agenda was not for lack of representation or opportunity. The principality had returned a majority of Liberal members committed to the agenda at every election since 1868 and the Liberal party had been in power for no fewer than fourteen of the intervening years. Nor was it the result of Conservative opposition, as, 'in spite of Tory obstruction, England has always had her wants attended to without delay'. Rather, the problem was the weight afforded to England and English opinion. 'The main factor in British legislation,' he argued, is 'not so much which Ministry is in office as what is required by England at the hands of the Ministry.'[31]

But the predominance of England, Lloyd George claimed, resulted in the suppression not only of Welsh legislative demands but of Welsh political life itself, whose distinct 'temperament' he defined as the immutable product of racial difference. He took aim at the inconsistency of those 'men in high positions' who, while denying Wales's 'national existence', spoke of the racial inferiority of Welshmen. Referring to Lord Salisbury, he remarked:

> He seems to think that race distinctions in Britain are a fact existent only for the display of an English Conservative's superior extraction... But a fact is a fact for all purposes. If a nation at all, then we are a nation to all intents. We cannot be an infirm race to point the moral of Unionist intellectual supremacy, and no race of any sort or kind to base a claim for self-government'[32]

Thirdly, Lloyd George challenged the idea that small nations were predestined to impotence and inefficiency in government. Ireland had already demonstrated as much with land reform, which he proffered as evidence of a small nation's capacity for progress rivalling that of England. That Irish land reform resulted from pressure on the imperial parliament by the Land League informed his vision of Cymru Fydd as a popular movement intended to leverage pressure on Westminster. Yet at the same time he was clear that the logic of Welsh self-government, like Irish Home Rule, remained undiminished by any concessions that Westminster might grant in individual policy areas. Concessions extracted through popular agitation were a poor substitute for permanent self-government, since the influence of such pressure on the imperial parliament was so unpredictable. It meant, in effect, that Welsh interests were subject to representative government on an arbitrary basis under the Union. By contrast, self-government ensured better government. In making this claim, his argument rested on the assertion that a provincial parliament possessed the necessary 'local knowledge' to develop legislation in a more timely and

---

[31] du Parcq, *Life*, vol. 1, 143; *Western Mail*, 5 Oct. 1894, 6.

[32] du Parcq, *Life*, vol. 1, 145; *South Wales Daily News*, 2 Dec. 1896, 6.

systematic way than an imperial parliament, which lacked local knowledge and in Britain's case was 'overweighted' with concerns on a global scale.

Nor was Ireland an example simply to inspire. Lloyd George found it important to distinguish between the two nations to expose ways in which Unionist objections to Irish Home Rule did not apply to Welsh Home Rule. Notwithstanding its interdenominational rivalry, Welsh society could be characterised as mercifully free of sectarianism. Compared to Ireland, 'Wales has no Ulster'. This ensured that the introduction of self-government to Wales would be a peaceful development, he insisted. There would be no cause for any group to fear religious persecution and no prospect of the 're-establishment of Roman Catholicism as the national religion'. Unionist opinion in Westminster would have no basis on which to fear collaboration between peaceable, protestant Wales and the subversive forces of Catholic Irish nationalism: 'Wales has a religion that would satisfy the fastidiousness of the most rabid Orangemen in the thoroughness of its Protestantism'.[33]

Government and Patriotism

Clearly, then, Lloyd George was no advocate for the Union in the form that it entered the twentieth century. His speeches portrayed the centralised unitary state as capable of injustice, through the 'oppression' of Welsh interests and the 'monopolisation' of Welsh resources. They referred to the goal of Welsh 'emancipation' in the same breath as the liberation of Germany from the 'Napoleonic yoke' and of Italy from Habsburg tyranny.[34] Yet he never advocated full independence for Wales, a prospect from which he explicitly sought to distance himself periodically. Responding to the common charge that dissolution of the Union provided the true motive behind home rule, he remarked in 1890: 'Who can point out in the speech of the wildest Welsh Nationalist a single passage that would indicate a desire for separation?'[35]

Indeed, by 1900 Lloyd George's career ambitions reached far beyond the principality. Writing to his wife following an encouraging meeting with Henry Massingham, editor of the *Daily Chronicle*, he enthused that he 'should take in hand the resurrecting of the Liberal party & do what Lord Randolph Churchill did for the Tory party'.[36] The Second Boer War provided an opportunity. His opposition to Britain's annexation of the Boer republics, and the ferocity of his attacks on his erstwhile radical hero, Joseph Chamberlain, the Liberal Unionist Colonial Secretary, brought him nationwide renown as a platform

[33] du Parcq, *Life*, vol. 1, 87–8; *South Wales Daily News*, 5 Feb. 1890, 6.
[34] du Parcq, *Life*, vol. 1, 142.
[35] *Ibid.*, 88.
[36] *Family Letters*, 112 (9 Sept. 1897).

Nation and Union in the Career of David Lloyd George   113

speaker of penetrating power. It cemented his reputation as the leading Liberal radical of his generation, a figure whom the next Liberal prime minister could scarcely overlook for ministerial preferment. After his appointment as President of the Board of Trade in 1905, biographers began to chronicle the story of Lloyd George's dramatic rise 'from village green to Downing Street', from Welsh rebel to British statesman. Further laudatory studies, as well as a biopic, appeared during his premiership.[37] These characterisations, as well as his own self-presentation, played an important role in demonstrating his unionist credentials in ways consistent with his earlier vision of Welsh self-government.

The defining feature of his unionism in these years was federalism. While the concept of federation was familiar to that generation of politicians for whom nation and empire were the subjects of so much contemporary commentary, the origins of Lloyd George's active interest in federal statecraft is somewhat diffuse. His travels to Germany, Switzerland and Canada, while not always intended as policy missions, introduced him to the great federal experiments of his time.[38] He hero-worshipped Abraham Lincoln as a war leader and as saviour of the US federal union, whose constitution was famously chronicled for English readers by his cabinet colleague, James Bryce, himself a supporter of Irish Home Rule who had previously lent his support to Lloyd George on the Cymru Fydd platform while remaining close to leading Unionists like Dicey.[39] As prime minister, he worked closely with the former High Commissioner for Southern Africa and founder of the Round Table group of imperial federalists, Alfred Milner, whom he appointed to the War Cabinet, and recruited Philip Kerr, editor of the *Round Table Journal*, as a private secretary. He thus became acquainted with other Round Table figures, among them F.S. Oliver, a Liberal Unionist Scot whose *Alexander Hamilton: An Essay on American Union* (1906) presented the US federal union as a guide to British imperial federation and

[37] In addition to du Parcq, *Life*, see for example J. Hugh Edwards, *From Village Green to Downing Street: The Life of the Right Honourable David Lloyd George* (London, 1908); Beriah Evans, *The Life Romance of David Lloyd George* (London, 1915); Harold Spender, *The Prime Minister: The Life and Times of David Lloyd George* (London, 1920); and E.T. Raymond, *Mr Lloyd George* (London, 1922). The biopic, *The Life Story of David Lloyd George* (dir. Maurice Elvey), was suddenly suppressed before its intended premiere in November 1918.

[38] John Grigg, *Lloyd George: the Young Lloyd George* (London, 1973), 127, 164, 249–54, 260–1; Kenneth Morgan, 'Lloyd George and Germany', *Historical Journal*, 39 (1996), 755–66.

[39] Kenneth O. Morgan, 'Kentucky's "Cottage-Bred Man": Abraham Lincoln and Wales', in Richard Carwardine and Jay Sexton (eds), *The Global Lincoln* (Oxford, 2011), 147; James Bryce, *The American Commonwealth* (3 vols, London, 1888); Christopher Harvie, 'Ideology and Home Rule: James Bryce, A.V. Dicey and Ireland, 1880–1887', *English Historical Review*, 91 (1976), 298–314.

114   *Geraint Thomas*

to the broader ideal of political union across multiple governments;[40] and Edward Grigg, co-editor of the *Round Table Journal* who would succeed Kerr as private secretary in 1920.

Despite the preoccupation of the Downing Street federalists with the consolidation of the empire, Lloyd George's engagement with federalism betray once more his concern to effect good government in domestic matters. This can be seen in his memorandum of August 1910, in which he advocated a coalition government to spearhead a programme of reforms to improve national efficiency and which historians have highlighted as premonitory evidence of his exceptional ambition.[41] In it he lamented the 'unsatisfactory' system of local government which overburdened the Imperial Parliament with responsibilities which could be 'more efficiently discharged by local bodies on a large scale' – that is, by devolved national parliaments.[42] It was that same quest for efficiency – manifested in growing frustration with Asquith's conduct of the war – that brought him into contact with Milner's circle, through a dining group convened by Leo Amery.[43]

So far as the policy of federalism had a direct bearing on the Union in these years, it was as a possible solution to the Irish question, its provision of self-governance promising to satisfy the Nationalists and its reaffirmation of the Union offering reassurance to unionist opinion, especially in Ulster. In 1916, having declined the position of Chief Secretary for Ireland when it fell vacant following the Easter Rising, Lloyd George was tasked by the cabinet to open negotiations with Nationalists and Unionists. In addition to suggesting that Home Rule could be brought into operation in Dublin during the war, he anticipated an Imperial Conference at which 'a constitution for the United Kingdom' would be discussed along federal lines.[44] His handling of the negotiations angered Conservative members of the cabinet, but the federal solution remained to the fore during his first term as prime minister. In April 1918 he instructed a cabinet committee under Walter Long to draft an Irish Home Rule Bill and gave it a wide remit to consider devolution for the UK as a whole. One influential member of the committee, Austen Chamberlain, viewed federalism

---

[40] Kidd, *Union and Unionisms*, 111–12.

[41] Savage, 'The Parnell of Wales'.

[42] 'Mr Lloyd George's Memorandum on the Formation of a Coalition Government', 17 Aug. 1910, as Appendix I in Charles Petrie, *The Life and Letters of the Right Honourable Sir Austen Chamberlain, vol. 1* (London, 1939), 387.

[43] *The Leo Amery Diaries, vol. I: 1896–1929*, ed. John Barnes and David Nicholson (London, 1980), 126–7.

[44] *The Crisis of British Unionism: Lord Selborne's Domestic Political Papers, 1885–1922*, ed. George Boyce (London, 1987), 173–4 (memorandum by Walter Long, 15 June 1916).

'as the only possible solution of the Irish question... the only thing which would make Home Rule safe & the only form of Home Rule which Ulster could be got to accept'.[45] Although aborted, the scheme highlights an important stage in Lloyd George's evolving appreciation of the Union. Gone was 'Home Rule All Round', the nationalist iteration of devolution, which had been replaced with 'federalism' as the unionist iteration of the same policy – a policy now justified as a means of consolidating the Union rather than as a vehicle for extending legislative independence to Wales. Thus, Lloyd George emerged from the war with his unionist credentials enhanced, enough that his early career could be rendered 'unionist' retroactively. 'It is a curious fact,' wrote his friend and biographer, Harold Spender, in 1920, 'that if Mr. Lloyd George had stood for Parliament in 1886, he would probably have been drawn by his sympathy for Mr. [Joseph] Chamberlain into the ranks of that small section of Radical Unionists who followed Mr. Chamberlain in his opposition to Gladstonian Home Rule, but afterwards, recoiling from open reaction, rejoined the Liberal Party – men like Sir George [Otto] Trevelyan'.[46]

Curiously, Lloyd George moved decisively away from devolution just as the policy appeared to command growing support in parliament and across the political parties. In June 1918 he received a deputation on the subject, comprising peers and MPs drawn from the Unionist, Liberal and Labour parties. He was told that 95% of Liberal party opinion backed the policy, as did around 150 Unionist MPs, with many more open to persuasion. Among the deputation was William Adamson, the leader of the Labour party, whose party conference passed a resolution that same week in favour of statutory legislative assemblies for England, Scotland and Wales.[47] This widening base of support for the policy reflected one of the deputation's main claims to the prime minister, that federal devolution now answered the mainstream concerns of 'the mass of the nation and not merely... the resentment and action of minorities'. The Irish situation once more demanded it, they argued, and so too would the global situation after four years of war, 'when all manner of questions about national self-determination are of the essence'. But it was the burden of imperial and domestic reconstruction, and the resulting 'congestion of parliament', that provided the greatest impetus. (This echoed the argument that Lloyd George himself had made in 1910.)[48] Questions of national finance, foreign and colonial policy, the

[45] *The Austen Chamberlain Diary Letters: The Correspondence of Sir Austen Chamberlain with his Sisters Hilda and Ida, 1916–1937*, ed. Robert C. Self (Cambridge, 1995), 80 (to Ida, 9 Mar. 1918).

[46] Spender, *The Prime Minister*, 52–3.

[47] *The Times*, 29 June 1918, 3.

[48] 'Mr Lloyd George's memorandum on the formation of a coalition government', 387.

armed services, the government of India, and relations with the self-governing Dominions – these alone would test the capacity of any single legislature. But additional responsibility for the specific reconstruction problems of England, Scotland, Ireland or Wales would break it. 'If Parliament... as now constituted, was to try and grapple with this stupendous task, we think it could only end in national disaster.'[49]

Lloyd George's reply is instructive. On the one hand, he expressed support for the principle of federalism and invoked with admiration the foresight of Chamberlain's federal alternative to Gladstone's Irish policy. In relation to reconstruction, he described as 'the purest commonsense' the case for delegating domestic policy to devolved parliaments, thereby enabling Westminster to devote itself more expertly to imperial and foreign affairs. On the other hand, he declined to commit the government: 'You cannot attempt a big measure which is highly controverted in the middle of a great war.' Whereas Scottish and Welsh opinion was settled, he claimed English opinion remained unclear – and, given England's relative size, 'that is really what matters.'[50] His cabinet colleague Christopher Addison recounted this as equivocation, or 'drift – with the Prime Minister, I am sorry to say, heading the drifters.'[51] But it is perhaps better understood as carefully choreographed stonewalling by a prime minister who needed to retain the goodwill of devolutionists and Unionist federalists but had himself come to disavow self-government for Wales and Scotland.

After all, this was Lloyd George, a proven master of ministerial initiative, whose distinctive method of policymaking was well developed by 1918. Its hallmark, namely the recruitment of external experts to whom responsibility would be delegated for developing policy, could be seen in his pre-war pension and national insurance schemes as well as in the areas of munitions, shipping, food supply and public health during the war.[52] In addition to Kerr, the secretariat contained two trusted figures amply qualified to explore devolution policy. One was Thomas Jones, assistant secretary to the cabinet and close confidant of the prime minister. The Welsh-speaking Methodist had until his appointment spent all his working life in Ireland, Scotland and Wales, served as the first secretary of the Welsh Insurance Commission up to December 1916, and edited the monthly

---

[49] 'Joint Deputation from the Houses of Parliament to the Prime Minister', 26 June 1918, Parliamentary Archives, Lloyd George Papers, LG/F/225.

[50] *Ibid.*

[51] Christopher Addison, *Politics from Within, 1911–1918* (2 vols, London, 1924), vol. 2, 246.

[52] John Turner, *Lloyd George's Secretariat* (Cambridge, 1980); John Turner, '"Experts" and Interests: David Lloyd George and the Dilemmas of the Expanding State, 1906–19', in Roy McLead (ed.), *Government and Expertise: Specialists, Administrators and Professionals, 1860–1919* (Cambridge, 1988), 203–23.

journal of 'national social progress' *Welsh Outlook* between 1914 and 1916.[53] The other was W.G.S. Adams, the Scottish-born Gladstone Professor of Government in Oxford and previously head statistician to the Irish Department of Agriculture in Dublin, and advocate of federalism.[54] Neither Jones nor Adams was instructed by Downing Street to develop schemes of devolution. Such work was instead carried out by a Speaker's Conference following a motion of the House of Commons. Its report of April 1920 contained detailed proposals on the allocation of powers to subordinate legislatures in England, Scotland and Wales, as well as alternative schemes for the composition of such legislatures which reflected the conference's divided opinion on the question.[55] When Lloyd George received a second deputation later that year, his response remained sympathetic but noncommittal.[56] Why?

Two contexts, both reflecting shifting imperatives at the centre of Lloyd George's career, suggest an explanation. The first is postwar international reconstruction. As Lord Riddell observed, great international disputes held a deep fascination for Lloyd George, who despite his relative lack of experience of foreign affairs embraced the role of global statesman.[57] This inevitably diverted time away from domestic affairs. Crucially, it also conditioned the terms on which the desirability and feasibility of federal devolution were now assessed, by advocates and opponents alike, as the twin projects of national self-determination and internationalism emanating from Versailles thrust the national claims and rights of small nations once more into debate. It was expressly as a Welshman that Lloyd George claimed special understanding of the national aspirations stirring within the territories of the collapsed empires of Europe. 'I am a member of a small nation myself,' he told Ignacy Paderewski, Prime Minister of Poland, 'and therefore I have great sympathy with all oppressed nationalities.'[58] But while celebrating patriotic fervour, he cautioned against the pursuit of unrestrained nationalist aspirations. This could lead to self-defeating overreach, as in the case of Lithuania, whose independence he

---

[53] Rodney Lowe, 'Jones, Thomas (1870–1955)', *Oxford Dictionary of National Biography*, 24 May 2007 version.

[54] Brian Harrison, 'Adams, William George Stewart (1874–1966)', *Oxford Dictionary of National Biography*, 8 Oct. 2009 version.

[55] 'Conference on Devolution. Letter from Mr. Speaker to the Prime Minister', 27 Apr. 1920, Cmd.692.

[56] 'Deputation to The Rt. Hon. David Lloyd George from Members of Parliament on Federal Devolution', 16 Dec. 1920, Parliamentary Archives, Lloyd George Papers, LG/F/225.

[57] *Lord Riddell's Intimate Diary*, 362.

[58] Quoted in David Lloyd George, *The Truth About the Peace Treaties* (2 vols, London, 1938), vol. 2, 998.

considered as ill-advised as independence for Wales.[59] Worse, it could lead to small nations seeking territorial expansion and the oppression of other races, the 'very tyranny which they have themselves endured for centuries'.[60]

Although the spectre of overreach now haunted Lloyd George's view of small-nation nationalism, he did not, for the time being, articulate any lessons that might apply to the nations of the UK. However, one prominent figure informally attached to the Downing Street secretariat did. Alfred Zimmern had been among Lloyd George's closest advisors during his rise to the premiership in 1916 and remained a close associate of Thomas Jones and David Davis, the prime minister's PPS who endowed the Woodrow Wilson chair in International Politics at the University of Wales in Aberystwyth, to which Zimmern was appointed in 1919. In June that year, as the Versailles conference neared its final stages, he addressed the National Conference on Self-Government for Wales held in Llandrindod Wells. 'The war', he stated, 'while it has brought many new states into existence in response to the cry of self-determination, has at the same time brought about conditions under which small states, whether new or old, are more dependent than ever before in history, upon the policy of their larger neighbours.' In such a world, political independence was a mirage in which the prospect of increased freedom soon faded and the reality of emasculation loomed. He invited 'any Welshmen who may be attracted by the political programme of Sinn Fein' to observe the Irish, or indeed the Estonian, delegation to Versailles, their 'supplicant guise' and 'painful weakness' standing in stark contrast to the integral position of Wales in the British delegation. His concluding advice was to delegate 'the sphere of government' to the empirical, unsentimental methods of public administration and to channel nationalist sentimentalism to the study and promotion of the nation's 'cultural inheritance'.[61] Once out of office, Lloyd George preached the same message to audiences in Wales, including at the National Eisteddfod in 1923, that Welsh patriotism served the nation's interests best through cultural than political aspirations.[62]

The second and related context is that of government. Given his experience of ministerial office, uninterrupted since 1905, Lloyd George's view of public administration could hardly be expected to survive unaltered from his time on the backbenches. Over this time his emphasis had shifted from a preoccupation

---

[59]   *The Deliberations of the Council of Four: Notes of the Official Interpreter, Paul Mantoux*, ed. and trans. A.S. Link (2 vols, Princeton, 1992), vol. 2, 308–10.

[60]   Lloyd George, *Truth About the Peace Treaties*, vol. 2, 998.

[61]   Alfred Zimmern, 'The International Settlement and Small Nationalities', address delivered to the National Conference on Self-Government for Wales, 9 June 1919, reprinted in *Welsh Outlook*, July 1919, 71–5.

[62]   For an English translation of the speech, see *The Times*, 10 Aug. 1923, 10.

with parliamentary government to a preoccupation with executive government, from the representation of grievances to the effective implementation of solutions. With this came a growing appreciation of the role of executive activism in addressing the particular interests of Wales within the unitary Union. Nowhere did he discover this more powerfully than in the field of education. Following the Liberal government's failure to pass its Education Bill in 1906, a flagship policy for Welsh nonconformists incensed by the provisions of the Conservatives' Education Act of 1902, Lloyd George – though operating from the Board of Trade – proved instrumental in establishing a Welsh Department of the Board of Education.[63] The department acquired responsibility for the administration and inspection of education at all levels in Wales, producing a distinctly Welsh provision and playing an active role in promoting Welsh-medium education. The department marked the first instance of administrative devolution to Wales, a practice extended to other policy areas with the establishment of the Welsh National Insurance Commission in 1911, the Welsh Health Service Insurance Commission in 1912 and the Welsh Office of the Board of Agriculture in 1919.[64]

Lloyd George considered this 'homespun' education among the finest achievements in the service of Welsh national interest. Addressing a conference of teachers in Llandudno in 1925, he attributed its success to the fact that the department had wrested 'control of Welsh education from Whitehall'.[65] Such anti-establishment asides at Whitehall and Westminster remained a feature of his speeches throughout his career, especially in Wales where they signified 'anti-Toryism' almost interchangeably. They served him well electorally and explain his considerable success in shaping the narrative of Welsh political debate into the 1930s.[66] But they obscure the extent and nature of his flight from radical nationalist to unionist.

* * *

In his account of Liberalism after 1886, Parry assesses the profound consequences of Gladstone's commitment to Irish Home Rule and his subsequent pandering to Welsh and Scottish nationalist sentiment. 'Passion had triumphed over reason; separation over assimilation; populist appeals over parliamentary

---

[63] Lloyd George to Herbert Lewis, n.d. Jan. 1907, National Library of Wales, Herbert Lewis Papers, D29.

[64] Peter J. Randall, 'The Origins and Establishment of the Welsh Department of the Board of Education', *Welsh History Review*, 7 (1975), 450–71.

[65] *Western Mail*, 8 June 1925, 6.

[66] Geraint Thomas, 'The Conservative Party and Welsh Politics in the Inter-War Years', *English Historical Review*, 128 (2013), 901–11.

120   *Geraint Thomas*

discussion... sentimentalism over science; "government by average opinion" over didacticism.' Diverted by the Grand Old Man's 'executive arrogance' and 'sense of Providential mission', Liberalism had abandoned its vision of statecraft as a self-consciously British cause.[67] Given his sustained critique of the Union, not to mention the self-belief that characterised his conduct in government, Lloyd George's career might easily have hastened this disintegration, leading not only to the Irish Free State but to a wider and systematic dismantling of the Union.

Yet the Anglo-Scottish and Anglo-Welsh unions survived unaltered. This was not on account of any diminution of nationalist outlook on Lloyd George's part. He remained a proud cultural nationalist his entire life, championing the Welsh language, promoting Welsh education, and upholding the public spirit of Welsh nonconformity long after the campaign for disestablishment was won and his own Christian faith started to dwindle.[68] He did more than any other politician of his generation to expand the bureaucracy of the central British state, yet by establishing official roles and structures for Wales and Scotland proved himself a devolutionist in the administration of some public policy. Nor, given how most Liberals, the Labour party and some Unionists were advocating a federal scheme by 1918, was it on account of immovable public hostility or the immutable absence of political opportunity.

Over the course of his career, Lloyd George the Welsh nationalist became, additionally, a Welsh unionist. For Saunders Lewis, the first President of Plaid Cymru, this career spent at the centre of the British state was a betrayal of the spirit of Cymru Fydd and stood in contrast to that of William George, the brother who stayed at home to run the family firm, served his country as educationist and county councillor, and remained an unreconstructed home ruler.[69] In reality, Lloyd George embodied what Colin Kidd labels 'analytic unionism' and Graeme Morton calls 'unionist-nationalism', which stood in contrast to the 'banal unionism' of those who never questioned the existence or justification of the Union.[70] It was arrived at not unthinkingly, and notwithstanding the vicissitudes of career and events, but by deduction. Lacking any particular point of conversion, it was a gradual and almost imperceptible process, yet one rooted in a reasoning that remained remarkably stable – namely a nationalist concern with what the Union ought and could secure for Wales as a distinct nation.

---

[67] Parry, *Rise and Fall*, 305–6.

[68] On his private religious beliefs, see George, *My Brother and I*, 270–2.

[69] D. Hywel Davies, *The Welsh Nationalist Party, 1925–1945* (Cardiff, 1983), 44. Although a Liberal, William George was present at several of the founding activities of Plaid Cymru in 1925–1926.

[70] Kidd, *Union and Unionisms*; Graeme Morton, *Unionist-Nationalism: Governing Urban Scotland, 1830–1860* (East Linton, 1999).

Part III

Ideas Over Time: Narratives of Change

Chapter 6

Politics, Rhetoric and the Serial Fluctuations of 'Small State' Ideology in the Long Nineteenth Century and After

Boyd Hilton

The closest Jonathan Parry has come to stating a credo is in a reference to his mentor Maurice Cowling's quest to 'capture the complex dynamic of political history and especially the relation between political tactics, languages and ideas'. As someone who knew him at close quarters, Parry can claim that Cowling's approach was 'more sophisticated than he managed to convey in print'.[1] Not without trepidation, he wrote *The Politics of Patriotism* (2006) to show how it should be done, though sadly Cowling did not live to see the result. The aim of this essay is to explore the same dynamic with reference to an area of policy that has hardly been central to either historian's concerns. Indeed, in his first monograph, published in 1986, Parry noted with satisfaction that the preoccupation of earlier historians with constructed economic ideologies such as 'interventionism', 'laissez-faire' and 'individualism' was now being treated with scepticism by his own generation. There was therefore no longer any need to highlight 'the danger of sailing the ship of "ideas" too near to the rocky shore-line of political reality... While rejecting the notion that elaborated theory can usually be assigned any very specific influence in the shaping of detailed policy, ... prejudices, and "ideas" in a less developed form ought not to be ignored by the political historian', and 'closer attention to the intellectual setting in which political activity took place is a necessary precondition for an understanding of the interest which politics evoked, the anxieties which it aroused, and the consequences of those anxieties for future developments'.[2] In terms of its subject

---

[1] Jonathan Parry, *The Politics of Patriotism: English Liberalism, National Identity and Europe, 1830–1886* (Cambridge, 2006), x.

[2] J.P. Parry, *Democracy and Religion: Gladstone and the Liberal Party, 1867–1875* (Cambridge, 1986), 4–5.

matter the present essay might seem to revert to a pre-Parry historiography, and certainly it could be argued that if there were any field in which elaborated theory was likely to impact on policy, then political economy was the most likely area in which to find it. However, there is very little elaborated theory in the following story of conflicting prejudices, rhetorics, narrative appropriations, and political contingencies.

My reference to 'small state' in the title might seem like an opportunistic riff on recent debates in the Conservative party, for example on the benefits of 'levelling up', helping 'the just-about-managing' and scattering the 'enemies of growth', three slogans related respectively to the policies propounded by Prime Ministers Theresa May (2016–19), Boris Johnson (2019–22), and Liz Truss (September–October 2022).[3] In fact, this essay was written in 2015, long before those debates, and delivered in Oxford as a 'Dacre Lecture' in honour of Hugh Trevor-Roper. Its starting point was a comment by the *Times* journalist Matthew Parris suggesting that 'the watershed, the real battle for the soul of twenty-first-century Britain [is] the size, reach and cost of the state'.[4] Parris's unusual terminology may have been an unconscious echo of Margaret Thatcher's determination to 'change the heart and soul' of the nation.[5] Like her he inclines to interpret the battle between 'big' and 'little' state as ideological,[6] and so it often seems when frozen at particular moments in time, but polemically the struggle goes back at least two hundred years. What Parris was really hearing were two traditional political tunes or earworms, modulating, syncopating, briefly harmonising, mostly discordant, occasionally cacophonous.

'Big' and 'Little' State Thinking in the Revolutionary Age

Traditionally, fiscal-military state mercantilism backed by economic and social constraints has been seen as a Hanoverian norm that came under increasing challenge from market theorists. Yet although a number of economic controls were dismantled in the later part of this period, historians such as Joanna Innes, Julian Hoppit, and David Eastwood have pointed to a reverse process involving new 'forms of government growth' and areas in which the province

[3]   Truss's spectacularly short-lived ministry might be seen as the apogee of the economic individualist position.

[4]   M. Parris, 'Message to Voters: It's the Austerity, Stupid', *The Times*, 4 Apr. 2015, 23.

[5]   Margaret Thatcher in *Sunday Times*, 3 May 1981, 35.

[6]   M. Parris, 'Tories do have an Ideology – and they'll need it', *The Times*, 1 Oct. 2010, 23.

Politics, Rhetoric and the Serial Fluctuations of 'Small State' Ideology   125

of legislation was 'amplified'.[7] If the focus of this essay was the nature of the state *as an agent*, it would be necessary to distinguish between various binaries such as central and local government spending and mandatory and permissive legislation. The focus here, however, is on opposing concepts of the role of the individual in society: should citizens be left to stand on their own feet and to make their own market choices, as Parris believes, or should the community constrain them? Thus, the references below to 'small state' strategies take in the whole gamut of free *market* policies: minimal state, exiguous welfare, balanced budgets, free trade and fixed currency (leading in modern parlance to globalisation), all contributing to a deflationary paradigm which increasingly influenced the official mind of policymaking from the 1820s. It was resisted by a 'big state' counter-paradigm that included not just protective tariffs but managed currency, generous welfare benefits, discretionary or 'real bills' banking, fiscal controls to nudge citizens into non-market led choices, and colonial preference. Both paradigms have since taken many sudden changes of direction due to contingent political events ('exogenous shocks') that were extraneous to the macroeconomic debate. New directions have required new rhetorical justifications, and these in turn have often led their proponents to act and argue in new and unanticipated ways.

Since prevailing economic theories usually serve to rationalise the material interests of a ruling group, it is unsurprising that eighteenth-century pro-market policy norms suited the demands of Whig commercial society. Facing acute fiscal problems in the aftermath of wartime spending, Walpole, Pelham and North all turned to retrenchment and the refinancing and redemption of debt. Pitt the Younger followed suit during his first decade in office but in 1794, with the outbreak of war, a fiscal crisis, revolutionary radicalism, food price inflation and widespread distress, he adopted diametrically opposite policies almost overnight. Economically these involved enhanced taxation and government borrowing, central requisitioning of grain and even some half-hearted attempts to control its price. Constitutionally they included paid Middlesex magistrates reporting to the Home Office alongside beefed-up policing in the metropolis, and the establishment of a home and foreign secret service. In the same year the totally unexpected refusal of jurors to convict in the case of key prosecutions for treason signalled the failure of traditional law and order policies, based on suspension of habeas corpus and on arbitrary and exemplary

---

[7]   Julian Hoppit, *Britain's Political Economies: Parliament and Economic Life, 1660–1800* (Cambridge, 2017), esp. 38–101, 277–325; Joanna Innes, *Inferior Politics: Social Problems and Social Policies in Eighteenth-Century Britain* (Oxford, 2009), 21–105; David Eastwood, '"Amplifying the Province of the Legislature": The Flow of Information and the English State in the Early Nineteenth Century', *Historical Research*, 62 (1989), 276–94.

punishments to deter the multitude. Over the next seven years Pitt embarked on what he himself agreed was a very 'un-English' (i.e. 'Continental') attempt to prevent disorder through a system of authoritarian social policing, using government spies, censorship and precise controls on public behaviour by pre-scribing exactly what was permissible in terms of outdoor meetings, publications, workplace combinations, and so forth.[8] It is beside the point to observe, as some historians do, that the repressive measures of the later 1790s rarely led to prosecutions,[9] since the whole point of *preventative* legislation, based on state cognisance and control, was to cow people rather than prosecute them. However, interventionism could be tender as well as tough, notably with the introduction of inflation-proof outdoor relief supplemented by child benefit. It is important to emphasise that the new approach to governance had nothing to do with either party politics or ideology. It was simply a way of coping in an emergency, a new common sense. It meant that Pitt's legacy at a practical level was ambiguous, hence the divisions among conservatives after his death. Whether or not the labels 'liberal' and 'high' tory are helpful, there was clearly a division between those who celebrated the Pitt of the 1780s and others who claimed the 'big state' mantle of the wartime Prime Minister.

The most significant consequence of the fiscal crisis was Britain's quarter-century off the gold standard (the 'Bank Restriction') from 1797. The currency question was ideologised in the crucial debates of 1811, when Huskisson's pro-bullion (pro-gold) deployment of Newtonian mechanics came up against Castlereagh's anti-bullionist theory of an 'abstract pound'.[10] It was then politi-cised as a result of the restoration of the gold standard ('resumption of cash payments') at the old par during 1819–21, a process which created winners and losers by deflating prices and raising the value of money. Overseas traders were mostly in the first camp along with rentiers and other creditors and persons on fixed incomes, while the unlucky ones included mortgagees and other debtors, wage earners and others with precarious incomes, and produc-ers dependent on the domestic market. Like the UK's recent membership of 'Europe', the Bank Restriction was a case of 'gradually in' but 'rapidly out', the pace of extraction causing much additional disruption to those in the losing camp. Resumption was sold in 1819 as a self-regulating 'small-state' policy inso-far as it guarded against official manipulation of the money supply by the Bank, the Treasury and international financiers such as Rothschild, yet the political

---

[8]   Roger Wells, *Insurrection: The British Experience, 1795–1803* (Stroud, 1983), 37–70, 143–245.

[9]   For example, Clive Emsley, 'An Aspect of "Pitt's Terror": Prosecutions for Sedi-tion during the 1790s', *Social History*, 6 (1981), 155–84.

[10]   Boyd Hilton, *A Mad, Bad, and Dangerous People? England, 1783–1846* (Oxford, 2006), 258–9, 324–5.

Politics, Rhetoric and the Serial Fluctuations of 'Small State' Ideology   127

forces had seemed stacked against the policy at first, and it took some artifice on the part of bullionist ministers – notably the blatantly false promise that the move would benefit agriculture – to win over a landed House of Commons. But though the decision was taken with MPs' fingers crossed and eyes closed, it set the country on the deflationary free-trade path.[11]

A more fortuitous reason for the bullionists' success was parliament's wholly unexpected decision to abolish the wartime income tax three years earlier. This was an exogenous factor in that it resulted from a Whig–Radical political coup and had not been wished for by either side in the monetary policy debate. The consequence was that public spending necessarily had to be forced down towards pre-war levels, which gave bullionists the upper hand over their opponents since they wished to raise the value of money by the same proportion. Fiscal tightening also made it essential to cut down on the cost of poor relief, which was set to spiral further in peacetime with the demobilisation of soldiers and sailors, yet it was justified morally in language which Duncan Smith would have appreciated.[12] 'Small state' politicians (including Peel) admonished citizens to stand on their own feet, but they realised that the populace could only be expected to postpone gratification (including parturition) if the economy operated neutrally according to market forces in a context of fixed exchange rates, thereby enabling citizens to predict the medium and long-term outcomes of their own behavioural choices.[13]

The polarised positions taken on monetary and welfare policy were paradigmatic in the sense of being integrated into wider world views and moral systems, but this was not yet so with respect to tariff policy in general or agricultural protection in particular. A programme of corn law reduction with clear practical aims was laid down by Liverpool's administration in 1821 and began to be put into effect in 1827–8. At that time it was expected to reach the final 'repeal' stage within about ten years, but it was put on hold in 1830 when almost five decades of what some historians misleadingly call 'Tory' government came to an end, and was not resumed until the same party, now properly called 'Conservative', returned to office under Peel in 1841. That party-political earthquake was mainly a response to Catholic emancipation, and therefore exogenous to arguments over the economy and state activity, and so too was the Whig Governments' neglect of free trade during the 1830s. It dismayed their liberal allies as well as their supporters in the large and newly enfranchised boroughs, but it was a political imperative given that their 1832 Reform

---

[11]   Boyd Hilton, *Corn, Cash, Commerce: The Economic Policies of the Tory Governments, 1815–1830* (Oxford, 1977).

[12]   As Secretary of State for Work and Pensions (2010–16), Iain Duncan Smith adopted a highly doctrinaire approach to welfare policy.

[13]   Hilton, *Mad, Bad, and Dangerous*, 326–8.

Act had increased landed representation in the Commons substantially. What the Whigs did instead is discussed below, but we should first consider the counterfactual: *what if* the 'Tories' had been able to secure repeal as early as 1837? Their landed supporters would have been angry and very likely the party would have split irrevocably, just as happened nine years later when Peel finally did repeal the corn laws. But at least in that case Peel's essentially pragmatic motives would have been evident to all. These were to safeguard food supplies at affordable prices for the low-waged, to prevent corn trade fluctuations from causing exchange rate instability, and to safeguard jobs in export industries. However, the Whigs' total neglect of the issue frustrated mercantile interests and led to the creation of the most significant extra-parliamentary pressure group in English politics before women's suffrage – the Anti Corn Law League run from Manchester. Thanks to the League and its leader Cobden, free trade became an ideological issue at last: first as a 'People's' revolt against aristocracy; second as a harbinger of universal peace and the brotherhood of man; and third, more relevantly, as a panacea that would lead to international economic specialisation, wealth creation and 'trickle-down', thus benefiting all classes of society and ultimately all nations.

Now, although Peel also craved corn law repeal, he had no truck with this Cobdenite analysis, not only because of the practical objectives outlined above but because his understanding of the natural world and of human nature was the antithesis of Cobden's.[14] Peel was adamant that neither corn law repeal nor deflationary free-market economics generally could ever *create* wealth. The great merit of those policies was that they might dampen speculative fever, hence the tight money policy of his Bank Charter Act which, had it operated as Peel intended, would have strangled the long mid-Victorian boom at birth. He did not object to growth on moral or aesthetic grounds, but simply that as a much older man than Cobden, with a Malthusian ecological mindset, he did not believe that sustained economic growth was possible, and the longer it continued the more dangerous would be the inevitable relapse. For booms were *always* followed by busts, the latter being in his opinion the salutary part of the equation. Indeed, the other great virtues of a free market for him were, first that it would create a just society in which the hardworking virtuous would be most likely to prosper while lazy cheats went to the wall, and second, that when hardworking virtuous types *also* failed, instead of blaming government policies for interfering with market supply and demand, they would recognise such blows for what they were: 'dispensations of Providence sent for some just but beneficent purpose, it may be to humble our pride or punish our unfaithfulness or to impress on us a sense of our own nothingness and dependence on His mercy'. Such statements should not be taken to imply that Peel repealed the

---

[14] Having already argued this point *ad nauseam*, I shall state it very briefly here.

Politics, Rhetoric and the Serial Fluctuations of 'Small State' Ideology 129

corn laws for ideological rather than practical reasons, simply that like every sentient person he had ideological preconceptions – what Parry referred to as 'prejudices' and 'ideas in a less developed form' – and that his were Malthusian not Cobdenite in economics, providential not utopian in temporal perspective, redemptionist not 'liberal' in theology.

Hence it is emphatically *not* the case that Peel aimed to 'lay the foundations of the prosperity which made Great Britain the workshop of the world' or 'remove the last barriers to economic expansion', yet far too many historians seem to agree with (respectively) Robert Blake and Norman Gash that his reasons for introducing free trade measures were the same as Cobden's.[15] To be fair to them, Peel seemed to endorse this view when he told the Commons just after repeal that credit for the measure lay with Cobden, not himself.[16] This has always seemed puzzling, especially as he hated the revolutionary Anti-Corn Law League, but Peel was fighting for his political life. The main and well-justified charge against him was that he had deceived his party at the previous 1841 election by falsely pretending to be a protectionist still. After coming out for repeal in 1845, he sought to rebut that charge by persuading his followers that he had genuinely changed his mind on repeal *since* 1841, and the best ways to do that were: first, to pretend that he had been converted by the Cobdenite doctrine of the market theory of wages as leading to a fairer distribution of rewards; and second (another red herring) to pretend that repeal might alleviate suffering in Ireland following the failure of the potato crop in 1845.[17]

The Politics of State Intervention during Boom and Depression, 1850–1906

Corn law repeal was not irreversible. It and the Bank Charter Act were widely blamed for the banking and financial crash of 1847–8 and many political pundits thought that there was a very real possibility as late as 1849–50 that the corn laws might return. Hence, when word got about that Disraeli had pronounced them 'not only dead but damned' in 1850 there was much grumbling

[15] Robert Blake, 'In the Top Half Dozen of History', *The Times*, 30 Nov. 1990, 14; Norman Gash, *Sir Robert Peel: The Life of Sir Robert Peel after 1830* (London, 1972), 598. For a more recent example see Douglas Hurd, *Robert Peel* (London, 2007), 4, 358–9, 395–7.

[16] *Hansard*, 29 June 1846, vol. 87, c. 1054.

[17] To be fair also to Peel, he acknowledged in 1846 that Ireland was more likely to suffer from corn law repeal than any other part of the UK, for the same reason that it had suffered most from his modest lowering of the corn law in 1842. The potato famine red herring was only trotted out in hindsight when he wrote his memoirs. See *Memoirs by Sir Robert Peel*, ed. Earl Stanhope and Edward Cardwell (London, 1856–7), vol. 2, 102–3 (on the market theory of wages) and 154–6 (on the Irish Famine).

among Conservatives, whereas when he confirmed the position in his 1852 budget there was hardly any protest, causing Brougham to comment that Protectionists had been wiped out like dinosaurs.[18] Instead, a rhetorical optimism of almost Truss-like proportions took sudden hold, including a belief that tax cuts would lead quickly to economic growth and social harmony. Peel's offer of belt-tightening austerity as a solution to the prospect of national bankruptcy lost its appeal when challenged by Cobden's vision of trade- and manufacturing-led growth. Now, optimism might have got Blair and Johnson a long way but by itself it does not invariably triumph. Nor can it be explained by the slight economic recovery of 1849 since that was hardly yet perceptible. 'This sucker could go down', said George W. Bush of the US economy following the collapse of Lehman Brothers,[19] and the Kwarteng–Truss Budget of 2022 demonstrated the point, but markets rarely go up anything like as quickly. What *can* go up almost overnight is national mood, and the most likely reason why Cobdenite optimism caught fire was because it chimed with a wholly unexpected burst of relief and elation. 1848 provided another exogenous shock, a wholly positive one.

It has long been a truism that the revolutions all over Europe in 1848 changed nothing. Britain alone had no revolution, which changed everything, if only because it had been widely feared that a proletarian rising in industrial Britain would be a hundred times worse than the peasant and bourgeois stirrings elsewhere. Chartism collapsed very suddenly in the high summer thanks to government repression,[20] but since the elite did not like to admit that Britain did repression, the collapse was represented as proof that the British people, who for more than fifty years had seemed so dangerous, were really law-abiding citizens. This led to much complacent 'Podsnappery' and a boosterish breast-beating that only increased after the stonkingly successful Great Exhibition of 1851. For the country to emerge from the perils of 1848 and to reach the sunlit peaks of 1851 was, in G.M. Young's words, like 'the opening of the city gates after a long and wintry siege', a very 'Maytime of Youth recaptured'.[21] The euphoria was fairly brief, thanks to misgovernment during the Crimean war followed by crisis in India, but it lasted long enough to validate free trade and by extension small state, free-market capitalism in the national psyche.

[18] F.W. Monypenny and G.E. Buckle, *The Life of Benjamin Disraeli, Earl of Beaconsfield* (London, 1910–20), vol. 3, 241.

[19] *New York Times*, 26 Sept. 2008.

[20] John Saville, *1848: The British State and the Chartist Movement* (Cambridge, 1987), 129–65, 200–29; David Goodway, *London Chartism, 1838–1848* (Cambridge, 2002), 68–96, 123–49.

[21] G.M. Young, *Today and Yesterday: Collected Essays and Addresses* (London, 1948), 32–3.

And by the time complacency did wear off, an alternative validation was ready to take its place in the form of the mid-Victorian boom, which by the 1860s was not only perceptible but palpable. Free trade in this period has been aptly described by Tony Howe as a 'secular religion of humanitarian cosmopolitanism',[22] though looked at in a different light it was perhaps not so much secular as based on a newly fashionable liberal-cum-incarnational understanding of Christianity as distinct from Peel's older faith based on individual conscience and responsibility. Another comfort blanket was the widespread notion of an evolving and improving universe, inferred from a wholly mistaken progressivist reading of the theory of evolution by natural selection.

Judged in macroeconomic terms the tension between 'big' and 'little' statism eased considerably during 1850–80. With a successful economy, a political consensus in favour of low taxation and a new culture of organised and effective charity (e.g. Peabody Trust 1862, Dr Barnados 1866, Toynbee Hall 1884), the country came closer than before or since to resembling that of the modern United States. These developments took most of the politics out of the annual budgets, at least until the agricultural depression after 1880 led to a squeeze on philanthropy. After that, social intervention became again dependent on the state, which inevitably led to party political wrangling over which type of tax should be imposed – direct, super, inheritance, import – in other words, which sections of the community should stump up most.

However, tussles over the size and scope of the state did not go away after 1850, they simply took a different form. The Whig ministers who came to power in 1830 ditched the previous government's moves in the direction of free trade, but more importantly they switched the battle between 'big' and 'little-staters' from economic to social policy. Instead of seeking to protect native industry, control the money supply and offer handouts to the poor, like the interventionist Tories of the 1820s, aristocratic Whig interventionists such as Russell and Morpeth promoted education, health, better working conditions and urban planning. And on the other side, free-market individualist ministers such as Althorp, Brougham and Poulett Thompson scored victories that were more social than economic, such as the deterrent New Poor Law and the rejection of wage protection for skilled handworkers. The interventionists argued that only centralised policies could alleviate the terrifying social conditions in industrial urban towns, while their opponents articulated a powerful and almost atavistic belief that England should remain a country of low taxation and autonomous local government. Peter Mandler has shown how free marketers had the upper hand in government during the early 1830s, how social interventionists wrenched control in 1835, lost it during 1839–46,

---

[22] Anthony Howe, *Free Trade and Liberal England, 1846–1946* (Oxford, 1997), 111–52.

and then appeared to dominate the first half of Russell's government, what with the limitation of working hours in certain industries in 1847, unrealised Irish plans for the compulsory purchase of reclaimed waste land on which to set up peasant proprietors, and the creation of a General Board of Health in 1848.[23] But then from this high water mark the forces of interventionism suddenly collapsed. Virtually unchallenged, Gladstone's 1853 budget established the Victorian minimalist state, based on low taxes, low welfare, low spending, balanced budgets and Treasury control.[24] As a result, much social spending was gradually transferred to local government, where it had to run the additional gamut of ratepayer scrutiny.

An obvious explanation of this swift turnabout relates once more to the income tax, the unexpected abolition of which had stymied interventionists in 1816. Peel restored it on a temporary basis in 1842, not to expand state activity but to eliminate the huge deficit left him by the Whigs. Unfortunately, his own spending on defence meant the deficit was handed on to Russell's government, which sought in 1848 to raise the rate at which the tax was levied from 7d to 12d in the pound. It was forced into a humiliating climbdown by a combination of Tories and Radicals, whose manoeuvres against a minority government were more politically than fiscally motivated. Charles Read has shown that financial constraints ruled out several positive measures of famine relief in Ireland,[25] as well as demoralising interventionist ministers and giving heart to the economy-minded Chancellor (Charles Wood) and Assistant Treasury Secretary (Charles Trevelyan). Gladstone's 1853 budget inaugurated a programme for extinguishing income tax by 1860, and though that proved impossible his famous speech which introduced the measure undoubtedly established retrenchment, austerity and effective audit as key indicators of good government across the political spectrum. Another symbolic landmark in the switch to 'small-state' government came with the abolition of the General Board of Health after only ten years. But while fiscal considerations were an important part of all this, so too was the mood music expressed in G.M. Young's metaphor about 'the opening of the city gates after a long siege'. The 'condition of England' did not suddenly mend at mid-century, nor did the UK suddenly become the workshop of the world, but contemporaries began to think these things were happening and went about their business more vigorously.

---

[23] Peter Mandler, *Aristocratic Government in the Age of Reform: Whigs and Liberals, 1830–1852* (Oxford, 1990).

[24] For the impact of that budget see H.C.G. Matthew, *Gladstone, 1809–1874* (Oxford, 1986), 103–48.

[25] Charles Read, *The Great Famine in Ireland and Britain's Financial Crisis* (Woodbridge, 2022), 103–83.

Politics, Rhetoric and the Serial Fluctuations of 'Small State' Ideology

During the last fifty years, a bias among historians in favour of Glad-stone[26] has led them to denigrate – or at least 'explain away' – the social policy achievements of the Disraeli and Salisbury Governments (1874–80, 1886–92, 1895–1902) in such matters as public health, safety at work, education, trades unions, labour, food adulteration and above all artisan housing.[27] As Joseph Chamberlain admitted publicly in 1892, 'while it has been the great glory of the Liberal Party... to leave the individual free to create the best of his talents and opportunities, to the Conservative Party belongs the credit for almost all the social legislation of our time'.[28] The policies themselves came partly from quasi-quangos like the Social Science Association, a body in which Conservatives, though fewer in number, often invested more wholeheartedly than Liberals (especially Gladstonians), but it also reflected the growing importance of Conservative businessmen in local government, especially in the North, men such as Richard Cross, the Home Secretary responsible for the social policy *annus mirabilis* of 1875. Admittedly, an instinctive dislike of centralisation meant that, rather than impose national taxes, Conservatives preferred permissive to mandatory legislation, rate support grants and allowing local corporations to borrow to invest – 'implicit *étatisme*' in Avner Offer's felicitous phrase[29] – but all things are relative. In a period when 'small state' thinking was the mantra of the day, Conservatives' social interventionism was domestically the main party-political dividing line.

A telling incident occurred in 1873 when Gladstone sacked Robert Lowe and made himself Chancellor of the Exchequer, in which capacity he lost the following year's general election after promising to abolish income tax without any explanation as to how he would pay for its loss. If he had been able to go ahead it would have been the biggest unfunded tax cut of all time, but then the policy was only emblematic, a way of saying 'boo' to nanny-statism. Since Gladstone and Lowe agreed on economic policy, historians have usually cited the latter's (greatly exaggerated) political blunders as the reason for his demotion, but in fact the cause of the rupture between the two men could not have

---

[26] For an example of pro-Gladstonian biography see Eugenio F. Biagini, *Gladstone* (Woodbridge, 2000).

[27] Note that the Radical A.J. Mundella's 1880 Education Act, though passed under an incoming Liberal Administration, in fact completed the Disraeli government's plans for free elementary education.

[28] Quoted in Richard Shannon, *The Age of Disraeli: 1868–1881* (London, 1992), 212. Perhaps historians, influenced by Robert Blake's magisterial *Disraeli* (1969), have resisted crediting Disraeli because it might seem to lend support to a fanciful older view that he remained a principled Young Englander at heart.

[29] Avner Offer, *Property and Politics, 1870–1914: Landownership, Law, Ideology and Urban Development in England* (Cambridge, 1981), 216, 403.

been more substantive. In the first place, and for all his hostility to spending on 'fripperies' like the Thames Embankment, Lowe's instincts on poor relief were much more generous than Gladstone's, and he was also willing to spend additional public money on health and education, including support for a plan by the Chief Medical Officer of the Privy Council (John Simon) to utilise the state's poor law institutions for purposes of preventative health measures. Yet perhaps more important were their disagreements over *how*, as well as how *much*, to spend. Lowe admired the 'brain-power' of medics, engineers and other trained professionals and wished to give them discretionary leeway to decide on necessary social remedies according to differing local contexts – in other words, to treat laws as 'plastic'. Gladstone condemned his approach as a licence to unaccountable individuals to spend public money, but less prosaically he believed that laws made by humans should adapt to a natural law that had been designed by an intelligence higher than that of any expert. In this view, social policy required adherence to the Chadwickian tradition of basing intervention on box-ticking, one-size-fits-all type rules. In 1870, for example, Gladstone and Lowe were agreed that evicted Irish tenants should be able to claim compensation for the 'improvement' made to the land during their tenancies, but differed over the best way of deciding on the appropriate amount. Gladstone insisted that this should be done according to bureaucratic formula – value of holding, length of tenancy, &c – whereas Lowe would have set up 'courts of conscience and conciliation' to examine each individual case in the broadest human terms and decide in an equitable way 'what is fair and just between man and man'. 'I think this sort of judicial dictatorship very much preferable to any attempt to remodel the law.'[30] In other words, his was an anthropological as distinct from a sociological approach, a distinction which had applied also to the struggles of the pre-1850 decades.[31]

Continuing addiction to the ideal of free trade meant that the United Kingdom did not, like other European countries, protect its arable farmers against the influx of American wheat in the later 1870s, a refusal that had

[30] B. Hilton, 'Robert Lowe as Chancellor of the Exchequer' in E.H.H. Green and D. Tanner (eds), *The Strange Survival of Liberal England: Political Leaders, Moral Values and the Reception of Economic Debate* (Cambridge, 2012), 59–60. I feel justified in repeating this paragraph from an earlier festschrift as I have never met anyone who has read the original.

[31] So, for example, Anti-bullionists had argued for banks to have discretionary authority to determine money supply as against allowing the exchange rate to monitor and respond to the specie flow mechanism. Supporters of outdoor poor relief had been willing for ratepayers' money to be spent at the discretion of magistrates and guardians, whereas under the 'marketised' New Poor Law (1834) relief, though minimal, could be triggered by individual paupers themselves.

Politics, Rhetoric and the Serial Fluctuations of 'Small State' Ideology   135

drastic consequences for Ireland especially. By the mid-1880s it was common ground that free-market capitalism was not serving that country's needs, and that public money would be required for such purposes as land reform and public works. Salisbury's Conservative administration responded by using British taxpayers' money to try to 'kill' Home Rule by bribery while Gladstonian Liberals promoted Home Rule as a way of allowing a devolved Dublin parliament to undertake any necessary interventions (and also, through direct taxation in Ireland, to pay back any loans taken out from Westminster for the purpose). In that way, Ireland would get the spending it needed without the Mother of Parliaments having to establish a mechanism and a precedent for economic intervention. This was a lucky break for the 'small state' cause since, if it had been the East Midlands (say) suffering from wretched poverty instead of an appendage like Ireland, direct intervention by parliament might have been unavoidable. The Home Rule crisis also gave rise to a flurry of 'high political' manoeuvring, but if A.B. Cooke and John Vincent (1974) are right, then rather than undermining the significance of Parris's dichotomy with respect to the size of the state, it reinforced it. The suggestion here is that Gladstone and Salisbury tacitly but deliberately colluded in promoting Home Rule as the great existential issue on which each side would fight to the death, in order to polarise politics along traditional religious and nationalist lines *and so prevent* the emergence of a social democratic, interventionist middle ground which was then being promoted by younger politicians in both parties, and not only with respect to Ireland.[32]

The Birmingham region had a long history of opposing small-state political economy, starting with the campaigns by Thomas Attwood for currency depreciation and real bills banking in the decades after 1819.[33] Free trade and gold were not highly controversial during the mid-Victorian boom, but during the downturn of the 1880s it was the West Midlands that led the calls for fair trade and bimetallism. Chamberlain's 'gas and water' socialism made Birmingham the model for proponents of big local government, which was seen as complementary to the development of a more interventionist government at national level.[34] Chamberlain's gravitation to the Conservative party had more to do with imperial and foreign obsessions and especially with Ireland, but a willingness to encourage a more active state was another factor. In 1903 he split

---

[32] A.B. Cooke and John Vincent, *The Governing Passion: Cabinet Government and Party Politics in Britain, 1885–86* (Brighton, 1974).

[33] David J. Moss, *Thomas Attwood: The Biography of a Radical* (Montreal, 1990), 56–99, 126–51.

[34] For links between Birmingham, tariff and social reform, and proto-Keynesianism, see Ewen Green's essay on Arthur Steel-Maitland in his *Ideologies of Conservatism: Conservative Political Ideas in the Twentieth Century* (Oxford, 2002), 72–113.

his new party by declaring in favour of protection, one object of which was to raise revenue for social reform on a national scale. The move proved disastrous at the 1906 general election, the outcome of which has always been seen as a triumphant victory for free trade. In a House with 569 MPs representing British constituencies, a Conservative majority of 215 at the dissolution gave way to a Liberal majority of 241, while the Labour party jumped from 2 MPs to 30. Since tariff policy was undoubtedly the most important issue in the election, with Liberals and Labour fighting to defend 'the Englishman's breakfast' and the 'cheap loaf', Frank Trentmann feels able to claim that Edwardian Britain was a 'Free Trade Nation'. According to him, free trade was 'uniquely central to national identity in Britain down to 1914'. It was a 'national ideology', integral to its 'democratic culture', and also 'a civilising mission… that traversed all classes, regions, and parties… to spread social justice, peace, and progress throughout the world'.[35] Such enthusiasm seems a throwback to the heroic days of the Anti-Corn Law League, and Trentmann's account of how the cause was mobilised convinces. But the original League had had to battle hard to get free trade accepted in the teeth of many entrenched forces of protectionism, and now in 1906 the free traders were again having to battle against an organised and articulate tariff reform lobby, as well as against much protectionist opinion. If Britain had still been a 'free trade nation', as it was in the third quarter of the nineteenth century, the political mobilisation which Trentmann describes so well would have been unnecessary.

Besides which, the 1906 election was an anomaly, a throwback to the eighteenth century during which only once, in 1708, did such an event lead to a change of government. The norm then was for governments to fall, often for 'high political' reasons, and for the new Ministry to call an election, relying on their newly-acquired access to levers of influence to increase their parliamentary strength. The same thing happened in 1906. Chamberlain's defection left the Conservative government so divided and demoralised that in December 1905 Prime Minister Balfour resigned. The Liberals took office and called an election a month later. Given that their opponents had so recently declared themselves unfit for office, the subsequent landslide was inevitable. Far from free trade winning it for the Liberals, the latter were gifted the victory, which thereby gave free trade a new lease of life, while also burnishing its populist credentials, which its proponents took advantage of to *create*, through its mobilisation, a good deal of genuinely popular enthusiasm.

---

[35] Frank Trentmann, *Free Trade Nation: Commerce, Consumption, and Civil Society in Modern Britain* (Oxford, 2008), 2–3, 8–19 and *passim*.

Twentieth-Century Echoes of an Old Debate

The twentieth-century story is much less neat, and not just because of the disruption caused by the exogenous super-shocks of two world wars. Hitherto, free *traders* and free *marketeers* had been broadly the same people, just as protectionists had been more inclined towards interventionism, but after 1906 'New Liberals' sought to combine free market economic policies with social intervention and increased direct taxation. Even so, the first third of the twentieth century was in important respects a playback of the previous one. As with the loss of the income tax in 1816, the retrenchment proposed by a government-appointed Committee on National Expenditure in 1922 (the famous 'Geddes Axe') inaugurated a politics of austerity which was embraced by Baldwin's Conservatives and tacitly accepted by MacDonald's Labour party, and only challenged belatedly by Lloyd George's admirers in the Liberal party. Meanwhile, fears of inflation plus unthinking nostalgia (especially on Churchill's part) prompted a restoration of the gold standard at the old par, turning 1925 into a re-run of 1819, with the same sectoral forces lined up as before: rentiers and the salariat in favour, and producers, wage-earners and debtors left badly out of pocket.[36] Unlike last time, however, a global economic crisis following the 1929 US stock market crash suggested that the main danger to middle-class incomes came not from inflation but from bankruptcy. It also put such strain on UK finances that MacDonald's Labour government, specifically installed to save the gold standard but reluctant to cut spending sufficiently, morphed into the 1931 National Government, which closed down not only on gold but on free trade and balanced budgets as well, the latter albeit in an experimental way. The 1930s also resembled the equivalent nineteenth-century decade, in that those calling for intervention on public works and the like lacked both the funds and the bureaucratic power to deliver such policies, while even full-blown deficit financing would have been ineffective given the small size of the national budget in relation to the economy at large.[37] In one other respect history repeated itself in reverse. Cooke and Vincent were cited above for their belief that in 1886 Gladstone and Salisbury had colluded to keep political conflict artificially *vertical* by focusing on issues of identity. Here they were almost certainly influenced by Cowling's opposite argument in *The Impact of Labour* (published three years previously in 1971), i.e. that during 1918–23 the Conservative and Labour leaderships schemed to make politics artificially *horizontal* – a trajectory from which neither Baldwin nor

---

[36] Robert W.D. Boyce, *British Capitalism at the Crossroads, 1919–1932* (Cambridge, 1987), 35–100, 299–301.

[37] Ross McKibbin, 'The Economic Policy of the Second Labour Government, 1929–1931', *Past & Present*, 68 (1975), 95–123.

MacDonald deviated during their subsequent periods as leader. Being committed to rival forms of corporate capitalism, tacitly but intentionally the two men conspired to ratchet up class rhetoric in their public statements because they knew such a discourse would deny the Liberal rhetoric of individualism any space of its own.[38]

The tension between 'big' and 'little' statism did not disappear after the Second World War, but it was largely depoliticised. This is not a reference to so-called 'Butskellism', the reality of which has been challenged,[39] but to Keith Middlemas's notion that key decisions were made in a 'corporately-biased' state by civil servants and their academic economist advisers.[40] In this scenario, 'demand-side' and 'supply-side' policies stood proxy for the big and little state, and an oscillation took place between them at regular intervals as each in turn was deemed to have failed in arresting comparative economic decline. Middlemas's key fact is that the policy turning points – viz. 1947, 1962, 1972 and 1976 – did not coincide with general elections or changes of government. The tacking motion just described may have been sensible given the nation's circumstances, but it must be a pity that the unprecedented bounty of North Sea oil fell exclusively in the lap of a government so committed to hard supply-side economics. Thatcher's commitment to monetarism may have had intellectual roots in Hayek, Sherman, Rand, *et al.*, and it may also have been adopted as a convenient weapon against Heath, but either way the lengths to which she pushed it (e.g. rate-capping), the bloated rhetoric she employed ('the Nanny State'), and the bitterness she provoked in opponents, all ensured that Parris's dichotomy came back into the centre of political argument.

Résumé and Reflections

It might seem inappropriate to write about the *course* of events since the 2016 referendum on membership of the European Union if only because the many bewildering shifts in policy, personnel and narrative justification give the impression that no one has been steering. When unanticipated contingencies succeed each other as rapidly as they have just done in recent years, the historian is naturally tempted to think: *What If?* If Johnson's coin had come down on the Remain instead of Leave side, would Brexit have won? Without the cameo roles played by Michael Gove and Andrea Leadsom, would not Johnson have become Prime Minister in 2016, and in that case would he not have negotiated

---

[38]   Maurice Cowling, *The Impact of Labour, 1920–1924* (Cambridge, 1971).

[39]   E.H.H. Green, 'Thatcherism: An Historical Perspective', *Transactions of the Royal Historical Society*, 9 (1999), 17–42.

[40]   Keith Middlemas, *Politics in Industrial Society: The Experience of the British System since 1911* (London, 1979), 20, 371–85 and *passim*.

Politics, Rhetoric and the Serial Fluctuations of 'Small State' Ideology

a more pragmatic version of Brexit than he eventually did? After Theresa May had manoeuvred the ball from the side of the scrum (to adapt Johnson's sporting metaphor), it was predictable that she would rely on her adviser Nick Timothy, an admirer of Joseph Chamberlain; but why did Timothy not see how much Chamberlain would have welcomed EU membership, being someone who supported social intervention and whose central aim was for the UK to belong to a large, autarchic economic bloc with an internal free market? It was also fairly predictable that May herself, having voted against Brexit, would feel compelled to be as rude as possible to Remainers, Europeans and the metropolitan elite. But perhaps her catchphrase 'Citizens of Nowhere' (first uttered at the Conservative Party Conference in 2016) would have died on her breath had David Goodhart not written *The Road to Somewhere*, a flawed but conceptually brilliant first draft of history which etched in the public mind the historically implausible notion that Brexit was the outcome of the 'long march of the left-behind'.[41] Also, by defining Remainers as *non*-citizens or 'Citizens of Nowhere', it became rhetorically possible to describe the votes of just 52 percent as being equal to 'the Will of the People'. That the campaign for a 'second referendum' (or so-called 'People's Vote') should turn out to be a case of the 'best' being the enemy of May's 'less bad' Brexit was, if not anticipated, at least unsurprising, unlike Johnson's capture of so many traditionally Labour-supporting 'red wall' seats in the north and midlands at the polls in 2019. Since that breakthrough was owing in large part to Jeremy Corbyn's disastrous leadership of Labour, it can be thought of as an exogenous shock, but it changed the rationale for Brexit, which was not now to turn London into 'Singapore-on-Thames', so much as to 'level up' the midlands and north, an aim which briefly seemed to reinforce the Goodhart thesis. Johnson's erratic behaviour while in office, and particularly in the context of the Covid-19 pandemic, was a shock to no one and entirely endogenous. And then, in the most bizarre twist of all, following Johnson's defenestration, Truss the former Remainer won the hearts of a large majority of Conservative members, not just by talking the Brexity language of low taxation but because the cut of her jib was that of a disrupter and a booster in the mould of Johnson and Nigel Farage. While Rishi Sunak, the once and continuing Leaver, repelled the same members by wearing a suit and adopting a style reminiscent of corporate nowhere, as well as by a commitment to economic responsibility which party members could barely distinguish from that of the hated metropolitan elite. In a joke of the day, however, Sunak's rejection lasted no longer than the natural life of an iceberg lettuce, and at the time of writing Conservative politics seem to be returning to a kind of normality, albeit a somewhat beleaguered one.

---

[41] David Goodhart, *The Road to Somewhere: The Populist Revolt and the Future of Politics* (London, 2017).

140   *Boyd Hilton*

But before we dismiss all this as Alice-through-the-Looking-Glass stuff, perhaps it was the pace of recent events rather than their sequence that was so unusual. If the long nineteenth-century story as outlined above could have been speeded up to the levels of today, when four minutes is a long time in politics, the unexpected impact of high political contingencies on the evolution of policy would have been just as apparent, as would the way in which policies pursued with one aim in mind could be hijacked to serve quite different ends, requiring different narratives or 'public doctrines'. Admittedly, the slower pace of old allowed longer life spans to successive policy options, such as free trade, the encouragement of private philanthropy and civic pride, and 'New Liberalism', but the mode in which – and the speed at which – narratives shifted when the time came for them to do so, was not very different.

To summarise the main points, a sudden emergency forced Pitt's new 'hands-on' technique of governing in the mid-1790s, but the new policies were nevertheless calculated and rational, whereas most of the later policy shifts were in economic terms random. Presiding at a time of post-war distress and dislocation, Liverpool's ministers were forced to emphasise their inability to 'buck the market' if only to absolve themselves of blame for the suffering. Meanwhile, the Whig-led Opposition attacked this *laissez-faire* approach and screamed at government to '*do* something'. When at long last they got the opportunity after 1830 they could hardly adopt the free-market lines that they had long denounced, much as their 'liberal' allies would have wished them to. Instead, they determined to tackle the wretched condition of large industrial towns, starting with municipal reform. There was a tincture of traditional Foxism behind this new Whig policy, but a compelling political factor was that as their landed support fell away, mainly on Church issues, they found themselves dependent on the middle-class electorates in boroughs such as Manchester and Leeds which they had created in 1832. Feeling let down, these towns eventually demanded corn law repeal, hence the Whigs' sudden and unconvincing tack on that issue in their 1840 budget. However, at that time only Peel, working surreptitiously for free trade inside the Conservative party, could have repealed the corn laws, and he did so with a sober – not-to-say pessimistic – concern for the 'just-about-managing' that today seems almost May-ite. However, a sudden wave of national self-regard due to geopolitical factors led Cobden's optimistic understanding of the free trade doctrine to suffuse the national consciousness. His market optimism ensured that the dominant Liberal governments of the third quarter-century, afforced by the adhesion of many Peelite economic liberals to the party, rejected the old Whig-inspired social reform, leaving a space for others to take it up. Logic might have suggested that this would be a Left-Liberal or Radical party, but the Conservatives defied logic by stubbornly clinging on to the role of official Opposition, despite losing not only most of their leadership after 1846 but also their main *raison d'être* in Protection. Hence

Politics, Rhetoric and the Serial Fluctuations of 'Small State' Ideology

it was they who stepped on to the vacant chess square labelled 'Social Reform'. By the 1880s that square was getting crowded with younger recruits from all parts of the House, prompting more traditional leaders to divert attention by 'making' Home Rule the great dividing line. Finally, in 1903–6 Conservative party splits led to a Liberal landslide which blocked what *had been* a rising tide of Protectionist opinion, leaving New Liberals to pursue welfare policies without revenue-raising tariffs. Imagine all of the above happening in the space of six years and in a context of 24 hours rolling news and social media!

It would be quixotic to attempt to interpret such an incoherent narrative as this essay contains, but – to return to the first paragraph – it may be possible to infer some insights into the relation between political tactics, languages and ideas as attempted by Maurice Cowling. It is routinely stated that Cowling's emphasis on day-to-day tactics and the pursuit of personal and party advantage at the expense of ideas 'takes the mind out of history'. That charge does stick (though not in a pejorative way) to the first volume of his trilogy on the 1867 Reform Act. Its emphasis on politics as a game for a limited number of players perfectly described the relatively serene politics of the period, when the leading politicians involved 'cannot usefully be said themselves to have wanted, desired, or believed anything except what was wanted by all other participants in the system', including of course the desire to come out on top.[42] However, Cowling's second volume on post-World War I politics (*The Impact of Labour*) and *The Governing Passion* by Cooke and Vincent on the Irish Home Rule crisis both covered highly fraught political episodes in which few players wanted exactly what others wanted, and in which the third and fourth estates also played important roles. As already indicated, the shrewdest politicians sought to manipulate the incoherent happenstances in a particular direction, largely by means of what Andrew Jones has called 'the use of words'.[43] Their object was to mould a public doctrine and thereby form a public opinion. In 1886 Gladstone managed to keep the vertical politics of 'small state' liberal individualism alive, and after 1918 Baldwin and MacDonald played craftily to smother the same. Cowling's final volume on *The Impact of Hitler* (1975) was not about manipulating events, but about how the retrospective public perception that Churchill had been overwhelmingly right, and Neville Chamberlain correspondingly wrong, over Hitler and the Munich agreement allowed a romantic form of 'big state' conservatism to relegate 'small state', economically liberal Conservatism for the generation prior to Thatcher. In other words, Cowling's aim was to discern a pattern among the clouds of 'contingent randomness', a

---

[42] Maurice Cowling, *1867: Disraeli, Gladstone and Revolution: The Passing of the Second Reform Bill* (Cambridge, 1967), 311–12.

[43] Andrew Jones, 'Where Governing is the Use of Words', *Historical Journal*, 19 (1976), 25–6.

quest which might almost be called 'putting the mind *into* history'. It partly explains why those later historians who have been to some extent inflected with Cowling's influence including Michael Bentley, Philip Williamson, David Craig, and – most pertinently in this context – Jonathan Parry, have invariably been concerned like him with mental states much more than with political snakes and ladders.

Chapter 7

The Socialist Lives of Beatrice Webb and Margaret Cole

Helen McCarthy

Beatrice Webb and Margaret Postgate first met during the summer of 1917, in the dingy Westminster offices of the Fabian Society. Beatrice, then in her late fifties and one of Britain's most famous socialists, decided to drop by unannounced, finding a mop-haired young woman playing tennis with a colleague using two flyswatters and a ginger biscuit. Beatrice did not – alas – record the incident in her famous diary, but upon Margaret it made the deepest impression. There entered, she recalled, 'a tall lady wearing a large and very ugly hat, with a beaked nose, a very thin pale face, a harsh high voice, and a bright commanding eye'. Beatrice looked 'infinitely old and frail', as though she might 'disintegrate if I sneezed or shouted suddenly'.[1] Sensing disapproval, Margaret fled the scene and learnt later that Beatrice had gone straight to the head of the Fabian Research Department – the Guild Socialist and Oxford historian, Douglas Cole – to warn him against allowing vivacious young women to lure his male employees into romantic entanglements. The veteran socialist's counsel was not heeded. A year later, Margaret Postgate became Mrs Douglas Cole.

Initially, Margaret shared Douglas's intellectual antipathy towards Beatrice and her husband Sidney Webb, yet before long, a friendship had struck up between the couples, and especially between the wives. Margaret, Beatrice wrote in November 1918, was a distinguished Cambridge graduate who had 'shocked us old folk with her daringly unconventional ways and rebellious attitude'. But she liked her: 'she has wit and reasoning power of an unusual quality, and she is fundamentally sweet-tempered and kind'.[2] In turn, Margaret developed a lasting admiration for Beatrice. Writing Beatrice's biography in 1945, two years after the latter's death, Margaret declared that she was 'the greatest woman I have ever known'.[3]

---

[1]   Margaret Cole, *Growing Up Into Revolution* (London, 1949), 65.
[2]   Diary of Beatrice Webb, 7 Nov. 1918 (all references are to the typescript diary, digitised at <https://digital.library.lse>).
[3]   Margaret Cole, *Beatrice Webb* (London, 1945), 5.

144   *Helen McCarthy*

These two socialist women were born more than three decades apart and achieved very different levels of public status during their long and active lives. Beatrice grew up in the era of Gladstone and Disraeli, the Scramble for Africa and the first stirrings of the women's suffrage movement. Margaret died in 1980, amidst industrial strife, Cold War tensions and the election of Britain's first female Prime Minister. Beatrice Webb's life has been written many times, whilst her contributions as a serious social policy thinker have been extensively studied.[4] Margaret Cole, despite a busy career as a writer, teacher and county councillor, is little known outside labour history circles and is the subject of just one compact biography.[5] Yet placing their individual lives into a single field of vision offers, as this chapter seeks to show, a fresh perspective on the development of socialism in modern Britain – one that places intimate human relationships at its heart.

In her recent book on the natural scientist Thomas Huxley (1825–95) and his grandson Julian Huxley (1887–1975), Alison Bashford suggests that a double biographical lens 'permits a kind of time-lapse over the nineteenth and twentieth centuries', allowing us to think of her two subjects 'as one very long-lived man'.[6] This chapter pursues a similar project, showing how, for all their differences of upbringing and temperament, Beatrice Webb and Margaret Cole were roped together by a shared commitment to living a fully socialist life. As young women, each travelled an intellectual and spiritual pathway towards socialism, and each sought to transpose her politics into an affective register through marriage to a socialist man. After meeting in 1917, these parallel trajectories meshed into an intergenerational friendship, and after Beatrice's death in 1943, Margaret continued to honour that bond through dedicated guardianship of the Webb legacy.

---

[4]   For biographical treatments, see Ruth Adam and Kitty Muggeridge, *Beatrice Webb* (London, 1967); Barbara Caine, 'Beatrice Webb and the 'Woman Question', *History Workshop Journal*, 14 (1982), 23–44; Deborah Epstein Nord, *The Apprenticeship of Beatrice Webb* (Basingstoke, 1985); Jane Lewis, *Women and Social Action in Victorian and Edwardian England* (Aldershot, 1991), ch. 2; Carole Seymour Jones, *Beatrice Webb* (London, 1992); Royden Harrison, *The Life and Times of Sidney and Beatrice Webb, 1858–1905, The Formative Years* (London, 2000). For evaluations of political and intellectual influence, see E.J.T. Brennan (ed.), *Education for Efficiency: The Contribution of Sidney and Beatrice Webb* (London, 1975); Alan McBriar, *An Edwardian Mixed Doubles: The Bosanquets Versus the Webbs* (Oxford, 1987); Lisanne Radice, *Beatrice and Sidney Webb* (London, 1984); Alan J. Kidd, 'The State and Moral Progress: The Webbs' Case for Social Reform c.1905 to 1940', *Twentieth Century British History*, 7 (1996), 189–205.

[5]   Betty Vernon, *Margaret Cole, 1893–1980* (London, 1986). She also has an entry in the *Oxford Dictionary of National Biography* (2004) written by Marc Stears.

[6]   Alison Bashford, *An Intimate History of Evolution: The Story of the Huxley Family* (London, 2022), xxi, xxii.

The analysis below explores each of these contexts – youthful journeys, political marriages, intergenerational friendship – by making use of the rich archival traces that each woman has left us. Writing was another shared passion, captured in the millions of published and unpublished words which Beatrice and Margaret put to paper either in partnership with their husbands or as sole authors. Their chosen forms and genres ranged from diaries and minority reports (Beatrice) to detective novels, book reviews and poetry (Margaret), whilst both published autobiographies and amassed an abundance of private correspondence, much of which in Beatrice's case has been edited and published.[7] From these sources we can reconstruct the duo's interconnected lives, teasing out new insights into how upper- and middle-class women were drawn into socialist politics in the late nineteenth and early twentieth centuries, how marriage functioned within the intellectual culture of the socialist left, and how other kinds of close personal relationships within and beyond families could nourish political commitments.

Beatrice and Margaret's stories do not light up every corner of this landscape, being neither of them involved directly in parliamentary or trade union politics, and exhibiting notably less interest in organised feminism or sexual radicalism than some socialist women of their class.[8] Their lives offer a window onto the world of the left's social elites, the kinds of people who, whatever the strength of their egalitarian zeal, lived in large, well-furnished houses and relied on servants, nursemaids and boarding schools to enable their political work.[9] Beatrice, famously, never learnt to boil an egg. Margaret sent her son to

[7] Beatrice Webb's papers, including the diary, form part of the Passfield Papers which comprise 126 boxes held at the London School of Economics. In 1978, Cambridge University Press published three volumes of Webb correspondence, Norman MacKenzie (ed.), *The Letters of Sidney and Beatrice Webb* (Cambridge, 1978, vols 1–3), whilst a four-volume edition of the diary, edited by Norman and Jeanne MacKenzie, was published by Virago between 1982 and 1985. Margaret Cole's papers are held alongside those of her husband, G.D.H. Cole, at Nuffield College, Oxford, while a file of Cole's personal correspondence with her close friend Francis Meynell can be found in the latter's papers at the University of Cambridge Library (Add.9813/C1/23).

[8] For example, Eleanor Marx, Barbara Ayrton-Gould, Vera Brittain, Dora Russell, Naomi Mitchison, Dora Montefiore, Edith Picton Turberville, Dorothy Jewson and Monica Whately, to name a few. See June Hannam and Karen Hunt, *Socialist Women: Britain, 1880s–1920s* (London, 1992), and Stephen Brooke, *Sexual Politics: Sexuality, Family Planning and the British Left from the 1880s to the Present Day* (Oxford, 2011).

[9] A very different picture of socialist activism emerges from the scholarship on working-class women in the Labour party, as detailed in Pamela Graves, *Labour Women: Women in British Working-Class Politics, 1918–1939* (Cambridge, 1994) and more recently in Stephanie Ward, 'Labour Activism and the Political Self in Inter-War Working-Class Women's Politics', *Twentieth Century British History*, 30 (2019), 29–52.

Winchester and her daughters to St Paul's. Yet this world, with its periodicals and pamphlets and seminars and summer schools, gave British socialism much of its intellectual character between the 1890s and the 1950s and maps the analysis pursued in this chapter onto Jonathan Parry's vision of politics as the interplay of people, institutions and ideas. How political lives are forged through personality, belief and circumstance is a core theme of Parry's work, developed most vividly in his writings on Benjamin Disraeli and Lord John Russell and in the many biographical sketches of notable political figures penned for the *Oxford Dictionary of National Biography* and the *London Review of Books* since the 1990s.[10] Inspired by Parry's example, this chapter brings into sharper focus the intimate bonds of marriage, friendship, loyalty and trust, and places women at the centre rather than the edge of the frame.

Journeys

Beatrice Webb was born in 1858, the seventh daughter of wealthy timber merchant Richard Potter. She spent much of her youth travelling between townhouses and country residences in preparation for the upper-class marriage market, although, like her sisters, she benefitted from a rich, if somewhat unstructured, education along the way, overseen by governesses and tutors at home.[11] Beatrice was encouraged to read widely and to discourse with the intellectuals who dotted the Potter social circle, including the philosopher Herbert Spencer, the naturalist Thomas Huxley, the eugenicist Francis Galton and the positivist Frederick Harrison. As for many women of her privileged class, Beatrice's political knowledge flowed from this membership of late-Victorian elites. Family history framed her understanding of the major currents of nineteenth-century politics: both grandfathers served as radical MPs in the 1830s and 1840s, while her father discarded this nonconformist dissenting inheritance two decades later by standing unsuccessfully as a Conservative by-election candidate.[12] As Beatrice approached early adulthood, both major parties, Liberals and Conservatives alike, were grappling with the new facts of

[10]   J.P. Parry, 'Past and Future in the later career of Lord John Russell', in T.C.W. Blanning and David Cannadine (eds), *History and Biography* (Cambridge, 1996), 142–72; Jonathan Parry, *Benjamin Disraeli* (Oxford, 2007). At the time of writing, Parry's tally of entries for the *ODNB* stands at thirteen. I count nine *LRB* pieces by Parry on biographical subjects, which include Lord Melbourne, William Gladstone and Joseph Chamberlain amongst others.

[11]   For a rich picture of this elite Potter girlhood, see Barbara Caine, *Destined to be Wives: The Sisters of Beatrice Webb* (Oxford, 1986).

[12]   Geoffrey Channon, *Richard Potter: Beatrice Webb's Father and Corporate Capitalist* (Newcastle-upon-Tyne, 2019).

The Socialist Lives of Beatrice Webb and Margaret Cole 147

mass democracy, from universal literacy and an expanding male working-class electorate, to the early stirrings of an independent labour and trade union movement.

This was the backdrop to a turbulent stretch for Beatrice following the death of her mother, Lawrencina, in 1882, when Beatrice rotated between playing hostess for her father and pursuing philanthropic work for the Charity Organisation Society (COS) in London's east end, to which she was introduced by her older sister, Kate (soon to be married to the Liberal MP, Leonard Courtney). The former duties led to a highly charged encounter with Joseph Chamberlain, then still a minister in Gladstone's Cabinet, for whom Beatrice developed a debilitating erotic obsession. Her work for COS meanwhile secured Beatrice a post in 1886 as investigator on Charles Booth's mammoth poverty survey of London, focusing on casual dock labour and 'sweating' in the east end tailoring trades.[13] From this research experience sprang Beatrice's first publications in the heavyweight periodical, the *Nineteenth Century*, and public recognition as an authority on the problem of low pay. As Beatrice narrated at length in her 1926 autobiography, *My Apprenticeship*, these were critical years which culminated in her conversion to socialism, and with it her decision to marry the Fabian economist Sidney Webb and devote her life to the 'brainwork' of the social policy expert.[14]

Margaret Postgate had a different journey into socialism. She grew up in Cambridge at the turn of the twentieth century, the eldest of six children born to J.P. Postgate, a distinguished Latin scholar and fellow of Trinity College. Her mother, Edith, had been taught by J.P. at Girton, and it was to Girton that Margaret went to read Classics in 1911, having spent four years of 'pure misery' at Roedean, an expensive girls' boarding school on the south coast.[15] Unlike that of Beatrice, Margaret's political education was slight up to this point; despite her parents' academic credentials, the Postgates were not, she recalled, 'a bookish household', and she certainly did not meet Cabinet ministers over the dinner table.[16] J.P. Postgate, like Richard Potter, was a Tory, although his 'strong political views did not impinge upon us, partly because we did not eat much with our parents, until his opinions clashed violently with those of his eldest son'.[17] Here Margaret was referring to her brother Raymond, who became a

[13] Lewis, *Women and Social Action*, ch. 2; Rosemary O'Day, 'Caring or controlling? The East End of London in the 1880s and 1890s', in Clive Emsley, Eric Johnson and Pieter Spierenburg (eds), *Social Control in Europe: Volume 2, 1800–2000* (Columbus: OH, 2004), 149–66.

[14] Webb, *My Apprenticeship* (London, 1926), ch. 7.

[15] Cole, *Growing Up*, 26.

[16] *Ibid.*, 12.

[17] *Ibid.*, 19.

conscientious objector during the First World War while at Oxford, on which grounds his father eventually disowned him.[18] It was, in fact, Raymond's imprisonment for his views in 1916 which Margaret identifies as the event which clinched her conversion to socialism, a process set in train at Girton by the works of J.A. Hobson, George Bernard Shaw and H.G. Wells. After listening to the judge pass sentence on her brother, she walked out of the courtroom 'into a new war – this time against the ruling classes and the government which represented them, and *with* the working classes, the Trade Unionists, the Irish rebels of Easter Week, and all those who resisted their governments or other governments which held them down'.[19] This declaration, compounded by Margaret's marriage to Douglas in 1918, led to the severing of relations between J.P. and his eldest daughter. Edith and the younger Postgate siblings were forbidden from visiting Margaret in London, a restriction only lifted in 1926 when J.P. was knocked off his bike by a lorry on King's Parade and died.

Raymond's sentencing was also instrumental in prompting Margaret to quit her 'safe, pensionable teaching post' at St Paul's Girls' School in exchange for £2 a week at the Fabian Research Department, a move facilitated by Raymond's Oxford contemporary, Alan Kaye. Founded five years earlier by the Webbs to bolster the Society's intellectual output, the Research Department had by 1917 fallen under the leadership of Cole and his Guild Socialist colleague, William Mellor, and it rapidly became Margaret's 'second University, taking up the major part of my time and thought, sleeping and waking for the next few years'.[20] She worked into late evening, 'until the last buses had all gone', copying out trade union reports, compiling the *Monthly Circular* of information on Labour questions and organising enormous volumes of press clippings. It was a convivial scene as Margaret paints it in her autobiography, full of comradely song, dinners in Soho and weekend hikes accompanied by lively recitations of verse. 'In effect, we lived as well as we worked together', Margaret wrote, 'with our eyes on the job, and almost oblivious of the events of the war'.[21]

Both women thus came to be absorbed in work and politics in the years before their marriages: Beatrice in the sweatshops and docklands of 1880s east London, Margaret in the offices and meeting-rooms of wartime Westminster. Each woman experienced this as a period of breaking free from (Conservative) parental authority coupled with new urban experiences, although this process appeared to be easier for Margaret, facilitated by a relaxed culture of workplace mixing at the Research Department and new opportunities for young

[18] John and Mary Postgate, *A Stomach for Dissent: The Life of Raymond Postgate* (Keele, 1994).

[19] Cole, *Growing up*, 59.

[20] *Ibid.*, 61.

[21] *Ibid.*, 72.

The Socialist Lives of Beatrice Webb and Margaret Cole   149

women to live independently in London. Margaret rented several flats with female colleagues which she used only 'for eating breakfast' because most evenings she was out: at socialist meetings, at the ballet or a wartime revue show, or attending a party at the Kensington studio of artist Stella Bowen, who lived with one of Margaret's Girton friends. Thirty years earlier, Beatrice's freedom of movement was more curtailed. As the oldest unmarried daughter, it fell to her to manage Richard Potter's ailing health and oversee the education of her younger sister, Rosie. Serious work for Booth was possible only when her married sisters temporarily stepped in to give Beatrice a 'holiday'. During those weeks away from the Potters, Beatrice stayed at the Devonshire House Hotel, a sober Quaker establishment in Bishopsgate, and was accompanied by male chaperones on her visits to industrial premises to collect facts and conduct interviews. Granted, the late-Victorian city was slowly bringing new forms of urban spectatorship into the lives of middle- and upper-class women, of which Beatrice, alongside other female investigators, writers and reformers of the 1880s and 1890s were beneficiaries. Yet, as Deborah Nord and Judith Walkowitz have shown, navigating this terrain called for caution, as London continued to be imagined as a place of sexual danger in which respectable, bourgeois femininity was perpetually at risk.[22]

This comparison of Beatrice and Margaret's access to the urban sphere suggests one context for women's political activism which was changing by the early twentieth century. Another was class. The Potters, as noted above, were a great deal wealthier than the Postgates and took a full part in the yearly rituals of London Society, which, in Beatrice's words, 'absorbed nearly half the time and more than half the vital energy of the daughters of the upper and upper middle class'.[23] A furnished house in some fashionable district of the city would be rented each spring for the Season, horses and a smart carriage would be procured, social calls would be returned, balls attended and, one by one, a Potter sister would be presented at court. Beatrice's turn came in 1876, a few months after her eighteenth birthday.[24] Marriage to Joseph Chamberlain, or someone like him, would have anchored her firmly in this elite milieu of social politics, where familial interests and political power were indivisible.[25]

[22] Deborah Nord, *Walking the Victorian Streets: Women, Representation and the City* (Ithaca: NY, 1995); Judith Walkowitz, *City of Dreadful Delight: Narratives of Sexual Danger in Late-Victorian London* (London, 1992).

[23] Webb, *My Apprenticeship*, 67.

[24] Caine, *Destined*, 52–3. For an excellent sketch of this world, see Leonore Davidoff, *The Best Circles: Society Etiquette and the Season* (London, 1973).

[25] The best account of this milieu is still Pat Jalland, *Women, Marriage and Politics, 1860–1914* (Oxford, 1986), but for a more recent deep dive into a single case, see Jennifer Davey, *Mary, Countess of Derby and the Politics of Victorian Britain* (Oxford, 2019).

As 'walking gentlewoman' to some 'great man', Beatrice might have become a skilled political hostess and chatelaine of a grand house, perhaps learning to give speeches to public meetings, as the wives of MPs were habitually doing by the 1880s.[26]

In Cambridge, by contrast, Margaret's social networks nested within the 'professional academic' habitus of the late-Victorian middle class. These families 'had nurses and servants and seaside holidays', and the children 'went to upper-class schools and had dancing and drawing classes', but they were not connected to landed aristocrats or captains of industry and had roughly similar incomes through their university stipends.[27] This, Margaret thought, produced an 'equalitarian society' amongst the university dons which fostered a 'natural bent towards equality' that pre-dated her socialist baptism of fire.[28] Of Beatrice's more elevated social origins Margaret was always keenly aware. 'There was a great deal in her make-up that was purely aristocratic, not to say arrogant', Margaret wrote in 1949, recalling the 'acid anecdotes' that Beatrice used to drop into conversation concerning upper-class contemporaries such as Margot Asquith, whom she loathed.[29]

Yet the sociability of Fabianism served as a partial solvent of these upper/middle-class distinctions, which were in any case beginning to blur by the beginning of the twentieth century through new combinations of money, titles and politics.[30] Beatrice waited for Richard Potter's death before marrying the lower middle-class Sidney in 1892, conscious that her unorthodox choice would distress him. She always felt the mild tug of disapproval from her sisters and their husbands when she brought Sidney to meet them (excepting perhaps Kate and Leonard Courtney, whose progressive Liberal politics made them more amenable to social intercourse with a hairdresser's son). The Webbs' house at 41 Grosvenor Street in Westminster was made by Beatrice into a space for a different kind of social politics, a venue for entertaining and 'permeating' along socialist lines made possible by an annual income from the Potters of £1,000,

---

[26] K.D. Reynolds, *Aristocratic Women and Political Society in Victorian Britain* (Oxford, 1998). Beatrice found public speaking very difficult in these early years. In 1887 she attended a public meeting of dock labourers in Canning Town 'but absolutely refused to speak' (*Diary*, 27 Nov. 1887), and three years later reflected: 'It will be a long time before I am fit for much in public speaking. I have no ease at present' (Diary, 12 Dec. 1890). Beatrice did eventually take on some of the public duties of the political spouse after Sidney became MP for Seaham in 1922. The 'walking gentlewoman' quote is from the *Diary*, 21 Oct. 1891.

[27] Cole, *Growing Up*, 9.

[28] *Ibid.*

[29] *Ibid.*, 136, 135.

[30] David Cannadine, *The Decline and Fall of the British Aristocracy* (London, 1990); W.D. Rubinstein, *Elites and the Wealthy in Modern British History* (Brighton, 1987).

The Socialist Lives of Beatrice Webb and Margaret Cole

plus whatever Sidney was able to earn from writing. From the mid-1920s, the Webbs added a second venue by purchasing a cottage, Passfield Corner, in Liphook, Hampshire, as their country retreat. To both houses were invited a cross-section of anyone the Webbs thought politically useful, from Liberal and Conservative party grandees to trade unionists and civil servants – and, after 1918, Douglas and Margaret Cole were included in their number.

William Whyte has suggested that aesthetic style as much as occupation or social origin united the intellectual elites of late-Victorian and Edwardian Britain. Good taste and a disavowal of the gaudy ostentation of the super-rich was the hallmark of the 'intellectual aristocracy', a phrase first coined by Noel Annan to describe a set of influential and interconnected family dynasties spanning academia, the professions and public service from the 1860s onwards.[31] We might identify Margaret and Beatrice (whose diary is a key source for Whyte) with a Fabian sub-strand of this tendency, perfectly exemplified in the manner in which both women furnished their homes. At 41 Grosvenor Road, Beatrice's regimen was for 'strict economy' of weekly expenditure amidst 'beautiful surroundings', an effect achieved through William Morris wallpaper and 'charming old bits of furniture' sourced from 'second-hand furniture shops'.[32] When the Coles moved into their rented house off the King's Road in Chelsea twenty-five years later, they put up Morris tapestry curtains and bought a solid oak cupboard and matching chest – the latter paid for with the ten-pound note received from the Webbs as a wedding gift.[33]

This small example suggests how a shared desire to live disinterested, socialist lives in service of the public good helped neutralise class and generational differences between these two Fabian women. Beatrice and Margaret's journeys into socialism were very different and took place thirty years apart, but they curved towards the same destination and at places they touched – most obviously, and most consequentially, in the decision that each woman made to turn their marriages into an extension of their politics.

Partnerships

In her diary, Beatrice described her engagement to Sidney Webb in 1891 as rooted in 'fellowship, a common faith and a common work'.[34] The couple had 'honestly only *one* desire: the commonweal', a sentiment engraved on their wedding rings the following year with the inscription *pro bonum publico* (for

---

[31] William Whyte, 'The Intellectual Aristocracy Revisited', *Journal of Victorian Culture* (2005), 15–45.

[32] *Diary*, dated Oct. 1893.

[33] Cole, *Growing Up*, 97.

[34] *Diary*, 20 June 1891.

the public good).[35] This kind of civic partnership was not uncommon amongst progressive intellectuals in the late nineteenth and early twentieth centuries. As Lawrence Goldman has shown, R.H. Tawney viewed his marriage to Jeanette Beveridge in much the same way (although Jeanette did not share her husband's conceptualisation of their union), and to this list of reform-minded couples we might add Charles and Mary Booth, Helen and Bernard Bosanquet, Samuel and Henrietta Barnett, and Lawrence and Barbara Hammond.[36] In the Labour movement, marriage and politics routinely mixed, especially following women's partial and then full enfranchisement after the First World War. Eleanor Lowe has established that nine of the 29 married women who stood successfully as Labour candidates at parliamentary elections between 1918 and 1970 were married to men who had themselves served, or would go on to serve, as MPs. In two further cases, women were married to other parliamentary candidates, and seven more had husbands who were elected councillors or notable party activists.[37] Whilst the Conservative and Liberal parties had their own traditions of political marriage, Lowe finds that Labour partnerships were distinguished by strong ideological commitments shared between spouses.

The marriages of Beatrice Potter (to Sidney in 1892) and Margaret Postgate (to Douglas in 1918) were socialist unions of a particular kind, both being essentially writing partnerships which sought intellectual, rather than electoral, influence.[38] The Webbs became famous for the massive body of work which they began to publish from the 1890s on subjects ranging from trade unionism and local government to the ownership of industry and Soviet Communism, a combined corpus exceeding five million words. What went into the production of these words Beatrice described intermittently in the diary and more systematically in a series of BBC radio talks delivered by her in the late 1920s and published as *Methods of Social Study* (1932). The routines she devised with Sidney for collecting material, organising notes and producing drafts have

[35] Eileen Yeo, 'Social Science Couples in Britain at the Turn of the Twentieth Century: Gender Divisions in Work and Marriage', in Annette Lykknes, Donald L. Opitz and Brigitte van Tiggelen (eds), *For Better or For Worse? Collaborative Couples in the Sciences* (Basel, 2012), 221–43.

[36] Lawrence Goldman, *The Life of R.H. Tawney* (London, 2013); Seth Koven, 'Henrietta Barnett 1851–1936: The (Auto) Biography of a Late Victorian Marriage' in Susan Pedersen and Peter Mandler (eds), *After the Victorians* (London, 1994), 31–53; S.A. Weaver, *The Hammonds* (Stanford, 1997).

[37] Eleanor Lowe, 'Love and Marriage in Party Political Cultures, 1918–1970' (unpublished PhD thesis, University of Cambridge, 2023).

[38] As previously noted, Sidney Webb served as an MP (1922–31) and as a Cabinet minister (1929–31), although he did so with reluctance and limited success. Douglas was adopted as a candidate in 1930 under pressure from the party, but ill health forced him to stand down before the 1931 election.

The Socialist Lives of Beatrice Webb and Margaret Cole   153

been of great interest to historians of social policy and social science, yet just as important was the function that writing played in the Webb marriage as a source of emotional – and, at times, physical – intimacy.

The work of co-authorship typically took place at Grosvenor Road (and later at Passfield Corner), and in the many properties that Beatrice and Sidney procured for working holidays, including the Argoed, a large country house in rural Monmouthshire owned by the Potters. It was here that Beatrice recorded the following diary entry for January 1897, when the Webbs were working on their magnum opus, *Industrial Democracy*:

> Have worked both together and apart, Sidney reading through the thirty volumes we brought with us on abstract economics, and writing, with occasional suggestions from me, the chapter giving our synthesis of the higgling of the market. Then he and I would write it out clearly – he criticizing my ideas; sometimes we would get at cross purposes – but our cross purposes would always end in a shower of kisses. I doubt whether two persons could stand the stress and strain of this long drawn-out work, this joint struggle with ideas, a perpetual hammering at each other's minds, if it were not for the equally perpetual 'honeymoon' of our life together.[39]

A few months later, Beatrice was happily installed in a rented cottage on the North Downs continuing the work:

> Glorious summer days. In excellent working form. Long mornings spent in work, recasting some of the chapters, filling up crevasses and thinking out the last chapter and foreshadowing the preface. Sidney sits at one table and I at another: the sun streams in through the dancing leaves. As fast as I can plan he criticises and executes, filling in his time with administrative work, but sacrificing everything to the book.[40]

Friends and associates confirmed this picture of loving co-production. George Bernard Shaw, who often stayed with the Webbs, described the couple's 'incorrigible spooning over their industrial and political science' in a letter to the actress Ellen Terry, giving a fuller account in the *Times Literary Supplement* shortly after Beatrice's death.

> I lived with them a good deal before my own late marriage, and was quite accustomed to be with them at work, and to see Beatrice every now and then, when she felt she needed a refresher (Sidney was tireless), rise from her chair, throw away her pen and hurl herself on her husband in a shower of caresses which lasted until the passion for work resumed its sway and

---

[39] *Diary*, 18 Jan. 1897.

[40] *Diary*, 24 May 1897. See also entry for 1 May 1897.

they wrote or read authorities for their footnotes until it was time for another refresher.[41]

Less demonstrative but still warmly convivial was the picture painted by Frank Galton, who worked for the Webbs as a research assistant at Grosvenor Road in the 1890s:

> I went to breakfast with them at 8am... After breakfast, not a long or heavy meal, we all smoked a cigarette together and discussed the coming morning's work... By nine o'clock the Webbs had started to work, seated each at one end of the table facing one another with the necessary books and paper at hand... [often] I was called down to join in the discussion with them... Sometimes these discussions became so interesting and absorbing that, even in winter, the fire in the room would go out and have to be relighted by one of the servants.[42]

These conversations were 'carried on in a lively and often high-spirited way', Galton recalled; on one occasion he was daring enough to crack a joke and Beatrice 'laughed gaily'.[43]

Finally, we can turn to visual evidence of the Webb marriage to confirm this picture of intellectual togetherness. Many photographic portraits were made of the couple over the decades. One of the earliest was taken at their first temporary home at Netherhall Gardens, Hampstead, featuring a seated Sidney, pen poised for writing, and Beatrice at his side, one hand on her husband's shoulder and the other fingering the enormous pile of papers on Sidney's desk (fig. 7.1). Beatrice's expression is strikingly demure; her eyes are cast downwards while Sidney stares levelly into the camera lens. This telling arrangement was reproduced in later portraits, which typically posed Sidney pen-in-hand and had Beatrice standing or sitting nearby, her gaze sometimes fixed on Sidney's papers and sometimes unfocused, lacking any obvious object. The undecidability of Beatrice's position in these photographs might be understood in terms of what Roland Barthes famously called the 'punctum', that is, the feature of an image that 'pricks' or 'punctuates' in ways that defy standard methods of interpretation.[44] Whether Beatrice was playing the role of wifely

---

[41] The letter to Terry is quoted in Cole, *Beatrice Webb*, 64. George Bernard Shaw, 'The History of a Happy Marriage', *Times Literary Supplement*, 20 Oct. 1945, 493. Beatrice makes references in the diary to 'intervals of human nature' during writing sessions with Sidney in the months before their marriage (see entries for 11 Aug. 1891 and 10 Oct. 1891).

[42] F.W. Galton, 'Investigating with the Webbs', in Cole, *The Webbs*, 32.

[43] *Ibid.*, 33.

[44] See discussion in Liz Stanley, *The Auto-Biographical I: The Theory and Practice of Feminist Auto/biography* (Manchester, 1992), 37–8.

Fig. 7.1. The partnership at work: the newly-wed Webbs photographed at their first home in Hampstead, north London, c.1894.

assistant to Sidney's dynamic intellect, or presenting herself as the creative visionary to his workmanlike scribe – both versions of herself which appear in the diary – are questions which would repay more detailed study as would a fuller scholarly engagement with the visual record of the Webb partnership.[45]

One obvious comparison is with the Coles, in whose marriage co-authorship was a similarly prominent feature, although the duo's publications were notably more eclectic than the Webb *oeuvre*. Margaret and Douglas jointly penned books on general political subjects, including *The Condition of England* (1937) for Victor Gollancz's Left Book Club, but they also edited volumes of romantic poetry, humorous verse and the writings of the early radical William Cobbett, plus over thirty detective novels. Images of the Coles are less abundant than

[45] Further research might throw light on the circulation and reception of Webb portraiture during and after the couple's lifetime, perhaps making use of the many photographs of Beatrice and Sidney taken by George Bernard Shaw in less formal settings. Some of these can be viewed at <https://digital.library.lse.ac.uk/collections/webb>.

Fig. 7.2. The Coles at home: Margaret and Douglas in their study in Hendon, north London, 1938.

for the Webbs, but those that exist produce a similar visual effect of intellectual partnership. Two portraits by the photographer Howard Coster in the late 1930s depicted the Coles at home in North London, first in quiet contemplation (Margaret sitting, Douglas standing) and later engaged in friendly discourse (their poses reversed).[46] Tellingly, Margaret included the second image (fig. 7.2) in the plate-section of her 1971 biography of Douglas, placing it across the page from William Nicholson's famous 1928 painting of the Webbs at Passfield Corner, in the process creating for her reader a near-seamless intergenerational collage of Fabian couples.[47]

[46] The first image appeared in 'The Coles at Home', *Bystander*, 20 Apr. 1938, 23 and was reproduced by Vernon in *Margaret Cole*, plate section. See also the image accompanying an interview with the Coles as fiction-writers included in Susan Hicklin, 'Behind the Who Dunnits', *Picture Post*, 9 Aug. 1952, 39–45 (image on p. 40).

[47] Nicolson's portrait, which depicted Beatrice and Sidney at home in Passfield Corner, was commissioned by the LSE to honour its founders and paid for by

The Socialist Lives of Beatrice Webb and Margaret Cole   157

It seems unlikely that this juxtaposition was unplanned, even though Margaret frequently denied that anything other than a superficial resemblance existed between the Coles and the Webbs. She insisted that she and Douglas wrote more as individuals than did Beatrice or Sidney, and that 'the many books, including the detective novels, which bear our joint name, are the result of combination (one hand writing either the whole draft or a chapter or more) and criticism, rather than collaboration of the kind which produced, for example, the [Webbs'] *History of Trade Unionism*'.[48] Differences of style and temperament explained 'why we are not a new edition of *Our Partnership*'.[49] Yet there can be no doubt that Margaret saw in the Webbs an ideal model of socialist marriage. She dedicated her 1938 study, *Marriage: Past and Present,* to Beatrice, 'in admiration of one of the best marriage partnerships I have ever known', and went further in her 1945 biography, concluding that the Webbs 'provided one of the most complete vindications of the institution of marriage that has ever been seen in public life'.[50] The Webb partnership is narrated as a highly sentimental love story in the screenplay which Margaret wrote around this time for a biopic based on Beatrice's life. In it she included tender scenes of youthful courtship – a lovestruck Sidney steals a furtive kiss from a framed photograph of Beatrice in the Potters' drawing room – and of companionship in old age – Beatrice grapples comically with Sandy, the Webbs' excitable dog at Passfield Corner, while awaiting Sidney's return from parliament.[51] These tributes gain greater poignancy in light of the difficulties in Margaret's own marriage, which provided close intellectual comradeship but not the affection or sexual intimacy that she craved.[52]

A relationship which proved more emotionally sustaining for Margaret was with her brother, Raymond, who, following his youthful experience of

---

subscription. See Sue Donnelly, 'The Webb Portrait', 11 Oct. 2016 <https:// blogs.lse. ac.uk/lsehistory/2016/10/11/webbportrait/>.

[48] Cole, *Growing Up*, 78. Margaret's claim is probably true for sole-authored published works, although looks less plausible once Beatrice's diary – all three million words of it – is added to the tally.

[49] *Ibid.*, 79. *Our Partnership* was a reference to Beatrice's second volume of autobiography which covered the first twenty years of the Webb marriage.

[50] Margaret Cole, *Marriage: Past and Present* (London, 1938); *Beatrice Webb*, 189.

[51] See draft screenplay, 'Beatrice Webb: Second Treatment', in Margaret Cole Papers, Nuffield College, G2.4.1.1. The film, perhaps unsurprisingly, was never made.

[52] Margaret had a long-running affair in the 1930s with Dick Mitchison, who was in an open marriage with Margaret's close friend, the writer and sex reformer Naomi Mitchison, a relationship discreetly hinted at in Vernon, *Margaret Cole*, 70–1, 75. In her biography of Douglas, Margaret described her husband, rather extraordinarily, as 'always under-sexed', remarking, 'If he had not married, I doubt very much whether he would have had any sex-life at all in the ordinary sense' (*Life of G.D.H. Cole*, 91).

conscientious objection, became a well-known journalist, writer and, latterly, food critic. Both he and Margaret wrote in the 1920s for *Lansbury's Labour Weekly*, the newspaper founded by George Lansbury MP, whose daughter Raymond married, and the siblings went together (without Douglas) on a fact-finding visit to the USSR for the New Fabian Bureau in 1932, and on a subsequent visit to Sweden five years later. From the mid-1930s the families lived in houses half a mile apart in Hendon, north London, and many Sunday afternoons were spent playing tennis followed by tea, often joined by other socialist friends.[53] When Raymond died in 1971, Margaret tried to articulate her sense of loss in a letter to her old friend Francis Meynell:

> You do understand so well – the close close relationship, personal, political & all – and above all the 'frame of reference' which, whether one met physically or not, was always <u>there</u> – much more than I had realised probably until he died. 'I must ask Ray about…'[54]

Had Sidney died first, one could imagine Beatrice Webb talking in these terms about her husband, but she never expressed comparable sentiments about any of her siblings, from whom she felt distanced owing to her socialist politics and decision to marry 'down'. 'My sisters no longer know me', she wrote in May 1893, 'they know only the shell with which I covered myself'.[55] Siblings arguably deserve far more attention than they receive from political historians, given how powerfully they could help to anchor a political life, as Raymond did for Margaret, or, conversely, make demands which bring family loyalties into conflict with political ideals, as Beatrice experienced with the Potters.[56] But whether it is husbands, brothers or sisters in focus, what this comparison of the Webb and Cole partnerships makes clear is that socialism, for both women, was lived through and given meaning by close personal relationships. The final section of this chapter explores how this shaped the bond between Beatrice and Margaret themselves – in life, and in death.

---

[53] John and Mary Postgate, *Stomach for Dissent.*

[54] Margaret Cole to Francis Meynell, 8 Apr. [1971], in Francis Meynell Papers, Cambridge University Library.

[55] *Diary*, 22 May 1893.

[56] A recent contribution which does take sibling relationships seriously is Lyndsey Jenkins, *Sisters and Sisterhood: The Kenney Family, Class and Suffrage, 1890–1965* (Oxford, 2021). See also Susan Pedersen's account of family politics in 'The Women's Suffrage Movement in the Balfour Family', *Twentieth Century British History*, 30 (2019), 299–320.

Friendships

The prospect of a close sympathy developing after the women's tense first meeting in 1917 seemed unlikely. As noted above, the Guild Socialists of the Fabian Research Department were hostile towards what they saw as the tyrannical bureaucratic tendencies of the Webbs, to whom Douglas had been serially unpleasant at pre-war Fabian conferences. Yet it was on cultivating him, the brilliant Oxford graduate, that Beatrice set her sights in the immediate post-war years, viewing Margaret, in the latter's own words, as 'a kind of umbrella which he had to be allowed to bring with him'.[57] Beatrice extended this attitude of dismissiveness to other young Fabian women, which Margaret attributed to a deeply-ingrained belief, instilled by anti-feminist figures like Herbert Spencer during childhood, in the superior intellect of men.[58] This gave the friendship which eventually bloomed between them a distinctive character. It was not rooted in the emotional intensities of the suffrage movement – about which Beatrice was ambivalent and Margaret mildly supportive – nor in the other forms of female community available to publicly-active women in the early twentieth century, from settlement houses to women's hospitals.[59]

The warming agent appears instead to have been repeated exposure leading to a creeping familiarity. Beatrice came to enjoy the company of the Coles. They were, she recorded in her diary for September 1926, 'always attractive because they are at once disinterested and brilliantly intellectual and, be it added, agreeable to look at'. Perceptively, she judged Margaret 'more human and more capable of affection and intimacy' than Douglas, 'but not so tenaciously clever or coldly incisive'.[60] By the 1930s, when the septuagenarian Webbs spent most of their time at Passfield Corner, it was Margaret's qualities which became the connecting element. Age recalibrates relationships in politics just as in other avenues of life, and Beatrice's advancing years seemed to bring out a tenderness in Margaret. She would sometimes visit without Douglas, bringing her son, Humphrey, instead, and in 1938 wrote Beatrice a warm, effusive letter to mark her eightieth birthday.[61] Margaret's autobiography includes a fond scene of visiting Passfield Corner one final time, long after the death of both Webbs, where she could 'almost see Beatrice standing at the door, among the heaths

---

[57] Cole, *Growing Up*, 135.

[58] Caine analyses this intriguing feature of Beatrice's character superbly in 'Beatrice Webb and the Woman Question'.

[59] Sandra Stanley Holton, *Suffrage Days: Stories from the Women's Suffrage Movement* (London, 1996); Martha Vicinus, *Independent Women: Work and Community for Single Women, 1850–1920* (London, 1985); Seth Koven, *The Match Girl and the Heiress* (London, 2014).

[60] *Diary*, 5 Sept. 1926.

[61] Vernon, *Margaret Cole*, 112; *Diary*, 23 Jan. 1938.

160   *Helen McCarthy*

and the rock-plants, with her eagle nose and a net cap over her straying white hairs, and her arms opened wide to embrace me.[62]

The posthumous care which Margaret showed Beatrice is perhaps the most striking feature of their friendship. Named an executor of the Webb estate in 1942, Margaret was entrusted by Sidney with Beatrice's diaries after she died the following April. All fifty volumes Margaret discovered neatly stacked in a corner of the cottage in brown paper wrappings, and she sat up that first evening until 4am trying to decipher their author's famously illegible scrawl.[63] This task was later shared with Barbara Drake, Beatrice's niece, with whom Margaret edited *Our Partnership*, the sequel to *My Apprenticeship*, but preparation of the diaries for publication Margaret did alone. Selections appeared in two volumes in 1952 and 1957 and picked up where the autobiographies left off, covering the years 1912–32. Alongside her biography of Beatrice and the never-to-be-made film script, Margaret also edited a collection of reminiscences of the Webbs by close friends and colleagues, *The Webbs and their Work*, contributed forewords to reprints of their books and, well into her own advancing age, wrote to newspaper editors to correct what she regarded as faulty information or misleading statements about her old friends. She clashed with a younger, less deferential generation of Webb scholars in the letters pages of *Encounter*, which published several articles in the late 1970s carrying accusations that Beatrice was anti-Semitic and that both Webbs held 'racialist' views.[64] To these charges Margaret sent spiky rebuttals, saving her deepest indignation for the remarks of conservative philosopher Shirley Letwin, whose 1965 book *The Pursuit of Certainty* denounced Beatrice's political thought as authoritarian and anti-liberal. Letwin referred to Beatrice's 'antipathy to all concrete human beings', a claim which Margaret declared 'stark nonsense', citing the Webbs' 'many generosities to those who opposed them and their kindness to those who sought their help'.[65]

The *Encounter* spat took a new turn in 1978 when George Feaver, a Canadian academic who had recently edited a re-issue of *Our Partnership*, published a long piece on the Webbs in which he criticised Margaret for omitting sections of Beatrice's travel diaries from her 1950s volumes and, more nastily, quoted Harold Laski's letter to R.H. Tawney at the London School of Economics, in which the former remarked that 'Mrs Cole has taken over [the Webbs'] legacy

---

[62] Cole, *Growing Up*, 137.

[63] Vernon, *Margaret Cole*, 113.

[64] See *Encounter*, May 1976, 91; Aug. 1976, 92; Sept. 1976, 89–90; Nov. 1976, 94–6; Jan. 1977, 93–5; May 1977, 93–4.

[65] *Encounter*, Jan. 1977, 95; May 1977, 94.

The Socialist Lives of Beatrice Webb and Margaret Cole   161

as a permanent source of income'.[66] Laski wrote these spiteful words in May 1949 in solidarity with Tawney over news of Margaret's forthcoming volume, *The Webbs and their Work*, a project which the two men felt to be both inappropriate, given her role as trustee, and inconsiderate of Tawney, who was in the early stages of researching a biography of Sidney (a plan he subsequently abandoned).[67] Margaret defended herself at the time and did so again to Feaver, pointing out that *Our Partnership* was edited at the express wish of Sidney and disclosing that the only Webb publication from which she had personally profited was her 1949 biography of Beatrice, and even then by 'not a great deal'.[68] Feaver struck back with a broader blow against Margaret's credibility as a Webb authority: 'Mrs Cole's writings on the Webbs are informed by her personal friendship and identity with Beatrice, and by the fact that, with her late husband, she was herself a principal player in a sort of second generation Webbian partnership on the political left'.[69]

Here, Feaver hit the mark, but what was intended as an insult inadvertently articulated a profound truth about the ties which bound these two women of the left, even in death. Margaret became to Beatrice (and, to a lesser extent, to Sidney) what the literary critic Ian Hamilton has called a 'keeper of the flame', personally invested in promulgating and defending a particular version of Beatrice's life.[70] It was a version in which Beatrice could be high-handed and scathing in her judgments of people who unimpressed her, yet displayed a 'fundamental good will and friendliness' and tried to help 'as far as she could, anyone who was really anxious to serve in the cause in which she had spent her life'.[71] It was a version in which Beatrice was the 'leading spirit' of the Webb partnership; she, not Sidney, Margaret avowed, identified the couple's signature subjects (cooperatives, trade unions, the organs of local government) and crystallised the 'Webb concept of society' as a functional organisation of citizens, consumers and producers.[72] In her many writings and lectures, Margaret strained to protect her friend from alternative 'myths' of the Webbs circulating

[66] George Feaver, 'The Webbs as Pilgrims', *Encounter*, Mar. 1978, 23–31 (Laski quote at p. 23).

[67] Laski's letter had recently come to light through a citation in Ross Terrill's biography of Tawney: *R.H. Tawney and His Times* (London, 1973). Terrill – like Feaver – evidently felt some sympathy for his subject over the affair.

[68] *Encounter*, July 1978, 93.

[69] *Encounter*, Sept. 1978, 94.

[70] Ian Hamilton, *Keepers of the Flame: Literary Estates and the Rise of Biography* (London, 1992).

[71] Cole, *Beatrice Webb*, 182. See similar sentiments rearticulated in *Growing Up*, 135.

[72] Margaret Cole, 'The Webbs and Social Theory', *British Journal of Sociology*, 12 (1961), 93–105, at 100, 101.

162   Helen McCarthy

after their deaths: Beatrice and Sidney as sly 'wire-pullers'; as bloodless bureaucrats; the 'two typewriters clicking as one', in A.G. Gardiner's famous words.[73] Doubtless, there was self-interest in Margaret's efforts to protect the partnership's legacy: to magnify the achievements of the Webbs was to bring Cole endeavours into focus too. But mostly Margaret did all this because she believed that she understood Beatrice in a way that others did not, and certainly not arrogant young men like George Feaver.[74] Mostly she did it because she cared.

* * *

It was often said of the Webbs that they lacked an intuitive grasp of the ordinary frailties and irrationalities of human behaviour. Their theories fixed too stubbornly on institutions, excluding from vision the psychically complex individuals who made those institutions live. They cared about 'town councils' rather than 'town councillors', as Sidney's Fabian colleague Graham Wallas once put it.[75] This chapter could be accused of doing the reverse by centring socialists at the expense of socialism, privileging people's feelings and relationships over their ideas. (It cares more, one might say, about Morris cushion-covers than about Marxist thought.) It is true that the preceding analysis has touched only briefly on the ideological content of Beatrice and Margaret's political writings, on the kind of socialism that they wanted to see come to pass in Britain. Nor has it detailed their formal contributions to the work of the Fabian Society, or each woman's place within the ecosystem of leftist groups for which Fabianism was a connective tissue in the early to mid-twentieth century: the Society for Socialist Inquiry and Propaganda, the New Fabian Research Bureau, the Socialist League, the Workers Education Association, the Left Book Club, plus, of course, the Labour party.

Yet these subjects become textured more richly when we run through them the threads of love, affection, loyalty and trust. What this chapter has sought to show is that ideas and actions in politics belong to the history of intimacy and friendship as much as they do to the study of parties, policymaking and political thought.[76] Like all the contributors to this volume, my account of Beatrice Webb and Margaret Cole's socialist lives sits firmly on the foundation

[73]   *Ibid.*, 102. These built upon the 'myths' that grew up in the Webbs' lifetime, as Deborah Nord discusses in *Apprenticeship*, introduction.

[74]   'I do not know whether Professor Feaver ever met her', Margaret wrote to the editor of *Encounter*, 'but I can assure him (and you) that I knew her pretty well, as my husband and I stayed several times at Passfield Corner' (Oct. 1979, p. 94).

[75]   Cole, 'Social Theory', 101.

[76]   A perspective brilliantly opened up in the series of articles on 'Radical Friendship' published by *History Workshop Online* in 2020 <https://www.historyworkshop. org.uk/archive/?s=%22radical+friendship%22>.

that Parry has built for us, in which political and intellectual cultures are produced by people connected by values, ideas and institutions. How individuals have seen the world and sought to act politically upon it is for the historian to recover as best they can. In this task, the youthful journeys, political marriages and enduring friendship of these two socialist women offers a powerfully illuminating case study.

Chapter 8

'Great Contemporaries' but Guarded Friends: Winston Churchill and G.M. Trevelyan Revisited[1]

David Cannadine

In his brilliant exploration of British Liberalism during the period 1830 to 1886, when it was the dominant force in the nation's political life, Jonathan Parry vividly celebrated the qualities that informed the 'good political leadership' displayed by the men of power. Among them were 'breadth of popular sympathy, self-confidence, courage and disinterestedness', as well as 'a cultured understanding of the relation between the present and the past', which was developed through the study of such subjects as history and literature. And underpinning and nurturing these modes of behaviour and of governing

[1] I am deeply grateful to Allen Packwood, Director of the Churchill Archive Centre, Churchill College, Cambridge, and to his staff, for their help and assistance in the preparation of this essay. Where I quote correspondence already published in printed sources, I have confined myself to providing the appropriate page references where full archival citations can be followed up; only in the case of direct quotations from archival collections have I provided full references. Throughout the notes, I have used the following abbreviations:

C	David Cannadine, *G.M. Trevelyan: A Life in History* (London, 1992).
CHAR	Churchill papers, Churchill College, Cambridge, up to 1945.
CHUR	Churchill papers, Churchill College, Cambridge, after 1945.
CPT	(Sir) Charles Phillips Trevelyan.
CPT	A.J.A. Morris, *C.P. Trevelyan: Portrait of a Radical* (Belfast, 1977).
CV I, pt. i, pt. ii	Randolph S. Churchill, *Winston S. Churchill*, vol. I, *Youth, 1874–1900*, Companion Volume, part i, *1874-1896*; part ii, *1896–1900* (London, 1967).
CV II, pt. i	Randolph S. Churchill, *Winston S. Churchill*, vol. II, *Young Statesman, 1900–1914*, Companion Volume, part i, *1901-1907* (London, 1969).

were dynastic connections and personal friendships, as well as shared educational backgrounds and membership of London clubs. According to Parry, Gladstone's messianic espousal of Irish Home Rule dealt this Liberal style of government a mortal blow that even the electoral landslide of 1906 could not long disguise.[2] Yet even as the lights of Liberalism faded politically, the afterlife of those Liberal assumptions and underpinnings was extensive, especially among those who belonged to the late-Victorian generation. Two such figures were Winston Spencer Churchill (born November 1874), and George Macaulay Trevelyan (born February 1876), and their guarded friendship offers one well-documented glimpse into the late-Liberal and post-Liberal worlds of British politics and culture.[3]

They were both descended from landed, titled families who had played significant parts in British, European and imperial history, and took pride and delight in their ancestors' many achievements. Churchill's dynastic heroes were the first Duke of Marlborough and his father, Lord Randolph, whom he celebrated and memorialised in two multi-volume biographies.[4] Trevelyan revered his great uncle, Thomas Babington Macaulay, his grandfather Sir Charles Trevelyan, and his father, Sir George Otto Trevelyan; Sir George wrote an extended life of Macaulay, and Trevelyan wrote an affectionate and admiring memoir of Sir George.[5] Churchill and Trevelyan both grew up with a liking for military history. They both attended Harrow School where they were taught to write English prose by the same master, Robert Somervell. And they were

---

CV V, pt. ii, pt. iii	Martin Gilbert, *Winston S. Churchill*, vol. V, *1922–1939*, Companion Volume, part ii, *The Wilderness Years, 1929–1935*; part iii, *The Coming of War, 1936–1939* (London, 1981, 1982).
GMT	George Macaulay Trevelyan.
M	Winston S. Churchill, *Marlborough: His Life and Times*, vol. I (London, 1933).
R	Peter Raina, *George Macaulay Trevelyan: A Portrait in Letters* (Edinburgh, 2001).
WSC	Winston S. Churchill.

[2] Jonathan Parry, *The Rise and Fall of Liberal Government in Britain* (New Haven & London, 1993), 1–7, 18, 304–11.

[3] Victor Feske, *From Belloc to Churchill: Private Scholars, Public Culture, and the Crisis of British Liberalism, 1900–1939* (Chapel Hill, NC, 1996), 137–227.

[4] WSC, *Lord Randolph Churchill* (2 vols, London, 1906); *Marlborough* (4 vols, London, 1933–8).

[5] G.O. Trevelyan, *The Life and Letters of Lord Macaulay* (2 vols, London, 1876); GMT, *Sir George Otto Trevelyan: A Memoir* (London, 1932).

both later admired, or disparaged, as the last 'Whig' historians.[6] Trevelyan was appointed Regius Professor of Modern History at Cambridge and subsequently Master of Trinity College; as the best-selling historian of his generation he combined academic pre-eminence and cultural authority in a uniquely resonant way, and in later life he was lauded as 'probably the most widely-read historian in the world'. Churchill's public life spanned sixty years, he was a heroic war leader and venerable peacetime prime minister, and he was regularly regarded in his seventies and eighties as 'the saviour of his country'.[7]

It is, then, something of an understatement to observe that Churchill and Trevelyan reached the peaks of their chosen professions, acquired large and admiring public followings along the way, and were, to borrow the title of one of Churchill's most appealing books, their own 'great contemporaries'.[8] Indeed, Sir John Plumb contended that Churchill was the only public figure 'for whom Trevelyan had an almost uncritical admiration throughout his life', and in support of this forceful claim, cited their 'strong Harrovian connection', their 'natural delight in history', their shared Edwardian liberalism and their common 'dislike' of appeasing Nazi Germany. All this, Plumb averred, meant they were 'life-long friends'.[9] But this was far from being the whole truth of things. To be sure, Churchill and Trevelyan knew each other a long time, and both were enthusiastic Edwardian Liberals; yet their friendship was more correct and distant than close and warm, and despite their undeniable affinities, they were in many ways different people from different worlds who lived different lives in different social milieux. They may have had some things in common, but by no means everything; and, *pace* Plumb, their differences were most in evidence during the 1930s, when they corresponded most extensively *and* also disagreed most fully – not only about history, but about politics, too.

Two Dynasties

For all their superficial similarities, Churchill and Trevelyan were scions of very distinct dynasties that by the nineteenth century were headed in notably contrasted directions. The Churchills came from Dorset and had exploded into greatness and grandeur because John Churchill won a succession of military

---

6   Mary Moorman, 'The Youth of an Historian: George Macaulay Trevelyan', *Contemporary Review*, 224 (1974), 248; R, 38, 42; WSC, *My Early Life* (New York, 1930), 16–17; GMT, *An Autobiography and Other Essays* (London, 1949), 11.

7   C, 18; Isaiah Berlin, *Mr Churchill in 1940* (London, n.d.), 39; A.J.P. Taylor, *English History, 1914–1945* (Oxford, 1965), 29 n. 1.

8   WSC, *Great Contemporaries* (London, 1937).

9   *The Collected Essays of J.H. Plumb*, vol. 1: *The Making of an Historian* (London, 1988), 225–6.

victories against the French at Blenheim, Ramillies and Oudenarde, and forged a continental 'Grand Alliance' against Louis XIV. In recognition of his exploits as a 'heaven-born general', he was created Duke of Marlborough, the highest rank in the British peerage, and was given abundant broad acres by the grateful Queen Anne to support his ducal dignities. His descendants resided at Blenheim, an Olympian house in Oxfordshire designed by Sir John Vanbrugh, that was one of the few non-royal and non-episcopal residences in Britain to be called a palace, and it was there that Winston Churchill was born, and later proposed to Clementine Hozier. The Trevelyans, by contrast, ranked significantly lower in the nation's titular and honorific hierarchy. They were West Country landowners (and West Indies slaveowners) who acquired by marriage a house and estate in Northumberland at Wallington, which was eventually inherited by Sir Charles Trevelyan, who was married to Macaulay's sister, and was created a baronet in 1874. But Wallington was nowhere near as grand as Blenheim, and unlike the Churchills, the Trevelyans belonged to the nation's service gentry, while also being strongly linked to the upper middle class.[10] Their relatives administered the empire in India, but in contrast to the great Duke of Marlborough, they never decided the fate of Europe, and they were far from being aristocratic grandees.

From these significant dynastic discrepancies, other divergencies followed. Despite his accomplishments on the battlefield, the first Duke of Marlborough was widely denounced by Jonathan Swift and Tory Jacobite pamphleteers as unprincipled, treacherous, disloyal and avaricious, a view repeated by Macaulay in his *History of England*.[11] Many of the great Duke's direct descendants were undistinguished and profligate, and during the nineteenth century, they were compelled to sell land in Wiltshire, Shropshire and Buckinghamshire, as well as the Old Master pictures that had been accumulated by the first duke, to pay their debts.[12] The younger son of the seventh duke, Lord Randolph Churchill, was widely regarded as erratic, irresponsible, unprincipled and opportunistic, and his political career crashed into ruin following his ill-judged resignation from Lord Salisbury's government in December 1886. Hence Gladstone's assertion that 'there never was a Churchill from John of Marlborough down that had either morals or principles'.[13] So it was scarcely surprising that when young Winston burst on the political scene in the 1900s, many thought him as

[10] Laura Trevelyan, 'My Family Owned 1,000 Slaves', *Guardian*, 25 March 2023; *CPT*, 2.

[11] Thomas Babington Macaulay, *The History of England from the Reign of James the Second* (4 vols, London, 1849–55), vol. 1, 460–2; vol. 2, 317; vol. 3, 437–8; vol. 4, 426 n. 1, 514; Maurice Ashley, *Churchill as Historian* (London, 1968), 138–9.

[12] David Cannadine, *Aspects of Aristocracy* (London, 1994), 133.

[13] R.F. Foster, *Lord Randolph Churchill* (Oxford, 1981), 127.

wayward, unstable and unprincipled as his father had been, and too self-centred and pushy for his own good. These criticisms and concerns seemed well borne out in May 1904, when Churchill left the Conservatives and joined the Liberals, which enabled him to obtain junior office late in the following year.[14]

By contrast, the Trevelyans were well-behaved, high-minded, secular evangelicals, driven by what George once described as 'an infidel sense of duty' (and perhaps by guilt that their forebears had been slaveowners).[15] As Assistant Secretary to the Treasury, Sir Charles Trevelyan sought to alleviate the worst excesses of the Irish Potato Famine, and as co-author of the Northcote-Trevelyan Report, he helped create a new-style bureaucracy based on character and competition rather than patronage and connection.[16] As an MP and imperial administrator, his brother-in-law, Thomas Babington Macaulay, supported parliamentary reform in Britain and legal and educational reform in India, and was widely recognised as the greatest British historian since Edward Gibbon. Trevelyan's father, Sir George Otto, was a Liberal MP from 1865 to 1897 and held office in all four of Gladstone's governments. He wrote a widely-read, multi-volume history of the American Revolution in addition to his life of Macaulay, and he was awarded the Order of Merit in 1911.[17] Whereas the Marlboroughs were poor dukes, with less than £40,000 a year from scarcely 20,000 acres, the Trevelyans were comfortably-off for gentry, with a similar acreage worth about £15,000 a year.[18] As George Trevelyan explained to his elder brother Charles in 1905, 'the world has given us enough money to enable us to do what we think right'. But this was not true of Winston Churchill, who was the son of an indebted father and spendthrift mother: 'we are', he had written to Lady Randolph in 1898, 'damned poor'.[19] Hence from an early age his efforts to become a successful, self-made writer, in the hope he might sustain an opulent lifestyle very unlike that of the austere and abstemious Trevelyans.

By the late nineteenth century, then, the Churchills seemed neither respectable nor reliable, whereas the Trevelyans epitomised decency and dutifulness. It was thus scarcely surprising that Winston Churchill and George Trevelyan

---

[14] Cannadine, *Aspects*, 137–8; Robert Rhodes James, *Churchill: A Study in Failure, 1900–1939* (New York, 1970), 14–16.

[15] Owen Chadwick, *Freedom and the Historian* (Cambridge, 1969), 29–30.

[16] Robin Haines, *Charles Trevelyan and the Great Irish Famine* (Dublin, 2004), 3–11, 544–56; Charles Read, *The Great Famine in Ireland and Britain's Financial Crisis* (Woodbridge, 2022), xii, 41–51, 105–6, 190–5.

[17] C, pp. 5–6; G.O. Trevelyan, *A History of the American Revolution* (3 vols, London, 1899–1905).

[18] John Bateman, *The Great Landowners of Great Britain and Ireland* (Leicester, 1971, reprinting 4th edn [1883]), 300, 448.

[19] R, 52; Cannadine, *Aspects*, 144.

Winston Churchill and G.M. Trevelyan Revisited   169

did not become friends while attending Harrow. In 1940, when Churchill appointed him Master of Trinity, Trevelyan claimed in his letter of acceptance that at school he had admired 'from a distance the driving force of your great character'.[20] But the phrase 'from a distance' was both revealing and accurate: for Churchill and Trevelyan were two years apart and placed in different forms and houses, and while they were both 'misfits', they were on very different political, academic and professional trajectories. Young Winston was a Tory Democrat like his father, and a generally undistinguished pupil, often near the bottom of his class. There was never any likelihood that he would win a place at university. He soon came to regret his lack of an Oxbridge education, and he only gained admission to Sandhurst at the third attempt and with the help of a crammer.[21] George Trevelyan, by contrast, was one of the few boys at Harrow who supported Gladstone and Irish Home Rule, and admitted to being something of a 'prig' and a 'swot'. He progressed with seemingly inexorable certainty to Trinity College, Cambridge, where his father and great uncle had been before him. He was recruited to the Apostles, took a First in the History Tripos in 1896 and was elected to a Fellowship at Trinity two years later.[22] At the same time, Churchill, having embraced a very different career, was soldiering on the frontiers of the British Empire in India and Africa.

Edwardian Affinities

The first recorded encounter between Churchill and the Trevelyans had taken place in 1887, when Charles Trevelyan, already at Harrow, had met Lord Randolph, who had brought young Winston to the school to sit the least demanding level of entrance examination, believing that any more taxing test would be beyond his son's capabilities. Churchill did not do well, being placed almost at the bottom in the lowest Form, as Charles later reported to his father.[23] In 1899, Charles Trevelyan was returned at a by-election as Liberal MP for Elland in Yorkshire, and at the subsequent general election, Churchill followed him into the Commons as Conservative MP for Oldham in Lancashire. By then, Trevelyan's opinion had softened. 'He is', Charles wrote to his mother, Lady Caroline, 'a big man', and 'whatever line he takes, he will always bring out the best and most reasonable side of it'. But he also shared the growing belief that, while Churchill possessed great gifts, he suffered, like his father, from serious failings of character and temperament, being both supremely egotistical and

---

[20] J.R. Colville, *The Fringes of Power: 10 Downing Street Diaries, 1939–55* (London, 1985), 253.

[21] WSC, *Early Life*, 16–17, 25, 113, 115; CV I, pt. ii, 725.

[22] GMT, *Autobiography*, 8–9, 13, 15, 20.

[23] *CPT*, 7.

'inordinately ambitious.'[24] Thereafter, Churchill distanced himself from the Conservatives, remaining committed to Free Trade while Joseph Chamberlain sought to convert the party to the cause of Tariff Reform.

When the Liberals took office in December 1905, Churchill was appointed Under Secretary of State for the Colonies, and Charles Trevelyan, who would only later be appointed to a junior post, hastened to congratulate him. Early the following year, Churchill published his life of Lord Randolph, and Trevelyan eagerly praised 'its literary merits.'[25] Despite his own disappointment, Trevelyan remained on good terms with Churchill as he was promoted to be President of the Board of Trade and Home Secretary, supporting his efforts at social and welfare reforms, and he wrote a warm letter of congratulation on Winston's engagement to Clementine Hozier.[26] But he also worried that Churchill was too belligerent as Home Secretary in his treatment of striking workers, and after he was appointed First Lord of the Admiralty in October 1911, relations between the two men further cooled. Abandoning his earlier commitment to economy and retrenchment in the armed services, Churchill massively expanded expenditure on the Royal Navy, and by early 1914, Charles Trevelyan had become increasingly concerned by what he regarded as his provocatively extravagant policy that would increase, not lessen, the likelihood of war with Germany.[27]

Throughout the years of Liberal ascendancy, Charles was the Trevelyan who maintained the closest relations with Churchill, but this was also when George Trevelyan first got to know him. In spring 1903, exactly a year before Churchill abandoned the Conservatives and joined the Liberals, he had committed his own act of apostasy, in his case academic rather than political, by resigning his Trinity Fellowship. Thanks to an allowance provided by his father, Trevelyan enjoyed the 'leisure, freedom and independence' that enabled him to renounce a conventional academic career, so he could devote himself to writing the sort of 'literary history' produced by his great uncle, but to which 'the critical atmosphere of Cambridge scholarship' was unsympathetic. He was also stirred by what he recalled as 'a young man's longing to be at least on the fringes of the great world of London', where Charles Trevelyan was already well established, and in 1904 he married Janet Penrose Ward, settling at Cheyne Gardens in Chelsea, where they soon started a family.[28] Trevelyan threw himself into the political and literary life of the metropolis, founding and editing a progressive

[24] *CPT*, 60.

[25] CHAR 2/24/48, CPT to WSC, 13 Dec. 1905; CHAR 2/26/22–24, CPT to WSC, 7 Feb. 1906.

[26] CHAR 1/73/92, CPT to WSC, 20 Aug. 1908.

[27] *CPT*, 56–7, 88–90, 102, 113–15.

[28] G.M. Young, *Last Essays* (London, 1950), 73; GMT, *Autobiography*, 19.

journal entitled the *Independent Review*, and teaching at the Working Men's College in Great Ormond Street. His Garibaldi trilogy, published between 1907 and 1911, celebrating liberalism and internationalism, provided a sort of historical validation for the progressive optimism of the times, and Asquith thought George Trevelyan 'the clever one', perhaps to differentiate him from his less able brother Charles.[29]

'Until the war of 1914', Trevelyan rightly recalled, 'I was a keen Liberal politician'. He had no wish to stand for parliament, but he claimed to have been a 'strong Liberal' since he was four years old, and thanks to his father had met Gladstone, and was well acquainted with such figures as John Morley and James Bryce. He was also an ardent champion of his brother's political career, campaigning with him at elections and sharing the general family disappointment that he had not been given office when the Liberals obtained power late in 1905.[30] Churchill regularly dined with the two Trevelyan brothers at Charles's London home, where he was 'always good company but invariably monopolizing the conversation'.[31] At such encounters, George Trevelyan may have come to share some of the reservations about Churchill that were already widely shared, but he strongly supported his efforts, in partnership with Lloyd George, to deliver the Liberal administration's social and welfare reforms. As he wrote to Charles in 1909, the two men were the 'very pulse' of the government 'machine', and their 'personal alliance' was a 'great piece of luck' in imparting dynamism and purpose in support of domestic progressive causes.[32]

The First World War abruptly ended these high Liberal hopes and Liberal political alliances. As a lifelong pacifist, Charles Trevelyan, like his brother Bob, was deeply opposed to Britain's involvement in the conflict: he resigned from the Liberal government in early August 1914, becoming a conscientious objector thereafter.[33] By contrast, Churchill was all for going into battle with the Germans, and hoped he might play a starring part in the ensuing drama, which meant his social relations with Charles Trevelyan were effectively ended. Much anguished, George Trevelyan disagreed with his two brothers because he believed that Prussian militarism, exemplified by Germany's unprovoked violation of neutral Belgium, had to be beaten if liberty in Europe were to be safeguarded.[34] But there was also a parting of the ways with Churchill. In December 1914, he was outraged by what he regarded as Churchill's concealment of the

---

[29] C, 61–3, 72; Michael and Eleanor Brock (eds), *H.H. Asquith: Letters to Venetia Stanley* (Oxford, 1982), 429.

[30] GMT, *Autobiography*, 9, 31.

[31] CV II, pt. i, 671; *CPT*, 68.

[32] C, 130.

[33] *CPT*, 118–20.

[34] R, 82–9; C, 78–9.

172   *David Cannadine*

sinking of the battleship *Audacious* by the Germans. The whole episode, he told his father, had 'gone far to shatter my belief in him'.[35] Thereafter, Trevelyan remained wary of Churchill, as instanced by their very different views of Mussolini during the 1920s.[36]

Interwar Divergences

Like many of their generation, Churchill and the Trevelyan brothers were disturbed and disoriented by the First World War and its aftermath, but they responded in different ways. Charles Trevelyan abandoned Liberalism and joined the Labour Party, briefly serving as President of the Board of Education in the two short-lived minority administrations formed by Ramsay MacDonald in January 1924 and June 1929. Churchill also gave up on the Liberals as, indeed, they had already given up on him, and by 1924 he had returned to the Conservative fold as Chancellor of the Exchequer in Stanley Baldwin's second administration. Churchill's prime purpose during the 1920s was to rebuild his reputation, having been made the scapegoat for the Dardanelles disaster, and for which he undoubtedly bore significant responsibility. Hence his multi-volume *The World Crisis*, which appeared between 1923 and 1931, described by Arthur Balfour as 'Winston's brilliant Autobiography, disguised as a history of the universe'.[37] George Trevelyan's response was different again. Disillusioned by Italy's embrace of Mussolini and subjugation to 'the obliterating steam-roller of Fascism', he wrote only one more book about the country of which he now despaired, concentrating thereafter on histories of England and biographies of Englishmen, which he wrote with 'a more realistic and less partisan outlook' than he had displayed before 1914.[38] Like Churchill, he, too, gave up on the Liberal Party and by the mid-1920s had become a supporter of the Conservatives.

Notwithstanding these new affinities and recent alliances, there remained significant differences between the two men. Churchill's relations with the Conservative party were never fully restored. His apostasy in 1904 had not been forgotten, and just as he had then left a party on the way down for one on the way up, so the same was thought to be true in the opposite direction twenty years later. His ambition and opportunism remained unappealingly undiminished,

[35]   C, 132.

[36]   C, 85.

[37]   WSC, *The World Crisis* (6 vols, London, 1923–31); Peter Clarke, *Mr Churchill's Profession: Statesman, Orator, Writer* (London, 2012), xiv.

[38]   GMT, *Autobiography*, 34, 38; *Lord Grey of the Reform Bill* (London, 1920); *British History in the Nineteenth Century* (London, 1922); *Manin and the Venetian Revolution of 1848* (London, 1923); *History of England* (London, 1926).

and although Churchill and Baldwin, like Churchill and Trevelyan, shared a Harrow connection, relations between the two men were never cordial. By the 1920s, Churchill had become a belligerent class warrior, denouncing the Labour party as 'unfit to govern', and adopting a hostile attitude towards the trade unions during the General Strike, whereas Baldwin sought to bind up the nation's wounds and promote social harmony. But Trevelyan greatly admired Baldwin, whom he regarded as 'the kindest Prime Minister who ever lived'. Both men were firm believers in the regenerative potential of the English countryside, and in what were termed 'spiritual values'. 'What a good Conservative', Trevelyan told Baldwin in 1935, 'Macaulay would have made if he had lived a few years longer'. That was the greatest compliment it was in his power to bestow, and the admiration was mutual. A year after the publication of Trevelyan's *History of England*, Baldwin appointed him Regius Professor of Modern History at Cambridge, where he resumed the Fellowship at Trinity College that he had relinquished in 1903, and returned to academe on generally better terms than Churchill had recently gone back to the Conservatives.[39]

By the interwar years, Churchill and Trevelyan were also moving in very different social circles with very different values. Churchill's friends were raffish buccaneers, among them Lords Birkenhead, Beaverbrook and Rothermere, along with Brendan Bracken and Robert Boothby. Trevelyan's friends were high-minded academics such as Gilbert Murray, H.A.L. Fisher, J.L. and Barbara Hammond and Sir John Clapham, and 'decent' politicians such as Lord Robert Cecil and Viscount Grey of Fallodon.[40] Churchill remained on friendly terms with Lloyd George, but Baldwin and Trevelyan had both come to dislike him as a corrupting and destructive force in public life, exemplified by the meretricious glitter of his postwar coalition and the scandals surrounding the sale of honours. Baldwin and Trevelyan were members of The Club, the most venerable dining society in London, where they mingled with cabinet secretaries, archbishops and private secretaries to the sovereign.[41] But Churchill, along with the future Lord Birkenhead, had created the Other Club in 1911, where they dined with press lords, artists and writers instead.[42] Trevelyan's life was 'inadequately warmed by self-indulgence', whereas Churchill once allegedly remarked that his tastes were very simple: 'I'm easily pleased with the best'.[43] It is impossible to imagine Trevelyan enjoying,

---

[39] R, 105; C, 160–1.

[40] GMT, obituary of Sir John Clapham, repr. *Autobiography*, 213–21.

[41] Cambridge University Library: Baldwin Papers: GMT to Stanley Baldwin, 17 June 1926.

[42] Janet Adam Smith, *John Buchan* (Oxford, 1985), 305–6; Martin Gilbert, *Winston Churchill and the Other Club* (London, 2011), 1–5, 243–60.

[43] C, 48; *Making of an Historian*, 181–2.

174   *David Cannadine*

as Churchill often did, lavish dinners at the Savoy Hotel, imbibing large quantities of champagne and brandy, gambling at the casinos on the French Riviera, or liking the *luxe* of the Hotel Mamounia in Marrakesh. Although he was much criticised and admired during his long and controversial life, no one ever claimed that Churchill was an upholder of 'spiritual values', whereas Baldwin and Trevelyan undoubtedly were.[44]

Contesting Macaulay's Legacy

Despite these growing divergencies, Churchill and Trevelyan continued to share a lifelong preoccupation with Macaulay, albeit in different ways and for different reasons. Churchill had first encountered him at Harrow, winning a prize for faultlessly reciting more than one thousand lines of Macaulay's *Lays of Ancient Rome*.[45] It was the beginning of a lifelong love-hate relationship. When seeking to fill some of the gaps in his education while a subaltern in India, Churchill had asked his mother to send him Gibbon's *Decline and Fall of the Roman Empire*, and Macaulay's *History of England* as well as volumes of his essays. They were essential works for anyone of Churchill's generation who wanted to be thought well-read, and Churchill later claimed that he was equally indebted to both authors.[46] To be sure, his family pride meant he was outraged at Macaulay's critical treatment of the great Duke of Marlborough and concluded that he was 'the prince of literary rogues'.[47] But Churchill was also captivated by the propulsive force and narrative velocity of Macaulay's prose. On the podium and on the page, both men were compulsive rhetoricians, with a shared and inborn sense of histrionics. Indeed, Churchill admitted to his mother that he sometimes yielded to 'the temptation of adapting my facts to my phrases'. Macaulay, he noted, was also 'an archoffender in this respect', and the same criticism was often levelled at Churchill throughout his political career.[48] Yet even in the final years of his peacetime premiership,

---

44 C, 155–8.

45 WSC, *Early Life*, 18; CV I, pt. i, 166, 170.

46 WSC, *Early Life*, 111–12, 211; CV I, pt. ii, 715, 724, 726, 733–4, 895; Roland Quinault, 'Winston Churchill and Gibbon', in Rosamond McKitterick and Roland Quinault (eds), *Edward Gibbon and Empire* (Cambridge, 1997), 317–332; Richard C. Marsh, *Churchill and Macaulay* (Ann Arbor, 2014).

47 WSC, *Early Life*, 112.

48 CV I, pt. ii, 933; David Cannadine, *In Churchill's Shadow: Confronting the Past in Modern Britain* (London, 2002), 94-95; John Clive, *Not by Fact Alone: Essays on the Reading and Writing of History* (New York, 1989), 73.

Henry Channon could also marvel at the skill with which Churchill could 'pour out' his 'Macaulay-like phrases' at the dispatch box to 'sublime effect'.[49]

So far as Gibbon was concerned, while Churchill learned prudent lessons from him about preventing great-power decay and avoiding imperial dissolution, he preferred Macaulay's exuberantly patriotic celebration of Britain's global greatness. To be sure, Macaulay was sometimes critical of those who had acquired Britain's imperial possessions, notably demonstrated in his critical essay on Warren Hastings. But he greatly admired the Earl of Chatham and generally approved of the Empire's 'civilizing mission'.[50] Indeed, Macaulay had played his own part in what he believed to be that ennobling enterprise during his time in India, and so, later, did Churchill, on the North-West Frontier, in the Sudan and in South Africa. Like Macaulay, Churchill occasionally expressed doubts about those entrusted with bearing Britain's imperial responsibilities, as in his condemnation of General Dwyer in the aftermath of the Amritsar 'Massacre' of 1919; but for the most part he remained a fervent believer in the justness and rightness of the British Empire throughout his life.[51] Indeed, Macaulay may well have been the author who had the greatest influence on Churchill and his continuing – if controversial – presence eventually loomed large in his fluctuating relations with Trevelyan.[52]

For Trevelyan, Macaulay was as much his family's ultimate hero as the great Duke of Marlborough was for Churchill. He had devoured the *History* and his father's biography long before he entered Harrow, and re-reading those canonical works remained an annual ritual. As a Trinity undergraduate, he walked past his great uncle's statue in the chapel, and one of the reasons he left Cambridge in 1903 was that he deplored the widespread hostility to Macaulay then in vogue in 'scientific' scholarly circles, exemplified by Sir John Seeley's view that his great uncle was 'a charlatan' – an insult Trevelyan neither forgave nor forgot.[53] All his life, he relished the genius of Macaulay's gifts: his stupendous learning, his incomparable prose, and the rich and varied career experience he brought to bear on his writings. He was often, Trevelyan believed, more fair-minded than his detractors asserted, and he was the first real social

[49] Simon Heffer (ed.), *Henry 'Chips' Channon: The Diaries, 1943–57* (London, 2022), 746, 916.

[50] Thomas Babington Macaulay, *Warren Hastings* (London, 1893 edn), 9–10, 18–19, 25–31; Edward Adams, *Liberal Epic: The Victorian Practice of History from Gibbon to Churchill* (Charlottesville, 2011), 260, 274–81.

[51] Jonathan Rose, *The Literary Churchill: Author, Reader, Actor* (London, 2014), 33, 61, 145, 166, 216–17, 222, 418.

[52] Lord Moran, *Churchill: The Struggle for Survival, 1940–1965* (London, 1966), 302, 320, 526.

[53] Chadwick, *Freedom*, 22.

176 David Cannadine

historian, who was as interested in the lives of ordinary people as in those of the high and mighty, as exemplified in the famous panoramic survey that formed the third chapter of his *History*. In writing about the past in ways that were both scholarly and accessible, Macaulay had made history an integral part of the public culture of Victorian England, and it was for the same purpose and audience that Trevelyan felt called to write in his own generation.[54]

Yet Trevelyan's relation with Macaulay was not uncritically admiring. In private and occasionally in public he admitted his great-uncle's faults. He was 'biassed, pugnacious, often impatient', he possessed an 'inherent over-certainty of temper, flattered by the easy victories of his youth', and his 'prejudices and his mistakes' were correspondingly glaring: his lack of training in rigorous methods of historical research, his eagerly mistaken deductions from the evidence, and his weakness in understanding human motivation. Although it was sometimes alleged that Trevelyan wrote his own books as if he had 'a bust of Lord Macaulay upon his desk', he soon gave up the jaunty exuberance that had characterised his first publication, *England in the Age of Wycliffe* (1899). Thereafter, he sought to make his prose more 'chaste' and 'poetic', and his mature style in his later books, which was often more elegiac and melancholy, bore little sign of Macaulay's incorrigible buoyancy.[55] Furthermore, unlike Macaulay (and unlike Churchill), Trevelyan was deeply sceptical of the British Empire and its 'civilizing mission'. He had opposed the Boer War, and he regretted that Britain had 'over a long period of time effected the violent seizure of an enormous portion of the globe'. And having lived through the horrors and traumas of the First and Second World Wars, he was unable to share Macaulay's nineteenth-century faith in the ever-onward march of progress.[56]

Marlborough Denounced and Defended

Although Macaulay's influence on Churchill and Trevelyan had begun early in their lives, it was at its peak during the 1930s, when Trevelyan published *England Under Queen Anne* in three volumes (1930–4) and Churchill his life of the Duke of Marlborough in four (1933–8). Both literary enterprises were acts of dynastic piety and represented the fulfilment of long-cherished personal ambitions. For many years, Trevelyan had considered writing a sequel to Macaulay's *History*, which had ended abruptly and unfinished on his death, having only reached the demise of William III in 1702. Once he had completed his own panoramic *History of England*, Trevelyan resolved to write a more detailed narrative, beginning where Macaulay had perforce left off, and this also seemed an

[54] C, 26–8.
[55] R, 64, 68.
[56] R, 54; C, 91.

Winston Churchill and G.M. Trevelyan Revisited 177

appropriately ambitious project once he returned to Cambridge.[57] Likewise, Churchill had been repeatedly invited to write the biography of the great Duke from the late 1890s onwards, and out of office with the Conservative defeat at the general election of 1929, he finally turned his attention to it, being allowed exclusive access to the Blenheim archives.[58] As a result, Churchill and Trevelyan found themselves competing in their family veneration, dynastic piety and ancestor worship, as they both engaged with Macaulay's earlier critiques of the great (or not so great) Duke.

Trevelyan published his first volume in 1930 and it was widely read and admired. 'I have just finished... *Blenheim*', Clementine Churchill wrote to her son Randolph, 'which I could not get on with at first, but when I got into the swing I wanted to go on and it suddenly stopped after Blenheim, just when I wanted to know what happened next'. Winston in turn urged the book's claims on Stanley Baldwin, believing it to be 'admirable'; and Ramsay MacDonald also read it.[59] One reason Churchill may have liked the book was that Trevelyan freely admitted the limitations of Macaulay's portrayal of Marlborough. He conceded that his great-uncle had adopted his 'unfavourable reading' of the Duke's 'motives and character' from the contemporary polemics of Swift and other Tory pamphleteers, and that his 'own over-confident, lucid mentality', meant he 'always saw things in black and white, but never in grey'. Trevelyan's Marlborough was very different from the treacherous, ambitious and avaricious figure that Macaulay had depicted and disliked. His undeniable conspiracies against James II 'saved England from the horrors of [another] civil war', and he was devoted to 'the liberties of England and the protestant religion'. His 'ambition saved his country and Europe' from domination by the France of Louis XIV, and for 'every guinea that his avarice drew from England, he gave back the value of a thousand'. He was an uxorious husband, and his soldiers loved him 'because he cared for their wants and led them to victory'. He was also 'patient, courteous, persuasive [and] humane', and as 'one of the first born of the Age of Reason', he was 'the armed champion of toleration and good sense'.[60]

Churchill did not get to *Marlborough* in a serious way until the early 1930s, since he had many other literary obligations to discharge (and for which he needed the money): two late instalments of *The World Crisis*, on *The Aftermath* (1929) and *The Eastern Front* (1931), as well as his beguiling autobiography, *My*

---

[57] GMT, *Autobiography*, 46.

[58] CV 1, pt. ii, 930.

[59] CV V, pt. ii, 145, 186, 200.

[60] GMT, *England Under Queen Anne*, vol. 1, *Blenheim* (London, 1930), 188–93; C, 116–17.

Early Life (1930) and a collection of essays, *Thoughts and Adventures* (1932).[61] But Trevelyan was eager for Churchill to get on with writing about the great Duke. 'I have always been very fond of all your books', he wrote in October 1930, on receiving a copy of *My Early Life*, 'as my father was of your life of yours'. He thought it Churchill's 'best book, at least I am enjoying it most of all'. And now, he continued, 'for the Great Duke! I can't tell you how much I am looking forward to it'. A year later, Trevelyan remained 'deeply interested to get authentic information' as to 'how *Marlborough* progresses', and he looked forward to 'seeing what you make of your great ancestor', in what Churchill was then projecting as being a two-volume work. And having recently acquired a 'letter which Lord Churchill [as Marlborough then was] had written to William of Orange on August 4 1688... offering his services for the coming revolution', Trevelyan allowed Churchill to quote and reproduce this correspondence in facsimile in his inaugural instalment.[62]

In summer 1929 Churchill had hired a young Oxford history graduate, Maurice Ashley, to undertake archival researches at Blenheim and elsewhere while he got on with his other books. By the first half of 1933, Churchill was finalising his first volume of *Marlborough*, and began the secondary reading on a period of English history with which he was unfamiliar.[63] He also corresponded with Trevelyan about some of the documents Ashley had unearthed. One of them, which he had discovered in the Royal Archives, suggested that the alleged *Memoirs* of James II, which had been used by Macaulay to discredit Marlborough, were in fact a forgery. Another was a copy of what was known as the Carmaret Bay letter, preserved in the Nairne papers in the Bodleian. Written in 1694, allegedly by Marlborough, it betrayed to the French the English plans for an attack on the port of Brest. But it seemed highly likely it was also a forgery. Churchill believed these documents showed conclusively that Macaulay was mistaken in relying on such tainted and hostile sources, although Trevelyan was more circumspect about Churchill's view of James II's *Memoirs*.[64]

In light of their cordial and collaborative correspondence, and of his own admission in *Blenheim* that Macaulay had been seriously at fault in his treatment of Marlborough, Trevelyan must have been taken aback by the ferocity of Churchill's unrelenting attacks on his great-uncle throughout his first volume, pursuing his quarry with an obsessional vengefulness in his determination to demonstrate that 'Truth' would 'fasten the label "Liar" to [Macaulay's]

---

[61] Clarke, *Churchill's Profession*, 138–44.

[62] CHAR 8/321, WSC to GMT, 19, 21 Apr. 1933; GMT to WSC, 21 Apr. 1933; CV V, pt. ii, 207, 513, 580; *M*, 272, and facsimile opposite.

[63] Clarke, *Churchill's Profession*, 159–60.

[64] CHAR 8/321, GMT to WSC, 16, 22, 29 Jan. 1933; WSC to GMT, 19 Jan. 1933; CV V, pt. ii, 514–15, 519–20.

Winston Churchill and G.M. Trevelyan Revisited   179

genteel coat-tails'. 'Our task', Churchill insisted, with all the righteous ardour of a prosecuting counsel, 'is to repel erroneous or exaggerated criticism, to separate censure from cant, to strip prejudice of its malignity, and to unmask imposture.'[65] In practice, this meant he repeatedly berated Macaulay with even greater zeal than Macaulay had criticised Marlborough: for his 'prejudice, bias and deliberate malice', for his 'pungent rhetoric and elaborate scorn', for his 'nimble, sharp, unscrupulous pen', for 'deliberately falsifying facts', for his 'libels and embroideries' and his 'many untruths', for twist[ing] history and reality to [Marlborough's] condemnation', for depicting the great Duke as 'odious' and a 'villain' by 'insulting' and 'blackening' his memory, and for creating a 'vast structure of calumny and distortion which has hitherto served as history'.[66] This was rhetorical overkill. Unsurprisingly, in thanking Trevelyan in the preface to his first volume, Churchill conceded that he 'may think some sentences I have written about Macaulay a poor return for his own historical reparations.'[67]

Trevelyan declined to review Churchill's initial instalment, but responded to it in a lengthy letter to the *Times Literary Supplement*, later reprinted in the final volume of *England Under Queen Anne*.[68] He began by expressing his 'great admiration' for 'the book as a whole and my earnest hope for its popularity and success', and his agreement with Churchill's 'general view both of the domestic and foreign questions of the time and of Marlborough's character'. He again admitted that 'Macaulay was wrong in his reading of Marlborough', and that this was 'the worst thing in his *History*', and he understood that 'Mr Churchill's family piety has aroused him to take revenge'. But Trevelyan also noted that for all his bluster, Churchill had coyly accepted most of Macaulay's facts: that Marlborough's patron was the man who kept his sister; that he took money from his mistress and invested it well; that he deserted James II when in his military service; that he did subsequently correspond with the Jacobites; and that 'many people in his own day thought ill of him'. Only in the case of the Camaret Bay letter did he accept that Churchill had overturned what Macaulay had written about Marlborough's alleged betrayal, and he undertook to make some modifications to *Blenheim* when it was reprinted. But as he pointed out, 'an historian who, before the days of our modern research, was deceived by these phenomena into thinking Marlborough a bad man was not necessarily dishonest'. Accordingly, Trevelyan urged that Churchill 'had no right' to call

---

[65] *M*, 146, 365; Ashley, *Churchill as Historian*, 138–42.

[66] *M*, 53, 64–5, 99, 143–44, 224 n. 1, 306, 363, 402, 427–8, 449–50; Clarke, *Churchill's Profession*, 163–5.

[67] *M*, 8.

[68] CHAR 8/323, GMT to WSC, 16 July 1933; WSC to GMT, 19 July 1933.

Macaulay a 'liar', since 'a 'liar' is a man who makes a statement that he knows to be false'.[69]

Churchill did not respond to Trevelyan's letter, while Trevelyan generously urged that 'our relations over this matter are perfectly open and friendly and will remain so'. Thereafter, their correspondence continued more easily, as Churchill moved on from Marlborough's controversial rise to power to his later military triumphs, about which Macaulay had not written. 'If you say', Trevelyan told Churchill at the end of 1933, 'you find it hard work to catch up and correct in the public mind so popular a writer as Macaulay, I am in the same difficulty in relation to you. Each of us has his ancestor's reputation to safeguard'.[70] Trevelyan read the proofs of Churchill's remaining three volumes, offering corrections, even as he vainly urged him not to print so many documents or to go on at a much greater length than he had originally intended. To be sure, his 'Marlborough must be the definitive life', but 'four vols', Trevelyan told Churchill, would make 'a very long book for folk to read in days to come'. But while Churchill proved incapable of taking this wise advice, and further delayed the completion of *Marlborough* by taking time out to produce *Great Contemporaries* (1937), he did pay tribute, in the preface to the third instalment, to 'the illuminating and impartial work of Professor Trevelyan'.[71] For his part, Trevelyan regarded volume two as 'a masterly work', not least because it was less 'necessarily apologetic' (i.e. polemical) than its predecessor; while he third instalment was 'the best volume so far'. As for the fourth: 'I most heartily congratulate you on the completion of this great work, a monument *aere perennius* both to yourself and to your glorious ancestor'.[72]

Despite the sustained and excessive outrage that Churchill had vented in his first volume, there was little real difference between what he and Trevelyan thought about Macaulay and about Marlborough. Macaulay, they both agreed, was often wrong about the great Duke, but some of his critiques were valid; and Marlborough, they both conceded, was neither unblemished saint nor

---

[69]   GMT, letter in the *TLS*, 19 Oct. 1933, repr. in GMT, *England Under Queen Anne*, vol. 3, *The Peace and the Protestant Succession* (London, 1934), 10–13. GMT's letter to the *TLS* was a distillation of several missives he had written to WSC: CHAR 8/324, GMT to WSC, 20, 27 Sept. 1933; 8, 17 Oct. 1933. For GMT's later modifications to *Blenheim*, see CHAR 8/504, GMT to WSC, 16 July 1935; WSC to GMT, 18 July 1935.

[70]   CHAR 8/324, GMT to WSC, 8 Oct. 1933; CHAR 8/325, GMT to WSC, 12 Dec. 1933; Ashley, *Churchill as Historian*, 143; Clarke, *Churchill's Profession*, 175.

[71]   CHAR 8/325, GMT to WSC, 30 Dec. 1933; CHAR 8/486 A–B, GMT to WSC, 31 July 1934, 5, 6 Aug. 1934; WSC to GMT, 7 Aug. 1934, 24 Sept. 1934; CHAR 8/530 A–B, WSC to GMT, 1, 19, 21 Aug. 1936; WSC to GMT, 21, 22, 29 Aug. 1936; CHAR 8/595, WSC to GMT, 15, 19, 26 Feb. 1938; Clarke, *Churchill's Profession*, 177–80, 187–9, 192–3.

[72]   CHAR 8/486 A–B, GMT to WSC, 5 Aug. 1934; CHAR 8/530 A–B, GMT to WSC 25 Aug. 1936.

incorrigible villain. And in different but equally significant ways, Trevelyan and Churchill both paid homage to Macaulay. In the first volume of *England Under Queen Anne*, Trevelyan provided a social panorama clearly modelled on the famous third chapter of Macaulay's *History*, and in the second volume, he furnished a similar account of early eighteenth-century Scotland.[73] Churchill was not interested in social history, but in *Marlborough*, as George Bernard Shaw pointed out, his prose sometimes read like a parody of Macaulay at his most histrionic, as in his floridly unforgiving portrait of Louis XIV, as 'the curse and pest of Europe', who 'disturbed and harried mankind during more than fifty years of arrogant pomp'.[74] Yet there was a further Churchillian indebtedness, albeit an ironic one. In the first volume of *Marlborough* he had denounced Macaulay for 'twisting' the evidence to align with his polemical purposes. But as he admitted to his research assistant, he approached his own task along identical lines. 'Give me the facts, Ashley', he once exclaimed, 'and I will twist them the way I want to suit my argument'.[75] For Churchill as for Macaulay, rhetoric often trumped reality.

Sir Edward Grey Rehabilitated

By 1934, Trevelyan had finished *England Under Queen Anne*, although Churchill had barely got started on *Marlborough*. Their subsequent correspondence on Macaulay and the great Duke remained current business for Churchill, but Trevelyan moved on to write the life of Sir Edward Grey, later Viscount Grey of Fallodon, who had died in 1933. Grey had been a long-serving Foreign Secretary in the Liberal governments of 1905–16, although neither Charles nor George Trevelyan had warmed to him then, regretting his earlier enthusiasm for the Boer War as a 'Liberal Imperialist' as well as the alliance he later negotiated with Tsarist Russia; and they had also feared he had made secret diplomatic and military agreements with France. But by the early 1920s, Edward Grey and George Trevelyan had become close friends. Like the Trevelyans, Grey was a Northumberland landowner; the Lord Grey who had steered through the Great Reform Act in 1832 was a kinsman, and Trevelyan had earlier written his biography.[76] Trevelyan and Grey of Fallodon shared a liking for the 'spiritual values' of country life and a loathing for the corruption that had become associated with Lloyd George after the war. Both were staunch supporters of the National Trust, and when Grey was installed as Chancellor of Oxford

---

[73] GMT, *Blenheim*, chs 1–4; *England Under Queen Anne*, vol. 2, *Ramillies and the Union with Scotland* (London, 1932), chs 10, 11.

[74] *M*, 258; Rhodes James, *Churchill*, 343; Clarke, *Churchill's Profession*, 173–4.

[75] Ashley, *Churchill as Historian*, 18; Clarke, *Churchill's Profession*, 168.

[76] C, 162; GMT, *Lord Grey*.

182   *David Cannadine*

University in 1929, Trevelyan was among those whom he nominated to receive an honorary degree. On Grey's death, his family invited Trevelyan to write his life – a venture into contemporary history and recent biography that he admitted was a 'new sort of thing' for him to do.[77]

Just as Churchill had sought to acquit Marlborough of the criticisms of Macaulay, so Trevelyan undertook Grey's biography to defend him from the sustained attacks Lloyd George had mounted in the *War Memoirs* he had begun publishing in 1933, where he denounced Grey as 'a calamitous Foreign Secretary, both before and during the war.'[78] 'It is a pleasure to all Grey's friends,' Lord Crewe wrote to Trevelyan in June 1935, 'to know that you are undertaking the book.' Recanting his earlier opinions, Trevelyan set out to show that, *pace* Lloyd George, Grey was better travelled than some critics had alleged, that he was zealous in his devotion to public duty, that he had not practised secret diplomacy, that he had sought to prevent war in 1914 rather than bring it about, that he was not to blame for the later failure of the allies to unite the Balkan nations on the side of the entente, and that he did not mishandle relations between the Russians and the Greeks. In demonstrating the inaccuracies and exaggerations of Lloyd George's recollections, Trevelyan sustained his criticisms less aggressively than Churchill had displayed in his pursuit of Macaulay. But he did allow himself two direct thrusts. 'Mr Lloyd George's great gifts,' he wrote of his account of events leading to the outbreak of war, 'are not strictly historical. He lives so keenly in the present that he cannot recall his own past'; and on another occasion he dismissed Lloyd George's biased recollections as being 'unworthy of the great part he has played in the world's affairs.'[79]

In addition to drawing on official documents and Grey's private papers, Trevelyan sought out the written recollections of those who had worked with Grey and thought well of him, some of which he reproduced at length in his biography. Among the people he contacted were Lord Crewe, Lord (Robert) Cecil – and Winston Churchill. In a letter of December 1934, Trevelyan noted that Churchill had published some of his letters to Grey in the early volumes of *The World Crisis*. 'Have you,' he asked, 'any of his to you that you would let me use?' He also wondered whether Churchill might be 'inclined to write me a couple of paragraphs or so... about him as a man and a statesman.'[80] In his reply, Churchill was 'delighted' to learn that Trevelyan had taken on the task.

---

[77]   C, 162.

[78]   David Lloyd George, *War Memoirs*: vol. 1, *1914–1915* (Boston, 1933), 53, 84–9; vol. 2, *1915–1916* (Boston, 1933), 133–9, 279–85, 298–9, 312; vol. 3, *1916–1917* (Boston, 1934), 31–2; T.G. Otte, *Statesman of Europe: A Life of Sir Edward Grey* (London, 2020), xxiv–xxv, 676–8.

[79]   GMT, *Grey of Fallodon* (London, 1937), 255, 257.

[80]   CHAR 2/234/4, GMT to WSC, 30 Dec. 1934.

Winston Churchill and G.M. Trevelyan Revisited 183

But, he continued, although he had 'a good many letters of Grey's', he did not think they would be of 'great consequence' for Trevelyan's biography. In any case, he possessed 'about forty boxes of papers and letters covering the pre-war period', and it would be 'practically impossible' for him to 'look them all through in this connection', although he might be willing to find any particular letter.[81] In fact, as it turned out the only substantive assistance Churchill gave was in response to Trevelyan's request to help date a photograph of Grey, his wife, Lord Haldane and Churchill himself, which he believed had probably been taken sometime between 1902 and 1904, but which Trevelyan reproduced dating it in 1901.[82]

Appeasement, War and Aftermath

The publication of *Grey of Fallodon* (1937) and the last volume of *Marlborough* (1938) signified the end of this detailed exchange between Churchill and Trevelyan. But it formed only a small part of Churchill's much larger Marlborough correspondence. For the first volume, he sent and received more than seven hundred letters in 1933 alone, including exchanges with such eminent scholars as Keith Feiling and Lewis Namier.[83] With historians as with hotels, Churchill was easily pleased with the best. The Churchill-Trevelyan letters were also noteworthy because of what they did *not* discuss. The 1930s were full of momentous events and ominous developments, but there was scarcely any mention of them in a correspondence that focused almost exclusively on history, Macaulay, Marlborough and latterly Edward Grey. Domestic politics scarcely intruded, and international politics not at all. Churchill once made the double-edged observation that 'most of the Tories of the present day seem uncommonly like their predecessors', and when Trevelyan suggested Churchill might follow *Marlborough* with a biography of Napoleon, 'in two volumes (no more)', he recognised it would only be possible 'if you are not back in office at some call of England's' – an outcome to which, in the light of his doubts about Churchill's judgment, he can scarcely have looked forward.[84]

For most of the 1930s, Churchill was an isolated and distrusted figure in public life. He had few friends in politics during his 'wilderness years', apart from Brendan Bracken and Robert Boothby, both of whom were deeply suspect and widely disliked, and although the non-political letters he exchanged with Baldwin, MacDonald and Chamberlain were affable when he sent them copies

---

[81] CHAR 2/234/2–3: WSC to GMT, 3 Jan. 1935.

[82] CHAR 2/258/6–7: GMT to WSC, 5 Sept. 1936; CHAR 2/258/23: WSC to GMT, 18 Sept. 1936. The image is printed in GMT, *Grey of Fallodon*, opposite 82.

[83] CV V, pt. ii, 515, 521; Clarke, *Churchill's Profession*, 126–7, 172–3.

[84] CV V, pt. ii, 784, 910, 917, 1153.

of his latest books, they deliberately and determinedly kept him out of successive National Governments. Churchill also lacked friends in the Commons: Conservatives and Liberals did not forgive his apostasy, and Labour MPs remembered his belligerent stand during the General Strike, denouncing him as a class warrior. His lengthy campaign against what eventually became the Government of India Act of 1935, his mistaken support for King Edward VIII, and his attacks on the policy of appeasing Nazi Germany aroused little popular support in the country and were widely regarded in political circles as further evidence that Churchill's judgment was incorrigibly faulty. *Pace* Sir John Plumb, this was also Trevelyan's view. As he wrote to his daughter Mary in the aftermath of Munich: 'I believe Churchill to be wrong again – as he was over India [and] the king business... He is always striking with immense emphasis the wrong nail on the head... And in military terms, he is always thinking wrong.'[85]

Whereas Churchill was politically isolated and apparently backing hopeless causes, Trevelyan had very good links to the National Government, of which he was a 'firm supporter'. He admired Sir John Simon, Foreign Secretary from 1931 to 1935, and Lord Halifax (holder of the same office, 1938–40), and he was especially close to his fellow Northumbrian and Trinity man, Walter Runciman. When he had been chosen by Asquith as President of the Board of Education in 1908, Runciman had engineered the appointment of Charles Trevelyan as his deputy. In 1931, he was brought back into the National Government, to Trevelyan's great delight, and in 1938 he was sent to Prague as an 'independent mediator' between the Czechoslovak Government and the Sudeten German Party.[86] In addition to being a friend and admirer of Stanley Baldwin's, Trevelyan was also a great believer in his successor. As he wrote to his brother Bob in October 1938, in the aftermath of Munich, 'Janet and I are Chamberlainites', and as he told Mary the same month, he was 'more grateful to Neville than to any other statesman in my lifetime.'[87]

Trevelyan's favourable view of Chamberlain and his colleagues was fully reciprocated, since *Grey of Fallodon* became one of the key texts for many members of the National Government, as Trevelyan's vindication of Grey's conduct between 1906 and 1914 was taken as providing historical validation for the policy that Baldwin and Chamberlain had been pursuing since 1935. According to Trevelyan, Grey had sought to maintain European peace by high-mindedly appeasing Germany; he had tried to ensure, if that policy failed, that Britain could count on continental allies, especially France; and he had been no less determined to carry a united nation into war against Germany if that ultimate

[85] C, 133–4.
[86] C, 132–3.
[87] R, 123; C, 134.

catastrophe could not be averted. During the late 1930s, this was once again government policy, and as Oliver Harvey (a junior official at the Foreign Office), Sir Nevile Henderson (British Ambassador in Berlin), and Anthony Eden (briefly Foreign Secretary) considered the similarities between their own difficulties in dealing with Germany and those Grey had faced a generation earlier, it was Trevelyan's book that enabled them to ponder these resemblances and affinities. There was also a further connection that could be drawn, for as another north country landowner, upholder of 'spiritual values', Chancellor of Oxford University and appeaser of Germany, Lord Halifax seemed to be Grey's natural successor in public life.[88] In 1938, Halifax succeeded Eden as Foreign Secretary, and early the following year, Trevelyan corresponded with him, still convinced that the Munich settlement had been right, but increasingly reconciling himself to the dismaying possibility that there might, alas, be another conflict with Germany after all.[89]

When that war finally came, Trevelyan felt obliged to recant his earlier views – at least to some extent. 'I don't think the Allies is the cause of God', he told Mary in March 1940. 'But I fear the other side is the side of the Devil.' Soon after, he admitted to his brother Charles that 'the late government and Baldwin's government have let us all down shockingly over re-armament... We have all been great fools'. He made the same point later that year to Eddie Marsh, a long-serving assistant to Churchill both inside and outside government. 'You may certainly take credit for your belief in *him* all along', Trevelyan told him. 'The country has for very good reason come round to your view.' In September 1940, Churchill appointed Trevelyan Master of Trinity, perhaps in part a belated gesture of magnanimity, if not to Macaulay then at least to his great-nephew. Later in the war, Trevelyan reaffirmed that 'Baldwin and Chamberlain and the 'appeasers', including to a considerable extent *ourselves*' had been wrong, while 'dire events' 'had... proved Winston right'.[90] But like many people who claimed to be in the know, he had not initially warmed to Churchill's appointment in May 1940. 'I have', he had told Mary, 'grave fears about him, but Halifax and Chamberlain may be able to look after him.' Although he recognised that he was 'a great parliamentarian', Trevelyan feared that 'lapses of taste are an essential part of Churchill, the price we pay for him'. He thought the prime minister's 'optimism' was 'subjective and temperamental', especially regarding the bombing of Germany, which he detested, and in late 1944, he was sure that Churchill was wrong over Greece, and that 'his obstinacy' was 'sometimes a blessing', but 'sometimes the reverse'.[91]

[88] C, 166–7.
[89] Cannadine, *Churchill's Shadow*, 194–8.
[90] R, 130, 194; C, 134–6.
[91] R, 149; C, 136.

186   *David Cannadine*

By spring 1945, Trevelyan had come to share the growing belief that Churchill had been a great wartime leader but that he was not the man to deal with the impending peace. He disliked the 'belligerent' tone of his first election broadcast, when Churchill predicted that a Labour victory would soon result in the country being overseen by 'some kind of gestapo', and he doubted that the Conservatives would benefit from the widespread feeling of 'excited gratitude' to the man who had won the war.[92] They did not, and Trevelyan accepted the voters' rejection of Churchill and Labour's landslide victory with a mixture of equanimity and enthusiasm. 'I like the result of the election', he told Bob: he did not see how 'a purely Conservative government could in the present conditions have turned out well', whereas the Labour leaders 'have now had some very realistic experience in government which they so sorely lacked before 1940'.[93] He hoped they would nationalise the mines, give independence to India and do something for the protection of the English countryside. They did all three, and in the case of the countryside, the major impetus came from Hugh Dalton, who had been a political protégé of Charles's during the interwar years, and whom Trevelyan much admired, since he had 'the right ideas and sympathies about the preservation of amenities'.[94]

The Labour government, Trevelyan believed, had done as well as it could in the difficult circumstances of austerity, and during what he feared was the broader decline of European civilisation brought about by the two world wars.[95] But he did not think Churchill would be more effective than Attlee and his colleagues. 'I doubt', he wrote to J.L. and Barbara Hammond in 1947, 'if Winston will make it any better if he gets in again.' Later that year, Baldwin died. Although Trevelyan had in retrospect become critical of Baldwin's handling of foreign affairs, he retained great affection for him. 'In a world of voluble hates', he observed at the first Trinity Commemoration held after Baldwin's death, 'he plotted to make men like, or at least tolerate, each other. Therein he had much success, within the shores of this island' – although not, he clearly implied, elsewhere in Europe. Trevelyan insisted that Baldwin remained 'the most lovable of prime ministers' – a verdict with which it seems unlikely Churchill would have agreed. 'It would have been much better', the latter had remarked earlier the same year, if Baldwin 'had never lived'. 'The candle in that great turnip has gone out', he opined on another occasion.[96] Trevelyan also remained in some ways an unrepentant Chamberlainite and man of Munich.

[92]   C, 136.

[93]   R, 150.

[94]   C, 176.

[95]   GMT, *Autobiography*, 49.

[96]   C, 161; Martin Gilbert, *In Search of Churchill* (London, 1994), 105–6; Nigel Nicolson (ed.), *Harold Nicolson, Diaries and Letters, 1945–1962* (London, 1968), 193;

In 1952, Viscount (previously Sir John) Simon published his autobiography, where he mounted a determined defence of the foreign policy of the National Governments. Trevelyan conceded that he had been 'perhaps a little too inclined to 'appeasement', but he 'certainly agreed' with Simon about Munich and found his own 'political opinions singularly like yours'.[97]

Yet Trevelyan also recognised that by 1945 Churchill had become a unique figure of world-historical renown, having seen off Hitler and Mussolini and outlived Roosevelt, and he was willing to acquiesce in this late-life apotheosis. He urged Lord Moran, Churchill's doctor, to keep a diary, since posterity would want to know as much as possible about him.[98] In 1946, Trevelyan presented Churchill with the original autograph letter of 1688 that he had allowed him to use as an illustration in the first volume of *Marlborough*, 'as a token of my personal gratitude to you for what you did for us in the war'.[99] He also told Churchill that 'Macaulay and you have much the same merits of style and composition as historians', adding rather archly, 'we will leave all the demerits to Macaulay!'[100] When he published his brief *Autobiography* in 1948, Trevelyan noted that *England Under Queen Anne* had been the 'chief historical work of my life', but that 'the two later volumes' had only enjoyed 'a fair sale', since Churchill's *Marlborough* 'no doubt competed' and 'of course, everyone wanted to read Winston'.[101] In April 1954, Churchill sent Trevelyan an autographed copy of *Triumph and Tragedy*, the final volume of his memoirs of the Second World War, and two years later, to mark Trevelyan's eightieth birthday, an appeal was launched in the columns of *The Times* from Cambridge to create a series of lectures in his honour. The letter described Trevelyan as 'one of our foremost national figures', who was, like Macaulay before him, 'the accredited interpreter to his age of the English past', and Trevelyan was 'honoured' that Churchill was among the signatories.[102]

Soon after, the diaries of Field Marshal Lord Alanbrooke were published, edited by Arthur Bryant, which recorded his often-stormy relations with Churchill when he was wartime Chief of the Imperial General Staff.[103] They

---

Philip Williamson, 'Baldwin's Reputation: Politics and History, 1937–1967', *Historical Journal*, 47 (2004), 141–5.

[97] C, 138.

[98] Moran, *Struggle*, xvi–xvii.

[99] C, 139; CV V, pt. ii, 513; CHUR 2/157 A–B: GMT to WSC, 13 May 1946, 2 July 1946; WSC to GMT, 3 July 1946.

[100] CHUR 2/1157A–B, GMT to WSC, 27 May 1946.

[101] GMT, *Autobiography*, 46.

[102] CHUR 2/536, GMT to 'the Prime Minister's Secretary', 26 Apr. 1954.

[103] Arthur Bryant (ed.), *The Turn of the Tide, 1939–1943* and *Triumph in the West, 1943–1946* (London, 1957–9).

were disapproved of by those to whom Churchill was by then an Olympian hero beyond criticism, but Trevelyan saw them differently. 'So far from lowering my estimate of Winston', he wrote to Bryant, 'the book, to me, has raised it.' Churchill was not, Trevelyan admitted, 'very considerate to his advisors', but he did ask for advice, 'and very often took it, sometimes contrary to what he had first thought himself.' This 'habit of taking counsel', he went on, 'combined with his own personal qualities, is what won the war'.[104] He also welcomed the appearance of the *History of the English-Speaking Peoples*, for the final revisions of which Churchill had re-read Trevelyan's *History of England*. The time would come, he told Churchill, when the public would 'stop reading us professional historians, but not you'. In 1961, Churchill and Trevelyan were among the first cohort of writers to be named Companions of Literature by the Royal Society of Literature.[105] When Trevelyan celebrated his eighty-sixth birthday in February the following year, Winston and Clementine sent him their congratulations and good wishes. 'A personal message from you', Trevelyan replied, 'is the greatest honour that an Englishman can receive on his birthday. I am deeply grateful for it.'[106] He died soon after, and Churchill followed in January 1965.

* * *

Such were the fluctuating contours of their longstanding relationship, as two New Liberals morphed into two old men, sometimes together, at other times, not. Beyond doubt, Churchill and Trevelyan 'knew' each other from the early 1900s to the early 1960s, but while they had both been well-born, it had been at different levels of Britain's complex social hierarchy. They both took pride in their ancestors, though Trevelyan was more critical of Macaulay than Churchill was of Marlborough. Churchill had changed parties to embrace Liberalism, whereas Trevelyan had inherited that creed from his father. They both became Conservatives during the interwar years, although Trevelyan was a more uncritical and comfortable Baldwinite than Churchill. While Trevelyan came round to Churchill in 1940 and was willing to join in the chorus of his late-life acclaim, he was never wholly reconciled, and he was more at ease with Labour after 1945. And although they met socially before the First World War, they do not seem to have done so thereafter: Churchill did not invite Trevelyan to Chartwell, and Trevelyan did not ask Churchill to Cambridge. Their passionate devotion to the past, and their shared belief that history was a vital component of national life and public culture helps explain their busy exchange of letters during the 1930s. But it was prompted by a coincidental convergence

[104] C, 139.
[105] C, 18, 139.
[106] CHUR 2/536, GMT to WSC and Lady Churchill, 15 Feb. 1962.

of writing projects, involving contentious issues about their ancestors, rather than another episode in a long, deep and abiding friendship.

As major public figures, with extensive family connections, Churchill and Trevelyan naturally knew many important people, but Churchill was too egotistical and self-absorbed to make many real friends, while Trevelyan's inimitable combination of 'barking shyness' meant he could be intimidatingly difficult to get to know.[107] But there was at least one well-documented Trevelyan friendship that was much closer than his relations with Churchill, and that was with John Buchan. They both loved nature and landscape as well as history and literature, distrusted 'intellectuals' for being foolish and irresponsible, believed in the importance of 'decency' in public life, and preferred Baldwin to Lloyd George (or to Churchill).[108] They saw each other socially, sometimes holidayed together, and their extensive correspondence was warm and amicable in ways that the Churchill-Trevelyan exchanges were not. Trevelyan dedicated *Ramillies* to Buchan, as 'a pledge of 'Union' and Friendship', while Buchan dedicated his biography of Sir Walter Scott to Baldwin and Trevelyan. When Buchan died in 1940, Trevelyan told his widow he could not 'remember anyone whose death evoked a more enviable outburst of sorrow, love and admiration' (and he was similarly effusive on the passing of other close friends such as H.A.L. Fisher and Roger B. Merriman).[109] By agreeable coincidence, the best recent treatment of Buchan's thought and world outlook is by Jonathan Parry, and that fine essay has greatly influenced what I have written here.[110]

---

[107] *Making of an Historian*, 7.

[108] Stefan Collini, *Absent Minds: Intellectuals in Britain* (Oxford, 2006), 124–6.

[109] Adam Smith, *Buchan*, 239, 272, 292, 341, 356, 359, 471; C, 9, 38–45; Cannadine, *Churchill's Shadow*, 201.

[110] J.P. Parry, 'From the Thirty-Nine Articles to the Thirty-Nine Steps: Reflections on the Thought of John Buchan', in Michael Bentley (ed.), *Public and Private Doctrine: Essays in British History presented to Maurice Cowling* (Cambridge, 1993), 209–35.

Chapter 9

What Happened to Political Nonconformity?[1]

Philip Williamson

The 'decline of political nonconformity' is a commonplace in political and religious histories of early twentieth-century England and Wales. As well as being an important historical occurrence in itself, it is integral to explanations of the decline of the Liberal party and the strengthened position of the Church of England after 1918.[2] Political nonconformity – or, in another contemporary term, the 'nonconformist conscience' – certainly declined as an organised electoral and political force. What is less certain is when decline started, why it occurred, and what happened to the politics of the nonconformists. The decline has been located in the 1930s, with nonconformity as a whole 'crumbling away' under multiple social, theological and political pressures.[3] More commonly it is dated from the 1920s, with a secularisation or 'desacralisation' of party politics, or greater state provision of welfare, or the replacement of Liberals by the Labour party, or the damaging effects of economic depression for chapels and denominations.[4] For some historians, it began during the First World War, with the challenges this brought for nonconformist values, or with the split among

---

[1] The following abbreviations are used in the notes: *FCC* for *The Free Church Chronicle* (the monthly journal of the National Council of the Evangelical Free Churches, hereafter NCEFC), and *FCYB* for *The Free Church Year Book* (annual report of the NCEFC and proceedings of its annual assembly). For 1923–9, the *FCYB* volumes in the British Library, cited here, contain mixtures of typescript and printed texts.

[2] E.g., Trevor Wilson, *The Downfall of the Liberal Party, 1914–1935* (London, 1966), 25–7; Matthew Grimley, *Citizenship, Community and the Church of England: Liberal Anglican Theories of the State between the Wars* (Oxford, 2004), 10–17.

[3] Adrian Hastings, *A History of English Christianity, 1920–1990* (London, 1991), 264–72.

[4] S.J.D. Green, *The Passing of Protestant England: Secularisation and Social Change, c.1920–1960* (Cambridge, 2011), 33–60; Peter Catterall, 'Morality and Politics: The Free Churches and the Labour Party between the Wars', *Historical Journal*, 36 (1993), 670–4; Ross McKibbin, *Classes and Cultures: England 1918–1951* (Oxford, 1998), 281–4.

Liberal politicians.[5] Others date it from the mid-1900s, as nonconformists became disillusioned with the Liberal government's failure to overturn measures of the earlier Unionist government,[6] or even as early as the 1880s, with the removal of their civil disabilities and the disintegration of a mid-Victorian nonconformist cultural 'synthesis'.[7] A complication is a tendency to conflate two types of decline, in chapel adherence and in political influence. Depending on which of these is given priority, the outcome can be different kinds of explanation: either general economic, social, political or religious changes, or decisions taken by nonconformists themselves.

Although connections between the decline of political nonconformity and the decline of religious nonconformity are obvious, their trajectories were not identical. Until at least the 1940s, organized nonconformity retained a political significance even as attendance at the chapels of the Congregational, Baptist, Methodist, Presbyterian and other denominations fell in numbers. Nor were the declines in either political or religious nonconformity straightforward or steady. They certainly did not seem so to nonconformist leaders. A striking feature of many of their statements from the 1910s to the 1940s is confidence in the prospects for their churches and their representative bodies. They were aware of losses and problems, but also conscious of gains and opportunities.[8] The numbers of worshippers in their chapels recovered for a period during the 1920s, while concerns that these numbers remained below the rate of population increase generated ambitious evangelistic, 'forward' and 'discipleship' campaigns.[9] Despite this relative decline in chapel adherence, nonconform-

---

[5]   Alan Wilkinson, *Dissent or Conform? War, Peace and the English Churches 1900–1945* (London, 1986), 54–5, 57–8; Alan Ruston, 'Protestant Nonconformist Attitudes towards the First World War', in Alan Sell and Anthony Cross (eds), *Protestant Nonconformity in the Twentieth Century* (Carlisle, 2003), 240–63. The war years are also emphasised in Ross McKibbin, *Parties and People: England, 1914–1951* (Oxford, 2010), 23–4.

[6]   John F. Glaser, 'English Nonconformity and the Decline of Liberalism', *American Historical Review*, 63 (1958), 352–63; Stephen Koss, *Nonconformity in Modern British Politics* (1975), ch. 5; D.W. Bebbington, *The Nonconformist Conscience: Chapel and Politics, 1870–1914* (London, 1982), 157–60.

[7]   Richard Helmstadter, 'The Nonconformist Conscience', in Peter Marsh (ed.), *The Conscience of the Victorian State* (Hassocks, 1979), 135–72.

[8]   David M. Thompson, 'The Older Free Churches', in Rupert Davies (ed.), *The Testing of the Churches 1932–1982* (London, 1982), 87–8, is a rare recognition of this point. See e.g. *FCYB 1920*, 38, 46, and *The National Free Church Council Annual Report 1934–5*, 5–7.

[9]   Robert Currie, Alan Gilbert and Lee Horsley, *Churches and Churchgoers* (Oxford, 1977), 25, 34, 143, 150; *FCYB 1920*, 38–40; *FCC*, Apr. 1921, 44–5, June 1921, 54–5, Sept 1921, 69–70; statement by NCEFC and denominational leaders, *Manchester Guardian*,

ist leaders obtained new positions of prominence in national life. They also remained active in national politics, continuing to issue statements on public affairs and to make representations to party leaders and government ministers.

'Decline' does not adequately describe what happened to political nonconformity during the interwar years. This is especially so if it leads to all the actions of nonconformist leaders, including the creation of alliances and unions among the denominations, being explained only as symptoms of weakness or efforts to stem or manage decline.[10] A less procrustean explanation is needed, to accommodate the mixed experiences of the nonconformist churches. This would place them in a fuller ecclesiastical and political context, and allow for more agency, not just by nonconformists themselves but also by the state and by their erstwhile opponents. What happened to political nonconformity is inseparable from the actions of governments, the monarchy, the Church of England and the Conservative party.

The Character of Political Nonconformity

A long historical perspective is helpful. For historians of twentieth-century Britain, political nonconformity begins with the general nonconformist revulsion and a passive resistance campaign against the Unionist government's provision of state aid to Church of England and Roman Catholic schools by the Education Act of 1902. This was followed by the National Council of Evangelical Free Churches (NCEFC) arranging an election pact with the Liberal party, its impressive electoral mobilisation through its 800 local councils, and the increase to 157 of the number of nonconformist Liberal MPs at the 1906 general election, contributing to a huge parliamentary majority for the Liberal government.[11] In 1908 a well-informed American scholar treated the NCEFC, like the Church of England, as part of 'the government of England'.[12] From such a position, any decline would indeed seem to be dramatic. Is, though, the political nonconformity of 1902 to 1906 the best expression of its character, and a sufficient indicator of party allegiances among nonconformist voters?

---

2 Jan. 1936, 6; Henry Townsend, *Robert Wilson Black* (London, 1954), pp. 74–83; Ian M. Randall, *The English Baptists of the Twentieth Century* (Didcot, 2005), 164–9.

[10] E.g. Koss, *Nonconformity*, 138–9. Koss's book, the standard study of twentieth-century political nonconformity, is relentlessly 'declinist' for the period from 1906. Its emphasis is on parliamentary candidates and MPs, and was written before historical interests expanded to include political and associational culture.

[11] Koss, *Nonconformity*, 38–75; Bebbington, *Nonconformist Conscience*, 76–9, 141–52.

[12] A. Lawrence Lowell, *The Government of England* (2 vols, New York & London, 1908), vol. 2, 380–5.

For nineteenth-century historians, the great age of political nonconformity was from the 1840s to the 1870s. Its main aim was religious equality, in the sense of removal of the historic disabilities and exclusions imposed by the state's establishment of the Church of England. The effect was a radical political agenda, a challenge to existing institutions and even at times to its obvious parliamentary allies, the Whig and Liberal parties. But as Jonathan Parry has argued, this radical nonconformity was contained by the pressures and conventions of party politics, as well as by the pragmatic concessions of governments and Anglican archbishops.[13] The removal of civil grievances was achieved through gradual adjustments, with the conservative purpose of forestalling even more radical pressures. This left what has commonly been taken to be political nonconformity's touchstone, disestablishment of the Church of England, and the issue of what nonconformist activists should do with the new position that their denominations had secured in public life.

In Wales, the Church of England ministered to only a minority of the population; the demand for disestablishment became integral to the nonconformist majority's sense of cultural and political as well as religious consciousness. No Liberal government could long ignore such a campaign for national justice. But within England, the Church of England was by far the largest *single* church – the nonconformists consisted of numerous denominations – and from the 1880s it generated new claims to be the national church, presenting itself as a pre-eminent expression of English tradition and identity.[14] Here disestablishment would face far greater resistance and have limited electoral purchase. For most nonconformists, a focus on English Church disestablishment came to seem a distraction from more spiritually urgent work. It became what Parry has called a 'ritual slogan': routinely emphasised as a fundamental principle, but usually dormant in practice.[15] The anti-establishment Liberation Society was marginalised, and disestablishment was not a leading concern of the activists who created the free church council movement in the 1890s. Only for brief periods did the issue flicker into some life, when nonconformists felt particularly provoked, as they were by Anglo-Catholic ritualism in the Church of

[13] Jonathan Parry, 'The Disciplining of the Religious Conscience in Nineteenth-Century British Politics', in Ira Katznelson and Gareth Stedman Jones (eds), *Religion and the Political Imagination* (Cambridge, 2010), 214–34.

[14] Arthur Burns, 'The Authority of the Church', in Peter Mandler (ed.), *Liberty and Authority in Victorian Britain* (Oxford, 2006), 197–200.

[15] J.P. Parry, 'Nonconformity, Clericalism and "Englishness": the United Kingdom', in Christopher Clark and Wolfram Kaiser (eds), *Culture Wars: Secular-Catholic Conflict in Nineteenth-Century Europe* (Cambridge, 2003), 179.

194   *Philip Williamson*

England during the late 1890s and by the 1902 Education Act.[16] By 1914, English nonconformist support for Welsh Church disestablishment was so tepid that for a period the Welsh free church councils seceded from the NCEFC.[17]

Instead, nonconformist activists were chiefly exercised by 'the nonconformist conscience', the concern to moralise public life and bring spiritual solutions to national problems, exemplified from the 1880s to the 1910s in numerous campaigns on social, imperial and international issues. David Bebbington has described the aims of particular nonconformist crusades as negative, to remove wrongs, but the general purpose was constructive, to create the conditions for a better society.[18] Nomenclature is important. As their civil disabilities were ended, the nonconformist denominations – which had already shed the term 'dissenters' – redefined themselves as 'free churches', free from earlier constraints but free also to advance the causes of religious and civil liberty, moral rectitude and social improvement. Negatives were replaced by positives: not opposition, but determination to contribute widely to public life, for the good of the whole nation and empire.

Nor were the free churches necessarily attached to the Liberal party. If their causes connected most easily with Liberal principles, they were pursued by what would later be called pressure-group politics: seeking to influence public opinion, parliament and government in general. In its origins during the 1890s, the free-church council movement was expressly non-partisan.[19] This was in part because some of its leaders, both ministers and laymen, disapproved of any identification of spiritual matters with commitments to a political party. It was also because not all free churchmen were Liberals. Some Wesleyan Methodists had long had Tory sympathies, and after the Liberal and nonconformist divisions from 1886 over proposed home rule (and Roman Catholic dominance) for Ireland, perhaps a third of free church voters supported the new alliance of Liberal Unionist and Conservative parties.[20]

From a late nineteenth-century perspective, then, political nonconformity looks different from how it can appear to twentieth-century historians. The national mobilisations which rallied most nonconformists to the Liberal cause

---

[16]   E.K.H. Jordan, *Free Church Unity: History of the Free Church Council Movement* (London, 1956), 32–3, 65–6; Bebbington, *Nonconformist Conscience*, 24–36; Bethany Kilcrease, *The Great Church Crisis and the End of English Erastianism, 1898–1906* (London, 2017).

[17]   Kenneth O. Morgan, *Wales in British Politics 1868–1922* (Cardiff, 1963), 266–7, 272; *Western Mail*, 11 July 1914, 7, and for re-affiliation, *ibid.*, 22 Mar. 1926, 7.

[18]   Bebbington, *Nonconformist Conscience*, 11–16, 156.

[19]   *Ibid.*, 61–75.

[20]   *Ibid.*, 88–96; David Bebbington, 'Nonconformity and Electoral Sociology, 1867–1918', *Historical Journal*, 27 (1984), 633–56.

in 1906 were exceptional and temporary, not a continuation or the beginning of a collective strategy of alliance with the Liberal party. The NCEFC's election manifesto stated that it was normally 'anxious to keep its treatment of political subjects entirely free from party considerations'; while it criticised Unionist measures, it made no explicit reference to the Liberal party.[21] The mobilisations were focused on the removal of particular provocations. Nor did the free church Liberal MPs elected in 1906 form a coherent parliamentary group, united in their policy commitments[22] – indeed, the definition of 'free church MPs' is itself a loose one, based on nonconformist family backgrounds rather than current connections with the chapels.[23] From 1905, the Liberal partisanship of free church representative bodies was steadily deflated. The slow process of the Church of England's revision of its liturgy tranquillised free church anxieties about ritualism for the next twenty years. Efforts to overturn the Education Act's religious provisions and other objectionable Unionist measures faltered before the obstruction of Unionist peers and the Liberal government's other policy preoccupations. What had for free churchmen been attractive moral solutions to social problems were overtaken by collectivist Liberal social reforms and new taxes, which attracted some but disturbed others. There were also renewed concerns that close associations with the Liberal party compromised their churches' spiritual and social missions and threatened unsettling party-political differences within their representative bodies, particularly after the creation of a distinct Labour party and the revival of the Irish home rule issue increased the potential tensions.

At this point, it is usual to cite an anonymous book, *Nonconformity and Politics*, which restated earlier arguments that politics was properly a matter for decision by individual citizens, not corporate action by churches.[24] But if the book was influential, this was for only part of its case. During the two general elections in 1910, the NCEFC took more care to emphasise that it was 'not allied to any particular political party', did not repeat its electoral arrangements with the Liberal party, and organised no national election campaigns of its own. But it did not cease to be engaged in politics. For both elections it published manifestos and issued over one million leaflets to guide free church voters on what it

---

[21] *FCC*, Feb. 1906, 37–8.

[22] D.W. Bebbington, 'The Free Church MPs of the 1906 Parliament', *Parliamentary History*, 24 (2005), 136–50. Another eight free church MPs were Unionists, and a further eight were members of the Labour party.

[23] The lists of free-church MPs (and parliamentary candidates) used by historians are chiefly based on optimistic attributions made by the free-church newspaper, *The Christian World*.

[24] 'A Nonconformist Minister', *Nonconformity and Politics* (1909): see e.g. Koss, *Nonconformity*, 102, and Bebbington, *Nonconformist Conscience*, 157–8.

considered to be the most urgent public questions, chiefly religious education, alcohol licensing, social welfare, and House of Lords reform.[25] Detachment from the Liberal party should not be confused with withdrawal from politics in general, either in 1910 or during the interwar years.[26] Free church representative bodies had resumed their position as pressure groups which sought action on national and international issues from politicians in all parties.

The Free Churches in Public Life

Free church leaders not only remained politically active; they also continued what David Thompson has described as 'the Free Church search for legitimation and social power'.[27] After the removal of their civil disabilities, their ambition was religious equality in its second meaning: ecclesiastical parity. Collectively their denominations had as many regular worshippers as the Church of England, and, they believed, were at least its equal in spiritual vitality, theological calibre and public service. Accordingly, they were entitled to a comparable position and influence in national life. In Wales, parity was achieved negatively by the disestablishment of the Anglican dioceses in 1920, creating an independent 'Church in Wales'. If in England compulsory disestablishment now seemed impossible or undesirable, there was an alternative: instead of the Church of England being levelled down, the free churches could be levelled up.

Successive free church consolidations – the creation in 1919 of a Federal Council of the Evangelical Free Churches (FCEFC, representing the denominations, rather than the NCEFC's membership of chapels and individuals), the union in 1932 of the Methodist connexions, and the merger in 1940 of the NCEFC and FCEFC as the Free Church Federal Council – were intended as much to strengthen the public position of their churches as to adjust them to changing religious and economic circumstances.[28] More important was external recognition. From the free churches' perspective, the institutions that

[25] *The Times*, 6 Dec. 1909, 10, and (with statement by the NCEFC secretary, F.B. Meyer) 29 Nov. 1910, 12. For renewed dispersal of free-church support across the political parties, see Neal Blewett, *The Peers, the Parties and the People: The General Elections of 1910* (London, 1972), 343–9.

[26] Jordan, *Free Church Unity*, 234–5, comments on the NCEFC's 'political inactivity' after 1918, and see also Bebbington, *Nonconformist Conscience*, 80, 160.

[27] David M. Thompson, 'The Unity of the Church in Twentieth-century England: Pleasing Dream or Common Calling?', *Studies in Church History*, 32 (1996), 527.

[28] See e.g. J.W. Ewing, the NCEFC president, in *The National Free Church Council Annual Report 1939–40*, 3: the union of councils would 'increase the power of the Free Churches to influence the life of the nation'.

could substantiate their national status were the government, the monarchy and the Church of England.

The First World War caused difficulties for the free churches' principled commitments to peace, voluntarism and individualism, but it also brought new public responsibilities. The German invasion of Belgium and violations of international law convinced most free churchmen that there was a 'call of God' to 'shatter a great anti-Christian attempt to destroy the fabric of Christian civilisation'.[29] For what they regarded as a righteous cause, the free churches became more favourable towards, more deeply involved in, and more valued by the state. They encouraged recruitment to the armed forces, promised the government their 'utmost support in the prosecution of all measures that are necessary and conducive to upholding... the ideals of Freedom, Humanity and International Law',[30] and joined in national days of prayer in support of the war effort, publicly approved or called by the king. The formation of a United Army and Navy Board of chaplains in 1915 had particular symbolic importance, in securing government recognition of the religious ministries for all their denominations.[31] With Lloyd George, the great political champion of free church causes, as prime minister, they felt themselves to be close to the heart of government.[32] After the Armistice, the free churches' contribution to the war effort was acknowledged by the attendance of the king, queen and royal family, the prime minister, many peers and MPs, and the lord mayor and corporation of London at their national thanksgiving service in the Royal Albert Hall. Free churchmen regarded this first royal presence at a 'nonconformist' service as momentous: for John Clifford, it represented an easing of the 'social stigma' on their denominations, and a new beginning 'in the relations of the State to "Dissent"'.[33] Royal recognition became common in other ways, including the award to leading ministers of the new order of Companions of Honour.[34] Since 1872 free churchmen had obtained official invitations to attend royal thanksgivings, funerals and coronations, but from the 1900s NCEFC and FCEFC wanted free church ministers to have an equal share in the conduct of all state religious

---

[29] Ruston, 'Protestant Nonconformist Attitudes', 243–5, 250, 255–8; K.W. Clements, 'Baptists and the Outbreak of the First World War', *Baptist Quarterly*, 26 (1975), 75.

[30] *FCYB 1917*, 26.

[31] J.H. Thompson, 'The Nonconformist Chaplain in the First World War: The Importance of a New Phenomenon', in Michael Snape and Edward Madigan (eds), *The Clergy in Khaki: New Perspectives on British Army Chaplaincy in the First World War* (Farnham, 2013), 17–39.

[32] Peter Shepherd, *The Making of a Modern Denomination: John Howard Shakespeare and the English Baptists, 1898–1924* (Carlisle, 2001), 99–101.

[33] *The Times*, 18 Nov. 1918, 10; James Marchant, *Dr John Clifford* (1924), 235.

[34] Clifford and W.R. Nicoll (1921), J.H. Jowett (1922), J.D. Jones (1927), J.C. Carlile (1929), Bramwell Booth (1929), J. Scott Lidgett (1933), and M.E. Aubrey (1937).

services, alongside Church of England clergy. After prolonged negotiations, it was a matter of celebration when at least more prominent parts were secured: in 1935 the FCEFC moderator read a lesson at the national service for George V's jubilee, and in 1937 free church ministers joined the ecclesiastical procession at George VI's coronation.[35]

From 1906 onwards, the Church of England's archbishops and bishops sought closer relations with the free churches, for mixed reasons: to advance shared religious and moral concerns, to contribute to the developing international ecumenical movement, to placate free church criticisms and to be better able to defend the Church's own interests. Free church leaders seized upon these opportunities for co-operation. Joint public statements, signed by the archbishops and moderators or secretaries of the NCEFC, the Baptist and Congregational Unions, Methodist connexions and other denominational bodies began to be published on a range of subjects, including temperance, Sunday observance, religious persecution, and international peace. Later, there were co-ordinated or joint calls for special prayers on matters of national concern, and for some occasions provision of the same texts of prayers for use in both Anglican and free church places of worship.[36] During the First World War, the NCEFC encouraged local 'united' free church and Anglican services for national days of prayer,[37] and in 1917 the archbishops accepted the suggestion of John Scott Lidgett, a leading Wesleyan Methodist and the NCEFC's secretary for public questions, for the creation of a joint standing committee of bishops and free church ministers on social and moral issues.[38] From 1919, the opening sessions of NCEFC annual assemblies, held in a different city or town each year, always included an address of welcome from the local bishop or archdeacon. Free church leaders were especially keen on protestant ecumenism: indeed J.H. Shakespeare, secretary of the Baptist Union and the NCEFC president in 1916–17, regarded his plans for a united free church – the origin of the FCEFC – as a step towards a larger union with the Church of England.[39] In preparation for a planned world ecumenical conference, another

[35] Philip Williamson, Stephen Taylor, Alasdair Raffe and Natalie Mears (eds), *National Prayers: Special Worship since the Reformation, Vol. 3: Worship for National and Royal Occasions in the United Kingdom 1871–2016* (Woodbridge, 2020) [hereafter *National Prayers, Vol. 3*], 10, 32, 49, 80, 222, 314, 330, 343.

[36] Philip Williamson, 'Archbishops and the Monarchy: Leadership in British Religion, 1900–2012', in Tom Rodger, Philip Williamson, and Matthew Grimley (eds), *The Church of England and British Politics since 1900* (Woodbridge, 2020), 57–79; *National Prayers, Vol. 3*, 187, 250–2, 314–15.

[37] *FCC*, July 1916, 95; June 1917, 83; July 1918, 95.

[38] Alan Turberfield, *John Scott Lidgett* (Peterborough, 2003), 229–31.

[39] J.H. Shakespeare, *The Churches at the Cross-Roads: A Study in Church Unity* (London, 1918), 166–87.

joint committee of bishops and free church ministers produced agreed principles on faith and church order, with the free church representatives going so far as to accept that a united English church might include episcopacy, if in a 'constitutional' form. These committees and further unofficial conferences contributed to the Anglican Lambeth Conference's appeal for church unity in 1920, and during the next two decades to discussions on reunion between the bishops and leaders of the FCEFC and NCEFC.[40]

The historical emphasis has been on the failure of these ecumenical efforts: the free churches refused episcopal re-ordination of their ministers, and the Church of England's convocations rejected intercommunion and interchange of preachers. But the Lambeth appeal and the subsequent discussions did produce valuable outcomes for the free churches. The Church of England now acknowledged that their denominations were *churches*, equivalent in character (though not, it later emerged, equal in adequacy) to itself. The archbishops and bishops publicly recognised free church ministries as 'effective ministries of grace' and presbyterial and congregational structures as rightful elements of church government.[41] Free church leaders also became used to correspondence with the archbishop of Canterbury and to meetings in Lambeth Palace.[42] Their enthusiasm – and gratitude – for this new relationship was palpable: their churches would 'gladly join with Anglican fellow Christians... not only in social and civic work, but also in common worship and in any form of religious fellowship which is open to us'.[43]

The national position of the free churches was now widely accepted. The government invited representatives of their denominations to the king's unveiling of the Cenotaph in 1920, and from 1923 to the annual national ceremony in Whitehall on Armistice Day. *The Times* listed ministerial appointments in the Baptist, Congregational and Presbyterian churches, adding to its long-standing reports of appointments in the Church of England.[44] From 1922 free

[40] G.K.A Bell (ed.), *Documents Bearing on the Problem of Christian Unity and Fellowship, 1916–1920* (London, 1920), 5–14, 54–56, 65–84; Thompson, 'Unity of the Church', 514–24.

[41] G.K.A. Bell (ed.), *Documents on Christian Unity 1920–4* (London, 1924), 3–4, 146–51, 152–3, 158–9, 164–5.

[42] Shakespeare, *Churches at the Cross-Roads*, 170, and see Turberfield, *Lidgett*, esp. chs 16–19.

[43] Joint FCEFC and NCEFC statement, 22 May 1921, in Bell (ed.), *Documents on Christian Unity*, 125.

[44] The notice of 'Free church pulpit changes', reprinted from *The Christian World*, appeared from February 1916 to March 1946: appointments in the Church of England continued to be listed until 1965. The periodic re-allocations among Methodist circuits received only occasional reports, as these were very numerous and occupied many columns: this soon proved to be impractical.

church ministers received prominent parts in the BBC's religious broadcasting, and NCEFC or FCEFC leaders joined Anglican archbishops and moderators of the Church of Scotland in conducting special BBC services for royal and national occasions. According to M.E. Aubrey, secretary of the Baptist Union, the broadcasting of religious services had ended a perception that free church people were 'necessarily of inferior religious and social standing'.[45]

Since the 1880s the free churches had ceased to regard themselves as outsiders.[46] Now their own estimations were validated by national institutions and, indeed, expressed in more general terms. Nonconformity was already central to Welsh national consciousness, and during the interwar years the free church tradition became integral to conventional accounts of English history and culture.[47] All this had political implications. The secularisation of party politics was not just a general effect of the First World War, completing the replacement of differences over religious and constitutional issues with disagreements over economic and social policies as the main distinctions between the political parties. It was also an outcome of the raised status of the free churches in public life, and especially the actions of leaders of the free churches and the Church of England: together, they removed denominational conflict from party politics. What happened was less a decline of nonconformist challenges to the Church than a confident free church desire for greater recognition and a cautious, whiggish, extension of Anglican accommodation.

The Politics of the Free Churches

Widening co-operation helped to overcome or soothe remaining points of political friction between the free churches and the Church of England. This was most evident on what had been the flashpoint in 1902. Religious education was the first business of the joint committee on moral and social questions.[48] During the 1920s, the NCEFC and the bishops encouraged a new approach: the negotiation by local educational authorities (LEAs) and local free church and Anglican ministers of regional 'agreed' or 'approved' syllabuses for religious instruction in state schools. By 1934 these had been adopted by two-thirds of the LEAs. Further arrangements in state schools and funding for church

---

[45] Kenneth M. Wolfe, *The Churches and the British Broadcasting Corporation 1922–1956* (London, 1984); *National Prayers, Vol. 3*, pp. lxxxvii–lxxxviii; *Church and State: Report of the Archbishops' Commission on the Relations between Church and State* (2 vols, London, 1935), vol. 2, 244.

[46] Parry, 'Disciplining', 224–5.

[47] Matthew Grimley, 'The Religion of Englishness: Puritanism, Providentialism and "National Character", 1918–1945', *Journal of British Studies*, 46 (2007), 891–8.

[48] Turberfield, *Lidgett*, 230–1.

schools continued to cause problems for successive interwar education bills, but consultations between the church leaders avoided political controversies and eventually produced a compromise, which became a central feature of the Education Act of 1944.[49] The new free church attitude also eased two new issues of potential conflict: in 1919 an Enabling Bill to allow the Church of England extensive self-government and a privileged parliamentary procedure, and in 1927–8 parliamentary measures to authorise revisions of *The Book of Common Prayer*, which re-ignited anxieties about Anglo-Catholic ritualism. In both cases, there were protests from the NCEFC and most of the free church denominational assemblies and executives. But these critical resolutions papered over internal divisions and did not disrupt the larger desire for continued co-operation. The Enabling Bill passed with private assistance from Lidgett and Shakespeare, and with the votes of most free church MPs, including even Lloyd George. Although prayer book revision was twice defeated in the House of Commons (by Anglican, Scottish, Welsh and Northern Irish as well as free church MPs), the free churches did not object when the archbishops ignored these defeats and permitted use of the revised book on their own authority. Still more significantly, neither episode provoked new free church agitations for disestablishment.[50] This issue was not quite dead: during the 1930s, the NCEFC's annual assemblies again passed resolutions calling for the Church's disestablishment and disendowment. But these no longer had a hostile political purpose. Free church leaders now wanted the Church itself to act, to remove the fundamental obstacle to reunion of the English protestant churches by accepting the logic of its self-government and undertaking voluntary disestablishment.[51] Yet as Matthew Grimley has observed, under the new threats of totalitarian and pagan regimes across Europe, they increasingly accepted the value of a national church – and in doing so, the claims of the Church of England to be this national church.[52] In 1953 the Free Church Federal Council declared that while continuing their churches' historic rejection of 'state *control* of religion', it 'welcomed state *recognition* of religion' and wanted to preserve 'the existing valuable cooperation between Church and State, in

---

[49] Marjorie Cruickshank, *Church and State in English Education* (London, 1964), chs 6–7; Stephen G. Parker and Rob Freathy, 'The Church of England and Religious Education during the Twentieth Century', in Rodger, Williamson and Grimley, *Church of England and British Politics*, 203–4, 206–8.

[50] Philip Williamson, 'The Church of England and Constitutional Reform: The Enabling Act in British Politics and English Religion, 1913–1928', *Journal of British Studies*, 62 (2023), 445–75; John Maiden, *National Religion and the Prayer Book Crisis, 1927–1928* (Woodbridge, 2009), 111–21, 158–61; Grimley, *Citizenship, Community*, 161.

[51] *FCC*, Apr. 1930, 8; Apr. 1931, 5; Apr. 1933, 4–5.

[52] Grimley, *Citizenship, Community*, 161–2.

which the free churches had come increasingly to share'.[53] The English free churches were finally at peace with the established Church.

While the original religious impetus of political nonconformity faded, during the interwar period its second element, the nonconformist conscience, remained vigorous and still commanded public attention. The NCEFC continued to have 'public questions' as a standing section in its annual report, to issue statements on public affairs, to publish general election manifestos, and to distribute lists of questions for parliamentary candidates. It still sent resolutions and deputations to government ministers. More frequently than before 1914, it asked MPs and peers to address its annual assemblies. The *Christian World, British Weekly, Baptist Times, Methodist Recorder* and other free church newspapers still commented extensively on political events, and regional and national newspapers continued to report political statements from NCEFC and denominational meetings. Free church opinion remained important for politicians, the more so because of the volatility of electoral and party politics during these years: prime ministers now accepted invitations to speak at NCEFC assemblies.

Longstanding moral crusades were continued, for Sunday observance, temperance and sexual 'purity', and against gambling. As these issues affected legislation or taxation as well as public morality, they remained significant for governments and parliament – and so well worth continued free church attention – but they had lost their purchase in party politics. Even many free church members must have considered the NCEFC president in 1922, Samuel Chadwick, to be out of touch when he asserted that the alcohol trade would be the dominant question at the general election of that year.[54] But free church representative bodies did move with the times, and address new and pressing public concerns.[55] In its 1918 general election manifesto, the NCEFC called upon the nation to 'take up... Social Reconstruction as an offering of thanksgiving to God' for victory in the war, with better provision for pensions, housing and health, prevention of unemployment, 'complete emancipation' of women, and 'a true partnership' between employers and workers.[56] From 1920 it welcomed the public works, slum clearance and house-building programmes of successive governments, but wanted them to be accelerated and expanded.[57] While

---

[53] Free Church Federal Council, *The Free Churches and the State* (London, 1953), 62–3 [emphases in original].

[54] *Westminster Gazette*, 21 Oct. 1922, 7.

[55] G.I.T. Machin, *Churches and Social Issues in Twentieth-century Britain* (Oxford, 1998), chs 2–4; Peter Catterall, *Labour and the Free Churches, 1918–1939* (London, 2018), ch. 2.

[56] *FCC*, Jan. 1919, 1.

[57] *FCC*, Dec. 1920, 134; Apr. 1923, 21–2; Feb. 1933, 1–2.

accepting a general need for retrenchment in public expenditure during economic difficulties, it opposed cuts in housing programmes and health policies as uneconomic and inefficient.[58] In 1929, it supported an 'inherent right' to work; in 1935 the chairman of the Congregational Union, Angus Watson, called for a £1,000m 'prosperity' loan to reduce unemployment.[59] The NCEFC condemned all forms of racial prejudice in the empire,[60] and supported constitutional reform in India. It protested against religious persecution in Soviet Russia and Nazi Germany. Above all, free church leaders welcomed new schemes for the avoidance of wars. They were early advocates of a League of Nations, and the free church councils and denominational bodies became very active recruiting agents for the League of Nations Union. In most years the NCEFC passed resolutions of support for the League's activities, for international arbitration, and for disarmament.[61] The nonconformist conscience remained vocal in interwar politics.

The NCEFC's leaders declared that it was 'not a political organisation',[62] and tended to describe economic issues as political matters on which they had no expertise. But as in 1910, such statements had specific meanings: to disclaim institutional involvement in *party politics*, and entanglements with particularly contentious party policies. Before the 1923 general election the NCEFC stated that it was 'both impossible and undesirable that the Churches as such could pass judgement upon the rival fiscal proposals [of] the different political parties'.[63] But neutrality in party politics did not preclude political activism where a general consensus existed among the churches on the moral and social aspects of public affairs, including economic issues. In these matters, the NCEFC appealed to all parliamentary candidates 'in the hope of securing agreement between all parties upon adequate policies'.[64]

A common historical criticism is that the resolutions and manifestos of the NCEFC and denominational bodies often consisted of generalities; but as the NCEFC president declared during the industrial disputes of 1926, they believed that the political function of the churches was 'to produce an atmosphere', leaving detailed proposals and legislation to the politicians.[65] National campaigns

---

[58] *FCC*, Oct 1924, 44–5; Apr. 1933, 2.

[59] *FCYB 1929*, 80; Machin, *Churches and Social Issues*, 46.

[60] *FCYB 1925*, 52.

[61] Keith Robbins, 'Free Churchmen and the Twenty Years' Crisis', *Baptist Quarterly*, 27 (1978), 351–2; Helen McCarthy, *The British People and the League of Nations* (Manchester, 2011), 87–9.

[62] *FCYB 1927*, 11; *National Free Church Council Annual Report 1938–9*, 3

[63] *FCC*, Dec. 1923, 49.

[64] *FCC*, Jan. 1919, 1; Dec. 1923, 50; Oct. 1924, 46.

[65] *FCYB 1926*, 76.

were still organised, for example a 'Warless World' movement in 1922–3, with the distribution of two million leaflets bearing a message of approval from the king, and a 'National Free Church Temperance Crusade' in 1930–1.[66] But there were now fewer of the agitations and the 'indignation' meetings that had characterised political nonconformity before 1914.[67] Instead, as Lidgett explained, the NCEFC leaders 'never ceased to make' free church views 'known in official quarters'; they were 'in constant touch with every government department in regard to every public question'. The new aim was 'to prevent mischief before it arises', which 'while quieter and less exciting work', could be 'more fruitful'.[68] Political methods had changed. This was pressure-group politics adjusted to the new mass democracy established in 1918: a larger and less religious electorate, new party conflicts, and a bigger state.

The free church councils and denominational leaderships not only spoke for themselves on many public issues; they also co-operated with other 'non-political' groups. These groups included Church of England bishops, who had now, in step with free church leaders, also detached themselves from party politics.[69] On occasion, they also included representatives of the Church of Scotland and even the head of the Roman Catholic Church in England and Wales. After 1918 joint statements and deputations with leaders of other churches became the chief means for the free churches to amplify their political opinions.[70] Free churchmen were also involved in numerous interdenominational bodies concerned with social issues. For example, the Baptist and Congregational ministers Hugh Martin and A.E. Garvie worked closely with William Temple in the Conference on Politics, Economics and Citizenship (COPEC) of 1924, whose work was publicised by the NCEFC and free church newspapers, and which accelerated the shift of ecclesiastical opinions from *laissez-faire* attitudes towards acceptance of a welfare state.[71] Free church leaders also participated in the proliferation of civic associations and campaigns that promoted public good causes in interwar Britain. They were especially prominent in the Peace Ballot movement and the Council

---

[66] *FCC*, Sept. 1922, 50; *Manchester Guardian*, 2 Dec. 1922, 7; *FCC*, Oct. 1930, 6–8.

[67] Bebbington, *Nonconformist Conscience*, 15–17, 154–5.

[68] *FCYB 1926*, 25–6.

[69] After 1914 the cliché of the Church of England as 'the Tory/Conservative party at prayer' is misleading: see Matthew Grimley and Philip Williamson, 'The Church of England, the British State and British Politics during the Twentieth Century', in Rodger, Williamson and Grimley, *Church of England and British Politics*, 2, 18–19.

[70] Williamson, 'Archbishops and the Monarchy', 65–70.

[71] *FCC*, Apr. 1924, 21; *FCYB 1925*, 52; *Christian World*, 10 Apr. 1924, 4–5; E.R. Norman, *Church and Society in England 1770–1970* (Cambridge, 1976), 279–313. Studies of COPEC invariably understate the free church contribution.

What Happened to Political Nonconformity? 205

of Action for Peace and Reconstruction, which had considerable effects for national politics in 1934–5.[72]

Free Church Voters

From all this, it is clear that post-1906 political nonconformity belongs more to the history of non-party voluntary associations as outlined by Helen McCarthy[73] than to the history of political parties within which it has usually been considered. Nevertheless, changing party allegiances among members of the free churches did have party-political consequences. It is a truism that free church votes became dispersed between the Liberal, Labour and Conservative parties,[74] although this glosses over vital features of interwar politics: there were often more than three parties, alliances among parties were formed at four of the seven elections, and there were two periods of coalition government, the last for most of the 1930s. The redistribution of party allegiances among free church men and women was complicated and accelerated by a prolonged reconstruction of the party system.

The free churches remained important for Liberal politics,[75] and Liberal politicians continued to address NCEFC and denominational meetings. When the NCEFC decided to appoint vice-presidents in 1928, these included Lloyd George. As is well established, in certain constituencies in England and Wales substantial numbers of free church voters remained loyal to the Liberal party, establishing pockets of Liberal electoral strength that were still discernible late in the century.[76] Otherwise, much of the historical focus has been on

---

[72] Martin Ceadel, 'The First British Referendum: The Peace Ballot, 1934–5', *English Historical Review*, 95 (1981), 810–39; Stephen Koss, 'Lloyd George and Nonconformity: The Last Rally', *English Historical Review*, 89 (1974), 77–108; Maurice Cowling, *The Impact of Hitler: British Politics and British Policy 1933–1940* (Cambridge, 1975), 10, 17–22, 36–41, 58, 79–81.

[73] Helen McCarthy, 'Parties, Voluntary Associations and Democratic Politics in Interwar Britain', *Historical Journal*, 50 (2007), 891–912, and McCarthy, 'Associational Voluntarism in Interwar Britain', in Matthew Hilton and James McKay (eds), *The Ages of Voluntarism* (Oxford, 2011), 47–68.

[74] For a denominational example, see D.W. Bebbington, 'Baptists and Politics since 1914', in K.W. Clements (ed.), *Baptists in the Twentieth Century* (London, 1983), 76–95. Before the 1929 general election, the *Christian World* on the first pages of three successive issues published appeals for free church support from the leaders of the Conservative, Labour and Liberal parties, in that order.

[75] Michael Bentley, *The Liberal Mind 1914–1929* (Cambridge, 1977), 191–204.

[76] E.g. Kenneth O. Morgan, 'Twilight of Welsh Liberalism: Lloyd George and the "Wee Frees", 1918–35', *Bulletin of the Board of Celtic Studies*, 12 (1968), 389–405; Barry Doyle, 'Business, Liberalism and Dissent in Norwich', *Parliamentary History*, 17 (1998),

the Labour party, in some early studies influenced by a preconception that it 'replaced' the Liberal party.[77] Many Labour party activists had at least free church backgrounds, and from 1924 the notionally free church Labour MPs exceeded the equally notional numbers of free church Liberal MPs. Some free church ministers were attracted by the Labour party's commitments to social reform, international peace and disarmament. Labour politicians had already spoken at NCEFC assemblies before 1914, and Ramsay MacDonald did so as Labour prime minister in 1924. Arthur Henderson, a Wesleyan Methodist lay reader, was another of the original NCEFC vice-presidents. But as Peter Catterall has argued, while many Labour politicians had some sort of connection with the free churches, it does not follow that the largest part of the free church vote now supported Labour.[78]

Labour replaced the Liberals only as the 'party of progress'. In the larger sense – dominance at general elections and in government – the Liberals were replaced by the Conservative party. A free church contribution to this success has increasingly been recognised, explained in large part by a continuing drift of middle-class free church voters towards the 'party of property', by absorption of free church men and women into 'apolitical' (but broadly Conservative) social associations, and by their growing fear of socialism, especially after the implosions of the Labour governments of 1924 and 1929–31.[79] But the Conservative party also acted in ways which made itself more attractive to members of the free churches. With the new agenda of party politics, it ceased to be closely identified with the Church of England, becoming more broadly protestant in character. Prayer Book revision could not generate renewed free church support for the Liberal party, as Lloyd George hoped, because the Conservative government treated it as an open question, and because parliamentary opposition to the measures was led not by Liberal MPs but by two evangelical Conservative ministers, including the home secretary.[80] Support for peace and disarmament was spread across the political parties, and the chief figure in

---

131–40; Garry Tregidga, *The Liberal Party in South-West Britain since 1918* (Exeter, 2000), 112–13, 155–7, 186, 203; Iain MacAllister, Edward Fieldhouse and Andrew Russell, 'Yellow fever? The Political Geography of Liberal Voting in Great Britain', *Political Geography*, 21 (2002), 421–47.

[77] E.g. Stephen Mayor, *The Churches and the Labour Movement* (London, 1967); Leonard Smith, *Religion and the Rise of Labour* (Keele, 1993); Koss, *Nonconformity*, 8, 10, 144, 147–51; Catterall, *Labour and the Free Churches*.

[78] Catterall, *Labour and the Free Churches*, 123–5, 213.

[79] Hastings, *English Christianity*, 267; Peter Catterall, 'The Party and Religion', in Anthony Seldon and Stuart Ball (eds), *Conservative Century: The Conservative Party since 1900* (Oxford, 1994), 647–9; Ross McKibbin, *Parties and People: England, 1914–1951* (Oxford, 2010), 91–5.

[80] McKibbin, *Classes*, 277–8; cf. McKibbin, *Parties*, 65, n. 93.

the League of Nations Union was a Conservative (and Anglican), Lord Cecil: in 1924 he became the first Conservative politician to speak at NCEFC assemblies. Seeking to capture Liberal opinion as well as cope with post-war problems, during the 1920s the Conservative party absorbed Liberal social policies. It also exploited Liberal party divisions. As with the Liberal Unionists from 1886, Conservative alliances with Lloyd George's National Liberals from 1918 to 1923 and with John Simon's Liberal Nationals during the 1930s facilitated conversions to Conservatism among their followers.

The formation and electoral perpetuation of the Conservative-dominated National coalition government in 1931 was especially influential. Its 'non-party' character and 'National' title had particular purchase in the free churches; the Liberal Nationals gave it a continuing Liberal presence; and its ministers included active and admired free church laymen, notably the Conservative, Kingsley Wood, and the Liberal Nationals, W.R. Runciman, Ernest Brown and Geoffrey Shakespeare (J.H. Shakespeare's son).[81] It was also important that the Conservative leader, Stanley Baldwin, had an unusually eclectic and ecumenical political appeal, and gave much attention to moral qualities in public life. Appealing directly to free church voters shortly after the formation of the first Labour government in 1924, he celebrated his own nonconformist heritage and presented the post-war Conservative party as both the natural heir to 'effete Liberalism' and the only effective barrier to socialism.[82] As prime minister in 1925 he became the second in what then became a series of Conservative ministers to address the NCEFC, with such success that he was invited to speak at fundraising occasions for Congregationalists and Baptists, and at commemorative events for Wesleyan Methodists, the Salvation Army and the Brotherhood Movement. By the 1930s, some free churchmen compared him to Gladstone in moral stature: he became, in Ross McKibbin's phrase, 'an honorary nonconformist'.[83]

A precise instance of changed free church loyalties since 1906 is the experience in 1935 of the Council of Action for Peace and Reconstruction, the last political initiative undertaken by Lloyd George in alliance with free church leaders and the editors of free church newspapers. For its historian, Stephen Koss, the Council's failure is explained by distrust towards Lloyd George's politicking, and the naivety of the free churchmen. But it is also testimony to the

---

[81] Catterall, *Labour and the Free Churches*, 29–40; Michael Goodman, 'A Faded Heritage: English Baptist Political Thinking in the 1930s', *Baptist Quarterly*, 37 (1997), 58–70.

[82] Speech to Nonconformist Unionist League, *The Times*, 9 Apr. 1924, 19.

[83] McKibbin, *Parties*, 91–2; Philip Williamson, *Stanley Baldwin: Conservative Politics and National Values* (Cambridge, 1999), 283–92, 349, 354–5; Catterall, *Labour and the Free Churches*, 35.

longstanding commitment of free church leaders to 'non-party' politics, their support for the National government, and their trust in Baldwin, who earlier in the year had again been invited to address the NCEFC assembly. Those free churchmen who signed the Council's manifesto supposed that the Council of Action was no more than a pressure group to encourage the government to take firmer action, and several had congratulated and praised Baldwin on his re-appointment as prime minister just a week before the Council's launch. Once it was grasped that Lloyd George intended to endorse parliamentary candidates standing against the government, it became apparent that many members of the free churches would not support the Council, and most of its free church leaders hurriedly restated either their party-political neutrality or their personal support for Baldwin. Even the sharpest critic of the churches' involvement in party politics praised the achievements of the National government.[84] By welcoming the results of that other free church cause, the Peace Ballot, announced during the same month, Baldwin deflated the Council of Action still further. Later in the year, by presenting the government's defence programme as reinforcement for collective security and the League of Nations, he reassured sufficient free church and Liberal opinion – assisted by a speech to the Peace Society, which had it printed verbatim in a leading free church newspaper[85] – to help the National government win a second large general election victory and a mandate for rearmament.[86]

* * *

The free churches suffered uncertainties and difficulties after 1914, but so did most other institutions. Despite their troubles, they now had prominent parts in religious and public life. By the 1940s, the free churches had in effect become partners – though junior partners – in a broadened Church establishment.[87] Their members were never united in their party allegiances: the extent of their support for the Liberal party from 1902 to 1906 was an exceptional reaction against unusually contentious Unionist policies. What declined from 1906 was *partisan* nonconformity. The characteristic style of political nonconformity was non-party pressure group politics, and this still gave the free churches political influence, as is evident from the continued attention they received from government ministers: free church council assemblies were addressed by

---

[84] Koss, 'Last Rally', 77–108; Aubrey in *The Times*, 27 June 1935, 18, and see W.M.S. West, 'The Reverend Secretary Aubrey, Part 1', *Baptist Quarterly*, 34 (1992), 204–12.

[85] *Christian World*, 7 Nov. 1935, 13.

[86] Philip Williamson, 'Christian Conservatives and the Totalitarian Challenge 1933–40', *English Historical Review*, 115 (2000), 630–4.

[87] Williamson, 'Archbishops and the Monarchy', 71–8.

Neville Chamberlain in 1940, R.A. Butler in 1943, Anthony Eden in 1944, and Clement Attlee in 1946.

A better description than 'decline' for what happened to political nonconformity during the interwar years is the term used by Alan Wilkinson: assimilation.[88] For him, the word had negative connotations, of concession, absorption and loss: it was his synonym for decline. Yet assimilation also has positive meanings, of acceptance, inclusion, even success, in forms which free church leaders had long desired: acceptance and inclusion were a vindication of their past struggles. Optimism about free church prospects was still possible amid a resurgence of state and public religiosity brought by the Second World War,[89] when free church leaders reached a peak of public prominence. But in the longer term, assimilation was corrosive. The nonconformist conscience became diffused in co-operation with other churches and with civic associations, and for the political parties members of the free churches ceased to be a sufficiently distinct body of political opinion. During the 1950s, assimilation really did mean decline: the free churches now accepted that losses in chapel membership and public influence were irrecoverable.[90]

---

[88] Wilkinson, *Dissent or Conform*, title of ch. 3; and see, similarly, Ruston, 'Protestant Nonconformist Attitudes', 240, 258–60.

[89] Michael Snape (ed.), *British Christianity and the Second World War* (Woodbridge, 2023).

[90] Thompson, 'The Older Free Churches', 89.

Part IV
Institutions

Chapter 10

Liberalism, the Law and Parliament in Modern British Politics

Ben Griffin

'If nineteenth-century Liberalism meant anything', Jonathan Parry has argued, 'it meant a political system in which a large number of potentially incompatible interests... were mature enough to accept an over-arching code of law'.[1] This has been a recurrent theme in Parry's work, but few historians have followed his lead.[2] Law was a vital concern for liberals, not least because by the middle of the nineteenth century they had come to understand it as a technology capable of effecting moral reform.[3] That is a subject of considerable importance, but in what follows we shall set it aside in favour of a less well-studied problem: how the boundary between law and politics was redefined in the long nineteenth century.

Abstractly, liberal governmentality has involved a desire to set limits to the scope of 'the political' by identifying areas of activity in which the authority to settle disputes is either delegated or abdicated by the sovereign power. Unlike absolutist, totalitarian, or theocratic regimes, liberal states deny that they are appropriate authorities to pronounce on the truth of scientific or religious statements. Similarly, when managing the allocation of resources, liberal states prefer to use market mechanisms instead of political processes. For this reason, the historical study of liberalism ought to be attentive to the how the boundaries of 'the political' have been created, maintained and policed. This

---

[1] Jonathan Parry, *The Rise and Fall of Liberal Government in Victorian Britain* (New Haven & London, 1993), 3.

[2] Jonathan Parry, *The Politics of Patriotism: English Liberalism, National Identity and Europe, 1830–1886* (Cambridge, 2006), 43, 49–52, 54, 72, 76, 84; 'Liberalism and Liberty' in Peter Mandler (ed.), *Liberty and Authority in Victorian Britain* (Oxford, 2006), 92, 94, 97. Cf. Margot Finn, 'The Authority of the Law', in *ibid.*, 159–78.

[3] Parry, *Patriotism*, ch. 2; Martin Wiener, *Reconstructing the Criminal: Culture, Law and Policy in England, 1830–1914* (Cambridge, 1990), 54; Ben Griffin, *The Politics of Gender in Victorian Britain: Masculinity, Political Culture, and the Struggle for Women's Rights* (Cambridge, 2012), 78–9.

is not least because liberalism's efforts to limit the scope of 'the political' has often involved removing whole classes of social relationships and contests over resources outside the sphere of 'the political', by identifying certain economic, sexual or racial hierarchies as 'natural' and therefore as non-contestable.[4] The boundaries of 'the political', it should be noted, are not conterminous with the boundaries of the state: much decision-making in the modern state is identified as administration rather than politics.[5] Precisely because the legal system has been identified as 'nonpolitical', historians have developed an array of terms to characterise the modern state (such as welfare state, warfare state, or fiscal-military state), none of which are capable of conceptualising one of its most important functions: dispute resolution through juridical process.[6] In short, liberalism has developed by identifying certain disputes as *political* problems, to be resolved by lobbying, petitioning, electioneering and voting, while other problems have been identified as *legal* problems, to be resolved by an entirely different set of mechanisms.

The desire to distinguish between law and politics has therefore been central to liberal modernity. The distinctiveness of this liberal vision can be seen if we think about how entangled law and politics were in the long eighteenth century. Gerald Postema has argued that the common law constituted 'the ruling political ideology' of the eighteenth century: one could not say that of the nineteenth century.[7] In the early modern period, James Hart has argued, law and politics were both 'part of the same process of government, transacted in the same form by the same individuals'.[8] This is clear if we consider the role of JPs and quarter sessions in county government.[9] Many magistrates simultaneously served as MPs, so that it would frequently have been difficult for local people to distinguish between law and politics as discrete forms of governance. Turning to the senior judiciary, common law judges were seen as representatives of the king's power in the early eighteenth century; they were expected to encourage

---

[4]   Brian Harrison, *Separate Spheres: The Opposition to Women's Suffrage in Britain* (London, 1978); Catherine Hall, *Civilising Subjects: Metropole and Colony in the English Imagination, 1830–1867* (Chicago, 2002).

[5]   E.g. Tom Crook, *Governing Systems: Modernity and the Making of Public Health in England, 1830–1910* (Berkeley, 2016), 296.

[6]   Ben Griffin, 'Paternal Rights, Child Welfare and the Law in Nineteenth-century Britain and Ireland', *Past & Present*, 246 (2020), 111–12.

[7]   Gerald Postema, *Bentham and the Common Law Tradition* (2nd edn, Oxford, 2019), 303.

[8]   James S. Hart, *The Rule of Law, 1603–1660: Crowns, Courts and Judges* (Abingdon, 2003), 61–2.

[9]   Norma Landau, *The Justices of the Peace, 1679–1760* (Berkeley, 1984); David Eastwood, *Governing Rural England: Tradition and Transformation in Local Government, 1780–1840* (Oxford, 1994).

loyalty to the monarch in their assize addresses, and to inform the government of the state of public feeling they encountered while on circuit. Indeed, David Lemmings has suggested that the Pelham ministry 'regarded their judges… as members of the government'.[10] It is no surprise then that the practice of elite politics took legal forms. Sir Lewis Namier argued that in the eighteenth century parliamentary politics were transacted, 'to a disastrous extent, in terms of jurisprudence': the Wilkes agitation, the impeachment of Warren Hastings, the treason trials of 1794, and Melville's impeachment come readily to mind.[11] It is of fundamental importance that politics was conducted very differently in the nineteenth and twentieth centuries. This points to a transformation in governmentality that has so far escaped scholarly attention.

Nineteenth-century liberals were so successful in establishing normative distinctions between 'the legal' and 'the political' that subsequent histories have often reproduced them uncritically. Judges and courts are almost entirely absent from most general histories of British politics. This is a mistake: the law is not politically neutral, judges are not disinterested arbiters, and why the public has been willing to cede so much power to a handful of unelected and unaccountable, elite, white men is an important historical question.[12] Moreover, given that studies of contemporary Britain have been troubled by the juridification of politics since the 1970s, we need to examine more critically the boundaries between law and politics that have supposedly been transgressed in recent years.[13] A first step will be to consider how those boundaries – first erected as *ancien regime* structures of governance – were reformed in the nineteenth century. The necessary implication is that the period between the dejuridification of eighteenth-century politics and the juridification of late twentieth-century politics forms a discrete phase of liberal modernity.

The distinctiveness of the relationship between law and politics in nineteenth-century Britain becomes clearer when compared with that found in

---

[10]   David Lemmings, 'The Independence of the Judiciary in Eighteenth-century England' in Peter Birks (ed.), *The Life of the Law* (London, 1993), 132, 146–7; Landau, *Justices of the Peace*, 46–8.

[11]   Lewis Namier, *The Structure of Politics at the Accession of George III* (2nd edn, London, 1957), 54.

[12]   Griffin, 'Paternal Rights'. Historians of labour, civil rights and gender have been more aware of the political role of the judiciary: e.g. John Griffith, *The Politics of the Judiciary* (5th edn, London, 1996); K.D. Ewing and C.A. Gearty, *The Struggle for Civil Liberties: Political Freedom and the Rule of Law in Britain, 1914–1945* (Oxford, 2000); Erika Rackley, *Women, Judging and the Judiciary: From Difference to Diversity* (Abingdon, 2013).

[13]   See especially Gunter Teubner, *Juridification of Social Spheres* (Berlin, 1987); Mark Bevir, *Democratic Governance* (Princeton, 2010), ch. 7; Fergal Davis, 'The Human Rights Act and Juridification: Saving Democracy from Law', *Politics*, 30 (2010), 91–7.

France (where post-Revolutionary politics was shaped by the administrative law enforced by the Conseil d'État), the United States (where battles between the executive and the Supreme Court have been central to politics since the early days of the Republic), or – most tellingly – Ireland. In Ireland, the legal system was consistently identified with the prejudiced exercise of power by a governing class, and Ireland's political struggles were conducted through the courts in a way that had no equivalent in England – most notably the trial of O'Connell in 1844, the role of the courts in the land question, and the judicial inquiry into Parnell's activities in 1888–9.[14] These comparisons indicate a need to understand how the boundary between law and politics in modern Britain came to be drawn where it was.

Part of the explanation comes from within the law itself.[15] The professionalisation of the law and the growing formalisation of legal education steadily increased the gulf between the trained lawyer and the country gentleman, whose legal knowledge derived from Burn's *Justice of the Peace* and Blackstone's *Commentaries on the laws of England*.[16] That gulf was widened further by the intellectual revolution that transformed the common law from the 1760s, as traditional doctrines and procedures were reconceptualised in terms of new 'scientific' rules and principles, and as printed law reports displaced older sources of law.[17] The result of these changes was to make legal discourse less accessible to the layman, and less usable within the political arena. For that reason, as Stefan Collini has noted, by the second half of the nineteenth century, lawyers who engaged in the political arena tended to draw more heavily on the linguistic arsenal of liberal moralism rather than the technical language of the law.[18] But these changes within the law were not the only forces at work. Politicians themselves were active in efforts to disentangle the 'legal' from the 'political'. Sometimes this was performative, as when the

---

[14] R.W. Kostal, 'Rebels in the Dock: The Prosecution of the Dublin Fenians, 1865–6', *Éire-Ireland*, 34 (1999), 70–96. I plan to write about the Irish experience at greater length in forthcoming work.

[15] The focus of this chapter is on politicians' efforts to separate law from politics: the legal profession's contributions to this project will be covered in my book *The Gender Order and the Judicial Imagination* (forthcoming).

[16] On professionalisation, see Raymond Cocks, *Foundations of the Modern Bar* (London, 1983); Penelope Corfield, *Power and the Professions in Britain, 1700–1850* (London, 1995); Patrick Polden, 'The Legal Professions', in William Cornish *et al.* (eds), *The Oxford History of the Laws of England* [hereafter *OHLE*], vol. XI 1820–1914: English *Legal System* (Oxford, 2010), 959–1222.

[17] Michael Lobban, *The Common Law and English Jurisprudence, 1760–1850* (Oxford, 1991); Polden, 'Legal Professions', 1211–22.

[18] Stefan Collini, *Public Moralists: Political Thought and Intellectual Life in Britain, 1850–1930* (Oxford, 1991), ch. 7.

Liberalism, the Law and Parliament in Modern British Politics

House of Commons refused to criticise the results of legal proceedings for fear of setting itself up as 'a court of unconstitutional appeal from the verdicts of juries and the judgments of courts of justice'.[19] In the remainder of this chapter, our attention will be on efforts by politicians to establish an institutional separation between law and politics, by removing judges from government, and from the House of Commons.

Problematising Judges in Parliament

In 1765 Blackstone's *Commentaries* declared that 'public liberty... cannot subsist long in any state, unless the administration of common justice be in some degree separated both from the legislative and also from the executive power'.[20] In this respect, as in many others, Blackstone was an outlier.[21] It is telling that this passage received short shrift from politicians like the Prime Minister, Lord Grenville, who in 1806 dismissed it as 'fanciful and impracticable'.[22] In that year, Grenville decided to appoint Lord Ellenborough, the Lord Chief Justice of the King's Bench, to the Cabinet as part of the 'ministry of all the talents'. The resulting controversy reveals great confusion about where the boundary between law and politics ought to lie, in part because new forms of liberal governmentality were having to work through early-modern institutional structures.

Ellenborough's appointment immediately attracted criticism from the Pittites. Walter Stanhope said that a judge 'should not only be above all bias, but above all suspicion of bias'.[23] Spencer Perceval asked whether 'the public, in troublesome times, such as, some years since, existed, when prosecutions were frequent against seditious persons, [would] be satisfied of the purity of that justice administered by a judge, the colleague of the Cabinet ministers, who thought prosecutions necessary'.[24] Castlereagh, for his part, asked how a judge in the Cabinet could be expected to deal with 'Libels on the government of which he forms a part; prosecutions against a colleague for malversation; trials for state offences, or questions connected with the construction of statutes in

---

[19] Sir James Graham: *Hansard*, 26 July 1842, vol. 65, c. 668.

[20] William Blackstone, *Commentaries on the Laws of England* (Oxford, 2016), vol. I, 173.

[21] Lobban, *Common Law*, 47–9.

[22] *Hansard*, 3 March 1806, vol. 6, c. 280; see also *ibid.*, 274 (Earl of Carnarvon); 295 (Mr Bond); 314 (Charles James Fox).

[23] *Hansard*, 3 March 1806, vol. 6, cc. 287–8, 291, 288.

[24] *Ibid.*, 334.

which the administration of the day take an interest'.[25] The 'respect and confidence of the public' was at stake – no small thing during the age of revolutions.[26]

But these criticisms did not find favour with the House of Commons. Indeed, 'Fox said he had never had a case more easy to defend.'[27] Stanhope had difficulty in finding someone in the House to second a motion critical of the appointment, and when he did, it was defeated by 222 votes to 64; in the Lords a similar motion was not even put to a vote.[28] For one thing, the examples of Hardwicke and Mansfield provided precedents for having a chief justice in the Cabinet.[29] More importantly, these debates illustrate how disentangling judicial functions from the executive required the emergence of modern institutional structures like the Cabinet. The central claim in Fox's speech was that 'there is nothing in our constitution that recognises any such institution as a Cabinet council'; there was only the Privy Council. Since judges were frequently privy councillors, the argument went, there was no irregularity in Ellenborough joining the government because that involved a commitment no different from that of a privy councillor.[30] Ellenborough himself made this argument in a letter to Perceval, when he complained that 'I am wholly at a loss to discover what duties in respect of advice to the crown are cast upon me in the character of, what is called, a Cabinet counsellor, which do not already attach upon me as a member of the Privy Council'.[31] Fox's claim that the Cabinet was not a feature of the constitution was subjected to considerable sarcasm from Canning; but the argument was nonetheless taken seriously because the Cabinet had only begun to emerge from the Privy Council in the middle of the eighteenth century, and it was not formally recognised until the early twentieth century.[32] The same argument was revived in 1832, when Lord Lyndhurst, at the time Chief Baron of the Exchequer, derailed the Reform Bill in the Lords, and then was called upon to advise the king about who should form the next government. Lyndhurst, like Ellenborough, argued that his oath as a member of the Privy Council required him to give political advice to the monarch, so he could not avoid

[25] *Ibid.*, 323.

[26] *Ibid.*, 325.

[27] Earl Russell, *The Life and Times of Charles James Fox* (London, 1866), vol. 3, 370.

[28] 'Spencer Stanhope (formerly Stanhope), Walter (1750–1821)', in R. Thorne (ed.), *The History of Parliament: The House of Commons 1790–1820* (London, 1986), vol. 5, 246.

[29] Lord Holland: *Hansard*, 3 March 1806, vol. 6, c. 278. Lord Sidmouth, *ibid.*, 269. The evidence for who had served in past Cabinets was disputed.

[30] Fox: *ibid.* cc. 309, 317–18. Cf. Sidmouth, *ibid.*, 270; Lord Temple, *ibid.*, 306.

[31] Ellenborough to Perceval, March 1806, Ellenborough papers, PRO 30/12/15/1, f. 22.

[32] Arthur Aspinall, *The Cabinet Council, 1783–1835* (Oxford, 1952).

Liberalism, the Law and Parliament in Modern British Politics 219

being a political actor.[33] While the Privy Council remained an important institution that exercised both executive and judicial functions, the boundary between law and politics was anything but clear-cut.

Nevertheless, in their attacks on Ellenborough's appointment, the Pittites had begun to articulate a recognisably modern distinction between law and politics that by the final third of the century had become the common sense of the political class. Although during the First World War the Lord Chief Justice (Lord Reading) combined his judicial role with special political duties, and Lord Cave served simultaneously as both home secretary and a lord of appeal between November 1918 and January 1919, these were regarded as exceptions to a rule that the judicial and executive functions should be kept separate.[34] The question became how far to apply the new principle that judges ought not to be active in politics. If strictly adhered to, that principle would have required the reform of a great many of Britain's governing institutions. There was rarely enough urgency for governments to spend political capital on such projects, but nevertheless one can trace a growing feeling that law and politics ought to be kept more separate than had hitherto been the case. An early indication was the creation of a specialist judicial committee of the Privy Council in 1833, to handle its legal business. Brougham and Langdale worked to separate the judicial and legislative functions of both the Lord Chancellor and the House of Lords in the 1830s and 1840s, and a concerted effort to reform the judicial role of the Lords was made in the 1870s. This fell through owing to Conservative opposition, but 1844 was the last year in which lay peers voted on an appeal in the House of Lords: henceforth the legal business of the House would be conducted only by trained lawyers.[35]

Reforming ambitions are most visible in the efforts to remove judges from the House of Commons. Senior English common law judges had been excluded from the Commons since 1605.[36] The exclusion of later creations, like the Vice-Chancellors, was ensured by legislation barring from the House of Commons those holding offices of profit under the crown; the Scottish judges were excluded from the Commons in 1733.[37] Nevertheless, many judges remained eligible to serve as members of parliament. MPs continued to serve as magistrates: both Richard Assheton Cross and John Davison, for example, served as Chairman of Quarter Sessions in their own constituencies during the

[33] *Hansard*, 17 May 1832, vol. 12, cc. 1001–2.

[34] Ewing and Gearty, *Struggle*, 82.

[35] Robert Stevens, *Law and Politics: The House of Lords as a Judicial Body, 1800–1976* (Chapel Hill: NC, 1978), 29–33, 47–67.

[36] John Hatsell, *Precedents of Proceedings in the House of Commons* (London, 4 vols, 1818), vol. 2, 29.

[37] *Ibid.*, 64. Lord Birkenhead, *Points of View* (London, 2 vols, 1922), vol. 2, 162–3.

parliament elected in 1868.[38] There were also many Recorders in parliament. Frederick Shaw, for example, sat for two Dublin constituencies between 1830 and 1848 whilst simultaneously serving as Recorder of Dublin, which made him the city's senior criminal judge. Similarly, in the 1830s, Stephen Lushington was simultaneously the Judge of the Admiralty Court and MP for Tower Hamlets – a constituency which sent a great deal of business to that court. From the 1820s to the 1950s there were repeated efforts to present the combination of judicial and legislative functions as a problem, and to address that problem by making judges ineligible to sit in parliament.

The first step in applying that principle came in 1821, with the exclusion of the Irish judges from the Commons.[39] In the 1810s and 1820s the status of the Welsh judges was fiercely debated, with critics complaining that Welsh appointments were a source of 'Old Corruption' used to bolster the influence of the Crown – a claim that was strengthened when Charles Warren, MP for Dorchester, threw over his old Whig friends and became a supporter of Lord Liverpool's ministry shortly after being named as the new Chief Justice of Chester in 1819. In response to the outcry, Wellington was forced to prioritise merit over considerations of patronage when making appointments to Welsh judicial posts, before abolishing Wales's separate judicature in 1830.[40] In 1835 the Municipal Corporations Act enacted that a Recorder could not serve as MP for the borough where he performed his judicial duties, and in 1837 the radical MP Daniel Harvey proposed (unsuccessfully) that Recorders be barred from parliament entirely.[41] There was a lot of concern about the Recorder of London, who was effectively a full-time judge at the Central Criminal Court, and in 1853, Joseph Hume introduced an amendment to disqualify that official from sitting in the Commons. Since the incumbent, James Stuart-Wortley, was an MP, he was able to offer his own defence; he pointed out that because he was not appointed by the Crown or paid out of the public purse, he was as independent as any other judge.[42] In 1833 a Select Committee recommended that the judges of the Admiralty Court and ecclesiastical courts should be ineligible for

---

[38] Cross: Joseph Foster, *Men-at-the-Bar* (London, 1885). Davison: *Law Times*, 46 (12 Dec. 1868), 106.

[39] Edward Porritt, *The Unreformed House of Commons: Parliamentary Representation before 1832* (Cambridge, 2 vols, 1903), vol. 1, 220.

[40] *Memoirs of the Life of Sir Samuel Romilly* (2nd edn, 3 vols, 1840), vol. 2, 292; Margaret Escott, 'How Wales Lost its Judicature: The Making of the 1830 Act for the Abolition of the Courts of Great Sessions', *Transactions of the Honourable Society of Cymmrodorion*, 13 (2007), 134–59; 'Warren, Charles (1764–1829)' in D.R. Fisher (ed.), *The History of Parliament: The House of Commons 1820–1832* (Cambridge, 2009), vol. 7, 656–8.

[41] 5 & 6 Wm. IV, c. 76, s. 103. Harvey: *Hansard*, 27 Feb. 1837, vol. 36, c. 1062.

[42] *Hansard*, 20 Apr. 1853, vol. 126, cc. 131–2.

Liberalism, the Law and Parliament in Modern British Politics 221

seats in parliament.[43] The Whigs were reluctant to act, but when the Conservative MP Lord Hotham proposed an amendment to bar the Admiralty Judge from sitting in the House of Commons in 1840, Lord John Russell reluctantly agreed to it, 'perceiving that the sense of the House was against him'.[44] In 1847 the new county court judges were deemed ineligible for seats in parliament, on the grounds that they were full-time jobs.[45] In 1853 Hotham tried a more ambitious reform, when he proposed to exclude from the Commons the Master of the Rolls, the Judges of the Ecclesiastical Courts in Canterbury, York and Ireland, and the Judge of the Admiralty Court in Ireland.[46]

The most striking proposal in Hotham's bill concerned the Master of the Rolls, the second most senior Chancery judge. The new mood can be seen from the fact that when Lord Melbourne offered Henry Bickersteth the Mastership of the Rolls in 1836, Bickersteth told him that he was 'on principle, opposed to the union of judicial and political offices in the same person'. He reluctantly agreed to accept a peerage, but only on the condition that he be considered 'wholly free from any political and party tie'.[47] That is telling, but so is Melbourne's bemusement at his scruples. Bickersteth's successor, Sir John Romilly, was not as high-minded, and combined his office with sitting as MP for Devonport, but Hotham's 1853 bill demonstrated how the tide was turning. Hotham argued that getting a seat in parliament would associate judges with all of the pandering, corruption and violence attendant on contested elections – especially now that nomination boroughs were no more.[48] He was supported by Sir Fitzroy Kelly (a future Chief Baron of the Exchequer who would himself later be accused of electoral bribery),[49] and the argument carried particular force because Romilly had lost his seat in 1852 after canvassing for voters in a manner that 'some people regarded... as a great scandal, and inconsistent with high judicial functions'.[50]

---

[43] 'Report of the Select Committee on Admiralty Courts' (Select Committee on Judges of Prerogative Court, Admiralty Court, Arches Court, and Consistory Court of London), *Parliamentary Papers* (1833) VII, 379.

[44] *Hansard*, 22 June 1840, vol. 54, c. 1411.

[45] Bankruptcy Act 1847 (10 & 11 Vict. c. 102); *Hansard*, 14 July 1847, vo. 94, cc. 321–2.

[46] *Parliamentary Papers* (1852–3) vol. 3, 757 (bill 195).

[47] Thomas Duffus Hardy, *Memoirs of the Right Honourable Henry, Lord Langdale* (London, 2 vols, 1852), vol. 1, 450–1, 453–4.

[48] *Hansard*, 3 March 1853, vol. 124, cc. 1000–1.

[49] Shimon Shetreet and Sophie Turenne, *Judges on Trial: The Independence and Accountability of the English Judiciary* (Cambridge, 2nd edn, 2013), 349–50.

[50] Kelly: *Hansard*, 13 Apr. 1853, vol. 125, c. 1084. On Romilly, see *Hansard*, 7 Feb. 1856, vol. 140, c. 326.

Whigs, Parliament and the Law

This project to differentiate law and politics more sharply was essential to modern liberal governmentality, but it was not a Whig project. The Whigs' ambition in passing the Reform Act had been to restore the authority of parliament by producing a House of Commons that was representative of all interests, and capable of effective government because it was well-informed about the issues facing the country.[51] It is notable that, when Lord John Russell returned to the issue of parliamentary reform in 1854, his bill would have created a new constituency representing the Inns of Court, to ensure that the legal profession had a voice in the counsels of the nation.[52] This vision of how parliament ought to function meant that the Whigs consistently resisted efforts to remove judges from the Commons, arguing that it was for the benefit of that House to be able to draw on their expertise. Melbourne made this case in 1839, when opposing the removal of the judge of the Admiralty Court from the Commons; that judge, he said, 'might, in certain matters give very important weight and authority to the opinion or decisions of the House of Commons' when considering 'the law of nations, and... the laws of other countries'.[53] In 1853 Thomas Macaulay warned that the tendency of bills like Hotham's was to weaken the House of Commons relative to the House of Lords, where the greater pool of talent and expertise would henceforth be found.[54] Consequently, he thought that they should remove the bar on the Judge of the Admiralty Court, the Lords Justices and the Vice-Chancellors from entering the Commons.[55] The debate on Hotham's bill took place against a backdrop of concern that the Commons was passing a great deal of muddled legislation, which is why, in 1856, Russell supported proposals to create a minister of justice to supervise new legislation.[56] Under those circumstances, the Whigs saw force in Russell's argument that, 'it was for the advantage of the constitution of this House, that there should be in it as many men of learning as the people would send to it'.[57] Ultimately, the Whigs argued, whether a man should be returned to the Commons was a matter for the voters.[58] Besides, Macaulay said, it was futile

---

[51] Parry, *Rise and Fall*, ch. 3.

[52] *Reynolds's Newspaper*, 5 March 1854, 7.

[53] *Hansard*, 13 Aug. 1839, vol. 50, c. 243.

[54] *Hansard*, 1 June 1853, vol. 127, cc. 1001–3.

[55] *Ibid.*, c. 1008.

[56] *Hansard*, 12 Feb. 1856, vol. 140, c. 652; 12 Feb. 1857, vol. 144, cc. 557–8.

[57] *Hansard*, 22 June 1840, vol. 54, c. 1411.

[58] Russell: *Hansard*, 13 Apr. 1853, vol. 125, cc. 1090–1; Ewart: *ibid.*, 1089; Labouchere: *Hansard*, 20 Apr. 1853, vol. 126, c. 136; Atherton: *ibid.*; Vernon: *ibid.*, 140.

Liberalism, the Law and Parliament in Modern British Politics   223

to insist on a conceptual separation of law and politics when 'the political and judicial... [were] interwoven from the top to the bottom of our system'.[59]

In the vote on Hotham's bill on 1 June 1853, 146 of those identified as Whigs, Liberals or Reformers voted against it, and only 15 in favour.[60] Among those 15 were Richard Cobden and several of his supporters, although those who self-identified as radicals were by no means all in favour of the bill and the independent Irish MPs were split 9 to 7 against. Followers of Lord Derby, on the other hand, overwhelmingly supported the bill: 81 voted for the bill and 26 against. The 'independent Conservatives' divided 13 to 9 against the bill, while nine self-proclaimed 'liberal conservatives' voted in favour of it. The 26 Peelites who voted all opposed the bill: presumably, this was the cost of keeping alive their coalition with the Whigs. It has been suggested that this was pure party politics: the Whigs were simply rallying behind their friend Romilly.[61] Certainly one can argue that the Conservatives were actuated by party motives. Without a deep commitment to the Whig vision of a reformed parliament, they had greater scope to insist on the exclusion of senior judges from the Commons; but they could do so knowing that there was no realistic prospect of carrying abstract principles so far as to endanger the judicial functions of the House of Lords or the presence in the Commons of Recorders or JPs. This gave them the flexibility to unite in support of proposals to separate law and politics opportunistically when it would embarrass the Grenville and Aberdeen governments.

The vote was also clearly influenced by the views of the many lawyers in the House reluctant to abolish forms of career progression from which they expected to benefit. They did not share the high-mindedness of the *Law Times*, which in 1852 had proposed disqualifying MPs from taking judicial office. The paper's ambition was to increase the influence of lawyers in parliament, by removing the suspicion that they were willing to subordinate principle to the pursuit of professional advancement; but the debates on Hotham's bill would have done little to dispel this impression.[62] Sir Fitzroy Kelly, for example, defended the presence of the Recorders in the Commons on the grounds that to exclude them would adversely affect men who hoped to advance their legal careers through politics.[63] Of those MPs who had received some kind of legal training, 26 voted for Hotham's bill while 49 voted against. The magistrates in

---

[59] *Hansard*, 1 June 1853, vol. 127, c. 997.

[60] Party identification has been taken from Michael Stenton, *Who's Who of British Members of Parliament: volume I, 1832–1885* (Hassocks, 1976); J.B. Conacher, *The Aberdeen Coalition, 1852–1855* (Cambridge, 1968), appendices A and B; J.H. Whyte, *The Independent Irish Party, 1850–9* (Oxford, 1958), appendices A–C.

[61] Birkenhead, *Points of View*, vol. 2, 170–1.

[62] *Law Times*, 8 May 1852, 42; 5 June 1852, 73; 18 Sept. 1852, 201; 29 Nov. 1856, 117.

[63] *Hansard*, 13 Apr. 1853, vol. 125, c. 1086.

the Commons divided 49 for to 69 against. The most significant supporter of Hotham's bill was Frederick Thesiger, the future Conservative Lord Chancellor. The bill was also supported by James Whiteside, a future Lord Chief Justice of the Queen's Bench in Ireland. Two Recorders backed the bill, as did the Chairman of the Cardiganshire Quarter Sessions and the Deputy-Warden of the Stannaries. On the whole, however, the men who were either judges at the time of the vote or who would go on to judicial appointments were hostile to the bill.[64]

The argument that the coherence of the Whig vote was caused by the party rallying to support Romilly cannot account for the consistency with which they had articulated their case over many years and in different contexts. It is therefore worth considering the Whig position in more detail by looking at Russell's views on the law, which illustrates a particular kind of Foxite complacency.[65] The 1865 edition of Russell's essay *On the History of the English Government* reassures the reader in a brisk sentence that the need to separate judicial from legislative or executive functions had already been accomplished during the reign of William III (conveniently ignoring Ellenborough's appointment). In Russell's view, the position of the judiciary thereafter posed no serious constitutional issues. Since the Glorious Revolution, Russell wrote, 'the character of English judges has been held in deserved estimation: – of their personal integrity, and their conscientious attachment to the law, no doubts or suspicions have been entertained.' The worst that could be said of them was that 'the judicial bias in political causes has been naturally and inevitably in favour of the Crown'; but this was a fault which 'was seldom pushed to any great extent, even in language, and never to any violent or palpable misconstruction of law'.[66]

Perhaps surprisingly, this complacency was widely shared, even among plebeian radicals. Sharply critical voices can be found, of course. In the 1790s, the radical John Thelwall had declared it 'impossible that anything like independency should exist upon the English bench', because a judge 'can have a pension, sinecure, or other emoluments held at the will of the king or his

---

[64] These included the future Chief Justice, Sir Alexander Cockburn; Sir Richard Bethell, the future Lord Westbury; the future Lord of Session, James Moncreiff; William Keogh, a future Judge of the Court of Common Pleas in Ireland; Viscount Monck, a future Lord Justice of Ireland; Joseph Napier, shortly to be Lord Chancellor of Ireland; Robert Philimore, a future Dean of the Court of Arches; and William Shee, a future judge of the Queen's Bench. They were joined by the former Recorders of Hull and Berwick, as well as the Recorders of Portsmouth, Weymouth and London.

[65] Fox's position can be found in J. Wright, (ed.), *The Speeches of the Right Honourable Charles James Fox in the House of Commons* (London, 6 vols, 1815), vol. 1, 3–6; vol. 4, 251–2, 256, 266, 429–31. Russell, *Life and Times*, vol. 2, 112.

[66] John, Earl Russell, *An Essay on the History of the English Government and Constitution* (London, 1865), 88–9.

ministers'. Moreover, 'the men who have the power of interpreting [the laws] are the very men who also have an interest in perverting the laws'.[67] But such statements never achieved much prominence. In the 1840s, the *Northern Star* confined itself to criticising individual judges rather than the legal system. This was partly because, as Wilfrid Prest has demonstrated, in the long eighteenth century the judiciary had shed a reputation for corruption.[68] But it was also because, in popular culture, juries were understood as having 'the authority to set aside laws and precedents deemed to be unconstitutional', and the judge's power was 'reduced to explaining the law'.[69] Thelwall's acquittal on a charge of treason in 1794 supported his claim that the 'manly intrepidity' of British juries could be counted on to frustrate 'all the machinations of courts'.[70] In this respect, Foxite views of the law were remarkably close to those of plebeian radicals. In Russell's 1865 essay on the constitution, he wrote that 'juries [were] in fact the real judges in England', because they had the power 'of refusing to put the law in force'.[71] This was no small reassurance because juries continued to play a prominent part in civil as well as criminal cases into the twentieth century.[72] There was therefore little reason to worry about conflicts of interest when judges sat in the Commons.

If Whigs and radicals agreed about the role of the jury, they were divided over a persistent tension in British constitutionalist thought between parliamentary sovereignty and the rule of law. As Trevor Allan has explained, the doctrine of parliamentary sovereignty 'appears to make the principle of the "rule of law" subservient to a fluctuating legislative majority', yet the rule of law suggests that there might be legal constraints on what parliament can do.[73] For most of the century after the Glorious Revolution, this tension had been

---

[67] Robert Lamb and Corinna Wagner (eds), *Selected Political Writings of John Thelwall* (London, 4 vols, 2009), vol. 2, 265.

[68] Wilfrid Prest, 'Judicial Corruption in Early Modern England', *Past & Present*, 133 (1991), 67–95.

[69] James Epstein, '"Our Real Constitution": Trial Defence and Radical Memory in the Age of Revolution', in James Vernon (ed.), *Re-reading the Constitution: New Narratives in the Political History of England's Long Nineteenth Century* (Cambridge, 1996), 33; John Brewer, 'The Wilkites and the Law, 1763–74', in John Brewer and John Styles (eds), *An Ungovernable People: The English and their Laws in the Seventeenth and Eighteenth Centuries* (London, 1980), 154–8.

[70] Lamb and Wagner, *Selected Writings*, vol. 2, 263.

[71] Russell, *Essay*, 199.

[72] Michael Lobban, 'The Strange Life of the English Civil Jury, 1837–1914', in John W. Cairns and Grant McLeod (eds), *"The Dearest Birth Right of the People of England": The Jury in the History of the Common Law* (Oxford, 2002), 173–216.

[73] T.R.S. Allan, *The Sovereignty of Law: Freedom, Constitution and Common Law* (Oxford, 2013), 1.

managed by a Whig consensus which made much of parliamentary sovereignty whilst accepting that there were constitutional principles which, if violated, would justify resistance.[74] After 1760, however, the potential incompatibility between the two became more obvious, as forms of radicalism emerged which claimed that the point of legitimate resistance had been reached, because the sovereign people were not effectively represented by the legislature.[75] Radicals embraced the idea that the legitimacy of laws made by parliament depended on their compatibility with common law principles derived from 'the law of nature'.[76] The 1832 Reform Act was the Whigs' attempt to reassert the claim of parliament to speak for the nation; but Radical dissatisfaction with that measure was further inflamed by Russell's Foxite enthusiasm for a more interventionist model of government.[77] The Whigs made strong claims for the reformed parliament's authority to legislate on a wide range of social and religious issues, but radicals responded by insisting that natural law placed limits on parliamentary sovereignty. So, for example, the firebrand Chartist orator J.R. Stephens cited Blackstone and other legal authorities to support his claim that 'The new poor-law bill... was an act of Parliament that ought not to be obeyed, for, being contrary to the laws of God, it was no law at all.'[78]

In contrast with this radical enthusiasm for natural law, Whig politics in the age of reform was strongly positivist, and this accounts for a rare breach in Russell's otherwise complacent view of the judiciary. In 1844, discussing the law of criminal conspiracy as it bore on Irish politics, he complained that it was no longer 'the ancient law of the land; it is not statute law, but law depending upon the decision and suited, according to the opinion of the judge, to the modern exigencies of society'.[79] That, in Whig eyes, was an illegitimate usurpation of parliamentary sovereignty. For the most part, however, the lawmaking activities of the judiciary was not an issue that gained much attention

---

[74] Jeffrey Goldsworthy, *The Sovereignty of Parliament: History and Philosophy* (Oxford, 1999), 196.

[75] Goldsworthy, *Sovereignty*, 204–20; Dickinson, *Liberty*, 221–4, 234.

[76] Michael Lobban, 'Custom, Nature and Authority: The Roots of English Legal Positivism' in David Lemmings (ed.), *The British and their Laws in the Eighteenth Century* (Woodbridge, 2005), 52–7; George Owers, 'Common Law Jurisprudence and Ancient Constitutionalism in the Radical Thought of John Cartwright, Granville Sharp, and Capel Lofft', *Historical Journal*, 58 (2015), 51–73, esp. 68.

[77] Parry, *Rise and Fall*, chs 5–6; Peter Mandler, *Aristocratic Government in an Age of Reform: Whigs and Liberals, 1830–1852* (Oxford, 1990).

[78] Josh Gibson, 'The Chartists and the Constitution: Revisiting British Popular Constitutionalism', *Journal of British Studies*, 56 (2017), 80.

[79] *The Times*, 14 Feb. 1844, 3.

from politicians in the nineteenth century, despite, for example, the dramatic changes to women's rights being made by the judges without parliamentary intervention.[80]

The crucial point here is that Russell's belief in the primacy of parliamentary sovereignty reinforced his willingness to see judges in the House of Commons. Given that it was parliament's role to make laws, he believed that the expertise of judges would be valuable in informing the House's decisions. This was not an abstract point: judges in parliament were active in promoting legal reforms. Consider Russell Gurney, Conservative MP for Southampton between 1865 and 1878, and Recorder of London between 1856 and 1878: in that latter capacity, he presided over cases involving married women's property rights and trade union rights, in which he thought the law operated unfairly; he responded by using his power as an MP to introduce legislation which changed those laws.[81]

The Failure of the Whig Vision

In the long run, however, the Whigs' reluctance to draw a sharp line between law and politics proved less influential than the Pittite vision articulated in the debates on Ellenborough's Cabinet appointment. This is for three reasons. First, the rise of party politics meant that the category of 'the political' became associated almost exclusively with forms of partisanship that were less compatible with judicial activity than the forms of partisanship that had prevailed hitherto. Consequently, discussions of judicial independence gradually shifted from a concern with independence from the crown to independence from party ties. The formalisation of party organisation, party funding and parliamentary whipping made it significantly harder to claim that a judge in parliament would not sacrifice his independence. Second, as noted above, the professionalisation of the law and the development of new forms of legal reasoning more sharply differentiated legal argument and political argument in their conceptual tools and frames of reference. Third, it is likely that the culture of the Liberal party changed as the number of MPs who were professional lawyers increased. In the 1820–32 parliaments the proportion of MPs with some legal training was almost 15 per cent; by 1886 this had increased to over a quarter, and they would have brought the culture of a newly professionalised occupation into the Commons with them – one which drew sharper lines between the 'legal' and

---

[80] Russell believed that improvements in law reporting meant judges could not easily deviate from precedents: *Essay*, 89. On judicial legislation eroding women's rights, see Griffin, 'Paternal Rights', 109–47.

[81] Mark Curthoys, *Governments, Labour and the Law in Mid-Victorian Britain* (Oxford, 2004), 87; Griffin, *Politics of Gender*, 66.

228   *Ben Griffin*

the 'political' than that of the older generation.[82] The distinction was expressed spatially, when in 1865 Parliament approved a plan to move the superior courts out of the Palace of Westminster to a separate site, with a new building that finally opened in 1882.[83]

Consequently, although attempts to institutionalise a separation of law and politics failed more often than they succeeded, they represented a growing tide of opinion which found expression in the proliferation of informal conventions to that end. MPs did not stop serving as magistrates, but the number of MPs who served as Chairmen of Quarter Sessions in their own constituencies declined appreciably in the twentieth century.[84] No Master of the Rolls sat in the Commons after Romilly lost his seat in 1852, and that exclusion was formalised by the 1873 Judicature Act. It also came to be accepted that the Recorder of London should not sit as an MP; and when, in 1922, the Lord Chancellor became aware that Sir Ernest Wild intended to continue as an MP while simultaneously serving as Recorder of London, he was successfully pressured into retiring from parliament.[85] In the same year, Lord Birkenhead said that:

> Sixty years ago it was not uncommon to find Judges sitting in the House of Commons. Gradually evolving a policy [...], those who were interested in our constitutional practice found that the only road alike of sanity and of safety was to exclude our Judges from all, even the slightest, participation in political affairs.[86]

These new sensibilities affected judges in the House of Lords as well as the House of Commons. Provoked by Lord Carson's speeches on the creation of the Irish Free State, Birkenhead laid down the principle that 'no Judge... has the slightest right to go upon a platform in the country and make political speeches.'[87] His position received significant support from Lord Curzon, who was 'astonished' that anyone would deny the existence of a 'convention that Law Lords and Lords of Appeal should not ordinarily take part in our political

---

[82]   Fisher, *History of Parliament: The House of Commons*, vol. 1, 259; W.C. Lubenow, *Parliamentary Politics and the Home Rule Crisis: The British House of Commons in 1886* (Oxford, 1988), 365–7.

[83]   David B. Brownlee, *The Law Courts* (Cambridge: MA, 1984).

[84]   This is based on a survey of Michael Stenton and Stephen Lees, *Who's Who of British Members of Parliament*, vols 2 and 3 (Hassocks, 1978–9).

[85]   *The Times*, 30 March, 1922, 12; *Report from the Select Committee on Offices or Places of Profit under the Crown*, P.P. 1940–41, III, 3, 20, 98; R.F.V. Heuston, *Lives of the Lord Chancellors, 1885–1940* (Oxford, 1964), 384. Chamberlain: *Hansard* (HC), 10 May 1922, vol. 153, cc. 2171–2.

[86]   Birkenhead: *Hansard* (HL), 29 Mar. 1922, vol. 49, c. 946.

[87]   *Ibid.*, 905.

Liberalism, the Law and Parliament in Modern British Politics 229

discussions and should dissociate themselves from any evidence of partiality or political partisanship'.[88]

Robert Stevens has shown how, in the early twentieth century, a backlash against Halsbury's partisan manipulation of the bench reinforced the desire to depoliticise the judiciary. As a result, judges went out of their way to avoid challenging the executive, and they embraced the formalist dogma that their role was not to make new laws but merely to interpret laws made by parliament.[89] Most significantly for our purposes, the pattern of judicial appointments changed. 'From 1905 onwards, and certainly after 1912', Stevens has argued, 'choosing High Court and Court of Appeal judges because of their political connections was effectively over'.[90] Whereas 58 per cent of senior judges appointed between 1832 and 1906 had once been MPs, a 2013 study found that since 1962 only one former MP had been appointed as a senior judge.[91]

Nevertheless, there were no more formal prohibitions on MPs serving as judges until the Second World War, when the employment of large numbers of MPs in war work prompted a desire to establish more clearly what kinds of jobs were compatible with parliamentary duties. In 1942 a select committee chaired by Sir Dennis Herbert made a series of recommendations; but owing to the pressures of war and reconstruction they were not implemented until 1957, having been updated in the meantime by a new select committee chaired by Sir Patrick Spens. The Herbert Committee advised extending the existing statutory disqualifications to include the Recorder of London, the Common Serjeant of London, the Judge of Appeal of the Isle of Man, and those stipendiary magistrates not already excluded.[92] The committee agreed that recorders should be allowed to serve as MPs, on the basis that they usually only sat as judges for a few days four times a year. The Lord Chancellor argued that he favoured allowing them to serve as MPs because the higher ranks of the judiciary were often recruited from among the recorders, and it was good for judges to have practical experience of the legislative process.[93] There was little appetite for disqualifying magistrates, but the Chairman and Deputy-Chairman of

[88] Curzon: *ibid.*, 961.

[89] Stevens, *Law and Politics*, 69; Robert Stevens, *The Independence of the Judiciary* (Oxford, 1993), 29, 32 and *passim*; Brian Abel-Smith and Robert Stevens with the assistance of Rosalind Brooke, *Lawyers and the Courts: A Sociological Study of the English Legal System, 1750–1965* (London, 1967), 121, 124, 134.

[90] Stevens, *Independence*, 40.

[91] Harold Laski, *Studies in Law and Politics* (London, 1932), 168; Ross Cranston, 'Lawyers, MPs and Judges' in David Feldman (ed.), *Law in Politics, Politics in Law* (London, 2013), 28–9.

[92] *Report from the Select Committee on Offices or Places of Profit under the Crown, P.P.* 1940–41, III, xxviii–xxix.

[93] *Ibid.*, 97.

London Quarter Sessions were thought suitable for exclusion because, like the Recorder of London, they had large criminal jurisdictions.[94]

By 1957 attitudes appear to have hardened further, as the list of disqualifying positions was extended to include the recorders of Liverpool and Manchester, as well as the Chairman and Deputy Chairman of Quarter Sessions in Lancashire; in addition, all paid Chairmen or Deputy Chairmen of Quarter Sessions were now to be disqualified from sitting for any constituency that overlapped with the area for which their court had jurisdiction.[95] The 1957 Act also disqualified Commissioners of Assize – barristers sitting in place of the judge on circuit. The judges of the many ancient inferior courts had troubled Lord Simon at a late stage of the Herbert Committee's deliberations. These included 'the Vice-Chancellor of the Palatine Court of Lancaster and the Judge of the Salford Hundred Court of Record…; the Judge of the Liverpool Court of Passage and the paid Chairman of the Lancashire Quarter Sessions…; the Judge of the Norwich Guildhall Court of Record …; and the Judges of the Tolzey court of Bristol and Derby Borough Court.'[96] Had those disqualifications been applied to the parliament elected in 1857, they would have excluded the MP for Leeds, Matthew Talbot Baines (Chairman of the Lancashire Quarter Sessions), as well as the MP for Rochester, John Kinglake (Judge of the Tolzey court). They would also have disqualified Thomas Chambers, the MP for Hertford who lost his seat in 1857, because he was Common Serjeant of London. The restrictions proposed in 1957 would also have prevented William Milbourne James, the Vice-Chancellor of the Palatine Court of Lancaster, putting himself forward as a Liberal candidate for Derby in 1857 and 1859, as well as stopping Edward James, Judge of the Liverpool Court of Passage, standing (successfully) in Manchester in 1865. Most of the positions that had troubled Simon in 1942 were added to the schedules of the House of Commons Disqualification Act in 1957, but many of these provisions were rendered obsolete by the 1971 Courts Act, which abolished many of the old inferior courts.[97] The law was therefore recodified in 1975 by the House of Commons Disqualification Act and Northern Ireland Assembly Disqualification Act. These various reforms show that a growing sensitivity to potential conflicts of interest between political and judicial roles gradually transformed the institutional relationships between law and politics. Taking these reforms together, we can see that, since the late eighteenth century, a profound change had taken place in the way that Britain was governed.

---

[94] *Ibid.*, xxv.

[95] 5 & 6 Eliz. 2. c. 20, first schedule, parts I and IV.

[96] *Report… on Offices or Places of Profit under the Crown*, 173.

[97] On the exceptions, see *Special Report from the Select Committee on the House of Commons Disqualification Bill, P.P.* 1956, IX, 98–9.

Liberalism, the Law and Parliament in Modern British Politics   231

* * *

This chapter has argued that the long nineteenth century saw the development of a new vision of liberal governmentality, which required a wholesale reform of Britain's governing institutions if there was to be a meaningful separation of law and politics. That project, pursued intermittently, and littered with awkward compromises, characterises a distinct phase of liberal modernity. Separating the judiciary from 'politics' has allowed judges since the 1950s to present themselves as above the political fray, and this has facilitated new governmentalities which have configured the relationship between law and politics differently. One example of this has been the increasing use of judges to chair Royal Commissions, departmental committees and public inquiries of major political significance.[98] Another example is the Heath government's unsuccessful plan to remove industrial relations into a depoliticised judicial realm through the creation of a National Industrial Relations Court in 1971.[99] Perhaps the most dramatic example of this new phase is the development of a body of public law in which the judiciary has sought to exercise far greater control over executive decision-making.[100]

In the long run, this revival of public law has once again blurred the boundary between law and politics. The early twenty-first century has witnessed a series of dramatic clashes between the executive and the judiciary that have no nineteenth-century equivalents – for example, the Supreme Court's unanimous decision that the prorogation of parliament in 2019 was unlawful.[101] The Human Rights Act (1998) has further accelerated the juridification of politics, by empowering UK courts to assess whether the acts of public authorities are compatible with the European Convention on Human Rights.[102] Some of the claims that have been advanced to justify this more interventionist role for the courts have envisaged the relationship between law and politics in a way strikingly different to that found earlier. A number of senior judges have described parliamentary sovereignty as a creation of the common law, suggesting that under certain circumstances the will of the courts might trump the will of an elected parliament.[103] It is difficult to imagine a position further from that of Lord John Russell.

[98] Griffith, *Politics*, 25–30; Shetreet and Turenne, *Judges*, 249–57.

[99] Griffith, *Politics*, 72–9.

[100] *Ibid.*, ch. 4; T.T. Arwind, Richard Kirkham, Daithí Mac Síthigh and Lindsay Stirton, *Executive Decision-making and the Courts* (Oxford, 2021).

[101] *R (Miller) v The Prime Minister* and *Cherry v Advocate General for Scotland*, [2019] UKSC 41.

[102] Davis, 'Human Rights Act'.

[103] For an assessment of the current position, see Jeffrey Goldsworthy, 'Is Parliamentary Sovereignty Alive, Dying or Dead?', *Public Law* (2023), 126–50.

The transformations described here have considerable importance for the way that we think about British political history. As a result of the boundary work described above, inequalities have been created and sustained in particular ways, and contests over power have been channelled down courses which would otherwise have been different. Just as important, studying this boundary work reminds us that the writing of political history assumes a subject of 'the political' which is itself historically contingent and unstable. Jonathan Parry is quite right to argue that the rule of law was central to nineteenth-century liberalism: but exploring what contemporaries meant by that requires us to unravel the concept of 'politics' on which so many of our histories have rested.

Chapter 11

The Backbenchers of the Nineteenth-century Commons: Activity and Accountability in the Age of Reform[1]

Kathryn Rix

In March 1833, shortly after the reformed Parliament first assembled, the political cartoonist 'H.B.' (John Doyle) published a cartoon entitled the 'March of Reform' (fig. 11.1). It depicted four former Tory MPs, all opponents of the Grey ministry's reform measure, looking on with suspicion and dismay as three newly elected Members – William Cobbett (Oldham), John Gully (Pontefract) and Joseph Pease (Durham South) – entered the Commons. While historians have long debated the 1832 Reform Act's implications, for contemporaries, as this image encapsulated, it 'provided a handy marker for a break from the past' and 'a starting point for new ideas of the nature of parliament and how it should be presented to the public'.[2]

The trio Doyle selected to symbolise reform's impact remained backbenchers throughout their careers, yet were notable figures at Westminster. Cobbett became as prolific with his Commons speeches as his radical journalism, making almost three hundred interventions during three sessions. The first Quaker to take his seat, the industrialist and railway pioneer Pease was commended by the parliamentary reporter James Grant as one of the 'most useful' members, present in the chamber 'from the beginning of business till the adjournment... all attention to what is going on'.[3] Although less vocal than Cobbett, he still managed over one hundred speeches in nine years. Described by Charles Dickens as 'a very well-known character', Gully's 'gentlemanly-looking' demeanour

---

[1] This chapter draws on the research of the History of Parliament's House of Commons, 1832–68 project. I wish to thank my colleagues Stephen Ball, Henry Miller, Philip Salmon and Martin Spychal for the references they have provided and am also grateful to Philip and Martin for reading a draft version.

[2] Joseph Coohill, *Ideas of the Liberal Party: Perceptions, Agendas and Liberal Politics in the House of Commons, 1832–52* (Chichester, 2011), 1.

[3] James Grant, *Random Recollections of the House of Commons* (London, 1837), 301.

Fig. 11.1. 'H.B.' [John Doyle], *March of Reform*, 1833. Lithograph.

in the Commons belied the background of this most unlikely parliamentarian, a publican's son who became a butcher, imprisoned debtor, champion prize-fighter, professional betting man and racehorse owner. Rumours swirled that he had only sought election to win a bet and would resign after taking his seat.[4] In fact Gully took his parliamentary career seriously, although he rarely spoke in debate, telling a fellow MP, 'I prefer to be a silent member. My duties are easily defined, to attend any Committee I am appointed to, and to be always in my place to record my vote'.[5]

From Gully's taciturnity to Cobbett's loquaciousness, MPs' activity levels in the chamber varied significantly, and this was equally true of the other aspects of parliamentary business Gully indicated: service in the committee rooms and votes in the division lobbies. In all these areas, MPs' performance of their duties at Westminster became far easier for those outside Parliament to analyse and

[4] George Newlin (ed.), *Everyone in Dickens* (3 vols, London, 1995), vol. 1, 52; Kathryn Rix, 'Gully, John', in Philip Salmon and Kathryn Rix (eds), *The History of Parliament: The House of Commons, 1832–68* (forthcoming).

[5] Lord William Pitt Lennox, *Celebrities I have Known* (2 vols, London, 1876), vol. 2, 247.

assess in the decades after 1832. This chapter will consider how and why this greater public scrutiny took place, and the implications of this process not only for the conduct of business within the Commons, but also for the relationship between MPs and their constituents. It will examine the reporting of debates, before focussing on a less well-studied aspect of MPs' activities, the recording of divisions. Both saw important changes during the 1830s, with the provision of a dedicated reporters' gallery and the publication of official division lists facilitating far greater publicity.

The Context of Change: The Reform Act and the 'Information Revolution'

These developments need to be understood within the wider context of parliamentary reform. Doyle's depiction of the upheaval in Commons personnel prompted by the 1832 Reform Act was echoed by the *Parliamentary Review's* report of the first day of the 1833 session, when 'a large portion' of the four hundred MPs present 'seemed to be strangers' and parliamentary veterans remarked upon the 'number of new faces'.[6] These impressions are confirmed by the statistics, with a far higher turnover of members in 1832 than at previous elections (Table 11.1). Well over one-third of those returned in 1832 had no prior parliamentary experience. While this had implications for the workings of the Commons, it is important not to overstate the impact reform had on its membership, for as Jonathan Parry notes, 'the act did not much alter parliament's social composition'. Over one-third of MPs elected between 1832 and 1867 had blood ties with the aristocracy, while 'the new boroughs returned men of great respectability'.[7]

Table 11.1. Turnover of MPs at General Elections, 1820–32.

Election	Members without previous parliamentary experience	As % of MPs
1820	87	13%
1826	143	22%
1830	141	21%
1831	116	18%
1832	248	38%

Sources: David R. Fisher (ed.), *The History of Parliament: The House of Commons, 1820–1832* (7 vols, Cambridge, 2009), vol. 1, 242; 1832 figures calculated by author.

[6] *The Parliamentary Review* (1833), vol. 1, 5.
[7] Jonathan Parry, *The Rise and Fall of Liberal Government in Victorian Britain* (New Haven & London, 1993), 99.

However, Parry also highlights that while the Reform Act was not expected to change Parliament's social structure, its Whig framers intended it to alter MPs' conduct and character, 'raising the standards of local propertied leadership' and thereby restoring public confidence in Parliament. Linked to this was an increasing sense among MPs that they should be seen as responsive and accountable to public opinion. For Parry, building 'a rapport with public opinion' in the more responsible parliamentary state created in 1832 was a central strand in the Liberal party's emergence.[8] While a core group of Radical MPs were most prominent in lobbying for parliamentary proceedings to be opened to greater scrutiny, their rhetoric about the importance of communicating with and being accountable to the public resonated with Liberals more broadly. However, the alterations made not only to the procedure and practices of the Commons but also its architecture, to facilitate what might be called a culture of accountability, affected MPs from across the political spectrum. They had to engage with changing expectations of MPs after 1832, if only to reject them.

Another key stimulus for this emerging culture of accountability was the 'information revolution' of the late eighteenth and early nineteenth centuries. The expansion of parliamentary reporting was an important aspect of this.[9] Select committees, royal commissions and the collection of statistics from local authorities all contributed to the 'accumulation of official knowledge' which Parry argues was instrumental in the greater systematisation of government, prompting reforms such as the abolition of thousands of sinecures as Lord Liverpool's ministry endeavoured to 'improve its reputation for efficiency, economy and morality'. Similar strategies guided the Whig governments of the 1830s, and the aim expressed by Lord John Russell in 1836 of 'introducing system, method, science, economy, regularity and discipline' into Britain's institutions was fundamentally intertwined with the conceptions of a more responsible parliamentary state outlined above, signalling a shift away from 'Old Corruption' and replacing 'arbitrary rule with system and accountability'.[10] This drive for efficiency and economy also affected the Commons, which appointed select committees in the late 1820s and early 1830s to examine its procedures and expenditure.[11]

A significant element of the 'information revolution' was the increased availability of statistics, which 'began to pour forth on a range of topics' in the 1820s and 1830s, aided by the establishment of statistical bodies within

[8]   *Ibid.*, 87–9, 131.
[9]   Peter Jupp, *The Governing of Britain, 1688–1848* (Abingdon, 2006), 206–7.
[10] Parry, *Rise and Fall*, 24–5, 35–8, 113–15.
[11] Kathryn Rix, '"Whatever Passed in Parliament Ought to be Communicated to the Public": Reporting the Proceedings of the Reformed Commons, 1833–1850', *Parliamentary History*, 33 (2014), 455–6.

Activity and Accountability in the Age of Reform   237

and outside government, and prompting the emergence of a 'new statistical culture'.[12] Statistics, together with cartography, underpinned the work of the boundary commissioners, whose appointment in 1831 marked 'the first major public indication' of the Whigs' commitment to deploying 'science, method and discipline' in government.[13] However, Lawrence Goldman has emphasised that despite a growing and almost universal enthusiasm for numbers, 'the development of statistics within early Victorian government was haphazard rather than planned, accidental rather than foreordained'.[14] Moreover, as Tom Crook outlines, while statistics became part of the apparatus of government, they could also be used to 'critique and assess' it, providing 'an essential tool of accountability'.[15] The recording and measurement of parliamentary activity, and the ways this was presented to the public, were influenced by these wider developments.

The 'Rage for Speaking' and Parliamentary Reporting

The most widespread and visible means through which MPs' parliamentary activities were publicised was newspaper reports of Commons debates. These formed the basis for the volumes compiled by Thomas Curson Hansard, who did not employ his own reporters until the 1870s.[16] Although there would be no official record of debates until 1909, this had been mooted long before. The Radical MP Joseph Hume noted in January 1832 that he had 'often' emphasised 'the inconvenience of leaving their debates to be published in an unauthorised form' and urged the appointment of official reporters. The Reform Act, with its expectations of an altered relationship between MPs and those they represented, gave a fresh impetus to calls for an official record, with the Tory veteran George Dawson suggesting in June 1832 that 'one of the first objects of a reformed Parliament should be, to take means that the reports of their proceedings should be sent forth to the public in an official shape'.[17]

---

[12] Tom Crook and Glen O'Hara, 'The "Torrent of Numbers": Statistics and the Public Sphere in Britain', and Tom Crook, 'Suspect Figures: Statistics and Public Trust in Victorian England', in Crook and O'Hara (eds), *Statistics and the Public Sphere: Numbers and the People in Modern Britain, c.1800–2000* (Abingdon, 2011), 10, 170–1; Lawrence Goldman, *Victorians and Numbers: Statistics and Society in Nineteenth Century Britain* (Oxford, 2022), xx.

[13] Martin Spychal, *Mapping the State: English Boundaries and the 1832 Reform Act* (forthcoming), ch. 3.

[14] Goldman, *Victorians and Numbers*, xix, 24.

[15] Crook, 'Suspect Figures', 173–4.

[16] Rix, '"Whatever Passed"', 456–7, 460.

[17] *Hansard*, 31 Jan. 1832, vol. 9, cc. 1035–6; 20 June 1832, vol. 13, cc. 908–9.

Hume briefly raised the possibility of an authorised record in 1833 and the issue was discussed at greater length in May 1834, when the language of parliamentary accountability was strongly in evidence. Hume's fellow Radical William Tooke, a leading light of the Society for the Diffusion of Useful Knowledge – a body epitomising the 'information revolution' – moved that the select committee on the business of the House consider establishing or encouraging the publication of 'an authentic report' of debates. He contended that since the House 'was responsible to its constituents... the fullest knowledge of what passed in Parliament should be communicated to the public'. Several Liberal MPs argued for the public benefit of an official record, outlining the problems in relying on press reports, which were selective, not always accurate, and often omitted proceedings on private bills and debates after midnight. Opponents countered that newspapers offered 'as long, as full, and as correct accounts as the public wanted', and that their editing of 'long and tiresome speeches, repetitions and inanities' was an advantage not only to the public, but also MPs, who might not appear in their best light if reported verbatim. An official record would create 'an authorized monopoly', and neither this nor the likely costs chimed with the prevailing ethos of removing monopolies and curtailing expenditure.[18]

The rejection of Tooke's motion cemented the significance of the press as a means of communication between Parliament and the public. This was embodied in the fabric of the Commons from the beginning of the 1835 session, when a dedicated reporters' gallery was installed in an advantageous position in the temporary chamber which MPs occupied after the devastating Westminster fire of October 1834. This replaced the unsatisfactory arrangement which since 1803 had allocated the remote and acoustically poor back row of the strangers' gallery for journalists, who sometimes found themselves competing with the public for seats.[19] The diarist Charles Greville recognised the symbolic importance of the reporters' gallery, seeing this innovation – which Charles Barry's new Palace of Westminster emulated – as 'a sort of public and avowed homage to opinion, and a recognition of the right of the people to know through the medium of the press all that passes within those walls'.[20] Another significant development was the expansion of the press after

[18] *Hansard*, 26 July 1833, vol. 20, c. 8; 22 May 1834, vol. 23, cc. 1228–48; Rix, '"Whatever Passed"', 460–1.

[19] Kathryn Rix, 'Rebuilding the Palace of Westminster: The Architecture of Representation in an Age of Reform, 1832–1868', in Edward Gillin and Harry J. Mace (eds), *Architectures of Empire: Buildings, Governance, and Power in the Age of Globalisation, 1800–2000* (forthcoming).

[20] Henry Reeve (ed.), *The Greville Memoirs: A Journal of the Reigns of King George IV and King William IV* (3 vols, London, 1874), vol. 3, 205.

newspaper stamp duty was cut to 1*d*. in 1836, allowing a growing audience to read fuller reports of parliamentary debates, as newspaper circulations and the number of pages per issue increased.[21]

The publicity given to debates was, however, a double-edged sword. There was recurrent criticism of 'the weight of parliamentary gabble' and 'excessive endless talking' in the reformed Commons.[22] Charles Williams Wynn, a veteran MP first elected in 1797, blamed this verbosity on 'the publication of debates', which made members 'anxious that their constituents should see that they took part in the discussion', irrespective of whether they had anything new to contribute.[23] The desire to be reported was such that in 1833 fraudsters exploited it by soliciting MPs' subscriptions to the non-existent 'Society of Special Reporters', which would supposedly ensure publication of their speeches.[24] Another long-serving MP, Sir Robert Heron, found the first reformed Parliament 'most disagreeable', as 'the Members are almost all seized with the rage for speaking, and persevere in making all sorts of motions, – many very absurd – to the interruption of most important measures'.[25] The statistics corroborate these impressions about the increased number of speakers after 1832. In 1828, 37 per cent of MPs were indexed in *Hansard*; in 1833, 60 per cent (395 MPs) featured. This did not change significantly before the Second Reform Act, with 418 MPs listed in 1863.[26]

As Heron suggested, this presented a major problem for the Commons. Ryan Vieira's work on parliamentary time has outlined the tension between MPs' desire to appear to their constituents as dutiful representatives, which prompted them to speak, and the efficient functioning of parliamentary business, which suffered as MPs' talkativeness put pressure on parliamentary time.[27] This prompted changes to procedure, notably regarding speeches on the presentation of petitions. These were restricted to morning sittings in 1833 and curbed completely in 1835, removing a key opportunity for MPs to speak.[28]

---

[21] Arthur Aspinall, 'The Reporting and Publishing of the House of Commons' Debates, 1771–1834', in Richard Pares and A.J.P. Taylor (eds), *Essays Presented to Sir Lewis Namier* (London, 1956), 239–40.

[22] *Douglas Jerrold's Weekly Newspaper*, 26 Aug. 1848, 1105; *Downpatrick Recorder*, 18 Oct. 1856, 2.

[23] *Hansard*, 20 Feb. 1833, vol. 15, c. 1013.

[24] *Essex Standard*, 6 Apr. 1833, 4.

[25] Robert Heron, *Notes* (London, 1853), 203.

[26] Gary W. Cox, *The Efficient Secret: The Cabinet and the Development of Political Parties in Victorian England* (Cambridge, 1987), 53.

[27] Ryan A. Vieira, *Time and Politics: Parliament and the Culture of Modernity in Britain and the British World* (Oxford, 2015), chs 1–2.

[28] Philip Salmon, 'The House of Commons, 1801–1911', in Clyve Jones (ed.), *A Short History of Parliament* (Woodbridge, 2009), 258.

240   *Kathryn Rix*

Parliamentary silence could therefore be presented to constituents as a virtue. Challenging criticism during the 1865 Renfrewshire election that he had not often contributed to debate, Michael Shaw Stewart observed, 'if every member of the House were to insist on making a speech... when should we ever get any work done?', and other MPs similarly asserted the benefits of holding one's tongue.[29] They were keen to emphasise, however, that taciturnity did not equate to neglecting their responsibilities. Henry Clifford, who rarely spoke in debate, assured his Hereford constituents in 1851 that 'he had never shrunk from work – work that did not come prominently before the public through the press. He had acted upon many committees... and had done his best to promote the interests of his constituents'.[30]

'If All Cannot Speak, All Can Vote': The Recording of Parliamentary Divisions

Given the pressures on parliamentary time, not to mention the lacklustre oratorical talents of some MPs, it was clearly not desirable that every member should intervene regularly in the chamber. But as the *Northern Star* observed in 1849, 'if all cannot speak, all can vote'.[31] Divisions were, alongside committee work, a key sphere of activity to which the significant number of MPs who were silent or rarely spoke in debate could point. Reviewing the 1833 session, Joseph Brotherton explained to his Salford constituents that he had not made many long speeches, but had voted in 120 divisions, while Lord George Paget asked the electors of Beaumaris in 1852 to 'look to his votes, for they would not see his speeches in Parliament', suggesting that if 'nine-tenths of the present speakers... were to adopt the same course... they would get through a great deal more business'.[32]

The Commons transformed its practices regarding the recording of divisions in the mid-1830s, making MPs' activity in this arena far more readily accessible to the public. This involved not only changes in procedure, but also alterations to parliamentary space. Until February 1836, the official record of divisions, published daily in the *Votes and Proceedings*, gave the number of MPs who voted on each side, naming only the tellers. Some division lists identifying every MP involved were published in the press, but since strangers, including reporters, were excluded from the chamber during divisions, this relied on the efforts of individual MPs, notably Hume, to collate and supply

---

[29]   *Paisley Herald*, 1 July 1865, 1. Thanks to Martin Spychal for this reference.

[30]   *Hereford Times*, 14 June 1851, 10.

[31]   *Northern Star*, 20 Oct. 1849, 4.

[32]   *Manchester Times*, 16 Nov. 1833, 3; *North Wales Chronicle*, 9 July 1852, 6. Thanks to Stephen Ball for the latter reference.

Activity and Accountability in the Age of Reform   241

them. Such lists were generally compiled only for important divisions, often confined themselves to listing the minority, and commonly prompted a flurry of corrections from MPs, whose anxiety to ensure their constituents received accurate information reflected the central place they felt their votes played in the relationship with those they represented.[33]

Shortly after the first reformed Parliament assembled, Radical MPs took action, with Daniel Harvey moving in February 1833 for an official published record of each division, listing every participant. His speech was permeated with the language of MPs' accountability to their constituents in the wake of the 1832 Reform Act, arguing that 'the due discharge of their duties mainly depended upon the fact, that the constituents were informed of what took place in that House... In a Reformed Parliament he believed, that all hon. Members would be desirous that their constituents should know how they voted'.[34] If MPs exercised restraint in not speaking unnecessarily, then the division lists were, in the view of another Radical, Benjamin Hawes, 'almost the only mode in which he could show to his constituents the part which he took in the Debates'.[35] Radical MPs were particularly keen to demonstrate their diligence to their constituents, and Brotherton was not the only MP who, in the absence of an official record, shared his own information about his voting habits. James Silk Buckingham circulated an exhaustive account to his Sheffield constituents following the 1834 session, which listed his votes, reproduced his speeches and outlined his attendance in the chamber and committee rooms, noting that he had 'rarely or ever quitted the House before midnight' and 'never occupied more than half an hour at any meal, nor slept for more than six hours at any one time since the session began'.[36]

Harvey's motion for official division lists was rejected, the key objection being that altering the method of taking divisions might consume more of that valuable parliamentary commodity: time. However, from the ministerial front bench Viscount Althorp sympathised with Radical concerns about accountability, concurring that 'every Member ought... to be responsible to his constituents as well as to himself'.[37] Harvey's fellow Radical, Henry Ward, who secured a select committee on the question in 1834, deployed the same rhetoric, arguing that 'without publicity, responsibility could not exist'.[38] This was one of several inquiries into Commons procedures in the first reformed parliament, in keeping with the prevailing desire for greater efficiency. Its preferred solution was

---

[33]   Rix, "'Whatever Passed'", 464–5.

[34]   *Hansard*, 21 Feb. 1833, vol. 15, cc. 1079–80.

[35]   *Hansard*, 11 Feb. 1834, vol. 21, c. 243.

[36]   *Sheffield Independent*, 30 Aug. 1834, 4.

[37]   *Hansard*, 21 Feb. 1833, vol. 15, c. 1083.

[38]   *Hansard*, 11 Feb. 1834, vol. 21, cc. 241–2.

242   *Kathryn Rix*

to construct a second division lobby, replacing the current practice which saw the presumed majority counted in the chamber and the presumed minority go out into the single Commons lobby. Yet the notoriously cramped space which the Commons occupied meant it refrained from recommending this. Instead, there was an unsatisfactory and swiftly abandoned experiment in July 1834 with a new method of taking divisions involving extra clerks.[39]

As with the reporters' gallery, the remodelling of parliamentary space after the 1834 fire facilitated change. Freed from the physical constraints of their old surroundings, another select committee secured by Radical MPs in March 1835 unanimously endorsed building a second division lobby for the temporary Commons. The Whig chancellor of the exchequer, Thomas Spring Rice, embraced the language of accountability when the committee's report was debated that May, agreeing that 'the whole body of the public, had a full and perfect right to be informed of all the proceedings of this House', and yielded to Radical pressure for action.[40] The second lobby was erected during the 1835–6 recess and the first division using the two lobby system to produce a full official division list took place on 22 February 1836. The Commons thereby assumed responsibility for compiling and publishing official division lists, an important landmark, especially given that it would be over seventy years before the same happened for its debates.[41]

The Implications of Official Division Lists

The Radical MP Richard Potter described the shift to official division lists as 'perhaps one of the most important measures ever sanctioned, as a check upon the conduct of members', claiming that 'the country is now beginning to think more of a man's vote than his speeches'. While information on MPs' voting habits had been available before 1836, through the press and publications such as Richard Gooch's *The Book of the Reformed Parliament* (1834), which tabulated each MP's votes in 116 selected divisions from the 1833 and 1834 sessions, the official lists offered the first complete record.[42] Moreover, although there were occasional inadvertent omissions, they could generally be relied upon for accuracy. This was significant, because errors in the unofficial lists had previously offered a loophole for MPs taken to task over their votes. In May 1834,

---

[39]   Rix, 'Whatever Passed', 467–9.

[40]   *Parliamentary Papers* (1835), xviii. 95–6; *Hansard*, 19 May 1835, vol. 27, cc. 1245–8.

[41]   Rix, '"Whatever Passed"', 469.

[42]   *Manchester Times*, 22 July 1837, 3; Richard Gooch, *The Book of the Reformed Parliament: Being a Synopsis of the Votes of the Members of the Reformed House of Commons upon all Important Questions* (London, 1834), 3–53.

for example, the Fifeshire MP James Wemyss had dismissed complaints that he had voted for the Grey ministry's proposals on church rates, objecting that 'the divisions are so inaccurately reported in the newspapers that on many occasions they are not worthy of notice'. Unimpressed by Wemyss's 'fudge' over whether he had actually opposed the government or merely abstained, the *Fifeshire Journal* reflected that 'inaccuracy of reporting is a very convenient scape-goat for public men'.[43]

Gooch's publication was cited in several constituencies at the 1835 election, and while references to it were rebuffed by challenges to its accuracy, they offered a foretaste of how the official lists might be used to take MPs to task for lax parliamentary attendance. In West Sussex, for example, Lord Surrey was greeted with a placard based on Gooch, stating his number of votes the previous session. Although he conceded that 'he might have attended his Parliamentary duties oftener', he declared this figure incorrect and promised to keep his own 'memorandum of his attendance and manner of voting'.[44] The fact that inaccurate division lists were 'frequently produced upon the hustings' in 1835 was skilfully used by Ward in his Commons arguments for official lists.[45]

The official lists made it more difficult for MPs to shirk responsibility by claiming their votes had been misreported, and much easier for the press and other publications to access, reproduce and interpret this information for the benefit of electors and the wider public. Given the growing enthusiasm for statistics, it is unsurprising that a prominent way in which this information was deployed was to calculate figures on MPs' parliamentary attendance. While MPs had previously faced scrutiny of their votes on particular issues, they were increasingly called upon to justify not only how they had voted, but also how often. One of the first publications to use the official lists systematically was *An Atlas of the Divisions of the House of Commons* (1836). It presented each MP's votes in a similar tabular form to Gooch, but unlike Gooch's partial record, included every division (195 from the 1836 session). It also added a novel feature, giving the total number of each MP's votes, which one reviewer tellingly described as 'a scale of diligence' for constituents to measure 'the conduct of representatives'.[46]

The press was the main conduit for informing the public on MPs' voting habits. Local newspapers usually focused on MPs from within their region, providing summaries throughout the parliamentary session of their votes on specific questions. As the *Atlas* indicated, the official lists also facilitated the compilation of annual statistics on each MP's attendance. The numbers of

---

[43] *Fifeshire Journal*, 10 May 1834, 3. Thanks to Martin Spychal for this reference.

[44] *Hampshire Telegraph*, 19 Jan. 1835, 1.

[45] *Hansard*, 4 Mar. 1835, vol. 26, c. 571.

[46] *True Sun*, 13 Jan. 1837, 3.

244   *Kathryn Rix*

divisions local MPs had attended each session were sometimes given within prose paragraphs, but more often tabulated. While MPs' names were sometimes presented alphabetically, it was increasingly common to see them ordered by their number of votes, effectively offering a league table of parliamentary assiduity. A ranked table – headed by the diligent Brotherton – of the votes of Lancashire's MPs in 1838, calculated from the division lists by a correspondent to the *Manchester Guardian*, was widely reproduced in the county's newspapers, where these annual tables became a regular feature.[47] Lancashire was by no means the only region where newspaper readers were offered this material: in 1849 the *Gateshead Observer* declared its tabulation of the votes of north-eastern MPs an 'annual custom', which, deploying the language of accountability, it described in subsequent years as a 'parliamentary audit' or 'reckoning day'.[48]

In the same vein, *The Spectator* deemed voting in divisions 'the tangible function of the Member' and 'the definite deed by which he is to be judged' when it published its alphabetical attendance list of every MP during the 1849 session, extracts from which were widely reproduced and analysed.[49] Press interest in measuring attendance continued into the 1850s, and was given a fillip by the efforts of the National Parliamentary and Financial Reform Association (NPFRA), whose register of MPs' votes could be consulted at its London office. Printed copies were gratuitously distributed, and the association published ranked attendance lists for the 1852–3 and 1854 sessions. Extracts from this register appeared in local newspapers on a weekly basis and the annual lists were widely dissected.[50] Attendance figures for 1856 collated by the 'statistical department' of the Administrative Reform Association (ARA) also generated considerable press comment.[51]

'The Inexorable Grip of the Statistician': MPs' Response to the 'Division-list Test'

It appeared that MPs could not escape what the *Morning Chronicle* dubbed 'the inexorable grip of the statistician'.[52] This chapter will conclude by considering how this statistical information was used, and MPs' response to such scrutiny. Press publication of attendance figures was commonly accompanied by editorial observations, flagging up examples of dedication and of dereliction of duty,

[47] *Manchester Guardian*, 12 Sept. 1838, 3.
[48] *Gateshead Observer*, 18 Aug. 1849, 2; 24 Aug. 1850, 5; 9 Aug. 1851, 5.
[49] *Spectator*, 13 Oct. 1849, 958–9.
[50] *Patriot*, 26 Sept. 1853, 5; *Morning Chronicle*, 15 Sept. 1854, 4.
[51] John P. Gassiot, *Third letter to J.A. Roebuck* (London, 1857).
[52] *Morning Chronicle*, 15 Sept. 1854, 4.

with the intention that these were remembered at future elections. Providing a ranked table of Lancashire MPs in 1838, the Liberal-supporting *Liverpool Mercury* wryly noted that the lacklustre attendances of Liverpool's Conservative 'misrepresentatives' were unlikely to endanger their health, Viscount Sandon having voted in 101 of 293 divisions and Cresswell Cresswell in just 47.[53] Although the radical-leaning *Norfolk News* denied wishing to 'pass sentence of condemnation' on Norwich's MPs, aiming 'merely to place before the public those details which enable them to form a correct judgment', its complaint that Norwich was 'wholly unrepresented' in more than four-fifths of divisions in 1850 left little doubt about the verdict to be reached on the inattentive Lord Douro (Conservative) and Samuel Peto (Liberal).[54] These newspapers were far from unique in viewing these figures through a partisan lens, but this was not just a matter of attacking opponents. Noting that of the entire Commons, only five Conservatives voted in more than half of divisions in 1836, compared with 34 'Destructives', the Tory *Hull Packet* bemoaned their lack of zeal in defending the Church and constitution.[55]

Attendance statistics were also deployed within wider critiques of the representative system. Reporting in its 1849 analysis that 'not half the Members attend half the divisions', the *Spectator* did not blame any particular party for 'excessive laxity of attendance', since 'all are alike demoralized', and contended that no suffrage reform would have much impact without 'a new spirit' in the exercise of the franchise and 'the representative function'. While foregrounding the deficient attendance of MPs with aristocratic connections, it was also unsparing of the supporters of the nascent parliamentary reform movement, noting that the 84 MPs who voted for Hume's 'Little Charter' that session had mustered an average of 138 absences from divisions.[56] This was somewhat ironic, given the efforts Hume and his NPFRA colleagues devoted to publicising MPs' voting records, in the hopes of encouraging the return of more members sympathetic to their aims. The same desire underpinned John Gassiot's 1856 statistics for the ARA, compiled to give the public 'easy and simple means' of forming opinions on their representatives at the impending election.[57] Like the *Spectator*, Gassiot focused not on specific votes, but the wider problem of 'indifference and negligence', which contravened the ARA's objective of improving the efficiency of the public service. MPs' absenteeism allowed

---

[53] *Liverpool Mercury*, 21 Sept. 1838, 6.

[54] *Norfolk News*, 24 Aug. 1850, 2.

[55] *Hull Packet*, 13 Jan. 1837, 1. Thanks to Stephen Ball for this reference.

[56] *Spectator*, 13 Oct. 1849, 960.

[57] *Morning Chronicle*, 29 Sept. 1856, 5.

'bad measures' to be carried, 'and good ones lost'.[58] Reflecting the association's concerns about the aristocracy's pervasive influence within government, he highlighted the inattentiveness of MPs connected with the aristocratic and landed interest, from whom it was 'hopeless' to expect 'business-like' attendance. He was more sanguine that 'the power of public opinion' could be wielded over those representing the 'independent' and 'popular' constituencies enfranchised in 1832.[59]

For some MPs and their supporters, particularly Liberals, the statistics provided welcome proof of their diligence, and were deployed in a variety of ways. At the 1852 Ashton-under-Lyne nomination, Charles Hindley's seconder boasted that his attendance the previous session had exceeded even the conscientious Brotherton's, while at the 1859 Finsbury contest, William Cox's supporters displayed placards at public houses showing his dedicated attendance.[60] Samuel Greer, one of the most attentive Irish MPs, 'was happy' to tell his Londonderry constituents in a review of his first parliamentary session in 1857 that he 'stood well' in the attendance tables, arguing that 'the member who was not faithful and diligent in attending to his duties as a representative ought to be called to account'.[61] Bombarding his Sheffield constituents with statistics at a meeting in November 1856, George Hadfield stated that he had voted in 702 of 908 divisions since his election in 1852, and had also attended the Commons on 145 days when no division took place, presented 495 petitions, accompanied 56 deputations to ministers and put his name to 14 bills.[62]

In contrast, other MPs rebuffed attempts to reduce their Commons contribution to mere numbers. While the official lists meant they could no longer claim their votes were misreported, MPs used other tactics when challenged about their attendance. At the 1847 Northumberland North nomination, Lord Ossulston was confronted with a placard showing that he had voted in only 47 of 610 divisions during his Commons career. Despite this meagre showing, which he blamed partly on 'foreign travel', he claimed to have voted 'in almost every important division', and this hustings intervention failed to change his habits, being the second least attentive north-eastern MP in 1850.[63] Seeking re-election for Lancashire South in 1837, Lord Francis Egerton rejected attacks on his poor attendance, insisting that 'the quantity of his votes was more than counterbalanced by their quality'. He disdained the idea of attending 'every

---

[58] *Stroud Journal*, 20 Dec. 1856, 6; John P. Gassiot, *Second letter to J.A. Roebuck* (London, 1856), 9–10.

[59] *Morning Chronicle*, 29 Sept. 1856, 5.

[60] *Manchester Examiner and Times*, 7 July 1852, 8; *Islington Times*, 30 Apr. 1859, 2.

[61] *Londonderry Standard*, 15 Oct. 1857, 2.

[62] *Manchester Examiner and Times*, 15 Nov. 1856, 12.

[63] *Daily News*, 9 Aug. 1847, 3; *Gateshead Observer*, 24 Aug. 1850, 5.

Activity and Accountability in the Age of Reform   247

paltry ring of the division bell', but would participate in key votes in defence of Church and crown. Yet his laxness continued as he toured the Mediterranean on his yacht for health reasons, voting nine times in 1839 and not once in 1840.[64] Egerton's son Algernon, who later represented the same constituency, was similarly dismissive when challenged about his attendance at the 1865 nomination, where his colleague William Legh tore up a card with their voting records, declaring that 'I do not care twopence for it'.[65]

Although these were Conservative backbenchers, misgivings about using the division lists to assess MPs' diligence were not confined to them. As Crook and O'Hara note, 'the very use of statistics in relation to political matters was questioned', and the attendance figures were no exception.[66] The *Globe* declared the ARA's attendance tables one of the 'most extraordinary... abuses of statistics'. While 'mechanical tests' of MPs' 'usefulness' might have 'a wonderful charm for the spirit of the age', it attacked 'the gross gullibility which will accept such palpably absurd arithmetical criteria'.[67] As *The Times* pointed out, by this measure, leading figures such as William Gladstone (who voted 58 times out of 198 in 1856) and Lord John Russell (with just 28 votes) would be found lacking.[68] MPs seized on such examples to defend their own record. Cautioning against 'attaching too much importance' to the 'Division-list Test', Viscount Newport, Conservative MP for South Shropshire, cited Russell's low attendance as proof that 'the division list was not one of the best tests of the efficiency of members of parliament'.[69]

An obvious issue with using divisions to gauge assiduity was that they measured only one aspect of parliamentary activity. The *Morning Chronicle* was not alone in mocking the idea that 'the whole duty of the senatorial man consists in walking in and out of the lobbies of the House'.[70] Reporting that Joseph Bailey was less attentive in divisions than other local MPs, *Berrow's Worcester Journal* observed 'in justice' to Bailey that 'his labours on Committees have been incessant' and that he had worked 'strenuously' regarding two bills of particular local interest, the Severn navigation bill and the Grand Connection railway bill.[71] William Brown ranked ninth on Lancashire's 1849 league table, but the *Liverpool Albion* was at pains to record that he was 'as constant an

---

[64] *The Times*, 13 July 1837, 3, and 3 Aug. 1837, 4; Kathryn Rix, 'Egerton (formerly Leveson Gower), Lord Francis', in Salmon and Rix, *House of Commons, 1832–68*.

[65] *Liverpool Mercury*, 18 July 1865, 6.

[66] Crook and O'Hara, '"Torrent of Numbers"', 4.

[67] *Globe*, 31 Mar. 1857, 2.

[68] *The Times*, 31 Mar. 1857, 9.

[69] *Shrewsbury Chronicle*, 2 Oct. 1857, 7.

[70] *Morning Chronicle*, 15 Sept. 1854, 4.

[71] *Berrow's Worcester Journal*, 27 July 1837, 3.

attendant... as any of those who appear to have voted more frequently', since his 'business habits and acknowledged shrewdness and capacity' made him greatly in demand for committees.[72] However, the *Spectator* argued that committee service could only explain so much, since Wednesday was the only day on which committees conducted business while the House was sitting, accounting for at most thirty absences from divisions per session. Moreover, those 'most exemplary' in committee work also voted most often.[73]

A more substantial concern was that numerical totals failed to differentiate the significance of particular votes. Faced at the 1841 Hertfordshire nomination with a placard comparing the Conservative Abel Smith's attendance record unfavourably with his Liberal opponent's, Smith's seconder proclaimed, 'we don't count the number of divisions – we look to the importance of them: we don't wish our member to sit through every paltry discussion – as though nailed to the benches'.[74] Looking at the 1856 rankings, the *Gateshead Observer* noted that divisions comprised the 'trivial and important, empty and substantial', while *The Times* recorded that 'the greater part of these Divisions were on private Bills, local Bills, Irish or Scotch Bills', as well as divisions on adjourning the House, measures already decided at other stages and 'purely vexatious' motions. Of the session's 198 votes, '50 are the very outside that an ordinary member... would find worth any consideration whatever'.[75] Another factor was that MPs could 'neutralise' the effect of their absence on a division's outcome by pairing, which went unrecorded in the official lists.[76]

There was some deliberation among MPs about whether they should vote on private bills which did not affect their constituencies. Despite the NPFRA's penchant for scrutinising division lists, its president Sir Joshua Walmsley told his Bolton constituents in 1850 that judging MPs by their voting totals was 'unjust and fallacious', since nearly half of divisions were on matters 'purely of a local character', urging them to consider instead how he had voted on 'those heart-stirring questions involving civil and religious liberty'.[77] At the 1857 Tower Hamlets election, when his patchy attendance came under scrutiny, Sir William Clay explained that 'he had constantly been in the library when divisions were called on some private bill, and, although to be present would only have cost a walk of ten yards, he had disdained so cheap a source of popularity. He could not think that 50 votes upon insignificant subjects were to be compared with a single vote upon an important question', while his fellow Liberal

---

[72] *Liverpool Albion*, 13 Aug. 1849, 8.

[73] *Spectator*, 13 Oct. 1849, 960.

[74] *Hertford Mercury and Reformer*, 10 July 1841, 2.

[75] *Gateshead Observer*, 2 Aug. 1856, 4; *The Times*, 31 Mar. 1857, 8–9.

[76] *British Banner*, 28 July 1852, 3.

[77] *Bolton Chronicle*, 12 Jan. 1850, 8.

Activity and Accountability in the Age of Reform 249

Charles Butler was unwilling to abandon important committee work to vote on 'every piddling bill, with which Tower Hamlets can have no concern'.[78]

Yet not everyone was convinced that MPs could be excused from voting on private bills. The *Spectator* declared that the railway and improvement measures which constituted the majority of them were important because they gave rise to 'endless jobbing' and 'corrupting influences', which the votes of 'independent members' could counter.[79] The *Northern Star* concurred, arguing that 'many of these so-called private Bills, affect the public more directly, more generally, and, in many cases, more mischievously, than any Government or public Act'.[80] As Salmon has shown, private and local measures outnumbered public acts by more than two to one throughout the nineteenth century, forming a substantial element of parliamentary business.[81]

There was, however, a wider issue at stake, namely whether MPs should vote on questions where they were not sufficiently well-informed. The Birmingham MP William Scholefield, notably hardworking in the committee rooms, countered criticism at the 1857 election that he and his Liberal colleague George Muntz had been 'exceedingly deficient' in their attendance, arguing that they had voted on questions of national importance and matters concerning their constituency, but deliberately 'walked out' when the division bell rang on private bills, since 'I will never vote on a bill unless I distinctly know what I am going to vote about'.[82] The Conservative MP for East Gloucestershire, Christopher Codrington, pursued the same course. He suggested that the Cheltenham MP Charles Berkeley, who boasted of his own superior attendance, voted daily on private bills merely 'for the purpose of getting his name in as many divisions as possible... to enable him to present a long list to his constituents'.[83] Using abstention on private bills to excuse poor attendance was not always persuasive, however. The *Inverness Advertiser* gave short shrift to Alexander Matheson's protests on the 1857 Inverness hustings that he had been unfairly accused of neglecting his Commons duties. He claimed that in 1854–5, before his wife's death curtailed his attendance, he had voted on every important issue, but left private bills to those 'who understood the local bearings'. The newspaper

[78] *Globe*, 31 Mar. 1857, 2; *Morning Advertiser*, 28 Mar. 1857, 3. Thanks to Martin Spychal for the latter reference.

[79] *Spectator*, 13 Oct. 1849, 968.

[80] *Northern Star*, 20 Oct. 1849, 4.

[81] Philip Salmon, 'Parliament', in David Brown, Robert Crowcroft and Gordon Pentland (eds), *The Oxford Handbook of Modern British Political History, 1800–2000* (Oxford, 2018), 89.

[82] *Aris's Birmingham Gazette*, 30 Mar. 1857, 1.

[83] *Gloucestershire Chronicle*, 10 Aug. 1850, 2.

retorted that only one in twenty divisions was on private legislation, printing a lengthy list of key votes from which Matheson was absent.[84]

Qualms about voting on matters they did not understand were not shared by those MPs who, in the words of Lord Francis Egerton, would 'tumble down out of the coffee or library room... to vote on every idle motion'.[85] The influx of MPs from the smoking room or Bellamy's refreshment room when the division bell rang, without having heard the preceding debate, was regularly commented upon, and undermined the contention that voting in a large number of divisions necessarily indicated dedication to parliamentary business.[86] Indeed the presence of members who treated the Commons 'as one of the best clubs in the kingdom', and were 'never on committees' but 'always ready for a division', led Charles Adderley to conclude on the 1865 North Staffordshire hustings that there could be 'no worse test of a man being a useful member of Parliament', since 'a man might attend every division... and be the idlest dog in the House'.[87] However, while MPs might challenge the 'Division-list Test' in various ways, it was hard to deny that low attendance figures indicated 'some degree of neglect' of their parliamentary duties.[88] Although it may have been a somewhat blunt instrument, it remained a useful tool of accountability.

* * *

The 1832 Reform Act ushered in a new era in terms of communication between Parliament and the public, as the rhetoric of parliamentary responsibility combined with the ongoing information revolution to encourage efforts to open parliamentary proceedings to greater public scrutiny. The opportunity which the remodelling of the Commons after the 1834 fire provided to incorporate the emerging culture of accountability within Parliament's fabric was readily taken advantage of by those advocating change. While it was Radical backbenchers who took the lead in driving this process, they garnered broader support from their colleagues within the nascent Liberal party, for whom, as Parry has outlined, a 'willingness to respond pragmatically to opinion' was a crucial signifier of identity.[89] Improved facilities for reporters and the publication of official division lists were not the only ways in which the growing desire to give greater transparency to MPs' activities manifested itself during the 1830s. In February

---

[84] *Inverness Advertiser*, 7 Apr. 1857, 5; Martin Spychal, 'Matheson, Alexander', in Salmon and Rix, *House of Commons, 1832–68*.

[85] *Morning Herald*, 4 Aug. 1837, 1.

[86] *Morning Post*, 22 May 1837, 5; *Freeman's Journal*, 19 Apr. 1843, 4.

[87] *Birmingham Daily Post*, 5 July 1865, 5.

[88] *Berkshire Chronicle*, 24 Sept. 1853, 5.

[89] Parry, *Rise and Fall*, 131.

Activity and Accountability in the Age of Reform 251

1836 the Commons stipulated that select committee minutes should record not merely the names of those appointed to them, as previously, but which MPs attended their sittings, as well as who questioned witnesses and how they voted in any divisions. This information was available to the press and public in the 'blue books', which, after prolonged lobbying from Hume, became more accessible following the Commons' decision in August 1835 that parliamentary papers should be sold to the public at the lowest price possible.[90]

As well as changes to procedure, physical space and practices at Westminster, these developments had an impact beyond the walls of the Commons, as the public gained a clearer picture of their representatives' activities in the chamber, committee rooms and division lobbies. The prevalent enthusiasm for statistics meant that a key way in which the official division lists were analysed by political activists and the press was to measure MPs' attendance levels, offering an apparently simple and regularly referenced test of commitment to their Commons duties. Although MPs challenged the use of these figures in various ways, extra-parliamentary interest in them was unabated, as indicated by the appearance in 1869 of *The Parliamentary Buff Book* (covering divisions from 1866–8), which Thomas Roberts, secretary to the Liberal Registration Association, published annually until 1881.[91]

While John Bright might tell his Manchester constituents at a public meeting in 1855 that they had gathered for 'higher objects' than 'the purpose merely of counting over the exact number of divisions' in which he had voted, his allusion to the attendance figures showed the extent to which this culture of accountability had permeated contemporary discourse.[92] As the deployment of these statistics by the NPFRA, the ARA and Thomas Roberts might suggest, it was Liberal activists who embraced this most readily, even though their own MPs were not immune from criticism on this score. Yet while the rhetoric of responsiveness and accountability was most closely associated with Liberalism, the growing visibility to the public of MPs' activity – or inactivity – at Westminster meant that Liberal and Conservative MPs alike faced changing expectations from their constituents about their role. They came under greater pressure to discuss and justify their conduct as representatives, not only in terms of their political opinions, but also their contribution to the business of the Commons. Whether they chose to reject it outright, challenge its assumptions or use it to their advantage, MPs of both parties had to engage with and respond to this new culture of accountability.

---

[90] *Commons Journal*, 91 (1836), 30; Rix, '"Whatever Passed"', 472.
[91] *Evening Standard*, 30 Aug. 1869, 8; *The Bookseller*, 5 Jan. 1882, 8.
[92] *Star of Gwent*, 27 Jan. 1855, supplement, 2.

Chapter 12

Lord Salisbury as Modern Political Man, c.1880–1902

Tom Crewe

Benjamin Disraeli went out in a blaze of publicity. As he lay dying at 19 Curzon Street in April 1881, 'half a dozen agency reporters were literally encamped on the doorstep, waiting for the first opportunity of capturing the fateful news, and for days they picketed the spot in relays'.[1] Undignified, but not surprising: British politics was increasingly within the purview of the public. With the benefit of our access to the archive, we know that Lord Salisbury, Disraeli's successor, fully appreciated the significance of the change; two months before, he told his son that 'Power is more and more leaving Parliament and going to the platform', echoing Gladstone who (understandably) had said much the same thing in 1880.[2] And yet, at the time of Salisbury's accession to the Conservative leadership, initially in conjunction with Sir Stafford Northcote, he was popularly imagined to be almost uniquely unfitted for the new political moment. For most commentators, he was still the young fogey of the 1860s, the man who had opposed the 1867 Reform Act – older now, but unrepentantly anti-democratic. As recently as 1873, Frank Hill expressed a belief that Salisbury had 'forfeited his place in history' and was to the right of Polignac, advisor to Charles X of France.[3] But by 1882, the *Hampshire Telegraph* was marvelling that 'to-day Lord Salisbury is more of a demagogue than Mr. Bright'.[4] In 1884, the *Western Mail* thought that contact 'with great gatherings of the people, and the necessity... of adapting himself to the changed conditions of political warfare in a state of society which has become wholly democratic, seem to have had a bracing and invigorating effect... and to have developed in him capabilities as a popular leader the existence of which had been previously unsuspected'.[5]

[1] F.J. Higginbottom, *The Vivid Life: A Journalist's Career* (London, 1934), 209.

[2] D. Steele, *Lord Salisbury: A Political Biography* (London, 1999), 142; J.H. Grainger, *Character and Style in English Politics* (Cambridge, 1969), 105.

[3] F. Hill, *Political Portraits: Characters of Some of Our Public Men* (London, 1873), 79.

[4] *Hampshire Telegraph*, 15 Apr. 1882, 4.

[5] *Western Mail*, 30 July 1884, 2.

Lord Salisbury as Modern Political Man 253

The shift in Salisbury's public image was drastic and long-lasting, yet the historiographical view has never quite caught up, always having more in common with Hill's verdict than that of the *Hampshire Telegraph* or the *Western Mail*. Salisbury's accommodation with democracy has been portrayed as grudging and partial, his contact with the populace limited and unenthusiastic. His physical size has been made to symbolise his distance from the public political world; he is figured as a lonely rock, an island unto himself, an 'Olympian'.[6] In his remote fastness, he generated respect but not love, admiration but not understanding.[7] His sheer heft stood for 'reassurance', 'stolidity', 'massive imperturbability'.[8] As far as Salisbury has been credited with playing a role in the phenomenal electoral success of the Conservative party after 1886, it has usually been as a savvy party manager, a behind-the-scenes tactician, rather than as a national leader making a highly visible effort to construct a 'popular Conservatism'.[9] E.H.H. Green, while praising of Salisbury's political achievement, saw it as a triumph of management, in the service of a negative rather than positive ambition: 'The Conservative leadership's determination to avoid rather than confront the mass electorate shows they did not seek to construct a "popular" party. Salisbury's strategy was to *control* and not practise popular politics.'[10] Such is the weight of this historiographical tradition that the one serious attempt to posit a revisionist interpretation of Salisbury's politics – by David Steele, as long ago as 1999 – has not noticeably shifted the terms of

[6] According to Peter Marsh, 'he could not derive strength for his claim to the leadership from any domestic constituency... He stood alone': *The Discipline of Popular Government: Lord Salisbury's Domestic Statecraft, 1881–1902* (London, 1978), 26. Richard Shannon asserts that Salisbury was 'protected by grandness and remoteness': *The Age of Salisbury, 1881–1902* (London, 1996), 399.

[7] Paul Smith notes that the public 'trusted and admired him, but they did not fully understand him, and they found him aloof': Smith (ed.), *Lord Salisbury on Politics: A Selection from his Articles in the Quarterly Review, 1860–1883* (Cambridge, 1972), 2.

[8] Shannon, *Age of Salisbury*, 501; P. Smith, 'Cecil, Robert Arthur Talbot Gascoyne, third marquess of Salisbury (1830–1903)', *Oxford Dictionary of National Biography* (2004).

[9] Marsh, *Discipline*, 131–42, 183–213; Shannon, *Age of Salisbury*, 98–132, 307–44, 422–34. Important work on popular Conservatism by Jon Lawrence, Paul Readman, Frans Coetzee, Matthew Roberts and Alex Windscheffel hardly mentions Salisbury. It has even been possible to deny Salisbury any credit at all. Robert Blake thought it 'would be hard to argue that the Conservative ascendancy from 1886 onwards owed any specific debt to its leader, whose real métier was in foreign policy': Blake, 'Introduction' in R. Blake and H. Cecil (eds), *Salisbury: The Man and His Policies* (London, 1987), 8.

[10] E.H.H. Green, *The Crisis of Conservatism: The Politics, Economics and Ideology of the British Conservative Party 1880–1914* (London, 1996), 126.

254   Tom Crewe

debate.[11] This essay makes a fresh effort, showing that Salisbury has been caricatured almost out of recognition, and was, in fact, an archetypal modern politician, utterly implicated in popular politics and in all that was most dynamic in British political culture in the last two decades of the nineteenth century. In doing so, it engages with one of Jonathan Parry's great concerns: the differing ways and means by which, to borrow a phrase from Maurice Cowling, a 'vicarious satisfaction at the leadership of the politicians who operated the system or claimed the right to operate it in the future' was inculcated in the British public over the course of the nineteenth century.[12]

The Creation of a Public Personality, 1880–6

After 1880, what most identified Salisbury in the eyes of his contemporaries as a changed character, and as a major political figure, was his adaptation to the platform. This was a cross-party trend in the years after the Midlothian Campaign. Hartington, who had made 14 public speeches on political topics in the decade 1870–80, made 64 in 1880–5; and Harcourt, who had made 17 speeches in the 1870s, made 37 in the following five years. But it was even more dramatic in the case of the Tories. Northcote gave 7 speeches in the 1870s, and 60 in 1880–5; Salisbury had made 10 public speeches in the 1870s, but between 1880 and 1885 he made 70.[13] (This is even more striking because neither Northcote nor Salisbury fought a contested election in the latter period.) Simply by taking to the platform with such frequency, Salisbury publicised his new accommodation of democracy. In his speeches he went further, asserting the value of meetings as legitimate expressions of public opinion; indeed, it was in this early period that he first began to suggest that they might be more representative of that opinion than a parliament elected in different circumstances some time previously.[14]

Crucially, it was also by means of the platform that Salisbury advertised *himself* for the first time. This mattered because the rise of the public speech had personalised politics, increasingly seen as the preserve of a small group of leading figures, those whose contending speeches (expressive of views, attitudes and character) were relayed to the public by an unprecedentedly

[11]   Steele, *Salisbury*, passim.

[12]   M. Cowling, *The Impact of Labour 1920–1924* (Cambridge, 1971), 7.

[13]   Author's calculations.

[14]   For Salisbury's arguments in the 1880–5 period, see *The Times*, 14 Apr. 1882, 6; 29 March 1883, 6; 23 July 1884, 10; 15 May 1884, 10. Salisbury's views on this subject are discussed in C.C. Weston, *The House of Lords and Ideological Politics: Lord Salisbury's Referendal Theory and the Conservative Party, 1846–1922* (Philadelphia, 1995).

Lord Salisbury as Modern Political Man 255

integrated national and provincial press. In August 1885, the *Glasgow Herald* looked forward to the months ahead:

> On Saturday, Lord Hartington will lead off, and, if he chooses, offer a criticism of Mr. Parnell's... programme... On Thursday and Friday of next week Lord Randolph Churchill, who has before now evidenced the pleasure it gives him to criticise Lord Hartington, will deliver a speech at Sheffield... Mr. Chamberlain will have a chance of criticising his critics... at Warrington on the next Monday. After that Mr. Chamberlain will have a lively time of it in Glasgow, in Inverness, and in South London. But Lord Randolph may have his revenge, for he is engaged to speak in Glasgow two nights after Mr. Chamberlain's speech in South London. The same night... Lord Rosebery ... will speak at... Inverness. After the other speakers fall into line, like Sir William Harcourt and Mr. Trevelyan, ultimately the ball may be tossed between Lord Hartington and Lord Salisbury. This will bring us into the middle of October. But by that time Mr. Gladstone... may revolutionise the whole political situation.[15]

To be one of these men, it was not enough to have the respect of parliament or decades of experience. You had to make a splash. In 1886, the *Pall Mall Gazette* stated matter-of-factly that to be 'interesting' was the 'one quality which in these days is essential to a democratic statesman'.[16] Henry Lucy's perception that it was possible for a public man to 'be a supremely great statesman and yet lack the qualities that give the public an interest in him' was accurate, and the consequences could be fatal.[17] They were fatal for Salisbury's co-leader, Northcote, notwithstanding his sixty speeches. Salisbury, by contrast, never failed to be interesting. If we are to understand his success in the crucial early years of his leadership, which saw him overturn old ideas about himself and establish his ascendancy over his party, we should pay close attention to the 'public personality' he projected from the platform.[18]

Salisbury was never a great platform *performer*. But he did not wish to be one. He has been portrayed as temperamentally unsuited to democracy on account of not being Gladstone – according to Michael Bentley, 'the more Gladstone turned politics into a language of popular inclusion, the more Salisbury deepened in his resentment' – but, in fact, not being Gladstone

---

[15] *Glasgow Herald*, 25 Aug. 1885, 4.

[16] *Pall Mall Gazette*, 6 Oct. 1886, 1.

[17] H.W. Lucy, 'The Earl of Rosebery', *Illustrated Magazine*, 105 (June 1892), 650.

[18] This is the concept used by Philip Williamson in his *Stanley Baldwin* (Cambridge, 1999), 14.

was Salisbury's whole point.[19] Before the Hawarden Kite went up, he was 'anti-Midlothian' in his chief orientations, denouncing 'those quackeries, those hollow sophistries, those plausible clap-traps by which the election of 1880 was won.'[20] He proposed an 'eminently national' Conservative policy – straightforward, sober, practical and patriotic – 'in contrast to the sentimental, cosmopolitan, poetical, philanthropic theories upon which Radicals are too apt to rely.'[21] Tories were sceptical of the value of excitement and emotionalism, and Salisbury presented himself as the antidote to both. Indeed, he literally embodied the essential elements of his political message. As the *Birmingham Post* noted in 1891, his 'bearing and... "platform manner" are perfectly expressive of his moral constitution and his intellectual method. Sober-spirited and intensely practical, he disdains the meretricious arts of the rhetorician.'[22]

Salisbury's rhetorical style was a perfect vehicle for an anti-Gladstonian politics. His caustic aggressiveness – his propensity to deliver 'his opinions in the plainest, least mincing of language' – was highly prized, understood as intended to re-energise the Tories after the disastrous defeat of 1880, a period when, as Salisbury's son Hugh remembered, '[Mr. Gladstone] threw a great shadow on the world.'[23] Salisbury's supporters were happy to credit the G.O.M. with superior charisma, preferring to note instead that Salisbury 'has to the reader, if not the hearer, an advantage... The length and intricacy of [Gladstone's]... sentences... are avoided by the Marquis, who... always manages to be pungent.'[24] Salisbury himself pointed up the contrasts, mocking Gladstone's 'pulpit style' and priding himself on his ability to call a spade a spade: 'You must not interpret Japanese by Chinese (loud cheers and laughter) – you must not interpret Mr. Gladstone's sentiments by the language of ordinary Englishmen.'[25] This distinction was ballast for his argument that only he understood the *real* concerns of the working classes, demanding 'practical' solutions to social problems, as in his famous speech at Newport in 1885.[26] One paper noted approvingly that 'his speeches bristle with facts.'[27]

---

[19] M. Bentley, *Lord Salisbury's World: Conservative Environments in Late-Victorian Britain* (Cambridge, 2001), 299.

[20] *The Times*, 31 Jan. 1884, 7.

[21] *Ibid.*, 30 Mar. 1883, 10.

[22] *Birmingham Daily Post*, 25 Nov. 1891, 5.

[23] *Dundee Advertiser*, 17 Mar. 1882, 2; H. Cecil, 'Lord Rosebery's Randolph Churchill', *Dublin Review*, 140, 280 (Jan. 1907), 146.

[24] *Dundee Courier*, 24 Nov. 1882, 4.

[25] *The Times*, 5 Nov. 1885, 8.

[26] For its importance, see Steele, *Salisbury*, 175–7.

[27] *Hull Packet and East Riding Times*, 1 Dec. 1882, 4.

Lord Salisbury as Modern Political Man   257

A.A. Baumann, a Tory MP between 1885 and 1892, observed wisely that Salisbury's 'contempt for popularity was... one of the sources of his power over the democracy'.[28] There were further ironies in Salisbury's position: he projected himself as Gladstone's opposite while employing the strategies Gladstone had first introduced into British politics, and while invading his home turf, choosing to speak most often in the industrial cities of the north and Scotland.[29] He represented a modern Toryism, accepting of democracy, and putting forward the party's message with all the vigour that a democratic audience required. Yet Salisbury has usually been understood as opposed to the 'Tory Democrat' Lord Randolph Churchill, who started the decade in near obscurity but by 1885 was widely viewed as an inevitable leader, able to insist on his inclusion within Salisbury's first Cabinet. The two men's fortunes were entwined first by Churchill's manoeuvrings over the procedures of the National Union, and then by his increasingly intolerable behaviour in government, resulting in his resignation in December 1886.[30] Bentley has written that Churchill's trajectory became Salisbury's 'in negative: the story of a man whose rise required Salisbury's fall'.[31] However, narratives that view the two men solely as backstage rivals have obscured their public congruity.

Churchill lavished praise on Salisbury in his notorious letters to *The Times* in 1883, crediting him with having 'agitated Scotland and arrested the attention of the Midlands'; it was Salisbury 'who fears not to meet, and knows how to sway immense numbers of the working classes, and who... can "move the hearts of households."'[32] Though sometimes seen as thinly-veiled self-advertisement, Churchill's comments can more sensibly be understood as an attempt to align himself with Salisbury in the public mind, as kindred spirits attempting to revivify Conservatism, doing battle in unfamiliar quarters. This was the impression made on the *Aberdeen Journal*:

> When the Liberal party comes to sum up its... gratitude to Mr. Gladstone, it may remember that it was during his Ministry that one Conservative statesman [Churchill] awoke unbounded enthusiasm in Radical Birmingham, and another [Salisbury] assembled vast crowds to applaud Tory speeches in Liberal Scotland.[33]

---

[28] H. Wolfe (ed.), *Personalities: A Selection from the Writings of A.A. Baumann* (London, 1936), 153.

[29] E.D. Steele, 'Lord Salisbury and His Northern Audiences', *Northern History*, 31 (1995), 230–1.

[30] Steele, *Salisbury*, 159–60, 206–9.

[31] Bentley, *Lord Salisbury's World*, 276.

[32] *The Times*, 2 Apr. 1883, 8; 9 Apr. 1883, 8.

[33] *Aberdeen Journal*, 3 Oct. 1884, 4.

Both men impressed on their audiences the need for improved party organisation. Churchill is much quoted on this subject, but it is easy to find Salisbury stating, for instance, that 'The energy, determination, and resolution to work together must spread throughout the Conservative ranks from end to end, and victory, when won, will be as much the work of the meanest and humblest worker... as of the most distinguished leader'.[34]

The two men offered similarly uninhibited critiques of the Gladstone administration – as early as November 1880, the *Hampshire Telegraph* stated that 'there is, in truth, very little to choose between them', observing that both 'are insolent, passionate, and vindictive'.[35] Both sneered at the 'sentimental' appeal of Gladstonian Liberalism, and projected plain speaking, practical personas appealing (in Churchill's words) to 'the common sense and the experience of England'.[36] They mocked the wishy-washy Whiggism of Hartington, Derby and Goschen, and both gave credit to Chamberlain for the courage of his convictions: Salisbury declared that 'Mr. Chamberlain is genuine... a Conservative is genuine; anything between them is hollow'.[37] Furthermore, as Steele notes, their legislative agendas were almost identical in this period, with Churchill's Dartford programme of 1886 being largely a restatement of Newport.[38]

Identifying Salisbury and Churchill as representing a common type allows us to situate the fate of Northcote in a wider context. Northcote's eclipse is traditionally seen in high-political terms: during the Cabinet-making of 1885 and 1886, Salisbury (recognised as *primus inter pares* by the Queen) proved amenable to Churchill's and then Goschen's demands for Northcote's dispatch. This narrative can be complicated, however, if we ask why Salisbury's action was attended by so few political risks, despite the fact that for the previous decade Northcote had occupied a leading position in the party. The answer lies not mainly in Northcote's weak parliamentary performances, but rather in his failure to develop a compelling public profile and attendant powerbase in the country.

Northcote could not project himself as capable of reinvigorating his party or leading the new democracy. In a period when Conservatives were thirsting for partisan politics, nothing could have been more damning than the *Sheffield Independent's* claim that 'Sir Stafford is generally so genial, so gentlemanly, and so courteous in his political antagonism... that there is hardly an advanced Liberal or ardent Radical who does not confess to a secret and quiet liking for

---

34 *The Times*, 8 Oct. 1885, 7.
35 *Hampshire Telegraph*, 24 Nov. 1880, 2.
36 *Morning Post*, 21 Nov. 1885, 8.
37 *The Times*, 5 Nov. 1885, 8.
38 Steele, *Salisbury*, 177.

Lord Salisbury as Modern Political Man 259

[him]'.[39] The truth was that Northcote – who possessed, according to James Bryce, the 'capacities of the administrator... blended with a philosophic judgment and a wide culture' – represented a political ideal prized in a pre-democratic age. As Bryce recognised, 'Vehemence in controversy, domineering audacity of purpose, the power of moving crowds by incisive harangues, were the qualities which the younger generation seemed disposed to cultivate... For such courses Northcote was not the man.'[40] Even Northcote's authorised biographer admitted that the 'age for which he was fitted ended ere he died.'[41]

When Gladstone complained of the Conservative party's direction in the 1880s, it was because he recognised that the values Northcote represented had lost their purchase; in his jaundiced judgment, 'Conservatism so-called in its daily practice, now depends largely on influencing public passion, and thereby has lost the main element which made it really Conservative, and qualified it to resist excessive and dangerous innovation.'[42] This was a backhanded tribute to Salisbury and Churchill, who together had worked to reinvent Conservatism as a combative and practical creed, unafraid of democracy and progressive reforms but bullish in its defence of institutions and of the British national (and imperial) interest. They shifted it away from its associations with rural docility and towards modern metropolises, in the process reimagining the working man as an oracle of common sense, rather than as a grubby would-be revolutionary.

It is easy in retrospect to see how completely Gladstone's conversion to Home Rule played into Salisbury's hands. He was able at once to unite with Chamberlain and others concerned that the Irish issue would forever block social reforms, and to depict appeasement of the Irish Nationalists as a diabolical extension of Gladstonian foreign policy principles into the politics of the Union. The view that Salisbury had only to react to Liberal schism and not 'muff his chances', in Robert Blake's phrase, misses how proactively he had already defined his own role and line of attack.[43] So much was this the case, that he could afford to dispense with Churchill when the opportunity arose. John Gorst testified to the solidity of Salisbury's self-transformation when he reflected that Churchill's resignation gave no cause for alarm. If it 'had indicated the Government was going back on those popular principles upon which they had assumed office, if it indicated that they were ceasing to prefer the

[39] *Sheffield Independent*, 25 Aug. 1884, 2.

[40] J. Bryce, *Studies in Contemporary Biography* (London, 1903), 226.

[41] A. Lang, *Life, Letters, and Diaries of Sir Stafford Northcote, First Earl of Iddesleigh* (2 vols, London, 1890), vol. 2, 317.

[42] Quoted in R. Shannon, *Gladstone: Heroic Minister, 1865–1898* (London, 1999), 336.

[43] Blake, 'Introduction', 8.

260   *Tom Crewe*

rights of the many to the privileges of the few, it would have been an event of the highest political importance' – as it did not, it was merely regrettable.[44] Salisbury's public presentation for the rest of his career was essentially a refinement on the themes he had made his own in the period 1880–86.

Salisbury and Popular Politics

So far, in considering Salisbury's modernity, I have emphasised his own agency. Yet, throughout his time as party leader, he was also acted on by a range of pressures which he had to accommodate, sometimes endure. The most powerful of these were generated by his position as party leader, as the scope of Salisbury's speaking commitments makes clear. He often spoke at dinners and banquets organised by associations, clubs and societies supportive of the Conservative and Unionist cause. For example, he was hosted (more than once) by the Constitutional Union, the Constitutional Club, the Junior Constitutional, the National Conservative Club, the Nonconformist Unionist Association, the Church Defence Institution and the Irish Loyalist Club.[45] He addressed eight of the National Union's annual conferences (in Newport, Oxford, Nottingham, Birmingham, Cardiff, Brighton and twice in London) as well as the Scottish conference in Edinburgh.[46] (In connection with a conference, Salisbury would usually stay in the area for several days: in Nottingham in 1889, for example, he attended nine separate events, and made seven speeches.)[47] Unsurprisingly, he also spoke regularly at Primrose League events, and in his capacity as Grand Master had the distinction of speaking 12 times to the annual Grand Habitation; such was the growth of the League's membership that the event moved from the Covent Garden Opera House to the Royal Albert Hall, where in later years Salisbury was addressing annually an audience of ten thousand.[48] He also

---

[44] *Freeman's Journal*, 14 Jan. 1887, 6.

[45] *Leeds Mercury*, 30 June 1886, 5 (Constitutional Union of Great Britain and Ireland); *Morning Post*, 23 May 1887, 6, *Belfast News-Letter*, 23 June 1894, 5 and 17 Dec. 1898, 5–6 (Constitutional Club); *Standard*, 30 Mar. 1883, 3 (Junior Constitutional Club); *Derby Mercury*, 9 Mar. 1887, 8 (National Conservative Club); *Morning Post*, 11 Nov. 1892, 2 and 1 Feb. 1896, 2 (Nonconformist Unionist Association); *Morning Post*, 15 June 1894, 4 (Nonconformist Unionist Association); *Standard*, 18 Feb. 1895, 3 (Irish Loyalist Club).

[46] *The Times*, 8 Oct. 1885, 7 (Newport) and 17 May 1886, 6; *Daily News*, 17 Nov. 1897, 4 (London); *The Times*, 24 Nov. 1887, 6 (Oxford); *Glasgow Herald*, 27 Nov. 1889, 9 (Nottingham); *Western Mail*, 25 Nov. 1891, 5 (Birmingham); *Standard*, 29 Nov. 1893, 3 (Cardiff); *Durham County Advertiser*, 22 Nov. 1895, 7 (Brighton). For the Scottish conference, see *Birmingham Daily Post*, 31 Oct. 1894, 5.

[47] *Glasgow Herald*, 18 Nov. 1889, 10.

[48] *Standard*, 20 May 1886, 5; *ibid.*, 21 Apr. 1887, 3; *ibid.*, 22 May 1889, 5; *Morning Post*, 22 Apr. 1891, 3; *Belfast News-Letter*, 7 May 1892, 5; *Morning Post*, 20 Apr. 1893, 2

Lord Salisbury as Modern Political Man 261

opened Hatfield to the party, for example inviting the delegates from an anti-Home Rule demonstration for an afternoon fete, at which he spoke.[49]

Of course, Salisbury also spoke at hundreds of events organised under the auspices of local Conservative associations, all over the country. The new importance of party volunteers in the wake of the 1883 Corrupt Practices Act and the 1884 Reform Act made it incumbent on leaders to travel widely, in order to reward efforts and encourage recruits with appearances and pep-talks.[50] It is also apparent that visits were eagerly sought out in the belief that they could boost the fortunes of the party on the ground – thinking of this kind drove one Scottish Conservative in late 1885 to demand that Salisbury 'save 4 or 5 seats by one appearance in Edinburgh', and Salisbury to remark on another occasion that 'I constantly hear appeals sent down from this place or that place, "For heaven's sake, send us a Cabinet Minister"'.[51] This reflected the national significance of A-list politicians, whose prominence and popularity warranted their intervention in the politics of individual constituencies or geographical areas, and it is certainly the case that platform appearances were plotted as part of a national party strategy.[52]

The new system of public debate was unavoidably and vitally bound up with the 'political visit' to a town, city or region. And, as a consequence, every plat-form speech existed at the centre of a penumbra of activities and experiences that acted to radically extend the reach of national politics across Britain, cre-ating a mass participatory political culture for the first time.[53] Salisbury played such an active part in this dynamic new culture that its main aspects can be documented with reference only to him.

We might logically begin with the train, which, post-Midlothian, remained a major political actor. As politicians wound their way around the country, stations were transformed into venues ripe with interactive possibilities.

---

and 20 Apr. 1894, 5; *Glasgow Herald*, 30 Apr. 1896, 3; *Western Mail*, 7 May 1897, 5; *Belfast News-Letter*, 5 May 1898, 3; *Standard*, 10 May 1900, 4; *The Times*, 8 May 1902, 8.

[49] *York Herald*, 25 Apr. 1893, 2.

[50] K. Rix, "'The Elimination of Corrupt Practices in British Elections?" Reassessing the Impact of the 1883 Corrupt Practices Act', *English Historical Review*, 123 (2008), 65–98.

[51] J.S. Napier to A.J. Balfour, 6 Nov. 1885, in R. Harcourt Williams (ed.), *The Salisbury-Balfour Correspondence: Letters Exchanged Between the Third Marquess of Salisbury and his Nephew Arthur James Balfour 1869–1892* (Ware: Herts, 1988), 125; *Standard*, 24 Nov. 1887, 3.

[52] See comments made by Balfour in *Aberdeen Journal*, 5 Dec. 1889, 5 and *Leicester Chronicle*, 11 Feb. 1893, 3.

[53] This argument is made in detail in T. Crewe, 'Political Leaders, Communica-tion and Celebrity in Britain, *c*.1880–1900', (unpublished PhD dissertation, Cambridge, 2015), 27–61.

262   *Tom Crewe*

Gladstone, as we know, turned such trips into an art form, garnering gifts and giving speeches at the drop of a hat, but he was far from unique.[54] In 1888, on a journey from Hatfield to Liverpool, Salisbury was greeted by crowds at Peterborough, Retford, Peniston and Godley Junction, among others.[55] Hundreds of examples might be provided to demonstrate the ways that station stops facilitated interaction: a politician could expect to be surrounded by people waving, cheering and hooting, pressing themselves up against windows and extending arms for handshakes. Entirely typical was Salisbury's experience when halting at Bedford on his way to Derby in 1887: he found his train carriage 'at once besieged by an enthusiastic crowd' and 'during the two or three minutes that the train remained in the station... was continuously occupied in shaking hands with those who succeeded in reaching the open window at which he was sitting'.[56]

In this way it was possible for a statesman to encounter hundreds of people before he had even left his train carriage. So common was this that individuals were sometimes begrudged attempts to evade notice. One moment, when Salisbury stopped at Retford in 1888, offers an insight into the characteristic feelings of expectation and obligation. A large crowd had gathered but Salisbury remained seated in his carriage, on account of a bad cold. This excuse was conveyed, but still there were 'repeated cries from the platform for the Marquess to stand up' and the chairman of the local Conservative Association 'asked his Lordship to be kind enough to do so, in order to gratify his friends. Complying with this appeal, the Marquess... rose in the carriage doorway' and remained in sight until the train moved off.[57] In its evocation of a political culture in which interaction between the public and politicians was coming to be seen as de rigueur, this example recalls another occasion when Salisbury declined to leave his carriage at a stop in Galashiels, prompting 'one of a noisy crowd of enthusiasts who had been vainly trying to arouse a response from the interior of the... saloon... to exclaim with scandalised indignation: "This is nae politics!"'[58]

It is unsurprising that, though attempts were sometimes made to organise red-carpet receptions for visitors, popular enthusiasm often prevailed over the best laid plans, as well as the forces of order. When Salisbury visited Glasgow in 1884, crowds began to assemble outside the station two hours before his

---

[54] For a fine example of a multi-part Gladstonian journey, see *Leeds Mercury*, 16 Sept. 1884, 8 and 25 Sept. 1884, 8.

[55] *Aberdeen Journal*, 12 Jan. 1888, 5.

[56] *Ibid.*, 20 Dec. 1887, 5.

[57] *Sheffield Independent*, 12 Jan. 1888, 3.

[58] Lady G. Cecil, *Life of Robert, Marquis of Salisbury* (4 vols, London, 1921–32), vol. 3, 115–16.

Lord Salisbury as Modern Political Man 263

expected arrival. Such was the excitement that the police turned a water-hose on the crowd, but this was not enough to discourage them and the ticketed reception was finally overrun by around fifteen thousand persons, 'crowding the platforms, clambering on the tops of carriages, and getting a footing anywhere.'[59] It is possible to find many similar occasions when squadrons of police and railway officials were simply swept aside by crowds determined to mob their favourite politician as he disembarked from his train.[60]

No matter how raucous, the arrival of a statesman was still only a precursor to their entry into the town proper, whether first headed for their place of temporary residence, a political club, or the venue at which they were to speak. When they finally escaped the station, the carriages of statesmen typically processed – or, occasionally, were dragged by their supporters – through packed streets decorated with flags, banners, illuminations and triumphal arches, often preceded by a musical band.[61] In 1893, Salisbury was accompanied into Preston by a procession of twenty carriages, and 'was accorded an enthusiastic welcome by large crowds lining the streets... to the Club.' He then 'went out onto the balcony, his appearance being greeted with loud cheering by a great crowd assembled in the street in front.'[62]

Platform speeches were delivered in the largest available venue in a given town or city – in municipal halls, corn exchanges, theatres, ice rinks and circuses. Audiences usually ranged from three thousand to five thousand, often drawing in people from the surrounding area, with special trains running to ensure their attendance.[63] They could be much larger. In Carnarvon in 1888, Salisbury spoke to nine thousand, and sometimes magnificent temporary venues were specially constructed – when he spoke at Nottingham in 1889 and Exeter in 1892 accommodation was made for audiences of over ten thousand.[64] If you were not lucky enough to have a ticket, further opportunities to access the experience existed for the thousands who crowded outside venues. When Salisbury entered the Drill Hall in Cardiff in 1893, 'the cheers were so boisterous

---

[59] *Liverpool Mercury*, 1 Oct. 1884, 6; *The Times*, 1 Oct. 1884, 5.

[60] For examples of Salisbury's receptions falling apart, see *Aberdeen Journal*, 20 Dec. 1887, 5; *Leeds Mercury*, 20 Dec. 1888, 7; *Pall Mall Gazette*, 28 Nov. 1893, 7.

[61] See, for example, *Morning Post*, 16 Apr. 1884, 2 (Churchill); *The Times*, 6 Oct. 1884, 4 (Hartington); *Sheffield Independent*, 17 Sept. 1885, 2 (Chamberlain); *Glasgow Herald*, 2 Nov. 1885, 9 (Rosebery); *Standard*, 2 Feb. 1888, 3 (Morley); *Standard*, 11 June 1889, 3 (Gladstone); *Glasgow Herald*, 9 July 1892, 4 (Harcourt).

[62] *Dundee Courier*, 18 Oct 1893, 3.

[63] As was the case when Balfour spoke at Northwich in 1892: *Glasgow Herald*, 24 June 1892, 9.

[64] *Morning Post*, 11 Apr. 1888, 4; *Glasgow Herald*, 27 Nov. 1889, 9; *Belfast News-Letter*, 3 Feb. 1892, 5.

264   *Tom Crewe*

that they were heard in the square without and were taken up by the huge crowd assembled there'.[65]

There is not space to dwell on the interactions between Salisbury and his indoor audiences. It will suffice to say that his 'conversational' manner – partly a consequence of his not preparing his speeches in advance – meant that he was remarkably responsive to interjections, often using them to develop a train of thought, or as the prompt for an amusing one-liner. For instance:

> [T]here is no political sentiment with which at this moment I more heartily agree than that I heard just now from the corner of the room, that 'Every day we are getting worse and worse'. (A Voice: 'It is quite true, Sir'.) (Laughter and cheers.) I know not who the prophet is (laughter) whose words I respect, but I humbly sit at his feet as the greatest teacher of political wisdom at this moment (laughter).[66]

Salisbury's daughter remembered an occasion when at the end of one of his speeches, 'the meeting broke and thronged towards the platform. "Don't stop them, let them come!" he said imperatively, and then stood forward, his own eyes shining with the contagion of feeling, while the long line of excited men leapt up one by one to the platform to shake him by the hand'.[67]

Many of those who swarmed outside venues did so in expectation of a statesman's leave-taking. A torchlit procession was favoured for an atmospheric evening exit; first pressed into the service of the traditional political class during the Midlothian campaign and still a 'novel sight' when Gladstone visited Leeds in 1881, it was assimilated into the visual repertoire of both parties over the decade.[68] Indeed, torches might only be the start: after giving his speech in Carnarvon in 1888, Salisbury returned to his residence for the night 'preceded by a torchlight procession... During their progress through the crowded streets fireworks were displayed from the ruins of the Castle, an immense bonfire blazed on a hill, and the fountain in the town was brilliantly illuminated with coloured fires'.[69]

During the daytime – before a speech, or on the following day – other formal activities might be planned, including more elaborate kinds of procession.[70]

---

[65] *Standard*, 29 Nov. 1893, 3.

[66] *The Times*, 23 Apr. 1885, 7.

[67] Cecil, *Life*, vol. 3, 34.

[68] *Daily News*, 8 Oct. 1881, 5. For examples, see *The Times*, 1 Nov. 1881, 10 (Harcourt); *Aberdeen Journal*, 31 Jan. 1884, 2 (Northcote); *Birmingham Daily Post*, 20 Mar. 1889, 5 (Salisbury).

[69] *Western Mail*, 11 Apr. 1888, 3.

[70] In 1887, Gladstone reviewed a procession of 35,000 people (excluding spectators) in Swansea: *Western Mail*, 6 June 1887, 5.

In Ireland, during visits undertaken at the height of the Home Rule debate, Unionist processions took militant form as 'march-pasts'. In April 1893, Balfour was the star of one such march in Belfast, which involved over 80,000 people.[71] Only the next month, Salisbury reviewed a parade in Derry, consisting of over 15,000 participants. One journalist reported an additional 25,000 spectators, noting that the overall total was larger than the population of Derry itself.[72]

Frequently, ceremonies were held for the presentation of addresses. In Norwich in 1887, Salisbury accepted 120 addresses in front of nearly 6,000 spectators and in Edinburgh in 1888 he received 500 in the presence of another 6,000.[73] The numbers virtually represented by these addresses are even more striking – the 151 addresses presented to Salisbury at Bristol in 1889, for example, represented over 51,000 members of the Primrose League.[74] At Oxford in 1887, one address among 500 represented 2,000 agricultural labourers; another represented 8,000 miners from South Wales; a third listed the names of 4,000 Durham miners.[75] On many of these same occasions Salisbury would visit the local Conservative club, sometimes to dine with its members, or to take a tour and deliver a short speech.[76] Over the years he formally opened Conservative clubs in St Albans, Swansea, Derby, Watford, Waterfoot and Preston, to list only a few.[77]

The final departure, heading back to the station, was often another significant occasion. As Salisbury drove up to Larne station in 1893, a gang of enthusiastic supporters 'attempted to unfasten the covering of the carriage, and in their efforts succeeded in smashing the ex-Premier's silk hat, a disaster which caused shouts of laughter, in which Lord Salisbury most cordially joined'.[78] A few days later on the same trip, Salisbury's departure from Derry was gatecrashed by a huge crowd which swamped his carriage as it came into the station: 'In the short distance he traversed between the entrance gates and the [station] platform he must have grasped the hands of hundreds. Directly the carriage drew up at the platform the crowd surged forwards, and as the

---

[71] *Dundee Courier*, 5 Apr. 1893, 3.

[72] *Morning Post*, 19 May 1893, 4.

[73] *Leeds Mercury*, 29 July 1887, 7; *Royal Cornwall Gazette*, 6 Dec. 1888, 7.

[74] *Western Mail*, 24 Apr. 1888, 3.

[75] *Dundee Courier*, 24 Nov. 1887, 3; *Morning Post*, 24 Nov. 1887, 2.

[76] E.g. he dined at the Bradford and County Conservative Club on a visit to the locality in 1895: *Leeds Mercury*, 23 May 1895, 5.

[77] *Aberdeen Journal*, 23 Sept. 1886, 5; *Western Mail*, 11 Jan. 1887, 2; *Birmingham Daily Post*, 20 Dec. 1887, 5 and 20 May 1889, 5; *Daily News*, 4 Dec. 1890, 3; *Birmingham Daily Post*, 18 Oct. 1893, 5.

[78] *Standard*, 24 May 1893, 3.

266   Tom Crewe

Marquess alighted they seized him bodily and carried him into the saloon.'[79] (It is worth noting that Salisbury then weighed over 18 stone.)[80]

It should by now be apparent that the platform brought statesmen into unprecedented proximity with the public: its processions, handshakes and verbal exchanges provided, in Joseph Meisel's phrase, 'an intimate form of mass politics for a society that had only barely become a mass polity.'[81] At the same time, these interactions functioned to enhance and advertise the legitimacy of the political class. To better convey the nature of this dual achievement, it is helpful to introduce the idea of 'manly flattery'. The phrase is John Morley's, who used it with reference to Gladstone's Midlothian campaigns: 'The only flattery in the... speeches was the manly flattery contained in the fact that he took care to address all these multitudes... just as he would have addressed the House of Commons.'[82] The institutionalisation of the platform after Midlothian, routinely figuring audiences around the country as both confidants and supreme arbiters, might be seen as 'manly flattery' writ large. Henry Jephson was surely on the mark when he suggested that, '[a]s individuals people feel themselves of little consequence, but a public meeting begets a sense of power, and to some extent also a sense of responsibility... There is... a sense of participating in Government which is pleasing to men's self-esteem. The Platform is, in fact, the outward and visible sign of their possession of power.'[83]

However, 'manly flattery' did not only amount to leading politicians taking the public into their confidence. They also had little choice but to adapt to the rough-and-tumble of popular politics. Thus their flattery of the democracy was manly in a more literal sense, requiring a considerable sacrifice of personal comfort and autonomy without loss of good cheer. Salisbury watched his police escorts dissolve and official receptions be crushed, permitted his train carriages to be invaded and his vehicles to be commandeered, and was frequently hemmed in and harassed by large crowds. He was forced to make speeches near-constantly, and spent hours standing to receive addresses he would never

[79]   *Ibid.*, 19 May 1893, 3.

[80]   Roberts, *Salisbury*, 572.

[81]   J.S. Meisel, *Public Speech and the Culture of Public Life in the Age of Gladstone* (New York, 2002), 274. Meisel is referring only to the platform speech itself, but his insight is more pertinent if extended to encompass the culture of the platform as a whole. It can also be noted that, clearly, the 'political visit' was the last safe harbour for traditional election practices, most of which had been declared illegal by the mid-1880s. This offers a sharp contrast to James Vernon's argument for the stamping out of popular election rituals by around 1867; see his *Politics and the People: A Study in English Political Culture 1815–1867* (Cambridge, 1993).

[82]   J. Morley, *The Life of William Ewart Gladstone* (3 vols, London, 1903), vol. 2, 589.

[83]   H. Jephson, *The Platform: Its Rise and Progress* (2 vols, London, 1892; 1968 edn), vol. 2, 602.

Lord Salisbury as Modern Political Man   267

read. Commentators recognised these interactions as feats of endurance. In 1887, Salisbury spent an hour and a half receiving 120 addresses in Norwich – a sympathetic journalist noted that 'his arm must have ached long before the pleasing duty devolving upon him was concluded'.[84]

Jon Lawrence has shown that preserving poise and good humour in the face of discomfort and disorder was part-and-parcel of electioneering, but it was equally fundamental to the culture of the platform.[85] This has important implications. For, if elections had traditionally upended the relations between politician and public in a ritual staging of the upper-class gentleman's ultimate but temporary reliance on the votes of his social inferiors, then the platform represented this state of affairs as permanent. By ceaselessly providing illustrations of politicians' 'manly flattery' of the populace, platform culture seemed to affirm that the balance of power had shifted irrevocably to the people, at the same time as it enabled the further advance of national parties and testified to the people's enthusiastic dependence on the leadership of an elite few. A piece of Unionist propaganda published in 1891, depicting Salisbury borne aloft on the shoulders of two working men, perfectly encapsulates this (fig. 12.1).[86] Unthinkable even two decades before, its internal referents were to the new world of popular politics, and to the new forms of legitimation it had made possible.

Salisbury and his Image

That image of Salisbury borne aloft might easily be dismissed as bearing no relation to reality – except, as we have seen, two years previously he really had been carried around on the shoulders of his plebeian supporters. It is a reminder that Salisbury's public activities were constantly receiving visual reinforcement: in the papers you could see pictures of him on the platform; processing alongside torchbearers; or surrounded by the crowd that had conquered Glasgow station.[87] This is one means by which the illustrated press reconfigured the visual presentation of the political class after 1880.[88] But of course, a *precondition* of so much of the popular response to Salisbury was visual recognition. At Ipswich, Salisbury was 'recognised without difficulty by

---

[84]   *Leeds Mercury*, 29 July 1887, 7.

[85]   J. Lawrence, *Electing Our Masters: The Hustings from Hogarth to Blair* (Oxford, 2009), 5. On the (class) dynamics of this process, see *ibid.*, 74–5.

[86]   *St Stephen's Review*, 25 April 1891.

[87]   *Illustrated London News*, 17 Oct. 1885, 391; *Graphic*, 3 June 1893, 393; *Graphic*, 11 Oct. 1884, 381.

[88]   For a detailed argument on this point, see Crewe, 'Political Leaders', 98–138, and passim.

Fig. 12.1. Tom Merry [pseud. William Mecham], 'One Flag, One Leader, One Voice!', *St Stephen's Review*, 25 Apr. 1891.

any who had seen the ordinary portraits of him', and at Birmingham 'a person who saw him for the first time after knowing him only through the agencies of the photograph and the newspaper press, would find him no wise different'.[89] Justin McCarthy remarked that 'No man has been better known, so far as personal appearance was concerned, to the general English public than Lord Salisbury. He has been as well known as Mr. Gladstone himself, and one cannot say more than that'.[90]

In other ways too, images of Salisbury aligned him with the new forms of public engagement. It was common to be photographed during (or explicitly for) a political visit, in order to document events for local and national audiences: Salisbury was photographed on his trip to Belfast in 1893 for example, the photo being reproduced in the pages of the *Illustrated London News*.[91] While any attempt to recover the 'careers' of photographs in popular politics is hampered by a lack of detailed evidence (their presence was likely taken for granted), the incidental evidence we possess is suggestive: when Salisbury left his train at Garston on a visit to Liverpool in 1888, '[amongst] the crowd his Lordship's portrait was being hawked at 2d each'.[92] We also know that photographs were sold outside platform venues, and could be taken inside by partisans.[93]

Salisbury's portrait was often emblazoned on badges and medals and worn by members of his audiences: when he spoke at the Ulster Hall in 1893 'not a few had pinned on their coats portraits on silk of the ex-Premier'.[94] At mass meetings Salisbury's portrait was often prominently displayed.[95] His portrait also featured in the magic lantern shows favoured by Conservative propagandists, and adorned party publications.[96] 'Salisbury Clubs' proliferated in the provinces, and surely most possessed a portrait, prominently displayed, of the leader for whom they were named.[97] His face also graced some Salisbury pubs.[98]

We think of Salisbury as fiercely private. But the reason he thirsted for privacy was because he was extraordinarily well-known. It was impossible

[89] *Ipswich Journal*, 29 July 1887, 8; *Birmingham Daily Post*, 25 Nov. 1891, 5.

[90] J. McCarthy, *British Political Leaders* (London, 1903), 47.

[91] *Illustrated London News*, 10 June 1893, 688.

[92] *Leeds Mercury*, 12 Jan. 1888, 7.

[93] E.g., *Aberdeen Journal*, 14 Oct. 1884, 3.

[94] *Standard*, 26 May 1893, 3; also *ibid.*, 27 Nov. 1893, 3.

[95] E.g. *Dundee Courier*, 30 Nov. 1888, 5; *Morning Post*, 29 Nov. 1893, 4.

[96] M. Pugh, *The Tories and the People, 1880–1935* (London, 1985), 90.

[97] Shannon, *Age of Salisbury*, 324. Visiting a new Conservative clubhouse in Watford in 1889, Salisbury 'was... shown over the rooms, for one of which he promised to provide his portrait': *Birmingham Daily Post*, 20 May 1889, 5.

[98] It still does in Covent Garden and Harringay, for instance.

270 Tom Crewe

for a man in his position to isolate himself from the public sphere; to imagine Salisbury as breathing only the rarefied air of Hatfield and the Foreign Office is to overlook fundamental aspects of his personal experience. He was one of the most famous men in the country, perhaps the world. He was pictured in his home; asleep in his train carriage; even riding his tricycle.[99] His daughter remembered that

> to walk with him in any populous place outside the metropolis... was a nerve wracking experience. One kept as long as possible to sheltered paths; the strained alertness of observation which began as soon as those were quitted for more peopled thoroughfares, and the dread with which the approach of every passing group of pedestrians was watched, were revelations of what the feelings of a fugitive from justice must be like.[100]

* * *

Salisbury, like other major late nineteenth-century politicians, was a celebrity. The new visibility fostered by the platform and the media, and the consequent sense of familiarity engendered in the public, had changed the criteria of success: the personal was political. Leaders became spokesmen and totemic personalities; they had to work hard and carry within themselves the elements of their party's appeal. This Salisbury did, and it is because historians have not paid sufficient attention to his *public* self-representation and political activity that he has been so badly misconstrued, and his achievement so underestimated. Indeed, it was only around the turn of the century, when age and poor health forced his retreat from the frontline, and his retirement came to be seen as inevitable, that commentators began to discuss him in the terms later taken up by modern historiography, as grand and remote. His retirement soon after the Queen's death, at the end of a sustained period of reclusiveness, allowed him to be described as belonging to a past era, when in fact he had helped usher in the new.[101]

Salisbury's achievement as a thoroughly modern politician did not pertain only to the Conservative party. When political leaders become celebrities, their prominence in popular culture allows them to function as foci for 'democratic engagement and investment, a resource for political imagination and implicit

---

[99] *Graphic*, 18 Oct. 1884; *Daily Graphic*, 24 Feb. 1890, 4; *Graphic*, 2 Nov. 1901, 580.

[100] Cecil, *Life*, vol. 3, 34.

[101] For Salisbury's turn-of-the-century reputation, see Crewe, 'Political Leaders', 177–8.

criteria for judging both the ends and means of political practice'.[102] To crowd outside a railway station or in a town square to catch a glimpse of Salisbury, to attempt to shake his hand, to listen to or read his speeches, to put a signature to an address, to buy his photograph or examine his portrait in the paper, to pore over an article about his home and habits, to form an opinion of him vis-à-vis his colleagues and rivals, was to be implicated in national politics and to be engaged by the political process. Salisbury projected an 'interesting' public personality in democratic Britain, and in doing so he helped to make democratic Britain a reality.

---

[102] J. Corner, 'Mediated Persona and Political Culture: Dimensions of Structure and Process', *European Journal of Cultural Studies*, 3 (2000), 401.

Chapter 13

Edward the Caresser: Monarchy and Religion in the Reign of Edward VII

Michael Ledger-Lomas

When G.K. Chesterton's editor rang him in the country on a lovely summer's night in May 1910, the telephone exchanges were so overloaded that he could barely make out a word. 'Stifled accents' on other lines were 'saying something momentous and unintelligible; it might have been the landing of the Germans or the end of the world'. Chesterton finally gathered that Edward VII had died and that he must rush back to London. Before he did so, he stepped into his garden, gazed at the stars and mused on the 'superstition' that the recent passage of Halley's Comet had portended the death of a prince. It was no less a stretch to believe that Edward's death would be decisive for the constitutional crisis over the Liberal budget then gripping Britain. Yet such superstitions were what religious Modernists said 'that dogmas are: mere symbols of a much deeper matter'. Rationalist critiques of popular monarchism would always miss the 'full mass of inarticulate human emotion' that it expressed.[1] Chesterton considered the shock at Edward's death a tribute to his immense affability. Yet, in emphasising the irrational feelings which propped up the throne, he was restating Walter Bagehot's now venerable thesis that monarchy relied on the 'credulous obedience of enormous masses'.[2] A century later, academic and popular commentary on the strange survival of British monarchy still invokes the obfuscatory irrationalism which supposedly protects it, whether in the form of invented archaisms or mediatised celebrity.[3]

---

[1]   G.K. Chesterton, 'The Late King: An Appreciation', *Illustrated London News*, 14 May 1910, 705.

[2]   Walter Bagehot, *The English Constitution* (1867) in Norman St-John Stevas (ed.), *The Collected Works of Walter Bagehot* (15 vols, London, 1965–86), vol. 5, 232.

[3]   Though subject to much historiographical challenge, David Cannadine, 'The Context, Performance and Meaning of Ritual: The British Monarchy and the 'Invention of Tradition', c. 1820–1977', in Eric Hobsbawm and Terence Ranger (eds), *The Invention of Tradition* (Cambridge, 1983), 101–64 still shapes popular discussion; Edward Owens, *The Family Firm: Monarchy, Mass Media and the British Public, 1932–53* (London, 2000) puts the case for media manipulation.

Monarchy and Religion in the Reign of Edward VII   273

The death of Queen Elizabeth II was a cue for much loose talk about Bagehot and 'magic'.[4]

Jonathan Parry subjected these claims to searching criticism in an essay of 2007, whose amused scepticism remains generative today, when an elderly male monarch has succeeded a popular, long-lived matriarch. He stressed instead the underlying rationality of acquiescence in the monarchy. What mattered was that the people accepted the legitimacy of the state, with the throne as its apex. Parry's interpretation was 'Whig' not just in its doubts about magic, but in its scepticism about royal agency. It was not the personalities or actions of Victoria or her successors which saved the throne, but a bigger phenomenon: the fading of radical allegations that institutions were obstacles to progress. Parry conceded that sovereigns played a role in this transformation: some managed to appear representative of their societies in certain ways. But the safest course was – and remains – 'blandness', which allows monarchy to roll along, more or less unnoticed.[5] My recent monograph on Queen Victoria adds to Parry's thesis the claim that the informed consent of religious communities – rather than Bagehot's magic or Chesterton's superstition – was vital to this considered acquiescence in monarchy. Their faith in Victoria naturally involved much projection, but it was hardly irrational. It rested on the perception that she was committed to the established churches, while honouring the liberties of Protestant and non-Protestant minorities. Victoria's courage under repeated bereavements also caused religious Victorians to see her as an icon of the sacrifices that her empire required and that in turn ennobled it.[6]

This essay tests these arguments on her successor. Is religious identification with monarchs possible when they are black sheep, rather than paragons? Heather Jones has shown that the First World War made George V into a self-denying Christian soldier and then the 'hierophant' of his mourning people. Yet she ascribes George's success not to the spiritual capital amassed by the dynasty, but to his personal puritanism and domesticity, which banished

---

[4]   Anna Whitelock, 'As a Historian of Monarchy', *Guardian*, 19 Sept. 2022 was one such effusion.

[5]   Jonathan Parry, 'Whig Monarchy, Whig Nation: Crown, Politics and Representativeness 1800–2000', in Andrzej Olechnowicz (ed.), *The Monarchy and the British Nation, 1780 to the Present* (Cambridge, 2007), 47–76 at 74. See also Parry, 'The Decline of Institutional Reform in Nineteenth-century Britain', in David Feldman and Jon Lawrence (eds), *Structures and Transformations in Modern British History* (Cambridge, 2011), 164–86.

[6]   Michael Ledger-Lomas, *Queen Victoria: This Thorny Crown* (Oxford, 2021). For pathos, see Joanna Lewis, *Empire of Sentiment: The Death of Livingstone and the Myth of Victorian Imperialism* (Cambridge, 2018).

memories of his father, a 'hedonistic playboy'.[7] Such a view reflects the reactions of contemporaries to the news that 'Edward the Caresser' had succeeded his virtuous mother.[8] A decade later, Chesterton's instant obituary of Edward stressed 'his unquestionable and positive popularity', but put it down to his 'interest in sport, good living, and Continental travel'. He had been a swell on the throne.[9] Edward's scholarly biographers have demonstrated that he was a more conscientious and interventionist ruler than such verdicts allowed. But they have said little of his piety: they suggest he presented himself as a majestic, masculine and cosmopolitan sovereign, defined not by dowdy domesticity but by cars, yachts and Continental ceremonial.[10]

Yet Edward's reign was more than a naughty interval between two sober sovereigns. This essay advances the improbable claim that it strengthened the monarchy's hold on religious audiences. In 1910, the radical baronet Wilfrid Scawen Blunt was amused to find the press and the churches mourning Edward as a 'Solon and a Francis of Assisi combined'.[11] If his piety had not existed, then it would have been invented. Victoria had worried about, without being able to resolve, the viability of established churches. When Edward took the throne, Protestant nonconformity remained an insurgent force throughout the United Kingdom. It was correspondingly important for the monarch to be a unifying symbol of national religiosity along lines laid down under Victoria. Her participation in the Kirk's worship had allowed her to be imagined as a protector of national Protestantisms rather than a narrowly Anglican figure. British – if not always Irish – Roman Catholics could believe she sympathised with them. Victoria stood not only for rival Christianities but for religion in general. Jews vocally venerated her, while her non-Christian colonial subjects presented her as a friend to their faiths when it suited them.[12] This expansion in the throne's spiritual base was a boost to the Church of England, which was tasked with solemnising moments in the monarch's life. Philip Williamson notes that while the personal piety of monarchs informed this close but flexible alliance between throne and altar, 'ascribed' piety would do.[13] This essay therefore starts

---

[7]   Heather Jones, *For King and Country: The British Monarchy and the First World War* (Cambridge, 2021), 16.

[8]   Henry James, quoted in Christopher Hibbert, *Royal Victorians: King Edward VII, his Family and Friends* (Philadelphia, 1976), 191.

[9]   Chesterton, 'Late King', 705.

[10]   See Jane Ridley, *Bertie: A Life of Edward VII* (London, 2013); Richard Davenport-Hines, *Edward VII: The Cosmopolitan King* (London, 2013).

[11]   Wilfrid Scawen Blunt, *My Diaries* (2 vols, New York, 1922), vol. 2, 307.

[12]   Ledger-Lomas, *Queen Victoria*.

[13]   Philip Williamson, 'Archbishops of Canterbury and the Monarchy: Leadership in British Religion, 1900–2012', in Tom Rodger, Matthew Grimley and Philip Williamson (eds), *The Church of England and British Politics since 1900* (Woodbridge, 2020), 62.

by asking what Edward's piety was and how it might have supported the monarchy's reputation as protector of religion. Through an initial and necessarily selective survey of printed sources, it then shows how religious professionals from across the British world gladly ascribed piety to him, in ways which advanced their national and spiritual agendas.

To insist on the power of the words and feelings of clerics requires taking a broader position on the liveliness of Edwardian religiosity. Did they still speak for a 'faith society'?[14] Reflecting on Edward's hieratic coronation, one journalist mused that 'even to the thinking part of the nation monarchy and government in general make no appeal whatever on religious grounds'. It was 'Utilitarian and Manchester philosophers' who had diminished the sacrality of monarchy, not Edward's Parisian morals.[15] A decade later, a writer impressed by the London crowds gathered for his funeral confided that he was often 'tempted to despair of religion'.[16] Such admissions reflect steep falls in measures of religious practice and affiliation in Edwardian society, especially in London.[17] But the social decay of churches was compatible with their centrality to public doctrine, especially in articulating visions of nation and empire. From the beginning of Edward's reign to its close, they choreographed feelings about the king, in the United Kingdom and still more so in the colonies.[18] Edwardian clergy may have fretted over what Hensley Henson, then a canon of Westminster Abbey, called the 'terrible phenomenon of expiring Christianity', brooding that cathedrals would one day become 'our Baalbec, our Ravenna, the memorials of a vanished life'.[19] But such disasters lay in the future. To sample the voluminous body of religious speech and writing on the Edwardian monarchy is to hear how loud the 'voice of the churches' remained.

'Always Go to Church': Edward VII's Religion

We should ask of Edward – as of most Victorian people – not if he was religious, but how he was so. His piety was elusive because it was not just undoctrinal, but unintellectual. Unlike his parents, he was not a reader. Victoria and

[14]   Clive Field, '"The Faith Society"? Quantifying Religious Belonging in Edwardian Britain, 1901–1914', *Journal of Religious History*, 37 (2013), 39–63.

[15]   'The Significance of the Coronation', *Saturday Review*, 9 Aug. 1902, 161.

[16]   'Summary', *Church Times*, 27 May 1910, 691.

[17]   Field, 'Faith'.

[18]   Philip Williamson and Joseph Hardwick, 'Special Worship in the British Empire: From the Seventeenth to the Twentieth Centuries', *Studies in Church History*, 54 (2018), 260–80.

[19]   Hensley Henson Journals, 18 Aug. 1901, 12; 21 July 1907, 234 <http://www.hensonjournals.org>.

Albert had been in a flap about Puseyism when they arranged Edward's education and so his tutors skimped on ecclesiastical specifics.[20] Although he is said as an adult to have engaged in regular private reading of the Scriptures, religion was about externals for him. 'Always go to church, wherever you are', he advised one niece – it was one of the unexciting duties he performed impeccably.[21] Although he became an avid motorist, on Sundays he put the car aside for a carriage ride to church, dressed in top hat and frock coat.[22] When he could not go to church – when on a boat going down the Nile, say – he would read the service. At Sandringham, he was unfailing, if perfunctory, in his attendance at the parish church he had filled with family memorials. John Edward Bodley, who weekended there in the mid-1880s, described the Sunday drill. The men set off for church half an hour after the women and loitered in the churchyard until the litany began. They then piled their walking sticks up and entered to hear a very short sermon.[23] Unexpectedly called upon once to preach before the king at the Chapel Royal, Alfred Ainger used 'clear articulation at motorcar speed' to finish his text in twelve minutes.[24]

Edward's wife Alexandra reinforced this unintellectual punctilio. Though brought up in Danish Lutheranism, her friendships with Viscount Halifax and the Gladstones gave her a penchant for high church worship. To Victoria's alarm, she took to worshipping at All Saints, Margaret Street, a bastion of Ritualism. Years later, All Saints reciprocated by marking her husband's death with a week of requiems.[25] Alexandra raised her children as loyal Anglicans, sometimes taking Prince George to task when he worshipped alongside German Lutherans. Albert Victor's death in 1892 heightened her churchiness, as she plunged into an obsessive round of services at Sandringham.[26] It was probably Alexandra's influence which led the couple to consult not one but two bishops on the question of whether they could take communion at the thanksgiving service for the Diamond Jubilee at St Paul's, despite not having had time for solemn preparation.[27]

---

[20]   Giles St Aubyn, *Edward VII: Prince and King* (London, 1979), 27; Philip Magnus, *King Edward the Seventh* (London, 1964), 6.

[21]   Princess Alice, *For My Grandchildren: Some Reminiscences* (London, 1965), 116.

[22]   C.W. Stamper, *What I Know: Reminiscences of Five Years in the King's Service* (London, 1913), 173–4.

[23]   Shane Leslie, *Memoir of John Edward Courtenay Bodley* (London, 1930), 96.

[24]   Edith Sickel, *Life and Letters of Alfred Ainger* (London, 1906), 305.

[25]   Georgina Battiscombe, *Queen Alexandra* (London, 1969), 56–7; *Church Times*, 13 May 1910, 633.

[26]   Battiscombe, *Alexandra*, 164, 176, 201.

[27]   George Browne, *Recollections of a Bishop* (London, 1915), 352–3.

Monarchy and Religion in the Reign of Edward VII   277

Edward's own faith was wreathed in cigar smoke rather than incense. It was manly and mildly anti-clerical. Bodley noted that on Sunday night he started billiards the minute the clock struck midnight Sandringham time (half an hour early, that is). He was struck by the billiards screen, on which caricatures of personalities in church and state were collaged with risqué images of bathing beauties.[28] In a rare intervention as Prince of Wales, Edward had presented a petition in the Lords in support of legalising marriage with a deceased wife's sister, a proposal which appalled high churchmen but which struck lay Protestants as an assertion of scriptural freedom. His freemasonry was another manifestation of this mood: in 1875, he became Grand Master of the Order of England.[29] Churchmen looked on Sandringham as liberty hall. When the Bishop of Peterborough preached there in 1873 – for 'twenty-three' minutes – he was nonplussed to find two Rothschilds at lunch, 'an ex-Jew, Disraeli', a Roman Catholic, 'an Italian duchess who is an Englishwoman, and her daughter brought up a Roman Catholic and now turning Protestant'.[30]

Edward's dynastic and social duties further militated against exclusivity. Though he lacked Victoria's fondness for Balmoral Castle, he visited it regularly and took care to worship with Presbyterians there. The enemies of Cosmo Gordon Lang, a high church Archbishop of York who had forgotten his Presbyterian roots, were grimly amused when he was forced to accompany the king to Crathie Kirk.[31] Edward was a holiday Lutheran too, accustomed to taking communion with his German relatives. He had notably done so for the confirmation of his nephew Wilhelm, who as Kaiser harassed him with appeals to the providential alliance between two nations of 'the same creed' as well as 'blood'.[32] Edward played on the emperor's religious Teutomania, enlisting courtier clergymen such as William Boyd Carpenter, the Bishop of Ripon, to preach to him about the virtues of peace.[33] Edward also attended rites of passage for Catholic and Orthodox peers and relatives. Charles Dilke spotted him at the Russian Embassy's chapel for the funeral of Alexander II (admittedly asleep) and he travelled to Moscow for Alexander III's funeral, enduring thirty-nine masses and winning admiration for the flair with which he crossed himself.[34]

---

[28] Leslie, *Bodley*, 96.

[29] Magnus, *Edward*, 163, 100.

[30] John Cotter Macdonnell, *The Life and Correspondence of William Connor Magee, Archbishop of York* (2 vols, London, 1896), vol. 1, 294.

[31] Henson Journals, 24 Jan. 1910, 40.

[32] Magnus, *Edward*, 128; Sidney Lee, *King Edward VII* (2 vols, London, 1925–7), vol. 2, 12, 135, 684.

[33] H.D.A. Major, *The Life and Letters of William Boyd Carpenter* (London, 1925), 232.

[34] St Aubyn, *Edward*, 297.

278 *Michael Ledger-Lomas*

Family ties might even make light of confessional identities. Alexandra had discounted the religious difficulties impeding Albert Victor's proposed marriage with the daughter of the Comte de Paris, an Ultramontane bigot. Lord Salisbury and his ministers, who considered that the match would endanger the Protestant standing of the monarchy, were staggered at Edward's notion that the bride might remain a Catholic if she allowed the Anglican upbringing of her children.[35] After the assassination in 1908 of Carlos I, King of Portugal, Edward braved the displeasure of the Protestant Alliance to attend a requiem for him – the first British sovereign since James II to attend a mass in England. Hardly a fortunate precedent, as Cosmo Lang commented.[36]

Edward's bonhomie enveloped privileged non-Christians too. He went to Leopold de Rothschild's wedding at a synagogue and took seaside strolls with Arthur Sassoon.[37] Admittedly, Edward's Philosemitism expressed sociability rather than principle. Despite lobbying by Jewish courtiers, he was reluctant to raise the issue of Russian pogroms against the Jews with Tsar Nicholas II.[38] As a peripatetic Prince of Wales, he had taken a polite interest in Ottoman mosques, Buddhist shrines, Hindu temples and Parsi cemeteries in the eastern Mediterranean and India.[39] It is true that as king his interest in imperial questions dwindled, just as he no longer travelled beyond Europe. Edward's distaste for bestowing the Garter on non-Christian sovereigns was one mark of these narrowing horizons – though he made an exception for the Mikado of Japan, who ruled a 'knightly people... as civilized as Europeans'.[40] Though considerate of religious scruples in dealings with Indian magnates, he understood his role as emperor of India as being a neutral arbiter between hostile Hindu and Muslim populations.[41] General Booth left an interview with Edward convinced that he modelled himself in this on William III, who 'suffered because he would not allow the religionists of his day to tear one another to pieces'.[42] Having tried to block the appointment of a Hindu to the Viceroy's Council because it would alienate Muslims, he opposed the appointment of a Muslim to the Judicial Committee of the Privy Council.[43] All the same, Edward did

[35] Magnus, *Edward*, 330.

[36] Almeric Fitzroy, *Memories* (6th edn, 2 vols, London, 1925), vol. 1, 341.

[37] J.P.C. Sewell (ed.), *Personal Letters of King Edward VII* (London, 1931), 165; Anthony Allfrey, *Edward VII and his Jewish Court* (London, 1991).

[38] Magnus, *Edward*, 407; Lee, *Edward*, vol. 2, 595.

[39] For references and discussion, see my 'HMS *Bacchante*: Religion, Time Travel, and the Victorian Monarchy', in Simon Goldhill and Ruth Jackson Ravenscroft (eds), *Victorian Engagements with the Bible and Antiquity* (Cambridge, 2023), 235–58.

[40] Ridley, *Bertie*, 454–5; Lee, *Edward*, vol. 2, 157, 311, 471; Magnus, *Edward*, 306.

[41] *The Memoirs of Aga Khan* (London, 1954), 75.

[42] Harold Begbie, *The Life of William Booth* (2 vols, London, 1920), vol. 2, 324.

[43] Lee, *Edward*, vol. 2, 387–8; Fitzroy, *Memories*, 387.

Monarchy and Religion in the Reign of Edward VII   279

not so much abandon an interest in other faiths as farm out that duty to other relatives, particularly his son and heir George. After Victoria's death, Edward dispatched him on an imperial tour, which ended with him holding a 'pow wow' with First Nations on the Canadian prairie and appealing to a shared belief in the 'Great Spirit'.[44]

'Holy Traditions of Royalty': Edward's Accession and Coronation

The religious sorrowing over Victoria, which Randall Davidson later recalled as 'more truly world-wide than any human sentiment has at one moment ever been' was of lasting benefit to her son, who now appeared before his people as a devoted mourner.[45] Preaching on Victoria's death at St James's Church in Toronto, Canon Edward Welch noted that in informing the people that his 'beloved mother' had passed away, Edward had given a 'glimpse into the character of that home circle of which she was the centre, and the influence of which has done so much to keep up the standards of English family life'.[46] Those standards mattered to Welch, a martinet who lectured Torontonians on gambling, female intoxication and spoiling their children.[47] The new king spent his reign patronising monuments to Victoria; he died before the scaffolding had come off her elaborate Memorial on the Mall.[48] Victoria's virtues supplied a template for expectations of him. Preaching in Westminster Abbey before the coronation, Frederic William Farrar dwelled provocatively on 'weak and foolish kings' who had once done 'incredible harm by their example'. His hearers could quiet their apprehensions with the thought that Edward and Alexandra would be inspired by their 'beloved and sorrowed mother' to preserve the 'holy traditions of royalty'.[49]

After a year of mourning, Edward inadvertently boosted his religious standing by nearly dying before the coronation planned for June. His rushed operation for an intestinal complaint caused its abrupt postponement; the final rehearsal in the Abbey became an improvised service of intercession.[50] Popular

---

[44] See Ledger-Lomas, 'HMS *Bacchante*', 257 for discussion and references.

[45] Randall Davidson, *From Strength to Strength: A Sermon* (London, 1902), 8.

[46] E.A. Welch, *A Mother in Israel: A Sermon Preached in St James's Church* (Toronto, 1901), 11.

[47] F.C. Macdonald, *Edward Ashurst Welch* (Cambridge, 1936), 38; 'The Gambling Evil', *Globe*, 25 May 1901, 14; 'Surfeited with Rubbish', *Globe*, 29 May 1905, 12; 'Drunkenness in Toronto Society', *Globe*, 7 Oct. 1907, 1.

[48] 'The Wayfarer', *Church Times*, 13 May 1910, 648.

[49] F.W. Farrar in *Sermons for the Coronation of King Edward VII* (London, 1902), 11–12.

[50] J.E.C. Welldon, *Recollections and Impressions* (London, 1915), 308.

reaction to the news was initially muted. Blunt found the benches of St James's Park to be no less packed than usual with courting couples.[51] In many places, communities pressed on with costly celebrations and enjoyed the bank holidays the king had already declared.[52] Yet preachers quickly manufactured emotional responses to his illness and recovery. His brush with death had turned a sensual Falstaff into a pale man of sorrows, who had put on the 'crown of thorns'.[53] Canon Newbolt later reminded the congregation at St Paul's Cathedral that as Christians they regarded suffering as a 'special badge of favour from God, bestowed on those whom the King delights to honour'. The British had not just affirmed the 'glory of our race' at the delayed coronation; they had crowned a man who came 'straight from the shaping tenderness of the loving hand of God'. Edward's illness reminded people of his record in fundraising for hospitals: on his recovery, he could 'sympathize even more than he did before' with suffering.[54] The creation of the King Edward's Hospital Fund with the backing of the Canadian millionaires Lords Strathcona and Mount Stephen backed up talk of his philanthropic record.[55]

Providence, not the doctors, had saved the king and admonished the nation. Arthur Winnington Ingram, the Bishop of London, later preached in St Paul's that his survival was proof that God 'does choose, discipline, and use nations to work out His great purposes for the world, and that such a nation is our own'.[56] He was reviving arguments advanced decades before at the national thanksgiving for Edward's recovery from typhoid fever. Speaking to shocked worshippers at the North London synagogue in June, the Chief Rabbi Hermann Adler similarly suggested that the postponement of the coronation was part of 'God's great scheme of training', which in ruining a pageant had removed the British from the 'snare' of 'overweening pride' in empire.[57] Preachers not only hailed the power of providence, but reminded people that whatever scientists said, their prayers determined its course, having now twice saved the king.[58] Edward endorsed that faith in a public letter which offered 'my deepest gratitude to Divine Providence for having preserved my

---

[51]   Blunt, *Diaries*, vol. 2, 29; Fitzroy, *Memories*, vol. 1, 91.

[52]   Ben Roberts, 'The Complex Holiday Calendar of 1902', *Twentieth Century British History*, 28 (2017), 506–7.

[53]   H.J. Wilmot Buxton, 'The Pure Crown', in *Sermons for the Coronation*, 90.

[54]   'The Anglo-Catholic Pulpit', *Church Times*, 15 Aug. 1902, 180.

[55]   *Church Times*, 6 Sept. 1902, 243.

[56]   Arthur Winnington Ingram, *The Faith of Church and Nation* (London, 1905), 133.

[57]   Hermann Adler, *Anglo-Jewish Memories and Other Sermons* (London, 1911), 131.

[58]   H.J. Wilmot Buxton, *Thankfulness: A Sermon on the Thanksgiving for the Recovery from Illness of His Majesty King Edward VII* (London, 1902), 8, 12.

life and given me strength to fulfil the important duties which devolve on me as Sovereign of this great Empire'.[59]

Anglicans hailed the 'chastened' quality of the rescheduled coronation and the 'subdued' rejoicing in the country.[60] Ecclesiastical sticklers were glad that the Abbey remained a 'sanctuary' throughout. Things had improved since Victoria's coronation day: there were no intrusive galleries; no gaudy draperies; no raucous parliamentarians. The only lapse was the temporary annexe adjoining the Abbey, tricked out with suits of armour like 'a blend of Earl's Court and Madame Tussaud'.[61] Admittedly, the coronation had been an improvisation on tradition. Its organising committee could draw on antiquarian works which recovered lost elements of the medieval rite. Yet Randall Davidson sought to accommodate a fidgety king by shortening the refurbished service.[62] The need to spare the royal convalescent forced further abbreviations in August. Its performance was also more chaotic than understandings of the Edwardian age as an apogee of royal ceremonial allow.[63] The determination of the Archbishop of Canterbury to act as the chief celebrant, despite advanced age and near blindness, necessitated his 'ridiculous' use of enormous scrolls, lugged around by the Bishop of Winchester, which he read out erratically.[64] He swayed before placing the crown on the king's head, misleading the musicians into a premature rendition of the National Anthem. The king had to help him to his feet after he gave homage and came close to being upended in the process. He also endangered the communion by nearly dropping the paten containing the wafers. George Bradley, the aged Dean of Westminster, was no less shaky, the chalice almost slipping from his hands.[65]

None of these wobbles detracted from the coronation's semiotic clout. In his official history of the coronation – a masterpiece of Edwardian baroque – John Edward Bodley feigned to believe that a 'special providence had watched over the ceremony' and averted fiasco. The moment at the end of the service when the king had greeted a spent Archbishop Temple, slumped in his 'medieval cope', was a scene from an 'ancient realm of the days when all the world was beautiful'. That was appropriate, because, as Bodley's narrative established, the coronation was 'essentially an act of religious consecration' which proclaimed

---

[59] Lee, *Edward*, vol. 2, 105.

[60] *Church Times*, 8 Aug. 1910, 144.

[61] 'The Sacring of Edward VII and Alexandra', *Church Times*, 15 Aug. 1902, 182.

[62] Peter Hinchliff, 'Frederick Temple, Randall Davidson and the Coronation of Edward VII', *Journal of Ecclesiastical History*, 48 (1997), 71–99.

[63] Cf. Cannadine, 'Context'.

[64] Fitzroy, *Memoirs*, vol. 1, 99.

[65] 'Sacring', 184; 'Correspondence', *Church Times*, 22 Aug. 1902, 192–3; 29 Aug. 1910, 215; Welldon, *Recollections*, 315.

the king as the 'sole anointed governor of the Church', a priest whose 'sanctity' surpassed that of his clergy.[66] Bodley was a Francophile aesthete and a tepid churchman with a Gibbonian scepticism of theology. Yet a stint working as secretary to Cardinal Manning, a consummate Ultramontane politician, had convinced him that churches were actually becoming more powerful in democratising societies.[67] Thanks to the Church of England, monarchical Britain enjoyed more stability than republican France, now at odds with the Papacy, or Caesarist Germany.[68]

Because churchmen were concerned that the coronation rite should not just cater to a taste for flummery, their sermons carefully explained its components, which they represented as a justification of royal power rather than a mystification of its sources.[69] They spoke of the coronation as a 'sacring' – a 'national act of worship to Him who is the source of all earthly authority', which placed the cross over the orb.[70] Sabine Baring-Gould argued that the king had not just been crowned but ordained as the 'minister of God in the State', a formulation which reflected the researches of antiquarians like himself as well as a distinctively Anglican conception of a monarch as the link between two autonomous entities, the church and state.[71] Others were still more theocratic, likening Edward to Solomon, who had been anointed by Zadok the Priest. Just as Solomon had inherited David's mission to complete the Temple, so Edward would keep building his mother's godly empire.[72]

Against this theological background, Bodley's claim that the coronation was a 'consecration of the imperial idea' reads as a rebuke to rather than an expression of imperial jingoism.[73] Recent commentary on the monarchy by historians has often concentrated on the symbolic cover it gave to imperial crimes, ranging from genocide to ecocide.[74] But this is – at best – the wisdom of hindsight. Edwardian clerics presented the monarchy as a spiritual brake on greed and racism, especially on new colonial frontiers in Africa. For them, the coronation was a reminder not to regard the 'stewardship of the world' as a mere 'prize'. Since Victoria's Jubilees, leading clergymen had warned that England,

---

[66] J.E.C. Bodley, *The Coronation of Edward VII* (London, 1903), 304, 316–17, 279.

[67] Leslie, *Bodley*, 405–11.

[68] Bodley, *Coronation*, 79.

[69] *Church Times*, 15 Aug. 1902, 163, 169–70.

[70] *Ibid.*, 8 Aug. 1902, 139.

[71] Sabine Baring-Gould, 'From Above', in *Sermons on the Coronation*, 75–6, 79.

[72] Hammond, *God*, 9–10; Augustus James Steed, *The Coronation of Edward VII: A Sermon* (London, 1902), 7; Wilmot Buxton, *Thankfulness*, 3.

[73] Bodley, *Coronation*, 43.

[74] Priya Satia, 'The British Monarchy Mortgaged our Collective Future', *Time*, 12 Sept. 2022 <https://time.com/6212672/queen-elizabeth-death-empire-climate-change/> was especially overheated.

Monarchy and Religion in the Reign of Edward VII   283

now as 'glorious in the midst of the seas' as 'ancient Tyre', risked 'what ancient Greeks called *hubris*'.[75] Duncan Bell has pointed out that Victoria became a 'patriot Queen' to settler publics, the personification of the virtues of dutiful-ness and self-abnegation that united their imperial polity and might prevent it from experiencing the fate of most empires: disintegration and decay. Yet although Bell emphasises the civic humanism that informed this idealisation of Victoria and her successors, it had an equally strong ecclesiastical component.[76] The coronation vividly exemplified the confident expansion of colonial Angli-canism: eleven colonial bishops attended, while the Bishops of Bath and Wells and Norwich, who featured prominently, had held colonial sees.[77] Edward's reign coincided with efforts to strengthen the Anglican communion, culmi-nating with the back-to-back staging of the Lambeth Conference and the Pan-Anglican Congress, the latter concluding with a garden party at Marlborough House. Henry Montgomery, secretary to the former and architect of the latter, had been the king's choice as prelate of the imperialist order of St Michael and St George.[78]

In an address to colonial troops the day after the coronation, Canon Welldon spelled out what churchmen took to be its lessons. At six foot five, Welldon was every inch the imperial prefect: before coming to the Abbey, which he viewed as the 'sanctuary' of the 'British race', he had been headmaster of Harrow School, then the Bishop of Calcutta, where he had been troubled by the moral and physical toll the Raj exacted on its rulers. These misgivings stole into his sermon, which assured the troops that 'you will never maintain empire without character, you will never maintain character without religion, you will never maintain religion without Christ'. They went home after a 'hallowing of the Empire', which their conduct must now sustain.[79] The next year Welldon took his words to heart, returning from a tour of the colonies buzzing with ideas on how to revive the church's influence there. Colonial Anglicans echoed Welldon in focusing anxiety on how to improve their conduct, rather than the king's. They often dwelled in doing so on the recent end of the South African War, whose sacrifices had engendered 'clearer, higher views of what the burden of Empire means'.[80]

---

[75] Bishop Percival (1897), quoted in William Temple, *Life of Bishop Percival* (Lon-don, 1921), 173; Ledger-Lomas, *Victoria*, ch. 8.

[76] Duncan Bell, 'The Idea of a Patriot Queen? The Monarchy, the Constitution, and the Iconographic Order of Greater Britain', *Journal of Imperial and Commonwealth History*, 34 (2006), 3–22.

[77] Bodley, *Coronation*, 289, 291, 403.

[78] Maud Montgomery, *The Coronation of Edward VII* (London, 1903), 64–7.

[79] Welldon, *Recollections*, 331, 214–15, 225, 530–1.

[80] J.B.C. Murphy in *Sermons on the Coronation*, 24; *Toronto Globe*, 11 Aug. 1902, 10.

The leaders of other denominations and faiths echoed this preaching in their distinctive accents. Despite heightened tensions between Church and nonconformity over Balfour's education bill, Free Church leaders were honoured guests in the Abbey; the procession with the regalia had sung Isaac Watts's *O God our Help in Ages Past* in tribute to 'English nonconformity'.[81] Some of their leaders had pushed for even greater recognition. General Booth urged his son Bramwell to insist on being allowed to attend in Salvation Army uniform.[82] Outside Ireland, Catholics uttered many hosannas over the coronation. Bishop Orth of Victoria, British Columbia, spoke of the 'unqualified, unreserved and undivided temporal allegiance' of Catholics to the king and their determination, 'if needs be, to sacrifice their dear lives on the altar of true patriotism'. They recognised Britain's constitutional monarchy as Catholic in its origins – Magna Carta being the 'pure outgrowth of Catholic canon law'.[83] The Chief Rabbi had preached on the 'essentially Hebraic character' of the coronation rite and gone to the Abbey; around the empire, loyal rabbis tackled allegations of their clannishness and lack of patriotism. What, asked one rabbi in Vancouver, could be more Jewish or more patriotic than singing God Save the King while wrapped in one's tallit and facing the Ark?[84]

'Unseemly Wranglings': Church and State in the Reign of Edward VII

Despite the symbolism of the coronation, Edward soon showed himself to be cautious, even passive, when it came to intervening in church and state. This was prudent. In seeking to save the established churches by championing their liberal factions, Victoria had failed to reckon with their increasingly pluralistic character. By contrast, when the *Illustrated London News* summed up religion in Edward's reign, it contrasted his 'high tone' with 'unseemly wranglings' over modernism and Ritualism in the church and the 'miserable strife' between Church and nonconformity over education.[85] Edward initially emulated Victoria in asserting himself in church patronage. With Davidson at his elbow – who quickly succeeded Temple as Archbishop – he seemed as keen on choosing bishops as diplomats or military men, recognising that the selection of congenial people was the best way for constitutional sovereigns to

[81] Bodley, *Coronation*, 244.

[82] Begbie, *Booth*, 239.

[83] *Victoria Daily Times*, 11 Aug. 1902, 8.

[84] I.H. Daiches, *Sermon on the Coronation of their Gracious Majesties King Edward VII and Queen Alexandra* (Leeds, 1902), 8; *Toronto Globe*, 11 Aug. 1902, 10; *Vancouver Daily Province*, 11 Aug. 1910, 9. See Philip Williamson, 'Special Acts of Worship in Anglo-Jewry 1700–1970', *Jewish Historical Studies*, 53 (2021), 1–33.

[85] 'Religion in the King's Reign', *Illustrated London News*, 17 May 1910, 63.

Monarchy and Religion in the Reign of Edward VII   285

shape policy.[86] Yet this interest tailed off after 1906, when Scots Presbyterian (Campbell-Bannerman) and Congregationalist (Asquith) prime ministers introduced a more partisan approach to patronage, which paid little heed to royal or clerical sensibilities. When Asquith appointed Lang as Archbishop of York, Percival of Hereford – who, as a radical Liberal in politics had looked forward to getting the post – lamented that the 'son of a Yorkshire congregational minister' had preferred the 'sacerdotal son of a Scotch Presbyterian Minister'.[87] But there was little the king could do. He and Davidson had already come off second best when Campbell-Bannerman wanted to install a vigorously Protestant Bishop of Chichester. After the king's private secretary, Lord Knollys, passed on their objections, Campbell-Bannerman's secretary mocked the notion that the king had his 'own ideas' and read him a lesson in parliamentary erastianism.[88]

Distanced from ecclesiastical patronage, Edward also sought to avoid controversies over church and state, or at least responsibility for them. The coronation summer had been dominated by Balfour's education bill, which had enraged nonconformists by putting church and Catholic schools on the rates. Meeting Edmund Knox to take his homage as Bishop of Manchester in 1904, Edward asked him lamely why 'no reasonable compromise' had appeared possible.[89] Two years later, further controversy arose over Augustine Birrell's failed education bill, which in contemplating the secularisation of public education enraged many churchmen and Roman Catholics. Edward considered it an imitation of French anti-clericalism, one likely to trigger 'political-religious warfare'.[90] He pushed forward Davidson as a mediator in the hope that he could repeat Archbishop Tait's management of tensions over the disestablishment of the Church of Ireland.[91] The king called on Davidson to conciliate again two years later when an equally abortive Liberal bill proposed to charge congregations with the cost of religious education.[92] Davidson's educational diplomacy was ineffective, but it reflected his broader strategy of avoiding confrontation with the Liberal government, while taking a lead on social and foreign policy matters in collaboration with Nonconformists.[93]

[86] Lee, *Edward*, vol. 2, 52. See Michael Bentley, 'Power and Authority in the Late Victorian and Edwardian Court', in Olechnowicz, *Monarchy*, 163–87.

[87] Leslie, *Bodley*, 412; Temple, *Percival*, 303.

[88] St Aubyn, *Edward*, 405.

[89] Knox, *Reminiscences*, 208.

[90] Magnus, *Edward*, 353.

[91] For which see Peter Marsh, *The Victorian Church in Decline: Archbishop Tait and the Church of England, 1868–1882* (London, 1969), ch. 1.

[92] Lee, *Edward*, vol. 2, 461, 659.

[93] Tom Rodger, 'The Politics of Church Defence: Archbishop Davidson, the National Church and the 'National Interest', c.1900–14', in Rodger, *Church of England*, 44–54; Williamson, 'Leadership', 65ff.

Edward's relationship with Roman Catholicism was no less reserved. As Prince of Wales, he had advertised his friendliness towards Roman Catholics, fraternising with popes and giving a wide berth to Canadian Orangemen.[94] Although Edward had been opposed to the disestablishment of the Church of Ireland and was hostile to Home Rule, he recognised the need to distance himself from the Protestant Ascendancy. There was to be no repetition of his 1885 tour of Ireland, when the '*lazzaroni* of Cork' had chucked onions at him.[95] Visiting Dublin in 1903, he spent his time 'saying polite things to Roman Catholic clergy and eating a series of enormous meals'. His tribute to the recently deceased Pope Leo XIII was well received.[96] When he called at Maynooth, he politely inspected a painting of his Derby winner, which the seminarians had put up in lieu of a Union Jack.[97] Edward's friendliness reflected his practice on the continent, where he golfed with Austrian monks and popped in on convents in Biarritz. A visit to the Grotto at Lourdes generated the apocryphal story that the Chaplain to the Irish Guards had been summoned to convert him on his death bed.[98]

Yet a concern for Protestant sensibilities curbed this gentlemanly pro-Catholicism. Mindful of the 'Nonconformist conscience', he had prevented the Catholic Madame Albani from singing at Victoria's funeral and struck out prayers for the dead from the service.[99] He had infuriated Catholics by obediently reading the accession declaration against the Mass – despite mumbling it in deference to their sensibilities. Rather than supporting open discussion and principled reform of the declaration thereafter, Edward hoped that the matter would go away: its revision had to wait for the accession of George V.[100] Edward was right to be sensitive, given the shower of Protestant petitions the issue generated from across the empire. When he called as king on Leo XIII in 1903, he was careful to agree with Balfour an etiquette that would give no cause for Protestant outrage.[101] A few years later, he passed on to his ministers the task of giving formal assent for his niece Ena's marriage to the King of Spain – and so to her conversion – after receiving 'hundreds of letters about it' from

[94]   Magnus, *Edward*, 36.

[95]   *Ibid.*, 189.

[96]   J.W. Mackail and Guy Wyndham, *Life and Letters of George Wyndham* (2 vols, London), vol. 1, 459.

[97]   Leslie, *End*, 61.

[98]   Stamper, *What I Know*, 336; Ridley, *Bertie*, 556–7.

[99]   Ledger-Lomas, *Victoria*, 270.

[100]   Fitzroy, *Memories*, vol. 1, 56; Lee, *Edward*, 25; J. Fewster, 'The Royal Declaration Against Transubstantiation and the Struggle Against Religious Discrimination in the Early Twentieth Century', *British Catholic History*, 30 (2011), 555–72.

[101]   Magnus, *Edward*, 310–11.

Protestant activists.[102] In the autumn of 1908, he was 'greatly cut up' by the Liberal government's failure to forbid a public procession of the Host through London to celebrate a Eucharistic Congress. Protestant activists already exercised by his attendance at the King of Portugal's requiem bombarded him with petitions. Although 150,000 Roman Catholics did in the end march (without a Host or vestments), the king continued to rail against Home Secretary Herbert Gladstone, whose 'Papist' leanings had blinded him to the 'sore feelings' bound to be aroused by this insult to 'national history'.[103] The mainstream press mocked the outcry of Protestant societies – making the king's touchiness stand out as an indication of his care to deflect 'responsibility' for religious controversy.[104]

Beati Pacifici: Mourning Edward

Christian responses to Edward's death in January 1910 showed that his considered inertia was no less effective than Victoria's ecclesiastical partisanship in winning the adherence of religious publics. His obsequies were more public and democratic than hers. Before his funeral at Windsor, he had lain in state at Westminster Hall, where officials ensured egalitarian access to the departed sovereign.[105] The mourning undoubtedly concerned this world rather than the next: like Victoria's, it feted the technological integration and affective unity of empire.[106] One Ottawa newspaper boasted that fifteen minutes after a cable with the news arrived, they had already printed a memorial edition and were handing it out on the streets.[107] Although Alexandra's private rites of mourning at Buckingham Palace had been protracted and churchy, the transfer of Edward's coffin to Westminster Hall and from thence to Paddington Station struck many as altogether worldly. A *Church Times* reporter regretted that the procession had been a 'mere review', a cavalcade with only a 'sorry display' of military chaplains.[108] Another correspondent, mixing with an irreverent crowd, remembered reading Bodley on the 'spiritual ideas' of the coronation

---

[102] Fitzroy, *Memories*, vol. 1, 280, 285; Lee, *Edward*, vol. 2, 514.

[103] Magnus, *Edward*, 402; G.I.T. Machin, 'The Liberal Government and the Eucharistic Procession of 1908', *Journal of Ecclesiastical History*, 34 (1988), 581–3; Carol Devlin, 'The Eucharistic Procession of 1908: The Dilemma of the Liberal Government', *Church History*, 63 (1994), 423.

[104] Lee, *Edward*, vol. 2, 661.

[105] John Wolffe, 'The People's King: The Crowd and the Media at the Funeral of Edward VII, May 1910', *Court Historian*, 8 (2003), 23–30.

[106] Ledger-Lomas, *Queen Victoria*, ch. 9.

[107] 'How Ottawa Received the News', *Saturday Evening Citizen*, 7 May 1910, 2.

[108] 'The Royal Obsequies', *Church Times*, 27 May 1910, 709.

288   *Michael Ledger-Lomas*

and lamented that no such treatment of the funeral would be possible.[109] The instant celebrity of the king's terrier Caesar, who appeared in prints trotting behind the coffin then straining at the leash as Edward's coffin steamed out of Paddington, was one marker of this sentimental rather than spiritual mood. His ghost-written memoirs were a great success.[110]

The church nonetheless choreographed mourning throughout his kingdom and empire. Parish and cathedral churches hosted services improvised in the days after his death, then organised to coincide with the funeral. The Church of England led such efforts, in concert with other Christian churches. Nonconformists were especially anxious to participate. The Booths dispatched a band to the courtyard of Buckingham Palace while Edward's body lay there, where they were photographed playing his favourite hymns, *Abide with Me* and *Nearer my God, to Thee*.[111] On the day of the funeral, four thousand Salvationists attended a service held by Booth at a hall in Clapton.[112] Presbyterians north of the border and Scots in the empire joined the Church in ringing their bells, while their preachers evoked their proprietorial relationships to the king. In Auckland, the minister of St David's, Khyber Pass exhorted his New Zealanders to pray 'as Scots and descendants of Scots' for 'one of their own church', whose first oath as king had been to maintain the Church of Scotland.[113]

Edward's consistent friendliness to Catholics paid off in a global wave of Te Deums and votive masses, with the hierarchy careful to explain that they could not offer requiems for a non-Catholic. The Archbishop of Montreal had been conducting a first communion for four hundred children when he got the news the king was gravely ill; he instantly had them bow their heads in prayer.[114] Catholic clergy across the colonies delivered florid eulogies, emphasising the 'tender regards' of the king for Ireland and his kindness to religious orders fleeing laicising France.[115] 'Since the Reformation, no king had been so loved by his Catholic subjects', claimed Father Ainsworth of St Mary's Church, Hokitika, a mining community on New Zealand's southern island settled by Irishmen.[116] Although such generosity was easier outside Ireland,

---

[109] 'In Hyde Park', *ibid.*, 710.

[110] Wolffe, 'People's King'; *Illustrated London News*, 28 May 1910, 813; *Caesar, Where's Master?* (London, 1910).

[111] *Illustrated London News*, 14 May 1910, 740; Begbie, *Booth*, 405.

[112] *The Times*, 23 May 1910, 20.

[113] *Auckland Star*, 21 May 1910, 8; 'Presbyterian Services', *New Zealand Herald*, 21 May 1910, 8.

[114] *Saturday Evening Citizen*, 7 May 1910, 11.

[115] 'Roman Catholic Cathedral', *The Press* [Canterbury, NZ], 9 May 1910, 11; *Evening Star*, 9 May 1910, 7; *Vancouver Daily Province*, 9 May 1910, 9.

[116] 'Pulpit Utterances' *West Coast Times*, 9 May 1910, 3.

Monarchy and Religion in the Reign of Edward VII   289

in Dublin Archbishop Walsh, no friend to the dynasty, put on a votive mass in the pro-cathedral.[117] If Catholics praised a friend, Jews around the empire lamented their protector, the Chief Rabbi hailing a new 'King Cyrus' for 'his hate of hate, his scorn of scorn, and his absolute freedom from racial and sectarian prejudice.'[118] Even the Theosophists joined in: in Dunedin, New Zealand they draped Edward's portrait in purple, noting that he had died on the same calendar date as Madame Blavatsky.[119]

Although religious mourning was not limited to settlers, the emphasis which reporting placed on the sorrow of colonised peoples should be seen as a kind of self-congratulation about the universality and benevolence of British imperialism. How wonderful, trilled a Presbyterian minister in Vancouver's newly built West End, to think that 'priests of many gods not of the Christian Trinity' in lands 'where the flag of Great Britain laps like a red tongue at the air' were praying for Edward's soul.[120] It permitted a safe exoticism: natives from India to Johannesburg were said to have blamed Edward's death on the passage of Halley's comet.[121] In New Zealand, Māori representatives waited on the Prime Minister, asking him to pass on their sorrow to Queen Alexandra in words which largely reproduced what local missionaries had already said.[122]

It is hard to know how accurately clerics represented the feelings of their congregations and nations about Edward. But rather than applying a hermeneutic of suspicion to their sermons, we can merely note here their clamorous unanimity, which conjured into existence the grief they claimed to describe. If preachers ignored Edward's vices, apart from the odd flinty Presbyterian glancing at the 'foolish noise' of his youth, they were realistic about his piety.[123] Many praised his churchgoing, but they were generally less interested in what he may have believed than in how religious causes had advanced under his mild aegis. The most significant was peace in Europe, a cause which now engaged many Christians beyond an initial core of radical Nonconformists.[124] The *Church Times* concluded that '*Beati Pacifici* is his most fitting epitaph.'[125] The fiery Baptist John Clifford agreed, telling Free Churchmen that Edward had fulfilled the 'supreme function of monarchy' in serving as the 'ambassador of peace among

[117] *The Times*, 21 May 1910, 9.

[118] *Ibid.*, 8.

[119] *New Zealand Times*, 9 May 1910, 8.

[120] *Vancouver Daily Province*, 9 May 1910, 15.

[121] For Johannesburg, see *Vancouver Daily Province*, 9 May 1910, 9.

[122] 'Tribute from the Maoris', *New Zealand Times*, 23 May 1910, 8.

[123] Dr Gibb at St John's, *Dominion*, 9 May 1910, 2; 'References at City Churches', *Evening Citizen* [Ottawa], 9 May 1910, 9.

[124] Paul Laity, *The British Peace Movement 1870–1914* (Oxford, 2001), 2, 117, 120.

[125] *Church Times*, 13 May 1910, 631.

the nations'. Across the British world, Professor Hewitson told the pupils of Knox College, Dunedin that he had fought the 'war spirit' which was 'the most glaring survival of barbarism and paganism in our modern civilization'.[126] The celebration of Edward the Peacemaker depended on an exaggeration of his role in making peace in South Africa and in the opaque conduct of continental diplomacy.[127] Yet it suited conceptions of the Empire as a satiated and civilised power, more concerned to spare lives than gain territory.

Even though Edward had disappeared at a moment of political peril, providence still cradled his peoples. Let them not think it was 'some blind force' which had taken him away, urged Lang.[128] At St Paul's Cathedral, Davidson presented the reign as a study in providence, which had commenced with a 'bit of "revelation" – the unveiling of the Divine guidance and discipline of our people's life', namely Edward's escape from death.[129] So vast was the empire, so great the potential for 'mistakes of sovereignty' that its survival must be due less to Edward's undoubted virtues than their prayers for God's favour, which was with them still.[130] Ministers throughout the British world sounded similar notes. At a non-denominational service held outside New Zealand's Parliament in Wellington, J. Kennedy Elliott mused on the 'stupendous difficulty' of filling Edward's place but took courage from the 'providential government of the universe'.[131]

* * *

This essay has evoked the ceremonial and sermonic structures which supported the Edwardian monarchy. It has suggested that the invocation of monarchy by religious communities was too fervent and pervasive throughout the British world to be shaken by any one monarch, let alone one as equable as Edward. Nor should this come as a surprise: in the decades before the First World War, godly or even sacred monarchies remained the lynchpin of empires everywhere from Habsburg Austria and Tsarist Russia to Meiji Japan.[132] In highlighting the contribution of religious thought and argument to popular monarchism in the British case, we must not push the argument too far.

---

[126] *Evening Star*, 9 May 1910, 7.

[127] See Roderick McLean, *Royalty and Diplomacy in Europe, 1890–1914* (Cambridge, 2001), which establishes Edward's activity in foreign policy but is less convincing about its effectiveness.

[128] *Church Times*, 13 May 1910, 633.

[129] Davidson, *From Strength to Strength*, 6.

[130] *Ibid.*, 13.

[131] 'United Service', *New Zealand Times*, 21 May 1910, 1.

[132] Dominic Lieven, *In the Shadow of the Gods: The Emperor in World History* (London, 2022), 382, 408–15, 423–7.

If Edward was no secularised king, nor was he consistently sacralised either. His obituarists understood this, presenting his piety as one compartment in a worldly life, which fitted alongside his more printable pleasures: yachting, shooting, motoring. His monuments were mainly secular: coronation halls, trees, fountains and statues; here and there a church window.[133]

If popular interest in Edward was not uniquely or even mainly religious, then nor did he always loom large in the inner lives of highly religious people, a group starting to fear they were in the minority. Although Hensley Henson officiated at his coronation and preached a funeral sermon at St Margaret's, Westminster on 'the Peacemaker', his journals of the reign barely mention him.[134] But then most people did not need to think about the British monarchy most of the time. Therein lay its strength. What counted for Edward, as for Victoria, was the inchoate, but justifiable conviction, to which the clergy inter- mittently gave utterance, that he sympathised with the varied aspirations of his varied peoples. Far from having to re-establish the monarchy's spiritual credit, George V inherited it. At his coronation in June 1911, Cosmo Gordon Lang, who would be instrumental in burnishing George's demotic credentials, deliv- ered a sermon on kingship.[135] His 'hallowing' proclaimed the 'sovereignty of service': God entrusted George to lead his people in 'one fellowship of common memories, common ideals, common service'.[136] Quickfire 'platitudes', groused Hensley Henson. Yet it is such platitudes, rather than magic, which explain the survival of the modern British monarchy to the present day.[137]

---

[133] James Gildea, *King Edward VII the Peacemaker* (London, 1914) contains a com- prehensive catalogue of memorials.

[134] Bodley, *Coronation*, 289; *The Times*, 9 May 1910, 9.

[135] Frank Mort, 'Safe for Democracy: Constitutional Politics, Popular Spectacle, and the British Monarchy', *Journal of British Studies*, 58 (2019), 109–41; Robert Beaken, *Cosmo Gordon Lang* (London, 2012), 70–1.

[136] 'The Sermon', *The Times*, 23 July 1911, 14.

[137] Journals, 22 June 1911, 231.

Part V

Britain in the World

Chapter 14

Irish Realities and British Liberal Self-deception: The Reaches and Limits of British Liberal Constitutionalism

John Bew and Paul Bew

How far does the experience of nineteenth-century British political history – specifically, the story of the Victorian 'liberal' tradition within it – contain insights for other political worlds, distinct by geography or time? To what extent can this political credo – one grounded in self-confidence, a story of national exceptionalism, a belief in 'progress', economic liberalism, the rule of law and good governance – be replicated in other settings or eras? How far have the errors, missteps, or limitations of this approach – not least its occasional tendency to allow moral righteousness and self-delusion to cloud its judgment – been truly internalised or understood by its admirers, as well as its critics? And was this vision of Britain and the world around it, which achieved a dominant political position at the height of the Victorian period, more vulnerable to rival or hostile political visions, domestically or internationally, or to the miscalculations of its own purveyors?

The political and discursive world described by Jonathan Parry – what might loosely be called the 'imagined community of liberal Victorian Britain' – certainly reaches further into the domains of other national stories than is sometimes recognised. In some cases, such as within the elites of the Italian national movement for example, this was because of a deep-seated admiration for liberal government and an economic model which saw Britain achieve faster sustained growth than any of its rivals. In others, it is because ideas about constitutional form and political economy that were predominant in Victorian Britain were not exclusive to Britain alone. J.G.A. Pocock has done more than any other historian to describe the existence of shared intellectual foundations across the broader Atlantic world – the outworking of ideas from classical republicanism, civic humanism and the common law tradition – which included the British Isles, Ireland and North America and later took root in different parts of the Commonwealth. To be clear, this is not to conjure up a story of 'British ideas' spreading across the English-speaking world and beyond, on account of their inherent attraction and superiority. It is instead to identify strands of a shared intellectual heritage which provided common assumptions and political belief systems; and which, in Pocock's rendering, should provide a counter to narrow or exceptionalist national stories (including the one which underpinned the self-confidence of Victorian Britain).[1]

The story of cross-fertilisation is of course further complicated by the story of Empire and indeed the messy internal story of the United Kingdom. In much of the Atlantic world – notably Ireland and the United States – the existence of the English language, shared intellectual traditions and an identifiable constitutional discourse, must be considered against an explicit rejection of British influence; and by the creation of new democratic foundations for the polity that replaced British rule. The failure of the experiment of achieving deeper political integration between England and its neighbours in a 'union' – something that cannot solely be reduced to an attempt by the metropole to assert control over its colonies – underscores the point. The experience of temporary political union undoubtedly shaped the political history of England and its neighbours, leaving a lasting impact on both. Historians of Ireland have acknowledged the impact of the British parliamentary tradition on the shaping of Irish nationalism, both in its pre- and post-independence forms. But the depth and reach of those connections – and the interaction between ideas, individuals and discursive frames – has not always been fully appreciated, owing to the ferocity of the rupture that subsequently occurred. And ultimately, the failure of the project of British state unionism in Ireland from 1801 makes it hard to dispute the view that the political culture of Ireland was just too different for full political integration to ever work, even if the 'what ifs' are entertained: 'what if Catholic emancipation had been granted alongside the Acts of Union in 1801?'; 'what if the land question had been solved earlier'; or, as this chapter will discuss, 'what if there had been an Anglo-Irish consensus built around a benign and moderate version of Home Rule in the 1880s?'

Meanwhile, as the latter half of the chapter will go on to discuss, the post-Revolutionary American national story is more coterminous to that of Victorian Britain in that it presented dilemmas that sprang up along with the accruement of immense national wealth and international power. Specifically, it threw up the types of challenges of statecraft that were well-understood in Victorian Britain. The process of consolidating or integrating domestic territories into a functioning polity or 'union' was the primary challenge, in which

---

[1]   J.G.A Pocock, *The Machiavellian Moment: Florentine Political Thought and the Atlantic Republican Tradition* (Princeton, 1975). See also Pocock's edited collections *Three British Revolutions: 1641, 1688, 1776* (Princeton, 1980) and *The Discovery of Islands: Essays in British History* (Cambridge, 2005).

violence played a significant role in state formation. Alongside this was the question of how to protect and promote essential interests in external relations with others, which involved dealing with those with rival interests and alternative belief systems and at seemingly different stages of historical development. In both the American and the British cases, then, a national story emerged that was fiercely contested at home and depended on unfavourable contrasts with others overseas. Protestantism – particularly in its evangelical forms – was an important part of the story here, adding moral zeal and a missionary spirit to those interactions. So too was a form of commercial behaviour, backed up by the threat of overbearing military force, that others regarded as particularly rapacious and anything but high-minded.

Historians of and thinkers about America's place in the world in the twentieth century – with some exceptions such as the theologian Reinhold Niebuhr, writer Walter Russell Mead and diplomat Henry Kissinger – do not give sufficient weight to the British Victorian experience which preceded it. This is chiefly because America's methods of projecting international power and influence were consciously distinct from the British Empire model, against which it had rebelled. But setting aside the structural debates about what is or is not an Empire – and how 'formal' or 'informal' its structures are – this misses the way in which the formation of *worldviews* in Victorian Britain prefigured America's own awaking to superpower consciousness. On the one hand, the way in which domestic political drivers, from Protestantism to liberal political economy, spurred a sense of exceptionalism and shaped engagement with the rest of the world echoes from one to the other. On the other hand, the way in which Victorian Britain wrestled with recurrent dilemmas of international statecraft – with a premium on 'prestige', debates about intervention in the affairs of other states and the projection of military force, and the assertion of other forms of ideological, religious and commercial power – foreshadowed much of the angst and internal division that characterised American foreign policy. Ultimately, the Americans followed the British in the story they told themselves about the attractiveness of the form of self-governance and commercial enterprise that their nations had pioneered and, to varying degrees and with peaks and troughs of enthusiasm, sought to encourage others to adopt.[2]

How many analysts of American power have read Parry's *The Politics of Patriotism*? Few enough, in all likelihood. Yet the book tells a story that has profound echoes of the way in which Britain's internal politics interacted with a sense of its place in the world; and in which they shaped each other. The story is not one of the outworking of grand theories of empire or geopolitical

---

[2]   See Walter Russell Mead, *God and Gold: Britain, America and the Making of the Modern World* (New York, 2007) and Kori Schake, *Safe Passage: The Transition from British to American Hegemony* (Cambridge, MA, 2017).

competition but of how a domestic political narrative, one that was fiercely contested within and between political parties and in the public sphere, shaped conceptions of international affairs and how to approach it. Once it had been achieved, this status became a huge weight of responsibility to manage and preserve. As Parry puts it, in language that could easily be transported to the American experience, Victorians considered their country to be 'the greatest power that the world had ever seen and expected that status to be maintained'.[3]

What were the essentials of this model? Many thought that the rise to power was an expression of the will of God, alongside which came responsibilities to act in a certain way. But equally it was based on a theory of political and economic success in which constitutionalism, free trade and commercial acumen, economic probity, liberalism and humanitarianism were essential parts. While the driving force was not fear of 'the other', British exceptionalism was enhanced by contrast with the experience of (Catholic) European nations on the continent, where a combination of religious and political despotism, constitutional instability and economic stagnation were often seen to prevail. For British Liberals, this was particularly important. In highlighting the things that made Britain different from the continent – more successful, prosperous and secure – they were of course highlighting the essentials of their own political credo, casting themselves as virtuous and patriotic. But to what extent was it the theory of change – a belief that political and economic liberalism was the path of modernity and therefore success – or the deftness of the statecraft that accompanied it that was most important? Were the things that created predominance and inspired envy in others more fragile than they seemed? And what if a Catholic political culture that seemed more akin to those on the continent became increasingly important in an essential part of the British polity itself?

What is certain is that the sense of self that developed alongside the democratisation of politics and the ascendancy of liberalism as the dominant political force in Victorian Britain was markedly distinct from European traditions of *raison d'état* and *realpolitik*. No cult of Machiavellianism emerged in Victorian Britain as it did elsewhere in Europe, particularly after the failure of liberalism in the revolutions of 1848.[4] Victorian liberalism had, in its self-image at least, rejected a narrow and selfish conception of the national interest. It held to a higher purpose in which notions of progress and humanity were not only

---

[3]   Jonathan Parry, *The Politics of Patriotism: English Liberalism, National Identity and Europe, 1830–1886* (Cambridge, 2006), 387.

[4]   J. Bew, *Realpolitik: A History* (Oxford, 2016); Christopher Clarke, *Revolutionary Spring: Fighting for a New World 1848–9* (London, 2023); J.P. Parry, 'The Decline of Institutional Reform in Nineteenth-century Britain', in David Feldman and Jon Lawrence (eds), *Structures and Transformations in Modern British History* (Cambridge, 2011), 164–86.

The Reaches and Limits of British Liberal Constitutionalism   299

deemed to be politically desirable outcomes but methods of effective politics itself. Much of this righteous *mentalité* could be explained by comparatively privileged historical and geographical circumstances. Here, once more, the similarity to the formation of the modern American worldview is striking. In the introduction to their influential 1956 edited collection on the *Anglo-American Tradition in Foreign Affairs*, Arnold Wolfers and Laurence Martin made the point that constitutional and political theories in the Atlantic world were marked by an experience of relative security. Thomas More's *Utopia* was a classic case in point. This could be contrasted with the continental European experience – where Machiavelli's *Prince* had an outsized influence – in which fear of invasion or tyrannical interference from an overbearing neighbour shaped thinking about statecraft in a more 'realist' direction. The result was a demarcation between an Anglo-American inclination towards a philosophy of choice versus a European inclination towards a philosophy of necessity.[5]

But what happened when this method of self-professedly humane and constitutional politics – and the associated self-confidence that came with it – began to run up against alternative realities? What happened when the assumptions of liberal progress were undermined by other intractable historical forces, or when the liberal 'playbook' was clearly inadequate to the task?

For all its critics, the liberal theory of domestic and international political change was an immensely powerful political force in its own right – comprising a form of political economy in sync with modernity, a coherence between domestic and international policy and a moral force that enabled it to become predominant. It is no surprise therefore that it has been reincarnated in different eras and different forms. However, its success was dependent upon a degree of self-knowledge, individual reasoning, deftness and prudence that was not so easy to sustain when the spotlight shone most brightly. It was not so vigorous a force in its own right to withstand the consequences of major political miscalculation.

The Limits of Liberal Reasoning: The Case of Home Rule

There has been no better chronicler of the multi-layered nature of the Victorian liberal worldview, including its limitations, than Jonathan Parry. The middle part of this chapter picks up the other element of Parry's thesis in *The Politics of Patriotism*, which also bookends his *Rise and Fall of Victorian Liberalism* – about the ways in which that liberal self-confidence began to unravel

---

[5]   Arnold Wolfers and Laurence W. Martin, *The Anglo-American Tradition in Foreign Affairs: Readings from Thomas More to Woodrow Wilson* (New Haven, 1956). See also Jonathan Haslam, *No Virtue Like Necessity: Realist Thought in International Relations Since Machiavelli* (New Haven, 2002).

in the 1880s, as a result of a combination of seemingly insoluble problems and, ultimately, fatally misbegotten political reasoning. What was distinguishing about those problems was that they required logical leaps that Victorian liberals could not or would not make without severely undermining their foundational assumptions. Using Parry's scholarship as an analytical basis, what follows examines Gladstone's decision to pursue Irish Home Rule and then makes some broader points about the limits of liberal reasoning and the other ingredients needed for effective statecraft.

As countless scholars have pointed out, the limits of British liberalism were most often exposed by the indissoluble nature of the Irish question. The fact that British authority in Ireland increasingly depended on oppressive methods that Britain decried elsewhere as despotism was a considerable rebuke to the national self-image. Alongside this was the double embarrassment of the apparent failure of enlightened and hard-fought legislation to address satisfactorily Irish concerns and ameliorate grievances – such as those relating to religion, education and land. In 1869 Gladstone pressed through the disestablishment of the Anglican Church in Ireland, and in 1870 he passed a major Land Act. J.J. Shaw's pamphlet, *Mr Gladstone's Two Irish Policies 1868 and 1886*, celebrated a policy of using Westminster reforms to bring about unity and equality of all creeds in Ireland. As Shaw described, these were deemed to be two measures that were shining examples of liberal benevolence. 'The policy seemed to us statesmanlike and liberal... It was to be carried out by bringing Irish law and Irish institutions into harmony with the interests and feelings of the great bulk of the Irish people'.[6]

In the aftermath, however, Gladstone's tone towards Ireland became increasingly impatient, as if irritated with the churlish Irish response to his far-reaching reforms. In 1871, in a speech in Aberdeen, he said:

> We are told it is necessary for Ireland to close her relations with the Parliament of this country, and to have a Parliament of its own. Why is Parliament to be broken up? Has Ireland any great grievances? What is it that Ireland has demanded from the Imperial Parliament, and that the Parliament has refused? It will not do to deal with these matters in vague and shadowy assertions. I have looked in vain for the setting forth of any practical scheme of policy which the Imperial Parliament is not equal to deal with, or which it refuses to deal with, and which is to be brought about by home rule.[7]

---

6   J.J. Shaw, *Mr Gladstone's Two Irish Policies, 1869 and 1886* (London, 1888).

7   *The Speaker's Handbook on the Irish Question by an Irish Liberal* (London, 1890), 164.

The Reaches and Limits of British Liberal Constitutionalism 301

And yet liberal angst about the Irish question grew more acute at a time of deep political debates about the state of the British Empire. In the second half of the 1870s, out of office from 1874, the Liberal Party began to develop a critique of what they saw as a cynical and jingoistic approach to imperial expansion under Disraeli. The pinnacle of this was Gladstone's Midlothian campaign of 1878–80, a critique of the ethics and wisdom of so-called 'Beaconsfieldism', which set the tone for the formation of his second administration from 1880 to 1885.

Here is where the tension between the liberal self-image and critique of imperialism and the reality of British rule in Ireland became most acute. From 1880, land agitation and agrarian radicalism became increasingly widespread across Ireland as British authorities struggled to assert control. How could Liberals lecture Tories about the ethics of liberal constitutionalism when Ireland was unravelling under their control? In theory the liberal promise of British constitutional benevolence always held out the promise of self-government for peoples under British rule. Could that be granted to Ireland at a time when violence and seemingly anti-constitutional methods were on the rise? How could a resort to oppression in Ireland be the answer alone?

For Parry, Gladstone's final 'conversion' to Home Rule in late 1885 can only be seen against this backdrop. It was a last attempt to rescue Britain's self-image and external reputation as a polity that sought solutions based on constitutional adaption and a sense of justice.[8] The reasoning that went into Gladstone's decision has been subject to as much scrutiny as the merits of the approach itself. In one version of liberal history, that failure to deliver on Gladstone's vision was the moment at which any prospect of keeping the Union together and preventing the further spiralling of the Irish question towards violence, revolution and civil war was lost. In 1938, J.L. Hammond published his famous book *Gladstone and the Irish Nation*, which remains the classic pro-Gladstone tome. It presents the first Home Rule Bill of April 1886 as a great act of lost statesmanship, representing the moral depth and political wisdom of high Victorian liberalism. In the words of Roy Douglas, another admirer, Gladstone 'possessed a vision and moral authority which few men in politics have ever approached. Nowhere was that better seen than on the question of Home Rule, Gladstone's determination to bring about was an exceptionally farsighted statesmanship'. 'A hundred tragic years on', he wrote in 1988, 'who today doubts that the rejection of Home Rule in 1886 was an unqualified disaster both for Ireland and for Britain?'[9]

---

[8] J.P. Parry, *Democracy and Religion: Gladstone and the Liberal Party, 1867–1875* (Cambridge, 1986).

[9] Roy Douglas, 'Riddle of the Whigs', *Times Higher Educational Supplement*, 10 July 1988.

Perhaps the most famous challenge to that classic interpretation was the publication in 1974 of A.B. Cooke's and J.R. Vincent's 'high politics' classic, *The Governing Passion: Cabinet Government and Party Politics in Britain, 1885–86*. Cooke and Vincent raised substantial doubts about Hammond's moralistic interpretation of Gladstone's decision making – revealing, for example, several less than elevated Gladstonian party-political calculations in the crisis of 1885–86. More nuanced was James Loughlin's 1986 account, *Gladstone, Home Rule and the Ulster Question 1882–1893*, which argued that there was no great Gladstonian moral conversion but rather a panicky decision based on a sequence of alarming reports on the social dissolution of Ireland (in 1885) from apparently reliable informants.[10]

And what of Gladstone's reading of Ireland itself? It is on these grounds, rather than the question of his motivations, on which it is most appropriate to judge the quality of his analysis and subsequent decision-making. Gladstone made much of his reading of Irish history. But as Parry first argued, and has been developed by one of the authors of this article, it is on this terrain that his intellectual rigour suffered, from his tendency to project the liberal story he wanted to tell back upon the evidence before him. On the one hand this was reflected in a failure to grasp the depth of resistance in Ulster to this conception of Home Rule. On the other was a reading of recent Irish nationalist history through the prism of Daniel O'Connell's opposition to the Union and what he saw as the 'genuine liberalism' of O'Connell. This created three additional blind-spots. The first was the social and economic circumstances that underlay the land agitation and the radicalism that it inspired. 'The land question far from its basis is an incidental, unhappy and hampering accompaniment', Gladstone reflected.[11] Conceivably, land was not the sole 'basis' of the Irish question but it was certainly not 'incidental' or 'hampering'. The second was a wilful blindness about the increasingly anti-constitutional and radical nature of Irish nationalism in which agrarian agitation, violence and disorder played a crucial part. And the third was the extent to which Protestant Ulster felt itself an integral part of the British constitutional, economic and religious project which was the foundation of Victorian self-confidence.

Gladstone had been troubled by nightmares occasioned by his role as a member of the cabinet which jailed O'Connell in 1844; now he exorcised these nightmares in spectacular fashion. Irish nationalism was a pure form of patriotism. Old questions about the nature of Catholic public opinion in Ireland – including those raised sharply by his own anti-Vatican pamphlets of the mid

[10] James Loughlin, *Gladstone: Home Rule and the Ulster Question 1882–1893* (Dublin, 1986), 177.

[11] H.C.G. Matthew (ed.), *The Gladstone Diaries, vol. 12, 1887–1891* (Oxford, 1994), 130 [4 July 1888].

The Reaches and Limits of British Liberal Constitutionalism   303

1870s – were suppressed in favour of a gamble on the 'migration' of the 'old spirit' and its effective permeation by the 'genuine Liberalism' of O'Connell. The leap is made all the more interesting because of the way in which Gladstone wrestled with Irish agrarian arrest at the time of the Land League, confronted by an increasingly radicalised Irish national movement and the imprisonment of Parnell. He had reluctantly acquiesced in the Coercion Act of 1881. And in April and May 1882 Gladstone entered into secret negotiations with Parnell which led to his release from internment on 2 May 1882. In effect, Parnell offered to wind down the agitation with the use of the men of violence who were prominent in this movement. It was strange then that the Irish question became for Gladstone a question of the destiny of liberalism, with all questions reduced to one: if Ireland could only be governed by authoritarian repressive means by Westminster surely the best outcome was self-government?

Once this leap was made, the history was retrofitted to support it. And so Gladstone now came to the retrospective conclusion that the attempt to integrate Ireland politically as part of a larger political union, abolishing the old Irish parliament, was itself an act of constitutional vandalism. Even to his closest friends, Gladstone was perceived now to have become obsessive about the bribery and corruption that enabled the passage of the Act of Union: 'worse than the French terrorists', he told Edward Hamilton, his private secretary. The idea here was that Jacobin Terror was morally superior to British terror in Ireland in 1798 and 1799. Yet Gladstone's reading of nationalist political culture, as based primarily on a legitimate constitutional critique of unionism, was in itself too dependent on the other tropes of O'Connell. He missed the other elements of the Irish nationalist story that had become increasingly important, particularly after the famine. Conveniently, perhaps, in Gladstone's attempt to essentialise O'Connellism as the essence of nationalism, there was no place for the anti-liberalism and anti-utilitarianism of the Young Ireland movement. In particular, there was no place for hugely influential figures like John Mitchel who had reconceptualised nationalism in an anti-O'Connellite way, accusing him of being too close to the Whigs among other sins. It was also the case that Gladstone's own anti-Vatican pamphlets of the 1870s had undermined the middle ground that the Irish Liberal Party attempted to cultivate in an Ireland increasingly divided on confessional grounds.[12]

Just as he had relied too much on the O'Connellite prism for his reading of Ireland, so Gladstone now repeated the same mistake with Charles Stewart Parnell. For Gladstone, Parnell's leadership of nationalism was a crucial but complicated vehicle for the delivery of his project, which included a considerable role for the landed interest in the proposed constitutional settlement.

[12]   P. Bew, *Ancestral Voices in Irish Politics: Judging Dillon and Parnell* (Oxford, 2023), 114–25 and P. Bew, *The Politics of Enmity, 1789–2006* (Oxford, 2007), 348–53.

Parnell's status as a Protestant landowner with relatively conservative views on the land question seemed to provide some reassurance. It is on these grounds that Parry's verdict on Gladstone's analysis is so damning:

> on almost every ground Gladstone's solution for Ireland was surely misconceived. It was founded on the notion (derived, like many of his wilder ideas, from historical reading) that the Irish nationalist dynamic could resolve social and religious tension and reconcile the people to the rule of property. So it ignored the Ulster problem; it tried to revive moribund landed leadership by proposing a separate assembly of property-owners; and, unwilling to countenance a proper federal system for the whole kingdom, it could not solve the difficulty of the relationship between Westminster, on the one hand, and the Irish MPs and Irish finance, on the other. By polarising politics around this unworkable solution, it retarded the settlement of the Irish question for years – until the stakes had become too high for a settlement at all.[13]

Tellingly, not everyone in Ireland was impressed by Gladstone's history, or his efforts to overlay his decision with such moral conviction. On 18 December 1889 Gladstone remarked to Parnell: 'I am certain Mr Parnell when you read Irish history you must have been deeply affected.' Parnell in his coldest tone replied: 'Mr Gladstone I never read Irish history.' As the Irish nationalist MP Jasper Tully wrote, 'It was like sticking a pin into a gasbag and letting all the gas escape. Gladstone's idea was that all he had to do was pour out a long string of platitudes, overwhelming with sympathy for Ireland.'[14]

In Defence of Social Imagination and an Ethical Theory of the State

The timing of J.L. Hammond's spirited defence of Gladstone's decision on Home Rule, written a year before the outbreak of the Second World War, is significant in its own right. It allows us to consider the ethics and purpose of Gladstone's decision-making about the state against a broader backdrop. Writing a year before, in 1937, Winston Churchill had offered the most searing critique of what he saw as a total failure of statecraft:

> Gladstone was blind to the claims and cause of Protestant Ulster resistance. He displayed an indifference to the rights of the people of Northern Ireland which dominated the liberal mind for a whole generation. He elevated the

---

[13] Jonathan Parry, 'Crawling Towards God', *London Review of Books*, 16 (10 Nov. 1994), 35.

[14] *Roscommon Herald*, 6 Jan. 1940, 4.

The Reaches and Limits of British Liberal Constitutionalism 305

myopia to the level of doctrinal principle. In the end we all reached together a broken Ireland and a broken United Kingdom.[15]

For all the flaws in his reasoning, Gladstone's record can easily be defended against some of Churchill's more severe criticisms. Churchill, who had become increasingly isolated for his own retrograde views on India over the course of the decade, had his own blind-spots. How, after all, other than by an offer of Home Rule, could the British policy have responded to the popular Irish vote in 1885–6 and the landside for the Irish National Party? And if the Hammond thesis fails on the basis that Gladstone's reasoning was poor and his analysis was selective, the 'high political' thesis – that cynical political considerations drove his decision-making – does not stand up to scrutiny either.

For the purposes of this chapter, the most interesting aspect of Gladstone's ruminations over Home Rule is that they pivoted around a moral theory of the state, based on a constitutional idealism as well as a strongly held liberal political economy. Specifically, in both his private reflections and his public attempts to explain his rationale, he appealed to a sense of 'atonement' for the wrongs committed by that state and sought a constitutional remedy. This goes back to the very core of the self-image of Victorian liberalism, its model of economic and political success and its relationship with the world around it.

When set in the Irish context, this ethical theory of the state was unable to find a formula to accommodate some uncomfortable realities – from ethno-religious rage, often expressed through violence, to unsustainable socio-economic imbalances. When set in an imperial context, as Gladstone also recognised, it abutted other behaviours – jingoism, commercial rapaciousness and hard national self-interest – that were difficult to reconcile with the prevailing self-image and the contrast drawn with other nations. And when put under the spotlight by juxtaposition with other European theories of state, it could be presented as hypocritical or even self-delusionary.

How then did the liberal Victorian conception of the state look to others, including those striving for their own national stories? For the champions of realpolitik and an unsentimental approach to statecraft, it was both misleading and flawed. The German historian, Heinrich von Treitschke, rejected the 'moral' conception that he also thought had infected German liberalism in the second half of the nineteenth century, in which the state is 'regarded as a good little boy, to be washed, brushed, and sent to school'. For Treitschke, the virility of the state was not defined by its constitutional mores but by its power, and its ability to harness national resources in pursuit of historical destiny. Worse still

---

[15] Winston Churchill, 'Joseph Chamberlain', *Great Contemporaries* (London, 1937), 88.

was the fact that this theory of state was now being presented as the basis of good relations between states, backed up by an insipid commercialism.[16]

For Treitschke, the primary progenitor of this delusion was liberal Victorian Britain. There had been a time, in the era of the Napoleonic wars, when Britain had spoken honestly about its pursuit of self-interest. He admired the statecraft of men such as Wellington, Castlereagh, Canning and Palmerston. In recent decades, however, Britain had become beholden to the 'self-satisfied' moralism and commercialism of the heroes of Victorian liberal Britain, such as Cobden, Bright and Gladstone. Now they lectured the world on humanity while expanding their commercial tentacles across the world.[17]

Indeed, Parry's more recent work on the expansion of the British empire in the Ottoman Middle East between 1798 and 1854 captures much of the hard-nosed way in which British strategic and commercial interests were pursued. As he argues, much of Britain's informal empire in the region had been established before the highpoint of Victorian liberal self-confidence and patriotic constitutionalism that he describes in *The Politics of Patriotism*. The largely non-ideological and non-idealistic motivations for this expansion were driven by a combination of commercial opportunity and in some cases personal interest. The seeds of Britain's approach to the Ottoman Empire – propping it up as the cheapest means of stopping other European powers coming into its sphere of influence – was well-established before Gladstone's criticism of Disraeli's imperial expansionism began in the 1870s. What is more, Parry's description of the nature of diplomacy in these environs eschews any overarching ideological rationale, though that is not to deny the importance of ideas in its formation. What he describes is a series of 'men on the spot', operating with considerable latitude and a sense of the national interest, exercising judgment and building networks, but with no major project or programme in mind.[18] It is an important counterpart to the sense of noble purpose and exceptionalism that Parry describes in his other works, in which ideas and a sense of a higher mission set the frame.

It is only when the story of British Victorian imperial power is told over the *longue durée* that a different perspective on it – as a more coherent exercise in the building and maintenance of international power – can be taken. In this regard, Treitschke's successor as the foremost German theorist of *raison d'état*, Friedrich Meinecke, came to a more nuanced view of the evolution of British power and the place of liberal ideals within it. The British had gained a vast

[16] Heinrich von Treitschke, *His Life and Works* (London, 2014), 158–92.

[17] H.W.C. Davis, *The Political Thought of Heinrich von Treitschke* (London, 1914), 35–8, 227–89.

[18] Jonathan Parry, *Promised Lands: Britain and the Ottoman Middle East, 1798–1854* (Princeton, 2022).

commercial empire through the most nefarious of means – from commercial avarice to the use of privateers and brute force. But having gained a position of hegemony, they showed an 'increasing tendency to change the sword of the naked power-policy, which the English always pursued, into the sword of the executor of the law – whether summoned to the task by God or by justice and morality'. In essence, they practised 'the most effective kind of Machiavellianism' in which power-politics and the ferocious pursuit of the national interest became 'unconscious of itself, and to appear (not only to others, but also to itself) as being pure humanity, candour and religion'.[19] This contained within it lessons that rivals must learn. 'Power politics and *Realpolitik*, once freed of universal principles – and universal principles are basically ethical principles – could easily degenerate into a... politics of violence'. 'Utilitarian and ethical motives must work in unison', argued Meinecke after the First World War, reflecting on the ability of the Anglo-Saxon powers to mobilise others in support of a constitutional ideal.[20] It was not lost on him that Woodrow Wilson, the man who set the agenda for the creation of a new international order after 1918, was a huge admirer of Cobden, Bright and Gladstone.

Yet, as Adam Tooze describes, Wilson was far more cautious about assuming this great responsibility than the high idealism of his famous Fourteen Points would suggest. Partly because of his admiration for Gladstone, he feared the military burden, financial cost and ethical dilemmas posed by the acquisition of such vast international power – and the effect it would have on constitutional health of the American republic.[21] Indeed, Gladstone would have baulked at Meinecke's description of British power – and his suggestion that high-minded Victorian liberal cant was deployed a guise for imperial self-interest. In truth, much of his political mission was geared towards the restraint of British imperial expansionism, owing to the spiralling costs and the deleterious effect he believed it had on British liberal constitutionalism. Yet for those looking at the accruement of such a vast expanse of British power over the course of the nineteenth century, they were all part of the same commercial-imperial complex. Despite the Midlothian campaign and the critique of Beaconsfieldism, the British empire continued to grow.

It was only after the passage of the high point of liberal Victorian self-confidence that a discernible strategic concept of liberal imperialism emerged – a reckoning forced by the challenge posed by rival great powers. Eyre Crowe's

[19] Friedrich Meinecke, *Machiavellianism: The Doctrine of Raison d'Etat and its Place in Modern History*, ed. Werner Stark (New Haven, 1957), 137, 157–62, 179.

[20] Quoted in Richard W. Sterling, *Ethics in a World of Power: The Political Ideas of Friedrich Meinecke* (Princeton, 1958), 202–4.

[21] This is a major theme of Adam Tooze's book, *Deluge: The Great War, America and the Remaking of the Global Order* (London, 2014).

famous memorandum of 1907 captured the specific nature of the British strategic dilemma, posed by the acquisition of 'vast overseas colonies and dependencies' and a naval and commercial reach that made the British Empire 'the neighbour of every country accessible by sea'. Under this pressure, Britain's support for liberal constitutionalism took on the form of a strategic necessity. This is because it was in Britain's selfish strategic interest to 'harmonise with the general desires and ideals common to all mankind' and closely identify with 'the primary and vital interests of a majority, or as many as possible, of the other nations'.[22] It was not long after that Churchill would claim that 'the fortunes of the British Empire and its glory are inseparably interwoven with the fortunes of the world'.[23]

It was the Anglophile American theologian Reinold Niebuhr who came closest to capturing something of the enduring appeal of the Victorian liberal ideal of the state in a world that did not follow liberal, enlightened rules. In his view, the key to political wisdom was the exercise of prudence rather than a retreat to the extremes of austere realism or zealous idealism. Niebuhr contrasted the failure of the German Empire, brought to a partly self-inflicted collapse in the last war, with the longevity and durability of the British one. Of course, the British were guilty of hypocrisy, cant and self-aggrandisement. But equally the Germans 'were too much philosophers and therefore too much absolutists to engage successfully in the relativities of politics'. Whether consciously or not, the British had a 'genius for politics' in their appeal to a higher ideal. 'Moral pretension is the baser part of that genius', Niebuhr conceded. Nonetheless, there was a nobler aspect to this form of reasoning – 'the ability to gauge the interests and reactions of other than your own group so that no interest is pursued until resentment against it issues in social and political violence'. In words that have echoes of Gladstone's reasoning over Home Rule, Niebuhr went on to muse: 'a politically-minded people, such as the British, can achieve levels of social imagination which give their corporate life a semblance of morality and a reality of political effectiveness'.[24]

* * *

[22] Eyre Crowe 'Memorandum on the State of British Relations with France and Germany', in G.P. Gooch and H.W.V. Temperley (eds), *British Documents on the Origins of the War* (11 vols, London, 1926–38), vol. 3, 397–420.

[23] Quoted in J. Bew, 'Pax Anglo-Saxonica', *American Interest*, 9 April 2015.

[24] Reinhold Niebuhr, 'Awkward Imperialists', *The Atlantic*, 145 (May 1930), 670–5. See also J. Bew, 'The Art of Imperial Politics and the Interminable Frustrations of History', in R. Lovin and J. Maudlin (eds), *The Oxford Handbook of Reinhold Niebuhr* (Oxford, 2021), 611–22.

The Reaches and Limits of British Liberal Constitutionalism 309

As Parry describes so elegantly, Gladstone got it wrong on Home Rule, largely through a jaundiced reading of history. It was, in Gladstone's defence, a sophisticated rather than a cynical decision; and one forced by the evident failures of liberal constitutional reformism and Victorian political economy to soothe Irish grievances and buy Ireland into the same vision of modernity and progress in which Gladstone so strongly believed. Nonetheless, it was a piece of poor political reasoning which contained within it less circumspection, self-awareness and prudence than was required for a decision of that momentous significance. Worse still, it jeopardised the very thing – the essential but fragile liberal constitutional equilibrium of the Union – that Gladstone believed was his country's greatest strength. And yet when all is said and done, the problem was not the motivation that underlay the attempt to solve the Irish question, so much as the quality of judgment behind the boldest attempt to do so.

In some manifestations, the story of Victorian liberal Britain enters today's world as a tale of political virtue and noble-minded idealism. Parry's critique of Gladstone's decision-making should warn us against that. In other forms, the story of British constitutionalism – its reaches and limits – takes on a certain priggishness about political propriety and 'properness', often seen when historians of modern British history comment on contemporary British politics and its perceived deviation from those standards (such as the commitment of leaders like Gladstone to study history). But perhaps the most useful lesson of Parry's work, seen in his cold-eyed dissection of the Home Rule decision, is that the choices made in politics should be judged by the extent to which they are able to digest and absorb the brusque realities of political life – not to attempt to transplant them with a more elegant and appealing thesis about how we got to this point, even when in support of an apparently nobler ideal.

Chapter 15

Latin America and British International Thought, 1880–1920

Alex Middleton

Independent Latin America contained philosophical and political problems that should have mattered to the British. It was built on revolution, republicanism and the crumbling of empires. It raised distinctive issues about the rule of law, race and slavery, and directive government and civilizational progress. And it was not an inaccessible abstraction. For most of the nineteenth century, Latin America was one of the principal extra-European spheres of British influence, investment and naval power. By the early decades of the twentieth century, Britain was in a struggle for mastery in the region with France, Germany, the United States and the rising nations of the Pacific. Yet eminent and not-so-eminent Victorians bemoaned national ignorance about the 'other America'. J.R. Seeley, giving his seminal 1883 lectures on *The Expansion of England*, reflected that few among his elite Cambridge audience would be likely to 'know anything' about the 'mighty revolutions' that had realised Latin American independence.[1] The diplomat Robert Grant Watson, writing the next year, lamented the egregious misunderstandings of Latin American politics and geography he had encountered among MPs and, perhaps more predictably, at a Harrow School speech day.[2] The statesman and jurist James Bryce was still protesting in 1921 that the Spanish American republics had not drawn the attention they merited from historians or political philosophers.[3]

This seeming disconnect between strategic significance and intellectual engagement raises two main questions for historians of the interfaces between ideas and politics. What impact, if any, did post-revolutionary Latin America make on British political thinking? And what can the nature of that impact tell us about the relations between the realities of global power, and the shaping of modern international thought?

---

[1] J.R. Seeley, *The Expansion of England* (London, 1883), 53.

[2] Robert Grant Watson, *Spanish and Portuguese South America during the Colonial Period* (2 vols, London, 1884), vol. 1, x–xii.

[3] James Bryce, *Modern Democracies* (2 vols, London, 1921), vol. 1, 209.

Latin America and British International Thought, 1880–1920

In setting out to navigate this territory, it is not obvious where to begin. Independent Latin America is a blank space in the historiography of modern British political ideas.[4] It does not appear in studies of imperial political thought and culture, or of ideas about international relations and internationalism. It is similarly absent from work on patterns of thinking about democracy, civilization, progress, political leadership and allied problems. Most historians working in these fields take the term 'America' to mean North America, and the concept of the 'Atlantic' as a shorthand for British-US connections. These habits persist despite the emergence of literatures which stress the impact of British ideas and models in Latin America, and which chart how interest in the region affected politics in other places, particularly the United States and France.[5]

It is, however, straightforward enough to explain why political and intellectual historians of modern Britain have overlooked Latin America. Its importance does not leap out from the standard sources. The region rarely became a divisive issue in domestic politics, or a subject of moralising campaigns, and leading political thinkers did not write about it. Bryce is the only well-known British public intellectual to have produced anything like a serious study, his *South America: Observations and Impressions* (London, 1912). The historiography of 'informal empire' also has something to answer for. Most authorities characterise Britain's 'informal imperial' presence in Latin America as a robustly practical enterprise, driven by appetites for trade, influence and profit, and make little allowance for the role of political visions.[6] So recent efforts to globalise the histories of modern British political and intellectual culture have turned towards other geographical areas, and frameworks of power relations, especially those contained by 'formal' empire.[7]

---

[4] 'South America' was the dominant Victorian and Edwardian shorthand for the whole region between the US-Mexican border and Tierra del Fuego, though most writers knew to distinguish 'Central' from 'South' America when necessary. 'Latin America', widely used on the Continent and in the Americas from the mid-nineteenth century, crept into British parlance from the 1880s and 1890s, becoming common only in the 1910s.

[5] For Latin American impacts on the US and France, see e.g. Caitlin Fitz, *Our Sister Republics: The United States in an Age of American Revolutions* (New York, 2016); Helen Delpar, *Looking South: The Evolution of Latin Americanist Scholarship in the United States, 1850–1975* (Tuscaloosa, 2008); Edward Shawcross, *France, Mexico and Informal Empire in Latin America, 1820–1867: Equilibrium in the New World* (Basingstoke, 2018).

[6] Historians of international law are a partial exception. See Lauren Benton and Lisa Ford, *Rage for Order: The British Empire and the Origins of International Law, 1800–1850* (Cambridge: MA, 2016).

[7] Alex Middleton, 'Victorian Politics and Politics Overseas', *Historical Journal*, 64 (2021), 1449–76.

This chapter is a study in the construction of an international political problem. It asks how the British political class understood independent Latin America, and why their attitudes changed over time. It centres on the period 1880–1920, and it makes two points. The first is that the British engaged substantially and to important effect with Latin American politics in the century following independence, and that this intellectual history needs to be reintegrated into our understanding of modern British thought. The chapter argues that this engagement became more concerted in the decades around the turn of the twentieth century, in ways that challenge assumptions about the imperial and international thinking of the late Victorians and Edwardians, and about British visions of 'America', the 'Atlantic', and 'informal empire'. Long assumed by the British to have been fated to eternal turmoil by the oppressions of materialistic and despotic Iberian imperial rule, after the 1880s an increasingly stable South America seemed to offer new political, mercantile and philosophical possibilities. The chapter's second point is that this reshaping of Latin America as a perceived problem in Britain was an Atlantic process. British ideas responded to new patterns of commercial, diplomatic and geopolitical ambition in the Atlantic realm. Visions crystallised, moreover, in response to large-scale circulations of people, texts and ideas, primarily between Britain, Latin America and the United States, but also touching France and Spain. The chapter takes Bryce's book, a subject of presumptive interest for historians of political ideas, as a case in point to illustrate these dynamics. Its broader contention, then, is that historians can better understand British international political ideas if we pay closer attention to the structures of global power politics and interstate connections that guided shifts in thinking. The category 'international thought' makes more sense when it encompasses international frameworks, as well as the substance of arguments and theories about international affairs.

Latin America and the Victorians

Latin American independence, settled by the mid-1820s in part thanks to Britain's diplomatic recognition of Brazil and the Spanish republics, seemed to create an embarrassment of new opportunities. It precipitated a rapid expansion of the British presence in the region, with traders, bankers, diplomats, engineers and travellers diffusing themselves around the new states. This osmosis was not purely 'informal', since Britain also had local territorial footholds, in the shape of British Guiana, British Honduras and later the Falkland Islands. In 1808, moreover, the British Navy had established a presence on the South American coast, centred after 1813 at Valparaiso in Chile. The naval connection was central in bringing elite families into contact with the Americas, and one of the second Earl Grey's sons not only served on the South America station,

Latin America and British International Thought, 1880–1920   313

but also wrote a history of Mexico. Deployments of British naval power on Latin American coasts and waterways, calculated to apply pressure for financial restitutions or commercial concessions, or otherwise to take sides in local conflicts, would pockmark the nineteenth century. So Britain was very active in the region.

Latin America was also, by the 1820s, an established subject of political reflection and speculation at home. Scottish Enlightenment historians and political economists had written extensively about the reaction of the New World on Europe, and about Iberian America's impacts on the Iberian Peninsula.[8] The British press energetically debated the independence struggles of the 1810s and 1820s, much of its coverage informed by the agendas of the numerous Latin American actors who gathered in London in this era, Simón Bolívar being the most celebrated. Among political philosophers, Jeremy Bentham and James Mill both took a serious interest in developments.[9] It seemed obvious to those writing in the revolutionary era that for geopolitical, commercial and intellectual reasons, Latin America would continue to feature prominently in British political culture in the decades to come.

Instead, until the 1880s, the British saw the problem of South America shrink within a much smaller compass. Early optimism about the region's potential for social progress faded after the collapse of a speculative bubble around mining stocks in 1825–6, and because of the perceived failure of most of the Spanish republics to achieve political stability. Bryce would later remark that the friends of freedom in Europe 'presently lost interest in communities which were not reflecting credit upon democracy', leaving the republics as a field of admonition and warning for conservatives, while the socialist, Scottish nationalist, and sometime Argentine cattle rancher R.B. Cunninghame Graham similarly noted that 'interest in them died out except for purposes connected with the Stock Exchange'.[10] This characterisation served a purpose for men trying to stress the originality of their early-twentieth-century books about South America, but it is accurate only up to a point.

There was never any shortage of public interest in Latin America's romantic leaders and more dramatic political developments. British newspapers and periodicals bulged with articles about, for instance, the impossibly arbitrary

---

[8]   Adam Smith, *An Inquiry into the Nature and Causes of the Wealth of Nations* (2 vols, London, 1776), vol. 2, 154, 161; William Robertson, *The History of America* (2 vols, London, 1777), vol 2, book 8; Henry Brougham, *An Inquiry into the Colonial Policy of the European Powers* (2 vols, Edinburgh, 1803), vol. 1, 370–500.

[9]   Jonathan Harris, 'An English Utilitarian Looks at Spanish-American Independence: Jeremy Bentham's Rid Yourselves of Ultramaria', *The Americas*, 53 (1996), 217–33.

[10]   Bryce, *South America*, 524; R.B. Cunninghame Graham, *A Vanished Arcadia: Being Some Account of the Jesuits in Paraguay, 1607 to 1767* (London, 1901), 6.

dictatorial regime of Dr Francia in post-revolutionary Paraguay, the Anglo-French intervention in the Río de la Plata in the 1840s, and France's spectacular and doomed attempt to impose a Habsburg prince on the reconstituted throne of Mexico in the 1860s. Polemicists attached these cases to partisan agendas, and used them to rationalise or to challenge despotic directive rule, 'gunboat diplomacy' and European imperialism.[11] There were also more deliberate attempts by British writers to yoke Latin America to serious political and intellectual projects. The political economist and Liberal MP John MacGregor was among the first to weld North and South America together analytically, in the service of a thesis about the dependence of modern civilization on free exchange, while the agenda of Arthur Helps's multi-volume work of 1857 is in its title, *The Spanish Conquest in America and its Relation to the History of Slavery and to the Government of Colonies*.[12] Most specialised early- and mid-Victorian British writing on Latin America, however, came from figures who had had spent long periods in the region, and who had ill-concealed personal axes to grind.[13] It remained unusual for educated British people to learn Spanish or Portuguese – hence the public confusion over Elizabeth Barrett Browning's 1850 *Sonnets from the Portuguese*, which she originally claimed were translations.[14] Between the 1820s and the 1880s neither Latin America as a whole, nor any of its constituent states, ever became a subject of regular, coherent political debate, on the model of more structurally significant foreign polities like France or the United States. The region lurked on the margins of Victorian global consciousness.

For most British commentators, for most of the nineteenth century, Latin America raised two main problems: one about its internal condition, and one about its external relations. The first problem was how to account for the apparent political failure of the Spanish republics. Why were they so prone to revolution, turmoil and civil war, and why did they seem unable to sustain free

[11] Alex Middleton, 'Britain and the Paraguayan Dictatorship, c.1820–1840', *Historical Journal*, 65 (2022), 371–92; David McLean, *War, Diplomacy and Informal Empire: Britain and the Republics of La Plata, 1836–1853* (New York, 1995); Alex Middleton, 'British Liberalism and the French Invasion of Mexico', *Journal of British Studies*, 62 (2023), 362–89.

[12] John MacGregor, *The Progress of America, from the Discovery by Columbus to the Year 1846* (2 vols, London, 1847); Arthur Helps, *The Spanish Conquest in America and its Relation to the History of Slavery and to the Government of Colonies* (3 vols, London, 1855–7).

[13] See e.g. J.P. and W.P. Robertson, *Letters on Paraguay: Comprising an Account of a Four Years' Residence in that Republic, under the Government of the Dictator Francia* (2 vols, London, 1838).

[14] Graciela Iglesias-Rogers (ed.), *The Hispanic-Anglosphere from the Eighteenth to the Twentieth Century* (London, 2021).

Latin America and British International Thought, 1880–1920   315

institutions? Competing answers to these questions emphasised different subsidiary dynamics, but there was general agreement on the basic cause, crossing party-political and philosophical lines. It stemmed from some of the essential precepts of Victorian political thought. The refined republican arrangements the successor states had tried to borrow from the US did not work in South America, because Spain had not trained its colonial subjects in self-government, or promoted the character and habits required for the successful operation of constitutional rule. In short, the Spanish crown's hoarding of despotic authority had doomed its portion of the Americas to instability. It was no more difficult to explain why the colonies had pursued separation after Napoleon Bonaparte's invasion of the Iberian Peninsula, since this was simply a natural response to centuries of unsympathetic, jealous, obscurantist, priest-ridden imperial rule. Explaining the condition of independent Latin America did not require a firm grasp of contemporary political sociology, but only a smattering of stereotyped imperial history.

Victorian writers typically developed their arguments about the fate of Latin America through contrasts with the historical experiences of North America.[15] They explained that where it was materialistic adventurers seeking silver who had invaded Central and South America, without any ambition to govern, it was clear-eyed Britons, experienced with self-rule and committed to the selective replication of European social structures, who had colonised the more successful North. This 'two Americas' model guided attention to the second great problem the British saw facing Latin America: the policy of the United States. What would be the future relationship between the continent's great power and its 'sister republics'? Would the US turn to conquest, to less direct forms of tutelage, to isolationism, or to other schemes entirely? And where did the malleable Monroe Doctrine stand in all this? After the US peeled away vast chunks of Mexico in the 1840s, British discussion of Latin America increasingly treated the region as a field on which other powers would compete, assimilating it to wider debates about the proper parameters of empire, expansion and commercial interest. Richard Cobden was one of very few prominent early Victorians who looked forward to the region taking an independent place in the global balance of power.[16]

None of the better-known Victorian thinkers visited Latin America, or subjected it to serious empirical study, but they did deploy conventional wisdoms about it as evidence for their political observations and theories. John Stuart

---

[15] Victorians rarely thought about Latin America in relation to the Caribbean, which had been an important dynamic in eighteenth-century writing, especially in relation to contraband commerce.

[16] Richard Cobden, 'Russia' (1836), in *The Political Writings of Richard Cobden* (2 vols, London, 1867), vol. 1, 275–8.

Mill pointed to its 'state of chronic revolution and civil war' as a consequence of a factionalised representative system, while Herbert Spencer cited its experiences to illustrate the outcome of mismatches between institutions and national character.[17] Walter Bagehot and Charles Dilke reflected on the region's unique 'experiments in mixing races'.[18] Lord Acton took a somewhat deeper interest in the emancipation of the Spanish colonies and its impact on the modern world, intriguingly suggesting that Britain's encouragement of Latin American independence would hasten the end of its own empire.[19] But this was exceptional among the age's luminaries, and it is striking that Latin America barely features in the pioneering later-nineteenth-century studies of comparative political science, even those of Seeley, despite his lamentations.[20] The assumption was evidently that it sat outside the relevant categories of political phenomena. This lack of a native philosophical industry manufacturing studies of Latin America helps to account for the remarkable longevity of Thomas Carlyle's vivid 1843 essay on the era of revolutions, 'Dr Francia'.[21] Despite its point being that nobody in Europe really knew what was going on in South America (a 'great confused phenomenon'), commentators continued to cite the piece as capturing something essential about the region into the twentieth century.[22]

From the outset, however, debates about Latin America crossed borders. Citizens of the United States provided the British with the most authoritative histories of Latin America, with W.H. Prescott's volumes on Mexico and Peru holding the field for decades.[23] One of the most influential 'two Americas' analyses was outlined by Alexis de Tocqueville in *Democracy in America* (1835), which explained the divergent trajectories of the continents by reference to climate as well as to the unsuitability of republicanism for South America, and

[17]   John Stuart Mill, *Considerations on Representative Government* (London, 1861), 72–3, and see also 'Coleridge' (1840), in *Collected Works of John Stuart Mill*, ed. J.M. Robson *et al.* (33 vols, Toronto, 1963–91), vol. 10, 117–64, 136; Herbert Spencer, *The Study of Sociology* (London, 1873), 275–6.

[18]   Quotation in Walter Bagehot, *Physics and Politics* (London, 1873), 68–9; C.W. Dilke, *Greater Britain* (2 vols, London, 1868), vol. 1, 279–80.

[19]   John Dalberg-Acton, 'Colonies', *The Rambler*, 6 (1862), 400; *Lectures on Modern History*, ed. J.N. Figgis and R.V. Laurence (London, 1907), 69–70. And see S. Paul Kramer, 'Lord Acton and Latin America', *Journal of Inter-American Studies*, 5 (1963), 39–44.

[20]   E.g. E.A. Freeman, *Comparative Politics* (London, 1873); J.R. Seeley, *Introduction to Political Science* (London, 1896).

[21]   [Thomas Carlyle], 'Dr. Francia', *Foreign Quarterly Review*, 31 (1843), 544–89.

[22]   E.g. 'The Emancipation of South America', *Saturday Review*, 75 (1893), 496–7; 'The Revolt of Spanish America', *Times Literary Supplement*, 24 Jan. 1918, 44.

[23]   W.H. Prescott, *History of the Conquest of Mexico* (3 vols, London, 1843); *History of the Conquest of Peru* (2 vols, London, 1847).

Latin America and British International Thought, 1880–1920   317

which imagined a future in which Latin America fell under US tutelage.[24] Contributions came also from other national quarters, with the French-sponsored Archduke Maximilian's sojourn in Mexico generating a series of accounts by members of his Austrian retinue, which London publishers had translated.[25] Those in Britain who needed to understand Latin America could easily draw on resources from overseas, which helps to explain both why the British did not at this stage invest significant quantities of intellectual capital in the subject, and why arguments emanating from different political cultures often looked so similar.

Rethinking Latin America, 1880–1920

A new constellation of attitudes took shape after about 1880. Economic circumstances had already begun to shift, with Acton observing in 1868 that parts of South America were expanding faster than the US in terms of population and trade.[26] But a turning point came at the time of the Saltpetre War of 1879–84 between Chile, Bolivia and Peru, a major regional conflict, which prompted a series of new reflections and investigations.[27] From that point forward, a consensus began to gather that Latin America was starting to emerge from its unprecedented political difficulties, and that its future was both an important and an uncertain question of international policy. Historians tend to think that when the British looked abroad in this era, they trained their eyes mainly on Europe, the European empires and the United States. Yet looking at the US around the fin-de-siècle also meant looking at Latin America. The journalist W.B. Duffield could not have written in 1880 what he wrote in 1903: that for Britain, the future of South America was 'the greatest political problem of the new century'.[28]

The resurgent political-cultural interest of this era took a number of forms. Scholarly work on Latin American history proliferated, notably the 1890s study produced by Edward John Payne, a Fellow of University College, Oxford, and a leading colonial historian.[29] Joseph Conrad's 1904 novel *Nostromo* promoted the region (or at least the fictional republic of Costaguana) into the realms

---

[24] Alexis De Tocqueville, trans. Henry Reeve, *Democracy in America* (2 vols, London, 1835), vol. 1, 7, 246, 252–3; vol. 2, 255–9, 443–50.

[25] E.g. Countess Paula Kollonitz, trans. J.E. Ollivant, *The Court of Mexico* (London, 1867); Max, Baron von Alvensleben, *With Maximilian in Mexico* (London, 1867).

[26] John Dalberg-Acton, 'The Rise and Fall of the Mexican Empire' (1868), in *Historical Essays and Studies*, ed. J.N. Figgis and R.V. Laurence (London, 1907), 143–4.

[27] E.g. A. Gallenga, *South America* (London, 1880).

[28] W.B. Duffield, 'German Policy in South America', *Monthly Review*, 10 (1903), 65.

[29] E.J. Payne, *History of the New World Called America* (2 vols, Oxford, 1892–9).

of great fiction.[30] From the beginning of the twentieth century the *Economist* and the *Financial Times* were crammed with articles about Latin American commerce and finance, while in 1910 *The Times* began a regular South America Supplement, which ran for forty-four issues, in response to 'the rapidly increasing importance of Latin America in the world's polity'.[31] The publisher T. Fisher Unwin commissioned a 'South America Series' which included heavy books on all the major republics, and literary reviews began to groan under the weight of 'the enormous body of literature devoted to this continent'.[32] In 1911 the Argentine Club was founded at premises in Mayfair, for those with links to Latin America, while 1912 saw a large-scale 'Latin-British Exhibition' held in White City, at which visitors could gaze down at Latin-American-themed exhibits from a vertiginous ride called the 'revolving flip-flap'.[33] Centenaries of revolutions and declarations of independence offered convenient opportunities for taking stock. The dark underbelly of Europe's commercial presences in the region also came into sharper focus. In particular, the 'Putumayo atrocities', a programme of murder and slavery pursued by the agents of the London-registered Peruvian Amazon Company, became a major public-political *cause célèbre* around 1910, campaigned against by the *Anti-Slavery Reporter*, investigated by Roger Casement, and probed by a parliamentary committee.

How do we account for this explosion of interest? Technological advances were part of it. J.A. Hobson argued in the 1890s that steamships, railways and telegraphs were prising South America open, creating new opportunities for capital and new options for foreign domination.[34] Latin America was the site of the most audacious engineering project of the age, in the shape of the Panama Canal, which did much to open new imaginative vistas. But the main reason is that the basic problem of Latin American government changed from the 1880s. It became possible to detect signs of greater stability and prosperity in most of the South American republics – a category which included Brazil after 1889 – if not in their less fortunate Central American counterparts. Even Mexico, long understood to be the most tortured of the Spanish successor states, found apparent relief from perpetual disturbance under the rigorous rule of Porfirio Díaz from the 1880s. The first of *The Times*'s South America Supplements in

---

[30] E.g. 'Nostromo', *Times Literary Supplement*, 21 Oct. 1904, 320. Graham Greene would go on to interpret Latin America more extensively from the 1930s.

[31] *The Times*, 28 Oct. 1913, 7.

[32] *English Review* (Nov. 1912), 684–5. For a comprehensive list of works on South America published in the US in the 1900s and 1910s, see Ernst B. Filsinger, *Commercial Travelers' Guide to Latin America* (Washington: DC, 1920), 580–92.

[33] Advert in *Sunday Times*, 26 May 1912, 5.

[34] J.A. Hobson, *The Evolution of Modern Capitalism: A Study of Machine Production* (London, 1895), 106–7.

Latin America and British International Thought, 1880–1920   319

1910 claimed that the continent had at last 'reached a stage from which it can advance', and specialist writers were at pains to stress that armed revolutions were no longer a daily occurrence.[35] This new state of things also magnified the philosophical interest of the region for defenders of republicanism and democracy, who had once held it at arm's length. This symbolic role grew during World War I, when Lord Cromer argued that the republics 'after a prolonged and very fiery trial, have justified democratic rule'.[36]

Relative stability and prosperity created new commercial and geopolitical dynamics. For many journalists and businesses, it was the 1820s all over again, as the idea took hold that Latin America represented a still-largely-untapped commercial opportunity. But this time there were more competitors for trade and political influence. German penetration was one fear, from the start of the twentieth century, not least because German agents were said to be better than their British counterparts at winning Latin American hearts and minds.[37] French projects remained a concern, especially since Paris had replaced London as the pilgrimage destination for Latin Americans visiting Europe in the decades since independence. Japan was suddenly a consideration as well, after its success in the 1904–5 conflict with Russia.[38] But the greatest perceived threat was, inevitably, from the US. Schemes of Pan-Americanism, encouraged by touring US Secretaries of State, grew in importance from the 1880s.[39] Already in 1890 Charles Dilke thought that the US was assuming a new role as patron of all the South American republics.[40] The Venezuela crisis of 1895, in which the US intervened under the aegis of the Monroe Doctrine in a dispute about the border between Venezuela and British Guiana, popularised this notion. Ultimately the US's turn towards formal imperial ambition, and apparently sharp diplomatic practice, seemed to throw the whole of Latin America into the balance.[41] British writers increasingly assumed that Central America, at the least, would succumb, formally or informally, to the domination of the US.

---

[35] 'The starting point of South America', *Times South American Supplement*, 1 (30 July 1910), 5; e.g. G.F. Scott Elliott, *Chile: Its History and Development* (London, 1911), 340.

[36] Cromer, 'South America', *Spectator*, 115 (6 Nov. 1915), 624.

[37] Cromer, 'South of Panama', *Spectator*, 116 (11 Mar. 1916), 350–2.

[38] 'Japan and Latin America', *Review of Reviews*, 44 (1911), 281.

[39] P.A.R. Calvert, 'Great Britain and the New World, 1905–1914', in F.H. Hinsley (ed.), *British Foreign Policy under Sir Edward Grey* (Cambridge, 1977), 382–94; Gordon Connell-Smith, *The Inter-American System* (Oxford, 1966).

[40] Charles Wentworth Dilke, *Problems of Greater Britain* (London, 1890), 98.

[41] R.B. Cunninghame Graham, 'Facts About Panama', *Saturday Review*, 114 (26 Oct. 1912), 513–5.

In international terms, there were two competing views of what might happen next. One was that Latin America would assume an independent place in the state systems of the future. In a speech at Lincoln's Inn in 1913, Bryce called South America 'the one Continent which stood almost wholly outside the web of international relations', but argued that finance reached where politics could not, and was binding it in to the international community.[42] Georges Clemenceau – whose little-studied book about his travels in Latin America was also translated into English – anticipated that the progress of its civilization would 'inevitably change the political and social equilibrium of the planet that to-day is still, in effect, European'.[43] The alternative view was that the region would come into the imperial orbit. J.A. Hobson's seminal 1902 *Imperialism* claimed, among its other contributions to political thought, that that the entry of the US into the struggle for empire 'throws virtually the whole of South America into the arena', since European powers with their 'vast economic interests' in the region were hardly likely simply to acquiesce in the expansion of US dominance.[44] Hobson was not alone in thinking this. It became almost a commonplace that after the partition of Africa, Latin America would be the next great scene of colonising energy. The London councillor and aspirant Liberal MP Henry Somers Somerset wrote in 1903 that 'equatorial America must be to the twentieth century what Africa was to the nineteenth'.[45]

These shifts in geopolitical assumptions had wider intellectual consequences. The period 1880–1920 saw the emergence of a distinctive British intellectual culture concerned with the politics, institutions and international relations of Latin America. This culture took shape, as ever, in close contact with work and agents from other countries, especially the United States, but not least from Latin America itself, with an increasing number of historical and sociological works written in Spanish translated into English and republished in London.[46] But it had a new and distinctive flavour. The figures involved are all now obscure. Many – like Charles Edmond Akers, the first name cited in the select bibliography of Bryce's study of South America – were *Times*

---

[42] 'The World's Destiny: What Will Happen in A.D. 2,000. Mr. Bryce's Prophecy', *Manchester Courier and Lancashire General Advertiser* (4 Apr. 1913), 8. See also L.T. Hobhouse, *Liberalism* (London, 1911), 47.

[43] Georges Clemenceau, *South America To-Day* (London, 1911), 11.

[44] J.A. Hobson, *Imperialism: A Study* (London, 1902), 235–6.

[45] Somers Somerset, 'Europe and South America', *Nineteenth Century and After*, 53 (1903), 586.

[46] E.g. An American, *The History of South America from its Discovery to the Present Time*, trans. Adnah D. Jones (London, 1899); F. Garcia Calderon, *Latin America: Its Rise and Progress*, trans. Bernard Miall (London, 1913).

Latin America and British International Thought, 1880–1920   321

correspondents who had been stationed in South America.[47] The most prolific writer of books on the region was W.H. Koebel, who began his connection with Latin America as a wine merchant, and who anticipated the historiography of 'informal empire' in publishing a propagandistic study of *British Exploits in South America* in 1917.[48] Perhaps the most intellectually serious British Latin Americanist was also the most eccentric, a figure called Charles Reginald Enock, who went to South America as a railroad and mining engineer, produced a string of authoritative regional studies in the 1900s and 1910s, and thereafter transformed himself into a Ruskinian sage, growing the appropriate beard and pursuing grand schemes to 'put the world in order'. He came to think that the world-historical significance of Latin America might be to introduce a new type of economic life, and his work on the region increasingly framed it in relation to the new 'science of humanity' he sought to develop.[49] These figures, and many others, argued among themselves and with their vastly more numerous US counterparts about the history and future of Latin America, but were all clearly conscious of speaking to a wider interested public as well.

The altered character of the Latin American problem after about 1880, especially the facts of relative political stability and intensified international competition for its trade, created new cultures of scholarship, commercial promotion and political argument around the region. But these remained, in societal terms, relatively specific and specialised cultures. Latin America still did not become a front-rank problem for the period's leading writers on politics and sociology, and it did not occur to most of the more illustrious Victorians who continued to write at length on democracy in the United States to turn their minds to the southern continent.[50] The one major exception to this rule requires closer consideration.

Bryce's *South America* in Context

James Bryce was the only eminent Victorian who tried to make sense of Latin America. He wrote and spoke about the region in various settings, but crystallised his ideas in his 600-page volume *South America: Observations and Impressions*, published in 1912. Most specialist studies of Bryce pass rapidly

[47]   Charles Edmond Akers, *A History of South America, 1854–1904* (London, 1904).
[48]   E.g. W.H. Koebel, *The South Americans* (London, 1915); W.H. Koebel, *British Exploits in South America* (New York, 1917).
[49]   Cf. C. Reginald Enock, *The Republics of Central and South America* (London, 1913), 520; C.R. Enock, *Spanish America: Its Romance, Reality and Future* (2 vols, London, 1920), vol. 1, iii.
[50]   Frank Prochaska, *Eminent Victorians on American Democracy: The View from Albion* (Oxford, 2012).

over the book, if they mention it, including those concerned with Bryce and 'America'.[51] Historians who deal directly with the volume assume it was a lonely island of Latin American interest in an ocean of British obliviousness.[52] We have seen that this was not the case, but of all the many studies of Latin America published during the 1880–1920 upsurge, Bryce's appears to have been the most widely discussed and read among the political class. Insofar as independent Latin America has played a role in modern British political thought in the conventional canonical sense, it clearly lies in Bryce's book, and the fact that someone of his stature undertook the enterprise underscores the cultural shifts of the period. What did the volume look to achieve?

The book arose partly as a matter of policy, and partly of scholarship. After establishing his reputation with 1883's *The American Commonwealth*, Bryce served in junior ministerial offices in Liberal governments, ending up as British ambassador to the United States between 1907 and 1912. He had by this stage conceived the project of a study of modern democracies, which in his view had necessarily to be based on first-hand experience. The opportunity to see Latin American republicanism at work was therefore unmissable, and he proposed to undertake a months-long trip, curving down the west coast of South America from Panama, returning via the east, and taking in eight of the continent's republics.[53] Edward Grey, the Foreign Secretary, approved the plan, which he thought might be useful for negotiating commercial treaties and assessing the extent of German penetration of the region.[54] Bryce thus brought British perspectives and agendas to the project. But he wrote up the book surrounded by Americans, and corresponded about it extensively with American experts. The volume, as a result, straddled US and British intellectual traditions.

Bryce had already committed himself to a series of positions on South America before he began his tour. Already in the 1880s he had asserted the potential significance of the western part of the continent as a field for capital and emigration.[55] By the 1900s, he considered the republics of South America

---

[51] Sometimes it does not even make the cut for bibliographies: e.g. John T. Seaman Jr, *A Citizen of the World: the Life of James Bryce* (London, 2006). The book deserves closer attention for what it reveals about the shape and changing nature of Bryce's thought, but that is not the focus here. The fullest existing treatment in this vein is Héctor Domínguez Benito, *James Bryce y los fundamentos intelectuales del internacionalismo liberal (1864–1922)* (Madrid, 2018).

[52] Itzel Toledo García, 'James Bryce's Analysis of Latin America in an International Perspective', *Terrae Incognitae*, 52 (2020), 90–2; Jonathan Madison, Eduardo Posada-Carbó and Adam Smith, 'Studying the Americas in the United Kingdom: A Preliminary Enquiry', *IdeAs: Idées d'Amériques*, 17 (2021).

[53] Bryce, *Modern Democracies*, vol. 1, vii. Bryce had already visited Mexico in 1901.

[54] H.A.L. Fisher, *James Bryce* (2 vols, London, 1927), vol. 2, 44.

[55] James Bryce, *The American Commonwealth* (2 vols, London, 1888), vol. 2, 403.

Latin America and British International Thought, 1880–1920   323

an exceptional political grouping.[56] Indeed, he repeatedly characterised 'the so-called republics of Central and South America' as military tyrannies, as places that were neither free nor orderly, possessing a low type of civilization, and where paper constitutions were rarely in normal action because of chronic disturbance.[57] It seemed likely to him from the 1880s that Central America would lose its independence in the face of a US advance, though he took the view that expansion would not be in the interests of the US, even if it was likely to benefit the regions appropriated.[58] Bryce had a clear understanding of why the republics had endured the many unsettled decades they had. His answer, developed in the typical fashion in a public address of 1905 by comparison with North America, was not race – race differences being 'nothing but the result of antecedent causes' – but history, and to some extent geography.[59] The fundamental problem, for Bryce, was the familiar one. Spain had gone to South America to enrich itself, not to colonise, and political training was therefore lacking in the peoples of the continent.[60] Bryce lamented in 1897 that Britain had not taken its early-nineteenth-century opportunity of 'conferring upon the temperate regions of South America the benefits of ordered freedom and a progressive population', perhaps purchasing Argentina from Spain and turning it into a 'second Australia'.[61] But he did not return to this intriguing theme.

Bryce's thinking evolved alongside the intellectual shifts of the fin-de-siècle, and he prepared his study in selective conjunction and consultation with other authorities on the region. His notes cite eighteen writers – nine British, eight American, and one French – and also highlight the utility of the publications of the Pan-American Union and the *Times*'s South America Supplements.[62] He was personally familiar with a number of the figures he identified. He corresponded extensively with Hiram Bingham, the pioneering US Latin American

[56] [James Bryce], 'The Study of Popular Governments. II', *Quarterly Review*, 203 (1905), 395.

[57] Bryce, *American Commonwealth*, vol. 2, 217; James Bryce, *Studies in History and Jurisprudence* (2 vols, Oxford, 1901), vol. 1, 253, vol. 2, 47–8.

[58] Bryce, *American Commonwealth*, vol. 2, 400; Fisher, *Bryce*, vol. 2, 44; James Bryce, 'British Feeling on the Venezuela Question', *North American Review*, 162 (1896), 148–9.

[59] 'North v. South America; A Remarkable Contrast; Address by Mr. Bryce, M.P', *Sunday Times*, 2 Apr. 1905, 7.

[60] James Bryce, 'The Migrations of the Races of Men Considered Historically', *Contemporary Review*, 62 (1892), 135; James Bryce, 'Some Reflections on the State of Cuba', *North American Review*, 174 (1902), 445–51.

[61] James Bryce, *Impressions of South Africa* (London, 1897), 589–90.

[62] Bryce, *South America*, 587–8. With one exception (see n. 64 below) the few additional works cited in the text but not in the notes were by writers of the same nationalities.

scholar and Yale professor (and later shortest-serving Governor of Connecticut); W.H. Koebel, the British journalist and writer, accompanied Bryce on part of his tour, and later gave the 'great ambassador' a warm review.[63] Notably, Bryce cited only one work in Spanish, even though he could speak the language, and that was translated from French.[64]

Bryce's stated motives for writing the book straddled the Victorian and Edwardian visions of the Latin American problem. He explained that his project was impelled by a desire, first, 'to learn the causes which produced so many revolutions and civil wars', and next by a sense that the republics 'were becoming potent economic factors in the modern world'.[65] He contended that he had something distinctive to add to the literature by combining first-hand observation with wider scholarship and reflection, adding that 'few of those who have read have travelled, and few of those who have travelled have read'.[66]

In practice *South America* had two linked sets of purposes, one political, one scientific. Its political objective was to vindicate a case about democracy. The book urged this case, which was brought out explicitly only towards the end, against a mostly nameless body of defenders of monarchism and conservatism, and opponents of liberty.[67] The only target the book actually identified was Henry Maine.[68] Bryce later suggested that the experiences of the South American republics had been the 'basis' of the case Maine had made against democracy in 1885's *Popular Government*.[69] It is true that in that work Maine had called the 'universal and scarcely intermitted political confusion' of South America a 'striking, instructive, and uniform body of facts', but he did not say much more than that, and the illustration was incidental to the book's wider philosophical arguments.[70] It makes sense that Bryce could not come up with a better straw man than this decades-old canard, given the more encouraging tenor of regional developments in recent decades. Bryce insisted nonetheless that the experiences of South America did not undermine arguments in favour of constitutional government. He argued that the moral of its history was, instead, that self-governing institutions should not be conferred on peoples

---

[63] W.H. Koebel, 'A Great Ambassador's Book on S. America', *The Sphere*, 51 (9 Nov. 1912), 152. Bryce did not mention Koebel's involvement in his tour.

[64] Romero's *Los lagos de los altiplanos*: Bryce, *South America*, 191; Fisher, *Bryce*, vol. 2, 49.

[65] Bryce, *South America*, xvii.

[66] *Ibid.*, 427.

[67] *Ibid.*, 524.

[68] *Ibid.*, 525.

[69] Bryce, *Modern Democracies*, 209–10.

[70] Henry Sumner Maine, *Popular Government* (London, 1885), 18–20.

Latin America and British International Thought, 1880–1920   325

unfit to use them.[71] Because the attempt to plant complex republican political institutions in unprepared ground could never have been expected to work smoothly, there was nothing discouraging in the history of the last century for the future of South America, or for democratic government in general.[72]

The second, scientific, purpose of the book was to explore the making of polities. Bryce's distinctive claim here was that South America was a laboratory of state formation, of a kind the world had never seen before and would never see again.[73] He argued that examining why the borders between the republics had fallen as they had, the forms of 'nationality' that had emerged, the roles political institutions had played, and the ways these dynamics interacted with race and racial mixture, could provide new insights into modern politics. Strikingly, given Bryce's jurisprudential expertise and the prominent role legal institutions had played in *The American Commonwealth*, he said almost nothing about the organisation of the law in South America, or its role in state-making. Perhaps he took the view that civilization in South America had not reached a stage where the theme was worth discussing. As Bryce had established well before he started on his travels, history and geography mattered far more than race in these developments, and he went on to claim that race sentiment was not a factor in South American politics.[74] He concluded optimistically about the future status of at least the more developed South American states in the modern world, though he considered the absence of religion as a basis for cohesion a misfortune.[75]

Bryce's book was not innovative. The other political-scientific topics he discussed – the identity of the 'Two Americas', urban development, etc. – had all been widely canvassed in the wider literature on Latin America in previous decades. Bryce spent considerable energy dismissing race as an explanatory factor in South American history – even stressing that the region's experiences proved that sharp racial divisions were not 'natural' – but this challenge was presumably more for his American audience than for the British, who had never laid much stress on the racial dimension.[76] In making this involved attempt to come to the root of the difficulties which had faced Latin America, moreover, Bryce ended up repeating the most commonplace argument of the last hundred years – that Spanish colonial administration had failed to train its subjects in self-government. Spain's rule had been 'the most ill-conceived

---

[71] Bryce, *South America*, 539.

[72] *Ibid.*, 570–3.

[73] *Ibid.*, 427.

[74] Viscount Bryce, *Race Sentiment as a Factor in History* (London, 1915), 6, 23–4.

[75] Bryce, *South America*, 583.

[76] US reviewers clearly found this argument more striking: e.g. L.S. Rowe, *Annals of the American Academy of Political and Social Science*, 45 (1913), 274–5.

326 *Alex Middleton*

and ill-administered scheme of government that selfishness and stupidity ever combined to devise'.[77] Specialist reviewers in the British press, like R.B. Cunninghame Graham, duly criticised Bryce's superficiality and his lack of attention to recent authorities, and concluded that the book 'contains nothing that can be counted new or in the least unknown'.[78]

Books do not have to be original to be important. Bryce was by the 1910s an Atlantic celebrity, and his status made the publication of *South America* an Atlantic event. It was published by Macmillan in both Britain and the United States in 1912, going through its first English print run in a month, and a slightly revised edition appeared early in 1913.[79] The book also received translations into French and Spanish soon after.[80] It was widely noticed in organs which did not usually cover Latin American literature, all reviewers agreeing that (what they called) the political-scientific chapters were the notable parts of the work, some claiming (wrongly) that it was the first study to treat South America as a whole since the eighteenth century. The *Spectator* called the book 'a much-needed corrective to this convenient fashion of dismissing half a continent', while the *Contemporary Review* pronounced it a classic of descriptive sociology.[81] British reviewers however complained that Bryce's diplomatic role prevented him from being forthright about his views of US policy, or about Latin Americans' attitudes towards their northern neighbour.[82] In the United States, *South America* was treated mainly as a contribution to political science, and often reviewed alongside other comparable books, including Georges Clemenceau's volume of 1911, *South America To-Day*.[83] It was treated with considerable respect, so much so that the political-scientific chapters were reissued by themselves in 1916.[84] Arthur N. Holcome, Professor of Government in Harvard, wrote in 1923 that it was Bryce 'who among modern political scientists

---

[77] Bryce, *South America*, 16. See also James Bryce, *University and Historical Addresses* (London, 1913), 139.

[78] R.B. Cunninghame Graham, 'Discretion', *Saturday Review*, 114 (5 Oct. 1912), 422–3.

[79] W.M.J.W., 'South America', *Gloucester Journal* (14 Dec. 1912), 8.

[80] James Bryce, trans. C. Gandilhon Gens-d'Armes, *Les républiques sud-américaines: les pays, les nations, les races* (Paris, 1915. 2 vols); James Bryce, trans. Guillermo Rivera, *La América del sud: observaciones e impresiones* (New York, 1914).

[81] 'South America', *Spectator*, 109 (5 Oct. 1912), 513; G.P.G., 'Mr. Bryce in South America', *Contemporary Review*, 102 (1 July 1912), 741.

[82] E.g. 'The Other Half of America', *Times Literary Supplement*, 559 (26 Sept. 1912), 384.

[83] E.g. Paul S. Reinsch, *American Political Science Review*, 7 (1913), 304–8.

[84] James Bryce, *The Rise of New Nations... Five Chapters Reprinted from 'South America: Observations and Impressions'* (New York, 1916).

Latin America and British International Thought, 1880–1920   327

of the first rank made the closest study of the Latin American republics.'[85] The American Jesuit magazine *America* did however launch a short-running campaign against Bryce's anti-Catholic slanders, which evidently eluded other reviewers.[86] In Germany, the *Zeitschrift für Sozialwissenschaft* pronounced the book 'ausgezeichnet.'[87] Yet the most striking aspect of *South America*'s reception was the response in South America. It was hugely enthusiastic, and highly engaged. A well-known British statesman reflecting on the continent and its cities was a significant cultural moment, and Bryce's book generated more fanfare than even Clemenceau's the previous year. This is noteworthy given the uniquely close cultural connections between Paris and the Latin American literary world. From Valparaiso, to Havana, to Rio de Janeiro, to Buenos Aires, and beyond, Latin American journalists publicised and criticised Bryce's arguments.[88]

South America was not a landmark. It did not say much that was new. And it did not replicate the impact of *The American Commonwealth* on the region it aimed to anatomise, though scholars in Latin America continued to read it for some years.[89] It also failed to inspire imitators, though this was partly because what it was to be a 'public intellectual' was changing rapidly in the early twentieth century, and political-sociological-travelogue volumes were falling out of fashion. Bryce himself maintained an interest in Latin America, tracking the emergence of genuine popular government in the 'temperate' states.[90] But when *Modern Democracies* eventually came out in 1921, the region was not a major part of the admittedly old-fashioned study, and no reviewer picked out the relevant chapter in the volumes.[91] The significance of *South America* lies in what it crystallised. It was written by an Anglo-Scots-Irish scholar and politician, educated in part in Germany, while resident in the capital of the United States. It gathered ideas and information produced within different national cultures, but particularised them in relation to schemes of political thinking its author had been developing for decades. It was read and criticised across

---

[85] Arthur N. Holcombe, *The Foundations of the Modern Commonwealth* (New York & London, 1923), 63.

[86] E.g. Henry Woods, 'South America Seen Through Mr. Bryce's Eyes', *America*, 8 (16 Nov. 1912), 128–30.

[87] Ernst Schultze, *Zeitschrift für Sozialwissenschaft*, 6 (1915), 422.

[88] Fuller critical treatments include C.S.V., *El Mercurio* (27 Dec. 1912), 5 [Valparaiso]; Antonio Valenzuela-Moreno, *Diario De La Marina* (9 Jan. 1913), 6 [Havana]; *O Estado De S. Paolo* (12 Dec. 1912), 1–2; *La Nación* (2 Nov. 1912), 10–11 [Buenos Aires]; *El Universal* (11 Dec. 1912), 1 [Caracas]; *Jornal Do Comercio* (14 Feb. 1913), 3–4 [Rio de Janeiro].

[89] García, 'International Perspective', 89–90.

[90] Viscount Bryce, *World History* (London, 1919), 17–18.

[91] Bryce, *Modern Democracies*, vol. 1, 7, 209–32, 493.

328   *Alex Middleton*

the Atlantic world. Even though other writers knew more and thought harder, we should nonetheless recognise *South America* as a revealing artefact in the intellectual turn towards South America in early-twentieth-century Britain, not least because it cannot be regarded in any simple way as a 'British' study.

* * *

Latin America was not a blank space on the map of modern British political thinking. Seeley and the diplomat Watson had a point when they complained that historical and political knowledge of Latin America was deficient among British elites in the early 1880s. But in the decades around the turn of the century, there emerged a sharper and more sophisticated interest in Latin America in British political and scholarly culture, which dealt both with the region's internal condition and its external relations. The substance of the ideas and schemes involved is important in itself, and needs to be reintegrated with wider understandings of nineteenth- and twentieth-century British political and international thought. But what is most striking about this shift is how it responded to global recalibrations and transcultural links. So Latin America has new things to teach us about the nexus between British politics, political ideas, and international policy – a set of interfaces which Jonathan Parry's work has done so much to conceptualise and clarify in other contexts, both European and now Middle Eastern. The present discursively focused chapter has only scratched the surface of these possibilities.

The emergence of a British intellectual culture around Latin America was mainly a response to transformations in geopolitics and diplomacy, and intensifying foreign competition in the region. Perceived threats to British interests, in a climate of growing uncertainty about how or whether Britain would maintain its accustomed global primacy, arrested attention in a way the quiet commercial and financial expansions of the previous half-century had not. It was a distinctive intellectual moment. After the adjustment of another Venezuelan border issue in 1903, British policy in the region declined in ambition and assertiveness, while dreams of renewed commercial hegemony evaporated after World War I, as the US asserted an unbreakable hold on the region. As intellectual life in Britain changed shape and increasingly fell behind the walls of universities, Latin America dropped off the agenda, especially after the Great Depression crushed the region's 'belle époque'. It would not be until after the Parry Report of 1965 that universities would finally institutionalise Latin American studies in Britain.[92] In the period *c.*1880–1920, however, the apparent threat to what had emerged as a precarious hold created a new market

---

[92] Gabriel Paquette, 'The "Parry Report" and the Establishment of Latin American Studies in the United Kingdom', *Historical Journal*, 62 (2019), 219–40.

Latin America and British International Thought, 1880–1920   329

for Latin American visions and prognostications. In this setting at least, then, 'informal empire' was not a purely practical and material activity. Instead, it was connected with wider and intricate constellations of ideas, which bridged commerce and politics and international relations in distinctive ways.

'British' thought about Latin America, however, was not coherently or autonomously British. It was characterised by seams and frayed edges. Deeply indebted to debates among United States scholars and commentators, responsive to the studies and agendas of French writers, and increasingly engaged with works by Latin Americans, British writing about the region formed part of a genuinely international set of political debates. These were shaped both by structural connections between public spheres, and by incidental cross-cultural journeys and exchanges. The composition, agenda and reception of Bryce's *South America* indicates how some of these border-crossing dynamics worked. The case highlights the need to work towards a more genuinely 'Atlantic' history of political ideas, which takes in the full range of the circuits and hubs scattered across the whole region, and which goes beyond the Anglo-US dynamics the label has so far tended to describe. It should also encourage us to think less myopically about the meanings of 'America' in modern British political and intellectual culture. The word was not simply a shorthand for the northern continent, but in many settings a relational concept, which covered Americas North and Central and South and Latin and archipelagic, and temperate and tropical and frigid, and which summoned up wider and longer-running debates about the identity of the 'New World' and the contrasting fates of its shifting subdivisions. Finally, and briefly, we might reflect on methodology. Canonical approaches to the history of political thought cannot detect the intellectual significance of Latin America in modern Britain. To determine how it mattered, we must look instead at the impressions left on broader political and press cultures, in combination with the ambitious empirical and theoretical works produced by forgotten regional 'specialists', who were often locally experienced and connected. This is true of other areas of the globe. In other words, the history of international political thinking might make more rapid progress if we were to look again at the masses of largely unexamined political-cultural evidence to which some historians were attempting to direct us more than forty years ago.[93]

---

[93] J.P. Parry, 'The State of Victorian Political History', *Historical Journal*, 26 (1983), 472, 484.

Chapter 16

Cambridge Beginnings, Oxford Departures: 'Liberal Education' and Imperial Legacies, 1945–70[1]

Susan D. Pennybacker

My book-in-progress, *Fire By Night, Cloud By Day: Refuge and Exile in Postwar London* considers the lives of individuals from India, South Africa and Trinidad who came to live in London for long and short periods after 1945. It explores their consequential relationships to metropolitan political culture.[2] The 'liberal education' offered in Britain and in schools and institutions of higher learning in the former empire, profoundly influenced many of these political agents.[3] The Universities of Cambridge, Oxford and London

---

[1] The author thanks: Mani Shankar Aiyar, Sana Aiyar, Manu Bhagavan, David Campion, Colin Darch, Pradip K. Datta, Julia de Nicola, Navina Haidar, Salman Haidar, Erika Huckestein, Jon Hyslop, Tom Jeffery, Sarah Limb, Ali Raza, Vikramditya Sahai, Anand Sahay, Rob Waters and Leslie Witz. The research for this essay received support from the S.C. Davis Endowment, History Department, Princeton University; the Fulbright-Nehru awards; the College of Arts and Sciences, University of North Carolina at Chapel Hill; and the School of Historical Studies, Institute for Advanced Study, Princeton.

[2] To be published by Cambridge University Press. Recent works that illustrate the divergent historiographical status of these issues include John Davis, *Waterloo Sunrise, London from the Sixties to Thatcher* (Princeton, 2022), Panikos Panayi, *Migrant City: A New History of London* (New Haven & London, 2020) and Rob Waters, *Thinking Black: Britain, 1964–1985* (Oakland, 2018).

[3] See Hilary Perraton, *A History of Foreign Students in Britain* (Basingstoke, 2014). Between 1946 and 1976, the numbers of overseas students in British universities, roughly 10% of the whole, grew from 7,000 to 34,000. US students first outdistanced India's historic lead in numbers, in 1961/2 (pp. 83, 86), when the humanities and social science still led the fields studied (p. 90). See also Marc Matera, *Black London: The Imperial Metropolis and Decolonization in the 20th Century* (Oakland, 2015), ch. 6; Sumita Mukherjee, 'Mobility, Race and the Politicisation of Indian Students before the Second World War', *History of Education*, 51 (2022), 56–77; Jodi Burkett, '"Unity in Struggle is our Strength": Sheffield University's Overseas Student Bureau and Internationalism at a Local Level',

were first destinations for several of the book's subjects. Two of those born in British India, Salman Haidar (1937–)[4] and Mani Shankar Aiyar (1941–),[5] arrived in Cambridge in the late 1950s and early 1960s. Martin Legassick (1940–2016)[6] and Colin Darch (1944–)[7] were British-born and arrived at Oxford in the same decade. Legassick grew up in South Africa and returned there, from exile, in 1991. Darch left the UK as a postgraduate and has spent most of his life on the African Continent.

Social History, 48 (2023), 140–61. Amartya Sen's *Home in the World, A Memoir* (London, 2021) recounts his student days at Trinity, Cambridge.

[4] Haidar is a former diplomat and Foreign Secretary of India (1995–7); he was High Commissioner to the UK in 1998. Born in 1937 in Madras, British India, he attended St Stephen's College, Delhi University (BA, English), and Magdalene College, Cambridge (MA, English). After a distinguished career, Haidar joined the Academy of Third World Studies at Jamia Millia Islamia at University in Delhi, and the Centre for Research in Rural and Industrial Development. He lives in Delhi.

[5] Aiyar is a former Indian Congress Party diplomat and Member of the Lok Sabha (the Indian Parliament, 1991, 1999, 2004 and 2010–16), where he represented a Tamil Nadu constituency. Born in Lahore, British India, he attended the Doon School in Dehradun; St Stephen's College, Delhi University (BA, Economics); and Trinity Hall, Cambridge (MA, Economics). From 1963 to 1989 he served in the Indian Foreign Service (and as ambassador to Pakistan in 1972), the Ministry of External Affairs, and in the Prime Minister's Office of Rajiv Gandhi (1985–9). In 1973, he married Suneet Vir Singh, and is a widely-published author and columnist with a special interest in nuclear disarmament. He founded the Indian *Society for Secularism*. Aiyar lives in Delhi.

[6] Born in Edinburgh and raised in South Africa, Legassick attended the University of Cape Town; Balliol College, Oxford (BA, History); and the University of California at Los Angeles (PhD, History). He held academic posts at the University of California at Santa Barbara, the Universities of London and Warwick, and at the University of Western Cape (UWC), where he was Professor Emeritus of History at the time of his retirement. He spent a decade outside the academy as an activist in the UK, before his 1991 return. He headed the South African Democracy Education Trust (SADET) and was a leading voice in eviction movements in post-1994 South Africa. The last of his extensive scholarly and activist publications was *Hidden Histories of Gordonia: Land Dispossession and Resistance in the Northern Cape, 1800–1990* (Johannesburg, 2016).

[7] Darch was born in Shropshire, grew up in London, and attended St Dunstan's College; Mansfield College, Oxford (BA, Germanic Philology, 1963–6); the former North Western Polytechnic, London (diploma in Library Studies); and the University of Bradford (PhD, Social and Economic Analysis). He served as an activist researcher, librarian, instructor and media broadcaster in Ethiopia, Tanzania, Mozambique, Zimbabwe and Brazil, and at the University of the Western Cape and the University of Cape Town. His publications as writer, bibliographer and editor have appeared in English and Portuguese. Darch lives in Cape Town. See <https://www.colindarch.info/>. All URLs in chapter accessed 1 Sept. 2023.

Jonathan Parry's recent historical scholarship dwells upon Britain and the Middle East in the nineteenth century,[8] work pursued in a university environment in which the legacies of empire are readily invoked as part of university policy, pedagogy, and fervent scholarly and activist agendas.[9] This essay explores the ways in which these four young men absorbed the mores and discourses of British political and student cultures of their day, taking what they witnessed in these institutions and in the increasingly volatile geopolitical era, back into the Global South. It proposes that the 'liberal education' received by these individuals contributed to their varied shifting worldviews and political activism, as liberal internationalists, secular humanists, Marxists, social democrats and anticolonial nationalists. Their paths tread upon those of some of Parry's own interlocutors, over a century later. Each had ties to notable women, both in the highest circles of politics and in their personal lives. The profoundly male-centered Oxbridge student cultures of the immediate postwar years emerge as frameworks for altered and self-questioning commitments, and for their urgent interests in the zones and circumstances of the former British empire and its rivals and opponents. The most conventional and elite British institutions trained and fostered dissenters, as did the elite schools and universities in the former empire, over decades. Here, the particular appropriations and refashioning of received wisdoms that occurred during the immediate postwar and Cold War era remain audible and distinct, as captured in the testimonies of these former Oxbridge students.

The Independence Generation: Haidar and Aiyar

Salman Haidar, the former Indian Foreign Secretary, and the first Muslim to hold the position, was born in Madras in 1937 and entered Cambridge in 1957. We spoke in New Delhi in 2013. His father, a professor of chemistry at Aligarh Muslim University in Uttar Pradesh, died when he was young. One of his uncles, a lawyer who lived in London, had offered some lectures in Islamic law at Cambridge before Haidar's own arrival. Haidar completed his first degree at St Stephen's College of Delhi University where he read English. He recalled, 'To "study abroad" meant going to England... Oxford and Cambridge had a huge hold on us... We were not rich, but [my mother] felt that it would be good

[8]   Jonathan Parry, *Promised Lands: The British and the Ottoman Middle East* (Princeton, 2022).

[9]   For a record of the 2015 protests, see Roseanne Chantiluke, Brian Kwoba and Athinangamso Nkopo (eds), *Rhodes Must Fall: The Struggle to Decolonise the Racist Heart of Empire* (London, 2018); and, for the policy debates, Aneta Hayes, *Inclusion, Epistemic Democracy and International Students: The Teaching Excellence Framework and Education Policy* (Basingstoke, 2019).

'Liberal Education' and Imperial Legacies, 1945–70   333

for me, and it would launch me well in life to go to Cambridge.'[10] His father had been there on an Honor Tata loan, in the 1920s.[11] Haidar followed him to Magdalene College: 'We were the last college to open our doors to women and immediately the academic performance of the college went up very substantially. Magdalene was better known for beagling and sports of that nature than for academic excellence, but once women came [1988], all that changed. Now it's a more normal college', he hastened to state when we spoke. Haidar read English, but, he explained, 'it wasn't confined to English Lit. as such, because we did something called the Moralists, which took us into doing Plato and philosophers, Greek and other philosophers.'[12]

I was anxious to hear about London, but he said that 'it was just a kind of way station for us at that stage. I got to know London much better, much later... As a student... I really looked to London as a Big Smoke and as a place that was away, because we were people from outside... Our world really was Cambridge. We lived in that... it was a very intense two years'. He completed his degree in what he regards as '[a time of] magnificent teachers.'[13] I asked if he felt he had been treated properly:

> I was treated... like anyone joining a college in Oxbridge in those days... with a kind of amiable neglect,... in the sense that it wasn't like Delhi University where you're ragged, or things are done to bring you into certain activities. Nothing of that sort. You're just thrown in and you found your own level. And you did what was interesting. There was a huge variety of activities, and I made friends, good friends, who remained friends through my life... it was an opportunity for an individual, for individuals to take or not to take. There are no compulsions. There is no sense of saying that 'this is correct, and you have to conform'.

Haidar reflected on both racial and class dynamics:

> I was up for two years which was good, but I remember... that while the racial prejudice was not important at that time, racial prejudice became more marked when mass immigration took place, and then, as an Indian, you tended to be typecast, or seen in a particular way... What did become more apparent was the social stratification of Britain itself... In your first year you were dazzled by what was going on... And for English students who were coming straight from school to have the liberation of being in

---

[10]   Interview with the author, New Delhi, 2013.

[11]   The Tata firm (1868–) offered awards that supported Indian students to attend Oxford and Cambridge.

[12]   Interview with the author, New Delhi, 2013.

[13]   *Ibid.*

a magnificent place like Cambridge was... a very important part of their growing up and of achieving themselves as human beings. As time went on and they became more aware and saw things beyond the classroom and beyond the lecture theatre and their tutorials... then, I think the sense of social differentiation became more apparent.[14]

No immigration bar yet existed that prevented him from staying in Britain when he finished in 1959.[15] Yet Haidar departed:

there was no real option. We were emotionally very strongly committed to India and coming and living and working here and the civil services were an obvious thing to do... Remember, [it was] the heyday of the Nehru era... His spirit was all over the country. And it really gave us pride... All these patriotic sort of urges... were common; [a] sense of Nehru's rhetoric still rings in people's ears, including mine, like 'temples of new India' and 'join in the great adventure of building a new India'... We felt that it was required of us.[16]

Haidar was posted briefly to London for his first assignment, where he met some British diplomats who were Oxbridge graduates. They envied India, saying: '"You have a purpose... You have a leader; you have a vision..." They were just sort of drifting.'[17] During the early period of Haidar's appointment to the Indian Foreign Service, he was sent to Egypt to learn Arabic, in part to enhance his Muslim identification, a role that did not reflect his own secular outlook and agnosticism. He resisted being typecast, recalling that he had not wanted 'to be treated as a Muslim'.[18] Haidar nevertheless went to Cairo, launching his career of consummate government service. He had married Kusum Bahl, a prominent Indian actress from a Hindu family trained at the *Ecole du Mime*, in addition

---

[14] *Ibid.*

[15] On the history of immigration, see Ian Sanjay Patel, *We're Here Because You Were There: Immigration and the End of Empire* (London, 2021): 'After the 1962 Commonwealth Immigrants Act, the right of entry into Britain referred in the first instance to "a person born in the United Kingdom"' (p. 7).

[16] Interview with the author, New Delhi, 2013. In inaugurating the Bhakra-Nangal Dam, in 1963, Nehru stated that 'This dam has been built with the unrelenting toil of man for the benefit of mankind and therefore is worthy of worship. May you call it a Temple or a Gurdwara or a Mosque, it inspires our admiration and reverence': <https://bbmb.gov.in/speech.htm>. Nehru's 'Tryst with Destiny' speech, of the night of Independence, in 1948, read: 'To the people of India, whose representatives we are, we make appeal to join us with faith and confidence in this great adventure. This is no time for petty and destructive criticism, no time for ill will or blaming others. We have to build the noble mansion of free India where all her children may dwell': <https://www.americanrhetoric.com/speeches/jawaharlalnehrutrystwithdestiny.htm>.

[17] Interview with the author, New Delhi, 2013.

[18] *Ibid.*

'Liberal Education' and Imperial Legacies, 1945–70   335

to Delhi University, the School of Dramatic Arts in Bombay and the British Drama League in London.[19] She later worked in UK Arts Council-sponsored theatre projects when she and her husband once more resided in London.[20]

In 2013, I also spoke with Haidar's colleague in government, the Indian Congress Party MP and former diplomat Mani Shankar Aiyar, former key aide to Prime Minister Rajiv Gandhi. Aiyar is also a writer and journalist. We met in New Delhi, and later, in Washington DC. He began: 'I am a midnight's child, so we had a lot of English people around us as I grew up.'[21] Aiyar was born in 1941 and was aged six at Partition. His father moved the family to Delhi from Lahore. He attended the Welham Preparatory School for Indian Boys at Dehradun, run by an Englishwoman, Hersilia Oliphant (1861–1963), who had served in a Voluntary Aid Detachment in the First World War.[22] Aiyar's teachers included a German Jewish refugee. He went on to the Doon School, nearby, which remains a training ground for elites in several professions, including those in politics. Aiyar arrived at Trinity Hall, Cambridge, two years after Haidar's departure:

> If there was a defining moment in my life, a real turning point in my life, it was Cambridge... I discovered that I had actually been brought up to be a kind of quasi-Englishman much more than I had been brought up to be a quasi-Indian. And there was a very strong emotional reaction to that, to return to India and search for my roots and get to know why I should be proud to be an Indian, a question that hadn't really bothered me at all until I went to England.[23]

For Aiyar and his fellows,

---

[19] Kusum Haidar's leading films include: *Kama Sutra: A Tale of Love* (1996), *Yeh Woh Manzil To Nahin* (1987), and *Amu* (2005). See <http://www.kusumhaidar.com/acting.html>.

[20] See *Song for a Sanctuary* by Rukhsana Ahmad performed at the Tara Arts Theatre in London, as part of the Arts Council Project of the UK. First performed in 1991, the play dramatised the non-fictional story of a wife's murder by her husband in an Indian women's shelter: <https://kalitheatre.co.uk/product/song-for-a-sanctuary/>.

[21] Interviews with the author, Washington DC, 2013. Aiyar referred, colloquially, to children born between midnight and 1am on 15 August 1947, the date and time of formal Independence, six years after his own birth. The term appeared as the title of Salman Rushdie's novel of 1981.

[22] See <https://livesofthefirstworldwar.iwm.org.uk/lifestory/5151351>. Oliphant was married to Sir Lyonel Felix Carteret Eugene Tollemache, a landowner and graduate of Jesus College, Cambridge.

[23] Interview with the author, New Delhi, 2013. See Aiyar's recently published memoirs for another account of his Cambridge years: *Memoirs of a Maverick, 1941–1991* (New Delhi, 2023), ch. 2.

America was on the fringes of our thinking, and Europe was not there at all... we equated England with the West and thought it was a great country and a good people. At the same time there was the sense that, what happens when I get there? I mean will they spot that I eat my peas with a knife? Do I know their etiquette? Would I know how to behave when I got there? Will they giggle at me for my solecisms?[24]

India's engagement with the Soviet Union was a pole of deep attraction for Aiyar's circles: 'There was a very strong pro-Soviet Union and therefore pro-socialist, pro-communist attitude in my generation of youth, and I represented an extreme form of that.' In January 1961, Patrice Lumumba was assassinated in the Belgian Congo,[25] while April of that year witnessed the Bay of Pigs invasion of Cuba, by US-sponsored forces. It was in this fraught global context that Aiyar set sail from Bombay to Cambridge, via Liverpool, in September 1961 – on the day that Dag Hammarskjöld, General Secretary of the United Nations, was killed in an air crash.[26]

Upon arrival in Cambridge, Aiyar was keen to meet British students. He had Indian friends and befriended many Pakistanis, 'but my first real acquaintances were the missionary types'. He was always strapped for cash, and attended the *War on Want* lunches, 'for their bread, cheese and butter'.[27] Aiyar had read economics at Delhi University and did so at Cambridge. He had been influenced by Marxist fellow students in Delhi who followed the new *China Quarterly* and was further transfixed by Maurice Dobb's *Soviet Economic Development since 1917*.[28] He sought out the meetings of The Cambridge Marxist Society.

[24] Interview with the author, Washington DC, 2013.

[25] Susan Williams, *White Malice: The CIA and the Covert Recolonization of Africa* (London, 2021).

[26] Susan Williams, *Who Killed Hammarskjöld? The UN, the Cold War and White Supremacy in Africa* (London, 2011).

[27] Interview with the author, Delhi, 2013. For *War on Want*'s history, see <https://waronwant.org/about/history>. The NGO was founded in 1951 after a letter to the *Guardian* written by publisher and former *Left Book Club* leader, Victor Gollancz, a Classics graduate of New College, Oxford.

[28] *China Quarterly*, founded in 1960, had covert CIA support in its early years, when published by the anti-communist Congress for Cultural Freedom. The revelation of its supporters led to the journal moving to the School of Oriental and African Studies (SOAS) in 1968; it is now published by Cambridge University Press. Dobb's study was published by Routledge in 1948.

'Liberal Education' and Imperial Legacies, 1945–70   337

But his greatest interest was in the Cambridge Union Society. Aiyar ran successfully for the Union executive at the end of his first term, when 'the absolute star of the political horizon, was Harry Pollitt's son, Brian', a Communist like his trade unionist father, and a student at King's College. Aiyar found Pollitt 'very persuasive rather than thundering, well-dressed always, but in a very modest working-class kind of way.'[29] Pollitt was impressive enough to moderates to contend seriously for the Union's presidency against an American. The latter was exposed as having corrupted the election, nullifying it, and John Gummer, subsequently chairman of the Conservative party, took the presidency, succeeded by Michael Howard, the future Tory grandee and party leader. But Pollitt captured the post soon after, in 1962.[30] Aiyar had tutorials with the economist Frank Hahn of Churchill College, who told him that Harold Macmillan's government was the worst 'since Lord Bute.'[31] He asked Hahn to arrange additional supervisions for him with Maurice Dobb.[32] 'He [Hahn] was most amused at the idea that I wished to be taught by the most raving, famous Communist of all.' But after the first couple of meetings with Dobb, Aiyar posed a troublesome question: 'Why has the Soviet Union occupied Hungary?

> [H]is answer was a ridiculous one. [Dobb] said, 'A socialist country by definition cannot be imperialist and therefore it's not an occupation'. It seemed to me to assume that I was an absolute cretin and that therefore it seemed to me that all those living in communist countries were being taken for cretins by a leadership which talked such blathering nonsense.[33]

Aiyar was further stunned when he found that Dobb didn't know Marx's articles on the Indian railways and the recent challenges to them, and he abandoned the tutorials.[34]

---

[29]   Interview with the author, Washington DC, 2013.

[30]   For the Union Society Presidents, see <http://www.martintod.org.uk/CambridgeUnionSocietyPresidents.html>.

[31]   Hahn came to Churchill in 1960, with a stint at the London School of Economics (1967–72) being followed by a return to Churchill, where he remained for the rest of his distinguished career. John Stuart, Earl of Bute (1713–92), was the seventh British Prime Minister, serving George III in 1762–3, a term of office that was rocked by scandal: his policy in the American colonies drew much ire, bringing the region closer to war and revolution.

[32]   Maurice Dobb (1900–76), was a CPGB member, a fellow of Pembroke College and then of Trinity College. On Dobb, see Sen, *Home in the World*, chs 13, 15–17, 21–24, 26.

[33]   Interviews with the author in New Delhi and Washington DC, 2013.

[34]   See Karl Marx, writings from the *New York Daily Tribune*, 10 and 25 June 1853: <http://users.sussex.ac.uk/~saff9/Marx%20100%20Folder/Marx%20100/original%20texts/Marx%20on%20India.htm>.

Meantime, Aiyar was cultivating strong relationships with the rising group of Conservatives in his cohort at the Union, the 'Cambridge Mafia'.[35] Some he has known for life, and he defended the Union's norms of civility and interaction as what he regarded as parliamentary in nature, at least in 2013. Aiyar felt no hostility toward him at Cambridge:

> At the back of my mind there was always the apprehension that because I came from a country that had been their colony only a decade earlier, and my color and my race and all that, that perhaps there would be some discrimination. But... I met nobody, absolutely nobody at Cambridge, who was actively nostalgic for the Raj.[36]

He was blunt in pursuing his Union ambitions. His first election speech was an intervention on the issue of whether Britain should join the European Economic Community (EEC):

> I advocated that instead of their [i.e. Britain] doing the stupid thing of joining five continentals whom they had been warned against since Palmerston's time, the sensible thing for them to do was to understand that the Commonwealth was going to grow, and that since the titular head of the Commonwealth was the Queen, they should join the Commonwealth group which would consist of a lot of Non-Aligned countries... instead of being the puppy dog of the United States of America, [chiding] 'You'll be an inferior. You'll be part of the group that comes in through the tradesman's entrance, but if you imagine that you can ever be equal to the United States, you're just completely misleading yourselves'.[37]

If Britain would not stand with the Soviet world, contended Aiyar, the country ought to stand with 'this emerging world that was increasingly coming up at that time'. He and his comrades inveighed against John Strachey's *End of Empire*, invoking Lenin's *Imperialism*,[38] and contending that Strachey had failed to identify 'neo-colonialism'.[39] The post-imperial era was not yet nigh, in Aiyar's view. He had also become convinced of his mission in India, invoking the reversals of identity embedded in his Indian upbringing:

---

[35] On the term and its references to the group of young Tories at Cambridge in Aiyar's time, see, e.g., <https://www.theguardian.com/politics/wintour-and-watt/2010/jun/30/kenneth-clarke-prisons-and-probation>.

[36] Interview with the author, Washington DC, 2013.

[37] *Ibid.*

[38] John Strachey, *End of Empire* (London, 1959); V.I. Lenin, *Imperialism: The Highest Stage of Capitalism* (London, 2010 [first Russian ed., 1917]).

[39] Interview with the author, Washington DC, 2013.

'Liberal Education' and Imperial Legacies, 1945–70 **339**

I realised with a shock... about a year into my being at Cambridge and becoming so much a part of the system... that I knew much, much, much less about India than I knew about England... I was a fanatical nationalist if you like, xenophobic almost... I was absolutely determined that I was not going to allow this bastardisation of my inheritance to continue, and that I just had to live in India, work for India, be in India.[40]

Aiyar joined the Indian Foreign Service in 1963, recalling, 'I became so proud of being an Indian because it enabled me to escape from this British-like identity, this "wog" identity, that was not being imposed on me, but which I had absorbed through the pores of my skin'.[41] His most noted role was as muse to Rajiv Gandhi, whom he had known very distantly as a younger fellow student at school and at Cambridge where Gandhi was at Trinity College, following after his grandfather Jawaharlal Nehru. In reflecting on Rajiv Gandhi in the wake of his assassination, Aiyar wrote of their mutual support for 'unity in diversity... the true enemies of our country are those who would deny primacy of place to the religious, linguistic and cultural minorities... in a bid to reserve the honour of being true Indians to those who belong to the major groupings'.[42] This reflected his deep commitment to secularism. In the Gorbachev era, he wrote of the 'feasibility of intensifying our time-tested relations with the Soviet Union' and of the danger of a new 'dictatorship of military powers', and was bent on 'pressing for a Non-Aligned movement in the New World Order'.[43]

A Liberal, Universalist Inheritance? Haidar and Aiyar

In his final hour with me, Salman Haidar offered forthright reflection on the years that followed Cambridge, when he lived in London for several long stretches. These conversations were in the last days of Congress Party rule before the onset of the present BJP Government. Haidar observed of Britain, in 2013, that 'a lot of encouragement has been provided and continues to be provided, to bring Indians into some prominence within British society'. In the 1990s, he had often heard British local government officials opine,

[40] *Ibid.*

[41] *Ibid.* In 2023, Aiyar added, in a statement to the author, that his entry into the Indian Civil Service in 1963, came only 'after crossing a series of security hurdles owing to his "red" image at Cambridge'.

[42] Mani Shankar Aiyar, *Remembering Rajiv, 1989–91* (Kolkata, 1992), 10, 11. The volume contains some pieces written for the Indian press, before Gandhi's murder. In these, he cites A.J.P. Taylor's *Origins of the Second World War* (1961), William Shirer's *Rise and Fall of the Third Reich* (1960) and E.H. Carr's *What is History* (1967); and he quotes T.S. Eliot, all signifiers of his Anglo-education (pp. 46, 56, 61).

[43] Aiyar, *Remembering Rajiv*, 16.

'we like Indians; they don't make trouble', spoken, with prejudice, by way of contrasting Indian reliability with the volatility of others of colour. Haidar underlined that these encounters had been before the advent of the 'Al-Qaeda era', and its 'impact on Muslim communities'. Indians and many Pakistanis, he maintained, had 'found what they were looking for in terms of professions they could carry on their backs... like medicine... they were always ready to move if they had to'.[44] An Indian Government official working in Britain asked Haidar to encourage Indians residing there 'to become councillors... they wanted them in the police... [and] to that extent... "multiculturalism" became a kind of slogan... not much more than a slogan, but there were some elaborate shows of [it]'.[45] Haidar spoke of the atrophy of India's relationship to the Labour party. The British Left had originally favoured Independence, and there had been an historic 'kind of intonation towards them'... but then, that 'special relationship between Labour and India, progressively disappeared'. The Tories, he said, 'were disdainful of "the wogs" and people like us, and the traditional English society was not that open. There were enlightened people of course, but generally there were certain reservations and barriers'.[46] Haidar observed that the deeper 'connections between Britain and India had been impaired'. He noted that the 'legacy' of Cambridge that did endure for him and others was that of the 'acknowledgement of British ways, cultural norms, language as a part of it as matters of value'. He eschewed 'the corporate and commercial relationships' between Britain and India that had taken on 'in British projection, a very, very important position... this is not the Britain from which India had absorbed a lot'.[47]

Haidar also spoke with the historian and Director of the Institute of Commonwealth Studies, Philip Murphy, in 2013. He once more posited the 'shrinking' role of Britain, favouring the drift of the Commonwealth when it was 'promoting national liberation' and 'non-alignment' as distinct from endorsing 'the Non-Aligned' as an organised geopolitical movement.[48] His typically wry sensibility was evident, his phrasing always prudent:

> let me say [of the Commonwealth] – to use an inappropriate word, it's been a civilising factor. It has helped to combat some of the great evils of the world – colonialism, apartheid, poverty, exploitation, and it has done this through consensus, not through brutality. I think it has not always

[44] Interview with the author, New Delhi, 2013.

[45] *Ibid.*

[46] *Ibid.*

[47] *Ibid.*

[48] Philip Murphy interview with Salman Haidar, Institute of Commonwealth Studies, Voice File, COHP, unpublished transcribed text, p. 2: downloaded from <https://sas-space.sas.ac.uk/6445/>.

successfully promoted democracy, but it has been on the side of democracy. It has kept that notion of rule by acceptance of the people before the Commonwealth, before itself, and has not contested it.[49]

Again, the moderation of Haidar's tone regarding Commonwealth endeavours, in 2013, bespoke a reasoned respect for a kind of pragmatism and regard for a democratic vision, in consonance with his years at Cambridge more than a half-century earlier. In his more characteristically strident, concluding words to me, Mani Shakar Aiyar invoked the 'East of Suez' debate,[50] declaring that

> it wasn't quite clear that Britain didn't have a role... They were very much present in a proxy form in Northern and Southern Rhodesia, in South Africa in a very major way... And now [2013], Britain is a huge irrelevancy, and tragically, with the Indian middle class coming to the USA for studies, and the Americanisation of India, people like me are becoming *Jurassic Park* – the Anglicised Indian.[51]

Aiyar's greater frustration with the loss of Britain's cultural prominence was in part a product of his critique of British foreign policy since Cambridge. The continuing imperial ambition, however quixotic, had rendered 'values' more suspect, for him.

Darch and Legassick: The British-born Left

Aiyar's contemporary, the linguist and bibliophile Colin Darch, was raised in London and attended the University of Oxford. Martin Legassick, the South African-raised Rhodes scholar who was born in Edinburgh returned to the UK to read physics, then history at Oxford, and forged an academic and activist career in Britain in exile, finally returning to South Africa in 1991.

Darch and I spoke in Cape Town in 2018, where he had moved from Mozambique, the theatre of politics and work that commanded the greatest commitment of his lifetime. He was born in 1944, to parents whose families had moved to London from Bristol and Wolverhampton. In Lewisham, he won an LCC scholarship to St Dunstan's, a minor public school:

> I went through that system – wearing a school blazer and all the rest of it... When I was still at school... I became oddly enough radicalised by a friend of mine who came from a left-wing family. My family were completely Conservative, Tory... Despite having the benefit of not having to pay for

[49] *Ibid.*, p. 11.
[50] i.e. the debate as to whether Britain still belonged East of the Suez Canal following defeat in the 1956 war.
[51] Interview with the author, Washington DC, 2013.

their kids' education, they still voted for the Conservatives all the time. This friend of mine... came from a left-wing family and he started explaining stuff.[52]

Darch won a scholarship to Oxford and was admitted to Mansfield College:

Before I went to university... I had a year to kill. There was a friend of mine from school who said, 'let's hitchhike around the Mediterranean'... We hitchhiked all the way across North Africa and Turkey. We went to Iraq. I was in Baghdad. I was in Damascus, Lebanon, all these places, and I fell in love with North Africa.[53]

Upon his return, he entered Oxford, and was involved in the most important of the Oxford organisations confronting racial discrimination locally, and in South Africa and in the United States:

I studied English literature for a year and then switched to what... was a kind of Germanic Philology... all Anglo-Saxon and old Norse... The thing I remember most about my undergraduate years at Oxford is rowing... that's what I did most of the time. I became much more progressive in those years... I joined a thing called JACARI which was the Joint Action Committee Against Racial Intolerance.[54] [Growing up], I didn't know any Black people, of course.... There was a Jamaican boy at school who was the son of some kind of a diplomat and he was the only Black person I had ever met. When I went to university, I met people... people from southern Africa doing master's degrees... Africans, mainly.[55]

And his love for traveling on the African Continent did not cease:

Every long vacation I spent hitchhiking, travelling around in Libya and Algeria and places like that, so my ambition immediately became, despite the fact that I was studying Germanic Philology [to find out] how [I could]... get a job in North Africa somewhere or in the Middle East. I really, really wanted to work there, to live there. Rewind a little. When I graduated, I worked in a stockbroker's in the City of London which drove me nuts. Eventually I went to the graduate career advice centre... run by the LCC... and they said, 'Have you ever thought of being a librarian?'... So, I worked for the London Borough of Camden Public Library system... They said to me 'you

[52] Interview with the author, Cape Town, 2018.

[53] *Ibid.*

[54] See <https://www.jacari.org/post/jacari-in-the-1960s>. On JACARI, see Stephen Tuck, *The Night Malcolm X Spoke at the Oxford Union: A Transatlantic Story of Anti-racist Protest* (Oakland, 2014), chs 3, 5.

[55] Interview with the author, Cape Town, 2018.

'Liberal Education' and Imperial Legacies, 1945–70   343

have to do a postgraduate diploma in Librarianship'... So, this was 1968, the English reflex to *soixante-huit*. We occupied the North Western London Polytechnic... The LSE came and advised us.[56]

Darch married Hilary Rampling, the daughter of an Irish Catholic CPGB central committee member, Tom Rampling; her mother was a first-generation East European Jewish immigrant and was also a CPGB member. In this adopted family context, Darch was becoming more generally active in London left politics. 'My father-in-law said, "don't join the [Communist] Party because then you are immediately flagged"'. Instead, Darch got involved in Left Labour and Communist neighbourhood-level work in a struggle over the control of the London Cooperative Society. His wife had some anarchist ties, dissenting from the nostrums of her household upbringing, and they lived in Stamford Hill in North London, home of a large Orthodox Jewish community. Darch was further influenced to study Ukrainian anarchism, after reading *Obsolete Communism – the Left-wing Alternative*, written jointly by Daniel Cohn-Bendit and his brother Gabriel, just after the events of Paris '68. But his ambition to live in North Africa and the Middle East took full hold and he got a job at the Haile Selassie I University in Addis Ababa, offered through the Association of Commonwealth Universities.[57] Sylvia Pankhurst's daughter-in-law, Rita Pankhurst, was the University's librarian. When he left Ethiopia, it was for Tanzania and then for Maputo, Mozambique. He entered the heart of the terrain of the 'proxy wars' in southern Africa.

Maputo became an important and precarious centre of expatriate South African presence.[58] In his work on the Soviet literature on Africa, completed from Maputo in 1980, Darch wrote of his 'own commitment to the materialist perspective as well as [his] many reservations about the way in which it has been manipulated in the Soviet Union and by Soviet scholars'.[59] After years spent working with the Mozambican political party of government, Frelimo, and after some time spent in Brazil, Darch left for Cape Town. In his work he memorialised the Frelimo leader Aquino de Bragança, who ran the *Centro de*

---

[56] *Ibid.*

[57] The ACU was founded in 1913, as the Universities Bureau of the British Empire. It is the world's largest international network of universities.

[58] Darch worked with South African Communist Party (SACP) leader Ruth First, who had been in exile in London, and was assassinated on 17 August 1982 in the Eduardo Mondlane University in Maputo by the South African Security Police (BOSS), while Darch was on her research team. On First, see Gillian Slovo, *Every Secret Thing: My Family, My Country* (London, 1997) and Susan Pennybacker, 'Fire by Night, Cloud by Day': Exile and Refuge in Postwar London, *Journal of British Studies*, 59 (2020), 1–31.

[59] Colin Darch, *A Soviet View of Africa: An Annotated Bibliography on Ethiopia, Somalia and Djibouti* (Boston: MA, 1980), xi.

Estudos Africanos at Eduardo Mondlane University, where he and South African Ruth First had worked alongside others; it was here that First was assassinated in 1982. Bragança and the Frelimo leader Samora Machel both died in a disputed plane crash in 1986. Darch and his co-editor wrote, in 2019, 'How then can we fail to conclude... in these dark times of deep pessimism and widespread distrust of arrogant power brokers – how much we miss personalities such as Aquino, generous, intelligent and committed to the democratic transformation of society?'[60]

Martin Legassick had been an important independent socialist voice in the British and South African academies, and on the streets in activist and workers' circles in South Africa, in the years long before and after the first ANC election victory of 1994. We spoke in Cape Town in 2005. Legassick entered political life in his undergraduate days at the University of Cape Town where he was active in Liberal party politics and influenced by the infamous shootings in Sharpeville in the Transvaal, just before he left for England.[61] He entered Balliol College, Oxford, planning to study physics. He recalled the Oxford Labour Club, a largely invisible Communist Party, and liberal American Kennedy supporters amongst his fellow Rhodes Scholars. The Committee for Nuclear Disarmament (CND) had impressed him as being the strongest of the movements of his day.[62] At the Oxford Union, Legassick and others heckled student Labour leaders who came to speak, including the future Foreign Secretaries Robin Cook (1946–2005) and Jack Straw (1946–), the latter also serving as Home Secretary. Legassick began to have contact with the nascent anti-apartheid movement in London, while continuing a course of independent debate and study in Oxford:

> I came in contact [at Oxford] with a number of South Africans who were liberals and we started discussing... the big issue around 1960/1961 [which] was the turn to the armed struggle of the ANC. And this was also affecting people in the Liberal Party... somebody gave me Che Guevara's *Guerilla Warfare* to read, and... stuff on global warfare, edited by an American, [and] put together... for counter-insurgency purposes... we had a discussion

---

[60] Colin Darch and Marco Mondaini (eds), *Independence and Revolution in Portuguese-Speaking Africa* (Cape Town, 2019), xxi. See also <https://cosmonautmag.com/2023/06/mozambique-colin-darch/>.

[61] Sixty-nine protestors were killed in a crowd of 7,000 at the police station in Sharpeville. Many more were injured as the police fired directly on unarmed demonstrators. Legassick stresses its influence in his masterwork, *Towards Socialist Democracy* (Scottsville, 2007), 1.

[62] For an excellent short account of the politics of the evolving Left at Oxford in the period, see Stuart Hall with Bill Schwarz, *Familiar Stranger: A Life between Two Islands* (London, 2017), ch. 9.

'Liberal Education' and Imperial Legacies, 1945–70   345

group [on] these questions about [the] force of South African violence... and the influence on me.[63]

In 1962, Legassick was asked by those with whom he had worked in Cape Town to represent the National Union of South African Students (NUSAS) in Europe, at conferences involving European, American and Iranian students. He met the ANC representative sent to Helsinki, the future South African poet-laureate, Mazisi Kunene (1930–2006), with whom he formed a strong bond.[64] He found himself defending armed struggle to the dismay of pacifists at the conference. Thereafter, Legassick began fundraising for Black South African students who wanted to come to England. I inquired about the depth of his social contact in these early years, with Africans within the university:

> You might go to dinner in the college hall with some African students, or they might come to your college. I can remember in the summer in '63, going to several parties, and one party in particular [that was] given by a Sierre Leonean student, that was in London. So, there was some social mixing, but... it wasn't full... you would meet and then you would part. On the other hand, with Mazisi Kunene, I became very, very close. I used to eat with him at Oxford, and spend time at his flat talking to him.[65]

He became an officer of an African Students' Society: 'All of this had a kind of radicalizing influence on me and made me think that I didn't want to pursue science as a career'. He would write that 'by the end of 1962, I regarded myself as a radical socialist'.[66]

The inaugural Rhodes Professor of Race Relations, an anti-apartheid South African Kenneth Kirkwood, suggested he go to Ghana to study with the Oxford Africanist, Thomas Hodgkin, in residence at the University of Ghana.[67] Before his departure, Legassick spent a summer working at the London ANC office in

[63] Interview with the author, Cape Town, 2005.

[64] Kunene taught at UCLA (1975–92) in exile. He first came to London in 1959, on an award for his writing as a university student in Durban, and studied at SOAS. In 1962, he began to represent the ANC in Europe.

[65] Interview with the author, Cape Town, 2005. See also Legassick, *Armed Struggle and Democracy: The Case of South Africa* (Uppsala, 2002), which states that the sabotage organization, the African Resistance Movement, attempted to recruit him at this time; Leggasick demurred, and remained loyal to the ANC (pp. 9–10).

[66] Legassick, *Towards Socialist Democracy*, 1.

[67] Hodgkin (1918–82) was the son of the Provost of The Queen's College, Oxford; both his grandfathers were historians of repute. He was an intermittent member of the CPGB and traveled from Balliol to Ghana to advise the early Nkrumah government. He was the spouse of the Nobel prize-winning chemist Dorothy Crowfoot Hodgkin (1918–82), of Somerville College, Oxford, whose PhD was earned at Newnham College,

346   *Susan D. Pennybacker*

Africa House in South Kensington, a property financed by the Ghanaian government. He recalled the excitement of the new Independence moment and the early popularity of Kwame Nkrumah. Once in Africa, he visited Algeria and became imbued with the spirit of revolution afoot on the Continent. His father died in South Africa, and his attendance at the funeral, traveling on a British passport, was the occasion for the security forces to interrogate him and to ban him from any future entry. He would not return until 1991. After his formative time in Ghana, Legassick would complete a PhD at UCLA, witnessing the mobilisations around Black Power and against the Vietnam War. He found his relations with African-Americans to be less formal than his past inter-racial encounters in England.[68]

He returned to London in 'the period of swinging London', with his partner, the American Audrey Anne Faren Rosenthal, who had also earned a History PhD at UCLA. They lived centrally and partook of the music scene of the day: 'We went to hear people like Jimi Hendrix and Pink Floyd [and] The Four Tops'. This was 1966–7:

> There is this Left, which is… reevaluating British Politics… as well as its relationship to the world, and… in terms of Third World things… it's mainly Vietnam… The Communist Party is in the anti-apartheid movement… together with the official Labour party… The anti-apartheid movement expects more of [Harold Wilson's] Labour government than it does of [a] Tory government. That's… the official protests, but I don't really think it's [all] really effective at this point. I don't think in '66–'67 there was any particular clique that is particularly concerned about South Africa apart from the anti-apartheid movement which is like a kind of 'official politics'. The Left is more diffusely concerned. It's really only… Soweto that puts South Africa back on the agenda.[69]

Cambridge (1937). Thomas Hodgkin pioneered the study of modern Africa in British universities.

[68] On Legassick in these years, see Roxanne Dunbar Ortiz: *Outlaw Woman: A Memoir of the War Years, 1960–1975* (San Francisco, 2001), Chs 2–3 and Epilogue.

[69] In 1967, he published a short study, *The National Union of South African Students: Ethnic Cleavage and Ethnic Integration in the Universities*, Occasional Paper No. 4 (African Studies center, UCLA, 1967), with a preface by his mentor, Professor Leonard Thompson of UCLA. He then co-authored an analytical survey of the student organizations and universities' political culture in South Africa, an expanded iteration of the first study, in 1968. See Martin Legassick and John Shingler, 'South Africa', in Donald K. Emmerson (eds), *Students and Politics in Developing Nations* (London, 1968), 103–45. The Soweto student uprising, and the scandalous shootings that occurred there, did not come until 1976.

In the London milieu in which she and Legassick were now active, Rosenthal agreed to travel anonymously to South Africa as a courier of information for the South African Defence and Aid Fund, headed by Canon Lewis John Collins of St Paul's Cathedral. She did several weeks of work there, posting information back. Shockingly, she died as she departed from South Africa with others in what was an uncommon crash of a South African Airlines flight, her sudden death an event of inexplicable loss for Legassick and the movement, its circumstances still unresolved for some.[70] Legassick returned to the University of California at Santa Barbara in one of the most confrontational periods of the US New Left, as America seethed with conflict. After two more years, when his academic position was not extended, he found work back at the University of London with Ford Foundation support during 1971–4, then secured a faculty position at the University of Warwick until he resigned in the early 1980s, to do fulltime political work, living on unemployment benefits.

Legassick became increasingly involved in the factional strife of the South African Left abroad as a critic of the ANC's posture toward the South African working class, and as the ANC and SACP continued a 'strategic' armed struggle. He was suspended from the ANC along with others, including the mathematician Paula Ensor (the future Dean of Humanities at the University of Cape Town). After his return, Legassick was destined to work as an independent activist and academician, his critical perspective on the successive ANC governments offered resolutely from without as he returned from Britain and took up a post at UWC.[71]

* * *

Colin Darch and Martin Legassick did not become diplomats nor South African MPs, but they departed from England with finality. Like Haidar and Aiyar, they remained imbued with both the provocations and the intellectual

---

[70] On Rosenthal, see Baxandale, *Outlaw Woman*, 63–4, 73–7. Recent reportage reveals the State's orders to search for her known and surveilled briefcase: <https://www.pressreader.com/south-africa/daily-dispatch/20190316/281625306629791>.

[71] For reflections on this history, see Martin Legassick, 'Armed Struggle in South Africa: Consequences of a Strategy Debate', in Henning Melber (ed.), *Limits to Liberation in Southern Africa: The Unfinished Business of Democratic Consolidation* (Cape Town, 2003), 156–77, and *Towards Socialist Democracy*, 1–11. Ensor, Robert Peterson and David Hemson, Legassick's fellow factionalists, were also banned from South Africa. Prime Minister Thabo Mbeki's biographer Mark Gevisser opines that the expulsion 'marked the ANC's definitive rejection of socialism' and 'severed the ANC's links to its most valuable and creative source of self-criticism': *Thabo Mbeki: The Dream Deferred* (Johannesburg, 2007), 474. He cites Mbeki's abject derision of and hostility toward the faction; Leggasick and Mbeki had known each other at Sussex University.

exposure that Oxbridge had afforded them. Haidar and Aiyar each reached pinnacles of the Indian political community in the era dominated by the rule of the Congress Party, yet they have now witnessed the fall from power of those representing the leaders of the Independence movements. Each figure continued an engagement with the problems of a social democratic order, as they faced the disorder and disenchantments of the years that ensued. Their intuitive struggles, in sharp difference and on common ground alike, bespoke their insistence on independent and forthright engagement, what Legassick had once, in youth, termed the generic 'liberal universalist tradition' of the English universities founded in his adopted South African homeland.[72] This inheritance was 'not enough', but, for these individuals, the evidence marshalled here suggests that it was immutable as an element of consciousness, and as a lifelong check upon autocracy in its various guises. 'Liberal education' begot radical futures, its lessons often unforgotten and remade, not least in attempts to extend its fertile pathways, to greater portions of humanity.

[72] Legassick, *National Union of South African Students*, 50. See Graeme C. Moodie, 'The state and the liberal universities in South Africa: 1948–1990', *Higher Education*, 27 (1994), 1–40. Moodie notes that 'in UCT and Wits "equality" did not extend outside the classroom to sports or social events'. For the NUSAS and liberalism, see esp. Saul Dubow, *Apartheid, 1948–1994* (Oxford, 2014), 128–9; for the South African Students' Organization (SASO) and its challenge to NUSAS, see *ibid.*, 160–1.

Chapter 17

The Curious Case of Wales's Statue to Henry Morton Stanley

Joanna Lewis

At 11am on Saturday 6 June 2020, a peaceful protest began in Denbigh, north Wales. Approximately fifty people had assembled in the town square to support Black Lives Matter.[1] Many were young and had gone down on one knee. Some also made a fist in the air whilst others held placards. However, everyone had their backs to a statue of the Victorian explorer, Henry Morton Stanley. By Monday an online petition demanding the statue be removed out of respect to the movement had attracted over a thousand signatures. The *Denbighshire Free Press* and *The Leader* covered the story, quoting the petitioners' reasoning: 'Stanley was known for his brutal treatment of Africans, to the extent that he used black children from his boat to calibrate his rifle sights when sailing down the river'; 'a statue to a man like that has no place in Welsh society in 2020. It is an insult to African people that it stands pride of place in the town.'[2]

Momentum gathered. The Bishop of St Asaph added his signature. A second petition called for the statue to be substituted with a permanent exhibition. Meanwhile its sculptor, Nick Elphick, from Llandudno, was left dumbfounded: 'I was like, what the fuck is going on', he told the *Daily Mail*.[3] He had spent two years crafting the tribute to Sir Henry but was now fielding an onslaught of online abuse. A Wetherspoons pub in Wrexham faced demands to change

---

[1]   <https://blacklivesmatter.com/> [All URLs in chapter accessed 9 Aug. 2022]. A Black Lives Matter Wales (*Bywydau Du O Bwys Cymru*) had been established to raise funds to support the Race Council Cymru.

[2]   '"No Place For it in Welsh Society"', *The Leader*, 9 June 2020: <https://www.leaderlive.co.uk/news/18506253.no-place-welsh-society---1-000-people-sign-petition-remove-hm-stanley-statue-denbigh-town-centre/>, quoting the *Denbighshire Free Press*. For the petition, currently at over 8,000 signatories, see <https://www.change.org/p/denbigh-town-council-remove-the-statue-of-stanley-from-denbigh-town-centre>.

[3]   *Daily Mail*, 20 June 2020: <https://www.dailymail.co.uk/news/article-8446735/>.

its name from The Elihu Yale.[4] And in Rhyl, three hundred people gathered in silent protest against racism in Wales. Denbigh Town Council quickly decided to have a vote on the statue, the date of which was put back to 20 June 2020, to allow time for consultation with the Welsh Assembly on the current thinking on statues. In the end, Councillors would vote by six votes to five, *not* to remove the statue.

There are many intriguing aspects to this story. The statue (fig. 17.1) was installed in 2010, well outside of the age of *statue-mania*.[5] Strong objections were raised at the time. Every year since its erection, a protest has been staged by a local artist. Dressed in Victorian funeral attire, Wanda Zyborska covers the statue in a giant black rubber sheath for 'The Annual Funeral Condom Re-Veiling'.[6] This is a reference to Stanley's role in setting up the Congo Free State for King Leopold of Belgium, whose colony brutally extracted rubber in the late nineteenth century.[7] If opposition to a commemorative statue was not new, neither was criticism of Stanley's 'methods'. These first surfaced during the 1870s. Details of the reasoning behind the negative views held by some of his peers were made available to the local council's committee during their 2020 deliberations by a group of academic historians. Moreover, during his life Stanley publicly denied he was Welsh and was disparaging about his fellow countrymen and women.

This chapter argues that these apparent inconsistencies and idiosyncrasies can be explained on the one hand, by the region's unique set of interactions since the 1870s with Stanley, his Welshness and small acts of remembrance; and on the other, by a conspicuous absence within those interactions, of an engagement with Empire. From the mid-Victorian period, a passionate struggle

---

4 The pub was named after Elihu Yale (1649–1729) in recognition of his generous benefactions. He had amassed a fortune from commercial activity in Madras and was buried in Wrexham, owning a large estate in the area. Allegations of his links to the slave trade circulated widely: <https://www.dailypost.co.uk/news/north-wales-news/wetherspoon-change-name-pub-whose-18387437>. See Elizabeth Keubler-Wolf, '"Born in America, in Europe Bred, in Africa Travell'd and in Asia Wed": Elihu Yale, Material Culture, and Actor Networks from the Seventeenth Century to the Twenty-first', *Journal of Global History*, 11 (2016), 320–43.

5 Defined as 'the nineteenth and early twentieth century craze for erecting statues of mostly male worthies in public locations', and a term first used in France in 1851: James Hall, 'At the mercy of the public. Is it necessary to kill some statues, or could we add to them?', *Times Literary Supplement*, 9 Apr. 2021, 12.

6 'Protestors to Cover H.M. Stanley Statue in Denbigh', *Denbighshire Free Press*, 15 Aug. 2018: <https://www.denbighshirefreepress.co.uk/news/16420475.protestors-cover-h-m-stanley-statue-denbigh/>.

7 Adam Hochschild, *King Leopold's Ghost: A Story of Greed, Terror and Heroism in Colonial Africa* (Boston: MA, 1998).

Fig. 17.1. Statue of H.M. Stanley, Denbigh.

was waged by the local press to have Denbigh and Wales recognised as part of the Stanley phenomenon, in the face of a perceived range of powerful forces working against this (including Stanley himself). Stanley's 'humble origins', evidence of class (English) prejudice against him, and a sense of him having privately kept in touch with family, were major factors that softened local feelings towards him. Overall, the most powerful and consistent driver of commemorative sympathies was of course religious feeling. That is until calls came for a statue in the early twenty-first century when, ironically, economics and external forces came into play. Nevertheless, such recent interventions were able to draw on these older local sentiments and conservative networks, as well as the historical absence of the presence of the British Empire, or any other empire for that matter, in public discussion of the explorer.

Background

Stanley was born in Denbigh, a market town and peri-rural community near the Clwydian Hills, North Wales. Denbigh's Welsh name *Dinbych* means little fortress. As the local tourist board cheerfully puts it: 'It is the home of princes and earls, rebels and revolutionaries where layer upon layer of history have shaped the architecture of the town and the character of the people.'[8] For the ruins of the once formidable hilltop castle are an iconic, brooding reminder of the brutal colonial subjugation of Wales by the English monarchy during the medieval period – the real 'Game of Thrones'.[9] The first castle was a residence of Prince *Dafydd ap Gruffudd* (and before that, a fortified garrison during the Roman imperial occupation). He would become the last native prince of an independent Wales. His assault on nearby Hawarden Castle in 1282 provoked the Plantagenet King, Edward I, into full-scale invasion. Violent retribution followed: *Dafydd* became the first nobleman to be hung until half-dead, then drawn and quartered. After a doomed second assault by the Welsh, Edward had the castle rebuilt as a fortress. The area continued to be a site of violent conflict up until the English Civil War. By the 1700s, Denbigh was home to a vibrant craft industry. This declined with the development of fossil-fuelled industrial manufacturing but by the 1860s, Denbigh had become the main centre of the Vale of Clwyd and was on the railway network. By the late-twentieth century, the impact of industrial decline more generally resulted in the closure

---

8   <http://www.visitdenbigh.co.uk/>.

9   For a twentieth-century example of anguished connections, see Mark Alan Rhodes, 'The Absent Presence of Paul Robeson in Wales: Appropriation and Philosophical Disconnects in the Memorial Landscape', *Transactions of the Institute of British Geographers*, 46 (2021) 763–79.

The Curious Case of Wales's Statue to Henry Morton Stanley   353

of the railway. The town's last main employer – a mental hospital – also shut its doors.

If the town's economic fortunes faltered, a lively interest in local history and genealogy had not.[10] A number of historical figures have connections with Denbigh including Robert Dudley, Samuel Johnson, Thomas Gee and Beatrix Potter. H.M. Stanley is Denbigh's most famous Victorian.[11] Born in 1841 and baptised John Rowlands, he was the eldest of four children born out of wedlock to Elizabeth Parry. Aged six, his mother placed him in the local workhouse where he stayed until aged fifteen. In 1859, whilst living with relations in Liverpool, he decided his miserable prospects would be improved if he worked his way to America as a cabin boy. Initially taken in by a shopkeeper, he fought for the Confederates in the American Civil War until his capture. Then he fought in the Union Army, after which he joined the US Navy in 1864, absconding in 1865. Next, he began chronicling the expansion of the American frontier in the 'wild west', quickly demonstrating a flair for journalism and accessible writing. His first major overseas expedition to the Ottoman Empire ended up in jail. This brought him to the attention of America's largest daily newspaper, the *New York Herald*.[12] One of his many derring-do missions was as correspondent accompanying a special force to the African kingdom of Abyssinia (Ethiopia) to liberate a group of hostages.

The newspaper assignment that changed his life was finding the missing Scottish explorer and missionary Dr David Livingstone still alive in central Africa. In 1871, Stanley sensationally succeeded where others had failed. Livingstone refused to return home with him in 1872, insisting on pushing on with his explorations, dying in the process in April 1873. Stanley resolved to 'finish' his work. The *New York Herald* supported Stanley's trans-African explorations. He found the source of the Congo River, traced its course, and survived three incredibly tough journeys through the notorious Ituri Forest, all of which earned him the appellation of the greatest European explorer of the day.[13] His achievements came to the attention of King Leopold II of Belgium,

---

[10] See for example, the wide-ranging subjects in the 2023 Denbigh Heritage Lectures: <http://www.visitdenbigh.co.uk/discover-denbigh/things-to-do>.

[11] The account that follows is drawn primarily from Felix Driver, 'Sir Henry Morton Stanley, 1841–1904', *Dictionary of National Biography* (Oxford, 2004). See also William Llewelyn Davies, 'Stanley, (Sir) Henry Morton (alias Rowlands, John) (1841–1904), Explorer, Administrator, and Author', *Y Bwygraffiadur Cymreig* <https://biography.wales/>.

[12] It boasted an impressive circulation of 84,000 in the 1860s: James L. Crouthamel, *Bennett's New York Herald and the Rise of the Popular Press* (Syracuse: NY, 1989).

[13] This contemporary acclaim has been revived in the most recent in-depth biography of Stanley: Tim Jeal, *Stanley: The Impossible Life of Africa's Greatest Explorer* (London, 2007).

354 Joanna Lewis

desperate for an empire. This resulted in a collaboration which helped establish the monarch's claim to territory and resources in central Africa, through treaties with chiefs, which in turn enabled the monarch to acquire – through other dubious methods – international recognition for his Congo Free State at the Berlin Conference of 1884–5. Stanley went on to publish numerous bestsellers, including *Into the Dark Continent*, a book which did much to popularise the term. He married late in life. Knighted in 1899, he died on 10 May 1904 aged 63, having been plagued by ill-health from his harsh life and travels. He was buried near his adopted home in Surrey (not in Westminster Abbey, next to Livingstone, which had been his wish).[14]

Putting Wales into the Story

The 2010 Stanley statue in Denbigh is in one sense a simple consequence of the fact Stanley was born in the town, baptised in the local church, and lived there until his mid-teens. However, Stanley's rise to international fame in the 1870s was as an *American* who had been adopted by a family whose surname he had taken out of respect and gratitude. His origin story became harder to sustain, thanks to the dogged efforts of the local press in North Wales.

The reasons for Stanley's denials have been the subject of speculation by biographers, who often interpret them as the consequence of multiple traumatic episodes during his formative years, based around rejection, hurt and humiliation. Being one of four children born out of wedlock to different fathers, as Frank McLynn puts it, 'was exceptional even for the fairly relaxed standards of the 1840s'.[15] His father, John Rowlands, showed no interest in his parental obligations so Stanley was brought up by his maternal grandfather. Soon after the latter's death, when Stanley was five, he was admitted to the workhouse (Rowlands died five years later of alcoholism). The admission entry described the young Stanley as 'a bastard of Denbigh parish' who had been 'deserted'.[16] Illegitimacy was a huge stigma. So, en route back to England in July 1872, after finding Livingstone alive in Africa, Stanley gave his first big celebrity press interview – an interview in which he was described as a prime physical

---

[14] For work by the UK's leading academic expert on Stanley, see Brian Murray, 'Building Congo, Writing Empire: The Literary Labours of Henry Morton Stanley', *Journal of English Studies in Africa*, 59 (2016), 6–17, and his *H.M. Stanley and Literature of Exploration: Empire, Media, Modernity* (forthcoming).

[15] Frank McLynn, *Stanley: Dark Genius of African Exploration* (London, 2004 edn), 16.

[16] Admission/Discharge Book, St Asaph Workhouse, 26 March 1845–24 June 1847. G/C/60/2, Flintshire Record Office, North East Wales Archives.

specimen of an *American*.[17] The *New York Herald* agreed: Stanley was a 'native American; Missouri, and not Wales is his birthplace'.[18]

However, the local press moved quickly to disprove that claim. A journalist at the *Carnarvon Herald* interviewed a landlady of the Cross Foxes Inn, Glascoed, near St Asaph, the reputed mother of Stanley. She produced photographs and two books bearing his signature. His real name was revealed as John Rowlands and her story was corroborated by the rector of Llanwyddan, and Sir Hugh Williams.[19] Another local man named Evans was also interviewed; he insisted Stanley was John Rowlands, 'born and bred in the Vale of Clwyd'. Evans claimed to have met him in Africa and recalled their singing Welsh songs together.[20] Regional papers excitedly ran with the headline: 'Mr Stanley. A Welshman.'[21]

Meanwhile, others went to press with the headline: 'Mr Stanley. Not a Welshman.' For Stanley himself was now denying he was Welsh through indirect means. The *Llangollen Advertiser*, amongst others, published the intervention of a Charles Ollivant from Cheshire who had written to Stanley about Evans's claims and – conveniently – offered 'an authoritative denial'. Stanley's signed response was reprinted in full in some newspapers. The Welsh newspaper claims were 'all bosh', Stanley insisted; 'I never knew a man named Evans, nor have I ever sung a Welsh song – not knowing anything of the language'; 'I say I am an American.'[22]

The debate then moved on somewhat. 'Is he a Welshman?', the *Carnarvon and Denbigh Herald* asked.[23] They had sent a journalist 'across the Rhuddlan Marsh' to interview the very same Mrs Jones who had the very same evidence to present. On the same day, the *Llangollen Advertiser* published more evidence he was born locally and had entered the workhouse, even returning there in 1866 to give inmates a treat and what in today's parlance might be described as a 'motivational talk'. This had been corroborated by a 'reliable woman' at the *Eisteddfod*, and a man who had spoken to Stanley on his return from Abyssinia. As the *Llangollen Advertiser*'s editorial concluded, it was 'remarkable' that despite all the proof, Stanley continued to repudiate his 'Welsh blood'.[24]

---

[17] Jeal, *Stanley*, 134.

[18] Tipyn O. Bob Peth, *Cambrian News and Merionethshire Standard*, 16 Aug. 1872, 3.

[19] Quoted in *Llangollen Advertiser*, 6 Sept. 1872, 3.

[20] *Cambrian News and Merionethshire Standard*, 30 Aug. 1872, 8.

[21] *Ibid.*

[22] 'Mr Stanley. Not a Welshman', *Llangollen Advertiser*, 30 Aug. 1872, 3.

[23] 'Is he a Welshman?' [from *Carnarvon and Denbigh Herald*], *Cambrian News and Merionethshire Standard*, 6 Sept. 1872, 3.

[24] 'Mr Stanley's Nationality', *Llangollen Advertiser*, 6 Sept. 1872, 3.

Yet sympathy for Stanley would persist. The *Llangollen Advertiser* accepted that Stanley owed his 'splendid achievements in Central Africa' to the 'training and development' he had received in America, but also thought that Wales could celebrate his achievements and be proud of him on 'cosmopolitan rather than national grounds'.[25] Such a temperate position had a number of possible roots. There was a sense, perhaps, that he was being humiliated by an anti-Welsh establishment with racist tones that non-Celts would not have to endure. Questions about his parentage were being put to him publicly in London, most famously and acridly by the eugenicist Francis Galton.[26] Added to that was the knowledge that Stanley had been subjected to professional derision on his return by various English institutions. The *Royal Geographical Society* had been particularly scornful. Taunts, jokes and quips published in metropolitan and American publications were reproduced in the Welsh press, which kept a close watch. These included an elaborate spoof in the *Spectator* at Stanley's expense;[27] and, in the American *Sun* newspaper, the publication of Lewis Noe's shocking account of Stanley's alleged sadomasochism towards him a few years before.[28] Stanley wrote at one point that 'my enemies command the entire press'.[29] This was not true. The local Welsh press reproduced positive coverage in the *New York Herald* (Stanley's employer) following the news that Queen Victoria had sent him a letter of thanks – a letter which caused the *Herald* to 'rejoice' at this 'generous tribute to American pluck and enterprise'.[30]

Family Matters

"Pwy bellach a wad nad yw efe yn Gymro, ac yn Gymro Cymreig?"[31]

Piecing together the details of Stanley's early life in Wales and evidence of his family connections and visits to the area became a local preoccupation for the next hundred years. Awkwardly for Stanley, he had visited Denbigh on a number of occasions between leaving for America as a teenager and setting out for Africa to find Livingstone. Nor did he cut ties with his family during the remainder of his life. And he would go on to marry a Welsh heiress. Thus, a

---

[25] 'Mr Stanley', *Llangollen Advertiser*, 30 Aug. 1872, 3.

[26] McLynn, *Stanley*, 212–13; Jeal, *Stanley*, 140–1.

[27] McLynn, *Stanley*, 225.

[28] *Ibid.*, 54–5, 217.

[29] Quoted in *ibid.*, 225.

[30] *Flintshire Observer, Mining Journal and General Advertiser*, 13 Sept. 1872, 2.

[31] 'Who shall now deny that he is a Welshman?': a quote from a correspondent published the day after his visit and published in the local newspaper *Yr Herald Cymraeg*, 16 June 1891, reproduced in Lucy M. Jones and Ivor Wynne Jones, *H.M. Stanley and Wales* (Hawarden, 1972), 30.

The Curious Case of Wales's Statue to Henry Morton Stanley   357

popular understanding of Stanley as a son of Denbigh, who privately may not have disavowed his Welshness, slowly incubated. This likely softened the antipathy felt by locals towards him, but not enough to generate calls for a public memorial during his lifetime or at his death – although a locally published history of his life in 1890, written in Welsh, *Hanes bywyd*, could be interpreted as the first step in this direction.[32]

Stanley's roots in Denbigh and his scandalous poverty in early life became known largely thanks to his family, childhood acquaintances, and an ex-girlfriend. Their collective willingness to show-and-tell meant alternative narratives fell on flinty ground in north Wales. For late in November 1872, John Camden Hotten sensationally published the story of his Stanley's life so far.[33] Teasingly, Hotten had used the pseudonym Cadwalader Rowlands.[34] This laying bare of what would have been viewed by many as his embarrassing, squalid origins provoked Stanley to write to *The Times* charging Hotten with 'unscrupulous conduct'.[35] Hotten replied, quoting from the book: 'Every statement made in the life has been supplied by Mr Stanley's relatives or friends – relatives who glory in his nationality'.[36]

Whilst the press only ever obliquely referred to the book, Stanley himself had left quite an implicating paper trail. He had signed the visitors book at Denbigh Castle in 1866. He had made a very public visit to the St Asaph workhouse in American naval uniform. Stanley had wanted to take a boy away with him 'into the world' but was prevented from doing since the boy was not legally old enough.[37] Stanley fell for a young Denbigh woman, a Miss Roberts. He wrote to her in March 1869, detailing, in monomaniacal style, 'my history': illegitimate, 'a waif cast into the world'; 'an outcast'; 'uncared for by all relations, by all humanity'.[38] The romance ended badly, and the letter would eventually go public.[39]

However, in the long term, these indiscretions helped transform him in local eyes – from a pathetic figure into a local boy who made it despite the hardship of his early life. For example, his 1869 letter to Roberts was republished in the *Abergele and Pensarn Visitor* in 1930. It also appeared in the 1972

[32] *Hanes bywyd Henry M. Stanley: yn cynnwys trem ar ei yrfa anturiaethus a'i archwiliadau llwyddiannus yn nghyfandir tywyll Affrica, at wasanaeth ei gydwladwyr* (Dinbych, 1890).

[33] Cadwalader Rowlands, *Henry M. Stanley: The Story of his Life from his Birth In 1841 to his Discovery of Livingstone, 1871* (London, 1872).

[34] Rowland was Stanley's original surname; Cadwalader in Welsh means battle-leader.

[35] *Cambrian News and Merionethshire Standard*, 22 Nov. 1872, 3.

[36] 'Mr Hatton' quoted in *Ibid.*, 22 Nov. 1872, 3.

[37] As alleged in Rowlands, *Henry M. Stanley*, 73.

[38] Jones and Jones, *Stanley and Wales*, 20–4.

[39] Jeal, *Stanley*, 146.

pamphlet, *H.M Stanley and Wales*, wherein Lucy Jones explained – generously – that Stanley's embarrassment about his early family history and the stigma of pauperism' resulted in him denying his Welsh origins for a time, but that 'this was only temporary'.[40] The pamphlet introduced Sir Henry as discover of Livingstone, founder of the Congo Free State, and heroic explorer of Central Africa. But these achievements were not elaborated upon. Instead, all local visits by Stanley were documented. 'He did not neglect his family', Jones insisted: his mother visited him in London in 1885, and he paid for her funeral and related expenses in 1886. And Stanley was allegedly once spotted reading a Welsh newspaper in a train in Bangor.[41] It seemed not to matter that Stanley wrote of how he regarded all nationalities as superior to the Welsh, and identified an unbridgeable chasm between him and Clwydian residents: 'They cannot understand why I should not be proud of this little parish world of North Wales, and I cannot understand what they see to admire in it.'[42]

'The Man Who Found Livingstone is Dead'[43]

Converting souls always mattered. Whilst the 2010 Stanley statue would become the most obvious and material of memorials, a longer history exists of formal and public occasions that commemorated Stanley's connections to the area, powered by Welsh religiosity which edged out the British Empire and related controversies. Welsh nonconformity as well as the Anglican church in Wales remained hugely grateful to Stanley for finding Livingstone – Christian missionary, anti-slavery icon and hero of the Victorian self-help manual – alive in central Africa.[44] This mattered more than Stanley's role in the workings of a remote and unrelatable colonial empire. It was a moral position with which local opinion was comfortable and confident. Newspapers from the time covered Stanley's enthusiastic speeches to various organisations – speeches in which he had routinely praised Livingstone for his commitment to evangelical work and endorsed the need to open Africa to Christianity and commerce.[45]

A narrative of the spread of Christianity in Africa thanks to the endeavours of men such as Stanley bedded down in the region throughout the remainder

---

[40] Jones and Jones, *Stanley and Wales*, 17.

[41] *Ibid.*, 17–26.

[42] Stanley quoted in McFlynn, *Stanley*, 215.

[43] 'Stanley', *Welsh Coast Pioneer and Review for North Cambria*, 13 May 1904, 16.

[44] On the outpouring of feeling towards Livingstone at his finding and then his death, see Joanna Lewis, *Empire of Sentiment: The Death of David Livingstone and the Myth of Victorian Imperialism* (Cambridge, 2017).

[45] For example, see 'Mr H.M. Stanley and the Missionaries; High Opinion of Livingstone; The Conversion of Africa', *Western Mail*, 29 May 1885, 3.

The *Curious Case of Wales's Statue to Henry Morton Stanley*   359

of his life. In June 1891, Stanley had visited North Wales to give a lecture in support of a Congo Training Institute based in Llandudno. The Institute was the dream of Baptist missionary Rev. William Hughes, who, not long after he had arrived in the Congo to proselytise, was forced to return to Wales because of ill-health.[46] He came home with Nkanak and Kinkassa, two Congolese 'boys' who had nursed him. They lived together at Colwyn Bay whilst Hughes tried to raise money for a centre that would, through assisted passages, host and train young men from the region. After an apprenticeship and having learnt English, they would return home. Stanley's June lecture pulled in an audience of four thousand. And, a month later, Hughes received the news that thanks to a request from Stanley, King Leopold had agreed that the institution could use the King's name as its patron.[47] A popular tourist guide soon described how African children, walking in the streets of Colwyn Bay, had become 'a feature of the place'.[48]

Thus, the Stanley who died in 1904 was the discoverer of Livingstone who 'pierced the utmost recesses of darkest Africa', opening up its centre for 'civilization'.[49] His death would not be an occasion to reflect on British colonialism, let alone the Belgian Congo and the atrocities under Leopold. Obituaries in the North Wales press varied, with detailed factual accounts of his life, borrowed from national newspaper coverage, giving way to distinctly local interpretations, including his denial of being Welsh. Short anecdotes or letters from locals about his mother or the workhouse visits and so on were published, *still* having to argue their case for his Welshness. The *Rhyl Journal* reproduced verbatim the letter Stanley wrote refuting the newspaper's claims, thirty years before.[50] Stanley's persistent refusal to 'acknowledge the stock from which he sprang' was damned in a *Welsh Coast Pioneer* editorial for being 'tantamount to a betrayal'; '*Cas gwr na charo'r wlad a'i macco*', the paper insisted: Stanley's 'greatness' would have more lustre in the eyes of his countrymen had he not concealed his 'Welsh peasant origin'.[51]

[46] Robert Burroughs, 'Imperial Entanglements of the Congo/African Institute, Colwyn Bay', in P. Fraiture (ed.), *Unfinished Histories: Empire and Postcolonial Resonance in Central Africa and Belgium* (Leuven, 2022) 103–20.

[47] The Institute folded in 1911, slowly bankrupted in the wake of various controversies and rumours of sexual misconduct: Christopher Draper and John Lawson-Reay, *Scandal at Congo House: William Hughes and the African Institute, Colwyn Bay* (Gwasg Carreg Gwalch, 2012).

[48] Extracted from John Heywood's *Guide Book to Colwyn Bay* (1892): <https://colwynbayheritage.org.uk/the-congo-institute/>.

[49] 'Stanley', *Welsh Coast Pioneer and Review for North Cambria*, 13 May 1904, 16.

[50] 'Stanley denies his nationality', *Rhyl Journal*, 21 May 1904, 6.

[51] 'Stanley', *Welsh Coast Pioneer and Review for North Cambria* (Rhyl Edition) 13 May 1904, 16. Translation: Hateful is the man who does not love his own people.

360 Joanna Lewis

Nevertheless, that 'greatness' was often elaborated upon at some length. He possessed 'an indomitable spirit'; he was 'one of the noblest and greatest men of action of the nineteenth century'; he was 'an organiser of victory' who 'won the most conspicuous victories of the century in the pioneer's battle against the primitive powers of nature'.[52] Echoing this theme, obituaries in the local English-speaking press were dominated by a sympathetic eulogy from the Bishop of St Asaph in his Sunday morning sermon, reproduced in full. Bishop Edwards had tied Stanley's achievements to 'the greatest event of the last 30 years... the opening out of Africa' which had 'no parallel in the world's history'.[53] He emotively recalled the 'the homeless childhood of this deserted Welsh boy'. There was a 'hardness and bitterness', he conceded; defects in his qualities 'like the greatest'. But, he continued, because Stanley achieved what he did *despite* his start in life 'we may well be proud to reckon him as true Welshman'.[54]

Yet by the late 1890s evidence of atrocities in the Congo Free State could no longer be ignored by the British government. In 1902 Roger Casement was dispatched to investigate and his damning report was published in 1904.[55] Rather than prompting reflections on the colonial controversies of the time, however, Stanley's death instead offered an opportunity to reflect on Welshness and being Welsh in the world. It was suggested that for Welshmen (no mention of Welshwomen) Stanley represented a living rebuttal of 'the taunt that men of Welsh stock had accomplished little or nothing beyond this tight little island... that Wales had given little or nothing to empire or to mankind... [that] the Celt... went forth to battles but he always fell away'.[56] Now, 'young Wales' should take inspiration from the greatest African explorer of the age:

> So far, Welshmen have been too contented with their limited surroundings; a narrow parochialism has led them to satisfy themselves with a pittance at home in preference to the conspicuous prizes which are to be won in the wider fields of the Empire and the World.[57]

---

[52] *Ibid.*

[53] Many local papers reproduced his Stanley sermon. See, for example, *Rhyl Journal*, 21 May 1904, 6; and 'The Passing of Stanley', *Welsh Coast Pioneer and Review for North Cambria*, 20 May 1904, 13.

[54] *Rhyl Journal*, 21 May 1904, 6.

[55] G. Kearns and D. Nally, 'An Accumulated Wrong: Roger Casement and the Anti-colonial Moments within Imperial Governance', *Journal of Historical Geography*, 64 (2019), 1–12. In 1905, the Congo Reform Association began lobbying for the Belgian Government to take over the territory and remove Leopold, which eventually happened in 1908.

[56] 'Stanley', *Welsh Coast Pioneer and Review for North Cambria*, 13 May 1904, 16.

[57] *Ibid.*

The reference to 'young Wales' was significant: these were years which saw a powerful Welsh Christian revival movement led by a 26 year-old former collier, Evan Roberts, whose modernisation, messaging and supernatural invocations were producing waves of new converts.[58]

Posthumously, Stanley spent the rest of the twentieth century comfortably occupying an uncontroversial and unremarkable place within the local moral economy. The workhouse he had been brought up in remained operational through to the 1930s. A new infirmary was built there in 1903, and in 1930 the workhouse was renamed the St Asaph Public Assistance Institution. This was in effect taken over by the NHS after the Second World War.[59] The site of the original workhouse became the H.M. Stanley Hospital in 1948.[60] Two other local commemorative gestures are worth noting. The first was an H.M. Stanley exhibition in 1972, held over 5 days in St Asaph Cathedral Museum (25–30 September). Including printed materials and relics, it was curated by the Flintshire Record Office and supported by the North Wales Association for the Arts. The Cathedral's exhibition committee consisted of a range of individuals and interest groups seeking to raise the profile of Stanley's connection to Wales. These included the former matron of the H.M. Stanley Hospital, Lucy M. Jones, and Ivor Wynne Jones, a popular local journalist, published historian and supporter of local tourism, known for 'fighting the cause of the underdog against the establishment'.[61] The second commemorative event took place five years later, in 1977, when a slate memorial plaque was installed in St Asaph's, to mark (belatedly) the centenary of Stanley's meeting with Livingstone. His name was accompanied with the all-important message: 'Born and bred in this diocese'.[62] This phase of local recasting was complete following a surge in interest in local family history and the establishment in 1980 of a lively society with an accompanying journal.[63] Soon two detailed and sympathetic accounts of Stanley's local family tree appeared in this same journal, the second revealingly entitled 'Elizabeth Parry of Denbigh, an Extraordinary Woman and H.M. Stanley, Her Son, an Extraordinary Man.'[64]

[58] J. Gwynfor Jones, 'Reflections on the Religious Revival in Wales 1904–05', *Journal of the United Reformed Church History Society*, 7 (2005), 427–45. I am grateful to Geraint Thomas for suggesting this.

[59] It closed in 2019 and the site was sold off for housing. There was at least one local road named after him – Stanley Mount – and a town house.

[60] Covering 16 parishes including Denbigh, it had been built at cost of £5,499 and was intended to house 200 inmates: <https://www.workhouses.org.uk/StAsaph/#Pre-1834>.

[61] 'Obituary – Ivor Wynne Jones', *North Wales Live*, 3 Apr. 2007: <https://www.dailypost.co.uk/news/north-wales-news/obituary---ivor-wynne-jones-2874794>.

[62] *Daily Telegraph*, 22 Jan. 1977, 8; 3 Feb. 1977, 16.

[63] *Hel Achau: Journal of the Clwyd Family History Society*.

[64] *Ibid.*, 15 (1985), 35–44.

Why a Statue?

The pressing need for a statue did not materialise until the publication of Tim Jeal's dramatically revisionist biography of Stanley, in 2006. Jeal had visited the town in 2004 to give a talk on Stanley in Wales, as part of a series of events to mark the centenary of his death. Speaking to the local press in 2008, to drum up support for a statue, Jeal explained how a local Stanley committee had been formed originally with the idea of raising funds to have the one in Kinshasa repaired and reinstalled, but the cost was too high, so instead, a statue for Denbigh was planned.[65] As soon as the plans became common knowledge following a planning application, 50 prominent figures signed a protest petition, citing Stanley's association with crimes against humanity, the support of a slave trade and British imperialism at its worst. Objectors included poet and activist Benjamin Zephaniah and Congolese Professor of History Georges Nzongola-Ntalaja.[66] Their complaint was in line with the direction of revisionist historiographical traffic on colonialism in the Congo and imperialism more generally.[67] It also aligned with Frank McLynn's two-volumed and reissued biography, the subtitle of which was *Dark Genius of African Exploration*. As the advertising blurb put it: 'Behind the public man lay a disturbed personality. A pathological liar with sadomasochistic tendencies, Stanley's achievements, he suggested, exacted a high human cost.'[68] More recently, the Ugandan historian Oduro Obura's study of Kalula, Stanley's young gun bearer who he brought to Britain, led Obura to raise serious questions about his relationships with young African boys.[69]

---

[65] 'Celebrate Our Greatest Explorer: There is no Statue in Wales of Henry Stanley, the Most Famous Welsh Explorer Who Ever Lived', *Wales Online*, 17 March, 2008: <https://www.walesonline.co.uk/news/local-news/celebrate-our-greatest-explorer-2189979>.

[66] 'Writers Join Protest Against HM Stanley Statue for Denbigh', *North Wales Live*, 1 Sept. 2010: <https://www.dailypost.co.uk/news/north-wales-news/writers-join-protest-against-hm-2744999>. Bangor University lecturer Dr Selwyn Williams set up the petition.

[67] Robert Gildea, 'Imperial Blether: How the British Fool Themselves About their Colonial Past', *Times Literary Supplement*, 18 June 2021, 22. For a Welsh example, see Chris Evans, *Slave Wales: The Welsh and Atlantic Slavery, 1650–1850* (Cardiff, 2010). For an alternative view see for example Robert Tombs, 'In Defence of the British Empire', *Spectator*, 8 May 2020, and his debate with Alan Lester on the British Empire and race: <https://blogs.sussex.ac.uk/snapshotsofempire/2022/02/01/the-british-empire-and-race/>.

[68] McLynn, *Stanley*. See cover blurb to 2006 edition.

[69] Oduor Obura, *Decolonising Childhoods in Eastern Africa: Literary and Cultural representations* (London, 2021).

The Curious Case of Wales's Statue to Henry Morton Stanley   363

Jeal, by contrast, focused on the personal archive of Stanley, held in Belgian archives to which others had not had access. He argued that Stanley had been duped by King Leopold; that Stanley's criticisms of the excesses of the Congo Free State had been underappreciated by historians; that Stanley had deliberately contributed to his pantomime villain persona in order to make Livingstone look good; and that Stanley had baulked at the unfair treaties made with chiefs for lands, warning junior colleagues not to treat locals in a racist manner.[70]

Before deciding on the statue, Denbigh Council went ahead first with a public consultation. Stanley as victim of a Belgian royal master manipulator, of English class prejudice, a man misrepresented and blamed for the excess of others, was perhaps appealing to a particular brand of the Welsh psyche. And certainly, from the couple of hundred responses, positive views were in the majority. The cause was taken up by local Plaid Cymru Councillor Gwyneth Kensler. She set up a Commemorative Group that pushed for the statute, drawing on a regeneration consultancy (Cadwyn Clwyd) for advice. Consequently, a bid was made to an EU Fund that awarded grants to address rural poverty. It was successful. Hence the £31,000 paid to sculptor David Elphick for a statue 'to boost tourism and economic growth', as the then Labour MP for Denbighshire explained.[71] The statue was commissioned and installed in 2010. Elphick chose to memorialise Stanley meeting Livingstone, and with it the famous phrase, which may not in fact have been spoken: 'Dr Livingstone, I presume'. The effect overall was flattering. A second monumental tribute to Stanley was installed at the site of the St Asaph workhouse early in 2011. This time, it took the form of a long obelisk decorated with images marking his life (see fig. 17.2). In 2019, the Stanley statue was chosen as the site to launch an election campaign by the local Brexit Party.[72]

Nevertheless, soon after Tim Jeal unveiled the statue in March 2011 it was subjected to protest. In October 2011, paint was daubed over Stanley's face; but the more dramatic and certainly more creative protest, that of the annual re-veiling of the statue in a rubber sheath, first took place in August 2011. Then

[70] 'H.M. Stanley Biographer Backs Planned Denbigh Statue', *North Wales Live and Daily Post*, 22 July 2020 <https://www.dailypost.co.uk/news/north-wales-news/hm-stanley-biographer-backs-planned-2751524>; and for national coverage see 'Row Over Statue of "Cruel" Explorer Henry Morton Stanley', *Daily Telegraph*, 25 July 2010 <https://www.telegraph.co.uk/news/worldnews/africaandindianocean/congo/7908247/Row-over-statue-of-cruel-explorer-Henry-Morton-Stanley.html>.

[71] Frances Williams, 'Stanley Statue: From Poor House to Power House', *Wales Arts Review*, 7 July 2020 <https://www.walesartsreview.org/poorhouse-to-powerhouse-denbighs-stanley-statue/>.

[72] *Ibid.*

Fig. 17.2 H.M. Stanley Sculpture, St Asaph.

The Curious Case of Wales's Statue to Henry Morton Stanley

came the Black Lives Matter and Fallism movements, that would, *inter alia,* result in the toppling of the large statue of Edward Colston, a prosperous slave trader who had lived in Bristol. Online and media protests in North Wales continued through June 2020 before the council met to review the statue. In the run-up to this meeting, four historians of exploration in late nineteenth-century Africa produced a document for the Council to consider. Organised by Dr Brian Murray, a leading expert on Stanley and his writings, the document made a number of claims. First, Stanley's methods of exploration were far more brutal than those of his peers: a case in point was the Bumbireh Massacre on an island in Lake Victoria, where he killed between 35 and 65 people, justifying his actions on the grounds that 'the savage only respects force'. Second, the document stated, there was substantial evidence that Stanley procured, deployed and cruelly treated African slaves, as he did for the Emin Pasha Relief Expedition (1886–9). Third, his writing popularised a particularly harsh form of racism, one which he especially applied to hunter-gatherers and forest dwellers. And finally, any criticism that Stanley may have made of Leopold towards the end of his regime was muted at best. Stanley did write a letter to *The Times* but excused the officers involved, citing how it was difficult to show self-restraint in dealing with such barbarians.[73] Yet, despite having received this evidence, the Council voted by a six to five majority to keep the statue.

Denbigh's Decision to Keep the Statue in 2020

A number of factors explain the Council's decision, beginning with local media coverage. The general line was that Stanley was controversial because of his association with King Leopold, for whom he had worked. (Murray responded privately by saying this reduced Stanley's involvement to 'an internship'.) There was little coverage in detail of the regular protests, namely Zyborska's annual condom re-veiling and associated 'funeral procession to draw attention to the millions of African people who died or were mutilated as a result of Stanley's exploits in the Congo rubber industry'.[74] Similarly, little detail was given of the criticism of Stanley during his lifetime, other than in the online petition. This had referenced the contemporary investigation of the British vice-consul in Zanzibar, John Kirk (1832–1922), who had found evidence of 'excessive violence, wanton destruction, the selling of labourers into slavery, the sexual

---

[73] Document in possession of author. In addition to Dr Brian Murray, the other contributors were Professor Dane Kennedy, Dr Adrian Wisnicki, and Professor Joanna Lewis.

[74] 'Protestors to Cover H.M. Stanley Statue'.

366   *Joanna Lewis*

exploitation of native women, sex trafficking, and the plundering of villages for ivory and canoes'.[75]

Sections of the media were taken with the position of Councillor Gwyneth Kensler, who urged, 'To get the true facts, not just claims, one must go to the primary sources and this is what Tim Jeal, the biographer of Stanley did; he was one of the first people to gain access to Stanley's archive in Belgium.'[76] And she suggested Stanley might well be the son of a single mother. Similarly sympathetic, Councillor Peter Scott was quoted as saying that a recent study had showed Stanley had left Leopold's employment eight years before the genocide had begun. In email exchanges, Jeal robustly rejected all academic objections, quoted from his biography and added it would be unwise in any case for an academic to say anything positive about Stanley in the current climate affecting universities. Nick Elphick's mother also set up a petition to keep the statue, on the grounds that Stanley's life offered hope to those who were poor or homeless; that they too could achieve despite the odds.[77]

Equally important was the argument put forward by pro-statue supporters that Congolese people themselves approved not just of the statue but of Stanley. The statue's sculptor claimed Stanley was still adored, and drew attention to a much publicised visit by an official delegation from the Congolese Embassy in 2016.[78] Photographs were republished of the then *Charges D'Affaires*, Madame Marie Louise Kafenge Nanga, shaking hands with the statue adorned with a fetching leopard-print hat among other items.[79] She even proposed Denbigh be twined with Boma, where Stanley had allegedly carved a house out of a baobab tree. Congolese Chief Thomas Bikebi, also director of an organisation led by sections of the UK Congolese Diaspora, had visited the area in 2018 to pay homage to the graves of the Congolese men brought to Colwyn Bay to study in the late nineteenth century.[80] Involved in both visits, and quoted in the North

[75] https://www.change.org/p/denbigh-town-council-remove-the-statue-of-stanley-from-denbigh-town-centre?redirect=false; '"No Place For it in Welsh Society"'.

[76] '"No Place For it in Welsh Society"'.

[77] https://www.walesartsreview.org/poorhouse-to-powerhouse-debighs-stanley-statue/.

[78] *Denbighshire Free Press*, 18 June 2020, https://www.denbighshirefreepress.co.uk/news/18525449.hm-stanley-sculptor-says-views-people-democratic-republic-congo-considered/.

[79] Aaron Evans, 'Denbigh's Sir Stanley Statue Row Continues as Meeting Over Possible Removal Looms', *Denbighshire Free Press*, 16 June 2020: https://www.denbighshirefreepress.co.uk/news/18520782.denbighs-sir-stanley-statue-row-continues-meeting-possible-removal-looms/.

[80] Zara Whelan, 'Why Congolese Tribal Chief Made Pilgrimage to Colwyn Bay Print Shop', *North Wales Live*, 1 Dec. 2018 <https://www.dailypost.co.uk/news/north-wales-news/congolese-tribal-chief-made-pilgrimage-15445337>.

Wales press in 2020, was a Congolese historian and writer, now based in Newport. Norbert X. Mbu-Mputu described Stanley as 'a man of his time' who should not be viewed as 'evil'.[81]

In 2021, the public was given 'the final say' on the statue, after the narrow Council vote to keep it in the town square. On 15 and 16 October, locals cast their votes, and 79.6 percent of those who voted wanted it to remain.[82] However, with turnout at just 8.8 percent, apathy over the statue was striking. It simply was not an issue. Opponents of the statue were branded as an extremist minority 'woke' brigade by supporters, but ultimately the vast majority of locals did not care to engage. One summed up the general mood: 'Weeks on end of posts about this bloody statue and the remove vote gets 20%. Either way I'm hoping for some peace and quiet from this crap now.'[83]

* * *

The reasons for there being no Stanley statue until the twenty-first century are more interesting than explanations for why a statue was installed just before the clock struck midnight for colonial statues. Stanley's denial of his Welshness and Wales's general lack of engagement with imperial triumph through his African exploration meant no statue ever appeared in the Victorian era of *statue-mania.* The local press was heavily engaged with outing him as a Welshman and residual anger about his denials was still felt at the time of his death. Nevertheless, there was sympathy for the workhouse boy who rose to fame; who experienced English prejudice and snobbery; whose family were poor and downtrodden. Small acts of remembrance, directed by the cathedral community around St Asaph, kept up a soft focus on Stanley as a facilitator of the spread of Christianity, supported by a local interest in history, heritage and genealogy. There would have never been a statue without interventions focused on promoting the area's connection with Stanley on the grounds of urban regeneration.

Ultimately, this episode is a history of the power of absences. It shows the importance of being sensitive to actual landscapes of historical memory that cast giant shadows from a deep colonial past – and not just the Victorian imperial one. Rural-facing Welsh regions were disconnected from the metropolitan

---

[81] Jez Hemming, 'Denbigh Councillors Vote to Keep HM Stanley Statue', *The Leader,* 25 June 2020 <https://www.leaderlive.co.uk/news/18540721.denbigh-councillors-vote-keep-hm-stanley-statue/>.

[82] 'H.M. Stanley Statue to Remain Outside Denbigh Library', *Denbighshire Free Press,* 27 Oct. 2021 <https://www.denbighshirefreepress.co.uk/news/19677149.hm-stanley-statue-remain-outside-denbigh-library/>.

[83] *Ibid*: comments.

centre, the imperial project and the high political preoccupations of its elite, as the general apathy to the statue's controversies show.[84] The region, like Wales as a whole, had its own historical colonial woes with permanent memorials burnished into the landscape itself, from ruined castles to exhausted mines: place-based markers of submission and extraction – a class-based identity formed around the downtrodden. The absence of a statue reflects the absence of past engagement in Wales with the history of the British Empire, as the eulogies around Stanley in 1904 suggest. Queen Victoria was never very enthusiastic about her Welsh kingdom, spending 'a paltry seven nights in Wales'.[85] Unsurprisingly, then, a supposed imperial figure of gargantuan impact and controversy, according to today's understanding, was historically far less understood as such from the Victorian age through to the twenty-first century.

In this regard, a number of Jonathan Parry's insights are useful in understanding why the British imperial 'project of empire' and corresponding preoccupations of a metropolitan, English elite appear to lack traction, even if Parry's work has been focused more on high politics, political parties and political culture. In his writing on Disraeli and England, for example, one can see how a particular, if not peculiar, set of 'beneath the surface dynamics' underscored the importance of local politics, traditions, community and identities, and not just British imperial ones.[86] (Even in 1880, Disraeli's raucous tub-thumping imperialism found limited purchase in England.) Similarly, in Parry's work on patriotism and national identity, it is domestic perceptions and the 'Irish Question' across the nineteenth century that dominate, not imperial ones. In the case of the Welsh, the construction of a national identity around an English empire was not a comfortable proposition. It was far more congenial to perch on the moral high ground of religiosity and superior evangelical zeal, and so to peck away at English superiority. Thus it was that modern empires were more peripheral in this region. After all, an older one still had a visible, felt presence, its living legacy expressed through class tension, and feelings of exclusion and humiliation, as the Stanley saga ultimately reveals.

[84] See Bernard Porter, *The Absent-Minded Imperialists: Empire, Society and Culture in Britain* (Oxford, 2006). Regions like Wales support his view, although the presence of empire and enthusiasm for it varied considerably across time, classes, cultures and geographies. More locally sensitive studies are needed.

[85] John S. Ellis, 'Reconciling the Celt: British National Identity, Empire and the 1911 Investiture of the Prince of Wales', *Journal of British Studies*, 37 (1998), 391.

[86] I am referring here especially to my 'take home' of a side theme from J.P. Parry 'Disraeli and England', *Historical Journal*, 43 (2000), 699–728; and Jonathan Parry, *The Politics of Patriotism: English Liberalism, National Identity, and Europe, 1830–1886* (Cambridge, 2006).

The story told here therefore supports the 'low impact' historiographical verdict on Britain and its empire. For Welsh non-elites, empire did not contribute to their lives in any great material or cultural way; neither did it have much impact on popular political discourse. Even iconic and controversial African explorers were not associated with empire in popular discussion. Therefore, Stanley did not function as a register of empire. Moreover, the controversies often surrounding Stanley – his methods and his role in empire building in Africa – were historically also absent too. If the Welsh were prodded into thinking about themselves in relation to the second British Empire, then an outstretched hand in friendship (as the 2010 Stanley statue has) would have suited them well. Religious nonconformist missionaries were spreading the gospel and literacy. They were learning local languages in India; they were being the right kind of settlers – *y Wladfa* – in Patagonia; and they were carrying out humanitarian work in Africa. All of this neatly converted into a view of the Welsh being mediators between the powerful and powerless; as setting an example to the English to be more compassionate, friendly and ethical imperialists.[87] They were too few on the ground to be responsible for anything very major or gruesome; too absent from the empire of military conquest and economic exploitation to carry much blame. Instead, Wales's smallness and the country's prior absorption into the United Kingdom meant that Welsh liberal politicians could even put forward Wales as model for colonial states to follow.[88]

The curious case of the statue to Henry Morton Stanley points to the way in which the British Empire was not generally part of Welsh people's lives nor identity, during its lifetime. Being a conquered, pacified people made the subject a bit awkward and embarrassing. Better to focus on the successes of spreading the Christian gospel and to sit tight and be practical. Being a smaller and poorer nation, in contrast – as always – to its imperial neighbour, Wales could show the way forward for other colonies in terms of the benefits, whilst sharing in imperial Britain's underlying ideologies. Far more concerning were events in Wales and Wales-England interactions. As Martin Johnes has argued, Wales has usually defined itself and been politicised against its larger

---

[87] See, for example, the exciting new work by Lucy Taylor, 'The Welsh Way of Colonisation in Patagonia: The International Politics of Moral Superiority', *Journal of Imperial and Commonwealth History*, 47 (2019) 1073–99; and – based on his forthcoming University of Swansea PhD – Rhys Owens, 'Not Only Settlers but Rulers: The Welsh and the British Empire', *Planet Magazine* <https://www.planetmagazine.org.uk/planet-online/244/rhys-owens>.

[88] Robert Crosby, '"A War for 'Small Nations": Wales and Empire from the Boer War to the Great War, 1899–1918 (unpublished dissertation, BSc International Relations and History, LSE, 2022). Winner of the 2022 History of Parliament Trust Prize for the Best Undergraduate Dissertation.

neighbour.[89] Anti-colonialism began and had ended at home. Yet ultimately one could argue that Stanley was engaged with sympathetically because of a Welsh version of its own coloniality: an imperialism of English slights, condescension and snobbery.

---

[89] Martin Johnes, *Wales: England's Colony? The Conquest, Assimilation and Re-creation of Wales* (Cardigan, 2019).

Jonathan Parry: List of Publications

This bibliography is arranged chronologically. It includes books, articles, essays, Oxford Dictionary of National Biography entries and Parry's contributions to the London Review of Books. Reviews of books in academic journals, blog posts and other shorter pieces are excluded.

1982
'Religion and the Collapse of Gladstone's First Government', *Historical Journal*, 25, 71–101

1983
'The State of Victorian Political History', *Historical Journal*, 26, 469–84

1984
'The Unmuzzling of Gladstone', *Parliamentary History*, 3, 187–98

1986
Democracy and Religion: Gladstone and the Liberal Party 1867–1875 (Cambridge: Cambridge University Press), 504 pp.
'High and Low Politics in Modern Britain', *Historical Journal*, 29, 753–70

1988
'Constituencies, Elections and Members of Parliament, 1790–1820', *Parliamentary History*, 7, 147–60

1991
'Gladstone and the Disintegration of the Liberal Party', *Parliamentary History*, 10, 392–404

1993
The Rise and Fall of Liberal Government in Victorian Britain (New Haven & London: Yale University Press), 383 pp.
'The Quest for Leadership in Unionist Politics, 1886–1956', *Parliamentary History*, 12, 296–311
'From the Thirty-Nine Articles to *The Thirty-Nine Steps*: Reflections on the Thought of John Buchan', in Michael Bentley (ed.), *Public and Private Doctrine: Essays in British History Presented to Maurice Cowling* (Cambridge: Cambridge University Press), 209–35

1994
'Footing the Bill', *London Review of Books*, 16:11 (9 June). Review of David Cannadine, *Aspects of Aristocracy: Grandeur and Decline in Modern Britain* (New Haven & London: Yale University Press)

'No Gentleman', *London Review of Books*, 16:12 (23 June). Review of Peter Marsh, *Joseph Chamberlain: Entrepreneur in Politics* (New Haven & London: Yale University Press)

'Crawling Towards God', *London Review of Books*, 16:21 (10 November). Review of H.C.G. Matthew (ed.), *The Gladstone Diaries, with Cabinet Minutes and Prime-Ministerial Correspondence,* vols XII–XIV (Oxford: Oxford University Press)

'Dear George', *London Review of Books*, 16:24 (22 December). Review of David Gilmour, *Curzon* (London: John Murray)

1995

'Duffers', *London Review of Books*, 17:18 (21 September). Review of David Kynaston, *The City of London. Vol. II: The Golden Years, 1890–1914* (London: Chatto)

1996

'Past and Future in the Later Career of Lord John Russell', in T.C.W. Blanning and David Cannadine (eds), *History and Biography: Essays in Honour of Derek Beales* (Cambridge: Cambridge University Press), 142–72

1997

'Holborn at Heart', *London Review of Books*, 19:2 (23 January). Review of Paul Smith, *Disraeli: A Brief Life* (Cambridge: Cambridge University Press, 1996)

'The Real Founder of the Liberal Party', *London Review of Books*, 19:19 (2 October). Review of L.G. Mitchell, *Lord Melbourne, 1779–1848* (Oxford: Oxford University Press)

1998

'Lord John Russell, first Earl Russell', in Robert Eccleshall and Graham Walker (eds), *Biographical Dictionary of British Prime Ministers* (London: Routledge), 151–61

1999

'Bovril and Biscuits: Mid-Victorian Britain', *London Review of Books*, 21:10 (13 May). Review of Theodore Hoppen, *The Mid-Victorian Generation, 1846–1886* (Oxford: Oxford University Press, 1998)

2000

(ed.) with Stephen Taylor, *Parliament and the Church, 1529–1960* (Edinburgh: Edinburgh University Press for the Parliamentary History Yearbook Trust), 193 pp.

with Stephen Taylor, 'Introduction: Parliament and the Church of England from the Reformation to the Twentieth Century', in Parry and Taylor, *Parliament and the Church*, 1–13

'Disraeli and England', *Historical Journal*, 43, 699–728

'Gladstone, Liberalism and the Government of 1868–1874', in David Bebbington and Roger Swift (eds), *Gladstone Centenary Essays* (Liverpool: Liverpool University Press), 94–112

2001

'The Impact of Napoleon III on British Politics, 1851–1880', *Transactions of the Royal Historical Society*, 6th ser., 6, 147–75

'Lord John Russell and the Irish Catholics, 1829–1852', *Journal of Liberal Democrat History*, 33, 9–12

2003

'Nonconformity, Clericalism and 'Englishness': The United Kingdom', in Christopher Clark and Wolfram Kaiser (eds), *Culture Wars: Secular-Catholic Conflict in Nineteenth-Century Europe* (Cambridge: Cambridge University Press), 152–80

2004

'Cavendish, Spencer Compton, Marquess of Hartington and Eighth Duke of Devonshire (1833–1908), Politician', *Oxford Dictionary of National Biography* (Oxford: Oxford University Press), print and online

'Disraeli, Benjamin, Earl of Beaconsfield (1804–1881), Prime Minister and Novelist', *Oxford Dictionary of National Biography* (Oxford: Oxford University Press), print and online

'Graham, Sir James Robert George, Second Baronet (1792–1861), Politician', *Oxford Dictionary of National Biography* (Oxford: Oxford University Press), print and online

'Hardy, Gathorne Gathorne-, First Earl of Cranbrook (1814–1906), Politician', *Oxford Dictionary of National Biography* (Oxford: Oxford University Press), print and online

'Layard, Sir Austen Henry (1817–1894), Archaeologist and Politician', *Oxford Dictionary of National Biography* (Oxford: Oxford University Press), print and online

'Lowe, Robert, Viscount Sherbrooke (1811–1892), Politician', *Oxford Dictionary of National Biography* (Oxford: Oxford University Press), print and online

'Manners, John James Robert, Seventh Duke of Rutland (1818–1906), Politician', *Oxford Dictionary of National Biography* (Oxford: Oxford University Press), print and online

'Morley, Samuel (1809–1886), Businessman, Politician, and Philanthropist', *Oxford Dictionary of National Biography* (Oxford: Oxford University Press), print and online

'Russell, John, Viscount Amberley (1842–1876), Politician and Writer', *Oxford Dictionary of National Biography* (Oxford: Oxford University Press), print and online

2006

The Politics of Patriotism: English Liberalism, National Identity and Europe, 1830–1860 (Cambridge: Cambridge University Press), 424 pp.

'Kebbel, Thomas Edward (1826–1917), Journalist', *Oxford Dictionary of National Biography* (Oxford: Oxford University Press), online

2007

Benjamin Disraeli (Oxford: Oxford University Press), 143 pp.

'Palmerston and Russell', in David Brown and Miles Taylor (eds), *Palmerston Studies* (2 vols, Southampton: Hartley Institute, University of Southampton), vol. 1, 144–73

'Liberalism and Liberty', in Peter Mandler (ed.), *Liberty and Authority in Victorian Britain* (Oxford: Oxford University Press), 71–100

'Whig Monarchy, Whig Nation: Crown, Politics and Representativeness, 1880–2000', in Andrzej Olechnowicz (ed.), *The Monarchy and the British Nation, 1780 to the Present* (Cambridge: Cambridge University Press), 47–75

2008

'L'histoire Politique de L'ère Victorienne: Nouvelles Tendances', *Revue d'histoire du XIXe Siècle*, 37, 71–86

2009

'Cowling, Maurice John (1926–2005), Historian', *Oxford Dictionary of National Biography* (Oxford: Oxford University Press), online [print, 2013]

2010

'Maurice Cowling: A Brief Life', in Robert Crowcroft, S.J.D. Green and Richard Whiting (eds), *The Philosophy, Politics and Religion of British Democracy: Maurice Cowling and Conservatism* (London: Tauris), 13–24

'The Disciplining of the Religious Conscience in Nineteenth-Century British Politics', in Ira Katznelson and Gareth Stedman Jones (eds), *Religion and the Political Imagination* (Cambridge: Cambridge University Press), 214–34

2011

'The Decline of Institutional Reform in Nineteenth-Century Britain', in David Feldman and Jon Lawrence (eds), *Structures and Transformations in Modern British History: Essays for Gareth Stedman Jones* (Cambridge: Cambridge University Press), 164–86

2013

'Steam Power and British Influence in Baghdad, 1820–1860', *Historical Journal*, 56, 145–73

'Patriotism', in David Craig and James Thompson (eds), *Languages of Politics in Nineteenth-Century Britain* (Basingstoke: Palgrave Macmillan), 69–92

2017

'Disraeli, the East and Religion: *Tancred* in Context', *English Historical Review*, 132, 570–604

'1867 and the Rule of Wealth', in Robert Saunders (ed.), *Shooting Niagara – and After? The Second Reform Act and its World* (Chichester: The Parliamentary History Yearbook Trust), 46–63

'Journeys Across Blankness: Mapping the Middle East', *London Review of Books*, 39:20 (19 October). Review of Daniel Foliard, *Dislocating the Orient: British Maps and the Making of the Middle East, 1854–1921* (Chicago: Chicago University Press)

'What's the Big Idea? The Origins of Our Decline', *London Review of Books*, 39:23 (30 November). Review of Simon Heffer, *The Age of Decadence: Britain 1880 to 1914* (London: Random House)

2018

'Christian Socialism, Class Collaboration, and British Public Life after 1848', in Douglas Moggach and Gareth Stedman Jones (eds), *The 1848 Revolutions and European Political Thought* (Cambridge: Cambridge University Press), 162–84

'Gladstone's First Government: A Policy Overview', *Journal of Liberal History*, 101, 12–19

2019

'Adrenaline Junkie: John Tyndall's Ascent', *London Review of Books*, 41: 6 (21 March). Review of Roland Jackson, *The Ascent of John Tyndall: Victorian Scientist, Mountaineer and Public Intellectual* (Oxford: Oxford University Press, 2018)

'Educating the Utopians: Parliament's Hour', *London Review of Books*, 41:8 (18 April). Review of David Brown, Robert Crowcroft and Gordon Pentland (eds), *The Oxford Handbook of Modern British Political History, 1800–2000* (Oxford: Oxford University Press, 2018)

'Policy Failure: The Party Paradox', *London Review of Books*, 41:22 (21 November). Review of Robert Crowcroft, *The End is Nigh: British Politics, Power and the Road to the Second World War* (Oxford: Oxford University Press)

2020

'Henry Layard and the British Parliament: Outsider and Expert', in Stefania Ermidoro and Cecilia Riva (eds), *Rethinking Layard 1817–2017* (Venice: Istituto Veneto di Scienze, Lettere ed Arti, 2020), 155–70

'Lord Aberdeen', in Iain Dale (ed.), *The Prime Ministers: 55 Leaders, 55 Authors, 300 Years of History* (London: Hodder & Stoughton), 199–207

'Harry Goes Rogue', *London Review of Books*, 42:3 (6 February)

'A Regular Grey', *London Review of Books*, 42:23 (3 December). Review of T.G. Otte, *Statesman of Europe: A Life of Sir Edward Grey* (London: Penguin Books)

'Briggs, Samuel (1776–1868), Merchant and Consul in Egypt', *Oxford Dictionary of National Biography* (Oxford: Oxford University Press), online

'Taylor, Robert (1788–1852), British Political Representative in Ottoman Iraq', *Oxford Dictionary of National Biography* (Oxford: Oxford University Press), online

2021

'Managing the Nation', *London Review of Books*, 43:6 (18 March). Review of Edmund Fawcett, *Conservatism: The Fight for a Tradition* (Princeton: Princeton University Press, 2020)

'Angelic Porcupine: Adams's Education', *London Review of Books*, 43:11 (3 June). Review of David S. Brown, *The Last American Aristocrat: The Brilliant Life and Improbable Education of Henry Adams* (New York: Scribner, 2020)

2022

Promised Lands: The British and the Ottoman Middle East (Princeton: Princeton University Press), 453 pp.

'To Serve My Friends', *London Review of Books*, 44:2 (27 January). Review of Mark Knights, *Trust and Distrust: Corruption in Office in Britain and its Empire, 1600–1850* (Oxford: Oxford University Press, 2021)

'Grumpy in October: The Anglo-French Project', *London Review of Books*, 44:8 (21 April). Review of Edward J. Gillin, *Entente Imperial: British and French Power in the Age of Empire* (Stroud: Amberley Publishing)

'Napping in the Athenaeum: London Clubland', *London Review of Books*, 44:17 (8 September). Review of Seth Alexander Thévoz, *Behind Closed Doors: The Secret Life of London Private Members' Clubs* (London: Robinson)

'Thirty-Eight Thousand Bunches of Sweet Peas: Lord Northcliffe's Empire', *London Review of Books*, 44:23 (1 December). Review of Andrew Roberts, *The Chief: The Life of Lord Northcliffe* (London: Simon & Schuster)

2023

'The Land Between Rivers', *History Today*, 73, 28–39

'Life on Sark: Sark's Self-governance', *London Review of Books*, 45:10 (18 May 2023)

2024

'The Third Earl Grey, Liberalism, and the British Empire', *Modern Intellectual History* (forthcoming)

'Carlyle, Parliament, and British Political Debate', *Carlyle Studies Annual* (forthcoming)

'John Robert Seeley, Liberalism and Empire', *Journal of Liberal History*, 122 (Spring 2024), 34–43

2025

'Britain and Europe, 1750–1900', in Lara Kriegel (ed.), *The New Cambridge History of Britain*, vol. 4 (forthcoming)

Index

Act of Union (1801) 12, 296, 303
  repeal of 129
Acton, John Dalberg, 1st Baron Acton
  46, 316, 317
Adams, W.G.S. 117
Adamson, William 115
Adderley, Sir Charles, 1st Baron Norton
  68, 250
Addison, Christopher 116
Administrative Reform Association 244
African National Congress (ANC) 344–
  5, 347
Aiyar, Mani Shankar 331, 331 n.5, 335–9,
  341, 347–8
Amery, Leopold 114
Amritsar Massacre 175
Anglo-Catholicism 193–4, 201
  See also Church of England
Annales school of history 41
Anti Corn Law League 128, 129, 136
anti-Semitism 67, 160
Apartheid 340, 344, 345–6
appeasement of Germany 166, 184–7
  See also under Churchill, Winston
    Leonard Spencer
Armistice Day 199
Arnold, Matthew 68, 106
Asquith, Herbert Henry 114, 171, 285
Attlee, Clement 186, 208–9
Attwood, Thomas 35

Bagehot, Walter 272–3, 316
Baldwin, Stanley 40 n.8, 97, 99, 103,
  137–8, 141, 177, 187
  and Englishness 9, 92, 97
  and religious nonconformity 10,
    207–8
  relations with G.M. Trevelyan 173–4,
    184–6, 189
Balfour, Arthur 136, 172, 265, 284, 285,
  286
Bank Charter Act (1844) 128, 129
Bank Restriction Act (1797) 126–7

Baptist Union 198, 200
Beaconsfield, Lord, *see* Disraeli,
  Benjamin, 1st Earl of Beaconsfield
Bentley, Michael 2 n.5, 6, 8, 142, 255, 257
Bew, John 12
Bew, Paul 12
Birkenhead, Lord, *see* Smith, Frederick
  Edwin, 1st Earl of Birkenhead
Birmingham 135
Bismarck, Otto von 21, 28, 32, 33, 35
Black Lives Matter 349, 263–5
Blenheim, Battle of (1704) 44–5, 49, 167
Bloch, Marc 18–19, 41
Boer War, second (1899–1902) 104, 112,
  176, 181
Bolshevism 97
Book of Common Prayer 201, 206
Booth, Charles 147, 152
Booth, William 278, 284, 288
  See also Salvation Army
'Brexit' 138–9
British Broadcasting Corporation (BBC)
  152, 199–200
Bryce, James 41, 42, 46, 47, 58, 104, 113,
  171, 259
  as British ambassador to the United
    States 322
  on democracy 313, 322, 324–5, 327
  on Latin America 310–12, 313, 320,
    321–28, 329
  tour of South America 322, 324
Buchan, John 7, 189
'Butskellism' 138

'Cambridge School' of the history of
  political thought 6–7
Cambridge, University of 7, 147, 150,
  166, 169, 173, 175, 177, 331, 332–4,
  335–9, 340
Cannadine, Sir David 38–9, 63
Carson, Lord Edward 228
Casement, Roger 318, 360
Catholic Emancipation 127, 296

Cavendish, Spencer Compton, 8th Duke of Devonshire 72, 254, 255
Cecil, Lord Robert, 1st Viscount Cecil of Chelwood 173, 182, 206–7
Chamberlain, Austen 114–15, 116
Chamberlain, Joseph 35, 72, 79–81, 112–13, 139, 147, 149, 255, 258
  and Irish Home Rule 115, 116, 259
  and social reform 133, 135–6
  and tariff reform 135–6, 170
Charity Organisation Society (COS) 147
Chartism 65, 130, 226
Chateau Gaillard 47, 49
Chesterton, G.K. 272, 273, 274
Church Defence Institution 260
Church of England 10, 190, 192–3, 195, 196–7, 198, 199–200, 204, 274, 282, 288
  debates over disestablishment of 193, 196, 201
Church of Ireland, disestablishment of (1869) 285–6, 300
Church of Scotland 200, 204, 288
Church in Wales 358
  disestablishment of 109, 120, 193–4, 196
Churchill, John, 1st Duke of Marlborough 44–5, 165, 167–8, 174, 175, 176–81, 182, 188
Churchill, Lord Randolph, see Spencer-Churchill, Lord Randolph Henry
Churchill, Winston Leonard Spencer 141, 165–6, 169, 170, 172–6, 181–3, 188–9, 308
  and appeasement of Germany 166, 183–5
  background and early years 167–9
  Chancellor of the Exchequer 137, 172
  Dardanelles 172
  General Strike (1926) 170, 173
  Ireland 304–5
  Second World War 185–8
  See also under Trevelyan, George Macaulay and Macaulay, Thomas Babington
Clapham, Sir John [J.H.] 41, 173
Clemenceau, Georges 320, 326, 327
CND, see Committee for Nuclear Disarmament

Cobbett, William 67, 155, 301
Cobden, Richard 23, 33, 128–9, 130, 140, 223, 315
Coercion Act (1881) 303
Cole, G.D.H. 143, 148, 151, 152, 155–8, 157 n.52
Cole, Margaret 10, 143–6, 159–63
  friendship with Sidney and Beatrice Webb 143, 159–60
  relationship with G.D.H. Cole 155–8
  upbringing and early life 146–51
Collingwood, R.G. 9–10, 41, 51, 55–6, 57
Collingwood, W.G. 41
Collini, Stefan 32, 216
Colston, Edward 364–5
  See also 'Fallism' movement
Committee for Nuclear Disarmament 344
Committee on National Expenditure (1922) 137
Commonwealth 338, 340–1
Communist Party of Great Britain (CPGB) 343, 345 n.67
Conference on Politics, Economics and Citizenship (1924) 204
Conservative party 94, 124, 127, 128, 133, 139, 140, 151, 173, 192, 194, 195, 233, 256, 259, 337, 340
  and religion 194, 204 n.69, 206–7
  divisions in 126, 135–6, 141
  electoral success of 92–3, 253–4, 269
  Salisbury and 260–2, 265, 269
Constitutional Club 260
Constitutional Union 260
constitutionalism 12, 298, 301, 306–9
Copley, John, 1st Baron Lyndhurst 218
corn laws 127–30, 136, 140
Corrupt Practices Act (1883) 261
Council of Action for Peace and Reconstruction 204–5, 207–8
Courtney, Leonard Henry 147, 150
Courts Act (1971) 230
Cowling, Maurice 4–6, 20, 22, 123, 137, 141–2, 254
Creighton, Mandell 40
Cross, Richard, 1st Viscount 133
Curzon, George Nathaniel, 1st Marquess Curzon of Kedleston 228–9
Cymru Fydd Society 102, 108, 110, 111, 113, 120

Dalberg-Acton, John, 1st Baron Acton, *see* Acton, John Dalberg
Dalziel, Henry 109
Darch, Colin 331, 341–4, 347–8
Davis, David 118
de Sélincourt, Hugh 9, 82–3, 87–90, 98–101
  early years 83–4
  literary inspiration 84–5
  the Great War and sport 90–2
  pastoralism 93–4
democracy 11, 21, 26, 253–5, 257, 258, 259, 266, 311, 313, 319, 321, 324, 340–1
  mass democracy, 83, 146–7, 204
Depression, *see* Great Depression
Derby, Lord, *see* Stanley, Edward George Geoffrey Smith, 14th Earl of Derby
devolution 114–17, 119
  Irish, see Home Rule
  Scottish 102–3 115–16, 120
  Welsh 102–3, 108, 109, 112–13, 115–16, 119, 120
  See also Lloyd George, David; Speaker's Conference on Devolution (1919)
disarmament 203, 206,
Disraeli, Benjamin, 1st Earl of Beaconsfield 67, 72, 78, 104, 108, 129–30, 133
  Gladstone's view of 306
  imperial policy 301, 307
  Jonathan Parry's work on 7, 17, 20 n.8, 146, 368
  public image of 252
Doyle, John ('H.B.') 233–5
Dr Barnardos 131

Easter Rising (1916) 114
ecumenicism 198–9, 207
Eden, Anthony 185, 209
Education Act (1902) 119, 192, 193–4, 195, 284, 285
Education Act (1944) 102
Education Bill (1906) 119, 285
Edward I 352
Edward VII 12, 274–5, 284, 290–1
  and religious minorities 285–7
  and Roman Catholicism 274, 277, 278, 284, 285, 286, 287, 288–9

coronation 279–84
death 272, 287–90
religious upbringing 275–9
Edward VIII 184
EEC, *see* European Economic Community
Egerton, Lord Francis 246–7, 250
Eisteddfod 105, 118, 355
elections, general, *see under* general elections
Elizabeth II 273
Enabling Bill (1919) 201
Escott. T.H.S 67
European Convention on Human Rights 231
European Economic Community (EEC) 338
European Union (EU) 138–9

Fabian Society 69, 143, 159, 162
'Fallism' movement 365
Famine, Irish, *see* Irish Famine
Feaver, George 160, 161, 162
Federal Council of the Evangelical Free Churches 196
federalism 102–3, 109, 113–17, 120
First World War 90–1, 93–4, 101, 114–15, 116, 118, 182, 197, 202
Fisher, H.A.L. 173, 189
Fox, Charles James 218
Free Church Council 193, 203, 204, 208
  in Wales 194
Free Church Federal Council, 196, 201
free trade 26, 33, 125, 127–9, 130–1, 134–6, 137, 140, 170, 298
Freeman, Edward Augustus 41–3, 47

Gandhi, Rajiv 335, 339
Gascoyne-Cecil, Robert, 3rd Marquess of Salisbury 11, 71, 72, 111, 133, 137, 167–8, 252, 254
  and democracy 254, 257
  and Home Rule 135, 259–60, 261
  and Midlothian Campaign 256
  and popular politics 253, 260–7
  platform speeches 254–6
  public image of 253, 257–60, 267–71
  'Salisbury clubs' 269

Geddes Axe, *see* Committee on National Expenditure (1922)
General Board of Health   132
general elections
  1835   243
  1857   249
  1874   133
  1880   256
  1892   109
  1895   75
  1906   136, 165, 192, 195
  1910   195–6
  1918   202
  1922   202
  1923   203
  1929   177
  1935   208
  1945   186
George V   198, 273, 286, 291
Gibbon, Edward   53, 168, 174, 175
Gibraltar, siege of (1704–5)   44, 45
Gaddis, John Lewis   47
Gladstone, William Ewart   9, 12, 21, 63, 133–4, 137, 141, 247, 258, 264, 300, 306–7
  and Hawarden   69, 72–9
  and Home Rule   12, 20, 119, 134–5, 165, 169, 259, 300–5, 308–9
  and Midlothian Campaign   107, 216, 254, 256, 264, 266, 301, 307
  public image of   68–9, 73, 78–9, 269
  public style of   252, 255–6, 257, 262
  See also Irish Land Acts
Glorious Revolution (1688)   224, 226
Gold Standard   126, 137
Gollancz, Victor   155
Gooch, Richard   242–3
Goodhart, David   139
Government of India Act (1935)   184
Great Depression   190, 328
Great Exhibition (1851)   130
Great War (1914–18), *see* First World War
Green, Alice Stopford   42
Green, E.H.H.   253
Green, John Richard   42–3, 44, 47, 49, 56
Grenville, William Wyndham, 1st Baron Grenville   217, 223
Grey, Sir Edward   173, 181–5, 233, 242–3, 322

Grigg, Edward   113–14
Grimley, Matthew   201

Haidar, Salman   331, 347–8
  British-Indian relations   339–41
  early life and education   332–5
Halifax, Lord, *see* Wood, Edward Frederick Lindley, 1st Earl of Halifax
Hansard, Thomas Curson   237
Harcourt, Sir William   253, 255
Hardy, Thomas   52
Hartington, Lord, *see* Cavendish, Spencer Compton, 8th Duke of Devonshire
Harvey, Daniel   220, 241
Hawarden, *see under* Gladstone, William Ewart
Heath, Edward   138, 231
Henderson, Arthur   206
Henderson, Charles   55–6
Herbert, Sir Dennis   229–30
high political history   4–6, 17, 20–2, 36, 63, 135, 140, 302, 305, 368
Hitler, Adolf   141, 187
Hobson, J.A.   148, 318, 320
Home Rule
  and Edward VII   286
  and First Home Rule bill (1886)   194, 322
  and Gascoyne-Cecil, Robert, 3rd Marquess of Salisbury   259, 265
  and Liberalism   12, 20, 119–20, 165, 299–305, 309
  and David Lloyd George   102–4, 111–17
  in political rhetoric and tactics   135, 141
  See also Gladstone, William Ewart
'Home Rule all round'   103, 109, 115
  See also federalism
Hotham, Beaumont, 3rd Baron Beaumont   220–1, 222, 223–4
House of Commons Disqualification Acts   230
House of Lords reform   196
Human Rights Act (1998)   231
humanitarianism   12, 131, 298, 369

income tax   127, 132, 133, 137
India   104, 115–16, 130, 167, 168, 184, 186, 203, 278, 305, 331 nn.4–5, 334–41

'information revolution' 236, 238, 250
Ingold, Tim 46, 54, 57
Ireland 129 n.17, 132, 134–5, 194, 216,
    221, 265, 286, 288, 296
    and image of the country house 65,
        67, 69, 73, 81
    and David Lloyd George 103, 108,
        111–12, 114
    and Liberalism 12, 299–305, 309
    See also Gladstone, William Ewart,
        Home Rule, Ulster
Irish Free State 103, 120, 228
Irish Famine 129 n.17, 132, 168, 303
Irish Land Acts 110, 134–5, 300
Irish Land League 111, 303
    See also Parnell, Charles Stewart
Irish Liberal Party 303
Irish Loyalist Club 260
Irish Parliamentary Party 109, 259, 304,
    305
Irish Universities Bill 34

Jeal, Tim 362, 363, 366
Jenkinson, Robert Banks, 2nd Earl of
    Liverpool 127, 140, 220, 236
Johnson, Boris 124, 130, 138–9
Joint Action Committee Against Racial
    Intolerance 342
Jones, Thomas 116, 118
Judicature Act (1873) 228
Junior Constitutional Club 260

Kelly, Sir Fitzroy 221, 223
Kerr, Philip 113–14
Keynes, John Maynard 103
Kidd, Colin 120
Koebel, W.H. 321, 323–4

Labour party 32, 35, 92, 120, 173, 190,
    340, 344, 346
    and activism 145 n.9, 152, 158, 162–3
    and devolution (1918) 115
    economic policy 137
    and general election (1906) 136
    and G.M. Trevelyan 172, 186
    and nonconformity 190, 195, 205–7
laissez-faire 33, 123, 140, 204
Lambeth Conference (1920) 199, 283
Land League, see Irish Land League

land reform 109–10, 111, 135
    See also Irish Land Acts
Latin America, see under Bryce, James
Law, Edward, 1st Baron Ellenborough
    217–19, 224, 227
Lawrence, Jon 36, 267
League of Nations 104, 203, 208
League of Nations Union 203, 206–7
Legassick, Martin 331, 331 n.6, 341–8
Leopold II, King of Belgium 350, 353–4,
    359, 363, 365, 366
Lewis, Saunders 120
    See also Plaid Cymru
Liberal party 11, 20, 23, 152, 172, 257, 301
    and devolution (1918) 115
    and nonconformity 192–6
    and reform of the Commons 236–51
    and the law 213–32
    and Welsh politics 109–12
    decline of 35, 190, 205–8
    economic and social policy 133–7,
        141
    See also liberalism, free trade
liberalism 8, 27, 30, 62, 258, 298
    and G.M. Trevelyan 166, 171
    and Ireland 295–309
    and the law 213–32
    and the work of Jonathan Parry 8,
        11, 12, 19–24, 32–7, 110, 119–20, 165,
        213, 295, 299–300, 301
    discussed in the work of European
        historians 24–32
    in Ireland 34, 302–3
Liberation Society 193
'linguistic turn' 2, 3, 36
Liverpool, Lord, see Jenkinson, Robert
    Banks, 2nd Earl of Liverpool
Livingstone, David 353–9, 361, 363
Lloyd George, David 9, 137, 171, 173, 182
    and the Boer War 104
    policy towards Ireland 109, 112–16
    political nonconformity 189, 197, 201,
        205–6, 207–8
    speech at Aberystwyth (1896) 102
    upbringing and influences 105–8
    unionism 113–17, 120
    views on Welsh self-government
        102–5, 109–114, 116–117, 118–120
Locke, John 24

London, University of 347
Long, Walter 114
Louis XIV, King of France 167, 177, 181
Lowe, Robert, Viscount Sherbrooke
133–4

Macaulay, Thomas Babington 165–6,
167, 168, 185, 188
G.M. Trevelyan's view on 173, 175–6
view of Marlborough 167, 174
as contested by G.M. Trevelyan and
Winston Churchill 176–81, 182
Winston Churchill's views on 174–5,
187
MacDonald, James Ramsay 103, 137–8,
141, 172, 177, 183–4, 206
Maine, Henry 324
Mandler, Peter 73, 131
Marlborough, Duke of, *see* Churchill,
John, 1st Duke of Marlborough
Massingham, Henry 112
McCarthy, Helen 10, 205
McKibbin, Ross 89–90, 97, 207
Meredith, George 53
Methodism 191, 194, 196, 206, 207
Middlemas, Keith 138
Mill, John Stuart 23, 25, 106, 315–16
Milner, Alfred 104, 113, 114
modernisation theory 19, 31–2
Mommsen, Wolfgang 33
monarchy 9, 12, 31, 272–91
Monroe Doctrine 315, 319
Munich Agreement, *see* appeasement of
Germany
Municipal Corporations Act (1835) 220
Mussolini, Benito 172, 187

National Conservative Club 260
National Council of Evangelical Free
Churches 193–4, 195–6, 197–9,
200
and disestablishment 201
and politics 195–6, 200–8
and religious education 192, 195–6,
200–1
and social reconstruction, 202
in the First World War 198–9
National Council on Self-Government
for Wales 118

National Industrial Relations Court 231
National Parliamentary and Financial
Reform Association 244
National Trust 40 n.8, 52, 53–4, 182
National Union of South African
Students 345
nationalism 21, 27–8, 105, 117–18, 135,
339
Irish 9, 27, 65, 104, 109, 112, 114, 259,
296, 302–4
Scottish 119–20
Welsh 9, 102, 104, 112, 119–20
See also Home Rule
National Government 137, 184, 187,
207–8
Nazi Germany 166, 184, 203
Nehru, Jawaharlal 334, 334 n.16, 339
New Liberalism 32, 35, 137, 140, 141, 188
New Political History 2, 5, 7
New Poor Law (1834) 131, 134 n.31
Nonconformist Unionist Association
260
nonconformity, 10, 107, 119, 120, 190–205,
274, 284–5, 286, 288, 289–90, 358,
369
Norgate, Kate 43
Northcote, Stafford, 1st Earl of Iddesleigh
252, 254, 255, 258–9
Northern Ireland 304–5
Northern Ireland Assembly
Disqualification Act (1975) 230
Norton, Lord, *see* Adderley, Sir Charles,
1st Baron Norton

O'Connell, Daniel 216, 302–3
Oliver, F.S. 113–14
Oxford, University of 83, 117, 182, 185,
331, 332–3, 341, 344

Palmerston, Lord, *see* Temple, Henry
John, 3rd Viscount Palmerston
Pan-American Union 323
Parnell, Charles Stewart 216, 255, 303–4
See also Irish Land League
Parry, Jonathan 4, 38–9, 65, 92, 189, 295,
306, 328, 332
and political history 6–7, 104, 110,
123–4, 129, 142, 146, 162–3, 165, 193,
213, 235–6, 250, 254, 298, 368

384 Index

Parry, Jonathan (*cont.*)
  on Home Rule   12, 119–20, 165, 299–304, 309
  on liberalism   8, 10–12, 17–24, 25–30, 32–7, 213, 232
  on monarchy   273
  on the nation and patriotism   8–9, 12, 62–3, 297–8, 368
Peabody Trust   131
Peace Ballot (1934–5)   208
Peace Society   208
Pedersen, Susan   5
Pitt, William, the Younger   10, 125, 126
Plaid Cymru   120, 363
Plumb, Sir John Harold   45, 166
Pocock, J.G.A.   6–7, 295–6
Pollitt, Brian   337
postmodernism   1, 2, 6
Powderham Castle   75
Power, Eileen   50
Powicke, F.M.   40, 50–1, 52
Pragnell, Vera   83–4
Primose League   65, 71, 260, 265
Primrose, Archibald Philip, 5th Earl of Rosebery and 1st Earl of Midlothian   79, 255
prorogation of Parliament (2019)   231
Pugh, Martin   71

rearmament, 208
reconstruction (post-war)   103, 115–16, 117, 202, 204–5, 229
Reform Acts
  1832   127–8, 140, 181, 218, 222, 226, 233, 235–7, 239, 241, 246, 250
  1867   4, 11, 141, 239, 252
  1884   20, 261
religion, *see* Anglo-Catholicism, Church of England, nonconformity, Roman Catholic Church, Roman Catholicism
revolutions of 1848   21, 130, 298
Roman Catholic Church   204
  and education   76, 192, 194
  See also Anglo-Catholicism, Roman Catholicism
Roman Catholicism   34, 112, 274, 277, 278, 284, 285, 286, 287, 288–9, 298, 302–3, 327
  See also Catholic Emancipation

Roosevelt, Franklin D.   187
Rosebery, Earl of, *See* Primrose, Archibald Philip, 5th Earl of Rosebery and 1st Earl of Midlothian
Round Table   113–14
Russell, John, 1st Earl Russell   7, 23, 131, 132, 146, 221, 222, 224–7, 231, 236, 247

Salisbury, Lord, *see* Gascoyne-Cecil, Robert, 3rd Marquess of Salisbury
Saltpetre War (1879–84)   317
Salvation Army   207, 284
Sandringham   73
Schwarz, Bill   38
Scott, Sir Walter   52, 189
Scottish Crofters Act (1886)   110
Second World War   138, 176, 186–7, 209, 229, 304, 361
secularisation   131, 190, 200, 285, 290–1, 339
Seeley, Sir John Robert   175–6, 310, 316, 328
Shaw, George Bernard   148, 153, 181
Simon, Sir John   134, 184, 207
Sinn Féin   118
Skinner, Quentin   6–7
slavery   61, 310, 314, 318, 358, 365–6
Smith, Frederick Edwin, 1st Earl of Birkenhead   173–4, 228
Social Democratic Federation   69
social reform,
  and the Conservative party   72, 135–6, 140–1, 259
  and the Labour party   206
  and the Liberal party   104, 141, 171, 195
Social Science Association, 133
socialism   10, 69, 87, 92, 135, 144, 146, 147, 148, 151, 158, 162, 206, 207
Society for the Diffusion of Useful Knowledge   238
South Africa   290, 331, 341–3, 344–8
South African Defense and Aid Fund   347
South African War (1899–1902), *see* Boer War
Soviet Union   97–8, 158, 203, 336–7, 339, 343
Speaker's Conference on Devolution (1920)   103
Spencer-Churchill, Lord Randolph Henry   112, 165, 167–8, 169, 170, 255, 257–9

Stanley, Edward George Geoffrey Smith, 14th Earl of Derby   66, 69–70, 72, 223, 258
Stanley, Sir Henry Morton   13, 349–52
   overseas expeditions   353–8
   statue of   358–70
   upbringing   352–3
   See also 'Fallism' movement
Steedman, Carolyn   51
Storrington (Sussex)   83–5, 88–9, 100–1
Sunak, Rishi   139

tariff reform, *see* free trade
Tawney, R.H.   54, 152, 160–1
temperance   109, 198, 202, 204
Temple, Frederick, Archbishop of Canterbury   281, 284
Temple, Henry John, 3rd Viscount Palmerston   21, 23, 68, 306, 338
Temple, William   204
Thatcher, Margaret   124, 138, 141
Tories, *see* Conservative party
Toynbee Hall   131
trade unionism   67, 145, 147, 148, 151, 152, 157, 161, 173, 227
Trevelyan, Sir Charles Edward   168
Trevelyan, Charles Philip   169, 170–1, 172, 184
   relationship with G.M. Trevelyan   171–2
   relationship with Winston Churchill   169–70
Trevelyan, George Macaulay   8, 38–41, 52–3, 165, 167, 168–9, 183
   and landscape preservation   39, 23–40 n.8, 53–4
   and Sir Edward Grey   181–3, 184–5
   and the 'poetry of history'   51–2, 53
   friendship with Winston Churchill   10, 165, 166, 170, 187–9
   historical imagination of   45–50
   love of walking   8, 39–40, 44, 45, 49, 54
   military historian   43–5, 166
   politcal views   39, 44, 169, 171, 173–4, 184, 185–7
   upbringing and early years   39–44
   See also under Macaulay, Thomas Babington

Trevelyan, George Otto   43–4, 115, 165–6, 168
Truss, Elizabeth   124, 130, 139

Ulster   114–15, 302, 304–5
unionism   9, 103–5, 108, 111–16, 119–20, 265, 296, 303
United States of America   113, 130, 131, 216, 338, 342, 347
   and Anglo-American ideas of superpower status   296–9
   and Henry Stanley Morton   353–6
   in British international thought   310–29
USSR, *see* Soviet Union
utilitarianism   275, 307

Venezuelan Crisis (1895)   319
Versailles, Treaty of   104, 117–8
Victoria, Queen   273, 274, 275–6, 283, 284, 356, 368
Vigo Bay, Battle of (1702)   45

Webb, Beatrice   10, 143–6, 149–51, 159–63
   early years, 146–7
   friendship with Margaret Cole   143, 159–60
   path to socialism, 147–8
   relationship with Sidney Webb, 151–8
Webb, Sidney   143, 147, 150–8, 160–2
Welfare State   204, 214
Welsh Department of the Board of Education   119
Welsh Health Service Insurance Commission   119
Welsh language   105, 107, 120
Whigs   8, 49, 68, 128, 132, 140, 221, 222–3, 225, 226, 227, 237, 303
Williamson, Philip   10, 142, 274
Wilson, Woodrow   118, 307
women's suffrage   2, 31, 128, 144, 159
Wood, Edward Frederick Lindley, 1st Earl of Halifax   184, 185, 276
Wordsworth, William   39, 52
World War One, *see* First World War
World War Two, *see* Second World War

Zephaniah, Benjamin   362
Zimmern, Alfred   118

Tabula Gratulatoria

Michael Bentley
John Bew
Ewen A. Cameron
David Cannadine
Paul Cavill
Matthew Cragoe
Tom Crewe
Graham Earles
Niamh Gallagher
Lawrence Goldman
Ben Griffin
Alana Harris
Boyd Hilton
Matt Innes
Stuart Jones
Mark Keatley
Joseph La Hausse de Lalouvière
Michael Ledger-Lomas
Joanna Lewis
Naomi Lloyd-Jones
Peter Mandler

Helen McCarthy
Max Middleton
Alex Middleton
Susan D. Pennybacker
James Raven
Paul Readman
Kathryn Rix
Robert Saunders
Ben Sayle
Peter Sloman
David L. Smith
Gareth Stedman Jones
Grant Tapsell
Stephen Taylor
Geraint Thomas
James Thompson
Martha Vandrei
Matthew White
William Whyte
Philip Williamson
Pembroke College, Cambridge

Printed in the United States
by Baker & Taylor Publisher Services